the complete
Supergardener

the complete
Supergardener

Alan Titchmarsh

CASSELL
ILLUSTRATED

FOR MY MOTHER,
WHO BOUGHT ME MY FIRST PACKET OF SEEDS,
AND MY FATHER,
WHO WAS RELIEVED TO HAND OVER THE SPADE

This edition first published in Great Britain in 2003 by Cassell Illustrated.
A division of Octopus Publishing Group Limited
2-4 Heron Quays, London E14 4JP

Original edition first published by Ward Lock 1983
Revised editions 1988, 1993, 1997, 1999

Distributed in the United States of America by Sterling Publishing Co., Inc.,
Sterling Publishing Co., Inc.,
387 Park Avenue South, New York, NY10016-8810

A CIP catalogue record for this book is available from the British Library

ISBN 1 844 03209 4

10 9 8 7 6 5 4 3 2

Printed in China

Contents

Introduction   6

PART I   THE BASICS

1   How to start   12
2   Plant propagation   20
3   The toolshed   28

PART II   THE PLANTS

4   Trees 38
5   Shrubs   52
6   Hedges   80
7   Climbers and wall plants   88
8   Roses   100
9   Border plants   112
10 Annuals, biennials and
    bedding plants   138
11 Garden bulbs   152

PART III   THE FEATURES

12 Rock gardens   166

13 Water gardens   178
14 Wildlife in the garden   188
15 Lawns   192
16 Patio gardening   202

PART IV   THE FOOD CROPS

17 Fruit growing   214
18 Vegetable growing   232

PART V   THE UNDER COVER GARDEN

19 Greenhouse gardening   250
20 House plants   268

PART VI   PESTS, DISEASES & DISORDERS   284

Index   300
Acknowledgements   304

Introduction

'The man who could call a spade a spade should be compelled to use one. It is the only thing he is fit for', said Oscar Wilde. So it is that gardeners have acquired a reputation as down-to-earth dullards who possess most of nature's secrets and few social graces. But the days of the crumbling conservatory presided over by a grumbling gardener have long since gone. The mystery of supposed 'green fingers' certainly lingers on, but folk who tackle the land with a handful of common sense as well as a bucketful of manure, will find that this oldest of crafts offers satisfaction and excitement as well as frustration and fury.

Don't believe that all expert gardeners have the patience of Job. Some of them are itching for their seeds to come up and grow into cabbages overnight; others want a mature garden in a matter of weeks. But all of them, if they have a feeling for the soil and for plants, will curb their impatience and learn that there's no rushing nature, though occasionally she'll let you cheat a bit.

I started gardening when I left school – having shown singular lack of success in any subject remotely academic. Off I plodded to the local nursery where I was astounded to find that someone would pay me to grow plants – something that I'd been doing in my spare time for the previous five years. Gardening doesn't grab everybody this way. Lots of folk look upon it as a chore that has to be done on a Sunday after the car has been washed. And it's easy to see why. They find that everything that shouldn't grow fast does – weeds, the hedge and the lawn – and everything that should be bursting into leaf and flower doesn't: the hastily planted tree, the summer bedding and the bulbs.

The secret of success is to adopt the right attitude to your garden. For a start, stop worrying about it, and stop worrying about what the neighbours will say if you don't cut the lawn or the hedge with monotonous regularity. Look upon your garden as a haven where you can escape the high-speed living of today; then the fact that things move slowly within its leafy confines will soon be welcomed as a positive advantage.

Hopefully *The Complete Supergardener* will give you a bit of inspiration as well as practical, down-to-earth advice. Everybody considers that their garden is a problem plot, so there are suggestions of plants that will put up with all sorts of soils and situations. If you've never lifted a spade before, you should still be able to understand what I'm rambling on about. Above all, remember that this is one man's choice of plants and one man's way of growing them, though both plants and techniques have been filched from other gardeners during the couple of decades that count as my apprenticeship in the craft.

I've had to garden, so far, on heavy clay in the north, on dust-like sand, and now on chalk, clay and flints in the south, so I know that time spent tending the earth is not always rewarded with bumper crops and a bounty of blooms. But the failures make the successes that much more enjoyable. If the book makes gardening seem faintly interesting and even encourages you to grow just one plant to perfection, then I'll be well pleased. I hope you will be too.

part I

THE
BASICS

Here you'll find sound
practical advice on the
essential elements of successful
gardening: planning,
techniques, propagation
and tools

A secluded haven, with outdoor dining area, has been created
in this small urban garden. Plants in containers can be moved
around to provide changing seasonal interest.

CHAPTER

1 How to start

Before you buy a plant or a packet of seeds, there are two vital preliminary stages in creating your dream garden: one is to draw up a plan; the other is to prepare your soil

It's a daunting prospect but an irresistible challenge – a weed-infested patch of earth from which must be sculpted a garden. So what should you do first? Most experts are united in their opinions on this: you must draw up a plan.

PLANNING YOUR PATCH

Say the word 'plan' to an architect and he'll immediately take out his pencil and a sheet of graph paper. The pencil will be of use to you; the graph paper is not essential. However, it is a good idea to consult with all members of the family so that you know just what they want of a garden: somewhere to sit, somewhere to play football, somewhere to put a swing or a sandpit, in fact it might seem at times as if there will be no room for plants. But don't make the mistake of thinking that gardens are planned on paper; I reckon the best ones are planned on soil. Get out there with an armful of bamboo canes and a hosepipe and draw patterns and shapes on the earth.

I'm not going to tell you much about the elements of garden design: there are a lot of them and they've been covered in depth in many books on garden planning. What I will say is that your garden should be both practical and pleasing to look at. If you want a formal plot (all circles and squares) then have one, but most folk like an informal scheme that utilizes gentle curves that are easy on the eye, sympathetic to plants, and totally divorced from the symmetry of motorways, traffic roundabouts and office layouts.

With your list of desirable attributes to hand you'll have fun plotting the shape of your potential garden. View it from all angles – both on the ground and from upstairs windows – and use your imagination to tell you that a bamboo cane will, in time, be a tree of sizeable proportions. Avoid fiddly corners on lawns (they'll be difficult to mow) and in beds (they'll be difficult to plant up), but make sure that one or two parts of the garden are invisible as you walk down it – that way you'll be drawn to explore the hidden nooks and crannies.

There are not many rules in gardening, but there are

What do you want from your garden?

Whether you are designing a garden from scratch or intend to make changes to an existing one, think carefully about what you want from your garden and work out how you can successfully achieve this before rushing out to buy new plants or to chop down unwanted shrubs. As well as making a list of desirable features, make sure that you know the aspect of your plot, as this will have a vital bearing on where some of the features can be situated.

A paved area is both attractive and functional, allowing access even when it is muddy elsewhere

A lean-to pergola, with climbing plants scrambling over it, provides privacy and shade on a patio

Before planting a tree, check the eventual height to ensure it will not outgrow the space available or cast unwanted shade

Site a play area within view of the house

For older children, a wild area provides a place for imaginative play within the safety of the garden

A waterfall cascades into the pool from an adjacent rock garden

Collect rainwater from a shed or garage roof by running a drain pipe into a water butt

A lawn with natural, sweeping curves sets off your plants and is more restful to the eye than a square or rectangular shape

A cold frame is useful for hardening off plants raised in the greenhouse

Site your garden pond in an open, sunny spot that is not overhung by trees. Moving water will require an electric power supply

A boundary hedge provides a haven for wildlife as well as an attractive backdrop to garden plants

Site your greenhouse in a well-lit sheltered spot, which is not overshadowed by trees or buildings

Grow runner beans on a tent-shaped support made from bamboo canes

Make your own compost in specially constructed bins into which organic waste is tipped and allowed to rot down

a few that will prevent disasters in garden design:

1 Make sure you know the aspect of your garden – a tall row of conifers planted on the south side will cast heavy shade over most of the plot. Find out where north is and plant with the sun's path in mind.

2 Garden features that need sun (a pond, a vegetable plot or a greenhouse) must be sited in the open.

3 Make sure that your soil is well drained and in good shape before you plant anything.

4 Be nosey. Look at gardens in your area and take note of plants that do well and those that don't. Avoid the poor 'doers' and save yourself some money.

5 Use trees and shrubs as the backbone of your planting scheme. Make sure that some of them are evergreens, and try to ensure that there's something to look at all the year round.

6 If you can't afford the time or money to plant all your garden at once (and few of us can), start in one corner and work slowly outwards. If you start near the house, you'll always have something to take your mind off the squalor that lies beyond.

7 Make it simple, sweeping and bold, even if the plot is small. Lots of twiddly bits will drive you nuts.

8 Remember that plant foliage is more important and

more enduring than flowers. The predominant foliage colour should be green (too many purples and greys will be overpowering), and each plant should be put next to a neighbour that in some way contrasts with or complements its shape, form or colour. It sounds a bit pretentious but it makes for much more impact than a jumbled scheme of assorted flowers.

Whatever design you settle on, don't make the mistake of thinking that one day your garden will be finished. No garden is a museum (those that are preserved as such invariably go downhill) and constant adjustment of shapes and replanting can be carried out when you tire of your original plantings. Mind you, the trees will appreciate being left alone.

LAND CLEARANCE

I'm afraid there's no magic formula – it's basically hard graft. For a start, all tall weeds, brambles and seedling trees should be hacked down as close to ground level as possible with a sickle, scythe or powered 'strimmer', and the compostable greenstuff stacked on the compost heap. Woody stems can be burned, but dry them off a bit first so that they don't smoke out the neighbours.

Next you have two options. If you're the patient sort, or it's an out-of-the-way spot, you can smother out deep-rooted perennial weeds by covering them with heavy duty black polythene for a season or two (for more details see p.18). Otherwise it's a matter of steadily digging over, removing the roots of perennial weeds as you go – painstaking work, but it will save all the time and trouble involved if neglected portions of root start to resprout. It's tempting to use a rotavator to turn over the soil. Do so if you're really short of time, but remember that the roots of pernicious weeds like bindweed will be chopped up by the blades, and each small piece will make a new plant. Added to this it is difficult to incorporate organic soil enrichment with a rotavator, and the soil is seldom cultivated as deeply as it is with a spade. Pay your money and take your choice.

When soil has been cleared and dug, keep an eye on it and deal quickly with any weeds that emerge. Better still, mulch it immediately with a 5–8 cm (2–3 in) thick layer of organic matter such as leaf mould, pulverized bark, compost or manure to prevent weed emergence. Neglect it and you'll have to do the whole job again – it's heartbreaking.

Don't overdo the hard work. A little slog every couple of days is better than one back-breaking blitz.

GETTING TO KNOW YOUR SOIL

Soil is pretty boring stuff on the face of it, but it is the staff of life as far as your plants are concerned. Remember: what goes in must come up – you only get out of your soil what you put into it.

The ideal garden soil is something called a medium loam. It exists but I don't know anyone who's got it! It consists of a mixture of sand, clay and rotted organic matter known as 'humus'. It doesn't become too sticky when wet nor too dusty when dry.

Sandy soils are 'light' and easy to work but they tend to be lacking in nutrients (which are rapidly washed through) and quick to dry in summer.

Clay soils dry like rock and become squidgy when wet. They are difficult to cultivate whatever the time of year. They are slow to warm up in spring, too.

Stony soils may be sandy or they may have a high proportion of clay.

Peaty soils are good to work, moisture retentive in summer, but they are inclined to be too acidic for certain plants.

Soil drainage

If soil drainage is poor you'll know about it: pools of water may lie on the surface, or the ground may be like a paddy field in wet weather. Where drainage problems are severe, some kind of piped, underground drainage system will have to be invested in, but such cases are, thank goodness, rare. More often than not, poor drainage is caused by the fact that the soil is almost pure clay, or because the surface has been compacted by heavy traffic, or because there is a hard and impenetrable layer in the subsoil. The way to deal with these problems is as follows:

1 Clay soil is easy to identify: it is rock-hard when dry and very plastic when wet. Rub it between your finger and thumb and it has a polished sheen. Improve its drainage by working in as much sharp sand, grit and organic matter as you can lay your spade on. All these materials will break up the clay and prevent the individual particles from adhering quite so firmly to one another. Winter digging allows frost to shatter clay but the effect is only temporary.

2 If the surface of the soil refuses to allow water to drain away, fork or dig over the area. If this is not possible – on a lawn for instance – spike the area deeply with a special aerator or a garden fork. Work grit and organic matter into the soil to prevent a recurrence of the problem.

3 If a 'subsoil pan' (a hard, impervious layer below the topsoil) is causing poor drainage, break up the stiff or rocky layer with a pick or a crowbar to allow water through. In large gardens the job might have to be done with a tractor attachment.

IMPROVING YOUR SOIL

Whatever your soil, the chances are that it needs improving. Sandy, stony or clay soil will be much easier to cultivate, and more conducive to plant growth, if some organic nourishment is added, not just at the start of cultivation but regularly over the years.

Manure and compost (of the well-rotted variety, see below) are the best kind of soil improvers, but leaf mould and composted bark will do wonders too if they can be supplemented with a sprinkling of general fertilizer (they lack the nutrients contained in compost and manure, which will fuel both beneficial soil bacteria and plants). A bucketful to the square metre (square yard) will do for all.

Dig in bulky enrichment like this during autumn and winter. Clay soils can be broken down and 'opened up' if plenty of grit and sharp sand is dug in. This stuff has a longer-lasting effect than organic matter, but will not have the same effect on soil fertility as good old muck – use both if you can.

Stones you will have to live with. Don't try to dig them all out – you'll be at it for ever. Instead, work in plenty of enrichment and let the plants' roots find their way around obstructions.

Making compost

There's real mystery attached to compost making, which is a shame because it puts a lot of people off. Don't be intimidated. Make yourself a couple of post and wire-netting enclosures 1.2 m (4 ft) square (or buy a proprietary bin) and start from there.

Line the first netting bin with newspaper (to prevent the sides of the heap from drying) and start off your heap. Tip into it anything organic (except waste food such as bread, meat and the like, which can tempt the odd rat or two). Grass clippings, vegetable tops, potato peelings, annual weeds, dead flowers, crushed eggshells, tea leaves and even a few torn up newspapers can be put into the bin, but make sure they are mixed together well. Trample the heap every time you add more. Concentrations of any one substance can slow down rotting. Over every 23 cm (9 in) layer sprinkle a little compost activator or sulphate of ammonia, and keep the top of the heap covered with a bit of carpet or sacking. Pour on a canful or two of water if the surface looks dry. Unfirmed and dry compost heaps don't rot. When the first bin is full, start to fill the second one.

Some compost buffs claim to have their stuff ready to use in a matter of weeks; I'd give it three to six months if I were you. Then it will be fairly brown, fairly crumbly and just the thing for any plant in any soil.

1 Make a post and wire-netting compost bin and fill it with vegetable waste. Mix everything together well and trample the heap every time you add more.

2 Scatter sulphate of ammonia or compost activator over each 23 cm (9 in) layer, and water in dry weather. Cover the heap with a piece of old carpet.

Sharp sand and grit can be added to peaty soils and liming may also be necessary.

Autumn leaves are a pain, but you can make them work for you too. Avoid the evergreen types, but put all others in black polythene dustbin liners that have been perforated at intervals to allow a little air circulation. Tread the leaves firm as the bag fills up (to expel air pockets), then seal the top. The leaves should be moist or rotting will not take place. It's fungi that break down dead leaves rather than bacteria, so adding sulphated ammonia won't help much.

Stack the bags in an out-of-the-way corner and crumbly leaf mould, ideal for a mulch, should be yours within about three months. Oak, beech and other small leaves are best; horse chestnut, plane and other toughies can be slower to rot down.

Acid or alkaline?

Don't worry about this complicated chemical state of affairs. Certainly it will affect the type of plants you can grow, but it is easy to discover the lime content – or pH value – of your soil. There are now plenty of soil-testing kits that allow a small sample of soil to be put in a test tube, treated with a special solution and checked against a colour chart to tell you its pH value. Lots of gardeners get by without ever knowing the pH of their soil, but it's fun to find out and it can save you a lot of frustration.

> "Choose plants that can cope with your conditions, rather than trying to change the status quo."

The desirable pH for most plants is between 6.0 and 6.5 on the pH scale. This is a slightly acid soil. Readings between 4.0 and 6.0 are very acid; and those between 6.5 and 8.0 are very alkaline (and probably very chalky). What does all this mean to you? Well, if your soil is very acid, rhododendrons, heathers and many woodland plants will be blissfully happy; almost all plants will grow well in a soil that is slightly acid. In alkaline soil, real lime haters will not thrive, but many plants will. Choose those that can cope with your conditions, rather than trying to change the status quo. Throughout the book I've indicated which plants are suitable for which conditions.

Making a chalky soil more acidic is not really practical in the long term, but acid ground can be ameliorated by the addition of ground limestone or chalk. Only on the vegetable plot is such adjustment made on a regular basis, when lime is applied in autumn several weeks after manuring (if you do the two jobs at the same time undesirable chemical reactions can take place). Brassicas (members of the cabbage family) in particular are best on a soil that is not too acid, and liming also discourages clubroot, that deadly disease that distorts their roots.

The kit you use to test your soil will indicate how much lime is necessary to bring an acid soil into a more hospitable state. If you can't be bothered with all this palaver, stick your nose over the fence and see what grows well in your neighbour's garden.

Using fertilizers

Cast your eye along the fertilizer shelf in a garden centre or hardware shop and you'll be surprised just how many different concoctions there are. Try to seek out those that are organic and which feed beneficial soil bacteria as well as the plants themselves. These are the fertilizers that are most useful:

Dried blood is high in nitrogen, which boosts plant growth. Leafy crops will enjoy it if it is hoed into the surrounding soil in spring and summer. Apply it at the rate of two clenched handfuls to the square metre (square yard) and use it only between March and August when plants are actively growing. It's also useful to keep bacteria fuelled within the compost heap.

Blood, bone and fishmeal is a general fertilizer that supplies the three most important plant foods – nitrogen for leaf and shoot growth; phosphates for root development, and potassium for flower and fruit production. Use it at the rate of one or two handfuls to the square metre (square yard) during the growing season and one week before sowing or planting. It is an organic fertilizer that encourages bacterial activity within the soil. Inorganic fertilizers (such as sulphate of ammonia) supply more concentrated nutrition that the plant can utilize more rapidly, but they make beneficial soil bacteria (which would otherwise break down the stuff) redundant. Use inorganic fertilizers to give crops a rapid boost, and organic fertilizers to improve fertility.

Growmore is an inorganic granular general fertilizer. It is readily available and reasonably priced but I find that blood, bone and fishmeal is more effective and a better tonic for the soil.

Bonemeal is high in phosphates but, to be fair, most of them are held onto so tightly by the soil that few are made available to the plants. Bonemeal is always recommended as a suitable fertilizer to dust around the hole when you're planting trees and shrubs, but in reality the plants probably see little benefit. Use it if it makes you feel better – I don't bother any more!

Rose fertilizer is just the job for getting plants to flower and fruit well, thanks to its high potash and magnesium content. Use it on well-established plants that are coming into flower or fruit – tomatoes, dahlias and other greedy types. Organic rose fertilizers are available.

Tomato fertilizer in liquid form is high in potash and can be diluted and used on *all* flowers and fruits. It is invaluable and quick-acting.

Foliar feeds are useful where growing crops need a quick boost. They are diluted in water and sprayed on to the foliage, preferably on a dull day. The leaves rapidly absorb the nutrients that perk up the plant. The effect is not as long-lasting as when fertilizers are applied to the soil.

Many gardeners are mean to their plants. Don't be: they need regular feeding just as we do. Give everything a dusting of general fertilizer every spring, and again in summer if you can.

WHY IS DIGGING NECESSARY?

A lot of folk are appalled at the thought of digging, but tackled a little at a time it's a grand way of getting a bit of exercise. Once you're into the rhythm of the job, you'll really enjoy seeing the fresh soil appearing in your wake. But until you've passed the pain barrier it's a real slog, so take it slowly and dig for just half an hour a day until you're ready for more.

But before you start, consider why digging is necessary. First of all it relieves compaction of the soil, so allowing plant roots to penetrate the soil more easily. It allows in air, which is as vital to plants as water, even around the roots. It improves surface drainage, allows weeds to be removed and organic enrichment such as muck and compost to be worked in. And dug soil looks good too!

There are those who advocate the 'no-dig' technique, in which the ground is never cultivated. Instead a layer of muck or compost is spread over the surface of the soil where it keeps down weeds, keeps in moisture and is incorporated by the worms. This is a fine system to adopt after an initial digging over if you have unlimited

---

Mulching and watering

A well-nourished soil that has been mulched is less likely to dry out than poor earth that hasn't, and it will grow better plants. If you can possibly afford to mulch your beds and borders, then do so. The job might cost you a few pounds but it will save you both labour and plants.

When to water is a vexed question. Forget all the old wives' tales and remember a few simple rules:

1 Water any newly planted tree, shrub or border plant thoroughly during its first season whenever the soil looks dry on the surface.

2 Water established ornamental plants thoroughly when they show signs of wilting.

3 Don't wait for vegetable or fruit crops to wilt before you water.

4 Don't use a watering can or an open-ended hosepipe to water garden plants. Invest in a sprinkler that can be attached to the hosepipe and leave it running over one patch of earth for at least two hours. That way the plants will be thoroughly soaked. Damping down the soil surface does more harm than good.

---

supplies of organic matter. Once any border or bed has been planted up it works a treat. On previously uncultivated ground and on the vegetable plot I'm not convinced of its usefulness, except in avoiding work. I'm all for short cuts where possible but, for me, digging is essential.

Digging techniques

There are two main methods of digging: single digging and double digging. Cynics assume that double digging is so called because it's twice as tiring as single digging. That's absolutely true, but the term was originally used to indicate that in double digging the soil is cultivated to a depth of two 'spits' or spade blades, while in single digging it's worked to a depth of just one spit.

Now there really is no need to double dig ground unless it is packed hard 30 cm (12 in) down and hasn't been cultivated for donkey's years. Even then I'd get out of double digging it if I possibly could. Only when trees and shrubs are to be established on really hard soil is double digging worthwhile – unless you aim to be a prize parsnip grower, in which case you can double dig your vegetable plot – but not every year, please!

Double digging If you're pining for exercise or genuinely feel that you have to double dig, this is how

Digging techniques

Double digging

1 Dig a trench one spit deep and 60 cm (2 ft) wide at one end of the plot and barrow the soil to the opposite end.

2 Fork over the base of the trench to the full depth of the tines, working in manure or compost.

Fill the last trench in the plot with the soil you removed from the first

3 Dig a second trench behind the first, throwing the soil, inverted, into the first trench. Continue to the end, filling the last trench with soil removed from the first.

Single digging

1 Excavate a trench one spit deep and 45 cm (18 in) wide at one end of the plot to be dug. Barrow the soil to the other end of the plot.

2 Throw plenty of well-rotted compost, manure or other organic material into the base of the trench.

In single digging, the soil is worked to just one spit (spade depth)

To bury short-lived weeds, invert the soil as you throw it forward into the trench in front

3 Dig up the soil immediately behind the trench and throw it forward, inverting it and removing thick-rooted weeds. When the second trench has been created, repeat the operation until the entire plot has been dug.

Cheat's digging

1 Start to dig across one end of the strip to be cultivated, lifting up each spadeful of soil, inverting it and throwing it forward a little so that a slight V-shaped trench is created. Remove any thick-rooted weeds.

2 Spread compost or manure along the sloping side of the soil facing you.

Remove any thick-rooted perennial weeds before throwing organic matter over the soil

3 Turn over another spadeful of soil across the strip and repeat the process. At the end of the plot only a slight depression will be left; this can be filled in when the soil is trampled immediately before planting or sowing. Continue digging to the end of the plot.

to do it: Start by excavating a trench one spit deep and 60 cm (2 ft) wide at one end of the plot to be dug; barrow the excavated soil to the other end.

Now fork over the base of the trench to the full depth of the tines of the fork – that way the soil is cultivated in two spits. Work in some compost or manure to perk up the earth.

Now dig another trench immediately behind the first, throwing the soil, upside down, into the first trench as you do so. This will bury any short-lived weeds such as groundsel and chickweed, but thick-rooted weeds should be pulled out or they will re-emerge later. Proceed like this until the end of the plot is reached. Then you can use the soil that you removed from the first trench to fill the last.

If the plot is quite wide divide it into two sections, down the centre, and take the first trench out at the end of one half only. Then, instead of barrowing the first soil to the other end of the plot, dump it at the same end of the other half. Now dig down one side and back up the other.

Single digging The difference with single digging is that the soil is dug to the depth of only one spit and the well-rotted manure or compost is scattered over the bottom of the trench rather than being forked into a second spit.

Cheat's digging I use this method all the time. It saves the onerous job of barrowing soil around and it allows manure to be spread easily in the upper soil where roots can get at it quickly (see box left).

THE BATTLE AGAINST WEEDS

Although never-ending, weed-control need not be as arduous as many folk assume. The cynic who is convinced that he'll have to spend most of his time in the garden bent double, pulling up nettles and dandelions, probably does just that. The sensible or idle gardener will look for measures that help to prevent the weeds re-emerging once the ground has been cleaned up.

Annual and perennial weeds

When you start to cultivate the soil try to eradicate weeds at the outset. There are two basic kinds: the annuals, which have small root systems but copious amounts of seed; and the perennials, which are often thick-rooted and persistent.

The annuals may not last long as individuals, but the old saying 'One year's seed, seven years' weed' shows that they can be as much of a pain as the longer-lived perennial kinds.

Always try to eradicate annual weeds before they flower. That way they'll have no chance to regenerate. The oldest and most obvious way of weeding is to pull or fork the plants from the soil. It's a practical proposition where ground is being dug or forked over, even though it might be arduous. Where annual weeds are a problem you can use a Dutch hoe. Push it over the soil so that it skims just fractionally below the surface to sever the top half of the plant from the roots. Carried out in dry weather it will leave the weeds to turn crisp on the surface. It's a useful technique on the vegetable plot.

Perennial weeds that are hoed will simply re-emerge from their fat roots, so you'll have to eradicate the underground parts too. Forking or digging them out is the best option if you want to plant up the area immediately and while it's hard work, it's also strangely satisfying when you survey the clean, nicely turned bed.

If you're not in any hurry to use a particular piece of weedy ground, smothering perennial weeds is a good option. A blanket of heavy duty black polythene excludes light and water so the weeds just don't stand a chance. It's an easy way to clear whole patches of uncultivated land, and especially effective for nightmare weeds like marestail (horsetail) and Japanese knotweed. Clear away the top growth then weigh down the sheeting firmly and leave it in place for at least one growing season, allowing two or more for the most pernicious weeds. It's handy in smaller areas too, particularly in the vegetable plot where it cuts out the need for hoeing or hand-weeding altogether.

Landscape fabric is another useful tool in your armoury of weed controls. It's porous, so plants can be easily fed and watered, but it presents an impenetrable barrier for weeds. It's useful in the kitchen garden for raising weed-free crops, and as a weed-suppressant for paths between beds. If you're making a new flower border you can enjoy years of no-weed gardening by

Natural weed controls - pros and cons

Heavy duty black polythene
Pro: Starves/smothers weeds completely. Invaluable for killing off the most troublesome weeds.
Con: Not very glamorous - where feasible disguise with soil or bark chips. Can take two or more growing seasons to kill pernicious perennial weeds.

Landscape fabric
Pro: Very useful in kitchen garden, new beds and borders, and on narrow vegetable garden paths.
Con: Looks a bit workmanlike – disguise with soil or bark chips in high profile areas such as flower borders.

Grassing down
Pro: Attractive solution if it fits in with short term design and long term plan.
Con: Can take several years to control deep-rooted weeds, and very regular mowing is essential.

Ground cover plants
Pro: Looks beautiful.
Con: Won't unfortunately smother out the most troublesome weeds such as bindweed, marestail and Japanese knotweed.

Troublesome perennial weeds

Deep-rooted perennial weeds are very persistent and can be difficult to destroy by manual methods, but barrier mulches will keep them under control.

Bindweed has an extensive root system that is difficult to destroy completely

Couch grass is fairly shallow rooting and can be dug out quite easily

Ground elder rapidly re-establishes itself from any piece of root that is left in the soil

COUCH GRASS

GROUND ELDER

BINDWEED   **MARESTAIL**

Marestail is difficult to eradicate because of its deep roots

Weed control checklist

- Hoe annual weeds regularly to prevent them from setting seed. Best done in dry weather.
- For easier removal of larger annual weeds, roots and all, hand-pull them when the soil is moist.
- Be scrupulous when digging out deep-rooted perennials. Overlooked portions of root can re-sprout.
- Don't overdo the digging. Set yourself a daily target for large uncultivated areas and take regular breaks.
- Anchor the edges of polythene sheeting very firmly, especially in windy areas. Old scaffolding planks are ideal.
- When planting up new borders using landscape fabric, set out the plants and move them around until you're satisfied with the overall effect. Much better than changing your mind half way through and ending up with lots of redundant holes in the fabric.

laying it over the whole bed and planting through it.

Grass is pretty good at smothering out weeds too and grassing down is a much more decorative solution than polythene for uncultivated land, particularly if it's in a spot that's visible from the house. Deep-rooted weeds will struggle under a blanket of turf, and regular mowing will eventually eradicate the most persistent of perennials. Once they have given up the unequal struggle, reclaim the land by simply skimming off the turf.

In ornamental beds and borders, ground-cover plants are invaluable for keeping weeds at bay. Their dense canopy shades them out, and many have tough rootstocks that form an impenetrable barrier. They're extremely decorative too, with many shrubs and roses fitting the bill, together with a superb selection of border plants (see p.136).

Weeding methods for different areas

Flower borders Among cultivated plants the best thing to do is to weed the soil properly during preliminary cultivations with the spade or fork and then, immediately after planting (when the soil is moist), lay a 5-8 cm (2-3 in) thick mulch of moist leaf mould, pulverised bark or other organic matter over the surface. Some of these materials may give rise to a few weed seedlings of their own, but such weeds are easy to pull up compared with heavy infestations on bare soil. Top up the mulch when necessary each spring. A closely planted bed or border will be less likely to support weed growth than one that is sparsely filled. The benefits of ground-cover planting coupled with regular mulching will save you hours of unnecessary hard graft.

When starting a border from scratch you can eliminate weeds altogether by laying landscape fabric. Make cross-wise cuts for the planting holes and tuck the flaps back round the newly installed plants.

Food crops Among certain fruit or vegetable crops (strawberries, for instance) you can lay a surface mulch of black polythene or landscape fabric, pulling the plants through small holes made at the required intervals. These barrier mulches are effective weed suppressers but won't win any prizes in the garden for its good looks.

Boundaries However weed-free your own garden, there's always the possibility of perennial weeds like ground elder and couch grass creeping in from neighbouring land. If it's a persistent problem, it would be well worth sinking an impermeable barrier such as thick polythene, vertically, to a depth of 45 cm (18 in).

Paths and patios When laying new paths and patios, take great care with the grouting so that weeds can't get a toe-hold. In established paving, remove weeds with a sharp knife or hooked patio weeder. This is more easily done when the ground is damp. If the grouting is very old and crumbly, re-grouting may be necessary.

For narrow paths between fruit and vegetable beds, eliminate weeds by laying landscape fabric. A scattering of soil or bark chips will improve the look of the path and help to prolong the life of the fabric by reducing wear and tear from boots and barrows.

If you feel you really must use a weedkiller (herbicide) to clear weeds from a new patch of land, then follow the manufacturer's instructions carefully.

THE NAMING OF PLANTS

I've no space to go into detail on plant names, but as I've used those terrifying Latin ones throughout this book I suppose I'd better make my excuses. They're a real mouthful but, unlike common names, they are standard wherever you might be. In China or Russia you could ask for *Alcea rosea* and get it; but they'd look puzzled if you asked for a hollyhock. Even within Britain, common names vary from county to county and some plants have no common name at all, so, to avoid any confusion, I've described the plants under their botanical names and given their common names alongside. Both are listed in the index.

CHAPTER 2

Plant propagation

Propagating your own plants, whether by seeds (bought or hand-gathered), cuttings or divisions, is surely the most fascinating and rewarding of all gardening activities

Most of us are compelled to propagate plants simply to save money, but the compulsion soon becomes an addiction when we find out how easy it is, and how satisfying, to raise a large number of plants with little effort and expense (putting aside the failures, that is). After centuries of gardening there are still a few plants that readily defy attempts at propagation, or which are extremely difficult to multiply in large numbers. This accounts for the relatively high price of certain trees and shrubs. Fortunately, most of the plant kingdom is more obliging and, provided the right conditions are created, most trees, shrubs, flowers and vegetables will increase happily.

There are two basic methods of increase: sexual reproduction (by seeds) and asexual reproduction (by vegetative means such as cuttings and divisions). Seed is a cheap and easy method for many plants, especially vegetables, and is the only way of increasing many annuals (plants that live for just one year before setting seed and dying). Seed-raised plants are almost always vigorous and disease-free.

Vegetative means of propagation must be used where no seed is set, or where such seed will not produce offspring identical to the parent, which is the case with many plant varieties and hybrids. Always take special care to ensure that plants from which cuttings are taken are healthy and disease-free or the problems will be inherited by the offspring.

GROWING FROM SEEDS

Rather like the lady who thought that beans only came out of tins, some folk seem to think that seeds only come out of packets. Don't forget that good seed can often be collected from many plants in the garden. Collected when fully ripe (the pods or capsules usually split at this stage, so you'll have to beat them to it), and stored in a cool, dry place, the seeds will often germinate well the following spring. Keep them in the fridge in an airtight container with a sachet of silica gel to absorb any moisture.

If you're buying seeds always go to a reputable seedsman. There are plenty of them about so it's not difficult. Nowadays all firms are bound by law to test their seeds and guarantee a high viability rate (percentage of germination). If the seeds don't come up when they've been bought from a reputable supplier, the chances are that either you've stored them in too warm a place or you've not given them the conditions they need. Don't rush to blame the seedsman before you check your own treatment.

F1 hybrid seeds are becoming more popular year by year. The first thing you'll notice about them is their price – they cost a bomb! The reason for this is that the seeds have been specially produced by crossing two selected plants known to produce a seed that yields vigorous and uniform offspring with certain desirable qualities – massive flowers or, in the case of a vegetable, whopping roots or leaves. For the home gardener, F1 hybrid flowers are almost always a good buy. F1 vegetables may not be. They tend to mature with amazing uniformity, providing you with a glut.

Don't save seeds from plants that are F1 hybrids – the characteristics they possess will be distributed unevenly in their offspring and you'll have a varied and probably inferior group of plants on your hands.

Pelleted seeds are simply ordinary seeds encased in a coating of clay, sometimes with a fungicide added to aid germination. They make space sowing easy, so cutting out the need for thinning, but they are pricey and, if the soil dries out in the slightest, they may fail to germinate. I never use them, preferring to pay less for a greater number of plain seeds that are not so finicky.

Germination requirements

All seeds need air, moisture and a suitable temperature to trigger off germination. Some also need light (primulas for instance) and should be sown on the compost surface rather than being given the usual burial. Many seeds need exposure to cold before they will germinate (a lot of hardy plants fall into this category), so autumn sowing is practised and the seeds are left in a cold frame during winter.

Some seeds have such tough coats that they have to be chipped a little to allow water to be absorbed; sweet peas are sometimes reluctant to come up unless you 'nick' them, but I've never found them to be difficult provided the compost is kept sufficiently moist.

Berries are usually 'stratified' before being sown. Spread them in alternate layers with sharp sand in a flowerpot during autumn and stand the container outdoors to be frosted all winter. Turn it out into a frame in spring, sift a little compost over the mixture and wait for germination. Some tricky blighters take several years to come up.

'How deep do I sow?' is a regular question. The answer is almost always to one-and-a-half times the diameter of the seed. Dust-fine seeds need no covering at all; large seeds such as beans and nasturtiums can actually be pushed down into the soil with your fingers. Always sow in moist soil but never in cold, soggy earth where the seeds will rot. Seeds sown late in warm soil will always overtake those put in earlier during unfavourable conditions.

Take out drills for vegetable seeds with a Dutch hoe or a draw hoe. Stand on the garden line to keep it firm while you draw away the soil to create a V-shaped channel.

Sowing in drills

Most vegetables are sown in straight lines in little V-shaped channels known as drills. The best way to create such drills is to fasten a taut garden line across the soil, resting on the surface, and to draw the soil away from the edge of it with a Dutch or draw hoe. Stand on the line to keep it firm. Sow the seeds thinly in the drill – by thinly I mean at least 0.5 cm (¼ in) apart – and then carefully return the soil to the drill with a rake. Label the row with the name and variety of the crop as well as the date of sowing.

Sowing broadcast

In the flower border, hardy annual flower seeds can be sown broadcast in irregularly shaped areas known as drifts. Rake the soil so that tiny furrows are left by the rake, and then scatter the seeds over the surface before raking once more in the opposite direction to cover them up.

Don't underestimate the value of thinning out seedlings; do it as soon as possible to give the chosen plants enough light and air to develop.

Sowing under glass

Under any kind of cover, be it greenhouse, frame or windowsill, seeds must be sown in pots of seed compost, not garden soil. However good your soil, it will not be open or well drained enough for plants in pots. Any proprietary seed compost can be used; it should be lightly firmed within the container before sowing so that it rests about 1 cm (½ in) below the rim to allow for a covering of compost and subsequent watering. Make sure the compost is moist before you sow the seeds.

> **"All seeds need air, moisture and a suitable temperature to trigger off germination."**

Now read the seed packet. Can you provide the right temperature for germination? The majority of plants you sow under protection will need a temperature of around 18-21°C (65-70°F), though one or two may need a little more heat.

Take the seeds out of the packet and place them in the palm of one hand. Tap the edge of this hand with the other so that the seeds are dislodged a few centimetres (inches) above the compost. They will fall and bounce on the surface, so becoming more evenly distributed. Don't sow too thickly. When you think you've sown enough seeds, return the rest to the packet and lightly sieve compost over those you have sown. Use a 3 mm (⅛ in) sieve and stop sieving as soon as the seeds disappear from view. Very fine seeds, like *Lobelia*, *Gloxinia*, *Begonia*, *Petunia* and *Calceolaria*, need not be covered at all except with a sheet of paper followed by a sheet of glass, which is a covering recommended for all seeds. The glass helps to keep the compost moist and the paper cuts down the sun's glare, as well as mopping up condensation.

Label the containers with variety and date and stand them in a warm place – ideally a propagator. These mini-greenhouses can be obtained in all shapes and sizes and at reasonable cost. If you're going in for a bit of propagating, you'll find that the kind that

Tap seeds from your palm so that they are evenly distributed over the compost.

Types of propagators

The cheapest propagator consists of a seed tray covered with a transparent dome that is fitted with small vents. An electrically heated panel can be positioned beneath the tray to provide 'bottom heat'. More elaborate structures can be made at home and fitted with thermostatically controlled solid warming cables. A polythene shroud will maintain humidity.

DOMED PROPAGATOR
WITH BASE HEATING PANEL

POLYTHENE-COVERED PROPAGATOR
WITH CONTROLLED HEATING PANEL

utilizes a plastic seed tray with a transparent dome and a heated base plate will suit you nicely without breaking the bank. Or you can stick to the airing cupboard if you don't mind compost-covered washing.

Check the pots every day and as soon as the first seedling in each container breaks the surface, remove the pot and stand it in a warm, well-lit place. Should the compost dry out, water it with a watering can fitted with a fine rose.

Seeds of hardy plants can be sown in pots of compost which are then stood outdoors in a garden frame. Spring is the usual time to sow, though many seeds are often best sown as soon as they are ripe – in summer or autumn. A cold winter may be just what they need to spur them into growth.

Pricking out

As soon as the seedlings are large enough to handle, they should be transplanted into seed trays where they will have more room to develop. Lever them from the compost in the pot with a pencil or small dibber, keeping as much compost around their roots as possible. Hold each seedling by one of its seed leaves, not its fragile stem, and lower its roots into a hole made

Prick out seedlings from the compost in which they are growing with a small dibber, holding each one by a seed leaf. Lower it into a pencil-hole made in the new compost and firm it in. Water the seedlings carefully but well.

in the compost with the point of the pencil. Firm the compost around the roots so that the seedling stands upright. Space the seedlings about 5 cm (2 in) apart on the square. Water them in when the tray is fully planted up. Grow the seedlings on until they are ready to be hardened off for planting out or potted up into individual containers. Pot plants such as geraniums

(*Pelargonium*) can be pricked out straight into 8 cm (3 in) pots to save time.

INCREASING STOCK BY DIVISION

This is one of the easiest means of propagating plants. Simple division, which is best carried out in autumn or spring where hardy border plants are concerned, involves the digging up and prising apart of established clumps. It sounds cruel but it does most plants the world of good. When you've dug up the clump, chop it into coconut-sized pieces with a spade, discarding the dead central portion (most perennials spread outwards and the old centre gradually dies). Make sure you replant the new plants at the same level as before. Water them well in times of drought. Autumn dividing pays dividends on any well-drained soil for the plants are ready to grow away eagerly come the spring, outstripping spring-divided plants by leaps and bounds. On clay soils, though, they may sit and sulk through the winter.

Irises and other plants that make rhizomes (fat stems at or just below ground level: see p.152) can also be divided. Irises are best split after flowering and fat, healthy rhizomes can be cut into individual portions, each bearing a fan of leaves. Shorten the leaves by half and replant so that the rhizomes sit just beneath the new soil surface.

It is always a good idea to clean up and enrich the soil before replanting your divisions, and it's a good idea to replant in a different spot, too.

Plants that produce suckers (shoots from the roots) can be propagated in autumn or spring by severing the new shoot with a few roots and replanting it where it is wanted. Plants grafted onto a different rootstock will, of course, produce suckers inferior to themselves, and these should be removed and discarded.

Tubers (see p.152) can also be divided, provided that each division has a portion of tuber plus a bud.

Any kind of plantlet, be it a strawberry runner or an offset of a *Sempervivum*, makes propagation easy. The youngster can simply be detached and encouraged to make roots of its own in a pot of compost or a bed of soil before being planted out independently. Alternatively it can be encouraged to form roots while still attached to its parent and then removed and transplanted afterwards.

TAKING CUTTINGS

There are three basic types of cutting: stem, leaf and root. All three types are removed from the parent plant and then encouraged to form either roots or shoots, whichever is lacking.

Stem cuttings

Stem cuttings fall into three categories, depending on the time of year at which they are taken and the consequent hardness of the wood.

Softwood cuttings are taken in spring and early summer and consist of healthy, vigorous shoot tips that are soft and pliable. The finished cutting should be 5-8 cm (2-3 in) long with two or three leaves at the top. The lower leaves should be removed and the basal cut made just below a leaf joint or node. Insert the cuttings to half their depth in a propagator filled with a half and half potting compost/sand mix, or around the edge of 10 cm (4 in) pots of the same medium. Bottom heat is helpful in rooting the cuttings quickly. This can be applied via a heated base plate below the propagator or with special soil-warming cables. Some cuttings, such as Impatiens, can even be rooted in jars of water stood on a windowsill. Only tricky cuttings need have their bases lightly dipped in hormone rooting powder before insertion.

Keep the cuttings shaded from brilliant sunshine – but not in the dark – while they root. Humidity is vital in preventing dehydration, hence the desirability of an enclosed propagator or a polythene bag over the pot. Most softwood cuttings root readily in a temperature of around 18°C (65°F). Growth of the shoots is a good indication of rooting and at this stage the plants should be knocked out of their containers and potted up

Taking hardwood cuttings

1 Hardwood cuttings of plants such as roses and gooseberries should be taken in autumn. Make them 20 cm (8 in) long and trim them above a bud at the top and below a bud at the base. Insert them to two thirds their depth in narrow trenches into which sand has been trickled.

2 Firm the sand around the stems of the cuttings, then replace the soil around them.

3 Tread the soil firmly back around the cuttings to exclude air pockets, and water them thoroughly.

Types of leaf cuttings

LEAF STALK CUTTINGS

Cut healthy leaves plus stalks from the parent plant. Insert the stalks in a pot filled with a sandy compost mixture

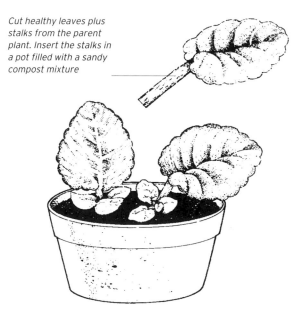

Leaf stalk cuttings of African violets (*Saintpaulia*) can be easily rooted in a mixture of potting compost and sand. Keep the cuttings warm while they root.

individually. Keep them out of bright sunlight for a few days until their roots are established.

Half-ripe cuttings During July and August the shoots of many plants (especially shrubs) begin to harden. At this stage, but while they are still relatively pliable, they are said to be half-ripe or semi-ripe. Cuttings taken at this time should be about 10 cm (4 in) long and prepared and inserted as for softwood cuttings. Half-ripe cuttings of hardy shrubs may also be inserted in a well-drained medium within a cold frame outdoors. Here they can stay until the following spring, when they can be removed and potted up or planted out. Those rooted in a propagator can be potted up and overwintered in a cold frame before being planted out the following year.

Some half-ripe cuttings are found to root better if removed from the parent plant with a heel of older wood. Tear them from the main stem and trim the heel to a length of 1 cm (½ in) before insertion. Many conifers root better with a heel.

Hardwood cuttings need no protection at all and they provide an easy means of increasing many deciduous shrubs, including roses (see box, left). Hardwood

cuttings are taken just as the leaves fall in autumn. Young, healthy shoots of pencil thickness should be selected. Trim them above a bud at the top and below a bud at the base so that they are about 20 cm (8 in) long. Roses can be left with two leaves at the top, should these still be present.

Insert the cuttings to two thirds their depth in narrow slit trenches into which a little coarse sand has been trickled. (The vegetable plot may be the most convenient spot for them.) Firm back the earth with your feet. The cuttings should root and grow during the following spring and summer and may be lifted and transplanted the following autumn.

Leaf cuttings

Some plants can be propagated from leaves without any vestige of stem at all (see box, below). Those of African violets (*Saintpaulia*) and others are removed from the plant, with their leaf stalks intact, and dibbed into a cuttings compost in a propagator. I've even rooted them in jars of water with the leaf blade supported over the water; the stalk is pushed through a piece of transparent clingfilm fastened over the top of the jar.

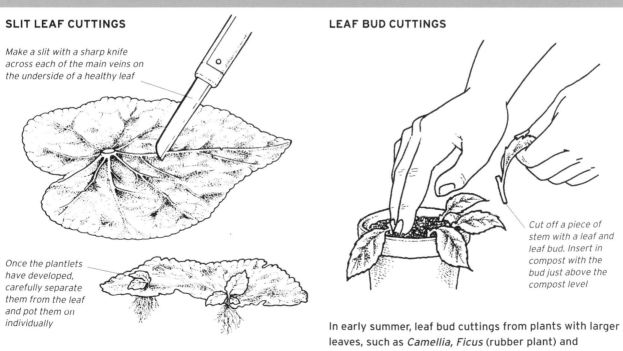

SLIT LEAF CUTTINGS

Make a slit with a sharp knife across each of the main veins on the underside of a healthy leaf

Once the plantlets have developed, carefully separate them from the leaf and pot them on individually

A leaf of *Begonia rex*, laid on the surface of moist compost and slit at the main veins, may produce a young plant at each of the slits.

LEAF BUD CUTTINGS

Cut off a piece of stem with a leaf and leaf bud. Insert in compost with the bud just above the compost level

In early summer, leaf bud cuttings from plants with larger leaves, such as *Camellia, Ficus* (rubber plant) and *Clematis* can be taken. Once the leaf stem has rooted, a tiny shoot will grow from the base. Leave the original leaf on until it begins to wither.

Leaves of *Begonia rex* can be cut up into postage-stamp-sized pieces and inserted into the rooting medium like gravestones; provided they are the right way up, they will root and send up youngsters from their bases. The entire leaf of the plant may be laid on the surface of the compost, slit at the main veins and kept moist. With luck plantlets will arise at the cuts.

Leaf bud cuttings include a small portion of stem and a bud. *Camellia*, *Ficus* (rubber plant) and even *Clematis* can be propagated from them. Early summer is generally the best time for this type of propagation.

Root cuttings

These are best taken during the plant's dormant season. Lift the plant to be propagated, wash its roots free of soil and then cut suitable roots (between knitting needle and pencil thickness) into 5 cm (2 in)

Lift the plant to be propagated, wash its roots, then cut suitable roots into 5 cm (2 in) sections

Be careful to plant the cuttings the right way up

Some plants can be propagated from sections of root that are removed and inserted in pots of compost.

long sections. To make sure that the roots are the right way up, make a flat cut at the top (the end which was nearer the parent) and a slanting cut at the base. Insert the cuttings in pots of seed compost, planting them vertically with the aid of a dibber. The top of the cutting should be level with the surface of the compost. Scatter a little sharp sand over the surface, label the pot and stand it in a garden frame or, if the plant is tender, in a propagator. If the compost is moist and the pot is kept lightly shaded, no water should be given until more roots are produced, probably after the shoots appear in early spring.

Not all plants can be propagated by root cuttings; I have indicated in the A-Z sections those that are.

LAYERING

Ordinary stems of garden plants can sometimes be encouraged to form roots if they are bent down and partly buried in the soil. The operation is usually carried out in early spring.

Find a conveniently long and supple stem. Trim off any leaves that occur between 15-38 cm (6-15 in) below the shoot tip so that a healthy cluster is left at the end of the shoot, with a bare length of stem behind. Bend the stem to the soil and make a slight wound in the bark at the point of contact, slitting the stem with a knife to make a tongue. Work compost and sand into the soil immediately below the cut, scoop out a 5-8 cm (2-3 in) hole and lay the cut portion in position. Pin it down with a piece of wire if necessary. Replace the soil and do not let it dry out.

Cut the new plant from its parent in the autumn and

With the stem bent to the soil, make a slight wound in the bark at the point of contact. Peg the stem down

Plants with suitably low-growing stems can often be propagated by layering. Make an incision in the shoot then bend it down and bury it in the soil, holding it firm with a peg. Sever the stem when the new plant is well rooted but leave for a few weeks before transplanting it.

Air layering

1 Make an upward cut in the stem and fill it with moist sphagnum moss.

Make an incision no more than 10 cm (4 in) below a healthy leaf

2 Wrap polythene around the cut area, tying the covering firmly at the bottom.

Push moistened sphagnum moss into the slit in the stem

Wrap the area around the slit in polythene, stuffed with moistened moss

3 Fill the polythene tube with more moist moss and seal the top. Keep the moss constantly moist. When roots are established the top part of the plant can be removed and potted up.

leave it for a few weeks before attempting to lift and transplant it. Alternatively wait until spring.

Tip layering can be carried out with plants such as the blackberry. Here the shoot is bent down to the ground and the top 10 cm (4 in) is completely buried. Once a new plant arises it can be transplanted.

Many tall house plants and shrubs can be air layered. At a suitable point in the stem - usually about 45 cm (18 in) from the shoot tip and a few centimetres (inches) below a healthy leaf - an upward incision is made, as for ordinary or simple layering. Sphagnum moss (available from florists) is moistened and pushed into the incision then padded around it. Polythene is bandaged around the moss and fastened top and bottom with sticky tape. Keep the moss moist and be patient. Roots are likely to be slow in coming, though the higher the temperature the more quickly they will

emerge. In most cases you may have to wait a year before the top half of the plant can be severed from the bottom and potted up on its own. Cherish it for a few months until it becomes established. The bottom part should grow away and become pleasingly bushy.

Plants such as heathers can be propagated by 'dropping'. Dig them up in spring and plant them again more deeply so that only the shoot tips can be seen. In autumn dig up the plants and cut off the shoot tips, which will have formed roots. Replant your new heathers in peat-enriched soil.

BULBS AND CORMS

Most bulbs and corms reproduce themselves naturally, though their rates of multiplication vary. I have no room here to delve deeply into the technicalities of 'scooping' and 'scoring' bulbs, which some aficionados may consider. It's a painfully slow job for use on bulbs that are otherwise hard to propagate in large numbers.

Where most gardeners can cash in is by growing on the smaller bulblets or cormlets produced around the base of larger flowering bulbs. A piece of good soil in full sun should be selected and, at the appropriate planting time, the babies should be set in the soil to twice their depth and allowed to grow on for another year or more until they reach flowering size.

Bulbils - the tiny bulbs produced on the stems of some lilies and one or two

Bulbils that form up the stems of certain lilies can be removed and grown on to flowering-sized bulbs.

other bulbs - can be similarly grown on in pots of sandy compost placed in a garden frame. Remove the bulbils from the plants as soon as they are ripe and press them into the surface of the pot of prepared compost, sifting a little sharp sand over them. Stand them in a garden frame for about a year and then transfer them to their flowering positions in the garden where they may need to grow on for at least another year. It's a job for the patient gardener, but a rewarding one. If your plants don't produce bulbils you may be able to induce them to do so by nipping out the flower buds before they open. Are you prepared to make the sacrifice?

3 The toolshed

Every job in the garden is made easier by having the right tools. If you choose them carefully and look after them well, they will last a lifetime

You might think that the best place to find a good set of garden tools is the garden centre or the local hardware shop, and sure enough that's where you'll come face to face with a showcase that rivals the Blackpool illuminations for brilliance. But how do you tell which tools are the best buy, and how do you know which are just expensive gimmicks that will end up gathering dust after their first disastrous try-out?

I reckon you'd do far better delaying a visit to the shop and going first to the garage or toolshed of an aged member of the family whose gardening days are numbered. There you might find a set of basic tools that have not only stood the test of time but which have been run in for you. Bright new spades and forks are all very well but they don't half take some breaking in. Until the blades and prongs have been honed to perfection by the soil, they are often difficult and exhausting to work with.

Should your aged relative decide that the tools cannot be parted with, cast your eye round local auction sales or secondhand shops for spades, forks, rakes and hoes that are well worn. Just make sure that in spite of their age the implements are still strong and that the handles have not cracked or become loose in their sockets. Years of use should have polished the shafts to a silken smoothness, but any splinters can easily be rubbed off with sandpaper. When all attempts at finding secondhand tools fail, then you can visit the local emporium – but beware of being bamboozled into buying something you don't need.

Here's my list of essentials that most gardeners can't do without. Buy them one at a time as you need them.

TOOLS FOR WORKING THE SOIL

Spade

However lazy you are, you'll have to dig sooner or later, even if you're only digging a hole for a tree or shrub. For this the spade is essential, but if your soil is really stony, a fork is much easier to use for general digging over. The spade has the advantage of being able to skim off surface weed growth before digging starts, and you can also use it for mixing composts and for edging the lawn if, like me, you're too mean to buy one of those special half-moon edging tools.

There are three sizes of spade: the standard digging spade has a blade measuring 29 x 19 cm (11½ x 7½ in); the medium spade 25 x 16.5 cm (10 x 6½ in); and the border spade 23 x 14 cm (9 x 5½ in). Pick the one that's most comfortable to use: even if you're in a shop, hold it as if you were about to dig, and go through the motions to see if it's well balanced and feels comfortable. The shaft should be smooth and splinter-free, the socket should be gently cranked to make for better leverage and any rivets should have smooth heads that do not chafe your hands. The handle at the top may be T, D, or YD-shaped (see p.30). Again, choose whichever feels the most comfortable, but be warned that the T shape can be more blister-making if you have tender skin. If your soil is very heavy, look for a spade with flattened treads on the upper edges of the blade – they'll be easier on your feet. You'd also be well advised to go for a medium-sized spade on very heavy soil, just to guard against strained muscles.

Most spade shafts are wooden, but some are made from tubular steel or alloy coated with polypropylene. The latter are likely to be more expensive. Nearly all spades and forks now have plastic handles at the top and, in spite of their appearance, they are usually comfortable and long lasting.

Another factor affecting the spade you choose is the size of your pocket. The most expensive tools are always made from stainless steel, but this is not essential and it can be rather heavy to work with. A good, well-balanced spade, which doesn't feel 'numb' or clumsy, will probably outlast you, so use your common sense when buying and come away with a well-made yet reasonably priced implement.

Fork

For digging stony or heavy soil, the fork is a better bet than the spade; for pricking over cultivated soil in beds and borders, it is essential. Use it, too, for moving compost and manure and for spiking the surface of the lawn in spring and autumn. When soil has been rough-dug, use the back of the fork rather like a carpet beater to smash up the clods. This action will produce a fine-textured surface, or tilth, without bringing stones to the surface – always a problem if you use a rake for the job.

As to construction, the same general rules apply as for the spade, but two sizes are widely available: the digging fork has a head 30 x 19 cm (12 x 7½ in) and the border fork measures 23 x 14 cm (9 x 5½ in). Both have prongs or tines that are square in cross-section. The potato fork has flattened prongs, supposedly to prevent damage to your spuds when they're being lifted, but I still manage to spear a few of mine whichever fork I use. Again, pick a fork that feels comfortable and not too heavy in your hands.

Rake

I reckon that the rake is the most over-used tool in the garden. True enough, it's vital for levelling soil before seed sowing, and it's helpful in clearing up leaves and debris, but it can produce unwanted results if it is used to break down the soil to a fine texture. It brings every available stone to the surface and causes the soil to cake in the first shower of rain. Use the back of the fork for breaking down the soil, and use the rake sparingly in long, sweeping motions to level the surface.

Your average rake has a handle about 1.5 m (5 ft) long and a 30 cm (12 in) wide head, equipped with 5 cm (2 in) teeth. Make sure the handle is smooth and splinter-free if it is wooden, and that the head is securely attached. Rakes with plastic-coated alloy handles are easiest to use, for they are light and less likely to dig up stones. They are also more expensive.

The wire-toothed spring-tined rake is the best tool for clearing up leaves and lawn mowings and for ripping the thatch, or dead grass, from lawns. It's not too expensive to buy and if you've a lot of grass (or leaves in autumn) I'd invest in one. Don't fall for the bamboo-toothed kind: this will hardly last for a season if you have powerful biceps.

> "There's nothing nicer than standing behind a sharp Dutch hoe as it smoothly chops through weeds in the flower border."

Hoe

You can get by with just one hoe - the Dutch hoe. This is the type that has a long handle and a head shaped like a horseshoe, with a band of metal across the open end. There's nothing nicer than standing behind a sharp Dutch hoe as it smoothly chops through weeds in the flower border or between vegetable rows. Used properly (and kept sharp with a file) it makes light work of weed control - the secret is to use it regularly every week or so and to let it skim over the surface of the soil. Avoid holding it at an angle so that it digs deeply. That way it's not half as effective at separating the weeds from their roots and they'll probably perk up after the next shower of rain.

When you use the Dutch hoe to clear away weeds you'll be moving backwards so that the soil you've just

Tools and equipment for garden care

What you need will depend on the size of your garden and what you plan to do in it. Before buying any tool or piece of equipment hold it and go through the motions of using it, to make sure that it is the right size and weight for you. Often well-honed secondhand tools are the best buy.

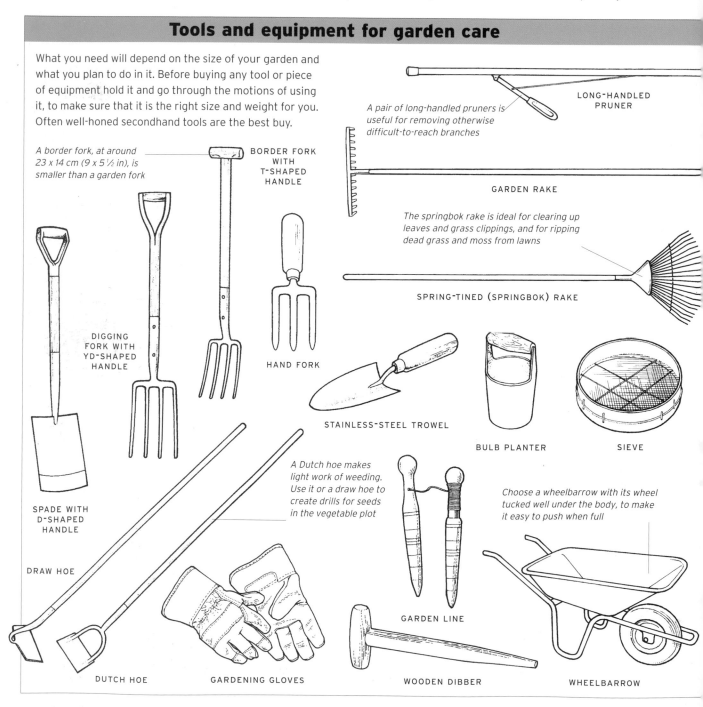

A pair of long-handled pruners is useful for removing otherwise difficult-to-reach branches

LONG-HANDLED PRUNER

GARDEN RAKE

The springbok rake is ideal for clearing up leaves and grass clippings, and for ripping dead grass and moss from lawns

SPRING-TINED (SPRINGBOK) RAKE

A border fork, at around 23 x 14 cm (9 x 5 ½ in), is smaller than a garden fork

BORDER FORK WITH T-SHAPED HANDLE

DIGGING FORK WITH YD-SHAPED HANDLE

HAND FORK

STAINLESS-STEEL TROWEL

BULB PLANTER

SIEVE

SPADE WITH D-SHAPED HANDLE

A Dutch hoe makes light work of weeding. Use it or a draw hoe to create drills for seeds in the vegetable plot

Choose a wheelbarrow with its wheel tucked well under the body, to make it easy to push when full

DRAW HOE

DUTCH HOE

GARDENING GLOVES

GARDEN LINE

WOODEN DIBBER

WHEELBARROW

worked on is left untrampled, but with the draw hoe (a flat-bladed hoe whose blade is at right angles to the shaft) you'll have to walk over the ground you've just scraped. If you're a keen potato and celery grower you'll find the draw hoe useful for earthing up.

Both hoes can be used for drawing drills (those little channels that are taken out against a taut garden line) for seeds. As with other long-handled tools, a smooth shaft and a secure head are the things to look for, plus a feeling of balance in the implement as a whole.

Although it's not strictly a hoe, I'll include the hand cultivator here because it's useful for perking up the soil between all manner of plants. Its head is claw-shaped, usually with three spikes, and it is pulled through the soil with jerky motions to break up the surface crust. Choose a small, lightweight version.

A pruning saw has a short blade, making it easy to use in awkward and confined situations

PRUNING SAW

GARDEN KNIFE

ANVIL SECATEURS

LIGHTWEIGHT GARDEN SHEARS

HOSEPIPE AND REEL

WATERING CAN

An oscillating sprinkler moves back and forth to soak a square or rectangular area, and can be adjusted to cover only half the area if necessary

OSCILLATING SPRINKLER

ROTARY SPRINKLER

The cheapest cylinder mower has side wheels and a rear grassbox; more expensive models have grass boxes on the front, large rear rollers and more blades to produce a finer cut

CYLINDER MOWER WITH REAR GRASSBOX

HOVER MOWER

A nylon cord trimmer is useful for cutting grass in awkward areas, such as around trees. It will also cut through quite thick, rough grass

PETROL-DRIVEN ROTARY MOWER

NYLON CORD TRIMMER

LONG-HANDLED EDGING SHEARS

HALF-MOON EDGING IRON

Trowel

There are some very poor trowels on the market that bend as soon as you show them a tough bit of ground. Play safe - lash out and buy a stainless-steel trowel; it's the only stainless-steel tool I possess, but I wouldn't be without it. Make sure the handle is smooth and that it fits your hand well and you'll not have to worry a jot about the blade - it will stay clean and sturdy whatever your soil. Short-handled trowels are much easier to use than the long-handled versions, which tend to wobble around. You'll need a trowel for planting everything from bedding plants to young vegetables, and it's a useful weeder in confined spaces.

Rod and line

Not a quick dissertation on fishing, but a note on two pieces of equipment that can be made at home. I do all my planting, both in the flower garden and on the vegetable plot, by eye, but if you don't know what 15 cm (6 in) or 30 cm (12 in) looks like, make yourself a measuring rod from a piece of 5 x 2.5 cm (2 x 1 in) timber marked with shallow saw-cuts at the appropriate distances - a little notch every 15 cm (6 in) and a larger one every 30 cm (12 in).

Two metal spikes (or lengths of broom handle) linked with 10 metres (11 yards) of stout nylon or hemp twine is just what you need to mark the position of drills being drawn on the vegetable plot and for cutting straight edges on the lawn. The line should always be kept as taut as possible when it's being used, and it should rest on the ground to prevent it from moving too much. Keep the line free of knots, which will throw the drill you are drawing with your hoe off course, and wrap it up after use to prevent it from being tangled by children or animals.

Dibber

This is perhaps the most traditional tool in the ancient gardener's armoury, but it's still valuable today. For transplanting or pricking out seedlings into trays, there's no finer dibber than a pencil. For transplanting cabbages and the like on the vegetable plot, an old spade or fork handle is what is needed: if you haven't broken a spade handle in years, go out and buy a new handle to use as a dibber.

With both kinds of dibber, the method of using the tool is the same: wiggle it around in the soil to make a hole; lower the roots into place, and push back the soil with the point of the dibber, firming it as you do so.

An old spade handle makes a handy dibber. Push it in and wiggle it around to make a hole; lower in the seedling, then use the dibber to firm back the soil.

Powered cultivator

The really pricey item in this section, the rotavator, is thought of by many gardeners as the only way of cultivating soil. Certainly it's quick and, even though it may pull your arms out of their sockets occasionally, it's easy to use. But it won't rid your ground of weeds and it doesn't work in organic matter very efficiently, so don't think that it replaces the spade completely. Used too regularly at the same depth it will cause a 'pan', or hard, impenetrable layer in the subsoil, so it is best used where its advantages outweigh its disadvantages. Use it for turning over the vegetable plot in winter or for cultivating ground that has been treated with a herbicide to kill off weeds.

It's seldom worth buying a rotavator unless you plan to use it at least once a week - hire it instead and let somebody else worry about the maintenance and storage. If you prepare all the patches of land you want cultivated in advance, you'll be able to romp away with the machine on the day it arrives.

All rotavated land becomes well aerated but rather fluffy so trample it well before you sow or plant to rid it of large air pockets.

TOOLS FOR CUTTING AND PRUNING

Secateurs

A good pair of pruning shears will help you with all cutting operations from flower gathering and deadheading to snipping out dead stems up to finger thickness. Don't try to cut stems fatter than this or you'll strain the secateurs and render them useless. There are several different designs, but the two basic kinds are those with a scissor action and those with what is described as an anvil mechanism. The first type cuts with a slicing motion and the second with a sharp blade that comes down against a flat metal surface. Both are reliable but the anvil type, in particular, must be kept razor-sharp if stems are not to be crushed and disease admitted. I've used a pair of Rolcut anvil secateurs for years and have found them very durable – sharpening is simple with either emery paper or a whetstone. Some secateurs must be returned to the manufacturer for sharpening, and those that look very glossy and are chrome-plated are best avoided – they can't keep an edge for half an hour.

By far the best secateurs (if you can afford them) are the type manufactured by Felco; they are superbly made and guaranteed for life – not a bad recommendation! Avoid at all costs those very cheap secateurs that look as if they are made of cast iron. They cut very badly, if at all, and are extremely uncomfortable to hold, trapping your fingers more times than not.

Pruners and lopers

Stems thicker than your finger are best cut with loppers – those long-handled pruners that have tougher blades than secateurs and which can produce more torque. If you have a garden full of shrubs and roses, a pair of loppers is a must.

With all pruning shears remember to cut back to a point immediately above a bud or a leaf to prevent die-back.

Knife

When I first went to work I was told by the foreman that my pocket should always contain a sharp knife, a piece of string and sixpence. The knife was for taking cuttings, the string was to hold my trousers up when all else failed, and the sixpence was for the foreman

A garden shed doesn't have to be an eyesore. This yellow-painted shed has a reclaimed stained glass window, and *Clematis montana* var. *rubens* clambering up the side.

himself! The knife I always had, but the other two were often missing.

Buy a good knife and it will last for ages; I still use the one I was given on my first day at work, and even then it wasn't new – the propagator decided he'd purloin the one sent for me and I could have his old one. I found I'd got the better of the deal for his old knife was nicely sharpened and well run in. Those sold as budding or grafting knives are good for general-purpose work and not too heavy. Do make sure you buy a knife that's specifically made for garden use, but not one of those with a blade you can see your face in – it will be the very devil to keep sharp. A good-tempered steel blade is what you should look for in a gardening knife, not a stainless-steel blade that's more at home on the dinner table. Always keep your knife sharp on a whetstone and keep it in your pocket.

Shears

A pair of general-purpose garden shears is always handy, whether it's for hedge clipping or for slicing off those tufts of grass that refuse to give in to the lawn mower. Wooden, polypropylene or tubular steel handles can all be comfortable, but check that your wrists are not jarred by the snipping action – rubber buffers between the blades are a help here. Go for carbon-steel blades and find a pair of shears that has a notch at the base of each blade to allow individual thicker stems to be cut.

In the interests of saving labour, I try to avoid creating bare edges to lawns, but if your garden is full of them, you'll find edging shears very useful. They have long handles, fitted with blades set at right angles, and they save you bending down to snip off overhanging grass. When you're buying a pair, the same considerations apply as for ordinary shears. When you're using them, try to get into the habit of holding the left hand still and moving just the right hand, which controls the upper blade. That way you'll achieve a more even cut, faster and with less exertion – not that this is the most exhausting job in the garden! (See p.82 for how to use electric trimmers.)

Rub the blades of your shears with emery paper after use; this will clear them of dried sap and keep them cutting cleanly.

WATERING EQUIPMENT

Watering cans

After years of using galvanized watering cans, most gardeners have switched to plastic. True, the plastic cans cannot be repaired easily, but they are much cheaper and lighter than their metal counterparts and more economical even if thrown away as soon as leaks develop. Long-spouted cans are always easiest to use, and a 10 litre (2 gallon) capacity can is best for general watering, though I'd plump for a 5 litre (1 gallon) can in the greenhouse for its ease of manoeuvrability. The sprinkler heads on the end of the spout are known as roses and brass ones are by far the best.

Use the can for watering anything, and fix the rose to the spout when watering in newly planted seedlings or small plants. A jet of water can flatten them or even wash them away but a gentle sprinkle gets them off to

the best possible start, tucking the soil around the roots with a minimum of disturbance.

Hosepipe

When you tire of using a can it's time you invested in a hosepipe. Only you will know how long a hose you need, but let me persuade you to buy one that's reinforced with nylon thread; it will last far longer than a plain plastic one even though it costs more at the outset. It will also be less likely to kink. Always coil up the hose when you've finished with it and store it out of direct sunlight. If it's left tangled, it will drive you batty every time you come to use it, and where kinks are formed the hose may eventually rupture.

Garden sprinkler

In the interests of spending more time in your deckchair and less time holding on to a hosepipe or watering can, invest in a garden sprinkler, which will do the watering while you stare at it. There are two types – the rotating sprinkler, which soaks a circle of ground, and the oscillating type, which moves back and forth to soak a square or rectangle. As most gardens are square or rectangular, rather than circular, the oscillating sprinkler is more useful (its back and forth motion is also quite soporific if you're trying to doze). Added to this, the oscillating type can usually be adjusted to cover only half the rectangle or square.

Both types of sprinkler apply water more effectively than any hosepipe because they create a fine rain that penetrates the soil very efficiently, getting the moisture to the plant's roots rather than caking the surface of the earth.

Some gardeners are frightened of watering plants in the garden, believing the old wives' tale that if you do the roots come up to the surface. This is rubbish. They will only come to the surface if you constantly keep the surface moist and allow the lower part of the soil to dry out. Give the ground a thorough soak for two hours with a sprinkler when necessary and you'll do the plants nothing but good. Plants hate drought; it stops them from growing, reduces their flowering and fruiting capabilities and may even kill them. So if it hasn't rained for a week or more in summer, and your soil is dry 5 cm (2 in) down when you scoop out a hole with a trowel, turn on the sprinkler. Your plants will show their appreciation while those of your superstitious friends peg out.

On a practical note, remember that in dry summers hosepipe-bans may be implemented in some areas.

Hand sprayer

Whether it's for perking up your house plants with a drop of fresh water, or for boosting them with a foliar feed, a small trigger-action hand sprayer is a useful bit of equipment. A 0.5 litre or 1 litre capacity sprayer (roughly 1 or 2 pints) is sufficient for most gardens, but if you have rolling acres and plenty of fruits, vegetables and flowering plants that would enjoy a foliar feed, a larger pump-up 5 litre (1 gallon) version may be more suited to your needs. For ease of use, choose a model with a carrying strap and long-reach lance. Telescopic lances are available too and are very useful for foliar feeding taller trees and shrubs without having to resort to a step ladder. Whichever size you use, wash it out thoroughly after use.

LAWN-CARE TOOLS

Lawn mower

Choose a mower that you find easy to work with and which cuts your grass adequately for your needs. Cylinder mowers give the finest results (the more blades there are in the cylinder the neater the finish) and are essential if you're out to create that bowling green lawn; in this case you can cut as low as 1 cm (½ in) or even 5 mm (¼ in) if you irrigate it regularly and only walk on it occasionally.

Rotary mowers are fine for most hard-wearing lawns, though it's a good idea to find a machine that is fitted with a grassbox. The rotary types won't give you the stripes you get from cylinder mowers, but they can cope with rougher, longer grass. Electric and petrol-driven versions are available.

Hover mowers are useful where the ground undulates too sharply for a wheeled mower and on banks where they can be swung, pendulum fashion, to cut quite long grass.

Be guided by information sheets and salesmen when you're buying a mower, but try, whenever possible, to

Electrical safety outdoors

- Make sure that all electrically powered equipment is fitted with a residual current device (RCD), which cuts off the supply as soon as a fault is detected.
- Avoid trailing leads, which may be tripped over or severed by moving blades.
- Never use electric tools when it is wet outside.
- Always disconnect the power supply before servicing powered equipment.
- Wear thick rubber-soled footwear when using electric garden tools.

arrange for a demonstration of one or two machines. The mower is the one piece of equipment I would advise you to buy new, and you might as well know what you're in for before you part with your hard-earned cash. Pick one that's comfortable to use, looks sturdily made, and has as wide a cut as possible to lessen the time you need to spend cutting the grass.

When your lawn has had its last mow of the season, clean the mower and rub it down with an oily rag before you store it in a dry shed or garage. Winter is the time to have it repaired – not spring when every gardener is beating on the workshop door begging for attention.

Electric strimmer

If you've plenty of trees set in grass, a nylon cord strimmer might be useful. This nifty little machine will cut off quite thick and rough grass right against the trunks with its whirling nylon thread.

WHEELBARROW

Not always essential in a small garden, the wheelbarrow is nevertheless a must where soil, leaves, lawn mowings and rubbish have to be carted any distance. There are all sorts of barrows, made of all sorts of materials, but the vital thing is that yours should be easy to push when full. Look for one that has its wheel tucked well under the body so that the weight is carried by the wheel and not by you. Ball-shaped wheels will travel over soft ground more easily than narrower types, but plastic bodies and wheels will not be as durable as those of steel, even though they have the advantage of being lightweight.

Buy a barrow that's large enough for your needs but small enough to go through your gate, and always store it under cover or tipped up so that water does not collect.

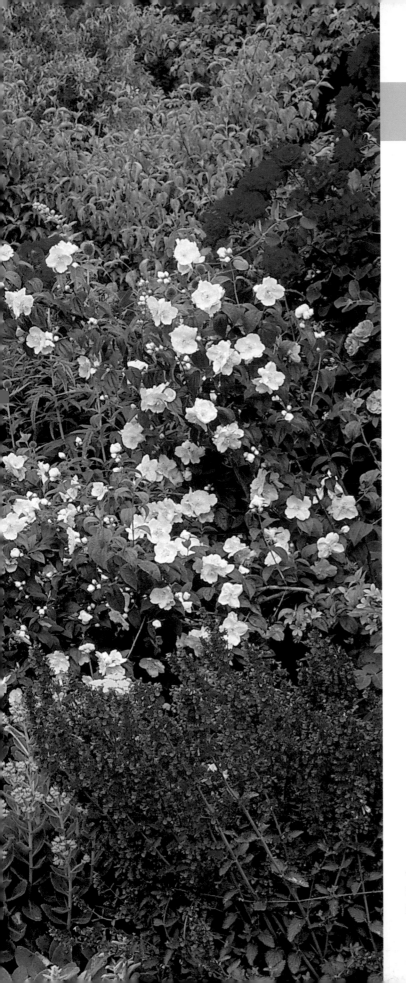

part II

THE PLANTS

Plants are what a garden is all about and this section will help you make your selections from the vast range that is available

This herbaceous border with its bold drifts of colour, including the purple spikes of *Nepeta sibirica* 'Souvenir d'André Chaudron', epitomizes the summer garden.

CHAPTER **4 Trees**

Carefully chosen trees create a natural framework in your garden, providing focal points to draw the eye, as well as all-year-round colour, form and fragrance

Why is it that many folk with small gardens are terrified of trees? I'll tell you why. It's because they've previously been in gardens where badly chosen trees have dominated the scene: casting shade over most of the plot, moving foundations with their roots, dripping water and leaves everywhere in autumn and threatening to fall onto the house in the first gale of winter. If only the right tree had been planted in the first place the story would be different, and the little job of leaf sweeping in autumn would be a modest price to pay for colour and form during the rest of the year.

So, if you're faced with a treeless plot, let me cajole you into planting a tree that will not foster your neurosis. You own the air space right up to the sky, and there really is no need to worry when the tree rises beyond head height. Provided it's one of the kinds I've recommended in the A–Z section at the end of this chapter, it will not endanger life and limb when planted in the right place.

There's much confusion between trees and shrubs, and some shrubs are often referred to as trees simply because they grow quite tall. But, strictly speaking, a tree is a plant that can reach a height of 5–6 m (15–20 ft) on a single woody stem. If your favourite tree is missing from my selection, take a look at Chapter 5 Shrubs to see if it belongs there instead.

The propagation methods used for increasing trees are exactly the same as for increasing shrubs. Details of the techniques involved are given in Chapter 2 Plant propagation.

HOW TO USE TREES

In a small garden there's only one way to use a tree, and that is as a single eye-catching specimen around which the rest of the garden revolves. Such a tree takes a lot of choosing: it should be of interest for as much of the year as possible; its shape should be desirable; it should not outgrow its situation; and it should be able to tolerate your garden conditions.

If you can fit in several trees, use them to carry the eye around the garden and to lift your gaze from flatter plantings below, and do try to have at least one tree under which you can sit.

In larger gardens, trees can be used as focal points, windbreaks and screens (on smaller plots their place will have to be taken by hedges, shrubs and fences) and as backdrops to plantings of shrubs and border plants.

WHAT TO LOOK FOR IN A TREE

When it comes to choosing a particular tree for a particular spot, there are quite a number of considerations to bear in mind.

Final size Uppermost in your mind should be the ultimate height and spread of the tree. Work out how much space you have to spare and select a tree that will fit the bill with a few feet to spare. Do this and you won't have to worry about pruning in the future.

Shape and habit Consider the shape and 'habit' of the tree and whether or not it will look right in your chosen spot. Do you want an upright columnar tree, a weeping tree, a round-headed tree, or one with branches that spread horizontally?

There are many varieties of *Prunus:* some are chosen for their flowers, some for their foliage and some, like *P. serrula* (Tibetan cherry), for their shining coppery bark.

Special features If you're planting just one tree, tick off its attributes and make sure that it offers as many features as possible. The ideal tree will have attractive foliage, colourful flowers followed by bright fruits, and bark that is good to look at in winter. All right, so your choice may not have all these characteristics but, unless it is exceptional in another area, always plump for a tree that offers at least two seasons of interest.

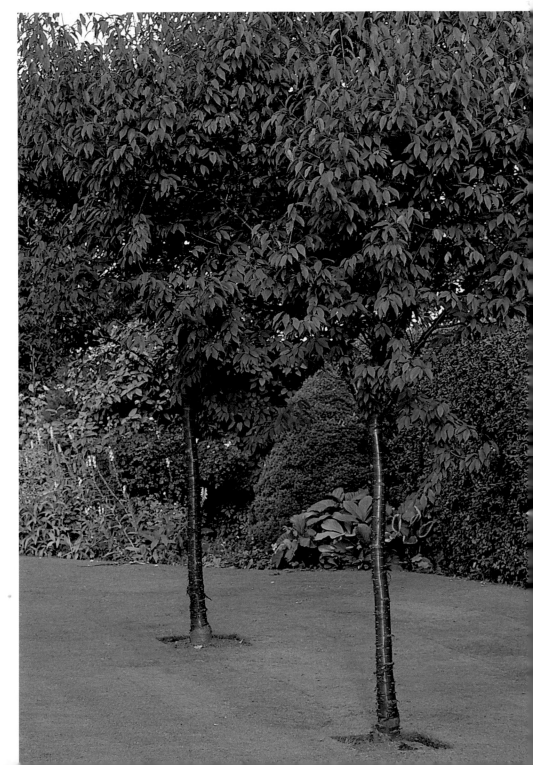

Local conditions Will the tree be happy in your soil and in the spot you've chosen for it? Check with the nurseryman and cast an eye round local gardens to get some idea of what grows well in your locality. If yours is an area of biting winds, it's no good choosing a tree with tender foliage that will be ripped to shreds in the first strong breeze. If your soil is chalky, don't plant a lime-hater.

Be adventurous Even though it's a good idea to be guided by what succeeds in your area, try to plant something a little out of the ordinary: not necessarily a tree that is difficult to grow, but one that doesn't crop up on every street corner. If you've room for only one tree, it seems a shame to plant a laburnum or a flowering cherry both of which can usually be seen in greater glory in a public park.

> "Try to plant something a little out of the ordinary... one that doesn't crop up on every street corner."

Choose a youngster When you're choosing your tree at the nursery – and you should always be able to pick the particular plant you want – go for one that has a strong central shoot or 'leader'; this will ensure that the tree will make a shapely specimen when it starts to grow away; and go for a youngster.

Not only are young trees a darned sight cheaper to purchase than their older relations, but they always establish themselves far more easily and quickly than tall, old ones; they don't need staking and their roots receive little check during transplanting. Sometimes you'll have to settle for an older plant of greater stature. You might think you've got a better deal at the outset, but during its first year the mighty specimen will grow slowly and can often be overtaken by a youngster, which may well develop both a better shape and a better root system.

WHEN TO PLANT

Trees growing in containers can be planted at any time of year provided the soil is in a workable condition. Don't plant them when the ground is so wet that it sticks to your wellies, when it is frosted hard, or when it is dust-dry in the heart of summer. Container-grown trees will be quite happy to wait until soil conditions are right.

Planting bare-root trees

Trees lifted from rows in the nursery are sold as 'bare-root' plants, because precious little soil is left clinging to their roots. The planting season for deciduous bare-root trees (those that lose their leaves in winter) is in the dormant season from November to March.

Planting balled trees

Evergreens are usually sold with their roots and surrounding soil wrapped in a piece of hessian. They are described as being 'balled' and are best planted in April and May when they can grow away actively, rather than in winter when they will sit sulkily in wet soil and a drying wind.

PLANTING METHODS

With the right tree selected for the right spot you can think about planting. But remember the general rules: the site should not be overshadowed; there should be plenty of room for growth; shelter should be provided from strong winds (in the early stages of growth); and the tree should be at least 4.5 m (15 ft) from any building. No tree should be planted on waterlogged soil, though *Salix, Metasequoia* and *Alnus* are all tolerant of poor drainage if you're stuck with a bog.

Planting after delivery

You can usually arrange a convenient delivery date with the nurseryman who (if he's worth his salt) will ship the plants to you in good condition. Any bare roots should have been wrapped in damp hessian or straw and polythene, and the branches should be tied together to prevent them from becoming damaged. Remove the ties and any straw from the branches, but leave the wrapping in place around the roots until you are ready to plant, if this can be accomplished within a day or two (if not, see Delayed Planting, below). Stand the trees in an unheated garage or shed.

Delayed planting

If the weather turns nasty and you can't plant for a few days, heel in the trees on a spare patch of ground. All this involves is digging out a hole, freeing the roots of any wrappings and packings and putting them into the hole. Replace the soil, and the roots will be kept moist until you are ready to plant. Don't position the trees upright; instead lay them on the ground, or at an angle of 45° so that they offer less wind resistance. I've left trees heeled in for far longer than I should (up to four

Tree planting

1 Excavate a hole that's amply big enough for the roots, knock in the stake and fork well-rotted manure or garden compost into the hole.

2 Trim off any damaged roots then lower the tree into the hole, making sure that there is room for the remaining roots to spread out without restriction.

3 Replace the soil, mixing it with extra compost or manure as you do so. Shake the tree up and down to make sure that soil is distributed around the roots.

4 Check that the old soil mark on the stem is level with the surface. Firm the soil and shorten the stake to 30 cm (1 ft) before adding the tie.

months) and they've come to no harm. Trees bought from garden centres will usually have to be collected. As most of them will be container-grown, the heeling-in precautions are not necessary.

BEFORE YOU PLANT

Preparing the site

With a bit of luck, any tree is going to be with you for a long time, so it's important to prepare the soil well so that it establishes itself quickly.

With both bare-root and container-grown trees, dig a hole one spit (spade blade) deep and 30 cm (12 in) wider all round than the roots or the rootball (the combination of roots and compost within the pot). Fork over the base of the hole and work in a bucketful of well-rotted manure, garden compost, or leaf mould dusted with a general fertilizer such as blood, bone and fishmeal. Mix some of this organic enrichment with the soil from the hole to perk that up, too.

Stakes for new trees

If the tree needs staking, now is the time to knock the stake into the hole; do it later and the roots will be disturbed. At least 60 cm (2 ft) of stake should be buried below ground level for stability, and the top of the stake should finish below the lowest branch of the tree. Stakes for trees should be about 5 cm (2 in) in diameter but they need not be treated with preservative; if the preservative is fresh it may harm the roots, and after two or three years the tree will be able to support itself anyway. A stake that rots after a year or two is a positive advantage, for it can be removed with little disturbance to the tree.

The current trend is for a short stake, emerging only about 30 cm (12 in) out of the ground. The theory is that this anchors the bare roots or rootball, while allowing the top growth to flex in the wind and so encourage rapid establishment of new roots below. Where children are at large, a long stake offers more protection to a newly planted tree.

Preparing to plant

I like to bung the roots of all bare-root trees and shrubs in a bucket of water for an hour prior to planting so that they don't have a chance to dry out. Cover the roots with damp sacking when you carry the trees to the planting site. A container-grown plant should be watered well an hour before planting, and the pot removed carefully at planting time. Any thick roots that

are obviously growing inwards can be teased out very gently; if just a fibrous rootball exists, leave it intact.

With a bare-root tree, remove the protective covering and examine the roots. Use a pair of sharp secateurs to trim off any thick roots that are more than 30 cm (12 in) long, as well as any roots that are torn or damaged. At the same time, snip off any broken or spindly shoots from the branch framework, making all cuts just above a bud. Forget to prune the branches and you may have to find a stepladder once the tree is planted. If there are any leaves or dead flowers present, remove those as well before planting.

PLANTING YOUR TREE

Stand the tree in the hole and check that when it is planted the old soil mark on the stem will rest just below the new soil level. Spread out the roots of bare-rooted specimens so that they are not all squashed together. Position a container-grown specimen so that it is upright and looks comfortable.

Now replace the soil gradually, adding compost or manure as you do so. With a bare-rooted tree, enlist a second pair of hands to hold the tree up and to jar it up

Staked and tied for stability, this is the same tree as on p.41, three months later. Make sure the roots never dry out, and slacken the ties as the trunk thickens.

and down so the soil shakes down around the roots. Firm the soil into place with your foot – stamping really hard so that no air pockets are left to cause problems of root drying. When planting is completed, leave a slight depression in the soil around the tree trunk so that water can be applied if necessary in dry weather.

Securing the tree

To fasten the tree to the stake, I prefer proprietary tree ties (plastic affairs with buckles) because they can be slackened when necessary; but if funds are short you can use rope cushioned with cloth,

When a long stake is used to protect trees exposed to children and ball games, position one tie just below the top of the stake and the other 30 cm (12 in) above soil level.

or even a pair of old tights. Position one tie about 30 cm (12 in) above ground level and another 2.5 cm (1 in) below the top of the stake. Ideally the stake should be on the windward side of the tree (south-westerlies are the prevailing winds in Britain) but I don't think that the life or death of your tree will depend on this.

Mulching and watering

Immediately after planting, and while the soil is nicely moist, spread an 8 cm (3 in) mulch of garden compost, manure or pulverized bark over the soil around the tree; a 90 cm (3 ft) diameter circle will be sufficient. Trees planted between April and October will almost always need to be watered in before this mulch is laid. Leave a hosepipe running on the soil at the foot of the tree for an hour, or give it at least three 9 litre (2 gallon) cans of water.

Aftercare of newly planted trees

Check the tree ties every month to make sure they're not constricting the stem. Slacken them if necessary.

Do make sure that the tree doesn't run short of water, especially during its first spring and summer. If the roots are allowed to dry out, you stand to lose a lot of money and a whole season's growth.

Trees that are bought as large specimens will often grow very slowly during their first few years. Some gardeners believe that they become 'bark bound' – the bark is so dry and hard that it refuses to allow the trunk to expand and grow. If you think that this is the case after a couple of years, try running a penknife down the length of the trunk so that the bark is split: old hands swear that this gives the tree a chance.

PRUNING

I'm not a great tree pruner: if a tree needs pruning when it's more than a few years old then the chances are that it has been planted in the wrong place. But in its formative years a young tree will need pruning to produce that bare stem and a good head of branches.

Early years

In the first two or three years of its life the tree is best left intact: the shoots that arise low down on the stem will encourage it to thicken and support the branches higher up. A tree with such a collection of lower branches is said to be 'feathered'.

If you want a tree that's furnished with leaves to ground level it's still best to remove the lowest branches so that those above can hang down a little. If this is the case the tree will look good and yet still have a strong trunk that may offer winter colour. As soon as your tree is about 2.5–3 m (roughly 8–10 ft)

In late summer, remove the lower branches of birch trees that need their canopies raised.

Use long-arm pruners to reach shoots that are too high to be removed with secateurs or short-handled loppers.

high, make sure that the lower 90 cm (3 ft) of stem is cleared of shoots: cut them off almost flush with the trunk. As the tree grows, trim off more shoots until you have the length of bare stem you require.

Trees bought as standards or half-standards should have their trunks trimmed of any emerging shoots. Standard trees are those with about 1.8 m (6 ft) of bare trunk; half-standards have about 1.2 m (4 ft) of trunk.

As with all rules there are exceptions. Trees with an upright columnar habit will never trail their branches to cover the trunk and you may prefer to let them retain all their stems right down to ground level.

Dealing with suckers

Any shoots that arise from below the ground are called suckers, and they should be pulled or cut away from the roots at their point of origin. If you let them remain, or cut them off flush with the soil, they'll develop into a disfiguring thicket. Suckers are an especial problem with some ornamental plums and cherries. Here the upper flowering growth has been grafted onto a rootstock that has no ornamental value whatsoever but which forms a healthy root system governing the vigour of the tree. If you leave suckers to develop on such trees, the upper portion may go into decline.

Pruning ornamental trees

The only regular pruning needed on most ornamental trees will be to remove dead wood. This is easiest to see in summer and can be cut off at that time, as can suckers. The removal of badly placed or dangerous

Pleached trees

Pleached trees create a wall or avenue of foliage when the branches, trained to intertwine horizontally, are in leaf. Young trees, with pliable stems, must be used.

First, erect a framework of uprights and horizontals: the uprights should be about 2.4 m (8 ft) apart. Plant a tree at the base of each upright. Tie in laterals at the height of the first row of horizontal supports and remove any lower side shoots.

The following year cut back the laterals to encourage new side shoots. Tie in new laterals to the next horizontal support. When the leader reaches the desired height, tie it to the top horizontal support.

Lime trees are one of the traditional choices for pleaching. Hard prune in winter and, in summer, prune back long growths to a well-placed bud.

branches may occasionally be necessary and this is done in the dormant season – November to March – when the sap is not rising.

Tree surgery

This grand-sounding term is usually applied to any kind of tree pruning. On a small scale you can do it yourself, but when large trees are creating a real problem then a reputable firm of tree surgeons should be called in to advise. Don't agree to let any bunch of cowboys tackle your trees. The sort of 'firm' that knocks on your door asking if you want your trees pruned is not the type to employ. True enough, they may be cheaper than a skilled firm of tree surgeons (who can be found in your Yellow Pages) but they'll leave you heartbroken.

Preventing wound infections

Trees have their own natural defence mechanism that helps to prevent wound infection. It is situated at the branch collar (a slight swelling or ridge of bark where the branch joins the trunk; the ridge starts in the crotch between branch and trunk). The tree will heal itself, without the need for wound paints, so long as you don't cut into this collar.

Remove long branches leaving a foot-long stump. Now make a clean cut at a slight angle away from the trunk; make it an equal but opposite angle to that made by the branch collar so that you won't breach the collar. Undercut the stump first to prevent the bark tearing when the main cut is made (see below for more details).

> **"If a tree needs pruning when it's more than a few years old then it's been planted in the wrong place."**

Removing odd branches

On smaller trees, where just the odd branch needs to be removed, you can tackle it yourself – although a second pair of hands is always helpful, whether it's to hold the ladder steady or to pass the saw. Small branches can be cut off in one go, but anything with a bit of weight to it should be dismantled from the tip inwards. Tie a rope to each section of branch that's being removed before you saw through the stem. Then the wood can be slowly lowered to the ground on the other end of the rope by your mate. That way no damage will be done to the lower branches by falling timber.

If you've a lot of trees you might be tempted by a chain saw, but I always use a bow saw for tree pruning; it is, by far, a much safer option than a chain saw. If you have to remove any branches larger than about 15 cm (6 in) in diameter, call in a professional tree surgeon.

1 Cut off heavy branches in stages. Support the weight of the one to be removed by running a rope from it and over a sturdy, higher branch.

2 Saw through the branch at least 30 cm (12 in) away from its junction with the trunk. That way you'll remove most of the weight before the final cut is made.

3 Undercut the stump flush with the trunk, then cut through from above to meet it. Neaten the surface with a knife and, if required, seal it with wound paint.

A-Z
of
garden trees

THIS IS A SELECTION OF WHAT I consider to be some of the best garden trees. I've left out the real giants – the oaks, beeches and cedars – and concentrated on those trees that are at home in gardens of modest size. They are not all dwarfs (such trees tend to be lacking in grace) but few of them should present any major problems provided they are planted in the right place.

The height and spread of each tree will depend entirely on the situation in which it is planted; the figures I have given are a rough indication of the ultimate sizes to help you decide if the tree will fit in your garden – remember that some trees will take an age to reach their ultimate height. Height is the first figure; spread the second.

Acer griseum
Paperbark Maple

6 x 4.5 m (20 x 15 ft)

A maple renowned for its glorious peeling bark of coppery bronze. The three-lobed leaves are orange-tinged on opening, later becoming green, and taking on fiery tints of scarlet in autumn.

Acer japonicum 'Vitifolium'
Downy Japanese Maple

4.5 x 4.5 m (15 x 15 ft)

This and its more shrub-like relation *A. japonicum* 'Aconitifolium' are two of the very best autumn-colouring plants in any garden. The leaves are deep-cut into seven or more lobes and are softly downy. They seem to catch fire in autumn, turning to shades of yellow, pink, orange and bright crimson.

Acer negundo 'Variegatum'
Box Elder

6 x 4.5 m (20 x 15 ft)

A maple whose foliage is striking in summer rather than autumn. The leaves are pinnate (like those of the rose) and edged with creamy white variegation. The whole effect is delicate and graceful. Occasional all-green shoots will arise and these should be cut out.

There's a form called 'Flamingo' that has pink variegation. It's a real beauty, but bad weather can cause leaf browning. This form is probably best grown as a shrub, by pruning hard each spring.

Acer pseudoplatanus 'Brilliantissimum'
Sycamore

6 x 4.5 m (20 x 15 ft)

A slow-growing beauty, this is a spectacular form of the sycamore whose leaves are shrimp-pink on opening, gradually turning yellow, then creamy white until they are eventually suffused with green. In spring and early summer it's a sparkling sight. Young specimens may burn a little in brilliant sunlight until their roots are well established.

Alnus glutinosa 'Aurea'
Golden Alder

4.5 x 3 m (15 x 10 ft)

The yellow-leaved form of the common alder is not as widely planted as it should be. It rarely exceeds 4 m (12 ft) in height, and keeps the yellow colouring of its leaves until late summer in a sunny, sheltered spot.

Arbutus unedo
Strawberry Tree

4.5 x 4.5 m (15 x 15 ft)

This superb evergreen is a slow grower but offers a number of attractive features. The bark is dark brown and peeling; white urn-shaped flowers are carried in clusters in autumn, and these are followed the next autumn by rough-skinned spherical fruits of bright reds, so that flowers and fruits are carried at the same time. The fruits are edible but tart – don't make a pie of them!

Betula ermanii
Erman's Birch

6 x 4.5 m (20 x 15 ft)

Anyone who plants the deformed Young's weeping birch (*B. pendula* 'Youngii') must be unaware of the four beautiful species mentioned here. This one makes a broad cone of growth and has bark that is white when young, and pink-flushed as it ages. The young stems are orange-brown.

Betula papyrifera
Paperbark Birch

10.5 x 4.5 m (35 x 15 ft)

A good 'peeler', this species has white bark marked with orange, pink or dark brown. Pure yellow autumn colour.

Betula pendula 'Laciniata'
(syn. *B. pendula* 'Dalecarlica')
Swedish Birch

10.5 x 4.5 m (35 x 15 ft)

Superb finely cut foliage carried on weeping stems and a good, white bark make this species an excellent choice where a bit of space is available.

Betula utilis var. jacquemontii
Kashmir Birch

6 x 4.5 m (20 x 15 ft)

The main branches and trunk are bright white or cream and the saw-edged leaves turn warm yellow before falling in autumn.

Cercis siliquastrum
Judas Tree
4.5 x 4.5 m (15 x 15 ft)

Slow growing and often seen as a shrub rather than a tree, *Cercis* is a fascinating plant. Its leaves are rounded and smooth but, before they emerge, the stems and even the old branches are smothered in rich pink pea flowers during May. These are followed in autumn by flattened pods of crimson-purple. It often grows rather lopsidedly but is still charming. Give it a sunny, sheltered spot and allow it a few years to settle in before expecting flowers – birds can eat the buds, so beware! Reputedly the tree on which Judas hanged himself.

Chamaecyparis lawsoniana
Lawson Cypress
9 x 3 m (30 x 10 ft)

Don't plant the boring ordinary species, but go for one of its varieties such as: 'Columnaris', upright and blue-grey; 'Ellwoodii', a rich green; 'Green Pillar', erect green fans of growth; 'Lanei Aurea' (syn. 'Lane'), the best yellow form; 'Pembury Blue', rich blue-grey. All these conifers are especially valuable for brightening the winter garden.

Crataegus laevigata 'Paul's Scarlet'
Paul's Scarlet Thorn
4.5 x 2.4 m (15 x 8 ft)

A welcome sight every spring, this hawthorn wreathes its branches in clusters of double pink blossoms. Plant it near shrubs that will please the eye later in the season when it's not much to look at.

Cunninghamia lanceolata
Chinese Fir
9 x 3 m (30 x 10 ft)

This is an unusual conifer that deserves greater popularity. It produces masses of narrow leaves, arranged rather like those of yew, but with an exceptionally shiny texture that is almost metallic. They turn bronzy in autumn and persist to some extent when dead. If you've room to experiment give it a try.

Davidia involucrata
Dove Tree, Pocket Handkerchief Tree
7.5 x 4.5 m (25 x 15 ft)

You'll need patience if you want to grow this tree: it can take 20 years to flower, but what a sight when it does! The shapely head of branches is furnished with bright green lime-shaped leaves and drips with white handkerchief-like bracts that surround the flowers. With luck it will bloom in its tenth year, but be prepared for disappointment. Flowering time is May.

Eucalyptus pauciflora subsp. *niphophila*
Snow Gum
6 x 4.5 m (20 x 15 ft)

This is the species I'd choose, though there are many on offer. The bark is a marbled python's skin of grey and pale orange, and the leaves are long, grey-green and sickle-shaped. The tree often leans appealingly and, like other eucalypts, it may be damaged in very severe winters, but regeneration from the base is common. Growth is rapid with all species, and young specimens should be planted from pots – older ones are difficult to establish. If the snow gum fails with you due to severe winters, try *E. gunnii* which is tougher.

Ginkgo biloba
Maidenhair Tree
7.5 x 3 m (25 x 10 ft) – larger with age

The maidenhair captivates all who set eyes on it. The fan-shaped leaves are rich green, turning to yellow before they fall in autumn, and the tree is of a convenient upright shape. It's the oldest tree in existence, dating back 200 million years.

Trees that thrive on most soil types

All the trees listed will grow on clay or chalky soil. Those marked ✳ are suitable for dry conditions, and those marked ◆ for cold sites.

- *Acer griseum* ◆
- *Acer japonicum* 'Vitifolium'
- *Acer negundo* 'Variegatum' ✳◆
- *Acer pseudoplatanus* 'Brilliantissimum' ✳
- *Alnus glutinosa* 'Aurea' ✳
- *Arbutus unedo* ◆
- *Cercis siliquastrum*
- *Chamaecyparis lawsoniana* varieties ✳◆
- *Crataegus laevigata* 'Paul's Scarlet' ✳◆
- *Cunninghamia lanceolata*
- *Eucalyptus pauciflora* subsp. *niphophila*
- *Ilex* x *altaclerensis* 'Golden King' ✳
- *Laburnum* x *watereri* 'Vossii' ◆
- *Larix decidua* ✳◆
- *Malus floribunda*
- *Malus* 'John Downie'
- *Metasequoia glyptostroboides* ✳
- *Picea breweriana* ◆
- *Picea omorika* ◆
- *Picea pungens* 'Koster' ◆
- *Populus* x *jackii* 'Aurora' ◆
- *Prunus serrula*
- *Prunus serrulata* varieties
- *Prunus* x *subhirtella* 'Autumnalis'
- *Pyrus salicifolia* 'Pendula'
- *Salix* x *sepulcralis* 'Chrysocoma' ◆
- *Sorbus aucuparia* 'Beissneri' ◆
- *Sorbus* 'Joseph Rock' ✳◆
- *Taxus baccata* 'Fastigiata Aurea' ✳◆
- *Thuja plicata* 'Zebrina' ✳◆

Gleditsia triacanthos 'Sunburst'
Honey Locust
4.5 x 2.4 m (15 x 8 ft)

Pretty as a picture from spring to autumn on account of its finely cut foliage of bright yellow that turns to fizzing lime-green as it ages. Along with *Robinia pseudoacacia* 'Frisia' it is one of the best yellow-leaved trees. Of the two it is the tougher and has smaller leaflets. The leaves turn butter-yellow before they fall in autumn.

Ilex x *altaclerensis* 'Golden King'
Variegated Holly
4.5 x 2.4 m (15 x 8 ft)

This is about the best variegated holly: its leaves, though not exceptionally spiny, are margined and splashed with bright butter-yellow. Remember that holly bushes are male or female and only the females carry berries. To add to the confusion 'Golden King' is a female and produces plenty of scarlet fruits in winter. It can be kept much smaller than its ultimate size by Christmas pruning. Other hollies are described in Chapter 5 Shrubs.

Laburnum x *watereri* 'Vossii'
Voss's Laburnum
4.5 x 3 m (15 x 10 ft)

In early June there is no finer sight than this tree, laden with its pendulous flowers of bright yellow. The green leaves that follow are a bit dull but at least this variety produces few of the poisonous seeds for which laburnums have become feared. Superb when trained over archways and pergolas.

Larix decidua
European Larch
6 x 3 m (20 x 10 ft) and more

Where you've a bit of room to spare, don't forget the larch. It's a pretty conifer that has soft, fresh green needles in spring and summer. In autumn they turn bright yellow before falling. Neat cones decorate the stems. Larch is a fast grower, and lovely when planted in groups: set the trees 3 m (10 ft) apart and plant them young.

Malus floribunda
Japanese Crab Apple
4.5 x 6 m (15 x 20 ft)

A wide-spreading tree that is truely magnificent in spring when it is smothered with white flowers opening from rich pink buds. For the rest of the year it's rather dull, so plant it where it can act as a backdrop for other plants when out of flower.

Malus 'John Downie'
Cherry Apple
4.5 x 3 m (15 x 10 ft)

A crab apple with reasonable white flowers and positively superb red and yellow fruits later in the season. They make delicious crab apple jelly if you can bear to rob the tree.

Metasequoia glyptostroboides
Dawn Redwood
9 x 2.4 m (30 x 8 ft) and more

A rotten Latin name for a lovely deciduous conifer. The dawn redwood was thought to be extinct until rediscovered in China in 1941, and now it graces many gardens worldwide. It makes a column of feathery bright green leaves that turn rich coppery shades before falling in autumn. The trunk and stems have russet peeling bark. Few gardens should be without it. Plant young specimens for quick establishment.

Morus nigra
Black Mulberry
3 x 4.5 m (10 x 15 ft) and more with age

The black mulberry makes a rounded, spreading tree with serrated heart-shaped leaves and a gnarled trunk. Red to black fruits are produced on trees over 20 years old and are only fit to eat when really ripe, at which time they fall from the tree. Can be propagated from branches about 1.5 m (5 ft) long, which are relieved of some of their smaller shoots and then pushed into the ground for one third of their length.

Nyssa sylvatica
Tupelo
9 x 3 m (30 x 10 ft) and more with age

For sheltered gardens where there is space to spare, this is worth planting simply for its autumn colour. The oval leaves are glossy and turn scarlet, orange and crimson in autumn – you'll see no brighter tree at that time.

Ostrya carpinifolia
Hop Hornbeam
4.5 x 3 m (15 x 10 ft)

Here's an oddity. A shapely, upright-growing tree with green hornbeam-like

Weeping and spreading trees

TREES WITH A WEEPING HABIT
- *Betula pendula* 'Laciniata'
- *Picea breweriana*
- *Pyrus salicifolia* 'Pendula'
- *Salix* x *sepulcralis* 'Chrysocoma'

TREES WITH A SPREADING HABIT
- *Acer japonicum* 'Vitifolium'
- *Arbutus unedo*
- *Cercis siliquastrum*
- *Eucalyptus pauciflora* subsp. *niphophila*
- *Malus floribunda*
- *Morus nigra*
- *Parrotia persica*
- *Prunus serrulata* varieties
- *Sophora japonica*

Trees with all-year-round interest

- Acer griseum
- Arbutus unedo ◆
- Betula ermanii
- Betula utilis var. jacquemontii
- Betula papyrifera
- Betula pendula 'Laciniata'
- Chamaecyparis lawsoniana varieties ◆
- Cunninghamia lanceolata ◆
- Eucalyptus pauciflora subsp. niphophila ◆
- Ilex x altaclerensis 'Golden King' ◆
- Picea breweriana ◆
- Picea omorika ◆
- Picea pungens 'Koster' ◆
- Prunus serrula ◆
- Salix x sepulcralis 'Chrysocoma'
- Salix babylonica var. pekinensis 'Tortuosa'
- Sorbus aucuparia 'Beissneri'
- Stewartia pseudocamellia
- Taxus baccata 'Fastigiata Aurea' ◆
- Thuja plicata 'Zebrina' ◆
- Trachycarpus fortunei ◆

◆ Evergreen

leaves among which hang hop-like fruits in summer. Planted behind lower-growing shrubs it makes a fascinating backdrop. Not spectacular but intriguing nevertheless.

Parrotia persica
Persian Ironwood
4.5 x 6 m (15 x 20 ft)

Here's a tree with more than one attribute. For a start the bark is marbled with grey and peels like a plane tree. In winter, tiny red spidery flowers (like those of the witch hazel, *Hamamelis*, to which it is related) bedeck the branches, and the leaves that follow start to turn reddish in summer, colouring brilliant orange, yellow and scarlet by autumn. A good backdrop to shrubs and border plants.

Picea breweriana
Brewer's Weeping Spruce
6 x 2.4 m (20 x 8 ft) more with age

A beautiful and statuesque conifer for the patient gardener. It makes a conical tree with graceful weeping branches, but it should be planted young and not expected to look at its best until it is almost 20 years old. If you want something to enjoy during your retirement, and you've a bit of space to spare, give it a try.

Picea omorika
Serbian Spruce
9 x 3 m (30 x 10 ft) and more

This is a better choice for the impatient gardener, for it is faster growing than *P. breweriana*. The branches droop but are not as pendulous as *P. breweriana*. The overall colour is a greyish green and the conical shape makes this one of the most handsome conifers of all.

Picea pungens 'Koster'
Koster's Blue Spruce
6 x 1.8 m (20 x 6 ft)

A conical conifer of blue-grey that will add a lift to green plantings. Excellent with a carpet of heathers surrounding it to make a bright winter garden.

Populus x jackii 'Aurora'
(syn. *P.* x *candicans* 'Aurora')
Variegated Balm of Gilead Poplar
9 x 2.4 m (30 x 8 ft)

A real stunner - from a distance or close to - where a variegated tree of stature is needed. It is the young foliage that's variegated - splashed with creamy white and tinged with pink. In small gardens it can be pruned hard each winter to encourage plenty of variegated shoots the next spring.

Prunus serrula
Tibetan Cherry
4.5 x 3 m (15 x 10 ft)

Plenty of small white flowers are produced in spring, but the reason why this tree is so popular is its shining coppery bark that glows in the sun. Plant it where hands can caress and polish its stems and peel off the older bark. Left untouched the trunk and branches may become dull and moss-covered unless plenty of bright sunshine strikes them.

Prunus serrulata
Sato Cherry, Japanese Cherry
Various sizes

There are dozens of flowering cherries so I've picked just a few of the very best. They are undoubtedly only of real value in spring when they bloom, but they flower with such generosity that they cannot be ignored. My selection would be:
'Amanogawa': 4.5 m x 60 cm (15 x 2 ft); upright with pale pink double flowers in April and May.
'Shirofugen': 7.5 x 7.5 m (25 x 25 ft); spreading, pale pink to white double flowers in May.
'Shôgetsu' (syn. 'Shimidsu'): 4.5 x 6 m (15 x 20 ft); spreading, double white flowers in May.
'Taihaku': (Great White Cherry) 6 x 6 m (20 x 20 ft); double white flowers in April, my first choice.
'Ukon': 6 x 9 m (20 x 30 ft); spreading, greenish white double blossoms in April and May.

In most varieties the foliage unfurls with or after the flowers and is tinged bronze. Most develop good autumn colour.

Prunus x subhirtella 'Autumnalis'
Winter Cherry
4.5 x 3 m (15 x 20 ft)

A fine back-of-the-border tree where during its dull summer season, it can act as a backdrop. When the summer border flowers fade, the bare branches of the tree erupt with pink buds that burst into white flowers. There's something to look at from October to April in most years.

Pseudolarix amabilis
Golden Larch
6 x 2.4 m (20 x 8 ft)

This lovely, large-leafed larch should be more widely planted. The deciduous leaves are fresh green in spring and summer, turning bright yellow before they fall in autumn. Give it a sheltered spot in full sun where its change of colour can be admired. Youngsters may be damaged by severe frosts.

Pyrus salicifolia 'Pendula'
Willow-leafed Pear
4.5 x 2.4 m (15 x 8 ft)

A good tree for a restricted space, but of muted rather than spectacular shades. The branches arch downwards and are clothed in narrow leaves of silvery grey, studded with small white flowers in spring. Cheer it up by planting colourful shrubs nearby!

Robinia pseudoacacia 'Frisia'
False Acacia
6 x 3 m (20 x 10 ft)

A favourite of mine, this tree is a stunning spectacle from June to September when its ferny leaves of brilliant acid-yellow stand out against summer skies of blue. Even when the sun is in they will brighten your garden. Compared with *Gleditsia triacanthos* 'Sunburst', this tree is more yellow and, I think, more graceful due to its tissue-thin leaves, which flutter gently in every passing breeze. On the downside, it has brittle wood and can suffer in colder areas.

The delicate, ferny leaves of *Robinia pseudoacacia* 'Frisia' remain acid-yellow throughout the summer, providing a brilliant spectacle.

Salix babylonica var. *pekinensis* 'Tortuosa'
Dragon's Claw Willow
9 x 3 m (30 x 10 ft)

Better where space is restricted, this willow has an upright habit and stems that are twisted like corkscrews, which accounts for the other common name of corkscrew willow. In summer and winter its contorted stems are visible, and the leaves are a fresh green. Raved about by flower arrangers.

Salix x *sepulcralis* 'Chrysocoma'
Golden Weeping Willow
9 x 9 m (30 x 30 ft) and more

This is not a tree for small gardens, in spite of the fact that it is often planted there. It is a fast-growing spreader that will rob you of light and shift your foundations if planted too close to your house. Only where there's a vast expanse of lawn, and preferably a lake, or at the very least moist soil, should it be planted. Then it can be allowed to make the magnificent specimen it deserves to be, with its living cascade of yellow stems, thickly decked with narrow green leaves in summer.

Cuttings root so readily that they can even be taken when they are broom-handle-sized and stuck into the ground to grow.

Sophora japonica
Pagoda Tree
6 x 4.5 m (20 x 15 ft)

Rarely planted but often admired, this has pinnate leaves like the rowan, and long clusters of creamy white flowers in late summer when it reaches a reasonable age. It is a tree of grace that relishes a warm, sunny spot.

Sorbus aucuparia 'Beissneri'
Rowan, Mountain Ash
6 x 3 m (20 x 10 ft)

This tree deserves a bright future in gardens for it offers orange-pink bark

Trees with attractive flowers or fruit

The following trees have flowers ✳ and/or fruits ◆ of note.

- *Arbutus unedo* ✳◆
- *Cercis siliquastrum* ✳◆
- *Crataegus laevigata* 'Paul's Scarlet' ✳
- *Davidia involucrata* ✳
- *Ilex* x *altaclerensis* 'Golden King' ◆
- *Laburnum* x *watereri* 'Vossii' ✳
- *Malus floribunda* ✳
- *Malus* 'John Downie' ✳◆
- *Morus nigra* ◆
- *Ostrya carpinifolia* ◆
- *Parrotia persica* ✳
- *Prunus serrula* ✳
- *Prunus serrulata* varieties ✳
- *Prunus* x *subhirtella* 'Autumnalis' ✳
- *Pyrus salicifolia* 'Pendula' ✳
- *Sophora japonica* ✳
- *Sorbus* 'Joseph Rock' ◆
- *Stewartia pseudocamellia* ✳

(especially stunning after rain or when a lawn sprinkler has played on it), reddish young stems and bright yellow autumn colour on its ferny foliage. Its habit of growth is attractive too – upright and broadly columnar – and it fits into the smallest gardens. A good choice if you've room for only one tree.

Sorbus 'Joseph Rock'
6 x 3 m (20 x 10 ft)

A stunning rowan of upright habit and with the usual ferny leaves. These take on fiery tints in autumn and are complemented by the generous crop of bright yellow fruits that persist when the leaves are shed. Birds hardly seem to touch them – a great advantage in gardens where fruits are gobbled as fast as they appear.

Stewartia pseudocamellia
4.5 x 2.4 m (15 x 8 ft)

A relative of the camellia, *Stewartia* makes a handsome tree with flaking bark, mottled purplish brown and buff and orange. White, yellow-centred flowers stud the branches in summer, and the leaves (oddly glossy on the undersides and dull above) turn brilliant shades of crimson and yellow in autumn. Plenty of attributes for a modest-sized tree. Sadly it won't put up with chalky soil and it prefers a shady situation to one in full sun.

Taxus baccata
Yew
6 x 6 m (20 x 20 ft)

An oppressive tree where space is limited, the green yew is best grown as a backdrop in large shrubberies. But the varieties 'Fastigiata Aurea' and 'Fastigiata Aureomarginata' (Golden Irish yew) are yellow and yellow-variegated respectively, making upright, towering minarets of growth. They cheer up any plot, especially in winter, and grow 3 m x 60 cm (10 x 2 ft).

Thuja plicata 'Zebrina'
Variegated Western Red Cedar
9 x 2.4 m (30 x 8 ft) and more

As an alternative to the variegated forms of the Lawson cypress, try this conifer. It makes an upright column of evergreen foliage banded with bright yellow. It is a picture in winter.

Trachycarpus fortunei
Chusan Palm
4.5 x 1.8 m (15 x 6 ft)

If you're feeling frivolous, try planting a palm tree! This one is surprisingly hardy in many parts of the country and makes a thick stem clad in 'coconut matting' and topped with a cluster of fan-shaped fronds. It will be some time before it reaches its maximum height.

CHAPTER 5 shrubs

Evergreen and deciduous, flowering and fruiting, with colourful foliage and attractive bark and stems, shrubs lend constant form and interest to any garden

Rightly described as the backbone of any garden, shrubs are indispensable. You don't have to pack your plot with gigantic bushes: there's a great diversity of shrub material from the positively dwarf to the gargantuan. The secret is to find the right shrub for your particular purpose, and the lists in the A–Z section of this chapter will enable you to do just that.

Shrubs are also good helpmates in keeping down weeds. There's nothing magical in this: in the early stages of establishment you'll have to do just as much weeding as in any other part of the garden but, when shrubs are close-planted, they will eventually form a thicket that beats the weeds, hides the bare soil and saves you work.

HOW TO USE SHRUBS

Providing form

One of the most important jobs for a shrub is to give form to your garden. Before buying consider the shape and style of any shrub, its ultimate height and its overall effect. Evergreens are valuable because they create structure in the garden all the year round, but plant too many of them and you'll be bored by an unchanging vista. The secret is to mix them up with deciduous kinds that lose their leaves. Do this and you'll retain form without sacrificing the freshness that spring brings to the garden.

Flowers, fruit and foliage

Remember that most flowering shrubs have only a brief season of glory – a month is good going when it comes to length of time in bloom. Position them where they will make a bright pageant in their flowering season, and then act as a plain backdrop to flowers that bloom later. Make them work for a living. A shrub that offers more than one attractive feature is often a better bet than one that puts all its floral eggs in one basket.

A word of warning about coloured foliage: don't overdo it. Green is the colour that should predominate in any garden. Go overboard on the purples and creamy yellows and you'll create a psychedelic nightmare. Choose a handful of bright-leaved shrubs to show off against the plainer kinds for a more spectacular effect.

Contours and focal points

In really small gardens you can avoid trees and select large or medium-sized specimen shrubs to act as your eye-catchers and focal points. I've recommended suitable choices in the A-Z section. Use all your shrubs with their contours in mind: try to create an undulating landscape, positioning the shrubs so that your eye is taken on a gentle tour, not flickering up and down as if you were looking at a castellated battlement. This may sound like pretentious clap-trap, but it makes for a more restful scene if the lines are gradual; then, when you aim to create an eye-catching contrast of form, such as an upright yew among a carpet of lower-growing junipers, you'll achieve the effect you want.

Forgotten art?

Topiary, the art of clipping shrubs into fanciful shapes, goes in and out of fashion, but it's always a useful pursuit if you can't afford to buy statuary for the garden. The secret of making topiary look good is to choose the right plants, and to put them in the right place. You'll have to be patient to succeed but, with plants like box, yew, *Lonicera nitida* and even the humble privet, you can make assorted ornaments that will cheer up odd corners of your garden. Even a simple pyramid of foliage is stunning in a well-chosen spot.

Creating mystery

To give shelter and privacy, shrubs are vital; more than any other plants, they enable you to create a garden that is three-dimensional. Try to turn your patch, however small, into a place that is a little mysterious. There should always be some part that is not quite visible, so that you're tempted to explore its hidden depths. With a bit of imagination you can make hidden crannies on a plot no bigger than 3 m (10 ft) square: I know it's possible, for I've done it!

CHOOSING A HEALTHY SHRUB

Container-grown plants

Container-grown shrubs can be bought and planted at any time of year – they are the stock-in-trade of the garden centre and are also available at nurseries.

Learn how to choose a good specimen. Look for a plant that is relatively young and in the peak of health. Don't go for an old and gnarled specimen even though it is larger and therefore more tempting than a youngster. It will probably have a spiralled mass of roots inside the pot and will resent disturbance. Its roots will also be reluctant to leave the safety of the rootball for the soil outside and the plant may sit and sulk rather than grow away.

That's not to say you should buy a plant that's only just been put into its container. No; it should be established and container-grown, but not decrepit.

Choose a shapely, symmetrical plant, furnished with branches down to soil level (unless it is meant to be grown on a bare stem). If it is a columnar grower, it should have a strong central shoot or 'leader'. The compost in the pot should not be dry; neither should there be a gap between compost and pot – a sure sign of previous drying out. Avoid pest- or disease-infected plants and those with brown-edged leaves.

Bare-root plants

Deciduous shrubs are sold for dispatch between November and March, the dormant season, when they can safely be lifted from the nursery rows and transported with little soil around their roots. If the shrub you order is to be delivered 'bare root' in winter, enquire if it is possible to select the plant you want; otherwise you'll have to rely on the reputation of the nurseryman. In general it is possible to transplant quite large bare-root shrubs, provided the nurseryman has occasionally undercut them to encourage the formation of a fairly compact rootball. This involves simply slicing into the soil along the rows of plants to sever any far-roaming roots. The job results in the development of more fibrous roots – always easier to deal with at planting time than those long roots that are almost as thick as broom handles.

> "More than any other plants, shrubs will enable you to carve out a garden that is three-dimensional."

PLANTING SHRUBS

The planting of shrubs is identical to the planting of trees except that staking to prevent wind rock will seldom be necessary (see pp.42–43 for details).

The spacing of shrubs gives rise to much argument. Some folk suggest that they are planted at their final spacing, to allow room for the expected spread; others suggest closer planting and a thinning out later on. I'd rather see the plants spaced out to allow for ultimate growth, and the gaps between them filled with short-term annuals or border plants that can easily be transplanted when the space they occupy is needed.

PRUNING SHRUBS

I think most gardeners hate pruning, probably because they're not quite sure what to do or when to do it. Calm yourself by remembering that the pruning of shrubs is usually necessary for three basic reasons: to remove dead or diseased wood; to keep a plant shapely and within bounds; and to encourage flowering. Some shrubs need hardly any pruning: they don't grow fast, are naturally shapely, seldom suffer from die-back and flower happily without being cut back. Others quickly become a thicket of flowerless stems where pests and diseases proliferate.

Vital techniques

I've given specific instructions on pruning each shrub in the A-Z, so I won't confuse you by rambling on generally here, except about pruning techniques. Never use anything but a sharp pair of secateurs for pruning, and take a pair of loppers (or long-arm pruners) to any stems thicker than your finger. Make all cuts directly above a leaf or bud: don't leave even a 1 cm (½ in) snag or 'finger' of stem behind - it will only die back and may allow disease to enter. Cuts larger than 2.5 cm (1 in) in

Transplanting an established shrub

Unless you are exceptionally clear-thinking and full of foresight when it comes to planting, you will occasionally make mistakes. The trouble is that you won't realize it straight away - only after two or three years when the scheme has matured will a plant scream out to be moved. Don't worry; you can still shift it with little danger to its constitution.

THE BEST TIME TO MOVE

Spring and autumn are the best times to transplant, though you can also do the job in winter if you don't mind working in cold weather. Evergreens prefer to be moved in April or May when the sap is starting to rise: it's the deciduous kinds that can tolerate a winter upheaval.

SEVERING THE ROOTS

Start off by taking your spade to the plant and cutting round it about 30-45 cm (12-18 in) away from the stem to sever out-growing roots. If the plant is very large it's a good idea to do this part of the operation some months in advance of the transplanting date. The plant can then recover from the shock while it still has a few roots pushing down underneath the rootball,

Once the rootball has been wrapped in a sheet of sacking or polythene, secure a stout stake to the stem. The shrub can then be lifted easily out of the hole.

and it will form a more fibrous network of roots above these, which can sustain it after transplanting.

WRAPPING THE ROOTBALL

When the sides of the rootball have been cut, push your spade underneath the plant to sever the anchor roots. Now swing the plant carefully to one side and tuck a sheet of sacking or polythene underneath it. Roll up the sheet to just half its size and push the rolled edge underneath the plant; then swing the plant back in the other direction and unroll the sheet so that the plant sits in its centre. Wrap the sheet around the plant as quickly and as tightly as possible, tie it or knot it, then, if it's made of sacking, soak it with a bucket of more of water.

RE-PLANTING

The plant can stand in a sheltered spot in its wrapping for several weeks if necessary, but for best results it should be planted in its new hole without delay. Stand it in the prepared hole, unwrap the sacking, swing the plant from side to side so that the wrapping can be removed, and then replace the soil, watering the plant in well if necessary. Anti-desiccant sprays can be used on conifers and evergreens before and after transplanting. These are proprietary solutions that can be sprayed onto foliage to prevent excessive water loss.

Snip out any dead or diseased stems as soon as you notice them, cutting back into healthy wood.

diameter can, if you wish, be painted with a proprietary wound sealant to prevent attack by fungus diseases. It's not the end of world if you don't do this because most wounds will heal naturally.

Know your shrub

Whatever else you do, don't tackle all your shrubs with the shears as soon as they get out of hand: you'll turn them all into flowerless lollipops. When you buy a shrub, make sure you know how big it'll grow and what pruning it needs, then you can plant with confidence, knowing that you'll get the best out of it without worrying that it will turn your garden into a jungle.

Renovating neglected plants

If you've taken over a garden that's already overgrown with shrubs, renovate them by thinning out the stems. Cut out all old and gnarled branches at ground level, leaving the young ones evenly spaced so that they can breathe and grow. If all the branches are old, cut out two thirds of them and leave the remainder. With any luck (and a bit of feeding) the plants will soon produce healthy young wood at ground level, and then the remainder of the elderly stuff can be cut out. This kind of pruning can be done in summer or autumn and winter. Dead or diseased wood on any shrub, or suckers from rootstocks (see pp.104–105), should be removed the instant they are noticed.

Finally, don't fall into the trap of thinking that because nature doesn't prune her shrubs you needn't. Take a look at a few shrubs in the wild and see how overgrown and full of dead wood they are. They make superb bird nesting sites in a wild part of the garden but they're not much to look at close to. If you can't bear pruning, there's only one thing to do and that's to select those shrubs that need no cutting back at all. They are clearly marked in the A-Z section.

LOOKING AFTER YOUR SHRUBS

Feeding and mulching

Don't forget that shrubs are just as hungry as other garden plants. Two or three handfuls of blood, bone and fishmeal scattered around each shrub in April will work wonders, especially if it's followed by a mulch of well-rotted garden compost or manure, or pulverized bark. The soil should be moist when you lay the mulch, and the mulch itself should be moist. That way the soil will be protected from excess drying out and weeds will be suppressed. Mulching saves a lot of hard labour.

Providing shelter

In particularly exposed places shrubs can be protected from winter winds by surrounding them with a 'tube' of sacking held in position by four stout canes or stakes, or by cutting the bottom off a plastic sack and slipping this over the canes.

A plastic sack with its bottom slit, held in place by four canes, makes an effective windbreak around a newly planted shrub.

PROPAGATION

It's always great fun to propagate plants. Though not all your cuttings may root, those that do will make all the fuss and bother worth while. All the plants mentioned in the A-Z section can be increased by at least one of these propagation methods: seeds, softwood cuttings, semi-ripe or half-ripe cuttings, leaf bud cuttings, hardwood cuttings, root cuttings, layering and division. Full details of all these methods are given in Chapter 2 Propagation.

A-Z
of shrubs

I MAKE NO APOLOGIES FOR THE shrub section being so long! The choice is wide and there are so many good garden plants among them that they must be done justice. It's a biased selection; they are all plants that I think deserve a space in your garden but, where the season of interest is limited or the plant has drawbacks, I've said so.

Make sure that any shrub will put up with the soil and situation you have to offer: I've indicated preferences and tolerances, and there are coloured boxes listing plants for particular situations, soils and characteristics.

The expected height and spread of each shrub is indicated with the height first and the spread second. Use it as a rough guide to work out whether or not you've room for the plant. The precise measurements will vary from place to place and from soil to soil.

Abelia x grandiflora
90 cm x 1.8 m (3 x 6 ft)

A spreading shrub with small, glossy, oval evergreen leaves and masses of pale pink flowers from summer to autumn. It's the length and timing of the flowering season that makes this a valuable shrub, rather than the spectacle of the individual blooms, which are quite small. Use it near the front of borders or to provide a muted background for more striking plants.
Likes a warm spot and well-drained soil. It may be cut back by frost in hard winters – try it at the foot of a warm wall. Tolerates heavy clay and chalk.
Prune after flowering, removing older stems that have carried blooms.
Propagate by cuttings of firm shoot tips in summer.

Acer palmatum varieties
Japanese Maple
Up to 3 x 4.5 m (10 x 15 ft)

Any gardener with an eye for form admires these supremely elegant plants. There are many varieties, of which these are some of the best: *f. atropurpureum*, with leaves that are burgundy-purple.
Dissectum Atropurpureum Group, the same but very finely cut like lace.
var. *dissectum*, with feathery green leaves.
'Osakazuki' is one of the best for autumn tints – the lobed green leaves are burnished rich, warm crimson.
'Sango-kaku' (syn. 'Senkaki') has stems of rosy pink and pale green leaves that turn orange-yellow in autumn.

All make shapely bushes or small trees that are ideal where space is restricted. They'll even grow in tubs.
Likes a sheltered spot where cold winds and early frosts will not damage their leaves. They don't like dry soils. Tolerates clay soil and occasionally chalky soil if the latter is enriched, but they fail in shallow earth over chalk.
Propagate with difficulty. Try layering a low-growing branch in spring; sow seeds outdoors as soon as they are ripe; bud onto seedling stocks in early spring if you are really keen.

Acer shirasawanum 'Aureum'
Japanese Maple
1.8 x 1.8 m (6 x 6 ft)

A real stunner that is ideal to use as a tree in a tiny garden. The fan-shaped leaves are a glorious acid-yellow when they unfold in spring and they retain much of their brilliance until they fall in autumn.
Likes a spot sheltered from winds and a soil that never becomes dust-dry.

Avoid frost pockets: the new foliage is sensitive. Tolerates clay soil and very occasionally chalky soil; worth a try if you're desperate and can improve the ground with organic matter.
Prune at your peril. Remove only dead wood and any inconveniently placed branches in autumn.
Prune/propagate as for *A. palmatum*.

Aloysia See p.92

Amelanchier canadensis
Snowy Mespilus
2.4 x 3.6 m (8 x 12 ft)

This is the name under which nurserymen sell their snowy mespilus, but botanists mumble that it's likely to be *A. laevis*. It doesn't matter. Either way you'll obtain a large shrub with oval deciduous leaves that take on dazzling tints of orange, red and yellow before they fall in autumn. Clusters of small white starry flowers are carried in spring so the plant has two seasons of interest, even if it's boring in summer. Position summer bloomers in front of it.
Likes any open spot in reasonable soil. Tolerates heavy or moist soil, and soils containing chalk.
Prune out a few old stems each winter.
Propagate by digging up and replanting suckers in autumn.

Aralia elata
Japanese Angelica Tree
3-6 x 3 m (10-20 x 10 ft)

You'll need plenty of space for this whopper, but it has such super architectural form that it's a must where a striking plant is needed. The massive leaves are usually about 90 cm (3 ft) long, but divided into many smaller leaflets. Watch out for the spines! Fluffy flower clusters of creamy green are carried in late summer, and the most striking sight is the variegated form 'Aureovariegata', whose leaves are edged with creamy white. Absolutely stunning.

Likes an open spot in any ordinary soil and plenty of room to spread. Tolerates heavy clay soil and chalk.
Prune out any unwanted stems and any dead wood in spring. Remove unwanted suckers, which these plants can produce rather too freely. Those from the variegated variety will be green-leafed, for it is grafted on to rootstocks of the true species.
Propagate by removing suckers from the true species or, if you've the patience, by grafting shoots of the variegated variety onto rootstocks of the true species in spring.

Aucuba japonica 'Variegata'
Spotted Laurel
2.4 x 2.4 m (8 x 8 ft)

Don't be put off this shrub by the fact that you've seen it, overgrown, in dingy shrubberies. As a single specimen in the right spot it has some sterling attributes: it is clothed with glossy yellow-spotted leaves all year round; it is easy to grow, shapely and produces fat red berries in winter if it's fertilized by a nearby male, which will hopefully be planted in someone else's garden. There are other varieties: some are spotted, some are plain; some are male (producing no berries) and some are female. Plant it where it can be admired from a window in winter.
Likes good soil and gentle (but not overpowering) shade. Tolerates clay, chalk, heavy shade and coastal exposure.
Prune only to remove unwanted branches in spring.
Propagate by cuttings of firm shoot tips in summer.

Berberis darwinii
Barberry
1.8 x 1.8 m (6 x 6 ft)

One of the best barberries, good in leaf and flower. The evergreen leaves are dark and glossy, like those of a miniature holly, and the orange

flowers, like tiny daffodils in close-up, absolutely smother the stems in spring. Thorny and impenetrable: wear gloves when you prune it! Good for hedges (see p.84).
Likes an open spot in any reasonable soil. Tolerates clay, chalk, dry soil, cold gardens, some shade and even coastal exposure, though it will burn in really severe salt-laden winds.
Prune carefully if you value your arms. Remove a few old stems each winter.
Propagate by cuttings of firm shoot tips in summer.

Bamboos
60 cm–3 m x 3 m (2–10 ft x 10 ft)

More folk should grow bamboos. There are midgets for small gardens and others that are so rampant they can only be let loose in relatively wild areas, but all produce a thicket of canes decorated with narrow leaves that may be dazzlingly variegated. These are my own favourites:
Fargesia murieliae (syn. *Arundinaria murieliae*): 3 m (10 ft), yellowish-green canes with arching tips clad in green leaves.
Fargesia nitida (syn. *Arundinaria nitida*): 3 m (10 ft), purplish canes and arching fronds of green leaves.
Pleioblastus auricomus (syn. *Arundinaria viridistriata*): 1 m (3 ft), devastatingly beautiful with short canes and leaves striped with fresh green and butter-yellow. The best for a small garden.

All are fun to grow in tubs and keep their leaves on throughout the year.
Likes sheltered spots in soil that is unlikely to dry out. Tolerates heavy clay and boggy ground and, surprisingly, relatively dry soil and shady sites under trees. They don't mind chalk and will also put up with coastal exposure, though they certainly grow better without it.
Prune out a few old and dead canes each spring. Leave some old wood to support the new and act as a windbreak.

Propagate by lifting and transplanting portions of the clump in spring or autumn.

Berberis x ottawensis f. purpurea
2.4 x 2.4 m (8 x 8 ft)

Also called *B.* x *ottawensis* 'Superba', this is a nicely vigorous, rather upright shrub whose leaves are a rich maroon-purple. The orange flowers look well against them in early summer, and tiny red berries follow. The leaves are shed in winter. Makes a good hedge. A good contrast to lower growing, grey-leaved plants.
Likes an open spot in any reasonable soil. Tolerates clay, chalk, dry soil, cold gardens and just a modicum of shade.
Prune out a few old stems each winter, or cut back really hard at that time each year to encourage the production of new plum-purple shoots from lower down. Very thorny, so beware.
Propagate by cuttings of firm shoot tips in summer.

Berberis x stenophylla
2.4 x 3 m (8 x 10 ft)

A spiny, arching thicket-former with tiny evergreen leaves and masses of scented orange-yellow flowers in spring. A really spectacular sight when in flower and one of the densest dog-proof hedges (see p.84).
Likes most sites and soils.
Prune by cutting out overcrowding stems in winter and by digging up unwanted suckers, which it produces generously.
Propagate by replanting the suckers, or by taking shoot tip cuttings in summer.

Berberis thunbergii
30 cm–1.2 m x 1.2 m (1–4 ft x 4 ft)

It is the forms of *B. thunbergii* that are valued for their eye-catching foliage. 'Atropurpurea Nana' is purple-leaved and only 30–60 cm (1–2 ft) high; 'Aurea' is also low-growing and has

acid-yellow leaves that turn to dazzling green later in the year; 'Rose Glow' is a real curiosity with young leaves splashed and marbled pink on plum-purple. Watch out for relative newcomer 'Bagatelle', which makes domes about 30 cm (12 in) high of dark maroon. All shed their leaves in winter and have unremarkable flowers, but the summer foliage effect is powerful.
Likes open but sheltered sites and reasonable soil. Tolerates clay, chalk and a little shade, but is not keen about dry soils in which it will grow rather slowly.
Prune only to remove dead or unwanted stems in spring.
Propagate by taking cuttings of firm shoot tips in summer.

Buddleja alternifolia
3 x 3 m (10 x 10 ft) or more

A graceful alternative to B. davidii, this species has an arching habit and narrow green leaves that are shed in winter. Lilac-pink flower clusters are carried right along the cascading stems in June, making the bush a real picture. Unlike B. davidii this species flowers on older wood, so don't prune it in the same way. It can be grown as a standard tree if trained to produce one fat stem from which the branches are allowed to cascade.
Likes full sun and a well-drained soil. Tolerates clay, chalk, dry soil, cold gardens and even a modicum of coastal exposure.
Prune out the older shoots once the flowers have faded. The stems produced through the rest of the

"A large shrub of box is crashingly dull, but smaller bushes kept close-clipped are fun."

Shrubs for ground cover

The measurement given after each plant is the recommended planting distance when the shrub is used in quantity as ground cover.

VARIETY	DISTANCE APART
Cistus	60 cm (2 ft)
Convolvulus	45 cm (18 in)
Cotoneaster dammeri	45 cm (18 in)
Cytisus (some)	45 cm (18 in)
Euonymus fortunei	45 cm (18 in)
Fuchsia	60 cm (2 ft)
Gaultheria (syn. Pernettya)	45 cm (18 in)
Genista (some)	45 cm (18 in)
Heathers	30 cm (12 in)
Hebe	45 cm (18 in)
Hedera	30 cm (12 in)
Hypericum	45 cm (18 in)
Juniperus	90 cm (3 ft)
Lavandula	45 cm (18 in)
Mahonia aquifolium	60 cm (2 ft)
Phlomis	45 cm (18 in)
Potentilla	60 cm (2 ft)
Prunus laurocerasus 'Otto Luyken'	60 cm (2 ft)
Rhododendron (some)	60 cm-1.5 m (2-5 ft)
Ruta	30 cm (12 in)
Salix	60 cm (2 ft)
Santolina	45 cm (18 in)
Sarcococca	45 cm (18 in)
Skimmia	60 cm (2 ft)
Symphoricarpos	60 cm (2 ft)
Viburnum tinus	60 cm (2 ft)
Vinca	45 cm (18 in)

summer will carry next year's crop of flowers.
Propagate by taking cuttings of shoot tips in summer, or by rooting hardwood cuttings outdoors in autumn.

Buddleja davidii
Butterfly Bush
3 x 3 m (10 x 10 ft)

Vigorous, eye-catching and easy to grow, the butterfly bush earns its name by acting as a hostelry to all manner of butterflies when its flower spikes open in July and August. The deciduous leaves are dark green on the upper surface and greyish below, and there are many varieties with flower spikes of pink, white, crimson, purple and violet. There are also two varieties with variegated leaves. Plant any of them at the back of a border or in gaps between paving stones on a patio to bring butterflies close to you in summer. Every garden should have one.
Likes full sun and a well-drained soil. Tolerates clay, chalk, dry soil, boggy soil, cold gardens and some coastal sites.
Prune hard back each winter, reducing the sideshoots (and even the main stems) to mere stumps to maintain a

vigorous and flower-laden bush.
Propagate by taking cuttings of flowerless shoot tips in summer and by rooting hardwood cuttings outdoors in autumn.

Buxus sempervirens
Box
Up to 3 x 3 m (10 x 10 ft) and more

A large shrub of box is crashingly dull, but smaller bushes kept close-clipped are fun, as are dwarf hedges around a kitchen garden (see p.84).
B. sempervirens 'Suffruticosa' is the miniature that grows to just 30–45 cm (12–18 in) tall and it can be clipped into tiny domes or cones in formal gardens, as well as being used as an edger. Try also the variegated varieties whose leaves are edged with creamy white.
Likes an open or shady spot in reasonably moisture-retentive soil. Tolerates clay, chalk, dry soil and shade.
Prune by clipping back in May. Excellent for topiary if you are a fan of vegetative peacocks and chessmen. Never cut back into very old wood.
Propagate by rooting cuttings of shoot tips in summer, or by dividing the dwarf kind in spring.

Calluna See Heathers

Camellia x *williamsii*
2.4 x 2.4 m (8 x 8 ft)

I reckon that this is the best of the camellias – evergreen spring-flowering shrubs with blooms as big as roses – for it sheds its flowers when they fade, rather than letting them turn brown on the plant, which is what happens with *C. japonica* (see p.92). The best variety is 'Donation', a double-flowered confection of pink.
Likes a peaty, moisture-retentive, lime-free soil and a spot in dappled shade. Avoid frost pockets or the blooms will be damaged as they unfurl. Tolerates bright sun provided that the soil does not become dust-dry. Will

tolerate occasional dryness at the expense of making growth.
Prune only when absolutely essential, removing old or badly placed stems after flowering in spring.
Propagate by inserting cuttings of firm young shoots in summer, or by layering suitably low-slung branches. Leaf-bud cuttings can also be taken.

Caryopteris x *clandonensis*
Blue Spiraea
90 cm x 1.5 m (3 x 5 ft)

Any shrub of modest size that extends the season of interest in a garden must be worth planting. So it is with the blue spiraea. The deciduous leaves are grey and roughly toothed, and from their axils spring fluffy clusters of blue flowers in late summer and early autumn. Butterflies love it. Superb with other grey-foliage plants and at the front of beds and borders.
Likes full sun and a well-drained soil. Tolerates dry soil, chalky soil and coastal exposure.
Prune back all the shoots quite hard each spring to encourage the production of healthy young growth.
Propagate by taking cuttings of shoot tips in summer.

Ceanothus See p.93

Chaenomeles See p.94

Chamaecyparis species
Cypress
Various sizes

There are dozens of different species and varieties of cypress with varying habits, from the squat to the columnar, and varying colours, from golden yellow to blue-grey. I've room to mention just a few favourites, but there are others recommended in Chapter 4 Trees too:
C. lawsoniana 'Gimbornii' is a 60 cm (2 ft) high dome of grey-green.
C. lawsoniana 'Minima Aurea' makes a yellow-tinged pyramid of 60 cm (2 ft).

C. pisifera 'Boulevard' grows into a 1.2 m (4 ft) high cone of steel-grey.
C. pisifera 'Filifera Aurea', for all its long name, is a squat spreader with leaves like strands of gold.
   They'll all provide you with year-round enjoyment.
Likes an open site in a humus-rich, well-drained soil. Tolerates clay soils, chalky soils, dry soils and cold gardens.
Prune only to cut out damaged or dead branches. 'Boulevard' can be lightly clipped in spring to encourage new growth and prevent browning.
Propagate by heel cuttings in summer.

Choisya ternata
Mexican Orange Blossom
1.5 x 2.4 m (5 x 8 ft)

If you want a shrub that really pays ground rent, this is a good one to choose. The fingered evergreen leaves are glossy and aromatic when crushed, and the flowers are certainly a lot like orange blossom. They are white, deliciously scented and carried in large clusters, first in late spring and then again late in summer. It's a shapely plant that is easy to grow in most situations. The variety Sundance has young leaves that are acid-yellow; *C.* 'Aztec Pearl' has finely cut leaves and pink-tinged white flowers.
Likes a sunny and sheltered spot in well-drained soil. Tolerates clay, chalk, shade and a certain amount of coastal exposure.
Prune out only dead or damaged branches in spring, along with any straggly shoots that make the bush unshapely. One or two old stems can be removed in spring to rejuvenate ageing bushes.
Propagate by taking cuttings of shoot tips in summer.

Cistus species and varieties
Sun Rose
Various sizes

These lovely sun-worshipping shrubs produce some of the best flowers of early summer: large round blooms seemingly made of crumpled tissue paper and centred with a boss of yellow stamens. Each flower is short-lived, but so many are carried that the bush performs well for several weeks. Often the rough, evergreen foliage is rather tacky to the touch. My favourite three are: *C.* x *cyprius*: to 1.8 x 2.4 m (6 x 8 ft), white flowers blotched with maroon at the base of each petal. *C.* 'Grayswood Pink': 60 cm x 1.2 m (2 x 4 ft), soft pink. *C.* x *purpureus*: 90 cm x 1.5 m (3 x 5 ft), rich pink, each petal blotched with maroon at the base.

Likes full sun and shelter. Tolerates dry soils, chalky soils and coastal exposure.

Prune out frost-damaged growth in spring.

Propagate by taking shoot tip cuttings in summer.

Convolvulus cneorum
60 cm x 1.2 m (2 x 4 ft)

Deservedly high-ranking among silver-leaved shrubs, this plant has none of the characteristics of its pernicious relative, the bindweed. It makes a sprawling bush with silver-haired spatula-shaped leaves, and the shoots are tipped with white, pink-backed trumpet flowers in summer. A gleaming 'evergrey' treasure.

Likes a warm, sunny, sheltered spot (preferably at the base of a south- or west-facing wall) and well-drained soil. Tolerates dry or chalky soil.

Prune out only stems damaged during winter. It is likely to be severely damaged, or even killed outright, by severe winters.

Propagate by layering suitable stems in summer, or by rooting cuttings of firm shoot tips in summer.

Cornus alba
Dogwood
90 cm-1.8 m x 1.8 m (3-6 x 6 ft)

Easily kept low, this shrub is available in many varieties. Here are three:

'Elegantissima' has cream-variegated leaves.

'Sibirica' has bright red stems to cheer you throughout the winter months when the leaves have fallen.

'Spaethii' has leaves freely splashed with butter-yellow.

Likes an open site and any ordinary soil. Tolerates boggy soil, clay, dry soil and chalky soil as well as cold and exposed situations. It also puts up with some shade, though the stems colour up best in full sun.

Prune by cutting back all stems really hard in early spring. This keeps the shrub low and produces plenty of new growth for foliage and stem colour. Cut back to ground level if you like.

Propagate by layering suitable stems (earth up around them to induce root formation); by taking cuttings of firm shoot tips in summer; or by inserting hardwood cuttings outdoors in autumn.

Cornus kousa
3 x 2.4 m (10 x 8 ft)

A real spectacle in June when the horizontal branches are decorated with flowers, each one surrounded by four white, pointed bracts. They nestle like doves among the green leaves. Superb autumn colour provides another good reason for growing the plant. The variety chinensis is rather larger altogether and supposedly freer flowering. I'd have either.

Likes a deep, lime-free soil and a situation in dappled shade. Tolerates quite heavy shade but hates shallow chalky soils.

Prune out any dead stems immediately.

Propagate by taking cuttings of firm shoot tips in summer, or by seeds sown in pots in a frame in spring.

Corylus avellana 'Contorta'
Corkscrew Hazel
3 x 3 m (10 x 10 ft)

The best time to look at this weird and wonderful shrub is in late winter and

early spring when the bare corkscrew branches are dripping with sulphur-yellow catkins. Its other common name of Harry Lauder's walking stick says it all. When the leaves appear, you'd rather forget about the plant: they are puckered and turned under at the edges as if being attacked by a hidden pest. Plant the shrub where summer flowers will mask its embarrassment at that time of year, but make sure you get a good view in winter.

Likes an open spot in well-drained soil. Tolerates clay, dry or chalky soils, and even those that are really damp. It also puts up with shade.

Prune only to remove overcrowding or dead stems in winter.

Propagate by hardwood cuttings in autumn.

Corylus maxima 'Purpurea'
Purple-leafed Filbert
3 x 3 m (10 x 10 ft)

It doesn't do to plant too many purple-leaved shrubs as the effect is rather oppressive, but this shrub must be one of the best. It sends up vigorous stems that are clothed in summer with coarse, bold leaves of deep plum-purple. Probably the largest-leaved purple foliage plant you'll find.

Likes a spot in the open or dappled shade in ordinary soil. Tolerates clay, chalk, dry soils, cold gardens and quite heavy shade.

Prune to remove a few older stems each winter to reduce the density of the thicket.

Propagate by layering or by removing and transplanting rooted suckers.

Cotinus coggygria
Smoke Tree
1.8 x 2.4 m (6 x 8 ft)

This shrub was designed by a sensitive architect: the rather thin leaves are

Sun-loving *Cistus* produces a plentiful supply of papery, pink, white or red flowers. This is *C.* 'Grayswood Pink'.

almost perfectly round, and the buff flowers are a cloud of fluff when they open in midsummer. By autumn they've turned smoke-grey. The bush is shapely, too, and wider than it is tall. Two superb purple-leaved varieties are available: 'Notcutt's Variety' and 'Royal Purple'. Both look terrific when planted near coppery roses such as 'Buff Beauty'. The true variety offers vivid autumn tints; the purple-leaved kinds not as bright, but they certainly make up for it in summer.

Likes well-drained soil and an open spot. Tolerates clay soil, chalky soil and cold gardens.

Prune only to remove one or two old stems and dead wood in late winter.

Propagate by cuttings of firm shoot tips in summer.

Cotoneaster species and varieties
Various sizes

This varied group offers something for almost every situation. They are valued for their foliage and winter berries, although their flowers are pretty spectacular, too. Briefly the ones that you'll find most useful are:
C. conspicuus 'Decorus': 1.8 x 1.8 m (6 x 6 ft), with arching stems clad in evergreen leaves and studded with bird-proof berries in autumn.
C. dammeri: an evergreen ground-hugger with white flowers followed by scarlet berries.
C. frigidus 'Cornubia': 3 x 3 m (10 x 10 ft), is semi-evergreen and laden with hefty clusters of red berries on its cascading stems – not so bird-proof.
C. horizontalis is another good ground coverer, but it is dealt with in Chapter 7 Climbers and Wall Plants. All of the cotoneasters are among the best berry bearers in any garden.

Likes well-drained soil and positions in the open. Tolerates any soil and any situation.

Prune only to remove unwanted or overcrowded growths in spring.

Propagate by rooting cuttings of firm shoot tips in summer.

Cytisus species and varieties
Broom
Various sizes

They don't look much in winter, but the brooms are a treat in spring and early summer when their wiry stems, upright or cascading, are plastered with bright pea flowers. There are many hybrids with flowers of crimson, orange, yellow and creamy white, some of them showing two distinct shades in the same bloom. I'd go for:
C. x *beanii*: 30 x 90 cm (1 x 3 ft), bright yellow and cascading.
C. x *kewensis*: 30 cm x 1.2 m (1-4 ft), creamy yellow flowers and rather more upright.

For brighter flowers I'd choose taller hybrids like 'Windlesham Ruby': 1.5 x 1.5 m (5 x 5 ft), bronze-red. Few of them will disappoint you, but in general all are short-lived. Be prepared to renew them every five to ten years, depending on their health.

Likes a sunny spot in lime-free soil. Tolerates clay soil, dry soil, and some chalky soils, though not those that are really shallow and poor. Also puts up with coastal exposure.

Prune out most of the flowered shoots when the blooms have faded. Failure to do this will produce an overcrowded bush with plenty of dead wood and little vigour. Try to avoid cutting back into really old wood.

Propagate by taking heel cuttings in late summer.

Daphne species and varieties
30-90 x 30-90 cm (1-3 x 1-3 ft)

Valuable little shrubs that flower in winter and spring with blooms that are deliciously scented. The mezereon, *D. mezereum*, 90 cm x 1.2 m (3 x 4 ft), with its pink or white flower cockades on bare stems in winter, is undoubtedly the most popular species, but there are others offering a greater season of interest. *D. odora* 'Aureomarginata': 1.2 x 1.5 m (4 x 5 ft), has evergreen leaves margined with cream, and clusters of pale pink perfumed blossoms in spring.
D. x *burkwoodii*: 90 cm x 1.2 m (3 x 4 ft), is good: a semi-evergreen, it carries pale pink flowers in May and June, extending your daphne season. No perfumed plot would be complete without them.

Likes to be planted when young in well-drained organically enriched soil that never dries out completely. Enjoy good light. Tolerates chalky soil, in the case of *D. mezereum* – the others don't like it much.

Prune out only dead shoots, nothing else.

Propagate by taking cuttings of firm shoot tips in summer.

Deutzia x *magnifica*
1.8 x 1.8 m (6 x 6 ft)

If you're planting a June border, don't forget the deutzias. This one, like most, grows upright before arching its stems to show off the double rosettes of white flowers against the green summer foliage. The flowering season is glorious but sadly brief and you'd be well advised to use the shrub where it can act as a green backdrop for brighter blooms in late summer. There are other species and varieties of similar build with flowers of pink or white.

Likes a sunny spot in any well-drained soil. Tolerates clay, dry or chalky soil and cold, exposed gardens.

Prune out some of the older shoots completely every year as soon as the flowers fade.

Propagate by taking cuttings of firm shoot tips in summer or by rooting hardwood cuttings in autumn.

Elaeagnus pungens 'Maculata'
Oleaster
2.4 x 3 m (8 x 10 ft)

Show-stopping in winter when the sun catches its leaves, this is a variegated evergreen that should be on the top of your list. Each oval leaf is margined

Shrubs for planting as single features

Where there is no room for a small tree, these shrubs can be relied on to act as focal points.

- *Acer palmatum* varieties
- *Acer shirasawanum* 'Aureum'
- *Aralia*
- *Buddleja alternifolia*
- *Camellia*
- *Chamaecyparis*
- *Cornus kousa*
- *Cotinus coggygria* varieties
- *Cotoneaster conspicuus* 'Decorus'
- *Elaeagnus pungens* 'Maculata'
- *Embothrium*
- *Eucryphia*
- *Fatsia*
- *Genista aetnensis*
- *Hamamelis*
- *Hibiscus*
- *Ilex*
- *Juniperus*
- *Laurus*
- *Lavatera*
- *Leycesteria*
- *Magnolia*
- *Mahonia* x *media* 'Charity'
- *Paeonia*
- *Pieris*
- *Pittosporum*
- *Prunus triloba*
- *Rhododendron*
- *Rhus*
- *Sambucus*
- *Syringa*
- *Tamarix*
- *Viburnum* (some)
- *Yucca*

with dark green and centred with a splash of bright yellow. Handsome all the year round, this shrub really comes into its own in the dreary months. A must for any 'winter garden'. The variety *E.* x *ebbingei* 'Gilt Edge' has yellow rims to its green leaves.

Likes any good soil and an open position sheltered from biting winds. Tolerates clay, chalk, dry soil, cold gardens and coastal exposure.

Prune out any shoots that revert to plain green, and remove or shorten unwanted stems in spring.

Propagate by taking cuttings of firm young shoots in late summer and early autumn.

Embothrium coccineum

Chilean Fire Bush

6 x 3 m (20 x 10 ft)

A gambler's treasure. A stunning tree-like shrub with semi-evergreen leaves and, in early summer, masses of fiery orange-red flowers that are long and thin and held in dense clusters along the stems. The Lanceolatum Group is

also good, but 'Ñorquinco' is breathtaking and can be seen thriving at Harlow Carr Gardens in Yorkshire.

Likes best a spot in woodland where organic, lime-free soil and dappled shade are found. Tolerates moist ground and cold gardens as long as some shelter can be provided from damaging winds.

Prune out only dead wood in winter.

Propagate by sowing seeds in a propagator in spring; cuttings of firm shoot tips (or root cuttings) can be taken in summer.

Erica See Heathers

Escallonia 'Donard Star'

1.8 x 1.8 m (6 x 6 ft)

I choose this variety as being representative of a group of plants that should be valued by more gardeners. They are of pleasing habit, bushy and upright or rather arching; most are clothed all the year round in shiny evergreen leaves, and all are generously decorated from summer to autumn with small but profuse flowers

of white, pink or deep rose. The cultivar 'Donard Star' has deep pink blooms.

Likes any reasonably well-drained soil and a position in full sun. Tolerates clay, chalky soil, dry soil and coastal exposure.

Prune out large portions of flowered growth completely once the blooms have faded. Sideshoots can also be shortened after flowering. After severe winters, any badly damaged growth can be cut out completely in spring as soon as new shoots can be seen growing away.

Propagate by taking cuttings of firm young shoots in summer.

Eucryphia x nymansensis 'Nymansay'

6 x 3 m (20 x 10 ft)

This has to be one of my 'Desert Island' shrubs. The upright branches on this tall bush or tree are clothed all the year round in dark evergreen leaves. In late summer, a feast of white flowers erupts all over them, each pristine blossom being centred with a tuft of fluffy stamens. The timing is as welcome as the spectacle itself – a sort of farewell to summer. Just the plant for the back of a wide border.

There's a handsome eucryphia planted outside the back door of Beatrix Potter's old home, Hill Top Farm at Sawrey in the Lake District, proving that some species (such as *E. glutinosa*) are tougher than many folk would have you believe.

Likes a moist, preferably lime-free soil that is never likely to dry out. Dappled shade is enjoyed too, but not heavy murk. This hybrid tolerates a chalky soil better than most eucryphias, and it will survive in fairly cold gardens provided that shelter can be given from biting winds.

Prune not at all, except to remove dead or damaged stems.

Propagate by layering suitable stems, or by taking cuttings of firm shoot tips in early autumn.

Euonymus europaeus

Spindle Tree

3 x 3 m (10 x 10 ft)

Doubly valuable in autumn, our native spindle tree colours its foliage well with tints of orange and crimson, and carries bunches of four-lobed fruits that are rich crimson-pink, splitting to reveal orange seeds. 'Red Cascade' is a particularly good form.

Likes any reasonable soil and a spot in full sun. Tolerates clay, dry soil, chalky soil and cold gardens. Will put up with shade but you won't get such good autumn colour.

Prune only to remove old and overcrowding stems and dead wood.

Propagate by hardwood cuttings or layering.

> "Most folk think of *Fatsia japonica* as a house plant, but it's as tough as old boots in the garden."

Euonymus fortunei 'Emerald 'n' Gold'

30 x 90 cm (1 x 3 ft)

A bright little carpeter with evergreen leaves that are blotched with butter-yellow and green. They take on pink tinges during cold winter weather, and the shrub will even scale walls if planted against them. There are other varieties of different habits and variegations, such as the green and white 'Emerald Gaiety'.

Likes ordinary soil and an open site. Tolerates most soils and situations.

Prune not at all, except to restrict its spread.

Propagate by cuttings of shoot tips in autumn or by layering.

Fatsia japonica

False Castor Oil Palm

1.8 x 1.8 m (6 x 6 ft)

Most folk think of this as a house plant, but it's as tough as old boots in the garden. True, it might be killed back to the stump by really severe winter weather once every five years, but it always seems to sprout again in spring, and in most years it will remain evergreen, those big, glossy, hand-shaped leaves forming a handsome mound of greenery. Starry white flowerheads are often carried in autumn. A plant has grown happily in my parents' garden in the Yorkshire Dales for over 30 years, and it's also an excellent choice for town gardens.

Likes good, moisture-retentive soil and full sun. Tolerates gentle shade, cold gardens, clay or chalky soil and coastal exposure.

Prune it not at all.

Propagate from shoot tip cuttings taken in summer, or by root cuttings.

Forsythia x *intermedia* 'Lynwood'

Golden Bells

2.4 x 2.4 m (8 x 8 ft)

All right, so forsythias might be in everybody's garden, but that's only because nothing else can touch them when it comes to brilliant spring colour! This, I think, is the best forsythia to grow as a shrub (see also Chapter 7 Climbers and Wall Plants). It makes an upright bush whose bare khaki stems cannot be seen in spring for the profusion of stemless yellow flowers. The large green leaves emerge to hide the fading blooms and provide pleasant verdure for the rest of the year when other plants are doing their stuff. Site it where you can admire it from a window on dull winter days.

Likes good, well-drained soil and a sunny spot. Tolerates clay and chalk and cold, exposed gardens, but don't plant it in shade or it won't flower at all well.

Prune it immediately after flowering, taking out completely those stems that have carried flowers. The shoots that form during the summer will carry next year's blooms.

Propagate by layering, by hardwood cuttings in autumn and by shoot tip cuttings in summer.

Fuchsia magellanica

varieties

1.8 x 1.8 m (6 x 6 ft)

The hardy fuchsias are a delight in summer and on into autumn, when their ballerina flowers drip from the arching, blushing branches. The blooms of this species have a petticoat of purple held below carmine sepals – a vibrant combination of colour found in few plants. The foliage of 'Versicolor' is a confection of green, pink and cream; var. *gracilis* 'Variegata' is similar but without the pink.

There are numerous hybrid hardy fuchsias (not to be confused with the more tender greenhouse kinds) but among the very best are 'Mrs Popple' – again with the carmine and purple combination and terribly generous with her flowers; and 'Mrs W. P. Wood', whose little blooms of blush-pink dangle like icicles from shapely bushes. In some years, or in cold gardens, the plants might be killed to ground level by winter frosts; but in milder areas they'll lose their leaves in winter and very little else.

Likes sunny spots in good, well-drained soil. Tolerates clay, chalk and coastal exposure.

Prune back to ground level in February in cold gardens or severe winters. Where the stems survive the winter, remove a few of the older ones in February and shorten all sideshoots to three buds. Earthing up with organic matter in autumn gives welcome frost protection to the roots and crown.

Propagate from shoot tip cuttings in summer.

Gaultheria (syn. *Pernettya*) *mucronata*

Prickly Heath

60 cm x 1.2 m (2 x 4 ft)

Knee-high thickets of tiny, pointed evergreen leaves don't sound very interesting, but smother them in purple, pink, red or white berries in autumn and you'll have a sight worth seeing. To get plenty of fruits you'll need several plants to ensure adequate pollination: some have predominantly male flowers, others female. There are named varieties offering berries of certain colours. Good under trees.
Likes peaty, lime-free soil and a spot in dappled shade. Don't let the earth dry out in summer. Tolerates clay and moist soils and cold, exposed gardens in light or heavy shade.
Prune hardly at all. It's sufficient to cut out unwanted stems at ground level in spring.
Propagate by division in spring or by shoot tip cuttings in summer.

Shrubs with evergreen leaves

- Abelia
- Aucuba
- Bamboos (some)
- *Berberis darwinii*
- *Berberis* x *stenophylla*
- *Buxus*
- Camellia
- Chamaecyparis
- Choisya
- Cistus
- Convolvulus
- *Cotoneaster* (some)
- *Daphne* (some)
- Elaeagnus
- Escallonia
- Eucryphia
- *Euonymus fortunei*
- Fatsia
- Heathers
- Hebe
- Hedera
- Hypericum
- Ilex
- Juniperus
- Laurus
- Lavandula
- Mahonia
- Myrtus
- Olearia
- Osmanthus
- Pernettya
- Phlomis
- Photinia
- Pieris
- Pittosporum
- *Prunus laurocerasus* 'Otto Luyken'
- Rhododendron
- Rosmarinus
- Ruta
- Santolina
- Sarcococca
- Skimmia
- *Viburnum tinus*
- Vinca
- Yucca

Genista species

Broom

Various sizes

There are four genistas I think you ought to know about, and each one is different. The giant of the race is *G. aetnensis*, the Mount Etna broom, which virtually makes a tree up to 4.5 x 3 m (15 x 10 ft) with wispy, semi-weeping stems, studded in summer with yellow pea flowers. Plant near a patio where it will cast the gentlest shade. *G. hispanica*: 30 x 90 cm (1 x 3 ft), is the spitting image of a miniature gorse, which is why it's

called the Spanish gorse. Its barbarous stems are interlaced with yellow pea flowers in late spring. *G. lydia*: 45 x 90 cm (18 in x 3 ft), is a cascading charmer for a bank or rock garden where its wiry stems drip with bright yellow blooms in spring. And finally *G. sagittalis*, 15 cm x 1.2 m (6 in x 4 ft), a carpeting curiosity with flattened, winged stems and the usual yellow flowers in early summer. Scrambling across rocks or paving, it's a real eye-catcher.
Likes sun and well-drained soil. Tolerates clay, dry soil and some chalky soils, though not the poorest and shallowest. Happy in coastal exposure.
Prune out most of the flowering shoots when the blooms have faded. Avoid cutting back into old wood. *G. aetnensis* can be trained to grow upwards in its youth, and as it matures no pruning is necessary, other than the removal of dead wood.
Propagate by sowing seeds in gentle heat in spring or by rooting heel cuttings in late summer.

Hamamelis mollis

Witch Hazel

3 x 4.5 m (10 x 15 ft)

A delight to the senses when the shuttlecock of bare branches is colonized by fragrant yellow spider flowers in winter. In the true species the blooms are bright yellow, radiating from a central bronze-red core, while in *H.* x *intermedia* 'Pallida' they are a soft sulphur-yellow, making them even more remarkable against a leaden sky. Some varieties, like 'Ruby Glow', have red flowers – a pleasant variation, but not so noticeable in dreary weather.

The marble-sized berries of *Gaultheria mucronata* (prickly heath) appear first in autumn, and last until the end of winter.

The large, hazel-like leaves unfurl in spring and take on rich autumn tints before they fall.

Likes good soil that's lime-free and not prone to drought. Tolerates clay soil and cold gardens.

Prune only to remove dead wood.

Propagate by layering suitable stems in spring or summer.

Heathers

Heath, Heather and Ling
15–45 cm x 90 cm (6–18 in x 3 ft)

I've cheated on the naming and grouped Erica (heath), *Calluna* (heather) and Daboecia (St Dabeoc's heath) together to make life easier. They can be had in flower in most months of the year, many of them have brilliant foliage that takes on vibrant tints of yellow, orange and mahogany red in winter, and all are superb ground coverers. Some species of Erica even tolerate chalky soil, the other two will not. I'll draw your attention to two really tall heaths that should be more widely planted: *E. lusitanica*, 3 x 3 m (10 x 10 ft), with wispy green leaves and tiers of tiny white flowers; and *E. arborea*, the tree heath, which is similar but even larger. Both bloom in spring and both need a warm, sheltered spot. They prefer warm coastal districts.

Likes acid, peaty soil that never dries out and an open site. Tolerates chalky soil (if you choose varieties of *E. carnea, E. x darleyensis, E. erigena* and *E. terminalis*), clay soil and dry soil. The dwarf species are happy in cold gardens.

Prune after flowering, lightly clipping over the foliate with shears.

Propagate by taking short stem cuttings in summer or by removing rooted layers.

Hebe species and varieties
Shrubby Veronica
30 cm–1.5 m x 2.4 m (1–5 x 8 ft)

Rather tender shrubs with opposite and decussate (criss-cross) leaves and bottle-brush sprays of flowers in summer or autumn. They are evergreen, and some species and varieties have coloured foliage – purplish on the undersides or glaucous grey all over. I'll recommend but three, for I've space for no more: *H.* 'Autumn Glory', 60 cm x 1.2 m (2 x 4 ft), is a valuable late summer and autumn bloomer with purple spikes and glossy green leaves; *H.* 'Great Orme', 75 cm x 1.2 m (2½ x 4 ft), although not as hardy as some, has slender spikes of such a lovely shade of pink that it's worth the risk; and *H. pinguifolia* 'Pagei', 30 x 60 cm (1 x 2 ft), makes hummocks of short grey leaves studded with white flowers in summer. The so-called 'whipcord' hebes are worth a try. Their leaves are strands of bronze- or golden-green growth, almost like a conifer, and they are hardier than the larger-leaved species. The most popular whipcord is *H. cupressoides*.

Likes warm, sheltered spots in well-drained soil. Tolerates dry soil, chalky soil and sometimes heavy clay too. They don't mind coastal exposure.
Prune out frost-damaged stems in spring when new shoots can be seen breaking from lower down. Cut back aged specimens into old wood in spring or summer; they will soon sprout up again. Remove one or two old stems each May and shorten the other growths by half. If you're lazy simply clip over the bushes lightly with

shears in spring. Very dwarf species need not be pruned annually.
Propagate by taking cuttings of shoot tips in summer.

Hedera varieties
Ivy
15 cm–15 m x 1.5 m (6 in–50 ft x 5 ft) or more

Although ivy is primarily thought of as a climber, it is invaluable as a weed-suppressing carpeter, particularly in shade and under trees. The varieties of *H. helix* are tremendously varied in appearance, having lobed evergreen leaves that may be dull and dark or shiny and vibrantly coloured in shades of cream, white, yellow and green. The best climbers are mentioned in Chapter 7 Climbers and Wall Plants, but here I would draw your attention to *H. helix* 'Arborescens', an adult form of the common ivy, with unlobed leaves and woody stems making a bush 1.5 x 3 m (5 x 10 ft). It is the form of ivy that often appears atop trees and walls when the younger stems have done the climbing. *H. hibernica* is unsurpassable as ground cover under trees, making a thick carpet of glossy green. This, too, has an adult

Hydrangeas are deservedly popular for their mass of either mop-head or lace-cap flowerheads. Both types are available in white, pink, red and blue.

form that is taller and more shrubby. *H. helix* 'Erecta', 45 x 90 cm (18 in x 3 ft), makes a neat, upright bush with leaves in tiered piles. It is a fine feature at the front of a border.
Likes most sites and soils – variegated varieties prefer good light to shade.
Prune most kinds by clipping over with shears in May. The arborescent (shrubby) kinds need no pruning.
Propagate by taking cuttings of shoot tips in summer: adventitious roots may already be present. Layers can be lifted and transplanted in spring.

Helianthemum See p.176

Hibiscus syriacus
2.4 x 1.8 m (8 x 6 ft)

No plant will tax your patience more than a hardy hibiscus. Just when you're about to give it up for dead in June, its grey stems will burst into life. The mallow flowers will appear among the leaves in late summer and autumn before the foliage falls and this lazy plant goes to sleep again. All varieties make upright bushes; 'Woodbridge' has rich rose-pink blooms, 'Hamabo' is white, and 'Oiseau Bleu' (syn. Blue Bird) a wishy-washy lavender; all are blotched with crimson at the base of the petals. At least the plants do make quite an effort when they're in bloom!
Likes a warm, sunny, sheltered spot in rich, well-drained soil. Best in the south of England. Tolerates clay, dry or chalky soils and warm coastal gardens.
Prune only to remove dead or damaged shoots in summer.
Propagate by taking shoot tip cuttings in summer or autumn and rooting them in a propagator. They can take an age to root. Layer suitable stems.

Hoheria See p.96

Hydrangea macrophylla varieties
1.5 x 3 m (5 x 10 ft)

There are two kinds of common hydrangea, the fat, mop-headed or

'Hortensia' varieties with their cob-loaf-like flowers of white, pink or blue, and the lace-caps with their flattened heads of tiny flowers surrounded by sterile florets with larger petals. The colour range is the same. All are deciduous and bloom in late summer and early autumn. Your local nurseryman will have his own favourites. Hydrangeas are enjoyed near front doors, especially in the southern counties, but they are also excellent in wide borders where they look good with ornamental grasses and other foliage plants.

Likes sunny spots, sheltered from strong winds, and a rich soil that is unlikely to dry out. Tolerates clay and chalk and very moist soils. Happy by the coast. Blue varieties colour best in acid soils: they usually turn pink in chalky soil. Water them with proprietary hydrangea colorant to help restore their cerulean qualities, or settle for a rosy glow.

Prune out weak and very old shoots completely in spring before growth starts. At the same time cut off the faded flowerheads above the topmost pair of fat buds. Single fat buds at the stem tips should not be removed for they are certain to flower.

Propagate by taking cuttings of firm shoot tips in summer.

Hydrangea paniculata
1.5 x 1.8 m (5 x 6 ft)

The white or pink-tinged flowers are more pyramidal in outline than those of *H. macrophylla*, though they are carried at the same time, in late summer and autumn. The variety 'Grandiflora' has the largest blooms and is rightly in demand. Plant it where you can get a good look at it during the flowering season.

Likes sunny spots and a good soil that's not likely to suffer from drought. Tolerates cold gardens more than the previous species. Also happy in clay and chalk.

Prune the shoots really hard back to

within 2.5 cm (1 in) of the main stem or ground level in late winter; this species flowers on shoots made during the current season, and if not pruned it gets taller and out of hand.

Propagate by taking cuttings of firm shoot tips in summer.

Hypericum species and varieties
St John's Wort
30 cm-1.5 m x 1.8 m (1-5 ft x 6 ft) or more

Sneers abound when hypericum is mentioned in high horticultural circles, but this is a deserving race of plants whose only failing is a desire to please (and an occasional attack of rust disease). *H. calycinum*, 30 cm x several metres (1 ft x several yards), is the rose of Sharon, a rampant spreader that is a boon to the gardener who wants a bright weed smotherer in dry soil under trees. It's semi-evergreen and carries plenty of yellow, shaving-brush-centred flowers in summer and autumn. *H.* 'Hidcote' is one of the best taller varieties at 1.5 x 1.8 m (5 x 6 ft). The yellow flowers are similar to the rose of Sharon but not so well endowed with central bristles.

Likes reasonably good soil and good light. Tolerates shade, clay, chalk and dry soils and coastal exposure.

Prune *H. calycinum* by clipping it back to within about 5 cm (a couple of inches) of ground level in spring, just before growth begins. At the same time, cut out completely any old and weak stems on *H.* 'Hidcote'.

Propagate by lifting and transplanting rooted portions of the plants in autumn or spring. Cuttings may be taken from the shoot tips of *H.* 'Hidcote' in summer.

Ilex aquifolium
Holly
6 x 3 m (20 x 10 ft) at least

As well as making excellent trees and hedges, hollies are very useful evergreen border plants, providing a

background of glossy green or green and yellow. Male and female flowers are carried on separate plants and only the females will carry berries, provided there is a male in the vicinity to pollinate their flowers.

Varieties of *I.* x *altaclerensis* are as good as those of the common holly, though their leaves are usually larger and less spiny. There are dozens of different variegations described in detail in nurserymen's catalogues: check the sex as well as the colouring.

Likes good, well-drained soil not prone to drought. Tolerates almost any soil and situation in sun or shade.

Prune to remove Christmas holly, or clip after fruiting to produce a formal shape. Regular pruning is unnecessary.

Propagate by shoot tip cuttings in a propagator in summer/autumn.

Jasminum See p.96

Juniperus species and varieties
Juniper, Savin
Various sizes

Fuzzy-foliaged conifers of upright or spreading habit, the junipers can be used either as elegant and deep ground cover or as columnar eye-catchers in flat border plantings. Forms of *J. horizontalis* and *J. sabina* (Savin) are among the best spreaders, sending out rocket-like growths over or above the ground. They grow to between 30 cm and 1.5 m (1 and 5 ft) high and to between 1.2 and 3 m (4 and 10 ft) across. *J. communis* provides plenty of upright forms, the favourite being the tiny *J. communis* 'Compressa', a bollard just 45 cm (18 in) high and 15 cm (6 in) across. The spreading forms are superb at covering manhole covers, even if they do make inspection a prickly job!

Likes soil enriched with humus. Tolerates any soil and situation except severe drought.

Prune only to remove dead wood.

Propagate by heel cuttings of young shoot tips in summer.

Kerria japonica 'Pleniflora'
Jew's Mallow
1.8 x 1.8 m (6 x 6 ft)

Nobody would recommend Kerria as a specimen front-of-the-border plant – its season is so short – but it is good at the back! Its wiry green canes are bare of leaves in winter and dotted with 3 cm (1 in) wide double chrysanthemum flowers of bright yellow in spring before the foliage unfurls. Soon it becomes an arching shuttlecock of green, but hardly a year goes by without its flowers drawing comments from gardeners unfamiliar with the spectacle. There is a single-flowered variety but it's not as good as the double.

Likes good soil and a sunny spot. Tolerates clay and chalky soil, some shade and cold, exposed gardens.

Prune out plenty of older stems completely as soon as the flowers fade.

Propagate by division or layering. Cuttings of firm shoot tips can be rooted in a propagator in summer.

Laurus nobilis
Sweet Bay, Victor's Laurel
Up to 15 x 4.5 m (50 x 15 ft)

Plant your own sweet bay and never buy another packet of bay leaves! Choose a young plant as older ones are prohibitively expensive. It's an evergreen, with leathery oval leaves that are aromatic and fruity flavoured when used in cooking. It can be left to grow unchecked, or clipped quite formally into a pyramid or lollipop – whatever takes your fancy. Only after many years and no clipping or pruning will it reach the given height.

Likes a warm, sheltered spot and a good soil that's not likely to dry out in summer. Drought or biting winds will burn the foliage. Tolerates sun or light shade, clay or chalky soil and coastal exposure.

Prune in spring or summer when necessary.

Propagate by taking cuttings of shoot tips in summer.

Lavandula angustifolia
Lavender
60 x 60 cm (2 x 2 ft)

Brushing past a bank of lavender on a warm summer's day is a treat to the senses. Nothing else has that sweet and fruity aroma.

Whichever variety you choose the plant will have downy grey foliage (though one or two are nearer grey-green) and spikes of purple-blue flowers on slender stems in summer. There are pink- and white-flowered forms, but both are remarkable for their insipidity. I'd go for 'Hidcote' as first choice and then, perhaps, Miss Jekyll's 'Munstead'.

The foliage is just as fragrant as the flowers, and the plants make unsurpassable edging to beds, borders and paths.

L. 'Helmsdale' is a lovely species with flowers that have 'ears'. It will survive mild winters.

Likes reasonably well-drained soil that is not heavily acid, and a spot in full sun. Tolerates dry soil and chalky soil.

Prune by clipping over the plants once the flowers have faded.

Propagate by taking cuttings of shoot tips in summer.

Lavatera x *clementii* 'Rosea'
Tree Mallow
2.4 x 2.4 m (8 x 8 ft)

A smashing shrub for a warm garden, I've never known any plant to be more generous with its flowers. They deck the downy grey stems from July to November – large pink mallow blooms that look a treat with the lobed, grey-green leaves. The shrub grows vigorously in any season, so give it plenty of space to spread its branches. Lovely against a south-facing wall of mellow brick.

Likes a warm, sheltered spot in full sun and a poor, well-drained soil. Tolerates dry or chalky soil and coastal exposure.

Prune hard back each spring, to

Shrubs for autumn and winter interest

These shrubs provide autumn and winter interest, having colourful berries, attractive bark or stems, or vibrant autumn foliage.

COLOURFUL BERRIES
- *Aucuba*
- *Berberis*
- *Cotoneaster*
- *Euonymus europaeus*
- *Gaultheria* (syn. *Pernettya*)
- *Ilex*
- *Leycesteria*
- *Mahonia aquifolium*
- *Sambucus*
- *Skimmia*
- *Symphoricarpos*

ATTRACTIVE BARK OR STEMS
- *Acer palmatum* 'Sango-kaku'
- Bamboos
- *Cornus alba* varieties
- *Corylus avellana* 'Contorta'
- *Deutzia*
- *Kerria*
- *Leycesteria*
- *Pittosporum*
- *Salix*

AUTUMN FOLIAGE COLOUR
- *Acer palmatum* 'Sango-kaku'
- *Acer palmatum* 'Ôsakazuki'
- *Amelanchier*
- *Berberis*
- *Cornus kousa*
- *Cotinus*
- *Euonymus*
- *Hamamelis*
- Heathers
- *Mahonia*
- *Ruta*
- *Viburnum*

ground level or to shoots breaking from mature stems.

Propagate from shoot tip cuttings rooted in a propagator in late summer. Plant a young specimen and be prepared to replace it after a few years: it may flower itself to death or, in the very cold parts of the country, be killed by severe winters.

Leycesteria formosa
Himalayan Honeysuckle
2. x 2.4 m (8 x 8 ft)

Here's a good plant for the impatient gardener. Each spring it sends up a number of bright green bamboo stems that arch at the tips. In July, August and September white flowers drip from the leaf-laden stems in long tassels, but you can hardly see them for the deep maroon bracts that overlap them. Black berries follow. Good for adding beefiness to a border.
Likes a rich soil in sun. Tolerates chalky soil, clay soil, shade and coastal exposure.
Prune everything to ground level in spring, in which case you'll have to make sure the plant is mulched annually with manure at the same time, or prune out older, flowered stems in spring, leaving just the healthy young ones.
Propagate by dividing clumps in spring and by digging up and transplanting self-sown seedlings, of which there will be plenty.

Lonicera See p.97

Magnolia species and varieties
2.4-6 m x 2.4-6 m (8-20 ft x 8-20 ft)

'Ooh' and 'aah' shrubs. There are two species of magnolia that are regularly planted; of these the commoner and, I think, the more beautiful, is *M. x soulangeana*. It makes a wide-spreading bush with upturned branches. Examine a plant in winter and you'll see silky hairy buds just waiting to do their stuff in spring.

Come April and May, with any luck, they'll erupt into white eggs and then burst into the typical waxy magnolia flowers. As they fade, the large green leaves will emerge to hide them. There are pure white varieties such as 'Alba Superba', but my heart belongs to 'Rustica Rubra' with its basal flushing of rosy purple.

The other magnolia of renown is *M. stellata*, smaller at 2.4-3 m (8-10 ft) round, and bedecked with starry white flowers earlier in spring. The trouble is that it is frequently burned by frost. *M. x loebneri* 'Merrill' is slightly later in bloom and also tolerates my chalky soil. All magnolias need plenty of room to spread.
Likes a sunny, sheltered spot in a good soil that's not chalky. Tolerates a little shade, clay or moist soil and chalky soil provided the topsoil is deep and suitably enriched.
Prune only to remove dead wood.
Propagate by layering suitable branches in spring.

Mahonia species and varieties
90 cm-2.4 m x 1.8 m (3-8 ft x 6 ft)

Architectural evergreen shrubs that add shape and form to the garden, as well as colour and perfume from their flowers. *M. japonica* is my first choice. Its large leaves composed of holly-like leaflets are held out at right angles to the stem, the top of which is decorated with long yellow flower tassels in winter. It is superbly scented. The mahonia most popular with landscape architects is *M. x media* 'Charity' - similar to M. japonica but rather more angular and a little taller at around 2.4 m (8 ft). For the improvement in architectural standing you'll have to sacrifice the scent. Everyman's mahonia is *M. aquifolium*, the Oregon grape - so called because of the black spherical fruits that follow the bunches of yellow spring flowers. It makes a 90 cm (3 ft) high thicket of growth on the poorest soil, and its leaves are burnished maroon in winter.

Use the first two as specimen plants, especially in town gardens, and the last as deep ground cover.
Likes any well-drained soil and a spot in dappled shade. Tolerates clay and chalky soil and heavy shade.
Prune only to remove dead wood or unwanted stems in winter or spring.
Propagate carefully: these shrubs have spiny leaves. Take shoot tip cuttings in summer, or layer suitable stems in spring. *M. aquifolium* can sometimes be divided in spring.

Myrtus communis
Myrtle
2.4 x 2.4 m (8 x 8 ft)

The sweetly scented myrtle is an old English garden plant that seems to have been unjustly neglected of late. The leaves are dark, glossy, evergreen and quite narrow but thickly carried on the stems of a dense bush. The flowers are white with a tuft of stamens in the centre: there is no daintier sight in the garden than a myrtle bush in flower. Plant one at the end of a border to act as a fragrant full stop.
Likes a warm and sheltered spot in well-drained soil (it's not a shrub for a cold, exposed garden). Tolerates dry soil, chalky soil and coastal exposure in the warmer counties.
Prune only lightly in spring to shorten unwanted stems.
Propagate by taking shoot tip cuttings in summer.

Olearia species
Daisy Bush
1.2-3 m x 1.8-3 m (10 x 6-10 ft)

Underrated shrubs with evergreen leaves and white daisy flowers. Great for adding form to a garden. *O. x haastii* has oval dark green leaves that are grey and downy beneath. Billowing heads of white daisies smother the plant in summer. It is the hardiest and the easiest of the bunch and grows to about 1.5 m (5 ft) high and 2.4 m (8 ft) wide. *O. macrodonta* is the biggest of my chosen three at up to 4.5 m (15 ft) high and across. Here the green leaves, downy beneath, are holly-shaped so that even when the summer flower display is over the bush is good to look at. *O.* x *scilloniensis* is 1.8 m x 1.8 m (6 x 6 ft), oval-leaved and a superb sight in flower with its long clusters of daisies. It is the tenderest of the three, but perhaps the most spectacular in bloom.

Likes warm, sheltered spots in sun and a well-drained soil. Tolerates coastal exposure, clay, dry or chalky soils.
Prune out unwanted shoots in spring; try to avoid leaving a cluster of stumps – thin the stems rather than chopping them all back. Leave unpruned if you like, but after a few years you might possess an overgrown bush.
Propagate by taking shoot tip cuttings in summer.

The sweetly smelling, dainty white flowers of *Myrtus communis* are set off to perfection by the glossy dark evergreen leaves.

Osmanthus delavayi

1.8 x 2.4 m (6 x 8 ft) or taller

Three paces after you've passed this shrub in spring you'll catch the most delectable scent – it travels at least that far on the air. It's a handsome bush with tiny evergreen leaves that are dark and glossy. The neat clusters of white tubular flowers nod from the stems to provide you with that spring treat when there's not much else to delight your nose. Best planted by a path to arrest your progress.

Likes a sunny spot in well-drained soil. Tolerates clay, chalky and dry soils and sheltered coastal gardens.

Prune out overgrown stems after flowering. Can train as a wall shrub.

Propagate by shoot tip cuttings in summer, or hardwood cuttings in the autumn.

Paeonia species and varieties
Tree Peony
1.5 x 1.5 m (5 x 5 ft)

Even when they've finished flowering these are handsome plants with a statuesque quality. They make long woody stems at the top of which their finely cut leaves radiate in a sort of Japanese style (in spite of the fact that they are from China!). *P. delavayi* var. *ludlowii* has sharp-toothed leaves of quality and yellow cup-shaped flowers in late spring. It looks good when planted in association with spiky leaved irises and round-leaved bergenias. The varieties of *P. suffruticosa* are certainly the most spectacular when in bloom. Their flowers are the size of dinner plates and may be single or double in shades of pink, yellow, crimson, lavender and white. My own favourite has single white flowers blotched at the base of each petal with deep maroon. There is always a central crown of stamens on the single varieties.

Likes a sheltered, sunny spot that is not liable to be frosted in spring. Organically enriched but well-drained soil. Tolerates chalky soil.

Prune out dead stems and one or two old stems after flowering.

Propagate by sowing seeds in spring, by rooting shoot tip cuttings in summer or by layering suitable stems.

Philadelphus species and varieties
Mock Orange, Syringa
1.8–3 m x 1.8–3 m (6-10 x 6-10 ft)

This plant is sometimes referred to as syringa, which is really the botanical name for lilac. However, they are indispensable shrubs for the flower border where they'll produce arching wands of headily scented white blossoms in early summer, if you choose the right varieties. My number one favourite is 'Beauclerk', the most powerfully perfumed of the lot. Its single flowers are flushed at the base of each petal with purple. 'Virginal' is the one to choose if you prefer double, pure white flowers. Both make good-sized bushes of considerable thickness. *P. coronarius* 'Aureus' produces creamy white flowers, but it's the acid-yellow foliage that makes it desirable. It retains its vibrancy well into summer and looks superb in a planting of golden-leaved shrubs, or where it can be placed against a contrasting purple-leaved plant.

Likes sunny spots in ordinary soil. Tolerates clay, dry and chalky soils and cold, exposed gardens.

Prune out all flowered stems as soon as the blooms have faded.

Propagate by taking shoot tip cuttings in summer or by rooting hardwood cuttings in autumn. *P. coronarius* 'Aureus' produces self-sown seedlings that are as brightly coloured as the parent.

Phlomis fruticosa
Jerusalem Sage
90 cm x 1.5 m (3 x 5 ft)

Patio gardeners can plant this shrub with confidence: it will not take up too much room and it will enjoy the sun and warmth. The evergreen grey-green leaves are densely felted, and from the shoot tips arise tiered yellow flowers in summer. The blooms are carried in whorls around the stem, each flower a little hooded masterpiece.

Likes a warm, sunny spot in well-drained soil. Tolerates dry or chalky soil and coastal planting.

Prune back the shoots in spring to buds that are opening lower down on the stem.

Propagate by cuttings of firm shoot tips in summer. Replace old plants every five years or so.

Photinia x *fraseri* 'Red Robin'
3 x 2.4 m (10 x 8 ft)

Don't gnash your teeth if you're on chalky soil and can't grow *Pieris* – grow *Photinia* instead. It's an evergreen shrub of considerable vigour and its leaves are long yet broad. In spring the young shoots are bright red, not quite as luminous as *Pieris* but not a bad compromise! White flowerheads appear in early summer: they're not much to write home about, but they do extend the season of interest.

Likes an open sunny spot that is not subject to spring frosts; any ordinary soil. Tolerates dry or chalky soil and clay.

Prune out a few old stems and shorten new ones to keep the bush shapely as soon as flowering is finished. Left unpruned the bushes can fall open.

Propagate by cuttings of firm shoot tips in summer.

Phygelius See p.98

Phygelius See p.98

Pieris formosa var. *forrestii*
Lily-of-the-Valley Bush
3 x 3 m (10 x 10 ft)

For reasons that are obvious even to the casual observer this shrub is almost always grown in gardens in its variety 'Wakehurst'. The young shoots that emerge over the dark evergreen leaves in spring are a rich and vibrant red. As they age, the bright shoots turn pink, white and then dark green. Long chains of white lily-of-the-valley flowers are carried at the same time. You can't deny that this shrub does its best to please. *P.* 'Forest Flame' is equally brilliant in leaf, but for flowers go for the heavily laden *P. japonica* 'Purity'.

Likes a peaty, leafy, lime-free soil and a sheltered spot in dappled shade. Tolerates little else.

Prune only to remove unsightly or damaged stems.

Propagate by layering or by taking cuttings of firm shoot tips in summer.

Pittosporum tenuifolium

4.5 x 3 m (15 x 10 ft)

Evergreens have a not altogether undeserved reputation for being dingy and oppressive, but this shrub dispels such maudlin thoughts. It has black stems, but there the sombre colouring ends, for the leaves are light green, glossy and wavy at the edges so that they constantly reflect the light. The variety 'Silver Queen' has brighter leaves still, edged with silvery white; but the crown for brilliance must go to *P.* 'Garnettii' (of hybrid origin), which has white variegation and pink flushing in winter. Purple-leaved varieties are also available. Super background shrubs that take on an important role in winter.

Likes sunny, sheltered spots in well-drained soil. Tolerates coastal exposure, for which they are famous, clay, chalk and dry soil.

Prune out dead wood, or shorten unwanted stems in spring. Otherwise leave untouched.

Propagate by cuttings of firm young shoot tips in summer.

Potentilla fruticosa varieties

Cinquefoil

60 cm-12 m x 12-18 m (2-4 ft x 4-6 ft)

Dumpy bushes, naked in winter but thickly clothed in fingered, silky haired leaves in summer, when they also produce their rounded flowers of yellow, white, orange, and now red. There are dozens of different varieties, and among the best are: 'Elizabeth',

primrose yellow; 'Jackman's Variety', bright yellow; 'Sunset', orange, fading to yellow; 'Abbotswood', white. The two newish arrivals, over which much fuss was made originally, are 'Red Ace', with vermilion-scarlet flowers, and 'Royal Flush', nearer to rose-red. Both are excellent in the right situation but, to use the words of the breeders, they 'fade in conditions of extreme heat, drought and wet'. As the British climate is almost always at some extreme or another the plants are a gamble. All varieties are well suited to being grown in small gardens and they tumble attractively over path edges and down banks.

Likes sunny spots in most well-drained soils. Tolerates dry, chalky or clay soil, cold, exposed and coastal gardens.

Prune out a few older stems each spring and shorten long youngsters at the same time.

Propagate by shoot tip cuttings in summer or by hardwood cuttings in autumn.

Prunus species and varieties

Cherry, Cherry Laurel, Almond, Peach, Plum.

Various sizes

I've mentioned the flowering cherries' value as trees in Chapter 4, and the cherry laurel as a hedger in Chapter 6; here I want to mention three species of Prunus that are valuable shrubs: *P. laurocerasus* 'Otto Luyken' is a sort of dwarf laurel 1.2 m (4 ft) high and as much across, with glossy evergreen leaves and white candles of flowers in spring – smart and shapely ground cover. *P. tenella* 'Fire Hill' stopped me in my tracks the first time I saw it. It is a bare-branched shrub in winter, but in spring its stems are plastered with starry pink flowers mixed with the bright green of the emerging leaves. It is a sprawling but erect-stemmed shrub 60 cm-1.2 m (2-4 ft) high and more across, and often known as the dwarf Russian almond. If you want a spring stunner, look no further.

P. triloba is another early bloomer, though not quite as reliable. In a warm, sheltered garden it will smother its stems with double rosettes of pink blossom. It makes an upright bush to 3 m (10 ft) or more and as much across, but pruning will keep it smaller. Florists sell it as a cut flower.

Likes most soils and situations, but the flowering types need good light and *P. triloba* grows best in warm, sheltered gardens. Tolerates most sites and soils but doesn't relish coastal exposure.

Prune 'Otto Luyken' of any unwanted branches in spring or summer. 'Fire Hill' can be relieved of a few old stems after flowering and any young ones can be shortened. *P. triloba* should be relieved of shoots that have flowered immediately the blooms fade; new stems sent up during the summer will carry next year's flowers.

Propagate by layering suitable stems. 'Otto Luyken' can be propagated from shoot tip cuttings in summer.

Pyracantha See p.98

Rhododendron species and hybrids (including **Azaleas**)

Various heights

I can't hope to do justice to the hundreds of different species of rhododendron and the thousands of different varieties, so I'll give you no more than a brief outline of the main types and their cultivation: that way at least you'll be able to keep the plant you selected at the nursery alive and well. Azaleas, by the way, are rhododendrons. The name is usually given to smaller-flowered rhododendrons and those that are deciduous. Apart from the countless species of rhododendron, the bulk of those that find their way into gardens are the evergreen 'hardy hybrids': hefty plants of strong constitution. But there are compact varieties too, and you should check with the nurseryman how high any plant will grow before you stagger home with it. Some of the 'azaleas' have delicious fragrances, especially the deciduous types, and many have flowers of almost luminous intensity. If your garden is really small, don't neglect the hybrids derived from *R. yakushimanum*, a diminutive plant that takes years to make a dome 90 cm (3 ft) high and as much across. Its hybrids are expensive but very choice. **Likes** a peaty, leafy, lime-free soil that is not likely to dry out in summer. Dappled shade is preferred to heavy gloom or full sun. Annual spring mulching is appreciated as are occasional waterings with iron sequestrene in the early years. Compact varieties can be grown in tubs provided they are never allowed to dry out. Tolerates clay soils and those that stay moist all the year round.

Prune only to remove dead or badly placed stems in spring.

Propagate by layering in spring and summer, or by taking cuttings of shoot tips in summer and early autumn and rooting these in a propagator.

Rhus typhina
Stag's Horn Sumach
3 x 3 m (10 x 10 ft)

Don't be conned into planting this shrub unless you've a bit of room to spare: it will eventually make a huge dome of growth smothered in ash-tree shaped leaves that are softly hairy. In autumn the foliage turns vivid shades of orange, yellow and red before falling to reveal the felted, antler-like stems. The autumn fruits are knobs of pink velour. The variety 'Dissecta' has more finely cut leaves than the true species and is deservedly popular for, with careful pruning it can be fitted into a small plot. A handsome architectural feature in the right place.
Likes ordinary soil and full sun. Tolerates chalk, clay and dry soil.
Prune away lower branches in the early stages of growth if a clean stem is required. If space is short and you

feel you must grow the plant, choose 'Dissecta' (syn. 'Laciniata') and prune back the sideshoots to three buds every March. In this way the plant can be kept down to about 1 m (3 or 4 ft).
Propagate by the removal of rooted suckers, which should be torn up anyway to prevent the formation of a thicket. Root cuttings can also be taken.

Ribes sanguineum
Flowering Currant
2.4 x 1.8 m (8 x 6 ft)

We used to have a flowering currant outside the back door when I was knee-high to the proverbial grasshopper and since then I've always had a soft spot for it. In winter it is bare, but in spring, along with forsythia, its blooms start to open, dripping from the branches like blobs of raspberry jam until they open into rich crimson-pink tassels. The sycamore-shaped leaves follow and have a thick aroma all their own. I love it; some folk hate it!

'Pulborough Scarlet' and 'King Edward VII' are the best deep pink varieties, and I've recently discovered the delights of a healthy pure white variety called 'Tydeman's White'. Lovers of golden foliage will appreciate the less vigorous 'Brocklebankii' with its luminous yellow leaves and pink flowers – a strident, and somewhat unsubtle, contrast. It brightens large pots and tubs on a patio.
Likes ordinary, well-drained soil and a sunny spot. Tolerates clay, chalky and dry soil, cold and coastal gardens, and a modicum of shade, though flowering will not be so spectacular. 'Brocklebankii' prefers gentle shade because of its yellow foliage.
Prune immediately after flowering, removing completely older stems that have bloomed. Can also be clipped formally and makes a good hedge. Clip after flowering.
Propagate by cuttings of firm shoot

tips in summer, or by hardwood cuttings in autumn.

Romneya coulteri
Tree Poppy
1.2 m x 90 cm (4 x 3 ft)

Do have a go with the tree poppy, even though it is a bit tender. It has the most sumptuous, finely cut grey foliage – not hairy but rather waxy – and its stems are topped in late summer and autumn with fragrant white poppy flowers, each one tissue-paper thin and centred with a doughnut of yellow stamens. In severe winters it may well be killed back to ground level, but it will still recover to flower the following year.
Likes a warm, sunny, sheltered spot, preferably at the foot of a west- or south-facing wall. The soil should be well drained and not too rich. Tolerates dry or chalky soil and a coastal situation.
Prune back to the nearest sprouting buds in spring.
Propagate by root cuttings inserted in boxes of sandy soil and placed in a frame in winter.

Rosmarinus officinalis
Rosemary
1.5 x 1.5 m (5 x 5 ft)

Rosemary must be at the front of a border: there you can brush past it and savour the savoury aroma of its narrow, dark, evergreen leaves as well as being able to pick it with ease for the roast lamb on Sunday. It is rather an upright plant, even though its stems often run along the ground before they start to ascend; it is especially vertical in the variety sold as 'Miss Jessopp's Upright'. In spring it carries masses of pale blue hooded flowers on its towering stems.
Likes a sunny, sheltered spot in well-drained soil. Tolerates dry soil, chalky soil, coastal exposure and colder weather than many folk would have you believe.

Shrubs with colourful foliage

GREY FOLIAGE
- Caryopteris
- Chamaecyparis pisifera 'Boulevard'
- Convolvulus
- Hebe pinguifolia 'Pagei'
- Juniperus (some)
- Lavandula
- Lavatera
- Phlomis
- Potentilla (some)
- Romneya
- Ruta
- Santolina

VARIAGATED FOLIAGE
- Aralia elata 'Aureovariegata'
- Aucuba japonica 'Variegata'
- Berberis thunbergii 'Rose Glow'
- Buxus sempervirens 'Elegantissima'
- Cornus alba 'Elegantissima'
- Cornus alba 'Spaethii'
- Elaeagnus pungens 'Maculata'
- Euonymus fortunei 'Emerald 'n' Gold'
- Fuchsia magellanica 'Versicolor'
- Hedera helix varieties
- Ilex x altaclerensis varieties
- Ilex aquifolium varieties
- Ruta graveolens 'Variegata'
- Sambucus nigra 'Variegata'
- Vinca major 'Variegata'
- Weigela 'Florida Variegata'

YELLOW FOLIAGE
- Acer japonicum 'Aureum'
- Berberis thunbergii 'Aurea'
- Chamaecyparis lawsoniana vars.
- Heathers (some)
- Philadelphus coronarius 'Aureus'
- Pleioblastus auricomus (syn. Arundinaria viridistriata)
- Ribes sanguineum 'Brocklebankii'
- Sambucus nigra 'Aurea'
- Sambucus racemosa 'Plumosa Aurea'
- Spiraea japonica 'Goldflame'

PURPLE OR RED FOLIAGE
- Acer palmatum f. atropurpureum
- Acer palmatum 'Dissectum Atropurpureum'
- Berberis x ottawensis f. purpurea
- Berberis thunbergii f. atropurpurea
- Corylus maxima 'Purpurea'
- Cotinus coggygria 'Notcutt's Variety' and 'Royal Purple'
- Photinia x fraseri 'Red Robin' (young leaves)
- Pieris formosa var. forrestii 'Wakehurst' and P. 'Forest Flame' (young leaves)
- Sambucus nigra 'Purpurea'
- Weigela florida 'Foliis Purpureis'

Prune out dead stems in spring; severe winters may lead to die-back but seldom to death, provided the soil is well drained. Straggly stems can be shortened in spring or summer. Replace old, worn-out plants with youngsters.
Propagate by taking shoot tip cuttings in summer.

Ruta graveolens 'Jackman's Blue'
Rue
45 x 60 cm (18 in x 2 ft)

Tidy, grey and acrid – it doesn't sound like much of a recommendation, but this really is a fine little shrub. The foliage is as finely cut as filigree, a really blue-grey, and topped with greenish yellow flowers in summer. It is virtually evergreen. There is also a variegated variety whose leaves are mottled green and cream. A super patio plant that is supposed to keep away flies: don't brush against it or the aroma will keep you away too, and may cause a painful rash.

Likes a chalky soil and a spot in full sun. Tolerates dry, non-chalky soils.
Prune back hard in spring, to within a few centimetres (inches) of ground level to encourage fresh, new growth.
Propagate by taking shoot tip cuttings in summer, or by inserting harder shoots outdoors in autumn.

Salix species
Willow
Various sizes

There are a number of low-growing willows, and some that are pruned to keep them short. The two I want to recommend are both naturally diminutive: *S. hastata* 'Wehrhahnii', 1.2 x 1.2 m (4 x 4 ft), has plum-purple stems that are gilded with the most beautiful catkins in spring before the leaves emerge. Pussy willow appears first – silver-grey and silky – then the yellow pollen lights up the whole plant. The foliage is plain green.
S. lanata, 60 x 60 cm (2 x 2 ft), has pussy willow, but here it is the grey-felted leaves that are the main attraction. Both plants have rather upright stems and are suited to being planted in restricted spaces.
Likes moist soil and a sunny spot. Tolerates clay, boggy and chalky soil and a modicum of shade. Happy in cold gardens.
Prune these two hardly at all. The removal of dead or badly placed stems in spring is all that is necessary. One or two old stems can be removed each year.
Propagate by hardwood cuttings in autumn.

Sambucus species and varieties
Elder
4.5 x 4.5 m (15 x 15 ft)

I'm a real fan of these beefy shrubs: they grow fast and furiously in most situations and are available in such variety of form that there's something to please every gardener. *S. nigra*, the common elder, has a superbly elegant form *laciniata* in which the leaves are finely cut to give a lacy look; 'Aurea' is yellowish in spring, becoming greener later; 'Guincho Purple' is a dusky plum-purple; and 'Albovariegata' is green edged with creamy white. All have the vigour you would expect of an elder, but they respond well to hard pruning so don't worry if your patch is small. *S. racemosa*, the red-berried elder, is rather less vigorous and most often seen in its variety 'Plumosa Aurea' with deeply slashed leaves of acid-yellow. It is as vibrant as any garden shrub, but I can't say in all honesty that the combination of luminous yellow leaves and bright red berries in autumn is a colour scheme of impeccable taste. Still, it is bright and the fruits don't set every year.

Likes any ordinary or moist soil that is not likely to dry out in summer and a spot in sun or dappled shade. Tolerates clay, chalky soil, boggy soil and heavy shade, though this is not to be recommended for the bright-leaved varieties. Cold, exposed and coastal situations are also tolerated.

Prune shoots hard back in late winter if growing in a confined space, otherwise allow the plant to grow freely, removing only badly placed and weak shoots.

Propagate from shoot tip cuttings in summer or hardwood cuttings in autumn.

Santolina species
Cotton Lavender
60 cm x 1.5 m (2 x 5 ft)

Endearing little shrubs with wispy foliage that is grey, feathery and highly aromatic – really fruity. They are evergrey and the shoots are topped in summer with yellow button-like flowers, if you let them run up high enough. I suggest you don't, for although the blooms are pretty in themselves, they weigh down the plant and pull it open, spoiling its shape. Sorry to be a spoilsport. Two varieties are commonly grown:
S. chamaecyparissus is the more

compact and wiry-stemmed of the two, and subsp. *neapolitana* is softer and a little more fluffy. Both make delightful dwarf edging when clipped or, if you insist on having those flowers, you can grow them next to a wide path so that they can tumble their blooms over the flagstones.

Likes sun and well-drained soil. Tolerates dry or chalky soils and coastal exposure.

Prune by clipping or snipping just before the flowers swell and open. Propagate from shoot tip cuttings in summer.

Sarcococca confusa
Christmas Box
90 cm x 1.8 m (3 x 6 ft)

This spreading evergreen is just like Osmanthus in one respect – its flowers have a perfume that will arrest you several paces after you've passed it by. The leaves are small, glossy and thickly packed on the stems, and the fluffy white flowers open in very early spring, filling you with optimism. A smashing plant for a border or bed beneath a window where its fragrance can drift up into the room.

Likes chalky soil and a spot in sun. Tolerates shade, clay and dry soil.

Prune only to remove dead wood in spring.

Propagate by removing and rooting firm shoot tips in summer.

Skimmia species and varieties
90 cm x 1.5 m (3 x 5 ft)

Council shrubberies are packed with skimmias, though usually the boring kinds that have few fruits and just a load of soot-laden evergreen foliage. The plain species, S. *japonica*, can be crashingly dull, but varieties such as 'Veitchii', a female with large red fruits in winter, and 'Rubella', a male with white flowers that are rosy pink in bud, will brighten any garden. Male and female flowers are carried on separate plants in the case of all varieties of

S. *japonica*, but subsp. *reevesiana* has the advantage of being both compact and hermaphrodite, which makes life easier. White flowers open in May and red fruits cheer up the plant in winter. A good choice for a bed or border that needs perking up in winter.

Likes ordinary well-drained soil in sun or light shade. Tolerates dry, chalky or clay soil, cold gardens and coastal exposure. subsp. *reevesiana* isn't keen on chalky soil; the others don't mind.

Prune only when the plants become straggly. Then a few stems can be shortened in spring to encourage branching from lower down.

Propagate by taking cuttings of firm shoot tips in summer.

Spiraea species and varieties
Various sizes

Lots of spiraeas are grown in gardens and a few of them are a bit dull, blooming for a brief spell in spring or summer and then packing up for the rest of the year. The two I'm going to recommend do that too, but at least their display is spectacular.
S. 'Arguta': 2.4 x 2.4 m (8 x 8 ft), is the bridal wreath, beloved of anyone with an ounce of sentiment or an eye for a graceful plant. Even if it doesn't flower for long at least it's a picture when it does: the arching branches are thickly dotted with tiny white flowers like miniature apple blossoms in spring. The small green leaves follow.
S. *japonica* 'Anthony Waterer' is altogether smaller at 60 x 60 cm (2 x 2 ft) and blooms in summer, producing flat-topped heads of rosy pink flowers. Another variety, 'Goldflame', has spring foliage that is bright yellow tinged with orange. At least one of them should grace your garden.

Likes ordinary soil that is not prone to dry out in summer, and a position in sun or dappled shade. Tolerates any soil and situation, though a few don't like chalk much.

Prune S. 'Arguta' by removing a few old stems completely after flowering.

Cut *S. japonica* down to within a few inches of soil level in spring.
Propagate *S. japonica* by division in autumn or spring; S. 'Arguta' from cuttings of firm shoot tips in summer.

Symphoricarpos species and varieties

Snowberry, Coral Berry

1.2-1.8 m x 1.2-2.4 m (4-6 ft x 4-8 ft)

You'll not find a thicker growing shrub than this; in any of its species and varieties it makes a dense, suckering bush ideal for bird cover and food, thanks to a plentiful supply of autumn berries. These follow the tiny white summer flowers. All the different kinds are deciduous, and all have plain but attractive leaves that are oval, fresh green and quite thin.

The largest and commonest species is the snowberry, *S. albus* var. *laevigatus* (often listed as *S. rivularis*). The fruits are almost as big as marbles and pure white. *S. orbiculatus*, the coral berry, is a small-fruited species with pink berries and it has been hybridized with snowberry to produce the Doorenbos Hybrids (x *doorenbosii*). These are without doubt the best garden plants of the lot, making rather small shrubs with large berries that may be white, pale or dark pink. 'Magic Berry' is rose-pink; 'Mother of Pearl', pink and white; and 'White Hedge' is pure white. All make good hedges and brighten up autumn borders. Those outside my study window are a-flutter with nectar-drinking moths on summer nights.
Likes ordinary soil that is not liable to dry out in summer, and a spot in sun. Tolerates clay, chalk, dry soil, moist soil, cold exposed and coastal gardens and heavy shade.
Prune to remove a few older stems each winter if you can get into the bush. Most folk give it up as a bad job: the bushes become so thick that pruning is impossible. Lazy gardeners rejoice!
Propagate by lifting and transplanting suckers in autumn or spring, or by hardwood cuttings in autumn.

Syringa species and varieties

Lilac

3.6 x 3 m (12 x 10 ft)

Brief but glorious – that's the lilac season. But what a show it is! In late spring the varieties of the common lilac, *S. vulgaris*, fill the air with pastel shades and sweet scents. Even though the season is short it's worth squeezing in one plant at the back of a border; out of flower it can act as a verdant backcloth to other blooms. The true species has pale, thinly furnished blooms, so avoid being palmed off with a plant of dubious origin. Settle instead for one of these: 'Madame Lemoine', double white; 'Charles Joly', double, deep crimson-purple; 'Masséna', single, deep purple; 'Maud Notcutt', single white; 'Primrose', single, pale yellow. There are other good named varieties and hybrids, too. *S. x hyacinthiflora* 'Esther Staley' is a single, warm pink. *S. x josiflexa* 'Bellicent' is an altogether more graceful plant than the common lilac, with flower trusses that consist of smaller florets. But it makes a superb shrub, blooming in late spring with the other lilacs, and arching its long, rose-pink flower spikes from the foliage. It's delectably scented and deserves a much greater popularity.
Likes ordinary well-drained soil and sun. Tolerates chalky soils; also clay. Usually happy in cold gardens.
Prune only occasionally, removing one or two older stems in winter.
Propagate by layering in spring, or by rooting cuttings of firm shoot tips in summer. Suckers can be dug up from plants on their own roots and transplanted. However, some nurserymen graft onto common lilac and any suckers that appear will be inferior. Remove and discard them.

Tamarix ramosissima

Tamarisk

3 x 3 m (10 x 10 ft)

Every September we spend a week in a house right on the Sussex coast; the garden gate opens onto the beach. It's a balmy time of year – the calm before the autumn storm – and the glorious tamarisks that surround and shelter the garden are at their best.

> **"Brief but glorious – that's the lilac season. But what a show it is... filling the air with pastel shades and sweet scents."**

Shrubs with scented flowers

There's much argument over which flowers in the garden are scented and which are not. I firmly believe that fragrance is in the nose of the inhaler – some scents seem overpowering to one nose and feeble to another. The few plants listed here should delight all olfactory glands. Any that are not listed can come as a gentle surprise to you!

- *Buddleja*
- *Choisya*
- *Daphne*
- *Hamamelis*
- *Lavandula*
- *Mahonia*
- *Myrtus*
- *Osmanthus*
- *Philadelphus*
- *Rhododendron* (some)
- *Sambucus*
- *Sarcococca*
- *Skimmia*
- *Syringa*
- *Viburnum* (some)

The heather-like grey-green leaves set off a treat the feathery spikes of pink flowers. The whole, massive bush is so ethereal that it looks as if it would blow away in the first sea breeze, but in reality it's as tough as old boots. The Sussex plant is the common tamarisk, *T. gallica* (see Chapter 6 Hedges), but perhaps a better choice for gardens is *T. ramosissima* (sometimes called *T. pentandra*), which is a little brighter and a fraction more shapely. It flowers at the same time as the common tamarisk and both are deciduous.

Likes sun and well-drained soil. Tolerates clay, dry and chalky soil, cold gardens and coastal exposure.
Prune shoots hard back in spring. Failure to do this may result in a straggly bush.
Propagate by hardwood cuttings in autumn.

Viburnum species and varieties

Various sizes

Here's a real jewel box of plants: some are deciduous and some are

Both *Vinca major* and the smaller *V. minor* make excellent ground cover plants that thrive in sun or shade and in most kinds of soil. This is *V. minor* 'Azurea Flore Pleno'.

evergreen; some have superb autumn colour; some produce fat flowerheads and others brilliant fruits. Here is the pick of the crop:
V. farreri (or *V. fragrans*) 2.4 x 2.4 m (8 x 8 ft) is a deciduous species whose bare, upright stems erupt with little pinkish white flower clusters in

winter. Catch its fragrance in a burst of watery sunshine and it will keep you going until spring. The leaves open after the flowers – bronze at first, changing to dull green.

V. x *bodnantense*, in its forms 'Dawn', pink, and 'Deben', pink in bud, white in flower, beats *V. farreri* by opening a month earlier, in October. It's a rather stiffer, more upright plant and its flowers are not quite as resistant to frost as those of *V. farreri*. *V. carlesii*, 1.5 x 1.5 m (5 x 5 ft), follows in spring, producing large, flat-topped clusters of gloriously fragrant pink and white flowers over the coarse green leaves. These will sometimes take on rich tints in autumn. 'Aurora' is its best variety – a real stunner.

V. plicatum in its forms 'Mariesii' or 'Lanarth' is a heck of a mouthful to quote to your nurseryman, but it will bring you a handsome, horizontally branched plant, naked in winter but furnished with deeply veined leaves in summer. Flat-headed flower clusters like those of a cream lace-cap hydrangea are arranged in rows along the shelf-like stems in late spring. A real treat that eventually makes a shrub 2.4 x 3.6 m (8 x 12 ft).

V. opulus 'Roseum' (syn. 'Sterile') is the snowball tree – so called because of its spherical heads of ivory-white flowers that are carried on the stems in early summer. It is deciduous, a splendid sight in flower, and a host to blackfly, so give it an occasional spray. *V. tinus* is that dingy-foliaged evergreen, but looks quite a treat in its pink-budded form 'Eve Price'. It grows about 1.2 x 1.8 in (4 x 6 ft) or more and blooms in winter and spring, so it's well worth bunging in a border even though its foliage is black as night.

Likes sun or dappled shade and a soil that is well drained yet never likely to dry out in summer. Tolerates clay, chalk (provided it is not shallow and dry), moist soil (*V. tinus* doesn't mind dry soil), cold gardens and shady spots.

Prune out a few old stems in later winter and remove dead wood as soon as it is seen. *V. tinus* withstands hard pruning or clipping in summer.

Propagate by layering, or by shoot tip cuttings taken in summer.

Vinca species and varieties
Periwinkle
15 cm x 1.8 m (6 in x 6 ft)

The greater periwinkle (*V. major*) and the lesser periwinkle (*V. minor*) are cheap and cheerful ground coverers that will seldom give you much trouble. They send their long, trailing shoots out over the soil to help smother weeds (eventually) and they brighten early summer with round, five-petalled flowers of blue, white or mauve. The difference in them lies in the size of their leaves. The best periwinkle of all is *V. major* 'Variegata', a vigorous beast with superb evergreen leaves that are fresh green splashed with creamy yellow. It makes a thick rug of growth.

Likes ordinary soil in sun or shade. Tolerates chalk, clay, dry soil, cold gardens and heavy shade.

Prune only to prevent unwanted spread.

Propagate by lifting and transplanting rooted portions – the plant's stems root as they creep.

Weigela
Bush Honeysuckle, Diervilla
1.8 x 1.8 m (6 x 6 ft)

It's impossible for me to think about *Weigela* without thinking about *Philadelphus*: they are both the first spectacular shrubs of late spring and early summer. *Philadelphus* has the edge when it comes to spectacle and perfume, but a well-grown, arching *Weigela* is very welcome in June when the bell-shaped flowers of white, pink or crimson appear. 'Bristol Ruby', deep pink, and 'Candida', white, are popular, but don't neglect the two other varieties that will cheer you up for the rest of the summer with their leaves of plum-purple, in the case of *W. florida* 'Foliis Purpureis', and creamy-edged in *W.* 'Florida Variegata'. Both harmonize with the pink flowers.

Likes ordinary well-drained soil and a place in the sun. Tolerates clay or chalky soils, a modicum of shade and even coastal or inland exposure.

Prune after flowering, removing older, flowered stems.

Propagate by cuttings of hardwood in autumn or shoot tips in summer.

Yucca filamentosa
Adam's Needle
90 x 90 cm (3 x 3 ft)

Stately plants with upright rosettes of spiky leaves; a must for a tropical effect. They grow slowly, eventually producing flower spikes on top of the rosettes – one spike on each plant. The blooms are beautiful, creamy white and carried thickly up the 1.5 m (5 ft) stalk in summer. Lovely in pots and tubs on patios, provided you don't walk into them! Be patient; your plant won't flower until it's a few years old.

Likes ordinary well-drained soil and sun. Tolerates dry and chalky soil and coastal exposure. These blighters are tougher than you'd think.

Prune to remove faded flower spikes.

Propagate by root cuttings or division; pot up or transplant suckers.

CHAPTER

6 Hedges

Whether marking boundaries, providing privacy and shelter, or dividing up different areas, hedges are a living feature of the garden and a haven for myriad forms of wildlife

In the quest for privacy (and perhaps to keep the dog in too) you may be tempted to plant a hedge – but before you do, make sure that you know exactly what you're letting yourself in for. The effect will be pleasing so long as you choose the right plant, but there are snags.

WHY PLANT A HEDGE?

The downside of hedges

On a very small plot a tall hedge can cut out light, so avoid planting a vigorous grower if your garden is very narrow. A deciduous hedge will let in just a bit more light in winter to brighten shady sites. The roots of any hedge will rob nutrients from adjacent flower borders; privet is a real brute in this respect and in my last garden I made vertical slits with a spade in the soil alongside the hedge and inserted old roofing slates to keep back the roots. Additional feeding of the border plants helps them to win the battle.

The most labour-intensive job of all is clipping: most hedges need at least two cuts a year and one or two, such as privet, will sometimes need three if you're a real stickler for neatness – I'm not!

The benefits

But in spite of all that, are still planted and are still appreciated. You soon tire of looking at a close-boarded fence, and so many of them pop up on housing estates nowadays that they can make the place look like a cattle market packed with pens. Fencing is pricey too.

A hedge will cut down wind, screen you from eyesores and the eyes of your neighbours, cut down noise and act as a lush green backdrop to other garden plants. It's also a haven for many forms of wildlife, from stick insects and moths to birds and mammals. With country hedgerows disappearing at the rate of hundreds of miles a year, planting a hedge will help to conserve a vanishing habitat. Wood-boring beetles are the only form of wildlife supported by a fence!

Don't think of a hedge as always being formally clipped. Some shrubs planted as hedges will grow best if lightly trimmed to shape rather than clipped flat, and many of them offer bright flowers and cheerful berries in addition to the usual leaves. One of these hedges is a far better bet in a small garden than the ubiquitous privet. The lists in the A–Z section offer suggestions for hedges that are colourful in leaf, flower and fruit. If your hedge has to act as a barrier to livestock go for a thorny one that will make a dense thicket. Recommendations are given for those too.

PLANTING YOUR HEDGE

Just like trees, hedges are usually in one place for a very long time. They say you can calculate the age of a hedge in the countryside by counting the number of different species of tree or shrub that are present: each one counts as a hundred years, so if you see a hedge with five different shrubs in it then it's 500 years old. A well-prepared planting site right at the start will give the hedge that kick in the pants it needs to establish itself with a view to outlasting you.

When to plant
Time of planting is as for trees and shrubs: November to March for bare-root plants; September or April/May for bare-root or balled evergreens; and any time of year for container-grown plants (provided the soil is not dust-dry, frozen or muddy). Just as with shrubs and trees, the roots of hedging plants should never be allowed to dry out. Heel them in (see p.40, Delayed planting) if they arrive before you are ready to plant.

Preparing the ground
One of the quickest and most successful ways to plant a hedge is to prepare a strip of ground along the line the hedge is to take. With bamboo canes and string, mark out a 60 cm (2 ft) wide strip of the required length. Dig it, working in two handfuls of bonemeal to each running 90 cm (1 yd), and any organic matter you can lay your spade on.

There's great satisfaction to be obtained from digging such a long, narrow strip because you can motor on at a rate of knots. When the strip is dug you can let it settle for a few days. Alternatively you can dig a trench along the line and return the soil at planting time, but don't let too much time elapse or the trench will become a muddy ditch.

Choosing hedge plants
Having decided on the type of hedge you want you'll have to locate the plants, and here one thing is vital – they should be young. Don't waste your money on tall plants just because they'll look good immediately after planting. Smaller plants will settle in much more quickly and even overtake taller ones after only a year or two. What's more they'll make a thick barrier right down to ground level, and that's the most important requirement of any hedge. They'll be cheaper too. So settle for plants about 30 cm (12 in) high, and buy enough to plant at the distance recommended in the A–Z entries. Most hedges are created by planting a single row of plants, but if you want to make an exceptionally dense thicket, plant two staggered rows 38 cm (15 in) apart.

Which plants?
Privet should be one of your last choices; look for something a little different that's going to offer you more than a green fence. Steer clear, too, of Leyland cypress (x *Cupressocyparis leylandii*) unless you've bags of room to spare. Where there's room for it to grow, it looks a treat, but in tiny gardens it soon outstays its welcome and fills the plot with gloom.

How to plant
Rig up a garden line along the strip to be planted and take out a hole for every plant (unless you're using the trench method). Trim broken roots from bare-root plants and spread out the remainder in the hole (see p.82). Return the soil, firming it into place with your feet, so that the old soil mark on the stem of the plant is just below the new soil level. With container-grown plants, water them an hour before planting. At planting time, remove the container and tease out any in-growing roots. Don't disturb the rest of the rootball. Plant so that the top of the rootball is just below the surface of the soil. Don't stint on the firming – really put the boot in. If you leave the soil light and fluffy, the roots might dry out, or on heavy soils the trench will act like a sump for the surrounding drainage water, drowning the roots.

> "Wood-boring beetles are the only form of wildlife supported by a fence."

Hedge planting

1 Dig a 60 cm (2 ft) wide trench along the line to be occupied by the hedge and fork some compost or manure into the base.

2 Trim back any thick or damaged roots on bare-root plants and keep them in a bucket of water until you're ready to plant.

3 Stand each plant where it is to be planted and feed back the soil, firming it with your foot. The old soil mark on the stem should match the new soil level.

Watering and mulching

Water the plants in if the soil is at all dry, and in spring spread a 5 cm (2 in) mulch of leaf mould, pulverized bark, well-rotted compost or manure over the soil – if you have any to spare. If not, keep a close watch on the soil and use a sprinkler to soak the earth when it starts to look dry. Drought will put paid to all your good work.

Autumn-planted hedges will need to be re-firmed into contact with the soil after frosts have lifted them – failure to boot them back in may result in death due to the roots drying out.

CARING FOR YOUR HEDGE

Immediate pruning

Immediately after planting, most hedging shrubs should be pruned to produce really dense growth at ground level. Forget to do this and you'll have a gappy hedge later on. Really vigorous growers such as privet, hawthorn, blackthorn, snowberry, tamarisk and Lonicera nitida should be cut back to within 15 cm (6 in) of ground level. Hornbeam, beech, hazel and flowering currant should have all their shoots cut back by one third of their length. Yew, laurel, holly, gorse, osmanthus, laurustinus and all conifers should have their sideshoots shortened a little, but their leading or topmost shoots should be left intact.

All other plants are best relieved just of long and straggling shoots, which should be cut back to a bud or leaf near the base of the offending stem.

Subsequent clipping

Subsequent clippings may have to be carried out twice a year: May and August are the best times. The traditional pruning tool for hedges is a pair of garden shears, which will make a neat job on most shrubs.

Using electric trimmers

Electric trimmers really do make life easier by clipping at a fast rate, but take care: one false move and you'll have made a hole in your hedge! Wear the trimmer cable over your shoulder to keep it out of the way of the blade – or, better still, invest in one of the special harnesses that can be worn to hold the cable out of the way.

Both shears and trimmers should be oiled after use and rubbed down with emery paper to free them of dried sap, which glues the blades together.

If you don't trust your eye when it comes to clipping the top of a hedge, fasten a taut line between two canes to mark the cutting line and clip to this.

If you can't rely on your eye when clipping, stretch a taut length of twine between two stakes to mark the cutting line (see picture opposite). Aim to create a hedge that is a little narrower in cross-section at the top than it is at the bottom. That way it will cast less shade and will be less likely to suffer snow damage. Don't be frightened of clipping hard in the early years: it will encourage the hedge to thicken up. The top surface of the hedge should also be trimmed back a little each time, even though it has not yet reached the required height. If you don't do this, the hedge will be even more likely to suffer from snow damage, its stems giving way under the lightest powdering.

Clipping informal hedges
Shears or electric trimmers are essential for clipping formal hedges with straight outlines, but informal hedges such as those of tamarisk, fuchsia, olearia, escallonia, cotoneaster and large-leaved plants such as laurel and aucuba are best pruned with secateurs, unwanted stems being snipped out above a bud or leaf. Where such hedges are very long then shears or trimmers can be used, but some sacrificing of form will have to be accepted.

Clipping flowering and fruiting hedges
Flowering hedges are always best pruned immediately after their blooms have faded; unwanted wood can be removed and the plants will still have time to produce stems that will carry next year's flowers. Do remember, berry-bearing hedges should be clipped after the fruits have fallen.

Disposing of clippings
Hedge clippings are difficult to dispose of. They won't really compost because they're too woody, and they produce foul smoke if burned. There are two ways of getting round this: either ferry them to the local tip in your car (or have a gentle word with your dustman to see if he is amenable to shifting bagfuls of chippings), or dry them out in a corner of the garden and then burn them. If the material is crisp and dry, it burns without too much smoke.

However if you have great swathes of hedging to deal with, it might be worth investing in a shredder. This will break down the clippings to the point where they will make a useful addition to the compost heap. The only drawback is that most shredders are incredibly noisy, so try to limit shredding sessions to sociable hours, or invest in one of the 'silent running' models.

RENOVATING AN OLD HEDGE

If you take on a battered old hedge that's riddled with holes you'll want to know what to do with it. Some hedges, such as laurel, privet and yew, will regenerate (produce new shoots) when cut back really hard into old wood. Others, such as box and most conifers, won't. Once the inner parts of conifer branches have gone crisp and brown there's little you can do to perk them up. It's far easier, provided you're not averse to hard labour, to dig out the plants and replant with something else after enriching the soil.

PROPAGATING HEDGES

Hedges can be propagated like other shrubs (see Chapter 2 Propagation), but there's a trick to growing privet, which any miser should know of. Get some hedge clippings - shoots that are firm and woody and about 30-45 cm (1½ ft) long are ideal - and strip off the lower leaves. Push the shoots into the soil for one third of their length along the line the hedge is to take. Stick one shoot in every 15 cm (6 in). Unless you're really out of luck, or you let the soil dry out, you'll soon have a privet hedge where once you pushed in your prunings.

Remove any plant debris too. Left to its own devices it will eventually form a dense mulch around the base which, especially on damp soils, can cause stem rot.

A-Z of **hedge plants**

Aucuba japonica
Spotted Laurel
Planting distance 60 cm (2 ft)
5 years to reach 1.5 m (5 ft)

Evergreen. Shiny green leaves spotted yellow in some varieties. This plant is well known for its Victorian effect (the Victorians loved it), which can put people off it, but it makes a handsome hedge when properly cared for and the spotted varieties are great for brightening up dark corners.
Prune in August with shears/trimmers and secateurs. Suitable for formal clipping or informal pruning.

Berberis darwinii
Barberry
Planting distance 45 cm (18 in)
6 years to reach 1.5 m (5 ft)

Evergreen. Dark green thicket plastered with orange flowers in April/May.
Prune in May, after flowering, with shears/trimmers. Suitable for formal clipping or informal pruning.

Berberis x *stenophylla*
Barberry
Planting distance 45 cm (18 in)
5 years to reach 1.5 m (5 ft)

Evergreen. Another spiny thicket-former; quite dog-proof. Masses of scented orange-yellow flowers in April/May.
Prune in May, after flowering, with shears/trimmers. Suitable for formal clipping or informal pruning.

Buxus sempervirens
Box
Planting distance 30 cm (12 in)
8 years to reach 1.5 m (5 ft)

Evergreen. Dense barrier of dark green leaves. Good variegated variety.
Prune in May and August with shears/trimmers. Suitable for formal clipping.

Buxus sempervirens 'Suffruticosa'
Dwarf Box
Planting distance 23 cm (9 in)
Grows to 30cm (12 in) maximum

Evergreen. Neat miniature for edging formal beds. Superb in kitchen gardens.
Prune in May and August with shears/trimmers. Suitable for formal clipping.

Carpinus betulus
Hornbeam
Planting distance 30 cm (12 in)
6 years to reach 1.5 m (5 ft)

A pleasant alternative to beech. Good, plain green leaves.
Prune in August with shears/trimmers. Suitable for formal clipping.

Chamaecyparis lawsoniana varieties
Lawson Cypress
Planting distance 60 cm (2 ft)
5 years to reach 1.5 m (5 ft)

Evergreen. Varieties like 'Green Hedger' are particularly good. There are also good yellow forms.
Prune in August with shears/trimmers. Suitable for formal clipping.

Corylus maxima 'Purpurea'
Purple-leafed Hazel
Planting distance 60 cm (2 ft)
4 years to reach 1.5 m (5 ft)

Bold leaves of dark plum-purple. Don't overdo it.
Prune in August with shears/trimmers and secateurs. Suitable for formal clipping and informal pruning.

Cotoneaster simonsii
Planting distance 45 cm (18 in)
5 years to reach 1.5 m (5 ft)

Evergreen. Boring green leaves but super white flowers and orange berries.
Prune after fruiting with shears/trimmers and secateurs. Suitable for formal clipping and informal pruning.

Crataegus monogyna
Hawthorn, Quick
Planting distance 30 cm (12 in)
7 years to reach 1.5 m (5 ft)

Thick and dog-proof. Flowering and fruiting restricted by pruning.
Prune in May and August with shears/trimmers. Suitable for formal clipping.

x *Cupressocyparis leylandii*
Leyland Cypress
Planting distance 75 cm (2½ ft)
3 years to reach 1.5 m (5 ft)

Evergreen. Don't use this unless you've room to spare. Quick and dense.
Prune in August with shears/trimmers. Suitable for formal clipping.

Escallonia rubra var. *macrantha*
Planting distance 45 cm (18 in)
4 years to reach 1.5 m (5 ft)

Evergreen. A marvellous hedge with shiny leaves and pink summer flowers.

Thorny hedges

The following are all suitable for forming a dense thicket to act as a barrier to pets and livestock.

- *Berberis darwinii*
- *Berberis* x *stenophylla*
- *Crataegus monogyna*
- *Ilex aquifolium* varieties
- *Pyracantha rogersiana*
- *Rosa eglanteria*
- *Rosa rugosa*
- *Ulex europaeus*

Prune after flowering with shears/ trimmers and secateurs. Suitable for formal clipping and informal pruning.

Euonymus japonicus

Planting distance 45 cm (18 in)
6 years to reach 1.5 m (5 ft)

Evergreen. Shiny green leaves, splashed with yellow in 'Aureus'.
Prune in August with shears/trimmers. Suitable for formal clipping.

Fagus sylvatica
Beech

Planting distance 30 cm (12 in)
5 years to reach 1.5 m (5 ft)

Common but lovely. Bright green leaves in spring; russet in autumn.
Prune in August with shears/trimmers. Suitable for formal clipping.

Forsythia x intermedia 'Spectabilis'
Golden Bells

Planting distance 45 cm (18 in)
4 years to reach 1.5 m (5 ft)

A bit overdone but unsurpassed for the spring brightness of its yellow blooms.
Prune after flowering, with shears/ trimmers and secateurs. Suitable for formal clipping and informal pruning.

Fuchsia magellanica

Planting distance 30 cm (12 in)
5 years to reach 1.5 m (5 ft)

Graceful and colourful with cerise and purple flowers in summer.
Prune in May with secateurs. Suitable for informal pruning.

Ilex aquifolium varieties
Holly

Planting distance 45 cm (18 in)
8 years to reach 1.5 m (5 ft)

Evergreen. Avoid the dark green types, which can be oppressive, and go for a variegated green and yellow variety.

Hedges that will grow anywhere

The following hedge plants do well on chalky or clay soils, on cold and windy sites, and on dry soil. Those marked ◆ also grow well by the seaside.

- Berberis darwinii
- Berberis x stenophylla
- Corylus maxima 'Purpurea'
- Cotoneaster simonsii ◆
- Crataegus monogyna ◆
- x Cupressocyparis leylandii ◆
- Euonymus japonicus ◆
- Ilex aquifolium varieties ◆
- Lonicera nitida ◆
- Potentilla fruticosa ◆
- Prunus x cistena
- Prunus laurocerasus
- Pyracantha rogersiana ◆
- Tamarix gallica ◆
- Taxus baccata
- Thuja plicata varieties
- Ulex europaeus ◆
- Viburnum tinus ◆

Prune after fruiting with shears/ trimmers and secateurs. Suitable for formal clipping.

Lavandula angustifolia
Lavender

Planting distance 30 cm (12 in)
Grows to 60 cm (2 ft) maximum

Evergreen. Superbly aromatic dwarf hedge for paths and borders, with spikes of purple-blue flowers in summer. 'Hidcote' is best.
Prune in August, after flowering, with secateurs. Suitable for informal pruning.

Ligustrum ovalifolium
Privet

Planting distance 30 cm (12 in)
4 years to reach 1.5 m (5 ft)

Evergreen. Overplanted and greedy. Plant the golden form if you have to.
Prune in May and August with shears/trimmers. Suitable for formal clipping.

Lonicera nitida

Planting distance 30 cm (12 in)
5 years to reach 1.5 m (5 ft)

Evergreen. A bit dull but reliable. Tiny, glossy, oval leaves.
Prune in May and August with shears/trimmers. Suitable for formal clipping.

Metasequoia glyptostroboides
Dawn Redwood

Planting distance 60 cm (2 ft)
5 years to reach 1.5 m (5 ft)

Unusual. Feathery foliage of fresh green. Super autumn colour.
Prune in August with shears/trimmers. Suitable for formal clipping.

Olearia x haastii
New Zealand Daisy Bush

Planting distance 30 cm (12 in)
7 years to reach 1.5 m (5 ft)

Evergreen. Leaves dark green above, grey beneath. White daisy flowers.
Prune after flowering with secateurs. Suitable for informal pruning.

Pittosporum tenuifolium

Planting distance 45 cm (18 in)
5 years to reach 1.5 m (5 ft)

Evergreen. Shiny, wavy edged leaves.
Prune in May with secateurs. Suitable for informal pruning.

Potentilla fruticosa

Planting distance 45 cm (18 in)
Grows to 90 cm (3 ft) maximum

Evergreen. A tumbling charmer with yellow, orange, white or red summer flowers.
Prune in May with secateurs. Suitable for informal pruning.

Prunus x *cistena*
Purple-leaf Sand Cherry

Planting distance 30 cm (12 in)
5 years to reach 1.5 m (5 ft)

Purple leaves and white spring flowers. Best kept to around 90 cm (3 ft).
Prune after flowering with secateurs. Suitable for informal pruning.

Prunus laurocerasus
Cherry Laurel

Planting distance 60 cm (2 ft)
3 years to reach 1.5 m (5 ft)

Evergreen. Victorian favourite. Shiny and green and good in the right place.
Prune in August with shears/trimmers and secateurs. Suitable for formal clipping and informal pruning.

Pyracantha rogersiana
Firethorn

Planting distance 45 cm (18 in)
4 years to reach 1.5 m (5 ft)

Evergreen. Dark leaves; thorny stems; cream flowers in summer, orange berries in winter.
Prune after fruiting with secateurs. Suitable for informal pruning.

Rhododendron ponticum
Common Rhododendron

Planting distance 60 cm (2 ft)
5 years to reach 1.5 m (5 ft)

Evergreen. Dingy of leaf but bright of flower in spring. Good in shade.
Prune after flowering with shears/trimmers and secateurs. Suitable for formal clipping and informal pruning.

Rosa eglanteria
Sweet Briar

Planting distance 45 cm (18 in)
3 years to reach 1.5 m (5 ft)

Deliciously aromatic leaves and pink flowers followed by hips.
Prune after fruiting with secateurs. Suitable for informal pruning.

Hedge plants with good flowers and fruits

The following plants all have either flowers ✳ or fruit ◆ of note.

- *Aucuba japonica* ◆
- *Berberis darwinii* ✳
- *Berberis* x *stenophylla* ✳
- *Cotoneaster simonsii* ✳ ◆
- *Crataegus monogyna* ✳ ◆
- *Escallonia rubra* var. *macrantha* ✳
- *Forsythia* x *intermedia* 'Spectabilis' ✳
- *Fuchsia magellanica* ✳
- *Ilex aquifolium* ◆
- *Lavandula angustifolia* ✳
- *Olearia* x *haastii* ✳
- *Potentilla fruticosa* ✳
- *Prunus* x *cistena* ✳
- *Prunus laurocerasus* ✳ ◆
- *Pyracantha rogersiana* ✳ ◆
- *Rhododendron ponticum* ✳
- *Rosa eglanteria* ✳ ◆
- *Rosa rugosa* ✳ ◆
- *Rosmarinus officinalis* ✳
- *Tamarix gallica* ✳
- *Ulex europaeus* ✳
- *Viburnum* ✳

Rosa rugosa
Ramanas Rose

Planting distance 45 cm (18 in)
5 years to reach 1.5 m (5 ft)

Fresh green leaves, mauve flowers, bright hips. Thorny as hell.
Prune after fruiting with secateurs. Suitable for informal pruning.

Rosmarinus officinalis
Rosemary

Planting distance 45 cm (18 in)
Grows to 1·2 m (4 ft) maximum

Evergreen. Aromatic leaves; blue flowers in spring.
Prune in May with secateurs. Suitable for informal pruning.

Tamarix gallica
Common Tamarisk

Planting distance 30 cm (12 in)
4 years to reach 1.5 m (5 ft)

Wispy leaved and beautiful. Fluffy pink flowers in summer. Try it.
Prune in May with secateurs. Suitable for informal pruning.

Taxus baccata
Yew

Planting distance 60 cm (2 ft)
8 years to reach 1.5 m (5 ft)

Evergreen. Green or gold variegated.

Prune in August with shears/trimmers. Suitable for formal clipping.

Thuja plicata varieties
Western Red Cedar

Planting distance 60 cm (2 ft)
5 years to reach 1.5 m (5 ft)

Evergreen. Aromatic feathery foliage, shinier than Lawson cypress.
Prune in August with shears/trimmers. Suitable for formal clipping.

Ulex europaeus
Gorse

Planting distance 45 cm (18 in)
6 years to reach 1.5 m (5 ft)

Evergreen. Bright yellow flowers smother thorny stems in spring.
Prune in May after flowering with secateurs. Suitable for informal pruning.

Viburnum tinus
Laurustinus

Planting distance 45 cm (18 in)
5 years to reach 1.5 m (5 ft)

Evergreen. Boring leaves brightened with white flowers in winter to spring.
Prune in May. Suitable for formal clipping and informal pruning.

For an aromatic evergreen hedge, try *Rosmarinus officinalis;* dwarf *Buxus sempervirens* is ideal for edging beds.

CHAPTER 7 Climbers and wall plants

The clinging and twining habit of climbers, in their rich variety of colour and foliage, gives them an enviable ability to transform charmless features into things of beauty

Houses without climbers always look naked to me. I think too many owners worry about the effect of roots on their foundations and of tendrils on their mortar, but, so long as the right plants are chosen and they are trained properly, the only worry will be an extra spider or two in your bedroom.

SITING CLIMBERS AND WALL PLANTS

Climbing habits

Take into account the habit of any climber or wall plant before deciding where you will grow it. Some of the plants recommended here are twiners, some have sticky pads or aerial roots that need a flat surface to hold on to, others simply scramble and ramble over a support system, and some won't climb at all: they just enjoy the sheltered atmosphere a wall provides.

Where to plant

Trees and some vigorous shrubs can certainly move foundations, but all the plants I've recommended here can be safely planted right up to your walls. Only on badly mortared walls and on pebbledash will clinging climbers ever do any damage. If your house is pebbledashed, rig up a support system that will take the weight of the plant so that the rendering does not peel off in one large sheet.

The right plant for the right wall

WALLS FACING NORTH OR EAST
- *Camellia*
- *Chaenomeles*
- *Clematis*
- *Cotoneaster*
- *Fallopia* (syn. *Polygonum*)
- *Garrya*
- *Hedera*
- *Humulus*
- *Hydrangea*
- *Jasminum*
- *Lathyrus*
- *Lonicera* (some)
- *Parthenocissus*
- *Pyracantha*
- *Tropaeolum*

WALLS FACING SOUTH OR WEST
- *Abutilon*
- *Actinidia*
- *Aloysia* (syn. *Lippia*)
- *Camellia*
- *Carpenteria*

There is no better climber than clematis for smothering a wall or arch with flowers. Varieties include this award-winning *Clematis montana* 'Elizabeth'.

- Ceanothus
- Chaenomeles
- Clematis
- Cotoneaster
- Cytisus
- Eccremocarpus
- Fallopia
  (syn. *Polygonum*)
- Fremontodendron
- Garrya
- Hedera
- Hoheria
- Humulus
- Hydrangea
- Jasminum
- Lathyrus
- Lonicera
- Magnolia
- Parthenocissus
- Passiflora
- Phygelius
- Pyracantha
- Ribes
- Solanum
- Vitis
- Wisteria

Climbing plants can also be used to hide the compost heap, to smother an unsightly garden shed, and to scramble through old and decrepit fruit trees that you can't bring yourself to chop down.

Arches and pergolas (a series of linked arches) are still found in many gardens, but it's time the arbour made a comeback. At one time, this shady retreat was found in every garden – an intimate corner where lovers billed and cooed and over which scrambled a profusion of carefree and colourful climbers.

If you've a sun-dappled corner, try making a three-sided enclosure of white-painted trellis fastened to stout posts. Several rails across the top will make a 'roof' over which honeysuckle, clematis or wisteria can cascade in summer. Smaller gardens can sport climbers on tripods among border plants, or in pots and tubs, which can be equipped with cane tripods or placed by walls fitted with horizontal wires or trellis.

A climber-covered tripod gives instant height to a border

A rustic arch, with climbers scrambling over it, adds charm to a simple gateway

A pergola provides the framework for a flower-covered walkway

Growing plants through shrubs and trees

Remember that many flimsy climbers like clematis can simply be grown alongside other garden shrubs and allowed to scramble through them. It's not a system for tidy-minded gardeners, but it's one for greedy types who can prolong the season of interest of a shrub when its own blooms have faded.

Before you chop down a gnarled and dilapidated tree, consider training a rampant climber through it to brighten its boring boughs. The following plants will happily scramble up through trees and shrubs:

- Clematis
- Eccremocarpus
- Fallopia (syn. Polygonum)
- Humulus
- Lathyrus
- Parthenocissus
- Passiflora
- Solanum
- Tropaeolum
- Vitis
- Wisteria

Shown here are three different types of support for climbing plants: tripod, arch, and pergola, each of which will make an attractive feature in your garden.

SITE AND SOIL REQUIREMENTS

There are climbers for walls of all aspects, sunny and shady; each entry in the A–Z section includes advice on this and other cultivation details, while lists throughout the chapter give recommendations for specific situations. What all the plants have in common is a desire for good growing conditions when they are first planted. Your kindness to them in their youth will nearly always be repaid by good growth later in life.

Improve the soil

The soil against a house wall is almost always bone-dry because it's in what is known as a rain shadow area. Dig it well before you plant, and enrich it with plenty of leaf mould, pulverized bark or, better still, well-rotted manure or garden compost. A dusting of blood, bone and fishmeal will also give encouragement to the roots.

Growing climbers in tubs

If climbers are to be grown in tubs, give them a good compost, such as John Innes No. 3 potting compost, over a drainage layer of pebbles. Make sure there are plenty of holes in the base of the tub to allow drainage, and make the container as large as possible if you want the plant to be in residence for some time. It's a good idea to remove 8 cm (3 in) of the old compost each spring and replace it with fresh.

PLANTING CLIMBERS

You can plant pot-grown climbers at any time of year, but they'll grow away best if introduced to their new site in spring when the soil is still a little moist. Bare-root climbers can be planted in autumn but, if the plant is the slightest bit tender, wait until spring.

Set the plants about 30 cm (12 in) away from the tree, shrub, wall, trellis or arch that is to act as the support system. That way the roots have a little more room to explore. Plant when the soil is moist, and water in well if necessary. Lay a 5 cm (2 in) thick mulch of organic matter immediately planting is completed to keep in moisture and keep down weeds.

PLANT CARE

Providing support

On walls and fences self-clinging climbers, such as ivy, will need no help at all, though you can paint the surface with manure-water if they refuse to cling at first. Other plants will need to be provided with either horizontal wires held at 30 cm (12 in) intervals, or with trellis. I prefer the wire system: it's cheaper and longer-lasting than trellis. Drill and plug the wall, then insert galvanized vine eyes that will support horizontal strands of plastic-covered wire. If your house wall is painted and will have to be re-painted in future, trellis supports will be better. Fasten the trellis to a batten frame, which can be hinged against the wall at the base and held with butterfly catches at the top. When painting is necessary, the entire framework can be carefully swung away from the wall: most climbers are more flexible than you might think.

Training and pruning climbers

All plants will need to be trained against the support system and their stems spaced out and tied in. I find that wire twist-ties (similar to the kind sold for sealing freezer bags) are the most convenient to use. Pinch out the shoot tips of young plants to encourage a branching habit and good wall coverage.

Detailed instructions on pruning are given in the A–Z section, but remember to use a sharp pair of secateurs or loppers and to cut back, without fail, to a healthy bud or to just above a leaf.

Watering and feeding

Don't, whatever you do, let the soil around the plant dry out during its first year of establishment. Soak it with a hosepipe when necessary and keep the mulch in place. Apply a fresh mulch each spring.

A good feed of a general fertilizer each April will work wonders: use tomato fertilizer to coax any flowering climber to bloom more freely (it contains lots of potash for flower and fruit formation).

Wall support systems

SUPPORTING PLANTS WITH WIRES

Stout horizontal wires fastened to the surface of a wall by metal vine eyes make a cheap, sturdy and unobtrusive support system for climbing plants.

SUPPORTING PLANTS WITH TRELLIS

On surfaces that have to be painted, train climbers against a trellis that is hinged to a batten on the wall. The trellis and plant can be swung away as necessary.

A-Z
of climbers and wall plants

AMONG THE CLIMBERS you'll find some real beauties, that are valued in leaf, fruit and flower. Don't stick solely to the common stuff: experiment a little with something unusual. All the plants featured here will give good value for money, but I've done my best to point out the drawbacks where they exist. If you're keen to try climbing roses look in the rose chapter for my favourite varieties.

Abutilon vitifolium
3-9 m (10-30 ft)

A little tender it might be, but this abutilon is a treasure worth risking. The leaves are maple-shaped and covered in soft down, and the mallow flowers are a delicate shade of lilac, darker in the variety 'Veronica Tennant', white in var. *album*. All three bloom in early summer and lose their leaves in winter.
Aspect south or west.
Likes sun and shelter and a rich, well-drained but not dry soil. Tolerates clay, dry and chalky soils and coastal exposure. Sometimes short-lived.
Prune out dead stems in spring and remove faded flowerheads.
Propagate by sowing seeds in heat during January, or by rooting cuttings of stem tips in a propagator in summer.

Actinidia kolomikta
1.8-2.4 m (6-8 ft), can reach 6 m (20 ft)

This climber needs patience. In the right spot, and when it's settled in, it will turn the tips of its green, heart-shaped leaves bright pink and white. Quite a spectacle. The flowers are insignificant and the leaves deciduous.

Aspect south or west.
Likes a sheltered, sunny spot and well-drained soil. Tolerates clay and dry soils, and enriched chalky soils.
Prune out unwanted growth in summer. Shorten sideshoots to two or three buds in winter and remove a few older stems, replacing them with young ones, which should be tied in.
propagate in summer by rooting shoot tip cuttings in a propagator or by layering suitable shoots.

Aloysia triphylla
(syn. *Lippia citriodora*)
Lemon Verbena, Aloysia
1.2 m (4 ft)

Never much to look at, this is a shrub valued for its strong citrus scent: crush the leaves and you'll get the full impact. It doesn't climb but certainly appreciates the shelter a wall can give. The leaves are deciduous (and useful for making pot pourri) and the pale lilac flower spikes are pleasing, though hardly spectacular, in summer.
Aspect south or west.
Likes sun and shelter and light, well-drained soil.
Tolerates dry or chalky soil and coastal sites.
Prune back dead stems to suitable buds in spring. Hard winters will kill the bush to ground level but it usually sprouts from below the surface. A thick winter mulch of dry bracken or straw will help to keep it alive.
Propagate by rooting cuttings of firm shoot tips in a propagator in summer.

Camellia japonica varieties
3 m (10 ft)

I've talked about *C.* x *williamsii*, which I think is a better plant for general garden cultivation, on p.59, but the varieties of *C. japonica* are worth growing on sunny walls, though not those that face east (the early morning sun might damage frosted buds). Their glossy evergreen leaves set off the waxy double or single flowers of red, white, pink or magenta that appear in spring. Ask your nurseryman to suggest suitable varieties from his stock.
Aspect north, south or west.
Likes well-drained, lime-free soil enriched with leaf mould. Apply diluted iron sequestrene in spring if the leaves are a bit yellow. Tolerates clay soil and sheltered coastal sites.
Prune out only unwanted or badly placed shoots in spring and shorten spindly shoots of older plants by half.
Propagate by taking leaf bud or shoot tip cuttings in summer and rooting them in a propagator.

Carpenteria californica
Californian Mock Orange
1.8-2.4 m (6-8 ft)

Not a climber, but a tender shrub

Plants for any situation

The following plants will do well in clay, chalky, or dry soils. Those marked ◆ will also thrive in coastal gardens.

- *Abutilon* ◆
- *Actinidia*
- *Chaenomeles*
- *Cotoneaster* ◆
- *Cytisus* ◆
- *Fallopia* (syn. *Polygonum*) ◆
- *Garrya* ◆
- *Hedera* ◆
- *Humulus*
- *Hydrangea* ◆
- *Jasminum* ◆
- *Lonicera*
- *Magnolia*
- *Parthenocissus*
- *Pyracantha* ◆

deserving a sheltered spot. The leaves are oval and evergreen, and the large, papery white, fragrant flowers are centred with a boss of yellow stamens.
Aspect south or west.
Likes light, well-drained soil, shelter and full sun. Tolerates dry or chalky soil and sheltered coastal gardens.

Camellia japonica will do well on a sunny wall, protected from frost and cold winds. Varieties available include this lovely pink *C. japonica* 'Tricolor'.

Prune out one or two older branches and any dead shoots in spring.
Propagate by shoot tip cuttings rooted in a propagator in summer. Sow seeds under glass in spring.

Ceanothus varieties
Californian Lilac
2.4-3 m (8-10 ft)

The upright habit of the ceanothuses makes them a good choice for walls. 'Delight' is a spring flowerer, and

'Autumnal Blue' adds colour to the latter part of the year. Both have rough, tiny evergreen leaves and soft blue powderpuff flowers.
Aspect south or west.
Likes sunny, sheltered spots and a well-drained soil. Tolerates dry or chalky soil and sheltered coastal sites.
Prune the flowering shoots back by half when the blooms have faded. Cut out dead stems in spring.
Propagate by rooting shoot tip cuttings in a propagator in summer.

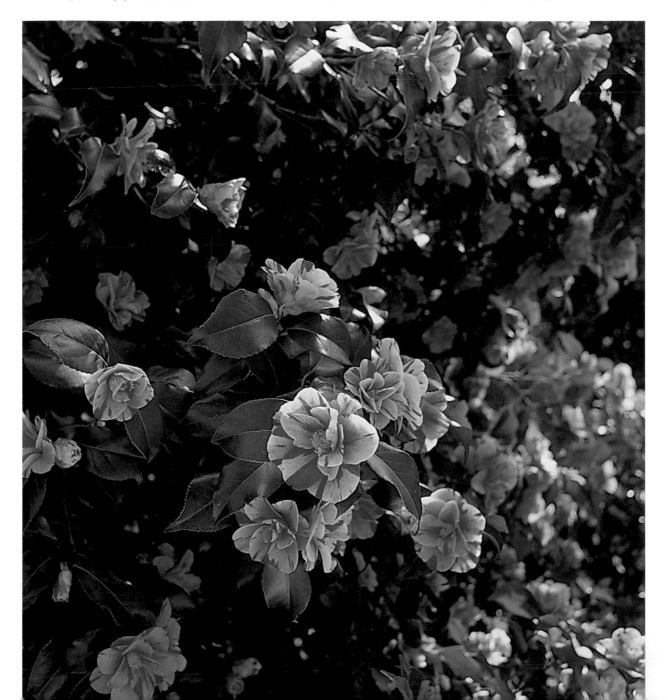

Chaenomeles species and varieties
Japonica, Japanese Quince, Cydonia
1.2–3 m (4–10 ft)

Indispensable spring flowers. Varieties of both *C. speciosa* (the earliest to flower, often starting in winter) and *C.* x *superba* are showy. All are deciduous and have apple-blossom-shaped flowers of red, white or pink. Among the best varieties of *C. speciosa* are: 'Brilliant' (scarlet); 'Moerloosei' (pink and white); and 'Nivalis' (white). *C.* x *superba* is especially good, and popular, in its variety 'Knap Hill Scarlet'. Most produce aromatic fruits that make sumptuous jelly.

Aspect north, south, east or west.
Likes a sunny site and well-drained soil. Tolerates dry, clay or chalky soil.
Prune by shortening sideshoots back to two or three buds after flowering.
Propagate by layering in spring or by rooting firm shoot tips in a propagator in summer.

Clematis varieties
Virgin's Bower
3 m (10 ft) plus

No garden should be without its complement of clematis, scrambling up walls, through trees and shrubs and over arches and pergolas. There are dozens of different varieties, most of them deciduous, which produce their wide-faced single or double flowers during spring and summer. Here's my pick of the large-flowered hybrids:
'Barbara Dibley': magenta; May, June and September.
'Barbara Jackman': lavender, striped magenta; May, June and September.
'Comtesse de Bouchaud': rose-pink; June to August.
'Elsa Späth': lavender-blue; May, June and September.
'Ernest Markham': magenta; June to September.
'Etoile Rose': deep pink, quartered bells with paler edges; June to September.

'Hagley Hybrid': shell-pink; June to September.
'Jackmanii Superba': violet-purple; July to September.
'Lasurstern': lavender-blue with wavy edges; May, June and September.
'Marie Boisselot': pale pink to white; May to October.
'Nelly Moser': pale pink-striped magenta; May, June, August and September.
'Vyvyan Pennell': bluish mauve; double in May and June, single in September.

For covering buildings, *C. montana* is a rampant white-flowered species, most frequently planted in its pink form var. rubens. Both are gloriously scented.

C. tangutica offers the best value of any clematis. It produces masses of bright yellow lantern flowers in summer and these are followed by fluffy spherical seedheads that persist through the winter. Grow it through a shrub or over a shed.

C. macropetala produces nodding double blooms of lavender-blue and white in May and June. It looks delightful in tubs and large pots.

Aspect north, south, east or west.
Likes its roots in cool, moist soil. Place flagstones or gravel over the soil around them. Most prefer their heads in the sun. Tolerates clay or chalky soil, and sheltered coastal gardens.
Plant where the soil around the roots will be shaded but the stems will be in full sun. Plant slightly deeper than the pot's soil level to avoid clematis wilt, and provide adequate support for the stems. Give all varieties time to settle in (up to three years) before expecting

Pruning clematis

GROUP 1
Prune only when they are becoming overgrown. Remove shoots that have carried flowers and any dead growth, as soon as the blooms fade.
● *C. montana*
● *C. macropetala*

To restrict the size or reduce overcrowding, thin out flower-bearing stems after flowering

Remove any dead or damaged stems, cutting back to a healthy pair of buds

them to produce masses of flower.
Prune clematis according to which group it is in. (See the chart above for all the varieties mentioned here.)
Propagate in summer by layering firm stems, or by rooting internodal cuttings in a propagator.
Diseases Clematis wilt may result in rapid collapse of the entire plant. Cut out any infected stems and wait patiently. In most cases the plant will re-grow, even if it has to be cut back to ground level.

Cotoneaster horizontalis
Fishbone Cotoneaster
1.8–2.4 m (6–8 ft)

Planted against a wall, this cotoneaster sidles up against it to quite a height, spreading out its fans of symmetrical branches. It decorates them with tiny green leaves in summer and red berries in autumn and winter.

GROUP 2

Remove dead or damaged stems in March and cut back all the rest to a pair of strong buds.

- 'Barbara Dibley'
- 'Barbara Jackman'
- 'Elsa Späth'
- 'Lasurstern'
- 'Marie Boisselot'
- 'Nelly Moser'
- 'Vyvyan Pennell'

Remove any dead or weak stems and cut back healthy stems to a pair of strong buds

GROUP 3

Cut all stems back to a healthy pair of buds 90 cm (3 ft) above ground level in March. Remove completely any damaged stems.

- 'Comtesse de Bouchaud'
- 'Ernest Markham'
- 'Etoile Rose'
- 'Hagley Hybrid'
- 'Jackmanii Superba'
- *C. tangutica*

Cut each stem back to a pair of strong buds about 1 m (3 ft) above soil level

Aspect north, south, east or west.
Likes ordinary well-drained soil. Tolerates dry, chalky or clay soil and coastal exposure.
Prune out only unwanted or overcrowding stems in spring.
Propagate by sowing seeds or by rooting cuttings of firm shoot tips in a propagator in summer.

Cytisus battandieri
Moroccan Broom
3–3.6 m (10–12 ft)

Take a sniff at the bright yellow cockade-like blooms of this open-growing broom and you'll detect the aroma of freshly cut pineapple. Early summer is the time of flowering, and the blooms are carried at the tips of stems that are clad in silky-haired deciduous leaves. Bees love it.
Aspect south or west.
Likes full sun and a sheltered spot in

well-drained soil. Tolerates dry, clay or chalky soil and sheltered coastal gardens.
Prune out one or two of the oldest stems each winter, and any that grow straight out from the wall. Never cut into the old wood.
Propagate by sowing seeds in spring, or by rooting firm shoot tip cuttings in a propagator.

Eccremocarpus scaber
Chilean Glory
Flower 3 m (10 ft)

Easy to grow and lovely when rambling through other shrubs. The green foliage is ferny and the tubular flowers are burning orange, decorating the plant from summer to autumn.
Aspect south or west.
Likes sun and shelter and light, well-drained soil. Tolerates dry or chalky soil; coastal exposure.

Prune out dead wood in spring. The plant will be killed back to soil level in severe winters.
Propagate from seeds sown in heat during spring.

Fallopia baldschuanica
(syn. *Polygonum baldschuanicum*)
Russian Vine, Mile-a-minute
6 m (20 ft) plus

The fastest climber of all, but one I can only recommend to the desperate gardener. It produces a rampant thicket of twining stems and a fluffy mass of creamy white flowers in summer and autumn. The arrowhead-shaped leaves are deciduous, leaving you to look at a mattress of brown stems in winter. But if you want a rapid grower, you can give it a go: it puts on a good 4.5 m (15 ft) each year and for a couple of months in summer it does look quite charming.

Aspect north, south, east or west.
Likes almost any site and soil.
Prune by clipping back any unwanted stems in early spring.
Propagate by rooting hardwood cuttings outdoors in autumn, or by rooting cuttings of firm shoot tips in a propagator in summer.

Fremontodendron californicum
Fremontia
3 m (10 ft)

A tender evergreen for gambling gardeners. The lobed leaves are a dreary dull green but the starry yellow flowers that appear in summer will make up for the foliar deficiency. Very classy.
Aspect south or west.
Likes full sun and shelter and a well-drained soil. Tolerates dry or chalky soil and sheltered coastal gardens.
Prune only to remove badly placed or dead branches in spring.
Propagate by seeds sown in heat in spring, or by cuttings of firm shoot tips rooted in a propagator in summer.

Garrya elliptica
Silk Tassel Bush
3.6 m (12 ft)

Funereal in leaf but fabulous in flower, the silk tassel bush produces living icicles of bloom in January and February. The grey-green catkins can be 15 cm (6 in) or more long and show up well against the deep evergreen foliage. A superb plant to position a floodlight beneath.
Aspect north, south, east or west.
Likes a sheltered spot in a well-drained soil. Tolerates dry, clay or chalky soil and coastal exposure. It may suffer in severe winters.
Prune out dead or out-growing, unwanted branches in spring. Otherwise pruning is not essential.
Propagate by layering low-hanging stems in autumn and by taking cuttings of firm shoot tips in summer any time of year.

Hedera species and varieties
Ivy
6 m (20 ft) plus

Valuable evergreens with leaves that may be finely cut, crimped or splashed with cream and yellow. They cling by means of tenacious aerial roots: avoid planting them against pebbledash, which they may pull off. All lend colour and form to the garden, especially in winter. (See Chapter 5 Shrubs for other varieties and uses.)

The small-leaved ivies are varieties of *H. helix*; among the best for walls are: 'Buttercup' young leaves bright yellow; 'Chicago' green leaves burnished purple; 'Glacier': green leaves edged with white; 'Königers Auslese' dark green fingered leaves; 'Oro di Bogliasco' (syn. 'Goldheart') dark green leaves with a yellow centre; 'Parsley Crested' green leaves with wavy edges.

Of the larger leafed ivies, the pick of the bunch is the lengthily named *H. colchica* 'Dentata Variegata': its foliage is attractively splashed and marbled with bright creamy yellow.
Aspect north, south, east or west.
Likes almost any soil and situation.
Prune mature plants by clipping them back with a pair of shears in spring every other year.
Propagate by rooting shoot tip cuttings in a propagator or outdoors in summer. Low-hanging shoots can be layered at any time of year.

Hoheria lyallii
3 m (10 ft) plus

Not half as widely grown as it should be, this shrub is a little tender and benefits from being sheltered by a wall. The deciduous, oval green leaves make a fine backdrop for the thick array of scented white flowers in summer. Try it in the open in sheltered gardens.
Aspect south or west.
Likes sun and a well-drained soil. Tolerates dry or chalky soil and coastal gardens.
Prune out dead wood and one or two older stems each spring.
Propagate by sowing seeds in gentle heat in spring, by layering in summer, or by rooting cuttings of firm shoot tips in a propagator in summer.

Humulus lupulus 'Aureus'
Golden-leafed Hop
4.5 m (15 ft)

This deciduous twiner is stunning in spring and summer when its acid-yellow vine-shaped leaves decorate the questing stems. It is good for brightening dingy corners, and superb with green-flowered euphorbias.
Aspect south, east or west.
Likes rich, well-drained soil and sun. Tolerates clay, dry or chalky soil.
Prune away all dead growth in spring: it usually dies back down to ground level in winter.
Propagate by division or seed in spring.

Hydrangea petiolaris
Climbing Hydrangea
Up to 15 m (50 ft)

If you like the bushy hydrangeas, then you must have a go with the climbing type. The leaves are similar but the stems are rather more tortuous and they are equipped with aerial

Climbers of special note

These climbers have either scented flowers or particular winter interest in the form of flowers and berries.

SCENTED BLOOMS
- *Carpenteria*
- *Clematis* (some)
- *Cytisus*
- *Hoheria*
- *Lonicera*
- *Magnolia*
- *Wisteria*

WINTER INTEREST
- *Chaenomeles*
- *Cotoneaster*
- *Garrya*
- *Hedera*
- *Jasminum*
- *Pyracantha*

CLIMBERS AND WALL PLANTS

CLIMBERS AND WALL PLANTS   **97**

roots that enable them to cling to walls. Large white flowerheads open in June.

Aspect north, south, east or west.
Likes rich and well-drained soil. Tolerates well-enriched dry, chalky or clay soils, and coastal exposure.
Prune out only unwanted or dead stems in spring.
Propagate by taking cuttings of firm shoot tips and rooting them in a propagator in summer.

Jasminum nudiflorum
Winter Jasmine
3.6 m (12 ft)

You'll see winter jasmine squirting through fences in cottage gardens all over the country, and billowing from walls, where it makes a thick mattress of dark green stems. The bright yellow blossoms are especially welcome, for they push out well in advance of the leaves any time from November to March.

Aspect north, south, east or west.
Likes almost any soil and situation.
Prune out flowered shoots immediately after blooming; that way you'll prevent the build-up of that thick mattress of flowerless wood.
Propagate by layering or by rooting hardwood cuttings in the open ground in autumn.

Lathyrus latifolius
Everlasting Pea
2.4 m (8 ft)

Here's something that makes a change from the annual sweet pea: it's a perennial version that will last for years. The foliage is typically pea-like, and the winged flowers are pink or white. Sadly it lacks the powerful fragrance of its annual relations.

Aspect south, west or east.
Likes rich, well-drained soil and sun. Tolerates clay or chalky soil.
Prune to ground level each autumn.
Propagate by division or seeds in spring.

Lonicera
Honeysuckle, Woodbine
6-9 m (20-30 ft)

The common honeysuckle (and there is none better) is *L. periclymenum*, sold in two varieties: 'Belgica' (Early Dutch) and 'Serotina' (Late Dutch). The first carries its pale yellow, pink-flushed flowers in May, June, and again in September, and the second blooms continuously from July to September. Both are deciduous. If you want an evergreen, try *L. sempervirens* with orange and yellow trumpet flowers. Sadly it lacks the fragrance of its leaf-losing relations. *L. japonica* 'Aureoreticulata' is a good honeysuckle for foliage: its semi-evergreen leaves are oval, fresh green and netted with yellow veins. All these honeysuckles will scramble and twine over anything put in their way.

Aspect *L. periclymenum* likes a south- or west-facing position; the other two will tolerate any aspect.
Likes rich, well-drained soil and shelter. Tolerates enriched clay, dry or chalky soil.
Prune out older, flowered growths of *L. periclymenum* and *L. sempervirens* immediately after flowering. Clip back *L. japonica* 'Aureoreticulata' in spring.
Propagate by layering or by taking cuttings of firm shoot tips and rooting them in a propagator in summer.

Magnolia grandiflora
Bull Bay, Laurel Magnolia
12 m (40 ft)

Now here's a stately wall plant. The leaves, as the second common name suggests, are evergreen and rather like those of laurel except that they often have the additional attraction of russeting on the undersides. You'll have to wait a good many years for the waxy cup-shaped flowers of creamy white to appear, but the plant is still

---

Plants with evergreen leaves	
● Camellia	● Hedera
● Carpenteria	● Lonicera (some)
● Ceanothus	● Magnolia
● Fremontodendron	● Passiflora
● Garrya	● Pyracantha

good to look at even when out of flower. The variety 'Exmouth' will bloom earlier in its life than the true species and flowers during summer and autumn. The blooms are scented (if any are within sniffing distance). For large walls only.

Aspect south or west.
Likes rich, well-drained soil and a sheltered spot. Tolerates enriched clay, dry or chalky soils.
Prune out only dead or badly placed branches in spring, otherwise leave it alone.
Propagate by spring layering.

Parthenocissus species
Virginia Creeper, Boston Ivy
12 m (40 ft) plus

The true Virginia creeper is *P. quinquefolia* with much divided green leaves that turn brilliant crimson before falling in autumn. *P. tricuspidata*, Boston ivy, is perhaps the better plant for most walls for it clings more efficiently, needing no support at all. The true Virginia creeper needs a few horizontal wires to give its scrambling stems a bit of a hand. Boston ivy has another advantage too: its maple-shaped leaves are glossy and even better equipped to show off their fiery autumn tints. Keep both plants away from pebbledash.

Aspect north, south, east or west.
Likes well-drained soil and a bit of sun for the best autumn colour. Tolerates clay, dry or chalky soil.
Prune in winter, clipping back any stems that are growing away from the wall and shortening any that are venturing where they are not wanted.
Propagate by layering in summer or

by rooting cuttings of firm shoot tips in a propagator in summer.

Passiflora caerulea
Passion Flower
6 m (20 ft) plus

In spite of its exotic appearance, the passion flower does well in many sheltered British gardens. It is a rampant climber, equipped with tendrils to speed it on its way. The hand-shaped leaves are evergreen and the white, blue-centred flowers are produced in summer, followed by orange, egg-shaped fruits if the weather is kind. They are edible but pippy.

The 'passion' referred to is Christ's passion, not some aphrodisiac property of the fruit. The five petals and five sepals represent the Apostles (minus Judas and either Doubting Thomas or Peter), the blue frill of filaments represents the crown of thorns, the five anthers the wounds, three stigmas the nails, the hand-shaped leaves are the hands of His persecutors and the tendrils the whip with which He was scourged.

Aspect south or west.

Likes sun, shelter and a well-drained soil. Tolerates dry or chalky soil and sheltered coastal gardens.

Prune in spring cutting back any long, trailing growths to within 10 cm (4 in) of the main stems.

Propagate by cuttings of shoot tips, which can be rooted in a propagator in summer.

Phygelius capensis
Cape Figwort
1.2–1.8 m (4–6 ft)

A pretty-flowered shrub that enjoys the protection of a warm and sunny wall. The leaves are unremarkable, but the flowers that appear in branched heads at the stem tips during summer are a jolly sight, little tubular red jobs like tiny trumpets. Tied in, the stems will grow to around 1.8 m (6 ft). Severe

winters will kill them back to soil level.

Aspect south or west.

Likes sun, shelter and well-drained soil. Tolerates dry or chalky soil and coastal exposure.

Prune back to ground level or to breaking buds each spring.

Propagate by removing suckers in spring, by sowing seeds in warmth in spring, or by rooting shoot tip cuttings in a propagator in summer.

Pyracantha species and varieties
Firethorn
4.5 m (15 ft)

Here's a plant that gives good value for money. The dark leaves are evergreen; creamy white flowers are produced in summer and are followed in autumn and winter by a heavy crop of berries: red in *P. atalantioides*, orange in *P. coccinea* 'Lalandei', and yellow in *P. rogersiana* 'Flava'. The birds love eating the berries, but if you enjoy their company does it matter? Yellow berries are the last to be taken.

Aspect north, south, east or west.

Likes ordinary well-drained soil. Tolerates dry, clay or chalky soil and coastal exposure.

Prune out only those stems that outgrow their allotted space. Prune after flowering but watch the thorns.

Propagate by rooting cuttings of firm shoot tips in a propagator in summer.

Ribes speciosum
Fuchsia-flowered Gooseberry
2.4 m (8 ft)

Tiny red tubular flowers, each with a central tuft of stamens, decorate the gooseberry-like stems of this wall shrub in spring, making it look as if it were hung with rosy icicles. The green lobed leaves fall in winter, but the spring show makes cultivation well worth while.

Aspect south or west.

Likes sun and shelter and well-drained soil. Tolerates dry or chalky soil.

Prune out any dead stems and one or

two older stems each winter. Shorten to two or three buds any shoots that grow out from the wall in summer.

Propagate by hardwood cuttings in autumn or by inserting cuttings of firm shoot tips in a propagator in summer.

Solanum crispum
Chilean Potato Tree
7–8 m (25 ft)

A pretty scrambler with purple and yellow tomato flowers any time between June and September. It looks delightful when allowed to wander through *Abutilon vitifolium*. The best variety is 'Glasnevin': hardier and even longer flowering than the true species. The foliage is deciduous and certainly nothing to write home about, but that doesn't matter if the plant is trained through another.

Aspect south or west.

Likes sun, shelter and a light, well-drained soil. Tolerates dry or chalky soil and sheltered coastal gardens.

Prune in spring, shortening all sideshoots to three or four buds. Cut out dead or unwanted stems at the same time. Such precise pruning is not necessary where the plant is grown through a shrub or tree.

Propagate by rooting cuttings of firm shoot tips in a propagator in summer.

Tropaeolum speciosum
Scotch Flame Flower
3 m (10 ft) plus

At Hidcote Manor in Gloucestershire, England, and Powys Castle in Wales you'll find dreary yew hedges brought alive by this nasturtium relative that loves to scramble through them. The fresh green hand-shaped leaves are almost as attractive as the tubular scarlet flowers; both are at their best in summer and autumn. The plant dies down completely in winter.

Aspect north walls and the shady side of shrubs.

Likes the cooler northern counties and a moist soil enriched with plenty

of leaf mould. Tolerates coastal sites.
Prune by cutting away all dead growth in winter.
Propagate by division or sow seeds in a frame in spring.

Vitis species and varieties
Vine
6 m (20 ft) plus

If you want a grape you can eat, on a plant that's ornamental, go for *V.* 'Brandt'. The leaves burnish well in autumn, and the black grapes are delicious at the end of a good summer. For bold foliage colour you'll not do better than the gross *V. coignetiae*, which has massive vine leaves coated in a light down. They turn vivid shades of orange and crimson before they fall to the ground in autumn.

Aspect south or west.

Likes sun and a rich soil. Tolerate enriched clay or chalky soil.

Prune by shortening the sideshoots to 8 cm (3 in) in winter. Can be left unpruned if growing rampantly over arbours and through trees.

Propagate by layering in spring or autumn or by taking cuttings of firm shoot tips and rooting them in a propagator in summer.

Wisteria sinensis
Chinese Wisteria
15 m (50 ft)

This plant brings back fond memories for me; it enveloped our first house, dangling its scented lilac-purple flower trails outside our windows so that the air was permanently scented during the month of May.

The deciduous leaves are pinnate (like those of an ash tree) and make a handsome fresh green covering for a house wall in summer even when there are no flowers are showing. There's a second, lighter flush of bloom later in the summer.

Give it a go over tall tree stumps, arches and pergolas and be patient – it may take a few years to settle in.

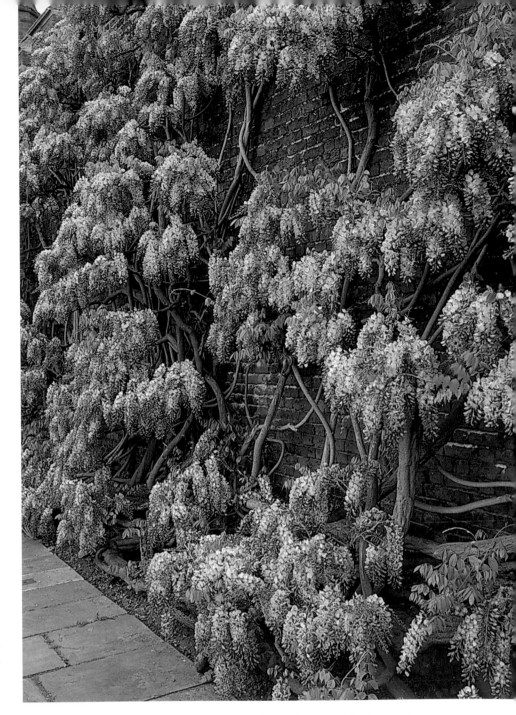

Correct pruning (and an occasional feed of tomato fertilizer, which has a high potash content) can encourage young plants to flower more easily.

If your plant still refuses to bloom after about five years, replace it with a wisteria that's been grafted from a free-flowering parent. Some forms are just shy of flowering and a real waste of time. Good ones are stupendous.

Aspect south or west.

Likes sun, shelter and a well-drained soil. Tolerates dry and chalky soil.

The fragrant lilac-purple flowers of *Wisteria sinensis* are a glorious sight in May and June, cascading over walls, pergolas and arches.

Prune first in July, shortening all unwanted shoots to about 15 cm (6 in). Prune again in January, shortening all sideshoots to four buds.

Propagate by layering in spring or summer. Cuttings of firm shoot tips can be rooted in a propagator in summer.

CHAPTER **8 Roses**

Available in a vast number of varieties, roses offer breathtaking colour and scent, glorious flowers, fruit and foliage, and types to suit every soil and situation

A friend of mine swears that roses grow in spite of their owners – perhaps that's why most gardeners hold roses dear to their hearts – but they also have romantic connections, delectable scents, glorious colours and one hundred and one uses.

Before you can even begin to choose a rose for your garden you really ought to know the different types that are available. Rose classification is complicated: the recently adopted system has 26 divisions, based on parentage, growth habit or flower type (see p.102). But for me and the average gardener, life has to be a little easier, so here's my simplified version, which I hope is clear and enables you to get the right plant.

DIFFERENT ROSE TYPES

Hybrid tea roses

The buffs now call these 'large-flowered roses'. The blooms are fat and fully double and are usually carried in small numbers at the tip of each stem. They will bloom from early summer until the frosts, and sometimes beyond, and the flowers tend to come in flushes. This is the type to grow for winning prizes; they also look fabulous in groups in beds or borders.

Large-flowered or hybrid tea roses are full centered and carried in small numbers on each stem.

Floribunda roses

Now known as 'cluster-flowered roses', these are bush roses with much-branched flower clusters at the stem tips. The blooms are usually rather smaller than those of hybrid teas. But don't make the mistake of thinking that all floribundas are single: some

Cluster-flowered or floribunda roses carry more blooms than hybrids.

of them have decidedly double blooms. The difference is in the size and quantity of flowers. They flower almost continuously through summer but are usually slightly less vigorous than the hybrid teas. They are the best choice for bedding.

Standard roses

Not recognized as a division, these are simply hybrid tea or floribunda roses (and very occasionally shrub roses) grown on a single, tall stem. They are used as specimen roses to add height to low plantings and should be supported by 2.5 x 2.5 cm (1 x 1 in) stakes that finish just below the head of branches. To my eye, standards look too artificial, but they do make rose-sniffing an easier pastime for those gardeners who have trouble bending down!

Miniature or 'patio' roses

Don't think that these are house plants. They might come in pots, but they will turn into spindly, fly-ridden thickets if you grow them indoors for any length of time. Planted out at the edges of beds and borders, on patios, and in tubs and windowboxes, they will perform well, making wiry little shrubs that are peppered with flowers right through the summer. They usually grow between 15 and 45 cm (6 and 18 in) high and some are good for ground cover. The secret of growing miniatures well in containers is to keep the compost gently moist at all times and to give the plants plenty of light.

Climbing roses

These are roses with long and questing stems that can be trained around arches, over pergolas, up walls and through trees. There are several groups of climbing roses, the most useful being the 'repeat-flowering climbers' that bloom right through the summer – unlike most rambler roses and many other climbers. 'Climbing sports' are derived from hybrid tea or floribunda roses which, for some reason best known to themselves, suddenly sent up a climbing shoot from an otherwise

Standard roses need to be supported; use two ties to hold stem to stake.

stocky bush. Gardeners over the years have propagated from these shoots, and we now have plenty to choose from – all can be easily spotted because they have the original rose name with 'Climbing' put in front; 'Climbing Ena Harkness' or 'Climbing Iceberg', for example. Sadly, climbing sports do not flower as freely as the bushes from which they were propagated. They usually have just one large flush of flowers in early summer.

I'll talk about pruning later, but the important thing about the climbing sports is that they should not be pruned too hard, otherwise they might lose their climbing tendency.

Rambling roses

Ramblers tend to have more lax stems than climbers. Like the climbers, they are useful when they can be planted against tall supports, but preferably not against walls where the lack of air circulation can encourage mildew.

They are especially good when planted at the base of old fruit trees and allowed to scramble through the branches above, giving them what appears to be a new lease of life. The flush of flowers is usually confined to a grand burst in early summer, and the blooms are usually relatively small.

Everyone's idea of the perfect country cottage, with roses cascading round the door.

Shrub roses

Here are to be found roses old and roses new, roses of history, and wild species. The term 'shrub roses' is a sensible one, for these plants should be grown as shrubs and not as rose bushes, and plenty are good for growing as hedges (see p.107). They vary enormously in shape and size and have minimal pruning requirements. Many of them have disease-resistant foliage, attractive fruits or 'hips', flowers that are fully double, or moon-faced and single, and the deepest, most complex scents imaginable. Recent developments in breeding mean that plenty of the newer shrub roses have a combination of delicate flower shape and colour and beautiful fragrance.

The disadvantages of shrub roses are two-fold: many of them have just one flush of bloom, in early summer, and many are quite large and look out of place in small gardens. But there are plenty of exceptions: there are repeat-flowering, and continuous-flowering shrub roses, and some that grow no more than 1 m (3 ft) high and as much across. You may have guessed from my enthusiasm that I rather like these roses.

SOIL AND CONDITIONS

Sun or shade?

There are a few roses that can tolerate shade but, in general, they like an open, sunny spot that's sheltered from direct wind. You'll often be told to avoid planting roses in frost pockets, but something has to be grown there and, quite honestly, roses are more reliable in such situations than most plants.

Soil type?

A common myth is that roses need heavy soil to do really well. In reality they'll thrive on any soil if you perk it up a bit before planting. You can double dig the site if you really feel better for such exercise, but single digging is all that's necessary on most reasonable soils (see p.16). Good drainage is essential, as it is for most plants, and work in as much organic matter as you can spare – compost, manure, or even crumbly leaf mould, plus a little fertilizer. The plants will be there for a long time so you might as well make them feel at home right away. I've seen 30-year-old roses blooming as happily as youngsters in a good soil that has been well prepared and looked after.

Avoid, if you can, planting new roses on ground that was previously occupied by old roses. The soil might be rather tired and in need of a change of crop.

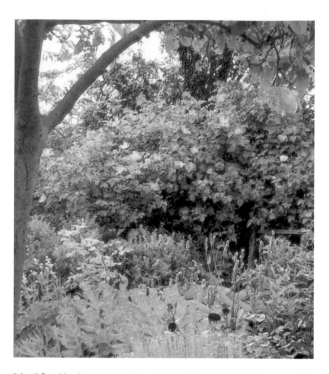

Ideal for the larger garden, scrambling shrub roses provide summer blossoms and autumn fruits.

How are roses classified?

Although they're avoided here, you will come across plenty of technical terms being applied to roses. Here's an explanation of some of them.

- Among the shrubs: **gallicas** descend from *R. gallica* and are quite compact; **albas** (with grey-green leaves) and **damasks** are noted for their fragrance, as are **centifolias** which also have many-petalled flowers; **moss** roses have hair-like mossy growths on their buds, stems and other green bits. You'll easily recognize them. **Rubiginosa** hybrids have apple-scented foliage and **pimpinellifolia** hybrids (or Scots briars) are prickly and grow in low mounds.
- Also among the shrubs are roses categorized as **bourbon, china, noisette** and **portland**. All these refer to something in their ancestry: the Noisette nursery in Paris, the French Iles de Bourbon, China is obvious, and the second Duchess of Portland.
- **Polyanthas** are shrubs or climbers related to the species *R. multiflora*. The flowers are in clusters.
- Everyone has heard of **tea** roses but there is no real explanation for the name. It could be the tea-like fragrance or the Fa Tee Nursery in China from where they were originally sold. **Hybrid teas** have teas in their parentage and the classic 'rose'-shaped flowers.

If there's an ideal pH for roses (see p.14) then it's in the region of 6.0 to 6.5, where most plants are happy. They'll still grow, though, on chalky earth, but plenty of organic matter will be appreciated.

BUYING ROSES

Container-grown roses You can buy and plant container-grown roses at any time of year, and the great advantage is that in summer you can see the plant in flower and check it for scent.

Bare-root roses are planted in the dormant season, from November to March. Specialist rose growers despatch most of their plants in this state, and they are undoubtedly the best source of supply if you want unusual varieties in first-class condition.

Pre-packed roses Sold in supermarkets and chain stores, pre-packed roses are not usually available in very wide variety, and they are seldom top quality bushes, but I've had some splendid plants that started life in this way. When it comes to price, the pre-packed roses are cheapest, followed by the bare-root plants. Container-grown roses are slightly more expensive: you'll have to pay for the privilege of planting at any time of year.

If you can see what you're buying, go for a shapely bush with at least three stems. If you can't you'll have to rely on the reputation of the grower. If you buy pre-packed roses, make sure they are recent stock and not starting to sprout in the bag.

HOW TO PLANT

The planting technique is exactly the same as that adopted for trees and shrubs (see p.40). Climbers and ramblers that are to be planted against walls, pillars or old trees should be given the same kind of support system and treatment as any other climber (see p.91). Plant hybrid tea and floribunda roses 60 cm (2 ft) apart when they are massed together in beds. Allow shrub roses sufficient room for their indicated spread.

ROSE PRUNING

The pruning of roses need not be the confusing job that it's made out to be. Approach your bush with the courage of your convictions, a sharp pair of secateurs and a clear idea of what you're setting out to achieve. The cardinal rule with all rose pruning is that cuts must be made cleanly and just above a bud; torn cuts will allow in disease, and long snags will simply die back. The different kinds of roses are pruned as follows:

Make a clean cut, just above an outward-facing bud

To prune a rose bush, cut out any dead, diseased, or weak stems, then any that cross the centre. Reduce the open framework that remains to knee height or just below.

Hybrid teas Immediately after planting bare-root hybrid teas, shorten all stems to 8-10 cm (3-4 in) above ground. It seems cruel, but it will force them into producing a healthy framework of new stems. Make clean cuts just above an outward-facing bud.

Container-grown roses planted during spring and summer are treated as mature plants by their first winter: prune between January and March as follows: first remove all dead wood, then any weak, diseased or crossing stems. Leave a cup-shaped frame of well-spaced branches. Cut all these stems back to just below knee height, above an outward-facing bud.

Remove one or two old branches from ageing plants every year so that a relatively young framework is maintained. If you can't find an outward-facing bud don't worry; find one that points anywhere other than right into the centre of the bush.

Floribundas Prune at the same time as hybrid tea roses, but not quite so low. Prune newly planted bare-root bushes back to 15 cm (6 in) and established bushes to just above knee height. Otherwise the technique is exactly the same.

Standard roses Depending on whether the variety is a hybrid tea or a floribunda, prune the branches as for bush roses (estimating the equivalent of knee height).

> "Approach your bush with the courage of your convictions, a sharp pair of secateurs and a clear idea of what you're setting out to achieve."

Miniatures and ground cover roses need little or no pruning other than the removal of dead or weak stems and shortening of overlong stems in March.

Shrub roses It is possible to make a real mess of shrub roses by pruning them, so I leave them entirely alone, apart from trimming away dead shoot tips in spring. Occasionally, old stems can be cut out completely, and it's a good idea to remember that total removal of a branch is always likely to produce a more shapely plant than if a branch is cut back by half or a third of its length. There are occasional exceptions to this rule, but not many. *Rosa gallica* 'Versicolor', for instance, can be grown as a small hedge and trimmed back by one third in spring to keep it neat. On most other varieties you must be much more circumspect.

Climbing roses There are several distinct groups of climbers and they all need slightly different pruning if you want to be really precise. However, it is perfectly possible to prune them all in the same way and get away with it, provided you're not too heavy handed. Simply cut off any dead shoot tips in March, and cut back to about 10 cm (4 in) any sideshoots that have previously carried flowers. One or two very ancient stems can be removed each year, but only when they are exhausted and flowering poorly. If in doubt, don't cut it out!

Rambling roses Most ramblers are pruned right after flowering, when a few very old and gnarled stems are cut out completely at ground level and new ones trained in to replace them. If few new ones have appeared, simply cut back lateral shoots that have flowered to within 10 cm (4 in) of the main stem. Hefty ramblers such as *Rosa filipes* 'Kiftsgate' need not be pruned as drastically (in fact you'll have a job to get at them if they're running through a tree); just trim out visible dead wood.

CARING FOR YOUR ROSES

Watering
Roses are deep rooted and, once established, are more capable of resisting mild spells of drought than most shrubs. During the first spring and summer after planting, however, soak the earth around them whenever it shows signs of drying out. Turn on a sprinkler if you can; otherwise, give each plant at least 10 litres (2 gallons) of water. In succeeding years the plants will only need soaking when drought threatens. It does pay off and can prevent the flowering season coming to an abrupt end.

Feeding
Like all plants that are generous with their blooms, roses like you to be generous with the fertilizer. Give them a good helping of general fertilizer such as blood, bone and fishmeal in April, scattering it onto the soil at the rate of two handfuls around each bush. In June a specially prepared rose fertilizer will help to give them a boost. One handful to each bush will be sufficient. The general fertilizer supplies all the major nutrients, but the specific fertilizer contains extra magnesium and potash, which keeps the bushes healthy and free-flowering. Hoe both fertilizers into the top few centimetres of soil.

Mulching
Just as with other shrubs, a mulch laid around your roses will retain moisture, keep down weeds and generally boost plant health. Pulverized bark or garden compost can be used, but well-rotted manure is certainly most enjoyed.

Deadheading
Unless the flowerheads eventually produce decorative hips, snip them off to save the plant's energy and to keep up appearances. Cutting the blooms of hybrid teas actually encourages them to form a second flush of flowers. If you don't cut the blooms for indoor decoration, a bit of light summer pruning won't go amiss – shorten the stems a little when the first flowers have faded.

Suckers are shoots that emerge from the rootstock of the rose. Remove them as soon as you see them by tearing them from their point of origin.

Sucker removal

Most roses are budded by the nurseryman on to a rootstock or briar because they can be grown to a saleable size more quickly in this way. Any shoots that emerge from the rootstock will be different in character and appearance from those that arise from the stems above ground. They can usually be differentiated from legitimate shoots by their paler colouring, lack of bronzing and, sometimes, by the presence of more leaflets (though this does not always hold good). Remove suckers as soon as they are seen or they will swamp the bush. Scrape away the soil at the base of the plants until the junction of sucker and rootstock can be seen. Tear away the sucker so that no part of it is left behind (see opposite).

Renovating old roses

Old bushes that have been allowed to grow unchecked can get into a sorry state. Ancient hybrid teas and floribundas can be renovated, if you fancy a challenge, simply by cutting out a portion of old and gnarled wood each year until sufficient new stems have been produced to take over completely. Shorten them gradually each year until they can be pruned to around the regulation knee height. You'll have to be quite patient but the results should be worthwhile.

Weed control

Mulching is the best answer, on several counts: it locks in moisture, thus reducing stress through any dry spells; over time, worms will drag the mulch down into the soil, helping to improve its overall condition; mulches that are relatively high in nutrients (well-rotted horse manure for instance) will provide a tasty snack for ever-hungry roses; and while weeds may gain a temporary footing, they're easy enough to pull out. Hoeing is the second best option but, if you do hoe, be careful not to damage the stems of your roses as this can stimulate the production of suckers and the tiresome work involved in removing them.

Underplanting

I don't much enjoy looking at bare soil, especially when it can be used to grow more plants. Some rose experts seem to like their rose beds bare of anything except

roses, but there's no reason why other low-growing plants should not make a pleasant carpet below them. You can choose all manner of things, but the following are especially good either as edgers or as carpeters: *Ajuga*, *Alchemilla*, *Arabis*, *Aubrieta*, *Dianthus*, *Geranium*, *Heuchera*, *Lamium*, lavender (edging), *Nepeta*, *Primula* (auriculas and polyanthus), *Pulmonaria*, *Stachys*, *Viola*, spring-flowering bulbs.

PESTS AND DISEASES

Roses can be regularly attacked by mildew, blackspot and greenfly (aphids). Other problems that may strike are rust, leaf-rolling sawfly, leaf-cutter bee, pincushion gall, capsid bug, caterpillars, froghopper (cuckoo spit), and die-back. All are covered in Part VI Pests, Diseases and Disorders.

It's a very depressing list, but your best ally is vigilance. If you deal with pest or disease problems promptly, they're much less likely to get a serious grip. So when you go out to smell the roses, give them a quick health check at the same time. In particular, watch for early infestations of aphids which, if left untreated, will cause horrible distortions of leaves and flowers.

PROPAGATION

Although the nurseryman propagates his roses by budding, it is much easier for the home gardener to increase his stock by taking hardwood cuttings in September or October. The plants may take a little while to come into flower (some of my shrub roses have taken five years) but there is no problem with suckers, and the technique is cheap and easy. All you need is patience. It is also easy to propagate climbers and ramblers by layering. Full details of propagation techniques are given in Chapter 2 Propagation.

Rose-care calendar

■ *March*	Complete pruning of established roses.
■ *April*	Apply general fertilizer; start spraying.
■ *May*	Look out for suckers and remove immediately.
■ *June*	Apply specific rose fertilizer to give roses a boost.
■ *July*	Deadhead hybrid tea and floribunda roses.
■ *August*	Apply general fertilizer.
■ *September*	Deadhead as necessary; tie in new shoots on climbers; watch out for diseases.
■ *October*	Take cuttings of species roses, ramblers, some floribundas and old roses.
■ *November*	Plant new roses as soon as they arrive.
■ *December*	Complete planting new roses during mild weather.

A-Z
of **roses**

OUT OF THE THOUSANDS OF roses available, these are the ones I'd take with me to a desert island. Other gardeners will have different favourites, but in my roses I look for vigour and shapeliness of the bush, good flower colour for as long a season as possible, and a sigh-provoking scent. Wherever possible, look for roses with leathery, disease-resisting foliage. Now and again some of these attributes may have to be sacrificed if a plant is stunning in other ways. I make no apologies for the fact that the shrub rose list is longer than the others – I love them best.

Roses that are particularly suitable for use as hedging or for planting in shady conditions, and those that are renowned for their fragrance are highlighted in the coloured boxes.

SHRUB ROSES

R. 'Abraham Darby'

Height 1.5 m (5 ft)   *Spread 1.5 m (5 ft)*

Repeat flowering, blended shades of pink to yellow, cup-shaped, double flowers; glossy dark green foliage; rich fragrance and moderate disease resistance.

R. 'Ballerina'

Height 1.25 m (4 ft)   *Spread 1.25 m (4 ft)*

Repeat flowering, masses of small, single pink flowers with a white eye; glossy green foliage; sadly only slight fragrance and moderate disease resistance.

R. 'Blanche Double de Coubert'

Height 2 m (6 ft)   *Spread 1.5 m (5 ft)*

Repeat flowering, pure white, semi-double flowers; rich green foliage; very fragrant; excellent disease resistance.

R. 'Buff Beauty'

Height 2 m (6 ft)   *Spread 2 m (6 ft)*

Repeat flowering, buff-orange, semi-double flowers; purplish green foliage; pleasant fragrance and moderate disease resistance.

R. 'Cardinal de Richelieu'

Height 1.25 m (4 ft)   *Spread 1 m (3 ft)*

Early summer flowering, mauve-purple, fading to dusky purple, double flowers; dull green foliage; very fragrant and moderate disease resistance.

R. x *centifolia* 'Cristata' (syn. R. 'Chapeau de Napoléon')

Height 1.5 m (5 ft)   *Spread 1.25 m (4 ft)*

Midsummer flowering, rich rose-pink, double flowers; mid-green foliage; pleasant fragrance and moderate disease resistance.

R. 'Complicata'

Height 2.5 m (8 ft)   *Spread 2.5 m (8 ft)*

Early to midsummer flowering, rich rose-pink single flowers with a white eye; mid-green foliage; slight fragrance; excellent disease resistance.

R. 'Cornelia'

Height 1.5 m (5 ft)   *Spread 2 m (6 ft)*

Repeat flowering, apricot-pink, fully double flowers; deep bronze-green foliage; very fragrant and excellent disease resistance.

R. 'Fantin-Latour'

Height 2 m (6 ft)   *Spread 1.5 m (5 ft)*

Early summer flowering, pale pink, flattened double flowers; dull green foliage; pleasant fragrance and moderate disease resistance.

R. 'Fru Dagmar Hastrup'

Height 1.25 m (4 ft)   *Spread 1.5 m (5 ft)*

Repeat flowering, pale pink single flowers; large red hips; rough bright green foliage; pleasant fragrance and excellent disease resistance. Also suitable for ground cover.

R. 'Frühlingsgold'

Height 2.5 m (8 ft)   *Spread 2 m (6 ft)*

Early summer flowering, bright primrose-yellow, semi-double flowers; light green foliage; pleasant fragrance and excellent disease resistance.

R. 'Frühlingsmorgen'

Height 2 m (6 ft)   *Spread 1.5 m (5 ft)*

Early and late summer flowering, rich pink single flowers with primrose-yellow eye; dull green foliage; pleasant fragrance and excellent disease resistance.

R. *gallica* 'Versicolor' (syn. R. *mundi*)

Height 1.25 m (4 ft)   *Spread 1.25 m (4 ft)*

Midsummer flowering, cerise-pink, striped white, semi-double flowers ; light green foliage; no fragrance and only slight disease resistance.

R. 'Geranium'

Height 2.5 m (8 ft)   *Spread 2.5 m (8 ft)*

Early summer flowering, bright red, single flowers; scarlet, flask-shaped hips; mid-green foliage; no fragrance but excellent disease resistance.

R. *glauca* (syn. R. *rubrifolia*)

Height 2.25 m (7 ft)   *Spread 2.25 m (7 ft)*

Midsummer flowering, rich pink, small, single flowers each with a white eye and yellow anthers; blue-grey, purple-

Shrub roses to use as hedging

SHRUB ROSE VARIETY	DISTANCE APART TO PLANT
R. 'Ballerina'	60 cm (2 ft)
R. 'Blanche Double de Coubert'	60 cm (2 ft)
R. 'Buff Beauty'	1 m (3 ft)
R. 'Complicata'	1 m (3 ft)
R. 'Cornelia'	1 m (3 ft)
R. 'Fantin-Latour'	1.25 m (4 ft)
R. 'Fru Dagmar Hastrup'	1 m (3 ft)
R. 'Frühlingsgold'	1 m (3 ft)
R. 'Frülingsmorgen'	1 m (3 ft)
R. gallica 'Versicolor' (syn. R. mundi)	60 cm (2 ft)
R. glauca (syn. R. rubrifolia)	1 m (3 ft)
R. 'Königin von Dänemark'	60 cm (2 ft)
R. 'Lady Penzance'	1 m (3 ft)
R. 'Maiden's Blush'	1 m (3 ft)
R. 'Marguerite Hilling'	1 m (3 ft)
R. 'Nevada'	1 m (3 ft)
R. 'Pink Grootendorst'	60 cm (2 ft)
R. 'Reine des Violettes'	1 m (3 ft)
R. 'Roseraie de l'Haÿ'	1 m (3 ft)
R. 'Scabrosa'	1 m (3 ft)
R. xanthina 'Canary Bird'	1 m (3 ft)

tinged foliage. Slight fragrance but excellent disease resistance.

R. 'Golden Chersonese'

Height 2 m (6 ft)   Spread 1.5 m (5 ft)

Late spring flowering, bright yellow single flowers; mid-green ferny foliage; pleasant fragrance and excellent disease resistance.

R. x *jacksonii* 'Max Graf'

Height 60 cm (2 ft)   Spread 2 m (6 ft)

Midsummer flowering, rich pink single flowers with a tuft of yellow stamens; mid-green foliage; pleasant fragrance and excellent disease resistance. Suitable for ground cover: the prostrate stems spread over the soil surface, rooting as they go.

R. 'Königin von Dänemark'

Height 1.5 m (5 ft)   Spread 1.25 m (4 ft)

Early summer flowering, pale pink, double, quartered blooms; pale green foliage; very fragrant and excellent disease resistance.

R. 'Lady Penzance'

Height 2 m (6 ft)   Spread 2 m (6 ft)

Early summer flowering, bright rose-pink single flowers, with tufted yellow stamens; good hips; the foliage emits an apple-like scent after rain; very fragrant; excellent disease resistance.

R. 'Madame Hardy'

Height 1.5 m (5 ft)   Spread 1.5 m (5 ft)

Midsummer flowering, pure white double flowers with a green button 'eye'; mid-green foliage; very fragrant and excellent disease resistance.

R. 'Maiden's Blush'

Height 1.5 m (5 ft)   Spread 1.5 m (5 ft)

Early summer flowering, blush-pink, double, quartered blooms; grey-green foliage; very fragrant and excellent disease resistance.

R. 'Marguerite Hilling'

Height 2.25 m (7 ft)   Spread 2.25 m (7 ft)

Early and late summer flowering, pink overlaid with deeper pink, semi-double flowers; mid-green foliage; slight fragrance and excellent disease resistance.

R. 'Mary Rose'

Height 1.25 m (4 ft)   Spread 1.25 m (4 ft)

Repeat flowering, rich rose-pink, double, cup-shaped flowers; rough, matt-green foliage; light fragrance and good disease resistance.

R. 'Nevada'

Height 2.25 m (7 ft)   Spread 2.25 m (7 ft)

Early and late summer flowering, creamy white, semi-double flowers; mid-green foliage; slight fragrance and moderate disease resistance.

R. 'Pink Grootendorst'

Height 1.25 m (4 ft)   Spread 1 m (3 ft)

Repeat flowering, rich pink, small double and frilly flowers in clusters; rough, rich green foliage; no fragrance but excellent disease resistance.

R. 'Reine des Violettes'

Height 2 m (6 ft)   Spread 2 m (6 ft)

Repeat flowering, violet-purple, double, quartered flowers with button eyes; grey-green foliage; very fragrant and excellent disease resistance.

R. 'Roseraie de l'Haÿ'

Height 2 m (6 ft)   Spread 1.5 m (5 ft)

Repeat flowering, rich magenta, fully double flowers; rough, rich green foliage; pleasant fragrance and excellent disease resistance. A tough shrub that will grow in poor soil and can withstand a maritime climate.

R. 'Scabrosa'

Height 1.25 m (4 ft)   Spread 1.25 m (4 ft)

Repeat flowering, mauve-pink single flowers; yellow stamens; good hips; rough, rich green foliage; pleasant scent and excellent disease resistance.

R. 'Stanwell Perpetual'

Height 1.5 m (5 ft)   Spread 1.5 m (5 ft)

Repeat flowering, blush-pink double flowers; grey-green foliage; pleasant scent; excellent disease resistance.

R. xanthina 'Canary Bird'

Height 2 m (6 ft)   Spread 2 m (6 ft)

Late spring flowering, small, single, bright yellow flowers; light green, ferny foliage; slight fragrance and excellent disease resistance.

HYBRID TEAS

R. Alec's Red

Height 1 m (3 ft)

Deep, rich red flowers; glossy green foliage. Very fragrant and excellent disease resistance.

R. 'Ena Harkness'

Height 75 cm (2½ ft)

Dark, velvety crimson flowers with sadly weak necks. Pleasant fragrance and moderate disease resistance.

R. Fragrant Cloud

Height 1 m (3 ft)

Geranium-red is the best description of the colour of the flowers; deep glossy green foliage. Very fragrant and moderate disease resistance.

R. 'Grandpa Dickson'

Height 1 m (3 ft)

Light yellow, massively full flowers; deep glossy green foliage. Slight fragrance but excellent disease resistance.

Shrub roses suitable for shade

All of the following shrub roses are suitable for growing in shade. Those marked with the symbol ◆ are also useful as ground cover.

- *R.* 'Blanche Double de Coubert'
- *R.* 'Complicata'
- *R.* 'Fru Dagmar Hastrup'
- *R.* 'Frülingsgold'
- *R.* 'Frülingsmorgen'
- *R. glauca (R. rubrifolia)*
- *R. x jacksonii* 'Max Graf'
- *R.* 'Lady Penzance'
- *R.* 'Maiden's Blush'
- *R.* 'Pink Grootendorst'
- *R.* 'Reine des Violettes'
- *R.* 'Roseraie de l'Haÿ'
- *R.* 'Stanwell Perpetual'
- *R. xanthina* 'Canary Bird'

R. Just Joey

Height 75 cm (2½ ft)

Coppery orange, medium-sized, veined red flowers; deep green foliage. Slight fragrance but excellent disease resistance.

R. Mischief

Height 1 m (3 ft)

Warm salmon-pink flowers; mid-green foliage. Slight fragrance and moderate disease resistance.

R. Pascali

Height 1 m (3 ft)

The best white flowered hybrid tea, this has glossy green foliage. Slight fragrance and moderate disease resistance.

R. Peace

Height 1.5 m (5 ft)

Huge pale yellow blooms edged with pink; deep glossy green foliage. Slight fragrance and excellent disease resistance.

R. Piccadilly

Height 75 cm (2½ ft)

Blooms carmine red above, yellow beneath; glossy purplish green foliage. Slight fragrance but excellent disease resistance.

R. 'Precious Platinum'

Height 1 m (3 ft)

Brilliant, rich red flowers; glossy green foliage. Slight fragrance but excellent disease resistance.

Roses for fragrance

All of the following roses are strongly fragrant. Those marked with the symbol ◆ also have excellent disease-resistance.

SHRUB ROSES
- 'Abraham Darby' ◆
- 'Blanche Double de Coubert' ◆
- 'Cardinal de Richelieu'
- 'Cornelia' ◆
- 'Königin von Dänemark' ◆
- 'Lady Penzance' ◆
- 'Maiden's Blush' ◆
- 'Madame Hardy' ◆
- 'Reine des Violettes' ◆

HYBRID TEAS
- Alec's Red ◆
- Fragrant Cloud
- 'Wendy Cussons' ◆
- Whisky Mac

FLORIBUNDAS
- Margaret Merril ◆

CLIMBERS
- 'Climbing Crimson Glory'
- 'Compassion' ◆
- 'Gloire de Dijon'
- 'Madame Grégoire Staechelin' ◆
- 'Zéphirine Drouhin'

RAMBLERS
- 'Albertine'

R. Rose Gaujard

Height 1 m (3 ft)

Flowers rich pink above, white beneath; deep glossy green foliage. Slight fragrance but excellent disease resistance.

R. 'Silver Jubilee'

Height 75 cm (4 ft)

Flowers in a mixture of pinks; glossy green foliage. Slight fragrance and excellent disease resistance.

R. 'Wendy Cussons'

Height 1 m (3 ft)

Very vibrant, rich cerise-pink flowers; deep glossy green foliage. Very fragrant and excellent disease resistance.

R. Whisky Mac

Height 75 cm (2½ ft)

Rich, coppery orange flowers; purplish green, glossy foliage. Very fragrant and moderate disease resistance. Very popular on account of its colour.

FLORIBUNDAS

R. 'Allgold'

Height 60 cm (2 ft)

Bright yellow, double flowers; glossy green foliage. Slight fragrance and excellent disease resistance.

R. City of Belfast

Height 60 cm (2 ft)

Bright scarlet, double flowers; glossy green foliage. Slight fragrance and excellent disease resistance.

R. Evelyn Fison

Height 75 cm (2½ ft)

Bright scarlet, medium-sized double flowers; deep glossy green foliage. Slight fragrance and moderate disease resistance.

R. Eye Paint

Height 1.25 m (4 ft)

Masses of small red, single flowers with white eyes; glossy green foliage. No fragrance but moderate disease resistance.

R. Iceberg

Height 1.25 cm (4 ft)

Plenty of pure white, double flowers; glossy green foliage. No fragrance but moderate disease resistance.

R. Lilli Marlene

Height 75 cm (2½ ft)

Deep red, double flowers with attractive petal formation; glossy purplish green foliage. Slight fragrance and moderate disease resistance.

R. Margaret Merril

Height 1 m (3 ft)

White, double flowers with a touch of blush; deep glossy green foliage. Very fragrant and excellent disease resistance.

R. 'Pink Parfait'

Height 1 m (3 ft)

Double flowers in a rich pink mixture; glossy green foliage. No fragrance but excellent disease resistance.

R. 'Southampton'

Height 1 m (3 ft)

Large, coppery orange, double flowers; deep glossy green foliage. Slight fragrance but great disease resistance.

R. Sue Lawley

Height 75 cm (2½ ft)

Semi-double, rich pink flowers edged with white; yellow stamens and a white eye; deep glossy green foliage. Slight fragrance but excellent disease resistance.

R. 'The Queen Elizabeth'

Height 2 m (6 ft)

Light pink, fully double flowers; deep glossy green foliage; good hedger. Slight fragrance but excellent disease resistance.

R. Trumpeter

Height 60 cm (2 ft)

Vibrant scarlet, double flowers; deep glossy green foliage. No fragrance but excellent disease resistance.

R. 'Yesterday'

Height 1 m (3 ft)

Rich lilac-pink and white, semi-double flowers; glossy green foliage. Pleasant fragrance and excellent disease resistance.

MINIATURES

R. Angela Rippon

Height 30 cm (12 in)

Salmon pink, double flowers; rich green foliage. Slight fragrance and excellent disease resistance.

R. 'Baby Faurax'

Height 30 cm (12 in)

Purplish pink, semi-double flowers; glossy green foliage. Pleasant fragrance; excellent disease resistance.

R. Darling Flame

Height 30 cm (12 in)

Vivid orange and yellow, double flowers; glossy green foliage. Slight fragrance and excellent disease resistance.

R. Magic Carrousel

Height 38 cm (15 in)

White, double flowers, deeply flushed pink at the edges; glossy green foliage. Slight fragrance but excellent disease resistance.

R. 'New Penny'

Height 23 cm (9 in)

Rich pink, double, rosette flowers; glossy green foliage. No fragrance but excellent disease resistance.

R. 'Rosina' (syn. R. 'Josephine Wheatcroft')

Height 38 cm (15 in)

Mid-yellow, double flowers; glossy green foliage. No fragrance but excellent disease resistance.

R. Snow Carpet

Height 15 cm (6 in)

White, semi-double blooms; deep glossy green foliage; a spreader that makes good ground cover. Slight fragrance but excellent disease resistance.

CLIMBERS

R. 'Aloha'

Height 2.5 m (8 ft)

Repeat flowering, rich rose-pink, double flowers. Slight fragrance but excellent disease resistance.

R. 'Bantry Bay'

Height 2.5 m (8 ft)

Repeat flowering, soft pink, semi-double flowers. Slight fragrance but excellent disease resistance.

R. 'Climbing Crimson Glory'

Height 3 m (10 ft)

Repeat flowering, deep red, double flowers. Very fragrant with slight disease resistance. Unfortunately, the flowers turn purple with age.

R. 'Climbing Iceberg'

Height 3 m (10 ft)

Repeat flowering, pure white, double flowers. No fragrance but moderate disease resistance.

R. 'Compassion'

Height 2.5 m (8 ft)

Repeat flowering, pink-flushed apricot flowers. Very fragrant with excellent disease resistance.

R. 'Danse du Feu'

Height 2.5 m (8 ft)

Repeat flowering, fiery scarlet, double flowers. No fragrance but excellent disease resistance.

R. 'Gloire de Dijon'

Height 4 m (12 ft)

Repeat flowering, large, buff to pale orange, old-fashioned, button-eyed, double blooms. Very fragrant with moderate disease resistance.

R. 'Golden Showers'

Height 2.5 m (8 ft)

Repeat flowering, bright yellow, double flowers; prolonged flowering season from June until the first frosts. Slight scent; excellent disease resistance.

R. Handel

Height 3 m (10 ft)

Repeat flowering, white, double flowers, boldly edged with deep pink. Slight fragrance but excellent disease resistance.

R. 'Madame Grégoire Staechelin'

Height 5 m (15 ft)

Early summer flowering, rich pink, double flowers with wavy-edged petals. Very fragrant with excellent disease resistance.

R. 'Mermaid'

Height 9 m (30) ft)

Repeat flowering, yellow, single flowers with amber stamens. Slight fragrance and excellent disease resistance.

R. 'Pink Perpétué'

Height 2.5 m (8 ft)

Repeat flowering, rose-pink, double flowers. Slight fragrance and moderate disease resistance.

R. 'Schoolgirl'

Height 3 m (10 ft)

Repeat flowering climber with apricot-orange, double flowers. Pleasant fragrance; excellent disease resistance.

R. 'Zéphirine Drouhin'

Height 3 m (10 ft)

Repeat flowering, thornless climber

with cerise-pink, semi-double flowers. A popular rose that is very fragrant with moderate disease resistance.

RAMBLERS

R. 'Albéric Barbier'

Height 5 m (15 ft)

Midsummer flowering, creamy yellow, double flowers with confused centres. Dark, glossy foliage. Pleasant scent and excellent disease resistance.

R. 'Albertine'

Height 5 m (15 ft)

Early summer flowering, pale pink, double flowers, tinged salmon. Dark

green foliage, reddish when young. Very fragrant; moderate disease resistance.

R. 'Félicité Perpétue'

Height 6 m (20 ft)

Midsummer flowering, creamy white, globular, double flowers. Slight fragrance and excellent disease resistance.

A profusion of pink roses provides a fragrant background to the mounds of magenta *Geranium* (cranesbill) and the pale green foliage of *Alchemilla* in this exuberant summer border.

R. filipes 'Kiftsgate'

Height 9 m (30 ft)

Midsummer flowering, masses of small, creamy white, single flowers. Slight fragrance but excellent disease resistance. The size of this lovely rose is legendary – plant it where it's got plenty of room to spread.

R. 'New Dawn'

Height 4 m (12 ft)

Repeat flowering, pale, blush-pink, double flowers. Pleasant fragrance and excellent disease resistance. This can be kept pruned as a shrub.

GROUND COVER

R. Blenheim

Height 1 m (3 ft)

Repeat flowering, palest blush, double flowers. Pleasant fragrance and excellent disease resistance.

R. Kent

Height 50 cm (20 in)

Repeat flowering, creamy white, double flowers. Slight fragrance but excellent disease resistance.

R. Pink Bells

Height 75 cm (30 in)

Midsummer flowering, clear pink, fully double. Slight fragrance but excellent disease resistance.

R. Red Meidiland

Height 75 cm (30 in)

Repeat flowering, deep red, white-eyed, single flowers. Slight fragrance but excellent disease resistance.

R. Suma

Height 60 cm (24 in)

Repeat flowering, deep pink, fully double flowers. Slight fragrance but excellent disease resistance.

CHAPTER 9 Border plants

Whether planted in an island bed, a mixed border, or in a formal herbaceous border, hardy perennials delight us by springing to life each year after their dormant period

Shrubs might be the backbone of the garden, but border plants flesh out the skeleton. Those that are covered in this chapter are the plants that the gardener calls hardy perennials.

WHAT ARE HARDY PERENNIALS?

'Hardy' means that the plants can stay outdoors all year round, usually putting up with the worst of the British weather; 'perennial' means that they will last indefinitely. True there are a few perennials that are short-lived, lasting maybe two or three years, but most of them will outlive you if you treat them well.

Hardy *herbaceous* perennials form the bulk of the A–Z section, and these are the tough, long-lived plants that die down to soil level each autumn, keeping alive through the winter by means of roots and resting buds at soil level. They may not have the year-round appeal of shrubs, but this gives them a different advantage: they provide seasonal change in the garden so that it's fresh whatever the time of year.

USING BORDER PLANTS

Flower beds and borders

The obvious place for your border plants is in a flower bed or border. The traditional herbaceous border has bitten the dust in all but the most stately of gardens, and it's been replaced by the mixed border, where shrubs, bulbs, bedding and border plants keep each other company in a longer lasting display; the old herbaceous border started its season of glory in late May or June and was spent by September.

There's an awful lot of fuss made about island beds nowadays. These are simply flower beds of regular or informal shape, around which you can walk. Planted up wisely, they show off border plants to perfection. The trouble is that there's seldom room for island beds in very small gardens, unless you want to turn your plot into something resembling a roundabout.

Where space is short, sweeping borders made as wide as possible are the best bet. You'll get plenty of plants into them and they'll be easy to work.

Planning ahead

Think carefully before you plant. Consider the characteristics of the plant and compare them with the characteristics of its neighbours. Bear in mind season of flowering, ultimate height and spread, and foliage, as well as flower colour.

It's a good idea to plant shrubs first and to fill in among them with border plants. The latter are easy to dig up and move when the space they occupy is needed by some expanding shrub. Not only will they tolerate disturbance, but they'll thrive on it. The tattiest border plants are those that are left alone, apart from agapanthus, peonies and one or two others that like to stay in one place for years.

Plan for a long display of colour, or for a burst of glory during one season. That revered gardener of the Victorian and Edwardian era, Gertrude Jekyll, had borders for every month of the year. Most small gardens would have a job to fit in all twelve, but it's no bad idea to set aside a patch outside a window that can act as a winter border; or another corner that billows with flowers in June. If you can't or won't do this, make sure that as one plant fades from its season of glory, there is another one nearby to take over and delight the eye. Remember that vivid colour isn't everything: one bright, bold bloomer set in front of some handsome or muted foliage shows up far better than half-a-dozen assorted flowers vying for attention.

Single-colour themes

The popularity of Sissinghurst Castle in Kent, and its 'white garden' in particular, has encouraged more gardeners to plant borders with a single-colour theme. Yellow, red, blue, grey or white schemes are great fun to create, but do make sure that other parts of the garden act as an antidote to these monochrome amusements, otherwise they'll eventually bore the pants off you.

Using height in the border

A traditional border relies on a carefully graded series of heights, moving from the shortest at the front to the tallest at the back. As many of the plants used are herbaceous, the full effect will not be seen until early or mid-summer. Bedding plants are included here, too.

In this island bed, low-growing perennials are blended with the occasional taller perennial or grass for impact, and bedding plants for variety.

Ground-cover planting

Some border plants are stately enough to be planted as individual specimens; others spread into a dense rug or canopy that will smother the weeds and ground once they are well established. Such ground-cover planting is useful, but it needs efficient maintenance in the early stages. For a start, the ground must be free of perennial weeds before planting. Watering will have to be attended to, and emerging weeds must be removed until the plants are large enough to do the smothering. Remember, too, that herbaceous ground-cover plants will disappear in winter.

Gravel beds

Gravel and cobble beds are great fun, very labour saving and will show off foliage plants to great effect.

All you need to do is cultivate the ground, plant your chosen specimens or arrangements, pat the soil level with the back of a fork, then lay 5 cm (2 in) of washed pea shingle or a layer of large pebbles or cobbles on top; this will keep down weeds and will always look smart. When you want to change or add to the planting, scrape away the gravel or lift off the cobbles, do your planting and then replace the stony mulch.

CHOOSING THE RIGHT SPOT

You probably won't have much choice when it comes to selecting a site for your bed or border. It is always recommended that hardy perennials are given a spot in full sun and a well-drained soil but, as the lists in the A–Z section show, there are plants for shade as well as sun, and some for heavy clay or chalk.

If you can't pick the ideal site, at least pick the plants that are ideal for your particular situation. Versatile as they are, few plants will thrive in really heavy shade cast by trees whose roots riddle the ground, or in very windy places. Only a handful will enjoy growing in really boggy soil. Do your best to improve the earth, whatever its composition.

PREPARING THE GROUND

Just because a plant is said to tolerate dry soil, it doesn't mean that if, on one baking summer day, you dig a hole in the dust and plant it, it will survive. Every plant needs a chance to establish itself before it can settle down and cope with inhospitable conditions.

Soil improvers

Whether you garden on clay, chalk, sand or dust, cultivate the soil well, and work in as much well-rotted garden compost, manure, spent hops, mushroom compost, pulverized bark or leaf mould as you can afford: a bucketful to each square metre (yard) of ground will do nicely. The last two contain few nutrients, so a dusting of general fertilizer can be scattered over them before they are dug in.

When to dig

Digging or forking is essential: it will enable you to remove thick-rooted weeds as well as letting in air and incorporating the organic enrichment. Living soil full of muck, bacteria and worms produces better plants than sterile, tired earth. Soil can be dug at any time of year, but heavy clay will be easier to work in late summer or early autumn when it's gently moist rather

than sodden or baked hard. Leave it through the winter and the frost will have broken it down into a crumbly soil by spring. Sandy soil can be dug in spring: it needs no frost to shatter it and it will only be compacted by winter rains and snow if dug earlier.

The no-dig technique

You might have heard of the 'no-dig' technique: it sounds appealing. If you decide to make a border without digging or forking the soil you'll first have to kill off the weeds by laying down an impermeable barrier of heavy duty black polythene for a season or more. Then an 8 cm (3 in) thick mulch of organic matter will have to be laid on the soil and the border plants planted through this into pockets of enriched earth below. It involves a lot of organic matter and I feel rather sorry for any plant that has to push its roots down into poor, compacted earth before it can think of enjoying life. It's digging for me.

PLANNING BEDS AND BORDERS

I've never been one for planning gardens in great detail on bits of graph paper, but it does help to sketch out some idea of the scheme when you're planting up a bed or border; then you can juggle the plants around in the cosy comfort of your fireside until you have the effect you want.

Planting in drifts

I've already mentioned the things you should bear in mind when deciding what plant goes where – height, spread, colour, shape, season of flowering – but remember, too, that the most impact is created by large patches of one particular plant. To this end, stately herbaceous borders possess drifts of three, five, or seven plants (odd numbers always seem to be the order of the day) of one particular species. In tiny gardens, or where the collecting bug has bitten, single

This luxuriant herbaceous border illustrates the effectiveness of planting in bold drifts of colours. In traditional style, the border graduates from smaller plants at the front to the tallest at the back.

plants can be used, but the effect will be more like a patchwork quilt. In cottage gardens there's nothing wrong with that.

In general, tall plants should be set at the back of the border, or the centre of a bed, and shorter ones at the front, but bring a few of the giants forward a little to vary the contours and to create hidden pockets. Even a border should hold a few surprises.

If you really can't be bothered to plan the scheme you can go to the garden centre and buy what's pretty. Bring the plants home and juggle with them on the soil around your existing border plants, but you'll still have to consider their height, spread and flowering season if you want good results.

Creating pleasing shapes

A final word on planning: consider carefully the design of the bed or border. It should be as large as your plot will allow, and arranged so that its shape can be appreciated. Curves should be gradual, to make them easy on the eye and on the mower. Lay a hosepipe on the ground to mark out the shape (soften it by running hot water through it first if necessary). Take out a strip of turf or a little V-shaped drill to mark the line, then start digging.

Where to buy the plants?

The garden centre might offer plants in flower, but seldom will it give you the choice that a specialist nursery offers. The larger, specialist firms do a healthy mail-order trade, and can be relied on to supply good, healthy plants. They will even replace plants that appear to be dead or damaged on arrival if they are informed immediately. Plan your border and buy the bulk of your plants from a specialist – the garden centre can be used for in-fillers. If you don't like that idea, then go along to the garden centre for a look round before planning your border to include only the stock they offer.

> "Bring a few of the giants forward a little to vary the contours and to create hidden pockets. Even a border should hold a few surprises."

PLANTING BORDER PLANTS

Container-grown plants

Almost all border plants sold in garden centres will be container grown; this means that they have been growing for some time in the pot in which they are sold. The advantage with this system is that the plants can be planted in your garden at any time of year provided the soil is not frozen, muddy or bone-dry.

Lifted plants

Plants bought from a specialist nursery by mail order, and plants obtained from friends, are usually lifted from the ground in October or November. If your soil is well drained or on the light side, this is by far the best planting season, for the plants will have time to sink their roots into the soil and become well established before growing away vigorously next spring. If your soil is heavy, avoid autumn planting. It's better to wait and get the plants in during spring when drainage is improving, rather than have them sit in a cold quagmire through their first winter.

How to plant

The planting method for both lifted and container-grown plants is the same. Scatter a handful of blood, bone and fishmeal over each square metre (yard) of soil and hoe it in. Make sure the plant's root system, or the compost in the container, is moist, and dig a hole with a trowel that will take all the roots, allowing an 8 cm (3 in) gap all round. Remove the pot if the plant is container grown and sit the rootball in the hole. Any large and obviously ingrowing roots can be gently teased out, but the rest should be left undisturbed. Spread out all the roots of plants that have been lifted from open ground. Replace and firm back the soil with your feet so that the old soil mark on the stem or crown of the plant is level with the new surface.

Water the plant in thoroughly if necessary, and don't let the soil around it dry out during the first spring and summer. Plant at a spacing that will allow the plant to grow to its full spread before meeting its neighbour, or plant a little closer and thin out later if you want to achieve the full effect more quickly; it will cost you money, though.

LOOKING AFTER YOUR PLANTS

Watering and feeding

Don't neglect your plants once you've bunged them in. Remove any weeds that might compete and water thoroughly with a lawn sprinkler in dry weather (unless the plants are tall or leafy and will be weighed down by water droplets: in this case support a hose, fitted with a sprinkler head, on the handle of a garden fork and let it play on the surrounding soil).

A sprinkling of blood, bone and fishmeal can be scattered on the soil around the plants in April and again in June if you're feeling generous and can get in to do the job. Hoe it into the surface.

Deadheading

Removing faded flowerheads from border plants can be a bore, but it will often encourage a second flush of bloom later in the season – it saves the plants the job

Supporting tall plants

Tall plants such as delphiniums will need individual cane supports for their stems: push a bamboo in by each spike as soon as it is 90 cm (3 ft) tall and gently tie the stem to it as it extends. Bushier plants can be held up either by proprietary wire plant supports such as Link stakes, or by pushing among them twiggy branches pruned from trees and shrubs in winter.

There's an excellent method of supporting border plants to be seen at Crathes Castle in Scotland; stout 2.5 cm (1 in) square dahlia stakes run around the border and black nylon netting with a 10 cm (4 in) wide mesh is stretched between the posts right across the border at a height of about 45 cm (18 in). When the foliage grows through the netting, the strands disappear but the plants are well supported.

Whatever kind of staking you use, make sure it's in position before the plants need it. You'll never get them to stand up properly once they've fainted. I've indicated in the A–Z section which plants need to be supported.

Knock in tall bamboo canes by individual delphinium spikes while they are quite small.

As the flower spike extends, tie it gently to the cane

A nifty support system used at Crathes Castle in Scotland. Wooden stakes support wide-mesh black nylon netting through which the plants grow.

of producing unwanted seeds. If the seedheads are needed for decoration or propagation, leave them be.

The benefits of mulching

If you can afford the time and money, then do lay a mulch of compost or pulverized bark over the soil in March each year, or even every other year if funds are short. It really does keep the soil in good condition (as well as suppressing weeds and holding in moisture) and the plants will enjoy the benefits, especially on sandy soils. After four years of trying to cope with a dry sandy soil, I resorted to spring mulching with bark while the soil was moist. That summer the plants grew as they had never grown before.

Renovating old plants

Apart from those plants that are indicated as being best left undisturbed, all border plants can be kept in good condition by regular division of the clumps. With age, the central portion usually dies out, and every three or four years such clumps should be lifted and divided into pieces as big as your fist before being replanted in freshly enriched soil. The dead central portions of each clump should be thrown away. Overgrown borders, inherited when you move house, can be completely renovated in this way in autumn or spring.

Dig up old clumps of border plants. Chop them into smaller lumps with a spade; discard the dead central portion and replant the youngsters.

Winter care

In winter, when the top growth of herbaceous perennials dies down, go over the border and chop off the stems at ground level. Leave 5 cm (2 in) high stumps and you'll stab your fingers when you come to do the job next year. One or two tender plants can be left with a little stem or foliage in place to give them a bit of frost protection, but most need no such coddling. When the stems have been chopped off, a light forking over will tidy the soil for winter.

A-Z of **border plants**

HERE I'VE INCLUDED NOT ONLY the floriferous border plants, but also a few ferns, bamboos and grasses, which provide a welcome change or a backdrop for the more blatant bloomers. Always consider foliage as well as flowers: choose a variety of foliage forms to provide interest while the plants aren't in flower. I've indicated how each plant can be increased: methods are given in the order of popularity with which they are used on each plant (see Chapter 2 Propagation for details on the techniques). I have also indicated which plants need staking for support. The measurements given throughout indicate the plant's ultimate height and spread.

Acanthus
Bear's Breeches
1.5 m x 90 cm (5 x 3 ft)

A. mollis has bold, arching, glossy green leaves that are deeply lobed. Those of *A. spinosus* are more finely cut. Prickly flower spikes of white and rosy purple appear in late summer.
Likes ordinary, well-drained soil and full sun. Tolerates gentle shade; dry, chalky and clay soils.
Propagate by division, root cuttings, seed.

Achillea
Yarrow
60 cm-1.5 m x 45 cm (2-5 ft x 18 in)

These are usually statuesque plants with flat heads of yellow flowers carried on feathery-leaved stems in summer. *A.* 'Coronation Gold' is mid-yellow: 90 cm (3 ft) tall; *A.* 'Moonshine' is sulphur-yellow: 60 cm (2 ft) tall. Both have greyish leaves. *A. filipendula* 'Gold Plate' is rich yellow and 1.5 m (5 ft) tall, and *A. ptarmica* 'The Pearl' has tiny double white rosette flowers on 60 cm (2 ft) stems.
Likes well-drained soil and full sun. Tolerates dry, chalky and clay soils; coastal gardens.
Staking required.
Propagate by division.

Aconitum
Monkshood, Wolfsbane
1.2-2.1 m x 60 cm (4-7 x 2 ft)

Towering plants with spires of hooded flowers – blue, pink, yellow or white in late summer. *A. napellus* is the common blue monkshood. The entire plant is very poisonous, as are all aconitums: avoid it where children are at large.
Likes moisture-retentive soil and full sun. Tolerates chalk, clay and shady spots.
Propagate by division, seed.

Agapanthus
Blue African Lily
60 x 60 cm (2 x 2 ft)

The 'Headbourne hybrids' are among the best and hardiest, producing rounded white or blue heads of 'lily' flowers on stiff stalks amid glossy strap-shaped leaves in midsummer.
Likes well-drained soil and a sunny, sheltered spot. Tolerates dry or chalky soil; coastal exposure.
Propagate by division, seed.

Ajuga
Bugle
15 x 90 cm (6 in x 3 ft)

Varieties of *A. reptans* are colourful carpeters making dense ground cover. Blue flower spires are carried in spring over leaves that are deep purple in the variety 'Purpurea', cerise, cream and pale green in 'Burgundy Glow', cream and green in 'Variegata', and purple with orange marbling in 'Multicolor'.
Likes moisture-retentive soil and gentle shade. Tolerates clay, chalk, heavy shade, sun (but not dry soil).
Propagate by division.

Alcea
Hollyhock
2.4 m x 90 cm (8 x 3 ft) plus

Tall spires of red, pink, yellow or white mallow flowers open in summer over clumps of lobed leaves. *A. rosea* has single and double varieties. Best renewed from seed every couple of years to keep rust disease at bay (those orange spots under the leaves).
Likes a sunny spot in well-drained soil. Tolerates clay soil.
Staking required.
Propagate by seed, divsion.

Alchemilla
Lady's Mantle
45 x 60 cm (18 in x 2 ft)

Scalloped green leaves covered in silky hairs hold water droplets like mercury. Fluffy lime-green flowerheads appear in summer. *A. mollis* is the commonest species and the loveliest. It seeds itself freely unless faded flowerheads are snipped off.
Likes gentle shade and a moisture-retentive soil. Tolerates sun, dry soil, chalk and clay.
Propagate by division, seed.

Alstroemeria
Peruvian Lily
60 cm-1.2 m x 45 cm (2-4 ft x 18 in)

Spectacular lily flowers are carried in large clusters atop narrow-leafed stems. The blooms are orange, marked

Lavender-coloured *Agapanthus*, orange-red *Alstroemeria* and deep pink *Phlox* provide the colour in this leafy border in Butterstream, Eire.

with brown lines in *A. aurea*, or salmon and pink in the beefier, more expensive, *A. ligtu* hybrids, which are trickier to grow. Plant them young and don't disturb. They flower in summer.
Likes a warm and sunny spot in well-drained soil. Tolerates a fraction of shade; dry or chalky soil; coastal exposure.
Staking required.
Propagate by division, seed.

Anaphalis
Pearl Everlasting
30 x 45 cm (12 x 18 in)

Neat stems clad in long, grey-haired leaves are topped with clusters of white, bead-like everlasting flowers in summer. The best species is *A. triplinervis*. Essential in any white garden or grey-foliage scheme.
Likes full sun and a soil not likely to dry out. Tolerates clay and chalky soils; gentle shade.
Propagate by division.

Anchusa
90 x 60 cm (3 x 2 ft)

True gentian-blue flowers are carried over hairy leaves in early summer. *A. azurea* (syn. *A. italica*) offers excellent value in the varieties 'Loddon Royalist' and 'Little John' – the latter grows to just 45 cm (18 in).
Likes well-drained soil and full sun. Tolerates clay and chalky soil.
Staking required.
Propagate by division, root cuttings.

Anemone
Windflower
1.5 m x 90 cm (5 x 3 ft)

Varieties of *A. x hybrida* are valued for their late summer and early autumn display of wide-faced flowers on tall branching stalks. 'Honorine Jobert' is white and 'Königin Charlotte' (syn. 'Queen Charlotte') is pink. There are others. All are good value when most plants are past it.

Likes a well-drained but moisture-retentive soil in full sun. Tolerates clay and chalky soil; some shade and coastal exposure.
Propagate by division, root cuttings.

Aquilegia
Columbine
75 x 45 cm (2½ ft x 18 in)

Bright border plants for early summer when their branched heads of bonnet-shaped flowers open above finely cut grey-green leaves. The blooms may be white, blue, pink, yellow and red. There are many hybrids. Most last only a few years but set plenty of seed and can be divided.
Likes ordinary well-drained soil in a sunny spot. Tolerates clay and chalky soils and gentle shade.
Propagate by seed, division.

Artemisia
Lad's Love
60 x 90 cm (2 x 3 ft)

The true lad's love, southernwood, or old man, is *A. abrotanum*. It makes a fruity-aromatic, feathery thicket of grey-green leaves. There are many other species, of which one of the best is *A. absinthium* 'Lambrook Silver' with exceptionally finely cut silver foliage. Grow any you can lay your trowel on. All are valued for their foliage.
Likes warm and sunny spots in well-drained soil. Tolerates dry and chalky soil; coastal exposure.
Propagate by stem cuttings, division.

Arum
Cuckoo Pint; Lords and Ladies
30 x 30 cm (12 x 12 in)

Our native cuckoo pint, *A. maculatum*, pops up all over my chalky garden, but *A. italicum* 'Marmoratum' is a better choice for most plots. The arrowhead leaves are veined with cream and, as in the native species, fat clubs of orange berries follow the spring arum flowers in late summer and autumn.

Likes a shady spot in moisture-retentive soil. Tolerates chalk, clay and full sun (but not drought).
Propagate by division.

Aruncus
Goat's Beard
2.1 x 1.2 m (7 x 4 ft)

Like a massive astilbe, *A. dioicus* (syn. *A. sylvestris*) has ferny dark green leaves, over which tower feathery plumes of creamy white flowers in summer. Give it room to show off.
Likes dappled shade and a moisture-retentive soil. Tolerates sun, quite heavy shade; clay soil.
Propagate by division, seed.

Asplenium
Hart's Tongue Fern
30 x 45 cm (12 x 18 in)

The crested forms of *A. scolopendrium* with their wavy-edged strops of lime-green leaves are grand front-of-the-border foliage plants. Protect them from spring frosts, which may burn the newly emerging leaves. Chop off old leaves in March.
Likes moisture-retentive soil. Tolerates sun or shade; clay, chalk and some dry soils.
Propagate by division.

Aster
Michaelmas Daisy
30 cm–1.5 m x 60 cm (1–5 x 2 ft)

Unsurpassable for late summer and autumn colour, most asters are super garden plants. The neat *A. amellus* is the shortest at 30 cm (12 in), and has varieties with purple, crimson, pink, violet and white flowers, as have most of the other species. There are dozens of different Michaelmas daisies in assorted shades and sizes, but *A. x frikartii* 'Mönch' is one to cherish. It has lavender-blue flowers from summer to autumn and lasts longer than any other aster I know.
Likes full sun and good soil. Tolerates

clay and chalky soils.
Staking required.
Propagate by division every 3 years.

Astilbe
False Goat's Beard
60 cm-1.2 m x 60-90 cm (2-4 x 2-3 ft)

All the varieties of *A.* x *arendsii* have ferny leaves and feathery plumes of white, pink, mauve or crimson flowers in summer. 'Fanal' is a popular one in dark crimson, while 'Irrlicht' is white with dark green foliage. 'Sprite' is a charming pink-flowered variety at just 23 cm (9 in). All are good by streams. The young foliage is often bronzed.
Likes moisture-retentive soil and sun. Tolerates shade; some chalky soils and clay soil.
Propagate by division.

Astrantia
Hattie's Pincushion, Masterwort
60 x 60 cm (2 x 2 ft)

Sterling plants with domes of fingered leaves from which spurt stems of starry flowers from early to mid-summer. *A. major* is the best white; *A. major* 'Rubra' has rich crimson flowers, and 'Sunningdale Variegated' has leaves that are splashed cream early in the season. *A. maxima* has pink flowers but a weaker constitution.
Likes moisture-retentive soil in sun or light shade. Tolerates quite heavy

shade; chalky, clay and some dry soils (where plenty of organic matter has been worked in).
Propagate by division, seed.

Ballota
60 x 60 cm (2 x 2 ft)

A straggly but endearing shrublet, *B. pseudodictamnus* has rounded leaves about 2.5 cm (1 in) across. Both they and the stems are thickly covered in white wool. The tiny mauve flowers are carried in compact clusters below the leaves but are hardly visible.
Likes sun and a well-drained soil. Tolerates dry or chalky soil.
Propagate by root cuttings.

Bergenia
Elephant's Ears, Megasea
30 x 60 cm (12 in x 2 ft)

Glossy leaves like table-tennis bats – and in some species just as big – and pink flower clusters on fat stalks in spring make this a cherished ground-cover plant. The most popular species is *B. cordifolia*, and its variety 'Purpurea' is one of the best bergenias for autumn colour, turning reddish purple. Evergreen.
likes sun and well-drained soil. A superb path-edger. Tolerates shade; clay, chalky or dry soil; coastal exposure.
Propagate by division.

Blechnum
15 x 90 cm plus (6 in x 3 ft)

The tiny evergreen fern *B. penna-marina* is neat ground cover at the front of a shady border where its upright fronds make a thick, dark rug.
Likes gentle shade and a peaty, leafy, acid soil. Tolerates full sun if kept moist at the roots.
Propagate by division.

Brunnera
45 x 60 cm (18 in x 2 ft)

A forget-me-not-flowered woodlander with heart-shaped green leaves. *B. macrophylla* blooms in spring and is available in three variegated varieties; 'Dawson's White', roughly bordered with creamy white; 'Hadspen Cream', with deeper cream variegation; 'Aluminium Spot' (syn. 'Langtrees') whose margins are spotted with silvery grey blobs. The last two are the best.
Likes a shady spot in organic, moisture-retentive soil. Tolerates dry soils (in the case of the true species and the variety 'Aluminium Spot').
Propagate by division, seed.

Calamintha
Calamint
30 x 30 cm (12 x 12 in)

Underrated edgers with aromatic leaves and small, hooded flowers carried in summer and autumn. *C. nepeta* has pale blue flowers; *C. grandiflora* has pink flowers. Good ground coverers.
Likes sunny spots in well-drained soil. Tolerates dry or chalky soil and shade.
Propagate by division, seed.

Campanula
Bellflower
Various sizes

I'd grow any campanula that came my way, but space allows me to mention just three. *C. persicifolia*, 90 x 30 cm (3 ft x 12 in), From evergreen clumps it

Border plants suitable for all soils

The following plants will do well in clay, chalky and dry soil. Those marked ◆ will also tolerate coastal exposure.

- Acanthus
- Achillea ◆
- Alchemilla
- Asplenium
- Astrantia
- Bergenia ◆
- Centaurea ◆
- Crocosmia ◆
- Cyanara
- Digitalis
- Dryopteris
- Echinops ◆
- Erigeron ◆
- Eryngium ◆
- Galega
- Geranium ◆
- Iris ◆
- Kniphofia ◆
- Lamium
- Lychnis ◆
- Paeonia
- Phlox
- Physalis
- Sedum ◆
- Solidago
- Verbascum
- Veronica

produces tall stalks of pale blue or white bells. *C. latiloba* 'Alba' is a queen among campanulas for shade, producing deep-toothed white bells up its 1.2 m (4 ft) stems in clumps 60 cm (2 ft) wide. *C. glomerata*, 45 x 60 cm (18 in x 2 ft), has densely packed heads of violet-blue, upturned bells. All these species bloom in early to mid-summer.
Likes sun and any well-drained but moisture-retentive soil. Tolerates dry soils (*C. persicifolia*), chalky soils (all), and shade (*C. latiloba*).
staking required.
Propagate by division, seed.

Carex
Sedge
30 x 30 cm (12 x 12 in)

Fountains of bright yellow leaves spurt up from the soil where *C. morrowii* 'Variegata' is planted. It's an ever-yellow plant to cheer you year round.
Likes moist soil and full sun. Tolerates clay, chalky soil (provided it's not dry) and a little shade.
Propagate by division.

Catananche
Cupid's Dart
60 x 45 cm (2 ft x 18 in)

Pale blue dandelion flowers on wiry stems are produced by *C. caerulea* in summer from a clump of narrow leaves. Plant it between beefier foliage plants. It can be short-lived.
Likes sun and a well-drained soil. Tolerates dry or chalky soil; coastal exposure.
Staking required.
Propagate by seed, root cuttings.

Centaurea
Cornflower, Knapweed
45–90 cm x 90 cm (18 in–3 ft x 3 ft)

Most gardens boast the spring- and summer-flowering *C. montana* with its spiky blue cornflowers and narrow grey-green leaves. More should give a home to the impressive *C.macrocephala*,

90 x 90 cm (3 x 3 ft), which has large leaves and hefty yellow thistle heads.
Likes sun and well-drained soil. Tolerates dry, chalky or clay soil; coastal exposure.
Staking required.
Propagate by division, seed.

Centranthus
Valerian
90 x 60 cm (3 x 2 ft)

The red valerian, *C. ruber*, is a summer beauty beloved of butterflies and gardeners. It makes an upright plant with deep pink flowerheads and there is also a white variety. Both will grow well in crevices in paving and walling.
Likes sun and a well-drained soil. Tolerates dry or chalky soils and coastal exposure.
Propagate by stem cuttings, seed.

Ceratostigma
Hardy Plumbago
90 x 90 cm (3 x 3 ft)

A rounded bush clad in coarse leaves and topped with bright blue flowers in late summer and autumn. *C. willmottianum* is not totally hardy and may be killed to ground level in winter.
Likes warm, sunny spots in well-drained soil. Tolerates chalky soil.
Propagate by stem cuttings, seed.

Cimicifuga
Bugbane
1.5 m x 90 cm (5 x 3 ft)

Tricky plants with ferny foliage and arching sprays of white flowers in late summer and early autumn. *C. racemosa* flowers earliest of all.
Likes shade and a rich, moist soil. Tolerates organically enriched chalk and clay soils.
Propagate by division, seed.

Convallaria
Lily-of-the-valley
23 x 90 cm (9 in x 3 ft) plus

A spreader with upright, pointed, oval

leaves and arching flower stalks that carry tiny white bells in spring. Headily scented. *C. majalis* is the true species, and it has several varieties including the pink-flowered var. *rosea* and the larger-flowered 'Fortin's Giant'. All spread greedily.
Likes dappled shade and well-drained soil. Tolerates full sun or heavy shade; dry or chalky soil.
Propagate by division.

Coreopsis
Tickseed
60 x 60 cm (2 x 2 ft)

The finely cut bright green foliage of *C. verticillata* sits like tangled wire netting below the orange-yellow daisy flowers that open from midsummer to early autumn. It's a showy but graceful plant for the front of a border.
Likes full sun and well-drained soil. Tolerates clay or chalky soil.
Propagate by division.

Cortaderia
Pampas Grass
2.4 x 2.4 m (8 x 8 ft)

Varieties of *C. selloana* are the most popular, producing plumes of creamy white flowers in early autumn once the plant is a few years old and well suited. Chop off dead foliage in spring.
Likes a sunny spot in light, well-drained soil. Tolerates some clay or chalky soils.
Propagate by division.

Corydalis
Fumitory
23 x 45 cm (9 x 18 in)

The finely cut green leaves of *C. lutea* make a fine foil for the spires of yellow flowers that bloom from spring to autumn. Good planted between paving stones.
Likes dappled shade and well-drained soil. Tolerates full sun; dry soil and chalk.
Propagate by seed.

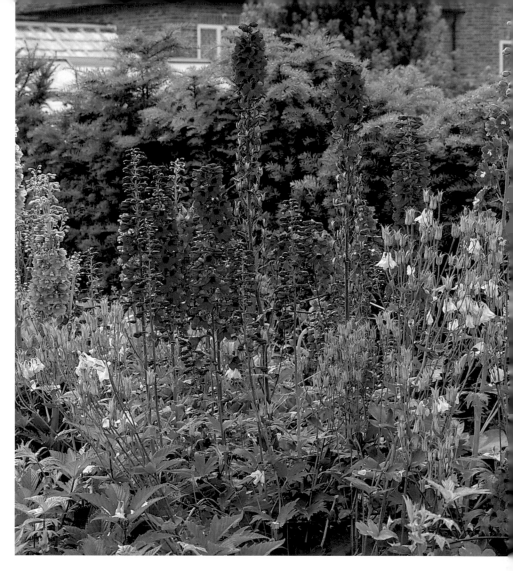

Crambe

1.8 x 1.2 m (6 x 4 ft)

The massive *C. cordifolia* produces hefty dark green leaves over which splay the billowing flower stems in early summer. The blooms are tiny and white, combining to form a dense cloud. For big borders only.

Likes a sunny patch of well-drained soil. Tolerates chalky and dry soils; coastal exposure (though strong winds may buckle its stems).

Propagate by division, root cuttings.

Crocosmia
Montbretia

60 cm-1.2 m x 60 cm (2-4 ft x 2 ft)

A popular late summer flower with grassy green leaves carried in dense, upright tufts. The flaring blooms are held on arching stems. Many varieites are shades of orange as in the common *C. x crocosmiiflora*, but yellows ('Golden Fleece' and 'Solfatare') and reds ('Lucifer' and 'Emberglow') are available. 'Lucifer' is a showy hybrid which starts to flower in June and carries on until late summer. It is tall at around 1.2 m (4 ft). Also worth mentioning is *C. paniculata* (Aunt Eliza); 1.2 m (4ft). Rather like a giant Montbretia this used to be called *Antholyza paniculata*, which explains its common name. The orange-red blooms appear in late summer. The leaves are broader and taller than those of most *Crocosmia* with marked pleating.

Likes sun and a well-drained soil. Tolerates dappled shade; dry, chalky and clay soils; coastal exposure.

Propagate by division.

Cynara
Cardoon

1.8 m x 90 cm (6 x 3 ft)

Stunning, arching leaves of grey are boldly cut, making *C. cardunculus* an exceptionally attractive foliage plant. Artichoke flowerheads appear on tall stems in summer. Cheap to grow from seed.

Likes sun and well-drained soil in a sheltered spot. Tolerates dry or chalky soil.

Propagate by seed, division, root cuttings.

Delphinium
Larkspur

1.8 m x 90 cm (6 x 3 ft)

The hybrids of *D. elatum* have become firm towering features in many gardens and always seem to be bracketed with lupins, although they are really quite different. The flower spikes rise from clumps of serrated leaves in summer, and have dozens of blooms ranging in colour from rich blue through paler shades to pinks, mauves and primrose-yellow as well as

Towering spikes of pale mauve and purple *Delphinium* and magenta *Alcea* (hollyhock) are punctuated with the pastel pink of *Aquilegia*.

white. The red delphinium, no doubt, will be with us shortly.

Likes sun and a rich, well-drained soil. Tolerates chalky and clay soils.

Staking required.

Propagate by division, seed.

Dianthus
Carnation, Pink

15-30 x 30-60 cm (6-12 in x 1-2 ft)

There are many named varieties of pink and border carnations and all make superb edgers for beds, borders and paths. Their spiky foliage is usually neat and grey, they bloom freely in summer, and they possess the

most exquisite scents. Varieties are available with crimson, pink, mauve, pale yellow and white flowers, single or double. Some are bicoloured.
Likes sun and well-drained chalky soil. Tolerates other well-drained soils if lime is added; coastal exposure.
Propagate by stem cuttings, seed.

Dicentra
Bleeding Heart, Lady in the Bath
45 x 60 cm (18 in x 2 ft)

The true bleeding heart is *D. spectabilis*, which has finely cut green leaves and arching stems of pink and white locket flowers in late spring. *D. formosa* is a smaller version with leaves like carrot foliage and more slender flowers. Among the best hybrids are 'Stuart Boothman', with filigree grey leaves and pink flowers in spring and summer, and 'Langtrees', grey leaved with white flowers tinged pink. 'Bacchanal' has dusky crimson flowers. The smaller versions grow to around 23 x 45 cm (9 x 18 in).
Likes gentle shade and moisture-retentive soil. Tolerates sun and chalky soil (provided the roots do not dry out) and clay.
Propagate by division in autumn or spring; be careful not to break the brittle roots.

Dictamnus
Dittany
75 x 60 cm (2½ x 2 ft)

Both *D. albus*, with white flowers, and its variety *purpureus*, with rich pink flowers, are superb border plants. The leaves are fingered and the flowers rather starry in appearance. They open in early summer and later form seed pods which give off a volatile oil. Hold a lighted match underneath them and, hopefully, you'll see a minute explosion! The plant is citrus scented.
Likes full sun and a well-drained soil. Tolerates dry and chalky soils.
Propagate by division, root cuttings, seed.

Dierama
Fairy Wand Flower, Angel's Fishing Rod
1.2 m x 90 cm (4 x 3 ft)

From a clump of grassy evergreen leaves the flower stems of *D. pulcherrimum* erupt in summer, carrying rich pink bell flowers on arching fusewire-thin stalks. Very graceful and always a conversation piece. The smaller *D. dracomontanum*, 30 x 30 cm (12 x 12 in), is similar but even more graceful and a good front-of-the-border plant. Plant in spring.
Likes full sun and a well-drained but moisture-retentive soil. Tolerates dry soil and chalk; coastal exposure. Be patient – it may die down after planting but will re-emerge.
Propagate by division, seed.

Digitalis
Foxglove
60 x 30 cm (2 ft x 12 in)

A pale yellow foxglove of modest height, *D. grandiflora* is a reliable perennial where most other foxgloves are biennial (p.150). The flower spikes shoot from downy, evergreen leaf rosettes in summer.
Likes organically enriched soil in dappled shade. Tolerates sun, quite heavy shade; dry, chalky or clay soil.
Propagate by seed, division.

Doronicum
Leopard's Bane
45 x 45 cm (18 x 18 in)

These bright yellow spring daisies are always welcome heralds of a new season and 'Miss Mason' is one of the best. Doubles like 'Frühlingspracht' (syn. 'Spring Beauty') are dazzling but look too much like a summer pot marigold. The rounded leaves are a good, fresh green.
Likes sun and well-drained soil. Tolerates gentle shade; clay and chalky soil.
Propagate by division.

Dryopteris
Male Fern
90 x 90 cm (3 x 3 ft)

The arching green fronds of *D. filix-mas* add an ethereal look to any border. Plant this fern where you can enjoy its form and where its mid-green fronds

can set off other plants. *D. affine* (Golden male fern) is similar with striking golden-brown midribs. Both also have varieties with twisted fronds for those who like something showy.
Likes shade and well-drained soil. Tolerates sun; dry, clay and chalky soils.
Propagate by division.

Echinacea
Purple Coneflower
1.2 m x 60 cm (4 x 2 ft)

Rich pink daisies are not plentiful in the garden but *E. purpurea* makes up for the deficiency by producing a good show over its green foliage in summer.

'Robert Bloom' is an exceptionally good variety of a dusky rose colour; it is long-flowering too.
Likes sun and a rich, well-drained soil. Tolerates chalk and well-worked clay.
Staking required.
Propagate by division, root cuttings.

Echinops
Globe Thistle
1.2 m x 60 cm (4 x 2 ft)

A real whopper of a border plant with finely cut dark green leaves (grey underneath) and spherical flowerheads of steely blue in late summer. *E. ritro* is the most popular species, but *E. bannaticus* 'Taplow Blue' is taking over from it and is even more vigorous at around 1.5 or 2 m (5 or 6 ft).
Likes full sun and a good, well-drained soil. Tolerates dry, chalk and clay soils; coastal exposure.
Staking required.
Propagate by dividing clumps in autumn or spring, or by root cuttings.

Epilobium
Rose Bay Willowherb
1.2 m x 30 cm (4 ft x 12 in)

When the Emperor of Japan came to Kew Gardens in 1971 he was offered any plant he wanted – and took away a packet of rose bay willowherb seeds. You might not want to plant this invasive, if beautiful, weed, but its white variety *E. angustifolium* var. *album* is a green-and-white-flowered treasure that is not so rampant. It flowers in late summer. Super in white borders.
Likes well-drained soil and sun or dappled shade. Tolerates clay and chalky soils.
Propagate by division, seed.

Growing to a height of 1.2 m (4 ft), *Echinops ritro* is a stunning plant for the back of the border, with its large, purplish blue, spherical flowerheads from July to September.

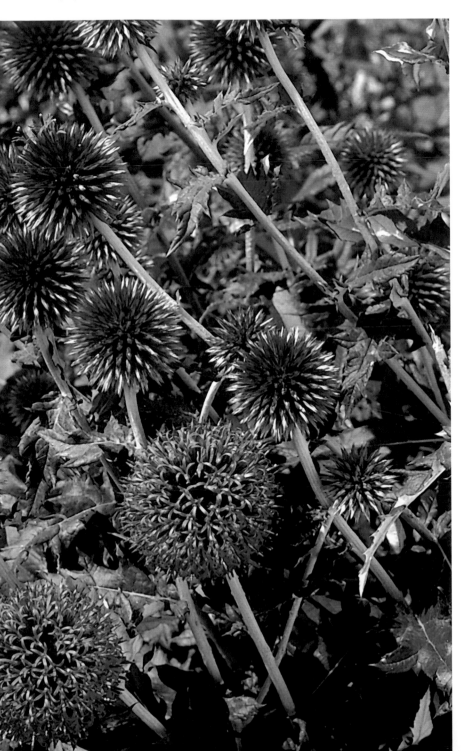

Epimedium
Bishop's Hat, Barrenwort
30 x 30 cm (12 x 12 in)

Whichever species you choose you'll inherit a fine ground-cover plant with mitre-shaped leaves that are often burnished with crimson when they unfurl in spring. The tiny, short-lived flowers may be red, yellow or white and they open in spring. The stems and stalks are stiff and wiry, an altogether admirable race of plants valued for foliage contrasts.
Likes some shade and a moisture-retentive soil. Tolerates sun provided it isn't dry at the roots; chalk and clay. Slow in dry soils.
Propagate by division.

Eremurus
Foxtail Lily
1.5-2.4 m x 60 cm (5-8 x 2 ft)

You'll find no showier border plants than the hybrids of eremurus that are now freely available. In early summer they send up rocket-like stems, packed for most of their length with starry flowers of white, pink, yellow or orange. The strappy leaves die down in summer so the plants should be clearly marked so that they are not disturbed by mistake. Mulch in winter.
Likes sun and well-drained soil; a sheltered spot. Tolerates nothing but excellent drainage; chalky soil.
Propagate by division, seed.

Erigeron
Fleabane
45-60 x 60 cm (18 in-2 ft x 2 ft)

Pretty daisies with petals of pink, mauve, violet or white, surrounding a central disc of yellow. They flower for a good two months in early to mid-summer. Pick from the varieties listed in nurserymen's catalogues.
Likes sun and well-drained soil. Tolerates clay, dry or chalky soil and coastal exposure.
Propagate by division.

Eryngium
Sea Holly
60 cm-1.2 m x 30-60 cm (2-4 x 1-2 ft)

No garden should be without sea hollies. From rosettes or clumps of leaves the branched stems erupt in summer carrying aloft spiky steel-blue flowers – a central knob of tiny florets is surrounded by a ruff of spiny bracts. The flowers are many and miniature on species such as *E. planum*, or large and spectacular in the fuzzy-collared *E. alpinum* or the more open-bloomed *E. x oliverianum*. Sneak the plants between other border inhabitants who will hold them up. They look silly staked. The plant known as Miss Willmott's Ghost is *E. giganteum*, a glorious silver-leaved sea holly of modest size 45 x 30 cm (18 x 12 in) but it is biennial. Grow it in spite of this minor drawback.
Likes well-drained soil and full sun. Tolerates dry or chalky soil and coastal exposure. Some can put up with clay.
Propagate by division, seed.

Euphorbia
Spurge
Various sizes

Classy plants with leaves arranged in spirals up the fleshy stems. The tallest and most stately is *E. characias*, 1.5 m x 90 cm (5 x 3 ft), most popular in its subspecies *wulfenii*. The flowerheads are the yellowish green so common in euphorbias. None is more luminous than those of *E. polychroma* (syn. *E. epithymoides*) 45 x 45 cm (18 x 18 in), which makes a neat, rounded dome of acidic yellow heads. *E. amygdaloides* var. *robbiae* 60 x 60 cm (2 x 2 ft) makes a dense, evergreen, weed-suppressing blanket of attractive growth. All these flower in spring and look terrific planted in front of the golden-leafed hop or near yellow-leafed shrubs. The stunning *E. griffithii* 'Fireglow' blooms in early summer, plastering its stems with rounded heads of brick-red blooms.

Likes sun and a good, well-drained soil. Tolerates shade; dry or chalky soil; coastal exposure.
Propagate by division, seed.

Fallopia
1.8 x 2.4 m (6 x 8 ft) plus

Unless you have plenty of room to spare, don't let loose the blighter *Fallopia japonica* 'Spectabilis' (syn. *Polygonum cuspidatum* 'Spectabile'): it's a close relative of Japanese knotweed. Where it can be entertained it will certainly entertain you in summer with its vigorous hollow stems that arch at the tips to show off the leaves. These are variegated green and creamy yellow with a tinge of pink, like some revolting foreign cheese. I can never make up my mind whether the plant is lurid or spectacular, but it always attracts gasps from onlookers.
Likes sun and moisture-retentive soil. Tolerates dappled shade and clay or chalky soils; sheltered coastal gardens.
Staking required by some.
Propagate by division.

Festuca
Fescue Grass
23 x 30 cm (9 x 12 in)

Big, blue-grey shaving brushes sprouting from the ground; that's the best description I can offer of *F. glauca*, the blue fescue. It's a neat foliage plant to squeeze into any bed or border and looks good among cobbles or gravel. It is evergreen but can be chopped to ground level in spring when tatty; it will soon sprout again.
Likes sun and well-drained soil. Tolerates dry or chalky soil; coastal exposure.
Propagate by division.

Gaillardia
Blanket Flower
75 x 45 cm (2½ ft x 18 in)

Bright-petalled double daisies of red, orange or yellow that are at their best

in summer. There are many varieties, but 'Mandarin' is one of the best; orange-red petals radiate from a central boss of mahogany-brown.
Likes light, well-drained soil and sun. Tolerates dry or chalky soil. Propagate by division, root cuttings.
Propagate staking.

Galega
Goat's Rue
1.2 m x 90 cm (4 x 3 ft)

This makes a thicket of vetch-like stems and leaves, decorated in summer with clusters of white, pink, lilac or pale blue pea flowers. It should be more popular. The varieties are derived from *G. officinalis*.
Likes sun and well-drained soil. Tolerates chalk, dry and clay and soils.
Staking required.
Propagate by division.

Gentiana
Gentian
60 x 60 cm (2 x 2 ft)

The willow gentian, *G. asclepiadea* looks a treat in late summer and early autumn when its arching stems produce pairs of blue trumpet flowers among the topmost leaves. The leaves are willow-shaped, which accounts for the common name. One of late summer's most cheering sights.
Likes rich, leafy soil and gentle shade. Tolerates sun (not drought); chalky soil.
Propagate by seed.

Geranium
Cranesbill
Various sizes

Vital plants in my garden where they make billowing flower-spotted ground cover from spring to autumn. Grow any of them – they're all worth a try. Among the best are: *G. macrorrhizum*: 30 x 60 cm (12 in x 2 ft), aromatic, pink or white. 'Claridge Druce': 45 x 90 cm (18 in x 3 ft), pink. *G. phaeum*: 60 x 30 cm (2 ft x 12 in), the mourning

widow, dusky purple. *G. pratense* 'Plenum Violaceum': 60 x 60 cm (2 x 2 ft), double blooms of violet and mauve. *G. psilostemon* (syn. *G. armenum*): up to 1.8 x 1.8 m (6 x 6 ft) usually less, magenta centred with deep purple.
Likes sun and well-drained soil. Tolerates shade; dry, chalky or clay soil; coastal exposure.
Staking required by *G. psilostemon*.
Propagate by division.

Geum
Avens
30–60 x 45 cm (12 in–2 ft x 18 in)

Most hybrid geums have double flowers of red, yellow, orange or pink, held like rosettes at the tips of sturdy stems. 'Mrs J. Bradshaw' is a good, solid red, and 'Lady Stratheden' a double yellow. *G. rivale* 'Leonard's Variety' is altogether more classy with its orange-pink bells that nod on 30 cm (12 in) stems. All bloom from early to midsummer.
Likes full sun and good, well-drained soil. Tolerates gentle shade; chalky or clay soil.
Propagate by division.

Glyceria
60 cm x 1.5 m (2 x 5 ft)

A clump of upright grassy leaves with blades that are boldly striped in white and green makes *G. maxima* var. *variegata* (syn. *G. aquatica variegata*) a must. It's a stunner and grows itself in any reasonable spot. It can be invasive.
Likes moisture-retentive soil and sun. Tolerates gentle shade; chalky or clay soil. Slow in dry soil.
Propagate by division.

Gunnera
Prickly Rhubarb
2.4 x 2.4 m (8 x 8 ft)

For massive gardens only. *G. manicata* makes gargantuan parasols of leaves, dull green above, lighter green below,

with prickly stalks. Best by a lake if you happen to have one. Protect the crowns with a bracken mulch in winter.
Likes rich, leafy, moisture-retentive soil; sun. Tolerates gentle shade.
Propagate by division.

Gypsophila
Baby's Breath
Various sizes

Billowing clouds of tiny blooms float over this plant in summer. *G. paniculata*, 1.2 x 1.2 m (4 x 4 ft), is white and single; 'Bristol Fairy', 90 x 90 cm (3 x 3 ft), is a double white; and *G.* 'Rosenschleier' (syn. 'Rosy Veil') a double pink. Can be short-lived.
Likes a warm, sunny spot in well-drained, chalky soil. Tolerates other well-drained soils; coastal exposure.
Propagate by seed, grafting (varieties).

Helenium
Sneezeweed
60–90 x 60 cm (2–3 x 2 ft)

Summer and autumn daisies of yellow, orange and mahogany-red. There are many varieties, all of which have a prominent central boss of yellow or brown. 'Butterpat', yellow; 'Wyndley', orange-brown; and 'Moerheim Beauty', mahogany, are particularly good.
Likes good, well-drained soil and sun. Tolerates clay or chalky soil.
Staking required.
Propagate by division.

Helleborus
Christmas Rose, Hellebore
30–60 x 30 cm (12 in–2 ft x 12 in)

By flowering in winter and spring this group of plants really earns its keep. *H. niger*, the Christmas rose, usually carries its waxy white saucers in January or February (unless it is cloche covered). *H. orientalis* is the undoubted aristrocrat with its many-flowered 30 cm (12 in) stalks, of creamy white, purple or purple-spotted blooms that precede the leaves.

H. corsicus is evergreen with spiny-edged fingered leaves, and in its second year each stem is topped with a cluster of pale green flowers. Most hellebores require a little patience while they settle in.

Likes gentle shade and well-drained but moisture-retentive soil. Tolerates sun; chalky or well-cultivated clay soils.
Propagate by seed, division.

Hemerocallis
Day Lily
60–90 x 60 cm (2–3 x 2 ft)

Grassy, fresh green leaves make a perfect background to the branched heads of lily flowers carried over them in summer. There are dozens of varieties with short-lived (but freely produced) blooms of yellow, orange, white, pink or mahogany-red. A good contrast for broader-leaved plants.

Likes sun and well-drained but moisture-retentive soil. Tolerate gentle shade; chalky or clay soils.
Propagate by division.

Heuchera
Coral Bells, Alum Root
30–60 x 45 cm (12 in–2 ft x 18 in)

Valued as pretty ground cover, the heucheras produce a thick pile of flowering-currant-shaped leaves over which are carried upright stems decorated with little bells of pink or red. The named varieties have now upstaged the true species. They bloom in early summer and some have leaves marbled bronze. 'Pewter Moon' is especially good in leaf.

Likes rich, well-drained but moisture-retentive soil. Tolerates sun or shade; chalky or clay soils; coastal exposure.
Propagate by division.

Hosta
Plantain Lily, Funkia
30–60 x 60 cm (12 in–2 ft x 2 ft)

Bold foliage plants of great merit. The leaves are always juicy and squeaky,

and tall stems of bell-shaped lily flowers tower over them in summer. The blooms are usually white or pale lilac in colour, but it is the leaves that are the main attraction. They die down in autumn to emerge afresh each spring. *H. sieboldiana* var. *elegans* has whopping blue-grey leaves that are rounded and ribbed; *H. fortunei* var. *albopicta* is striped and blotched with butter-yellow on green in spring, fading to green later; *H. crispula* has narrower leaves, twisted at the edges and margined. with creamy white. Of the many good newcomers 'Frances Williams' is strikingly bold. It has the size and colour of *H. sieboldiana* var. *elegans* but with a pale yellow margin.

Likes gentle shade and a rich, moisture-retentive soil. Tolerates sun (but not dryness); chalky or well-worked clay soil.
Propagate by division, seed.

Incarvillea
45 x 30 cm (18 x 12 in)

The rich pink trumpets of *I. delavayi* blow a colourful fanfare from the tops of sturdy stalks in early summer. The much-divided leaves are deep bronzy green. Spectacular in sheltered gardens.

Likes sun and a well-drained soil. Tolerates dry or chalky soil.
Propagate by division, seed.

Iris
Flag
Various sizes

Sword-like or grassy leaves and bright, often bearded flowers combine to make the irises indispensable garden plants. The German bearded irises, which are available in a tremendous variety of colours, make that brilliant June display of bloom; their glaucous leaves are still useful later in the season for foliage contrasts. Prolong the season with *I. unguicularis* (syn. *I. stylosa*) in dry soil at the foot of a sunny wall. Its grassy leaves remain all the year round, but from November to February it can produce pale violet-blue flowers to brighten your winter. Starve it and don't disturb it. *I. pallida* in either its white-variegated or yellow-variegated leafed forms is a superb foliage plant, and *I. foetidissima* is the species that has those fat seed pods that burst to reveal orange seeds in autumn.

Likes well-drained soil, especially if it's chalky; full sun. Tolerates gentle shade (*I. foetidissima* and *I. pallida*); dry or clay soils; coastal exposure.
Propagate by division, seed.

Specimen plants

These are plants that strike me as having such good form and appearance that they are worth planting as eye-catchers in a bed or border, or as single specimens on patios or in gravel and cobble beds. Not all of them are huge; some are small and capable of being fitted into the tiniest back yard.

- Acanthus
- Aruncus
- Carex
- Cortaderia
- Cynara
- Dierama
- Dryopteris
- Euphorbia
- Festuca
- Glyceria
- Gunnera
- Hemerocallis
- Hosta
- Iris
- Kniphofia
- Macleaya
- Matteuccia
- Persicaria (syn. *Polygonum*)
- Phormium
- Polygonatum
- Rheum
- Rodgersia
- Sedum
- Smilacina
- Stipa

Kirengeshoma

90 x 60 cm (3 x 2 ft)

Not half as widely grown as it should be, *K. palmata* has rich green, paired leaves show off a treat the upside-down shuttlecock flowers of pale yellow that dangle from branched, purple-flushed stems in late summer and early autumn.

Likes a rich, moisture-retentive and lime-free soil in dappled shade. Keep it sheltered from strong winds. Tolerates full sun if it's not dry at the roots.
Propagate by division, seed.

Kniphofia
Red Hot Poker

Various sizes

Striking plants with sceptre-like flower stems that appear from early summer to autumn depending on the species or variety. The leaves are grassy and make a massive clump. Most varieties have red and yellow flowers, but there are some with pale yellow or green flowers, and a good race of miniatures that can be easily fitted into the small garden. *K. uvaria*, 1.5 m x 90 cm (5 x 3 ft), is the common autumn-flowering poker, but try 'Little Maid', 60 x 30 cm (2 ft x 12 in), with its pale yellow flowers; 'Green Jade', 1.2 m x 60 cm (4 x 2 ft), with cool green blooms, and 'Strawberries and Cream', 45 x 30 cm (18 x 12 in), pale yellow and rich pink, all raised by Beth Chatto.

Likes full sun and well-drained soil. Tolerates dry, chalky or well-worked clay soil; coastal exposure.
Propagate by division.

Lamium
Deadnettle

30 cm x 1.2 m (12 in x 4 ft)

As a ground-cover plant at the front of a border *L. maculatum* has little competition. Choose a variety such as 'Chequers' with white-striped leaves and rich mauve hooded spring flowers, or 'Beacon Silver' with leaves almost entirely silver-green. *L. galeobdolon* (syn. *Galeobdolon luteum, Lamiastrum galeobdolon*) is a firework plant – light the blue touch-paper and stand back. *L. g.* subsp. *montanum* 'Florentinum' has trailing stems clad in green, grey-spotted leaves, with yellow flowers in early summer. Once established it is unstoppable and thrives where little else will grow. All are evergreen.

Likes any well-drained soil and sun. Tolerates heavy shade; dry, chalky or clay soil.
Propagate by division, stem cuttings.

Lathyrus

45 x 45 cm (18 x 18 in)

L. vernus is a neglected plant that should soon make a comeback. Over a mound of finely cut leaves it produces plenty of pinkish purple pea flowers in spring. There are several varieties, among which is 'Alboroseus' with pink and white flowers. Give it a try.

Likes sun and well-drained soil. Tolerates dry or chalky soil; coastal exposure.
Propagate by division.

Leucanthemum
Shasta Daisy

90 x 90 cm (3 x 3 ft)

The white, thick-centred shasta daisy used to be called *Chrysanthemum maximum* and is now *L. x superbum*, also known by the name of one of its varieties 'Esther Read'. One of the best white flowers of summer and a vigorous clump former.

Likes full sun and a well-drained soil. Tolerates clay or chalky soil and coastal exposure.
Staking required.
Propagate by division.

Liatris spicata
Kansas Gayfeather

60 x 30 cm (2 ft x 12 in)

L. spicata has shiny, narrow leaves that make a bold tuft of growth, and in summer it sends up pokers of fluffy pink flowers. Butterflies love them. 'Kobold' is a good purplish pink variety, and 'Alba' is white.

Likes sunny spots in well-drained soil. Tolerates dry or chalky soil.
Propagate by division.

Linaria
Toad Flax

90 x 30 cm (3 ft x 12 in)

The spires of *L. purpurea* pop up all over my garden and will do so for ever: the plant seeds itself freely. The stiff stems sport spirals of narrow grey leaves and are topped with spikes of tiny purple snapdragon flowers – pink in the variety 'Canon Went', which seems just as prolific and comes true from seed. Good in paving stone crevices and walls and flowering freely from early to late summer.

Likes sun and well-drained soil. Tolerates dry and chalky soil; coastal exposure.
Propagate by seed, division.

Linum
Flax

45 x 45 cm (18 x 18 in)

If you want a good sky-blue flower, look no further than *L. narbonense*. Its bell-shaped blooms decorate the wiry stems for several weeks in summer. It can be rather short-lived.

Likes sun and a well-drained soil in a sheltered spot. Tolerates dry and chalky soils.
Propagate by seed, stem cuttings.

Liriope

30 x 30 cm (12 x 12 in)

I'm never quite sure whether I like the appearance of *L. muscari*, but it's so useful that it's worth a mention. It makes a clump of darkest green, grassy leaves that arches into a small fountain, and in autumn stiff stalks appear carrying pale purple blobs of flowers.

Likes sun or shade (will tolerate dry shade under trees) and good, well-drained soil. Tolerates well-worked clay or chalky soil.
Propagate by division.

Lobelia
Cardinal Flower
90 x 30 cm (3 ft x 12 in)

As distinct from the bedding lobelia, *L. cardinalis* produces tall stems thickly set with scarlet flowers in summer. *L. fulgens* is similar but redder in leaf.
Likes sun and rich soil that is unlikely to dry out. Tolerates dappled shade and well-worked, enriched, chalky soil.
Staking required.
Propagate by division, seed.

Lupinus
Lupin
1.2-1.8 m x 60 cm (4-6 x 2 ft)

George Russell, an assiduous Yorkshireman, raised many different

Lupins, delphiniums, irises and pyrethrums epitomize the luxuriance of high summer.

varieties of tall-spired lupin with towers of close-packed pea flowers in shades of blue, pink, red, yellow, mauve, purple and white. They were all grown on allotments and he wouldn't take a penny for them from any nurserymen; instead he distributed them free of charge. We still have many of his excellent varieties, at their best in June. The blooms look well over the fingered green leaves that hold water drops in their centre like globules of mercury.
Likes good, well-drained soil and full sun. Tolerates well-worked clay soils and, reluctantly, organically enriched chalk. On shallow chalk they sulk.
Propagate by stem cuttings, seed, division.

Lychnis
Maltese Cross
90 x 30 cm (3 ft x 12 in)

There are two species of lychnis that have particularly striking flowers in summer. *L. coronaria* makes upright branching stems covered all over with white down; the leaves are felted too. Atop the stems are magenta flowers in early summer. *L. chalcedonica* has plain green leaves and stems topped with clusters of zingy scarlet flowers – there is no truer red in the garden. Place them carefully to avoid clashes.
Likes sun and a well-drained soil. Tolerates dry, chalky or clay soils and coastal exposure, though they appreciate shelter from strong winds.
Staking required.
Propagate by division, seed.

Lysimachia
Loosestrife, Creeping Jenny
Various sizes

The yellow loosestrife, *L. punctata*, makes a clump 60 x 60 cm (2 x 2 ft) and sends up stems of starry yellow flowers in summer. *L. nummularia* is a sprawling plant with tiny rounded leaves the size of a new penny. Little yellow cup-shaped flowers appear in

the leaf axils in early summer. The variety 'Aurea' has leaves of an eye-catching acid-yellow. All are rampant.
Likes moisture-retentive soil in dappled shade. Tolerates chalk and clay; sun but not drought.
Staking required by *L. punctata*.
Propagate by division.

Macleaya
Plume Poppy
2.4 m x 90 cm (8 x 3 ft)

The dusky green, lobed leaves of *M. microcarpa* (syn. *Bocconia cordata*) are grey beneath and flash brightly when disturbed by wind. The plumes of orange-pink flowers appear in summer and are most attractive in the variety 'Kelway's Coral Plume'. A hefty plant that suckers freely.
Likes well-drained soil in a sunny, sheltered spot. Tolerates dry or chalky soil.
Staking required.
Propagate by division, root cuttings.

Malva
Mallow
1.2 x 1.5 m (4 x 5 ft)

The easiest mallow to get hold of is *M. alcea* var. *fastigiata*, which produces upright stems decorated with round, pink flowers in summer. *M. sylvestris* 'Primley Blue' deserves to be better known, for it makes a spreading, vigorous plant that carries myriad soft blue flowers from early summer to autumn. Give it room to spread. Rust disease can sometimes attack and it can be short-lived.
Likes sun and well-drained soil. Tolerates chalk and well-worked clay.
Propagate by stem cuttings.

Matteuccia
Ostrich Plume Fern
60 x 60 cm (2 x 2 ft)

Shuttlecocks of bright green fronds in spring make *M. struthiopteris* (syn. *Struthiopteris germanica*) one of the

most striking ferns, if one of the most unpronounceable. It is superb grown in small colonies.
Likes dappled shade and leafy, moisture-retentive soil. Tolerates well-enriched chalk or clay; sun and heavy shade.
Propagate by division.

Meconopsis
Himalayan Blue Poppy, Welsh Poppy
Various sizes

The Welsh poppy, *M. cambrica*, 30 x 30 cm (12 x 12 in), is the easiest to please, seeding itself around so freely that it amounts to a weed in my garden. But its bright yellow poppy flowers are a treat in late spring.

The coveted blue poppy, *M. betonicifolia* (syn. *M. baileyi*), 1.2 m x 30 cm (4 ft x 12 in), is a showstopper, producing branched heads of almost luminous blue flowers in early summer. But beware: there are wishy-washy varieties, and the plant's performance varies from garden to garden, as does its length of life – many of the other species are monocarpic, which means they flower once and then die.
Likes dappled shade and a rich, lime-free soil. Best in the cooler northern counties. Tolerates full sun if happy at the roots.
Propagate by division, seed.

Milium
Bowles' Golden Grass
60 x 60 cm (2 x 2 ft)

A superb yellow-foliage plant, *M. effusum* 'Aureum' was spotted by that Enfield plantsman E.A. Bowles, which accounts for its common name. It makes dainty, arching clumps of acid-yellow leaves, which produce airy flower stems in summer. It seeds about freely.
Likes gentle shade and a well-drained soil. Tolerates dry or chalky soil and full sun.
Propagate by division, seed.

Mimulus
Monkey Flower
30-90 x 60 cm (12 in-3 ft x 2 ft)

There are lots of different monkey flowers with fleshy green leaves and trumpet flowers of red, yellow or orange, often contrastingly spotted. They bloom in summer and especially enjoy being planted by water.
Likes sun and moisture-retentive soil. Tolerates dappled shade, chalk and clay; coastal exposure.
Staking required by taller varieties.
Propagate by stem cuttings, division, seed.

Monarda
Bee Balm, Bergamot, Oswego Tea
60 x 60 cm (2 x 2 ft)

Crush the leaves of monarda and you'll smell Earl Grey tea! The aromatic foliage is just one of the attractions; the main benefit is the summer display of hooded flowers carried in tiers around the stems. 'Cambridge Scarlet' is the best variety with rosy crimson flowers; 'Croftway Pink' is a good paler pink, and 'Prärienacht' (syn. 'Prairie Night') a violet-purple.
Likes sun and well-drained but moisture-retentive soil. Tolerates chalky or clay soils.
Propagate by division.

Morina
90 x 30 cm (3 ft x 12 in)

The leaves of *M. longifolia* are just like those of a glossy thistle – don't uproot the plant by mistake when it's young. Later the leaves are longer and more handsome: then you'll have no difficulty in distinguishing them. The flower spikes of hooded white blooms appear above the leaf rosettes in summer. They turn to deep rose-pink as they age. This is a plant deserving greater popularity, and one of my all-time favourites.
Likes sun and well-drained soil in a sheltered spot. Tolerates chalk and

well-worked clay soil; coastal exposure.
Propagate by division, seed.

Nepeta
Catmint
45 x 60 cm (18 in x 2 ft)

Our cat loves this plant so much that she chews it off at ground level every time it tries to emerge. *N. x faassenii* is the one you want. Its aromatic leaves are dusky grey and it has long stems of lavender-blue flowers in summer. *N.* 'Six Hills Giant' is the most robust variety.
Likes sun and well-drained soil. Tolerates dry or chalky soil.
Propagate by division, stem cuttings.

Oenothera
Evening Primrose
23-45 x 60 cm (9-18 in x 2 ft)

The bright yellow cup-shaped flowers of *O. macrocarpa* are held on 23 cm (9 in) stems right through summer, making this grand for the front of a border and a long-lasting display. Taller varieties like 'Fireworks' (correctly *O. fruticosa* 'Fyrverkeri') 45 x 45 cm (18 x 18 in), with masses of yellow flowers and orange buds are even more showy.
Likes full sun and well-drained soil. Tolerates dry and chalky soils; coastal exposure.
Propagate by division, seed.

Paeonia
Peony
60-90 x 90 cm (2-3 x 3 ft)

Fleeting but fabulous, the spring-flowering Chinese peonies make a stunning show before any summer flowers have time to compete. There are dozens of varieties with double or single blooms of white, pink, crimson and magenta, and single kinds with crested centres. Pick where you like from nurserymen's pictures. Try *P. mlokosewitschii* (you'll have to point at the name if you can't say it). It makes a glorious show of golden goblets centred with yellow stamens and a red 'eye' in May.

Likes full sun and a rich, well-drained soil, especially if it's chalky. Tolerates dry or clay soils, provided the latter is well worked. Plant peonies and leave them: they don't like disturbance.

Propagate by division.

Papaver
Poppy
90 x 90 cm (3 x 3 ft)

The varieties of *P. orientale*, the oriental poppy, are flowers of June. It's a relatively brief display but one that is truely dazzling. The massive bowl-shaped blooms of orange, salmon, pink, scarlet or white are centred with a crown of black stamens and may be contrastingly blotched or picotee edged. Others have frilly-edged petals. 'Marcus Perry' is a good orange; 'Mrs Perry' a warm salmon-pink; and 'Picotée' is white-edged with orange; 'Black and White' is just as its name.

Likes sun and well-drained soil, especially if it's chalky. Tolerates dry soil.

Staking required.

Propagate by division, root cuttings.

Penstemon
60 x 45 cm (2 ft x 18 in)

Many penstemons are rather tender, but there are now a good few hybrids that can be gambled with as hardy plants in the milder counties. All carry their foxglove-like flowers on elegant spikes and bloom generously from mid- to late summer. 'Andenken an Friedrich Hahn' (syn. 'Garnet') is rosy red; 'Apple Blossom' has pale pink flowers with white throats; 'Sour Grapes' is lilac-purple; and 'Schoenholzeri' (syn. 'Firebird') is scarlet. There are other varieties with pink and salmon flowers.

Likes a warm, sunny, sheltered spot in well-drained soil. Tolerates dry or chalky soil and warm coastal gardens.

Propagate by stem cuttings.

Persicaria (syn. *Polygonum*)
Knotweed
Various sizes

Make a point of exploring this tribe: it offers such a varied and valuable collection of plants.

P. bistorta 'Superba', 75 x 90 cm (2½-3 ft), is a spring beauty with green, dock-like leaves over which tower pink pokers. It continues to throw up a few blooms right through summer.

P. campanulata, 90 x 90 cm (3 x 3 ft), is a more frothy treasure with dusky green leaves and branched flowerheads of miniature blush-pink bells from summer to autumn.

P. milettii, 45 x 60 cm (18 in x 2 ft), is the brightest persicaria I know, with deep rose-red flower spikes carried over lush green leaves in summer.

Likes sun and good, moisture-retentive soil. Tolerates dappled shade and clay or chalky soils; sheltered coastal gardens.

Staking required by some.

Propagate by division.

Phlox
1.2 m x 60 cm (4 x 2 ft)

Essential ingredients of a summer border, the varieties of *P. paniculata* are lovely plants with fat, rounded heads of flower, each bloom often being marked with a darker central eye. They'll flower from mid- to late summer, in shades of pink, crimson, lavender-blue, mauve, violet-purple and white. Take your pick from the glowing descriptions in nurserymen's catalogues. If your plants develop puckered, twisted leaves and swollen stems they've fallen prey to eelworm. Dig them up, take root cuttings (all else will be affected), and replant your new plants in uninfected ground.

Likes sun and well-drained soil. Tolerates dry, chalky or clay soil but only if all three are enriched with organic matter and well worked.

Staking required.

Propagate by root cuttings, division.

Phormium
New Zealand Flax
60-90 x 60-90 cm (2-3 x 2-3 ft)

Certainly among the most spectacular foliage plants in the border, the phormiums send up great sword-leafed fountains of tough foliage that may be rich bronze or striped with green, cream, orange and red. There's a new vogue for these plants, which are hardy (forms of *P. cookianum*) or on the borderline of hardiness (*P. tenax* varieties). There are now plenty of named varieties of varying heights. Use them for evergreen foliage contrasts.

Likes sun and a warm, sheltered spot in well-drained soil. Tolerates well-worked clay or chalky soil; coastal exposure in the milder counties. *P. tenax* varieties are only reliably hardy in southern counties.

Propagate by division.

Physalis
Chinese Lantern Flower
60 x 60 cm (2 x 2 ft)

No flower arranger will want to be without this plant in the garden. In autumn the stems of *P. alkekengi* var. *franchetii* are hung with Chinese paper lanterns of bright orange. They keep their colour when dried. An easy-to-grow treasure.

Likes sun and a well-drained soil. Tolerates dappled shade; dry, chalky or clay soil.

Staking required.

Propagate by division.

Physostegia
Obedient Plant
75 x 60 cm (2½ x 2 ft)

Here's a curiosity; the obedient plant produces densely packed flower spikes in late summer, and each of the tiny tubular blooms can be nudged on its stalk to any position you want – hence the common name. *P. virginiana* has two good varieties: 'Vivid', which is rich

mauve-pink, compact at around 45 x 45 cm (18 x 18 in) and particularly late, flowering in early autumn; and 'Summer Snow', a white form.
Likes sun and a good, well-drained soil that's not likely to dry out. Tolerates clay and chalky soils; coastal gardens.
Propagate by division.

Platycodon
Balloon Flower
30-45 cm x 45 cm (12-18 in x 18 in)

The inflated buds of balloon flower are pushed up over the greyish leaves where they open out into beautiful campanula flowers in mid- to late summer. *P. grandiflorus* has several varieties, of which 'Mariesii' is a good sky-blue, and *albus* a dainty white with blue veins. Good front-of-the-border plants which are fun to 'pop'.
Likes sun and a rich, well-drained but not dry soil. Tolerates clay and chalky soils.
Propagate by division, seed, stem cuttings.

Polemonium
Jacob's Ladder
60-75 cm x 75 cm (2-2½ ft x 2 ft)

Attractive flowering and foliage plants with pinnate leaves carried thickly on upright stems that are topped with lavender-blue flower clusters in early summer. *P. caeruleum* is the commonest species; its white form is particularly lovely. *P.* 'Pink Beauty' is mauve-pink, while 'Lambrook Mauve' produces masses of bell-shaped lilac-mauve flowers. All can be short-lived.
Likes sun and a rich, moisture-retentive soil.Tolerates shade; chalky and clay soil.
Staking required.
Propagate by division (regularly).

Polygonatum
Solomon's Seal
60 x 60-90 cm (2 x 2-3 ft)

I'm lucky enough to have this plant

growing wild in my garden and it looks a treat in late spring when its arching stems drip with tiny ivory bells. The bold leaves sprout from the stems like wings. A fine foliage plant for use with other bold beauties like hostas and sword-leafed irises. The British native is *P. multiflorum. P. x hybridum* is beefier.
Likes shade and a leafy, moisture-retentive soil. Tolerates chalk and well-worked, enriched clay.
Propagate by division.

Potentilla
Cinquefoil
45 x 60 cm (18 in x 2 ft)

There are lots of hybrid herbaceous potentillas that can be used to bring brightness to beds and borders in summer. They offer double or single flowers in shades of red, yellow, orange and salmon carried on floppy stems over fingered, downy leaves. 'William Rollison' is a favourite double red, and 'Yellow Queen' a double yellow. The doubles last longest.
Likes sun and a well-drained soil. Tolerates dry or chalky soil and coastal exposure.
Staking required.
Propagate by division.

Primula
Polyanthus
Various sizes

The polyanthus is the pride of spring in most folk's gardens, making neat mounds of primrose leaves that are iced with red, orange, yellow, blue or white flowers over many spring weeks. The plants grow to maybe 23 x 30 cm (9 x 12 in) but repay annual division after flowering. Try also the choice 'Guinevere' (syn. 'Garryarde Guinevere') which has pastel pink flowers and bronze-burnished leaves. The candelabra primulas come in all sorts of colours, carrying their blooms in tiers up stems that may be anything from 30-90 cm (12 in-3 ft) tall.

P. japonica, P. pulverulenta, P. chungensis and *P. bulleyana* are good examples, and *P. sikkimensis* has nodding clusters of sulphur-yellow bells. The others may be yellow, red, pink, orange, crimson, magenta or white. At Harlow Carr Gardens near Harrogate they look better than anywhere else. Late spring and early summer is their season of glory.
Likes sun or dappled shade and a leafy, peaty, moisture-retentive soil. Tolerates clay soil and chalky soil (though the candelabra types prefer acid ground and sometimes fail on chalk).
Propagate by seed, division.

Pulmonaria
Lungwort, Soldiers and Sailors
30 x 90 cm (12 in x 3 ft)

The lungwort is one of the earliest and most reliable flowers of spring. Its nodding clusters of pink and blue flowers unfurl in March and look a treat with hellebores. As they fade, the

> "No garden should be without sea hollies... the branched stems erupt in summer, carrying aloft spiky steel-blue flowers."

bold, oval leaves, splashed with silver-grey, push up to take their place.
P. saccharata is the type best in leaf, but for flowers (without the foliage spotting) try *P. rubra*, which has glorious, large, rich pink blooms especially early in the season. *P. angustifolia* 'Munstead Blue' has especially good blue flowers. There are huge numbers to choose from; visit a specialist nursery to make your choice.
Likes gentle shade and a moisture-

retentive soil. Tolerates clay and chalky soils; full sun but not drought. **Propagate** by division.

Rheum
Rhubarb
2.4 x 1.5 m (8 x 5 ft)

The bold maroon leaves of *R. palmatum* 'Atrosanguineum' (syn. 'Atropurpureum') take some spectators aback in spring when they unfurl from huge scarlet buds of rather rude appearance. But soon the deeply cut rhubarb leaves assume stately proportions, eventually being accompanied by a towering rose-red flower spike in summer. By then the upper surfaces of the leaves are dull green, but the ruddiness remains beneath.
Likes dappled shade and a rich, moisture-retentive soil that's not likely to dry out. Tolerates full sun (but not drought), clay and chalky soil.
Propagate by division.

Rodgersia
Rodger's Bronze Leaf
90 x 90 cm (3 x 3 ft)

Imagine some bronze horse-chestnut leaves stuck on 60 cm (2 ft) stalks and pushed into the soil and you have some idea what rodgersia looks like, except that it is rather more graceful than my crude description implies. *R. pinnata* 'Superba' is perhaps the best form, and it carries frothy plumes of pink flowers over its leaves in summer.
Likes dappled shade and a rich, moisture-retentive soil. Tolerates well-worked and enriched clay or chalky soils; full sun but not dry soil.
Propagate by division.

Rudbeckia
Coneflower, Black-eyed Susan
75 x 60 cm (2½ x 2 ft)

More bright summer daisies with vivid yellow flowers with a prominent brown centre. 'Goldsturm' (its full name is the mouthful *R. fulgida* var. *sullivantii* 'Goldsturm'!) is the most popular variety and blooms from mid- to late summer. 'Goldquelle' starts and finishes rather later.
Likes sun and a well-drained soil. Tolerates clay or chalky soils.
Staking Requires staking.
Propagate by division.

Salvia
Sage
Various sizes

The ornamental sages are a varied bunch, among the best of which are *S. nemorosa* 'Lubecca', 60 x 60 cm (2 x 2 ft), with slender spikes of violet-blue in summer and 'Oestfriesland' ('East Friesland') which has bracts of pink and purple that persist after the flowers have faded; and a lovely grey-foliaged plant, *S. argentea*, which produces a rosette of large, rumpled leaves covered in silky white wool. When the flower spike appears the leaves become a greyish green, so try to chop off the stalk as soon as you see it emerging. Older leaves can be cut off too. Best treated as a biennial on heavy soils; longer-lived on lighter earth.
Likes full sun and a well-drained soil. Tolerates dry and chalky soils; coastal exposure.
Staking required by all taller varieties.
Propagate by seed, division.

Saponaria
Soapwort, Bouncing Bet
75 cm x 1.2 m (2½ x 4 ft)

Buy a plant by the name of *S. officinalis* 'Rosea Plena' and you'll own a glorious late-summer bloomer that produces masses of double pale pink campion flowers over a thicket of mid-green

leaves. It starts in midsummer and doesn't finish until autumn. A treat with blue-grey foliage like that of *Hosta sieboldiana*. Not suitable for tidy gardeners.
Likes sun and well-drained soil. Tolerates dappled shade; chalk and clay soils.

Late summer colours glow in this border in Waterperry Gardens, Oxfordshire: *Sedum* 'Herbstfreude', golden *Rudbeckia* and purple and mauve *Aster*.

Staking Requires staking.
Propagate by division.

Scabiosa
Scabious

60 x 60 cm (2 x 2 ft)

Pale blue scabious always brings back

memories of my grandfather, who grew the plant as a cut flower on his allotment. 'Clive Greaves' is the best variety of *S. caucasica*, and it produces masses of sky-blue-petalled flowers with their complicated white and lilac-pink centres in summer. The green leaves stay low and are finely

cut. Scabious is particularly lovely among silver-foliaged plants.
Likes sun and well-drained, especially chalky, soil. Tolerates well-worked clay; coastal exposure.
Staking required.
Propagate by division.

Sedum
Ice Plant, Stonecrop

30 x 45 cm (12 x 18 in)

Grow a patch of *S. spectabile* at the foot of a buddleja and you'll have a combination of plants that butterflies find irresistible. The grey-green succulent leaves start to push up in spring, making the plant a fine foliage subject. In late summer and autumn the flat flowerheads of dusky pink open to attract your eyes and the insects. From the human point of view 'Brilliant' is a good form with flowers of a warmer and rather deeper shade of pink, while *S.* 'Herbstfreude', rather better known as 'Autumn Joy', is deep pink, ageing to coppery red, and apparently less popular with butterflies.
Likes full sun and a well-drained soil. Tolerates dry or chalky soils and well-worked clay; coastal exposure.
Propagate by division, stem cuttings.

Sidalcea

90 x 90 cm (3 x 3 ft)

Like elegant miniature hollyhocks the sidalceas are bright clump formers for summer borders. They produce lowering stems of mallow flowers at their best in the glorious pink of 'Rose Queen' or the rather shorter 'Loveliness'. There is also a smaller flowered white species, *S. candida*. The rich pinks are derived from *S. malviflora*.
Likes full sun and a well-drained but moisture-retentive soil (they resent dryness at the roots). Tolerates chalk and well-worked clay.
Staking required by taller varieties.
Propagate by division.

Plants for ground cover

The measurement given after each plant is the recommended planting distance when large numbers are used for ground cover. All the plants listed, apart from

Kniphofia and *Nepeta*, will grow in shade: entries in the A-Z section give more a precise indication of the type of shade the plants can tolerate.

VARIETY	PLANTING DISTANCE	VARIETY	PLANTING DISTANCE
● Acanthus	90 cm (3 ft)	● Glyceria	60 cm (2 ft)
● Ajuga	23 cm (9 in)	● Hemerocallis	60 cm (2 ft)
● Alchemilla	30 cm (12 in)	● Heuchera	30 cm (12 in)
● Aruncus	60 cm (2 ft)	● Hosta	60 cm (2 ft)
● Astilbe	45 cm (18 in)	● Kniphofia (some)	60 cm (2 ft)
● Astrantia	45 cm (18 in)	● Lamium	45 cm (18 in)
● Bergenia	45 cm (18 in)	● Liriope	30 cm (12 in)
● Blechnum	30 cm (12 in)	● Lysimachia	30 cm (12 in)
● Brunnera	30 cm (12 in)	● Nepeta	60 cm (2 ft)
● Calamintha	30 cm (12 in)	● Persicaria	
● Convallaria	23 cm (9 in)	(syn. Polygonum)	60 cm (2 ft)
● Corydalis	23 cm (9 in)	● Primula	23 cm (9 in)
● Crocosmia	30 cm (12 in)	● Pulmonaria	45 cm (18 in)
● Doronicum	45 cm (18 in)	● Saponaria	30 cm (12 in)
● Epimedium	30 cm (12 in)	● Stachys	30 cm (12 in)
● Euphorbia	60 cm (2 ft)	● Tradescantia	45 cm (18 in)
● Geranium	45 cm (18 in)	● Viola	23 cm (9 in)

Smilacina
False Spikenard

90 x 60 cm (3 x 2 ft)

Take the stems and leaves of Solomon's seal (*Polygonatum*) and the creamy white flower plumes of an astilbe; fasten the two together and you've got smilacina. It's a superbly attractive plant at its best in spring. The scent is deliciously overpowering.
Likes shade and leafy, well-drained lime-free soil. Tolerates well-worked clay.
Propagate by division.

Solidago
Golden Rod

60 cm-1.8 m x 60 cm-1.8 m (2-6 x 2-6 ft)

Railway embankments countrywide are decorated with the sceptre-like stems of golden rod in late summer and autumn, so happy is it to colonize any ground. Don't let the tall and dead-bottomed stems of sooty yellow flowers put you off growing the better varieties, which are brighter and less rampant. 'Goldenmosa' has an elegance and bright colouring that few others can rival. At 75 x 60 cm (2½ x 2 ft) it fits into any garden.
Likes sun and well-drained soil. Tolerates dry, chalky and clay soil.
Propagate by division.

Stachys
Betony, Lamb's Ears

45 x 60 cm (18 in x 2 ft)

There are two good species here: *S. macrantha* 'Superba' has toothed green leaves and dense heads of mauve-purple hooded flowers in summer. It makes deep ground cover and is smart without being prissy.

My second choice is *S. byzantina* (syn. *S. lanata*, *S. olympica*) – the white and woolly lamb's ears, tongues or lugs (depending on your part of the country). It makes a rag-rug of leaves over which tower spikes of tiny mauve flowers, interspersed with leafy bracts. Beth Chatto offers a variety known as 'Cotton Boll', whose flower clusters are orbs of white velvet dotted up the stem. These summer blooms are a treat and sadly lacking in the dreary 'Silver Carpet', often recommended as ground cover. It gets mildew and dies out in places and so needs frequent lifting and dividing.
Likes full sun and a well-drained soil. Tolerates partial shade (*S. macrantha* only), dry and chalky soils; coastal exposure.
Propagate by division.

Stipa
Feather Grass

1.8 x 1.2 m (6 x 4 ft)

You'll find lots of grasses down at the garden centre, but few of them are more deserving of a place in your garden than this one. It is a massive, elegant, oat-like grass with arching tufts of narrow green leaves over which hover the bronze flowerheads in summer. *S. gigantea* is a bold, yet graceful grass that glints in the sun. The heads turn strawy as they age. Don't be without it if you can spare the space it requires.

Likes full sun and a well-drained soil. Tolerates dry and chalky soil.

Propagate by division.

Thalictrum
Meadow Rue
90 cm–1.5 m x 60 cm (3–5 x 2 ft)

Feathery mounds of columbine foliage, finely cut and grey-green, are topped in summer with airy sprays of fluffy flowers. The blooms are lilac-pink in *T. delavayi* (syn. *T. dipterocarpum*) and even more fluffy in 'Hewitt's Double'. These lovely plants pay ground rent amply on account of both foliage and flowers.

Likes sun and well-drained but moisture-retentive soil. Tolerates dappled shade; well-worked clay and chalky soils.

Staking required.

Propagate by division, seed.

Tradescantia
Spiderwort, Flower of a Day
60 x 60 cm (2 x 2 ft)

The varieties of Andersonia Group are lush border plants with succulent stems and long, fresh-green leaves. In summer and on into autumn the stems are topped with three-petalled flowers of purplish blue – at least that's the colour of the type most frequently seen in gardens. Go to a nurseryman and you can choose from 'Osprey', white; 'Purewell Giant', magenta; and 'J. C. Weguelin', pale blue; as well as that good dark blue 'Isis'.

Likes sun and well-drained soil. Tolerates dappled shade; well-worked clay and enriched chalky soils (they fail on poor, shallow chalk); coastal exposure.

Staking required.

Propagate by division.

Tropaeolum speciosum See p.98

Trollius
Globe Flower
60–90 x 60 cm (2–3 x 2 ft)

That bright yellow spherical flower of spring, *T. europaeus*, is a good streamside plant where its flowers are shown off well against a mound of rich green buttercup leaves, but the king of the race is *T. chinensis*, a bright orange spring and summer bloomer with flowers that are composed of an outer cup and an inner tuft of spiky petals. There is no brighter orange in the garden.

Likes sun and moisture-retentive soil. Tolerates dappled shade; well-worked clay and chalky soil but never drought.

Propagate by division.

Verbascum
Mullein
45 cm–1.8 m x 30–90 cm

Many mulleins are biennial and die after flowering, but a few will stay with you for years. *V. chaixii*, 90 x 60 cm (3 x 2 ft), whose yellow blooms are spotted in the centre with purple, and its white-flowered version 'Album', are good garden plants. Varieties like 'Gainsborough' (soft yellow) and 'Helen Johnson' (warm brown) are not reliably perennial but can sometimes be increased by root cuttings.

Likes sunny spots in well-drained soil. Tolerates dry and chalky soil and well-worked clay.

Propagate by seed, division, root cuttings.

Veronica
Various sizes

If you're seeking upright spires of blue summer flowers, you can safely plump for veronicas. *V. spicata*, 60 x 60 cm (2 x 2 ft), offers them, and provides additional shades in its varieties 'Barcarolle', rose pink, and 'Rotfuchs

(syn. 'Red Fox'), deep rose. 'Icicle' will give you white spikes.

Likes sun and a well-drained soil. Tolerates dry, clay or chalky soils; coastal exposure.

Staking required by taller varieties.

Propagate by division.

Viola
Violet, Pansy
30 x 90 cm (12 in x 3 ft)

Charming plants, violas can grow in the tiniest, dimmest corner. I'll pick just two. *V. cornuta*, the horned violet, makes sprawling clumps of green leaves alive with pale lavender or white flowers in summer. Clip over the plants in late July and they'll bloom again in autumn. *V. riviniana* Purpurea Group (syn. *V. labradorica* 'Purpurea'), much neater at around 10 cm (4 in), makes carpets of maroon leaves, studded with lavender-purple flowers in spring.

Likes dappled shade and a well-drained but moisture-retentive soil. Tolerates heavy shade or sun; chalky or well-worked clay soil.

Propagate by division, seed, stem cuttings.

Zantedeschia
Arum Lily
90 x 60 cm (3 x 2 ft)

Bold, lustrous, juicy green arrowheads of leaves and white vase-shaped flowers centred with a yellow club-like spadix are the hallmarks of *Z. aethiopica*. It will bloom annually in summer in sheltered gardens. Its variety 'Crowborough' is apparently more tolerant of dry soils. Both need the winter protection of dry straw or bracken until well established.

Likes sun or gentle shade and a moisture-retentive, preferably boggy soil. Tolerates ordinary well-drained soil but not drought; coastal exposure.

Propagate by division, root cuttings, seed.

CHAPTER 10 Annuals, biennials and bedding plants

Annuals and biennials are the cheerful summer visitors, bringing a splendid variety of colour, form and texture to borders, windowboxes, hanging baskets and tubs

Take some blue lobelia and some white alyssum and plant them alternately along the edge of a flowerbed. Plant behind them a dense array of orange French marigolds, and behind these a forest of scarlet salvias, perhaps with a fuchsia or *Senecio cineraria* to act as a dot plant. And there you have it: the typical bedding out scheme. Nothing in the garden will be brighter – and nothing will be less inspiring!

PLANNING COLOUR SCHEMES

Persuading gardeners to be adventurous with their bedding out might have been the eighth labour of Hercules, so difficult is it to accomplish. Now I'm not sneering at lobelia, alyssum, French marigolds and salvias (even though I have to try really hard to like the last two), I'm sneering at the way they are used. People who'd never dream of painting their house in red, orange and blue, will use such contrasts in their garden. But it's much more fun to think of a different colour scheme for your bedding every year and to avoid planting in serried ranks as though your bedders were advancing troops clad in their ceremonial colours. Plan each bed or border with a particular colour theme: it will have tremendous impact. If you insist on a rainbow border, then plan one on paper so that the colours are displayed gradually as you round a corner or progress along the bed; that way the spectacle can be fun, rather than a reason for putting on your dark glasses.

The beauty of bedders

But before all dedicated bedders flip over a few pages, I'll cool down and sing the praises of a grand bunch of plants. Annuals, biennials and bedding plants are invaluable for their cheapness, cheerfulness and

Consider flower and foliage contrasts when planting annuals; here sweet pea is set off to perfection by the golden foliage of *Gleditsia triacanthos* 'Sunburst'.

speedy growth: They are nearly all raised from seeds, which gives a deep sense of achievement; they are valuable gap-fillers, especially in new gardens when the more permanent shrubby occupants have not yet filled their allotted space; and they offer a surprising variety of form, texture and colour.

WHAT ARE BEDDING PLANTS?

The names given to the different groups of bedding plants (any temporary garden occupant) can be confusing, but basically this is what they mean:

Annuals For a start, annuals are those plants that complete their life cycle – from seed to flowering and setting new seed – within the space of a year. If you want a quick mnemonic, think of *Beano* and *Dandy* annuals: both last for just a year.

Hardy annuals Hardy annuals are the bold little blighters that can be sown outdoors in April to bloom *in situ* in summer. Some are so tough they can be sown outdoors in September to struggle through the winter and flower quite early the following summer. Doesn't this make them biennials? No: they are still flowering within 12 months of being sown.

Half-hardy annuals are more lily-livered. They need

to be sown in pots in a greenhouse or porch or on a windowsill where they can be coaxed into action with a little warmth. As soon as they emerge they need pricking out (that strange phrase that brings a smirk to the novice's cheeks) into seed trays, and growing on, before being hardened off (that is, gradually accustomed to outdoor temperatures). These are the plants that are bought by the boxful from garden centres and greengrocers all over the country in early summer. Only when all danger of frost is past can they be planted out.

Tender annuals fall into much the same category, though often these are grown in a greenhouse for all their brief lives. If you simply cannot provide these plants with the protection they need to germinate, don't worry. Some of them can be sown outdoors in late May as for hardy annuals. They'll flower later, but are nonetheless welcome for that.

Biennials Most of the plants grown as biennials are truly perennials. Take the wallflower for instance: it will make a small shrub if grown on for several years, but it won't be as plastered with flowers as it was in its youth. True biennials complete their life cycle within the space of two years. They are sown during one year and grown on to flower and set seed the next. Here we are not talking so much about calendar years as about 12-month periods. Most biennials are sown in May to bloom the following May and June before they seed themselves and die off, probably during the summer. The whole episode probably takes about 14 months, but this varies from plant to plant.

Other bedding plants Gardeners love exceptions, and there is a host of superb bedding plants that are really tender perennials: pelargoniums (geraniums), greenhouse fuchsias and the like. These must be overwintered in a greenhouse or on a windowsill where the frost can't get at them. Most can be propagated from cuttings each spring or autumn, so youngsters can be used each year, instead of the ancient gnarled parents who have just about exhausted themselves during a summer of over-generous blooming.

> "Plan each bed or border with a particular colour theme: it will have tremendous impact."

RAISING THE PLANTS

The techniques for raising the plants from seed vary according to the plants' hardiness and length of life. The following are the methods used for each group:

Hardy annuals

These plants are sown in prepared patches of soil in beds and borders, usually among the permanent inhabitants, but there's nothing to stop you from having a bed devoted entirely to them. Fork over the earth in March and scatter over it a dusting of blood, bone and fishmeal at the rate of about a handful to the square metre (square yard). Don't add too much manure or compost: it turns the plants into Billy Bunters – fat and full of leaf, but short on flowers.

Preparing the soil April (and May for later flowers) is a good time to sow, for by then the soil has usually warmed up a little but is still moist. Rake over the soil to break it down a little (don't over-rake or the surface will cake in the first shower of rain) and mark out the area to be occupied by each plant. Use a rake handle or a trail of sand to show the shape of each drift.

Planning your border You can plan your border or bed in advance on a sheet of paper if you like, or rely on inspiration when you're out in the garden. Either way, try to place most of the taller plants at the back of the bed and the smaller ones at the front, but vary this arrangement occasionally and bring tall plants forward. They will create bays in the bed and make for a few surprises: the smaller plants crouching behind them will be revealed as you stroll along.

Sowing the seed First, draw the rake across each drift to leave tiny furrows. Scatter the seeds over the surface and lightly rake in the opposite direction to cover them. That's all they need, apart from labelling. Failures usually occur either as a result of the seeds being buried too deeply, or because they've been allowed to dry out during germination. Keep a watering can or lawn sprinkler handy and soak the soil before it has a chance to dry out. There's a chance that cats might patronize the area for their vital functions. Twiggy pea sticks laid on the ground will discourage them. (Remove these after germination.)

Thinning out When the seedlings emerge they'll need thinning out to give the survivors room to grow. Thin them twice: once to a spacing of 5 cm (2 in), and finally, when they are touching again, to the spacing recommended in the A-Z section. Instead of pulling up the unwanted seedlings, pinch them off at soil level. This prevents the roots of the remaining plants from being disturbed. Or dig them up with a trowel: they'll often transplant quite well to fill other gaps.

Providing support Most annuals can support themselves. Some can't. Push twiggy pea sticks among the feeble kinds when they are 15 cm (6 in) high; they'll soon grow to mask the supports.

Half-hardy annuals

Half-hardy annuals are sown in pots, usually during March, in a greenhouse or on a windowsill. Scatter the

Sowing hardy annuals

Hardy annuals can be sown directly in the garden. Rake over the surface of the soil to break it down, then lightly rake again to create tiny furrows.

Annuals that need supporting, such as chrysanthemums, sunflowers, poppies, and sweet peas, can be held up unobtrusively if a few twiggy branches are pushed into the soil around them when they are about 15 cm (6 in) high. Don't overdo it!

Mark out with trails of sand, or with the rake handle, the areas – or drifts – to be occupied by each plant. Scatter the seeds thinly and evenly over the surface of the soil.

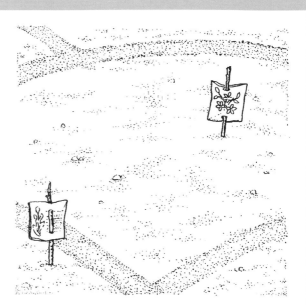

Lightly rake in the opposite direction to cover the seeds; label each drift. Make sure that the soil is kept moist during germination. Plastic netting will deter birds.

seeds thinly on the surface of moist seed compost that has been firmed down to 1 cm (½ in) below the pot rim. Dust-fine seeds such as begonias and lobelia need no further covering, but most seeds can be lightly covered with sieved seed compost. Place a label in the pot, cover with a sheet of glass or polythene, then place a piece of newspaper over it. Stand the pots where they can be kept at a temperature of around 18–21°C (64–70°F). Check them every day and remove glass and paper as soon as the first seedling breaks the surface. Water by immersing the pot to half its depth in water whenever the surface of the compost is beginning to look dry.

Pricking out Transfer the seedlings to trays of potting compost with a pencil, carefully lifting them individually and making a hole into which the roots can be lowered. Firm the compost around each seedling and then water them in.

Hardening off Grow the seedlings on in gentle heat and good light until early May, when they can be gradually accustomed to the temperatures outdoors: stand them out during the day and bring them under cover at night. By late May (or early June in the cooler north) they can be left outdoors all the time, for by then all danger of frost should be past and they are ready to be planted out.

Planting Plant them with a trowel (after giving them a really good soak in their trays) at the distances recommended in the A–Z section. Water them in with a lawn sprinkler left running for a good two hours, and soak them again at any time when the earth around them starts to look dry. Forget to water and you'll have wasted your time – they'll turn crisp and die.

Biennials
Biennials are usually sown on the vegetable plot where they can be trickled thinly into drills and transplanted to a wider spacing of 15–23 cm (6–9 in) when they are large enough to lift with a trowel. Sow during May and June, and the first transplanting can be carried out in July – still in rows on the veg plot. In September the plants can be dug up and planted at their final spacing in beds and borders. Most biennials are grown for spring bedding schemes but there are exceptions and these are indicated in the A–Z section.

Tender perennials
Tender perennials are usually planted out, along with the half-hardy annuals, in late May or early June, and lifted and brought under cover during September before the frosts strike. Their cultivation is covered in Chapter 19 Greenhouse Gardening.

A-Z
of
annuals, biennials and bedding plants

IN THIS A-Z SECTION, THE plants are arranged alphabetically in their respective groups, according to whether they are hardy annuals, half-hardy annuals or biennials.

HARDY ANNUALS

Hardy annuals are grown in profusion all over the country, but what they're called varies from one place to another – common names are anything but common! They are also often sold under a wide variety of names, including common names and old names. When buying seeds, be ready to look under all the different names given here. You may have to do some detective work to get the right thing.

I have included here some charming flowers that are facing extinction. They are still to be had for a few pence but, if gardeners don't do something about it soon, a host of beautiful hardy annuals will disappear from the seed catalogues, leaving us with more and more petunias and French marigolds. Try to grow a few of these before the seedsmen scrap them because of lack of demand. (See the list on p.146 for those most in need of your patronage.)

Adonis aestivalis
Pheasant's Eye

Height 45 cm (18 in)

Final spacing 23 cm (9 in)

Feathery leaves and scarlet, black-eyed flowers.
Sow in spring/autumn.

Agrostemma githago 'Milas'
Corn Cockle

Height 90 cm (3 ft)

Final spacing 23 cm (9 in)

Lovely pink blooms pencilled with darker streaks.
Sow in spring/autumn.
Staking required.

Amaranthus caudatus
Love-lies-bleeding

Height 90 cm (3 ft)

Final spacing 60 cm (2 ft)

Oval green leaves and drooping velvet tassels of crimson or green.
Sow in spring.

Amberboa moschata
(syn. *Centaurea*)
Sweet Sultan

Height 45 cm (18 in)

Final spacing 23 cm (9 in)

Starry cornflower-like blooms of purple, yellow, pink and white.
Sow in spring.

Anchusa capensis 'Blue Angel'

Height 23 cm (9 in)

Final spacing 30 cm (12 in)

Spreading domes of blue forget-me-not flowers.
Sow in spring.

Argemone mexicana
Prickly Poppy

Height 60 cm (2 ft)

Final spacing 30 cm (12 in)

Prickly, thistle foliage; yellow flowers.
Sow in spring.

Asperula orientalis
(syn. *A. azurea*)
Annual Woodruff

Height 30 cm (12 in)

Final spacing 23 cm (9 in)

Pale blue, tubular flowers carried in rounded heads. Tolerates some shade.
Sow in spring.

Atriplex hortensis var. rubra
Orach

Height 1.2 m (4 ft)

Final spacing 45 cm (18 in)

Dock-like flowerheads and leaves of deep maroon.
Sow in spring.

Bassia scoparia f. trichophylla
(syn. *Kochia trichophylla*)
Burning Bush

Height 60 cm (2 ft)

Final spacing 45 cm (18 in)

A bushy plant producing columns of green turning red in autumn.
Sow in spring.

Brassica oleracea
Ornamental Cabbage

Height 30 cm (12 in)

Final spacing 45 cm (18 in)

Cabbages with cream, white or pink hearts. Stunning!
Sow in spring.

Calendula officinalis
Pot Marigold

Height 30 cm (12 in) plus

Final spacing 23 cm (9 in)

Well-known, pungent, cream, yellow or orange daisies.
Sow in spring/autumn.

Centaurea cyanus
Cornflower

Height 90 cm (3 ft)

Final spacing 23 cm (9 in)

Sprays of blue, white or pink fluffy flowerheads are produced atop

slender upright stems.
Sow in spring/autumn.
Staking required.

Chrysanthemum carinatum

Height 60 cm (2 ft)

Final spacing 30 cm (12 in)

Single daisies with distinct bands in orange, yellow, red and white. around the central eye
Sow in spring/autumn.
Staking required.

Clarkia amoena

Dwarf clarkia varieties, Godetia

Height 30 cm (12 in)

Final spacing 15 cm (6 in)

Wide-faced blooms in shades of pink, red and white.
Sow in spring/autumn.

Clarkia unguiculata

(syn. *C. elegans*)

Height 60 cm (2 ft)

Final spacing 23 cm (9 in)

Double varieties are best. They produce rosettes of pink, mauve or crimson blooms.
Sow in spring/autumn.
Staking required.

Consolida ajacis

Annual Delphinium, Larkspur

Height 90 cm (3 ft)

Final spacing 23 cm (9 in)

Tall, slender plants with feathery leaves and long spires of blue, pink, violet or white flowers.
Sow in spring/autumn.
Staking required.

Convolvulus tricolor 'Blue Flash'

Height 15 cm (6 in)

Final spacing 15 cm (6 in)

Blue trumpets with yellow and white centres.
Sow in spring.

Coreopsis tinctoria

Height 30 cm (12 in) plus

Final spacing 23 cm (9 in)

Single yellow flowers with red centres. Very bright.
Sow in spring/autumn.

Crepis rubra

Hawksbeard

Height 45 cm (18 in)

Final spacing 15 cm (6 in)

Endearingly dainty pink 'dandelion' flowers.
Sow in spring/autumn.
Staking Requires staking.

Dimorphotheca sinuata

Star of the Veldt

Height 23 cm (9 in)

Final spacing 15 cm (6 in)

White, yellow or orange daisies.
Sow in spring.

Dracocephalum moldavica

Dragon's Head

Height 60 cm (2 ft)

Final spacing 15 cm (6 in)

Spires of hooded lavender-blue flowers. Aromatic.
Sow in spring.
Staking required.

Echium vulgare

Viper's Bugloss

Height 30 cm (12 in)

Final spacing 23 cm (9 in)

Violet-blue cup-shaped flowers among fluffy buds.
Sow in spring/autumn.

Emilia coccinea (syn. *Cacalia*)

Tassel Flower

Height 45 cm (18 in)

Final spacing 15 cm (6 in)

Fluffy 'composite' flowerheads of burning orange.
Sow in spring.

Eschscholzia californica

Californian Poppy

Height 30 cm (12 in)

Final spacing 15 cm (6 in)

Lacy foliage and poppy flowers of red, pink, yellow, orange or white.
Sow in spring/autumn.

Gilia capitata

Height 60 cm (2 ft)

Final spacing 23 cm (9 in)

Masses of pale blue, five-petalled flowers. Ferny foliage.
Sow in spring/autumn.

Gypsophila elegans

Height 45 cm (18 in)

Final spacing 15 cm (6 in)

Delicate sprays of tiny white or pink flowers.
Sow in spring/autumn.
Staking required.

Helianthus annuus

Sunflower

Height 3 m (10 ft) plus

Final spacing 60 cm (2 ft)

Massive yellow or orange daisies atop gigantic stalks.
Sow in spring.
Staking Requires staking.

Iberis

Candytuft

Height 30 cm (12 in)

Final spacing 10 cm (4 in)

Lance-shaped leaves, and clusters of flowers in white, pink, lilac or carmine.
Sow in spring/autumn.

Ionopsidium acaule

Violet Cress

Height 8 cm (3 in)

A carpeter with plenty of pale lilac flowers. Enjoys a little shade.
Sow in spring/autumn.

Lathyrus odoratus
Sweetpea
Height 1.8 m (6 ft) plus
Final spacing 30 cm (12 in)

Fragrant pea flowers; assorted colours.
Sow in spring/autumn.
Staking Requires staking.

Lavatera trimestris
Mallow
Height 60 cm (2 ft)
Final spacing 30 cm (12 in)

Trumpet-shaped flowers of pink ('Silver Cup') or white ('Mont Blanc') on a bushy plant. Sun or light shade.
Sow in spring.
Staking required.

Layia platyglossa (syn. L. elegans)
Tidy Tips
Height 30 cm (12 in)
Final spacing 15 cm (6 in)

Yellow daisies whose petals are tipped with white.
Sow in spring.

Legousia speculum-veneris
Venus's Looking Glass
Height 30 cm (12 in)
Final spacing 10 cm (4 in)

Violet-blue flowers with white eyes.
Sow in spring/autumn.

Leptosiphon
Stardust
Height 10 cm (4 in)
Final spacing 5 cm (2 in)

Small flowers of orange, red, cream or yellow are produced over needle-like leaves.
Sow in spring.

Limnanthes douglasii
Poached Egg Flower
Height 23 cm (9 in)
Final spacing 10 cm (4 in)

Feathery green leaves and two-toned white and yellow blooms (hence the common name). The flowers are highly attractive to bees.
Sow in spring/autumn.

Linaria maroccana 'Fairy Bouquet'
Toadflax
Height 23 cm (9 in)
Final spacing 10 cm (4 in)

Tiny snapdragon flowers in a bright range of colours.
Sow in spring/autumn.

Linum grandiflorum 'Rubrum'
Scarlet Flax
Height 30 cm (12 in)
Final spacing 10 cm (4 in)

Single wide-faced, bright red flowers.
Sow in spring.

Lobularia maritima
Sweet Alyssum
Height 10 cm (4 in)
Final spacing 15 cm (6 in)

Pink, white or violet scented flowers in dense bunches.
Sow in spring/autumn.

Limnanthes douglasii **is a delightful edging plant.**

Lonas inodora

Height 30 cm (12 in)

Final spacing 15 cm (6 in)

Clusters of bright yellow powder-puffs.

Sow in spring.

Malope trifida

Height 75 cm (2½ ft)

Final spacing 23 cm (9 in)

Single mallow flowers of pink, white or crimson.

Sow in spring.

Matthiola longipetala subsp. bicornis (syn. *M. bicornis*)

Night-scented Stock

Height 23 cm (9 in)

Dingy lilac, strongly perfumed at night.
Sow in spring, mixed with Virginian stocks.

The glowing colours and parasol-shaped leaves of *Tropaeolum majus* (nasturtium) edge this border, with spikes of purple *Nepeta* behind.

Mentzelia lindleyi

(syn. *Bartonia aurea*)

Height 45 cm (18 in)

Final spacing 23 cm (9 in)

Deeply cut leaves and a profusion of scented, pointed-petalled yellow flowers with feathery stamens.

Sow in spring.

Moluccella laevis

Bells of Ireland

Height 90 cm (3 ft)

Final spacing 23 cm (9 in)

Spires of white flowers that fall to reveal large, green, cockle-shaped calyces borne on graceful stems.

Sow in spring.

Nemophila menziesii

Baby Blue Eyes

Height 15 cm (6 in)

Final spacing 8 cm (3 in)

Carpeter with sky-blue flowers centred with white.

Sow in spring/autumn.

Nicandra physalodes

Shoo-fly Plant

Height 75 cm (2½ ft)

Final spacing 30 cm (12 in)

Pale lavender and white flowers; inflated seed cases.

Sow in spring.

Nigella damascena

Love-in-a-mist

Height 45 cm (18 in)

Final spacing 15 cm (6 in)

Feathery foliage and blue, white or pink flowers. The driedseed heads are popular with flower arrangers.

Sow in spring/autumn.

Papaver rhoeas Shirley Series

Height 60 cm (2 ft)

Final spacing 15 cm (6 in)

Lovely poppies of pink, yellow, orange and red. *P. rhoeas* 'Mother of Pearl' has flowers in pastel colours.

Sow in spring/autumn.

Staking required.

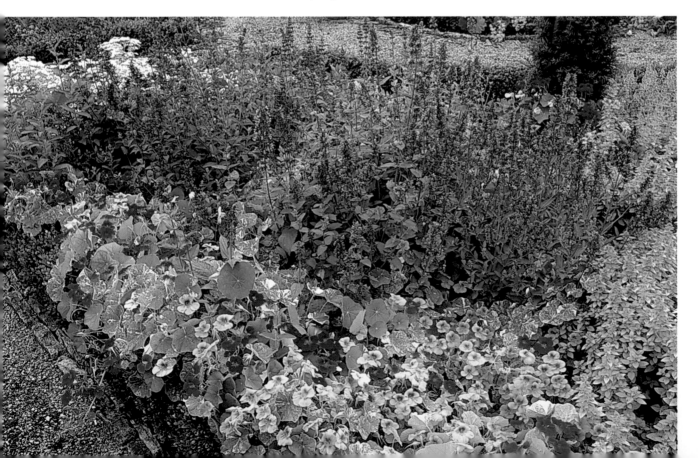

Papaver somniferum 'Paeony Flowered'
Opium poppy

Height 1.2m (4 ft)

Final spacing 23 cm (9 in)

Double, peony-like blooms with frilly-edged petals in a wide range of colours.

Sow in spring/autumn.

Staking required.

Perilla frutescens var. crispa

Height 60 cm (2 ft)

Final spacing 30 cm (12 in)

Deeply cut purple foliage – like a dark coleus.

Sow in spring.

Phacelia campanularia

Height 23 cm (9 in)

Final spacing 8 cm (3 in)

Pure gentian blue bells with bright yellow stamens – indispensable.

Sow in spring/autumn.

Reseda odorata
Mignonette

Height 30 cm (12 in)

Final spacing 10 cm (4 in)

Fluffy rusty-orange flowers; strongly perfumed.

Sow in spring.

Rhodanthe chlorocephala subsp. rosea (syn. Acroclinium rosea)

Height 45 cm (18 in)

Final spacing 23 cm (9 in)

Dainty pink and white 'everlasting' flowers.

Sow in spring.

Staking required.

Rhodanthe manglesii (syn. Helipterum manglesii)

Height 30 cm (12 in)

Final spacing 15 cm (6 in)

Dainty pink 'everlasting' daisies.

Sow in spring.

Use them or lose them

Here is a selection of beautiful hardy annuals that desperately need your patronage: do try to grow some of them before the seedsmen decide to remove them from their catalogues because of lack of demand.

- *Adonis aestivalis*
- *Agrostemma githago* 'Milas'
- *Argemone*
- *Asperula orientalis*
- *Crepis rubra*
- *Dracocephalum moldavica*
- *Echium*
- *Emilia*
- *Gilia*
- *Ionopsidium*
- *Layia elegans*
- *Legousia speculum-veneris*
- *Leptosiphon*
- *Limnanthes*
- *Linaria maroccana* 'Fairy Bouquet'
- *Linum grandiflorum* 'Rubrum'
- *Lonas inodora*
- *Malope*
- *Mentzelia*
- *Nemophila*
- *Nicandra*
- *Phacelia campanularia*
- *Reseda*
- *Saponaria vaccaria*
- *Silene coeli-rosa* 'Blue Angel'

Rudbeckia hirta
Coneflower

Height 60 cm (2 ft)

Final spacing 15 cm (6 in)

Orange ('Marmalade') or mahogany ('Rustic Dwarf') daisies.

Sow in spring.

Salvia viridis
Clary

Height 45 cm (18 in)

Final spacing 15 cm (6 in)

Tall spires of pink, white or blue bracts.

Sow in spring/autumn.

Saponaria vaccaria 'Pink Beauty'

Height 60 cm (2 ft)

Final spacing 15 cm (6 in)

Plenty of dainty pink flowers.

Sow in spring/autumn.

Staking required.

Silene coeli-rosa 'Blue Angel'
(syn. *Agrostemma, Lychnis, Viscaria*)

Height 30 cm (12 in)

Final spacing 10 cm (4 in)

This is worth growing, despite the botanists trying to give it a personality disorder by calling it all the names under the sun. Five-petalled lavender-blue flowers. Thrives in sun or partial shade.

Sow in spring.

Tropaeolum majus
Nasturtium

Height 30 cm (12 in)

Final spacing 30 cm (12 in)

Parasol-shaped leaves and red, orange or yellow flowers that will grow in poor but free-draining soil.

Sow in spring.

Tropaeolum peregrinum
Canary Creeper

Climber

Fingered green leaves and frilly yellow flowers.

Sow in spring.

Staking required.

Xeranthemum annuum

Height 60 cm (2 ft)

Final spacing 15 cm (6 in)

'Everlasting' daisy flowers of pink, yellow and white.

Sow in spring.

Staking required.

HALF-HARDY ANNUALS

These slightly tender plants are available in greater variety than you'd think. Steer yourself away from the commoner types to those that are less frequently planted. Generally, those varieties described as F1 hybrids are more expensive than all others, but they usually offer superb value for money, producing high quality and uniform plants. I have indicated which plants can be sown outdoors and, again, be prepared to look under all the names I have listed to find seeds.

Ageratum houstonianum
Floss Flower

| Height 15-23 cm (6-9 in) |
| Spacing 15 cm (6 in) |

Hairy green leaves topped with fluffy lavender-blue or white pom-poms.

Amaranthus tricolor
'Illumination'

| Height 75 cm (2½ ft) |
| Spacing 45 cm (18 in) |

Brilliant leaves marked red, bronze, yellow and green.

Anagallis 'Coerulea'

| Height 15 cm (6 in) |
| Spacing 15 cm (6 in) |

True blue, large pimpernel flowers over green domes of foliage.
Sowing Can be sown outdoors.

Antirrhinum majus
Snapdragon

| Height 15-90 cm (6 in-3 ft) |
| Spacing 23 cm (9 in) |

Lipped, tubular flowers of every hue except blue or green.

Arctotis
African Daisy

| Height 45 cm (18 in) |
| Spacing 23 cm (9 in) |

Vibrant daisies of red, orange, yellow, pink or white.

Sow these outdoors

- *Anagallis* 'Coerulea'
- *Aster*
- *Brachyscome*
- *Bracteantha*
- *Cleome spinosa*
- *Dorotheanthus*
- *Gourd*
- *Limonium*
- *Matthiola*
- *Mimulus*
- *Nolana* 'Lavender Gown'
- *Phlox drummondii*
- *Portulaca*

Aster

| Height 30-45 cm (18 in) |
| Spacing 23 cm (9 in) |

Double or single daisies in a wide range of colours.
Sowing Can be sown outdoors.

Begonia semperflorens

| Height 15 cm (6 in) |
| Spacing 15 cm (6 in) |

Shiny leaves of green or brown; red, pink or white flowers.

The fluffy pink blooms of *Ageratum houstonianum* 'Bavaria' flower freely throughout the summer.

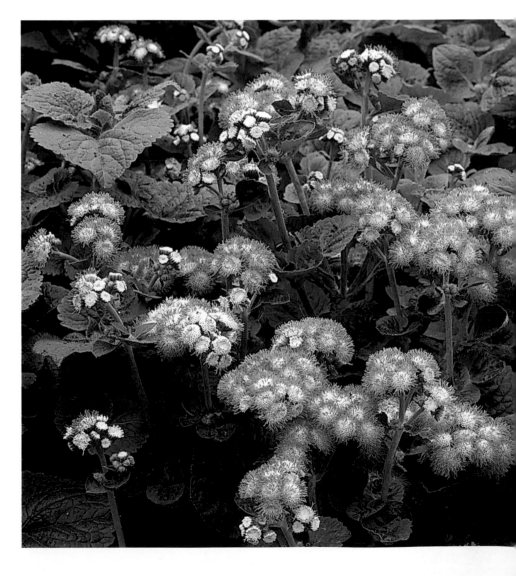

Brachyscome iberidifolia
Swan River Daisy
Height 15 cm (6 in)
Spacing 10 cm (4 in)

Finely cut leaves and blue or white daisy flowers. Tolerates a certain amount of drought.
Sowing Can be sown outdoors.

Bracteantha (syn. *Helichrysum*)
Strawflower
Height 45 cm (18 in)
Spacing 15 cm (6 in)

'Everlasting' flowers of orange, yellow, red and white. There are many named varieties of varying heights.
Sowing Can be sown outdoors.

The single, dahlia-like flowers of *Cosmos* seem to float above the delicate ferny foliage.

Calandrinia umbellata
Rock Purslane
Height 15 cm (6 in)
Spacing 15 cm (6 in)

Neat tufts of hairy foliage topped with rich crimson-magenta cupped flowers.

Calceolaria integrifolia 'Sunshine'
Height 23 cm (9 in)
Spacing 23 cm (9 in)

Bright yellow pouch-like flowers over green leaves.

Centaurea cineraria
(syn. *C. gymnocarpa*)
Height 45 cm (18 in)
Spacing 30 cm (12 in)

Finely cut grey leaves; an exceptional foliage plant.

Cleome spinosa
Spider Flower
Height 75 cm (2½ ft)
Spacing 30 cm (12 in)

Spidery flowers of pink or white on thorny, statuesque plants.
Sowing Can be sown outdoors.

Cosmos bipinnatus
Cosmea
Height 60-90 cm (2-3 ft)
Spacing 23 cm (9 in)

Single 'dahlia' flowers of red, yellow, orange, pink or white.

Dahlia
Height 30 cm-1.2 m (12 in-4 ft)
Spacing 30 cm (12 in)

Fleshy leaves and double or single mixed flowers. 'Redskin' is 45 cm (18 in) tall. It has flowers in mixed colours over bronze-purple foliage.

Delphinium grandiflorum 'Blue Butterfly'
Height 45 cm (18 in)
Spacing 30 cm (12 in)

Tall spires of rich blue flowers.

Dianthus caryophyllus
Height 45 cm (18 in)
Spacing 15 cm (6 in)

'Annual' carnations of mixed colours. The Lillipot Series is an F1 hybrid mixture; pricey but very showy. Height 20-25 cm (8-10 in); spacing 23 cm (9 in).

Dianthus chinensis Heddewigii Group
Pink
Height 15-30 cm (6-12 in)
Spacing 15 cm (6 in)

Brilliant annual pinks of red, pink, white and bi-coloured flowers; there are also some superb F1 hybrids: try 'Queen's Court'.

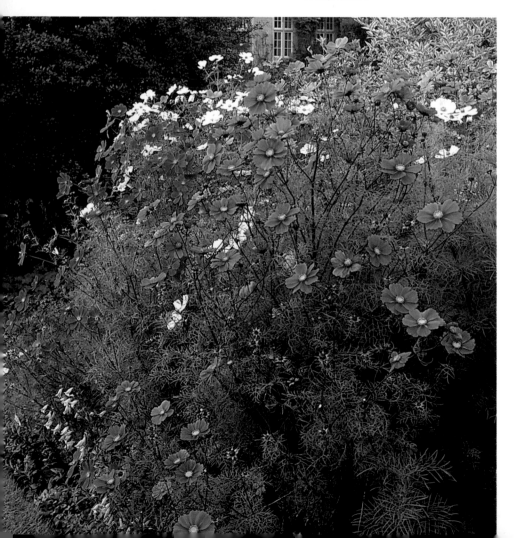

Dorotheanthus (syn. Mesembryanthemum)
Livingstone Daisy

Height 8 cm (3 in)

Spacing 15 cm (6 in)

Orange, pink or yellow daisy flowers.
Sowing Can be sown outdoors.

Gaillardia
Blanket Flower

Height 30-60 cm (12 in-2 ft)

Spacing 23 cm (9 in)

Double or single daisies of orange, red and yellow.

Gazania

Height 30 cm (12 in)

Spacing 15 cm (6 in)

Single starry daisies often bi-coloured in red, orange and yellow. Give it sun.

Gourd

Climber

Spacing 30 cm (12 in)

Cucumber-like vine with decorative fruits of orange, yellow and green.
Sowing Can be sown outdoors.

Heliotropium arborescens
Cherry Pie, Heliotrope

Height 45 cm (18 in)

Spacing 30 cm (12 in)

Lilac-purple scented flower clusters.

Impatiens
Busy Lizzie

Height 23 cm (9 in)

Spacing 23 cm (9 in)

Fleshy leaves and stems; red, white, orange or magenta flowers.

Ipomoea
Morning Glory

Climber

Spacing 30 cm (12 in)

Trumpets of sky-blue or carmine.

Limonium sinuatum
Statice, Sea Lavender

Height 45 cm (18 in)

Spacing 23 cm (9 in)

Branched sprays of pink, blue, white or yellow 'everlasting' flowers.

Lobelia

Height 10 cm (4 in)

Spacing 10 cm (4 in)

Lipped flowers of blue, white or carmine over fresh green leaves. Also available as a trailer for hanging baskets or windowboxes.

Matthiola incana Ten Week Stock
Gilly flower, Stocks

Height 30 cm (12 in)

Spacing 23 cm (9 in)

Ten Week Stock produces columns of fragrant magenta, purple, yellow, pink or white double flowers. Other types include Cinderella Series which is 20-25 cm (8-10 in) high.
Sowing Can be sown outdoors.

Mimulus
Monkey Flower

Height 30 cm (12 in)

Spacing 15 cm (6 in)

Red, orange or yellow trumpets, often spotted. Tolerates a little shade.
SOWING Can be sown outdoors.

Mirabilis jalapa
Four o'clock Plant

Height 45 cm (18 in)

Spacing 30 cm (12 in)

Scented red, yellow or white trumpets open in late afternoon.

Nemesia

Height 23 cm (9 in)

Spacing 23 cm (9 in)

Large-lipped flowers of red, yellow, orange or white.

Nicotiana
Tobacco Plant

Height 30-75 cm (12 in-2½ ft)

Spacing 23 cm (9 in)

Fragrant starry flowers of red, yellow, green or white.

Nolana 'Lavender Gown'

Height 15 cm (6 in)

Spacing 15 cm (6 in)

Mounds of lavender-blue flowers centred with white and yellow.
Sowing Can be sown outdoors.

Penstemon

Height 60 cm (2 ft)

Spacing 23 cm (9 in)

Spires of colourful foxglove flowers.

Petunia

Height 23 cm (9 in)

Spacing 23 cm (9 in)

Huge trumpets, some fully double, in assorted colours; some are striped.

Phlox drummondii

Height 15-30 cm (6-12 in)

Spacing 15 cm (6 in)

Dense heads of 'primula' flowers in assorted colours.
Sowing Can be sown outdoors.

Portulaca grandiflora
Purslane

Height 15 cm (6 in)

Spacing 15 cm (6 in)

Succulent leaves and double or single 'poppy' flowers in mixed colours. Good for a dry, sunny bank.
Sowing Can be sown outdoors.

Ricinus communis
Castor Oil Palm

Height 90 cm (3 ft)

Spacing 90 cm (3 ft)

This is really a shrub and it produces

large hand-shaped leaves of dark green or bronze.

Salpiglossis sinuata
Painted Tongue
Height 60 cm (2 ft)
Spacing 23 cm (9 in)

Trumpets of mixed colours contrastingly veined; stunning.

Salvia splendens
Height 30 cm (12 in)
Spacing 30 cm (12 in)

'Blaze of Fire' has green leaves and scarlet flower spikes. Recent breeding has produced the Phoenix Series, Salsa Series and Sizzler Series, all in a wide range of colours. 'Blaze of Fire' is still one of the best though.

Sanvitalia procumbens
Height 15 cm (6 in)
Spacing 23 cm (9 in)

Black-eyed, starry yellow daisies on compact plants.

Scablosa
Pincushion Flower, Scabious
Height 60 cm (2 ft)
Spacing 23 cm (9 in)

Dainty double flowers of pink, crimson, white or lavender. Thrives best in full sun.
Sowing Can be sown outdoors.

Senecio cineraria
Dusty Miller
Height 30 cm (12 in)
Spacing 30 cm (12 in)

'Cirrus' has densely felted foliage; 'Silver Dust' has fine filigree leaves.

Tagetes hybrids
African, Afro-French and French Marigolds
Various heights

African marigolds have double flowers of orange or yellow; they are the pompom-type blooms. To 60 cm (2 ft) high; space them 30 cm (12 in) apart. Afro-French and French marigolds are usually less pompom-like. Afro-French marigolds are 45 cm (18 in) high and need to be spaced at 23 cm (9 in). They are very floriferous. 'Nell Gwynn' is one of the best.

French marigolds are neat aromatic plants with small double blooms of orange and yellow. They vary between 10 and 30 cm (4-12 in) and need to be spaced at 15-23 cm (6-9 in).

Tanacetum parthenium 'Golden Ball' (syn. *Matricaria*)
Feverfew
Height 30 cm (12 in)
Spacing 30 cm (12 in)

Rounded plants covered in yellow 'button' flowers

Tanacetum parthenium 'Golden Moss' (syn. *Pyrethrum*)
Height 10 cm (4 in)
Spacing 15 cm (6 in)

Fluffy acid-yellow leaves; yellow and white daisies.

Tithonia rotundifolia
Height 1.2 m (4 ft)
Spacing 45 cm (18 in)

Single bright orange 'dahlia' flowers on tall stems.

Ursinia
Height 30 cm (12 in)
Spacing 23 cm (9 in)

Dazzling daisies of orange, yellow or red.

Verbena
Vervain
Height 23 cm (9 in)
Spacing 23 cm (9 in)

Clustered flowerheads of red, violet, pink or white.

Zinnia
Height 30-60 cm (12 in-2 ft)
Spacing 23 cm (9 in)

Double round-petalled flowers in mixed colours – even green!

BIENNIALS

Do remember that all these plants are sown one year to grow and flower the next. A great many of the plants grown as biennials are truly perennials and I have indicated in the entries where this is the case: if you like you can leave these to grow on for another year or so.

Bellis perennis
Double Daisy
Height 15 cm (6 in)
Final spacing 15 cm (6 in)

Neat double daisies with white, pink or crimson pompoms. True perennial.
Sow in June.

Campanula medium
Canterbury Bell
Height 75 cm (2½ ft)
Final spacing 23 cm (9 in)

Thick spires of pink, white or lavender bellflowers.
Sow in June.

Dianthus barbatus
Sweet William
Height 45 cm (18 in)
Final spacing 23 cm (9 in)

Clustered heads of crimson, pink or white flowers, often bi-coloured. Some are sweetly scented. True perennial.
Sow in June.

Digitalis
Foxglove
Height 90 cm-1.5 m (3-5 ft)
Final spacing 30 cm (12 in)

Tall spires of pink, mauve, yellow or white bells. Some are perennial.
Sow in May.

Dipsacus fullonum
Fuller's Teasel

Height 2.4 m (8 ft)	
Final spacing 60 cm (2 ft)	

Towering flowerheads with spiny blooms that dry well.
Sow in May.

Erysimum x *allionii*
(syn. *Cheiranthus*)
Siberian Wallflower

Height 30 cm (12 in)	
Final spacing 30 cm (12 in)	

Orange-yellow flowers. True perennial.
Sow in June.

Erysimum cheiri (syn. *Cheiranthus*)
Wallflower

Height 30-45 cm (12-18 in)	
Final spacing 30 cm (12 in)	

Gloriously scented in red, yellow, pink, orange and mauve. Best massed in single colours. True perennial.
Sow in May.

Lunaria annua
Honesty

Height 60 cm (2 ft)	
Final spacing 23 cm (9 in)	

Mauve flowers followed by translucent 'pennies' that dry well.
Sow in June.

Matthiola incana **Brompton Stock**

Height 45 cm (18 in)	
Final spacing 23 cm (9 in)	

Columns of mauve, pink, magenta, violet or white flowers. True perennial.
Sow in June.

Myosotis sylvatica
Forget-me-not

Height 30 cm (12 in)	
Final spacing 15 cm (6 in)	

Sprays of pale blue, pink or white.
Sow in June.

Papaver nudicaule
Iceland Poppy

Height 75 cm (2½ ft)	
Final spacing 23 cm (9 in)	

Single, papery blooms of pink, orange, yellow and white. True perennial.
Sow in May.

Penstemon

Height 30-60 cm (12 in-2 ft)	
Final spacing 23 cm (9 in)	

Spires of foxglove flowers in mixed colours. True perennial.
Sow in May.

Verbascum
Mullein

Height 1.2-1.8 m (4-6 ft)	
Final spacing 60 cm (2 ft)	

Tall spires of yellow, orange or white

White *Antirrhimum* and *Digitalis* (foxglove), yellow *Achillea*, and creamy white Siberian wallflower blend together in this gravel garden.

flowers. Some species are perennial, others true biennials.
Sow in May.

Viola x *wittrockiana* varieties
Pansy

Height 15-23 cm (6-9 in)	
Final spacing 15 cm (6 in)	

Wide-faced blooms in assorted colours, some in single colours, others with strong or subtle central markings. You are spoilt for choice with these pretty flowers. Especially good are the Universal strains, which flower in winter as well as spring and summer. Tolerates some shade. True perennial.

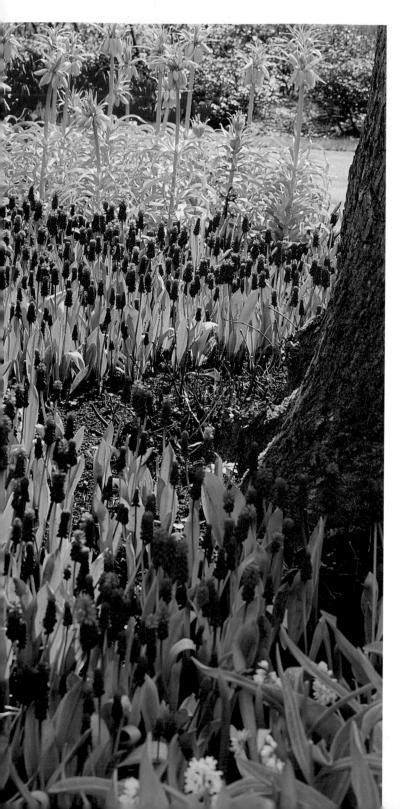

CHAPTER 11 Garden bulbs

Unmatched for their ability to provide year-round colour – not just in spring – bulbs are also obliging enough to reproduce themselves with very little help from us

Every bulb is a do-it-yourself kit. Packed inside it are roots, shoots, leaves and flowers – all you have to do is add water and stand well back... well, almost.

WHAT ARE 'BULBS'?

First let's clear up the confusion that exists between bulbs, corms, tubers and rhizomes. I've included plants that arise from all four of these 'storage organs', so it's only fair to tell you how they differ. Basically they are all designed for food storage: like a camel's hump, they keep the plant alive during its dormant season, while it's resting and not growing.
Bulbs (e.g. daffodil) are condensed shoots or buds. They have a flat bottom called the base-plate, which is really the stem. The fat scales that arise from this are modified leaves and, with any luck, they shield a central flower bud. The roots emerge from the base-plate as soon as moisture is placed within their reach.
Corms (e.g. crocus) are modified stems. Roots appear from the base, and buds and shoots from the tip.
Tubers may be swollen stems, as in the case of the potato, or swollen roots, as in the case of the dahlia. The potato shows it's a stem because buds appear all over it; they only appear at the top of a dahlia tuber.
Rhizomes (e.g. large-flowered border iris) are underground stems that usually grow horizontally, just below the surface of the soil.

CHOOSING GARDEN BULBS

Most folk buy their bulbs from chain stores. There's nothing wrong with this provided the bulbs are not old stock. However, you'll have a much wider choice if you order from a specialist catalogue. If you're buying bulbs over the counter, check that they are firm and a good size. One or two types of bulb, such as snowdrops, snowflakes and cyclamen, are best bought 'in the green' – as growing plants. They resent even slight desiccation and will receive less of a check if they are planted when in leaf. Sadly they are usually more pricey when sold like this, and you may think it's worth

Types of bulbous plants

BULB

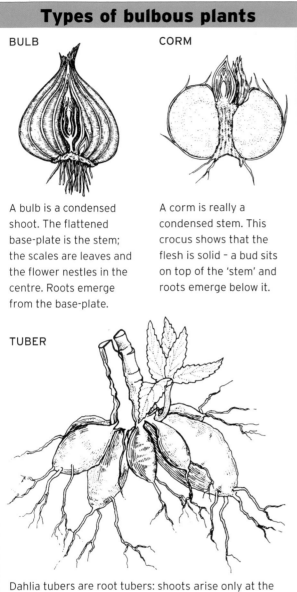

A bulb is a condensed shoot. The flattened base-plate is the stem; the scales are leaves and the flower nestles in the centre. Roots emerge from the base-plate.

CORM

A corm is really a condensed stem. This crocus shows that the flesh is solid – a bud sits on top of the 'stem' and roots emerge below it.

TUBER

Dahlia tubers are root tubers: shoots arise only at the top, so it's vital that a bud or shoot is attached to any parts of the tuber removed for propagation.

RHIZOME

A rhizome is a flattened stem that grows on or just below the surface of the soil, such as this flag iris.

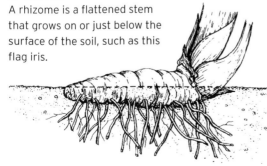

risking the loss of a few dry bulbs if the prices are markedly cheaper.

WHERE TO PLANT BULBS

The most obvious place to plant bulbs is in the flower border among herbaceous plants and shrubs. This is undoubtedly the best home for them in small gardens, because bulbs that are to remain in the garden undisturbed must be allowed to make plenty of foliage for at least six weeks after the flowers have faded. During this period they will look untidy, but this is masked to some extent by the growth of border plants and shrubs. If you chop the foliage off instantly after flowering, you're stopping the plants from building up their food reserves. Tie the leaves with elastic bands or string and you're still impeding feeding, for they need light in order to manufacture food. No: take a firm hold on your tidy-mindedness and let the bulbs go mad for six weeks, then, in most cases, you can chop off the leaves. Mind you, it's a good idea to mark the site they occupy to prevent accidents with a hoe or fork.

Most bulbs are happy left in the soil, in which case they are said to be 'naturalized'; those that are not, and which need to be dried off and ripened, can be dug up as soon as the flowers fade and brought into a dry shed or garage. As soon as their foliage dies off, they can be cleaned up and stored in a cool, dry, dark, frostproof place until planting time the following year. I've indicated which bulbs need this treatment under the individual entries in the A–Z section, so you need worry no more about it here.

Naturalizing bulbs in grass

Naturalizing bulbs in grass (planting them in haphazard formations and letting them grow on undisturbed) is an attractive proposition, but one I would not recommend in small gardens. After they've flowered the grass around them, along with their foliage, must remain uncut for six weeks, and the untidiness and restriction of movement on the lawn may be something you cannot cope with. Where you have space to let a little of your lawn run riot for a few weeks in spring, nothing looks nicer and more promising of a flower-filled summer to come.

Growing bulbs in beds and borders

Spring-flowering bulbs planted in beds with other temporary occupants, such as wallflowers, forget-me-nots, dwarf double daisies and polyanthuses, are always lifted after flowering so that the bed can be made ready for its summer occupants. I always find this a rather tiresome exercise and would rather fit these bulbs into pockets in a mixed border where they can be quickly replaced after flowering without having to clear the entire bed.

Container-grown bulbs

Pot-grown bulbs should be every gardener's joy; they can be fitted into the smallest garden or even onto a windowsill. The time at which the bulbs are potted up will depend on their time of flowering, but don't be conned into thinking that all pot-grown bulbs must be planted in bulb fibre. They'll usually do far better in John Innes No. 1 potting compost, preferably – but not essentially – with a little sharp sand added.

True bulb fibre (a mixture of peat, charcoal and crushed oyster shell) was originally developed for use in containers with no drainage holes, such as the bowls in which most folk plant hyacinths. The charcoal and oyster shell kept the mixture 'sweet' in the face of bad drainage. Today most bulb fibres are nothing more than

peat plus a few nutrients; they do nothing to ameliorate the conditions prevalent in a holeless bowl and seem to have become simply a moneymaking proposition for enterprising compost merchants. Spurn them in favour of John Innes, which will feed your bulbs and keep them in good condition, allowing them to be planted out in the garden after blooming to give pleasure in future years.

PLANTING BULBS IN CONTAINERS

When you plant large bulbs in containers, leave their 'noses' just showing through the surface of the compost. Smaller bulbs and corms, such as crocuses, can be planted just below the surface. There's a neat trick you can try with daffodils and narcissi (daffodil, by the way, is simply the common name for any narcissus with a large trumpet). Spread 5 cm (2 in) of compost in the bottom of the pot, cram in a layer of bulbs, add a little compost and then cram in a second layer before topping up with compost, leaving the noses of the top layer showing. You'll get twice as many flowers from your pot than if you use a single layer of bulbs.

To get as many daffodils as possible from one pot, plant a double layer of bulbs, positioning the upper layer so that the shoots below can squeeze past those above. A few crocks placed in the bottom of the container will improve drainage.

Choosing bulbs for your garden

Different bulbs are suited to different situations, though the majority will grow well in ordinary well-drained soil. Almost all bulbs will rot in soggy earth, so it's always worth improving matters with grit, sharp sand and organic enrichment such as leaf mould or peat; too much manure can cause leafy growth at the expense of flowers.

TO NATURALIZE IN GRASS
- *Crocus*
- *Fritillaria meleagris*
- *Galanthus*
- *Narcissus*
- *Scilla*

FOR ROCK GARDENS
- *Allium* (dwarf types)
- *Anemone*
- *Crocus*
- *Cyclamen*
- *Eranthis*
- *Erythronium*
- *Galanthus*
- *Iris* (dwarf types)
- *Leucojum autumnale*
- *Muscari*
- *Narcissus* (dwarf types)
- *Tulipa* (dwarf types)

FOR BEDDING SCHEMES
- *Crocus*
- *Dahlia*
- *Gladiolus*
- *Hyacinthus*
- *Muscari*
- *Narcissus*
- *Tulipa*

FOR GENTLE SHADE
- *Allium moly*
- *Anemone blanda*
- *Anemone nemorosa*
- *Colchicum*
- *Cyclamen*
- *Eranthis*
- *Erythronium*
- *Fritillaria meleagris*
- *Leucojum*
- *Scilla*

Bulbs for containers

- *Anemone* (some)
- *Chionodoxa*
- *Crocus*
- *Galtonia*
- *Hyacinthus*
- *Iris* (dwarf types)
- *Lilium*
- *Muscari*
- *Narcissus*
- *Nerine*
- *Ornithogalum*
- *Tulipa*

In general, pots with drainage holes are always more satisfactory than bowls without them, unless you take exceptional care not to overwater.

Temperature and light

All bulbs appreciate eight weeks of cool temperatures and darkness after potting. You can stand them outdoors and cover them with peat and ashes if you like (it's what the old gardeners used to recommend), but it's far easier to keep them in a cellar or coal shed, or to stand them outdoors and cover them with black polythene. Whatever you do, don't put them in the airing cupboard: your washing will get dirty and your bulbs won't enjoy the heat. They need cool conditions for the first two months so that they can establish their root system; only then can they take more heat, and this should be applied very gradually; bring them first into a cool room (if you're flowering them indoors) and then into a warmer one if you must. Most will bloom better and last longer in well-lit but cool rooms.

Bulbs grown in tubs, pots and windowboxes outdoors need none of this coddling; simply treat the bulbs as though they were being planted in the ground, but use John Innes No. 2 potting compost plus a little sharp river sand for extra drainage.

PLANTING BULBS OUTDOORS

All outdoor bulbs are best planted with a trowel. As a general rule they should be covered with soil to twice their depth. That is, if a bulb measures 5 cm (2 in) from tip to toe it should be planted in a hole 15 cm (6 in) deep.

Bulb-planting tools that take out a core of soil are useful for planting large numbers of bulbs in grass, but they are hell to use effectively on stony soil. If you do use one, take out all your holes first, push your bulbs in and then replace the divots.

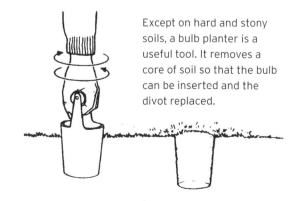

Except on hard and stony soils, a bulb planter is a useful tool. It removes a core of soil so that the bulb can be inserted and the divot replaced.

Save time when planting bulbs in grass by lifting a flap of turf. With a trowel, plant the bulbs in the soil below, then replace the turf and firm it into place.

I find it easier when naturalizing bulbs in grass to lift up a a small flap of turf, plant the bulbs underneath it, using a trowel, then replace the flap and firm it into place.

Never plant bulbs too shallowly. It's one of the greatest causes of failure. Shallow-planted bulbs will often refuse to flower well because they are short of water and nutrients. Seldom can a bulb be planted too deeply – unless you're daft enough to plant a tiny snowdrop 30 cm (12 in) under.

If you're planting bulbs among spring bedding plants, put the plants in first and the bulbs in afterwards – that way they won't be disturbed by the trowel.

IMPROVE FLOWERING BY FEEDING

People are as rotten to their bulbs as they are to their lawns: they often completely forget about feeding. You'll have better flowers each year if you treat your bulbs to a square meal of general fertilizer as the flowers fade. A light dusting of blood, bone and fishmeal will do them nicely. Lack of food will often cause 'blindness' (failure to flower), especially in bulbs that grow among grass, which robs them of food anyway; but dry springs can also be responsible for the failure of flower formation. If you can find the time, water your spring-flowering bulbs well during a parched April and May – you might notice a difference the following year.

PROPAGATION OF BULBS

Almost all bulbs are obliging enough to reproduce themselves without any help from us, but I have included a few tips on encouraging them to increase in Chapter 2 Propagation.

A-Z of **garden bulbs**

THIS SECTION INCLUDES THE bulbs, corms, tubers and rhizomes that are grown in the garden or in containers outdoors – although some of them can be brought indoors during their flowering season.

Some bulbous plants are so commonly grown as border plants that I have sneaked them into that chapter: if the plant you seek is not here, check to see if it is included in Chapter 9 Border Plants.

Where a specific planting depth is given for a bulb, it refers to the depth of the hole that should be taken out to plant the bulb in, not to the distance from the tip of the bulb to the soil surface.

Allium
Ornamental Onion

Most of these don't smell too strongly of onions unless they're bruised, so don't be put off. They are a tremendously varied and valuable bunch of plants, which can be relied on to bring colour to the garden from spring to autumn. They vary in stature from the very small to around head height, and many have attractive seedheads. I can mention just a few – the ones I'd grow in preference to all others. Some species (none of those that are mentioned here) can become annoying weeds.
A. bulgaricum (now *Nectaroscordum siculum* subsp. *dioscoridis*): 1–1.2 m (3–4 ft); towering heads of drooping creamy flowers striped with green and tinted purple; superb seedheads like

The huge mauve-pink flowerheads of *Allium cristophii* tower above the foxglove-like spires of *Penstemon glaber* and the woolly grey leaves of *Stachys byzantina* in this border.

Bavarian castles; summer flowering; likes sun and well-drained soil.
A. cristophii (syn. *A. albopilosum*): 45 cm (18 in); football-sized flowerheads composed of glistening, mauve-pink metallic stars; dries strawy brown; summer flowering; loves sun.
A. giganteum: 2 m (6 ft); lilac-purple ball-shaped flowerheads on top of its tall stems in early summer; likes sun or very gentle shade.
A. karataviense: 20 cm (8 in); remarkable as its spherical flowerheads of dirty pink nestle between a pair of very broad grey-green leaves in late spring or early summer; likes sun and good drainage.
A. moly: 30 cm (12 in); clusters of starry yellow flowers; early summer flowering; naturalizes well in sun or light shade.
A. oreophilum (syn. *A. ostrowskianum*): 15 cm (6 in); cheap and easy to find; rosy pink flower clusters in early to mid-summer; prefers well-drained soil and sun.
Plant in autumn or as soon as bulbs become available; cover all bulbs to twice their depth. Rich soil preferred.
Suitable for naturalizing, rock gardens (dwarf species), shade (as indicated); most adore sun.
Propagate by division of bulbs in summer.

Amaryllis belladonna
Belladonna Lily

This is the only true amaryllis (the 'amaryllis' with the massive, exotic blooms that your granny grows on her windowsill every year is really called *Hippeastrum*) and it's a bulb to treasure. It produces green, strap-shaped leaves and, once it is happy, a flowerhead carrying several large,

pink, white-flushed flowers shaped like gigantic stars. It grows to about 60 cm (2 ft) high and flowers in autumn. There are darker-flowered forms and a good white. Only in a sun-baked border will it thrive and become reliably perennial. In colder counties it may be killed in severe winters, and it will not tolerate poorly drained soil. Leave clumps undisturbed for many years for best results. Good against south- and west-facing walls. Feed with blood, bone and fishmeal in late summer and cover with dry straw or bracken in winter.

Plant in summer 15 cm (6 in) deep and 30 cm (12 in) apart. The leaves die down altogether in summer.

Propagate by division of established clumps in summer.

Anemone
Windflower

Little charmers of small stature but considerable impact. The Mothering Sunday bunches of anemones are generally the De Caen Group (single) and St Brigid Group (double) varieties of *A. coronaria* with flowers of red, pink, white, mauve and lavender-blue. They grow to around 30 cm (12 in) high and will bloom in spring (if planted in October), summer (if planted in April), or late summer and autumn (if planted in June). Give them a well-drained soil that has been laced with a little garden compost.

A. blanda, 10 cm (4 in), is my own favourite. It has starry wood-anemone flowers of white, pink, blue or, in the variety 'Radar', rich magenta. This last-named is iniquitously expensive; the others are very cheap. All flower in early spring and will multiply into large colonies if left alone in any decent soil; they can even be planted in grass.

A. nemorosa, 10 cm (4 in), is our native wood anemone with finely cut leaves and white flowers flushed mauve on the outside. It has a double form and a glorious lavender-blue variety called 'Robinsoniana'; both flower in spring and enjoy a peaty, leafy soil.

Plant both these species in autumn, 8 cm (3 in) deep.

Suitable for naturalizing in sun or gentle shade, or for growing in pots, but keep them cool. Good in rock gardens and under shrubs and trees, but avoid really dry soils.

Propagate by division of the tubers after flowering.

Camassia
Quamash

Variable but always beautiful bulbs with starry flowers in tapering spires. *C. cusickii*, 75 cm (2½ ft) high, is usually pale blue, and *C. quamash* (syn. *C. esculenta*), 45 cm (18 in) high, is usually darker blue, but both vary considerably in colour depending on source of supply. Both flower in summer and both deserve to be more popular.

Plant in autumn, 15 cm (6 in) deep and as much apart.

Suitable for naturalizing in beds and borders where they can be left undisturbed. They enjoy full sun and a moisture-retentive soil with a bit of body. They resent drought.

Propagate by sowing seeds outdoors in spring (they take three or four years to come to flowering size), or by division in autumn, though increase is slow.

Chionodoxa forbesii
Glory of the Snow

Grows without any fuss at all. It makes 15 cm (6 in) high arching stems of starry blue and white flowers in spring, and produces tufts of glossy green leaves.

Plant in autumn, 8 cm (3 in) deep.

Suitable for naturalizing in beds and borders, for rock gardens and for planting in pots, tubs and window boxes. They enjoy sun or gentle shade and any reasonable soil.

Propagate by division after flowering.

Colchicum
Meadow Saffron, Naked Ladies, Autumn Crocus

It's a shame about the third inaccurate common name. If ever you want to know whether or not you've got a colchicum or a true autumn-flowering crocus, count the stamens: crocuses have three (and a shorter name); colchicums have six (and a longer name). Some species flower in spring, but the most popular are the autumn bloomers such as *C. autumnale*, 15 cm (6 in), with its dainty crocus-shaped flowers of lilac-pink. *C. speciosum*, 23 cm (9 in), is better still and a good deal beefier – absolutely breathtaking in flower. It has various varieties with lighter and darker blooms. There is also a glorious double called

'Waterlily', which is a warm pink. Some species, such as *C. aggripinum*, have blooms that carry a chequered pattern (the experts refer to them as 'tessellated'), and the species that flower in winter and spring, including a rare yellow one, should be fitted in where there is room. Remember that all have vast leaves like huge leeks that push up after the flowers. If the foliage can be masked by shrubs and border plants, so much the better.

Plant in late summer 15 cm (6 in) deep and as much apart; plant spring-flowering kinds in autumn.

Suitable for naturalizing in beds and borders, under trees and among shrubs. They enjoy a rich, leafy soil, preferably organically mulched, which is not likely to become baked in summer. Bulbs of *C. autumnale* can be stood, quite dry, on a windowsill in late summer where they will flower with no attention whatsoever. Plant them out afterwards.

Propagate by seeds sown outdoors in summer (allow three to four years for flowering) or by division in summer. Most folk simply buy in more bulbs.

Crocus

I hardly know where to begin with the crocuses, they are such a delightfully varied bunch. I've never been a fan of the fat Dutch hybrids, but I rave over the smaller varieties of such species as *C. chrysanthus*, 5–8 cm (2–3 in), that flower in spring. Try the warm yellow 'E. A. Bowles', or 'Ladykiller' with white petals flushed purple on the undersides. *C. ancyrensis*, 8 cm (3 in), is a good orange-yellow that can be in flower in winter in pots or outdoors. By far the best naturalizer is *C. tommasinianus*, 8 cm (3 in), whose amethyst-purple buds spear the soil in late winter before opening in the sunshine like floral stars. There are several species that flower in autumn – some in September and some in October and November – and it's time more folk knew about them:

C. kotschyanus (syn. *C. zonatus*), 10 cm (4 in), pale lilac; *C. niveus*, 10 cm (4 in), white with red stigmas; *C. nudiflorus*, 15 cm (6 in), deep violet-purple; *C. speciosus*, 10 cm (4 in), pale mauve: all are good outdoors or in pots.

Plant or pot up in late summer (for autumn-flowering kinds) or autumn (for spring-flowering kinds). Plant 5 cm (2 in) deep and 8 cm (3 in) apart.

Suitable for naturalizing in grass or beds and borders, even under trees and shrubs. Good in the rock garden and in containers. If you plan to bring the containers indoors when the crocuses are in flower, try to keep them cool. In the garden leave the bulbs undisturbed to multiply on their own. All will tolerate any ordinary, well-drained soil.

Propagate by seed if you've the patience: it will be two or three years before the progeny flower. Most gardeners buy in new bulbs and leave their existing ones to increase naturally by both division and seed.

Cyclamen
Sowbread

It's not the large, pot-grown cyclamen so popular at Christmas that can be grown outdoors, but the smaller hardy species such as *C. hederifolium* (syn. *C. neapolitanum*). It grows just 8 cm (3 in) or so high, produces its pretty reflexed-petalled flowers of warm pink from summer to autumn, and then a show of marbled heart-shaped leaves.

Plant the tubers while they are growing, for preference, or take a gamble and hope that dry ones (which you can buy from department stores and garden centres) will succeed. Plant the tubers so they rest fractionally below the surface of the soil.

Suitable for dappled shade under trees and shrubs, and shady pockets on the rock garden. They like a peaty, leafy soil that doesn't dry out.

Propagate by sowing fresh seeds in pots of compost in a cold frame.

Dahlia

The dahlia is a tuber that can grow happily outdoors in summer, but which needs frost protection in winter. There are hundreds of different varieties with flowers in 'pompon', 'cactus' and 'decorative' shapes, in shades of red, orange, yellow, mauve, purple and white. The stems and foliage are juicy and succulent and the plants may grow anything from 45 cm to 1.5 m (18 in to 5 ft) tall.

Plant dormant tubers 15 cm (6 in) deep in late April or early May; young plants in late May or early June. Stake the plants as they grow. Feed fortnightly in summer and control earwigs (p.294), which will nibble both flowers and leaves.

Suitable for beds and borders in full sun. The soil should be rich: work in plenty of compost or manure and a dusting of blood, bone and fishmeal before planting. Water well in dry spells. When the stems are blackened by autumn frosts, lift the plants, cut off the top growth and store the tubers in an airy, cool but frostproof place in trays of dry peat. If you're idle you can risk leaving them in the ground outdoors, in which case mulch the soil above them with a thick layer of compost, manure, straw or bracken. Prepare for total losses in severe winters.

Propagate by taking cuttings from tubers boxed up in compost, watered and kept warm in a greenhouse during early spring. Alternatively, divide these tubers into sections (each with a shoot) as soon as they start to sprout. Grow on a little in heat and plant out when danger of frost is past.

Eranthis hyemalis
Winter Aconite

These pretty yellow buttercup flowers, each with a green ruff, are welcome heralds of spring, flowering in February just 8 cm (3 in) above the cold, damp soil.

Eranthis hyemalis (winter aconite) creates a mass of gold only 10 cm (4 in) from the ground.

Plant growing plants if you can find them; if you can't, plant dry tubers in autumn and be prepared to wait a few years for the plants to settle in and flower well. Plant 8 cm (3 in) deep and 10 cm (4 in) apart.
Suitable for naturalizing in rock gardens or in beds and borders under trees and shrubs in sun or dappled shade. Really dry soils will not be appreciated.
Propagate by division of tubers after flowering.

Erythronium
Dog's Tooth Violet, Trout Lily

Grey-green, liver-spotted leaves and pink or white pagoda-shaped flowers make *E. dens-canis* a popular plant. It grows just 15 cm (6 in) high, but there are taller species such as *E. tuolumnense* at 25 cm (10 in), which has glossy green leaves and yellow flowers. All bloom in spring, and all are well worth growing.
Plant growing plants in spring or, if this is not possible, dormant, but not

totally desiccated, corms in late summer. Plant 8 cm (3 in) deep and 10 cm (4 in) apart.
Suitable for dappled shade under trees and shrubs in a peaty, leafy soil that is never likely to dry out. Happy in shady pockets on the rock garden. A light mulch of leaf mould or pulverized bark will be appreciated after flowering. Once established the corms resent disturbance.
Propagate by division after flowering.

Fritillaria
Crown Imperial, Snakeshead Fritillary

The stately *F. imperialis*, with its 1 m (3 ft) stem, pendant orange or yellow bells and topknot of leafy green bracts, is a startling feature in the May garden and is criticized only for its foxy odour. The daintier *F. meleagris*, 23 cm (9 in), is altogether more coy, with nodding chequered bells of dusky plum-purple, pink or creamy white. Its leaves are narrow and grassy, unlike those of the crown imperial, which radiate in whorls from the thick stem.
Plant bulbs of *F. imperialis* 15 cm (6 in) deep on their sides; those of *F. meleagris* the right way up, 10 cm (4 in) deep and as much apart. Plant both in autumn.
Suitable for rich but well-drained soil in full sun for *F. imperialis*; moisture-retentive soil in dappled shade for *F. meleagris*. Both are best left undisturbed after planting; the snakeshead fritillary can even be naturalized in grass.
Propagate by seeds sown in a garden frame as soon as ripe. A job for the patient gardener – others will buy in fresh bulbs.

Galanthus
Snowdrop

The common snowdrop is *G. nivalis*, usually at its best during February, when its green and white ballerina flowers dangle from 15 cm (6 in) stems.

There are dozens of other species and varieties with quaint markings and broader leaves; some of them possess delightful scents, and some flower earlier, even in autumn if you choose the right species. Many are expensive to buy, but the double form of the common snowdrop is cheap and produces masses of tulle-petticoated flowers at the same time as the true species.
Plant growing plants 'in the green' immediately after flowering if you can. Dry bulbs can be planted in autumn but may not establish so quickly. Plant the bulbs 8 cm (3 in) deep and 5 cm (2 in) apart.
Suitable for naturalizing in beds and borders under trees and shrubs and in grass. Happy in full sun or dappled shade. Good in rock gardens.
Propagate by dividing mature clumps after flowering.

Galtonia candicans
Spire Lily

Stately spires of creamy-white bells 1 m (3 ft) tall are the trademark of galtonia. The blooms are deliciously fragrant and open in July or August.
Plant in spring 15 cm (6 in) deep and as much apart.
Suitable for well-nourished and well-drained soil in beds and borders among summer-flowering perennials and shrubs. Full sun is essential. Galtonia can also be grown in pots for room decoration. Plant one bulb, with its nose just showing, in a pot of compost in autumn. Keep it cool and dark for eight weeks and then gradually introduce to light and warmer temperatures. It will flower in spring.
Propagate by the removal of offsets in autumn.

Gladiolus
Sword Lily

Sword-leafed plants with tapering spikes of wide-faced flowers in shades of red, yellow, orange, pink, mauve and white, as well as a rather lurid green. There are many different forms with strangely shaped flowers such as the 'butterfly' types. They grow to 30 cm–1.5 m (12 in–5 ft) high and flower in summer. Most are not winter hardy and have to be lifted, dried and stored before frosts have a chance to kill them, but *G. communis* subsp. *byzantinus*, 60 cm (2 ft), is a magenta-flowered species that can survive outdoors all the year round. It's daintier and flowers earlier, in June.

Plant *G. communis* subsp. *byzantinus* in autumn 8 cm (3 in) deep and 15 cm (6 in) apart. Plant the hybrid types at intervals between March and May for a succession of flowers. Set the corms 10 cm (4 in) deep and 23 cm (9 in) apart. The hybrids will need staking as soon as the flower spikes appear. Feed fortnightly in summer.

Suitable for rich and well-drained soil in full sun. Water well in dry spells. Six weeks after flowering lift the hybrid varieties, cut off the foliage 2.5 cm (1 in) above the new corm, remove the old corm, which will be a shrivelled button below the new one, and store the new corms in seeds trays kept in a cool, dry, frostproof place in winter.

Propagate by planting 'cormels' (tiny corms that form around the main one) and allow them to grow on to flowering size. Plant them in spring.

Hyacinthoides (syn. *Endymion*)
Bluebell

This is the native British bluebell, *H. non-scripta*, along with its relation the Spanish bluebell *H. hispanica*. Both have variants with white and pink flowers, but the Spanish bluebell is more imposing at around 30 cm (12 in) high and can be a thug.

Plant both types in autumn to twice their depth.

Suitable for naturalizing in grass and woodland. (Avoid planting the Spanish bluebell in native woodland.)

Propagate by division after flowering.

Hyacinthus
Hyacinth

Unsurpassed for fragrance, the hyacinth is part of the Christmas tradition. The dense spikes of bloom may be rich rose-red, pink, blue, salmon, pale yellow or white. 'L'Innocence' (white), 'Jan Bos' (rich pink), 'Ostara' (blue), and 'City of Haarlem' (pale yellow), are probably the most popular varieties. All bloom in winter (in pots) or in spring (outdoors) and are around 25 cm (10 in) high. plant prepared bulbs in pots or bowls of compost in late August and September for Christmas flowers.

Plant one variety to each pot to make sure that all the bulbs flower simultaneously: mix your colours, and blooming may be staggered and less effective. Keep the pots of bulbs cool and dark for eight weeks, bringing them indoors when the flower spikes can be seen nestling among the leaves. Ordinary bulbs can be planted in bowls at the same time but they will not flower quite so quickly.

Plant outdoors during September and October, setting the bulbs 10 cm (4 in) deep and 15 cm (6 in) apart. The bulbs are so expensive nowadays that few folk can afford to grow them outdoors except in tubs and windowboxes.

Suitable for beds and borders, pots, tubs, bowls and windowboxes. Plant pot-grown bulbs in the garden when the flowers fade. If the soil is well nourished and in full sun they should bloom again in succeeding years, but plant them a good 10 cm (4 in) deep.

Propagate by scooping and scoring if you're really mean (see Chapter 2 Propagation). Otherwise save up and buy in more bulbs.

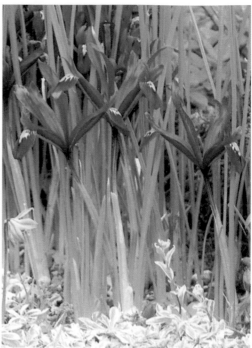

Dwarf bulbs such as *Iris reticulata* and *Scilla sibirica* take up little space but add much-needed colour to the winter border.

Iris

In January, February and March, when most gardeners' hopes are at a low ebb, the varieties of *I. reticulata* burst into flower. Their blooms may be blue or violet in various intensities, and are almost always attractively etched with yellow and white. They're just 15 cm (6 in) tall, but if you can get your nose down to them (or if you grow them in a windowbox at nose level) you'll detect a sweet scent in the winter sun. *I. histrioides* 'Major' is another must. It's slightly shorter but rather larger flowered and coloured blue and white. The foliage follows the flowers and, in all the varieties, is grassy and not too untidy. The Dutch, Spanish and English irises are all much taller at around 45 cm (18 in) and bloom in late spring or early to mid-summer. They are valuable and easy plants that are ignored by too many gardeners.

Plant the Dutch types to bloom in May, the Spanish to bloom in June, and the English to bloom in June and July, offering flowers of blue, violet, yellow and white.

Plant in autumn 8 cm (3 in) deep. Space the dwarf types 8 cm (3 in) apart and the taller varieties 15 cm (6 in) apart.

Suitable for beds and borders in full sun (taller varieties) or rock gardens in full sun (dwarf varieties). All appreciate a gritty, well-drained soil. The tall varieties can be lifted and divided every three years in autumn, the others are best left undisturbed. The dwarfs can also be grown in pots for winter colour indoors. Keep them cool at all times.

Propagate by division of established clumps in autumn.

Leucojum
Snowflake

There are three snowflakes grown with frequency by discerning plantsmen: the summer snowflake, *L. aestivum*, 45 cm (18 in), green-tipped, white bells in late spring and early summer; the spring snowflake, *L. vernum*, 30 cm (12 in), similar flowers in early spring; and the autumn snowflake, *L. autumnale*, 15 cm (6 in), a dainty miniature with reed-like leaves and papery white or pale pink bells in autumn.

Plant the spring- and summer-flowering species in early autumn, the autumn-flowering species in late summer. Alternatively, plant 'in the green' after flowering, as for snowdrops. Plant 10 cm (4 in) deep and as much apart. Both *L. aestivum* and *L. vernum* appreciate a leafy, moisture-retentive soil, while *L. autumnale* likes something grittier and well drained. All are happy in full sun or dappled shade.

Suitable for beds and borders and, in the case of *L. autumnale*, rock gardens. The bulbs may not flower in their first year.

Propagate by lifting and dividing mature clumps of bulbs after flowering.

Lilium
Lily

How can I even begin to tell you about lilies in such a small space? I can't, but I can perhaps persuade you to try them in beds and borders among your herbaceous plants and shrubs, and in pots on a patio or doorstep. They possess starry, bell-shaped, trumpet or turk's cap flowers in a wide colour range, and some fragrances that surpass anything that comes out of a bottle. If you've never grown lilies before, start off with *L. regale*, 1.2 m (4 ft), which has white and pale yellow trumpets flushed with purple on the outside, and *L.* 'Enchantment', 60 cm (2 ft), whose vibrant orange blooms are dotted with brown. Don't be put off by the daunting mystery that surrounds the lily: some are difficult, it's true, but others are easy if you meet their simple requirements.

Plant these two in October or in spring, as soon as the bulbs become available. Plant them 15 cm (6 in) deep and 20 cm (8 in) apart. They need a well-drained soil that is not prone to drought in summer. Winter sogginess will encourage rotting. Alternatively, pot up the bulbs in autumn in gritty compost – one bulb to a 13 cm (5 in) pot or three to a 20 cm (8 in) pot. Cover the bulbs with 8 cm (3 in) compost. Keep cool and dark until growth begins, then gradually introduce to light and warmth. Water carefully at all times: little will be needed until the plants are growing well. Outdoors and in pots the plants may need staking. Plant out potted bulbs in the garden after flowering.

Suitable for beds and borders in well-drained soil and full sun or dappled shade. Many can be grown in pots. Some lilies hate chalk, others don't much care for acid ground; some are 'stem rooting' and need to be planted quite deeply, others, like the madonna lily, need shallow planting in late summer. If you want to know more, get hold of a book devoted to the subject.

Propagate by seed or by the removal and growing on of bulb scales or bulbils – those little bulbs that appear in the leaf axils of some species. (See Chapter 2 Propagation for details.)

Muscari
Grape Hyacinth

Easy spring-flowering bulbs with spires of blue or white flowers held on stout stalks 15 cm (6 in) long. The commonest species is *M. armeniacum*.

Plant in autumn 8 cm (3 in) deep and 8 cm (3 in) apart.

Suitable for beds and borders, tubs, windowboxes and pots. Ordinary soil and full sun are appreciated. There is no need to disturb the bulbs once they are planted, but should they become all leaf and no flower in succeeding years, dig them up in June and discard all but the largest bulbs, which can be replanted in freshly fertilized soil.

Propagate by division after flowering.

Narcissus
Daffodil

There are hundreds, and maybe even thousands of narcissus varieties that are valuable to stately gardeners and windowbox owners alike. Catalogues offer a vast choice of form and colour: large- and small-cupped varieties, doubles and singles, and even blooms that are pale green or salmon-pink. I'll leave you to pick your favourites, but will sneak in a recommendation for the dwarf varieties such as *N. asturiensis*, *N. bulbocodium* and *N. cyclamineus* and some of their hybrids such as 'Little Witch', 23 cm (9 in), and 'Tête-à-Tête', 15 cm (6 in) (both yellow), which are marvellous for rock gardens, pots and windowboxes. All bloom in spring. Cottage gardeners should not be without 'Telamonius Plenus' (syn. 'Van Sion'), the double yellow daffodil; and orchard owners can carpet the ground around their trees with the headily fragrant Old pheasant's eye (*N. poeticus* var. *recurvus*), which has white petals

and a tiny red and yellow centre. Both are just over 30 cm (12 in) tall.
Plant in September and October, 10 cm (4 in) deep in beds and borders or 15 cm (6 in) deep if naturalizing in grass. The miniature varieties should be planted 8 cm (3 in) deep. All varieties can be planted 8 cm (3 in) apart. Plant in groups, not lines. Alternatively plant the bulbs in pots (see p. 154 for details) in autumn for winter flowering indoors. The varieties 'Soleil d'Or' and 'Paper White' are often potted for Christmas flowering.
Suitable for beds, borders, rough grass, rock gardens (dwarf varieties), pots, tubs and windowboxes. Pot-grown plants can be planted out in the garden after flowering. All appreciate full sun and a well-drained soil. Feeding with a balanced general fertilizer, such as blood, bone and fishmeal, after flowering will encourage regular blooming. Dry springs may account for 'blindness' (lack of flowers) the following year.
Propagate by division after flowering.

Nectaroscordum See *Allium*, p.156

Nerine bowdenii
Diamond Lily

Find this September-flowering bulb a sheltered patch of well-drained soil in full sun and it will demand little attention. It will gradually make a congested clump of bulbs from which

"In January, February and March, when gardeners' hopes are at a low ebb, the varieties of *Iris reticulata* burst into flower."

will spring branched heads of rich pink, wavy-petalled flowers at the end of summer, followed by a small forest of glossy green strap-shaped leaves. The flower stems are about 45 cm (18 in) high, and the leaves persist through winter, dying down in early summer.
Plant in late summer, positioning the bulbs just below ground level.
Suitable for light, well-drained, even dry soils in full sun. A spot at the foot of a south-facing wall is ideal and the plants will usually come through the winter unscathed, though they may suffer in the north and in sticky earth. They can also be grown in pots of gritty compost and protected from winter cold and wet in a frame. Withhold water in summer when the leaves die down. Repot in late summer when the bulbs become overcrowded. Those growing in the garden seem to flower best when jammed close together. Protect them from slugs and snails.
Propagate by division of clumps in late summer.

Ornithogalum umbellatum
Star of Bethlehem

A neat and cheerful little plant with branched heads of white, starry flowers that are green on the undersides. They are carried on top of 23 cm (9 in) stalks in April and May and make a pretty edging to a bed or border. They open late morning and close again in the afternoon, but they're nice when they're out!
Plant in autumn, 8 cm (3 in) deep and as much apart.
Suitable for ordinary soil in sunny beds, borders or containers.
Propagate by dividing clumps after flowering.

Schizostylis coccinea
Kaffir Lily

Rich pink, starry flowers emerge at the top of slender stems in autumn to make the kaffir lily a valuable border

flower. There are several named varieties such as 'Viscountess Byng' and 'Mrs Hegarty' that are paler than the true species. All are around 45 cm (18 in) tall and have grassy leaves.
Plant in spring, 8 cm (3 in) deep and as much apart.
Suitable for warm and sunny borders at the foot of south- and west-facing walls. In cold districts protect with straw or bracken in winter.
Propagate by division of mature clumps in spring.

Scilla
Squill

The two squills most commonly planted are *S. siberica*, 10 cm (4 in), and *S. bifolia*, 15 cm (6 in), both of which have rich blue, bell-like flowers in spring.
Plant in autumn to twice their depth.
Suitable for bed and border edgings. They do not need to be disturbed once planted.
Propagate by division after flowering.

Sternbergia
Lily of the Field, Winter Daffodil

Like a vivid yellow crocus to look at, *S. lutea*, 10 cm (4 in), blooms in autumn and then sends up a neat fountain of lustrous green 'daffodil' leaves. Sometimes it is reluctant to flower but if planted deep enough and allowed a year or two to settle in it should oblige.
Plant in late summer, 15 cm (6 in) deep and 10 cm (4 in) apart.
Suitable for sunny spots in well-drained soil, preferably at the foot of a warm wall where it will receive a welcome baking in summer.
Propagate by division in late summer.

Tulipa
Tulip

As popular and as varied a race as *Narcissus*, with almost as many variations. The hybrids are classified in different groups that vary in stature and time of flowering; it's possible to have tulips in bloom from late winter to late spring. Pick the hybrid types for bedding schemes – the Darwin hybrids have long stems and will bloom at the same time as wallflowers – and the smaller species for rock gardens. Colourful catalogues will give you more detailed information on varieties than I can hope to here, but let me urge you to have a bash with the miniatures like *T. clusiana*, 23 cm (9 in), white, flushed red outside, late April; its variety *chrysantha*, 15 cm (6 in), red and yellow, mid-April, and *T. tarda*, 10 cm (4 in), yellow and white, April. The varieties of *T. kaufmanniana* and *T. greigii* are stocky, large flowered and have leaves attractively streaked with maroon. At 23 cm (9 in) high they are the best types for container planting. There are many others that will delight you year in, year out.

Plant in October or November – no earlier, and the deeper the better. Plant the miniatures 15 cm (6 in) deep, and the larger hybrids 23 cm (9 in) deep if you want to avoid lifting them every year. I've known them to flower annually at this depth undisturbed for 30 years. Plant in pots at the same time, just covering the noses of the bulbs. Keep cool and dark for eight weeks, then bring into the light. Avoid a dramatic rise in temperature.

Suitable for bedding, naturalizing in beds and borders (where their foliage will not give offence), tubs, pots and windowboxes. Dwarf species look good in the rock garden. If tulips are used in

a spring-bedding scheme that has to be shifted to make way for summer flowers, lift the bulbs, leaving their top growth intact, and lay them in a trench on the vegetable plot, replacing some soil over the bulbs. When growth dies down, lift and strip the bulbs of their foliage before storing them in a cool, dry place. Discard the small bulbs and retain only the larger, flowering-sized bulbs for planting next year. Dry out

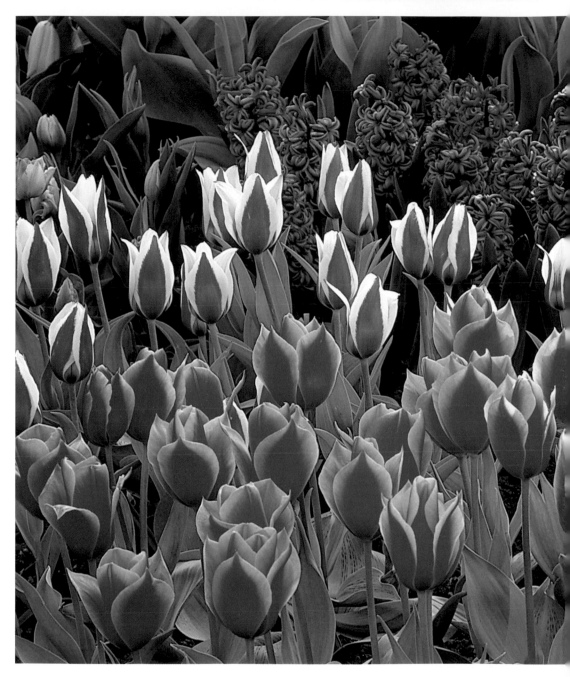

Massed tulips and hyacinths provide a gloriously colourful and fragrant spring display in beds, borders, and containers, welcoming us back to the garden after the dark winter months.

pot-grown bulbs after flowering and treat as for lifted bulbs.

Propagate tulips by dividing bulb clusters in summer and growing on the small bulbs.

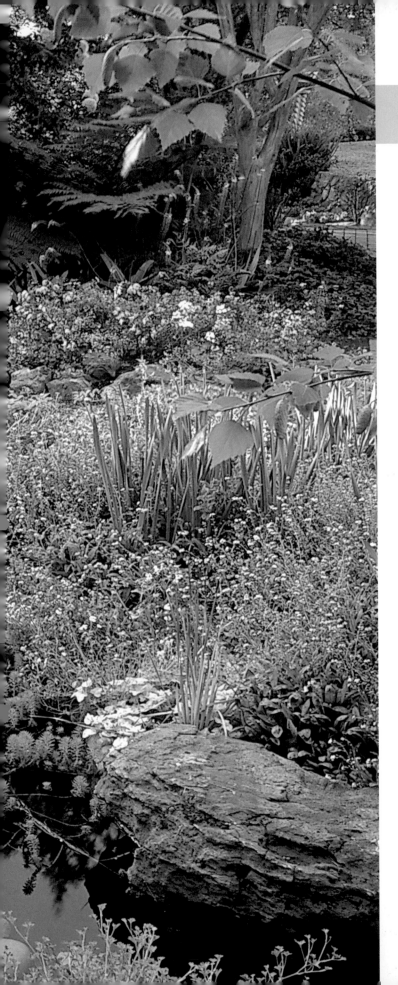

part III

THE
FEATURES

The features that we
incorporate into our gardens
are as vivid an expression of
personality as the plants that
surround them

This enchanting stretch of water winds its way through the
dense planting around its edges, givng it a wholly natural
charm that is attractive to both humans and wildlife.

12 Rock gardens

An open, sunny site and good drainage are the essential elements for creating a rock garden to grow a delightful collection of alpines and rock plants

Every gardener has his favourite plants: alpines and rock plants happen to be mine – even though they are regularly rivalled by roses, shrubs, house plants, border plants …

If I do nothing else in this chapter I'd like to encourage you to grow alpines anywhere but on rock-studded mounds that look like large graves. Alpines mostly come from mountainous areas so it may seem natural to create mini-Alps in the garden, but this is really not necessary. They are shown off and grow happily in rock beds (raised or flat), sinks and troughs as well as in properly constructed 'rock outcrops' that fit most naturally into banks or undulating ground.

WHERE TO SITE YOUR ROCK GARDEN

Whatever feature you decide on, the site should be open and sunny. There are one or two alpines that like a shady spot, but the vast majority need all the light they can get. Avoid a site that is overhung by trees or the plants will be dripped on all the year round and smothered with leaves in autumn.

Some shelter from strong winds is desirable and the patch of ground should not be in a frost pocket (a hollow that collects cold air). Most alpines flower in spring and will be damaged if frosted at that time.

As well as hating bad drainage, the plants dislike winter wet. Most of them are protected in the wild by a thick, dry blanket of snow. In Britain they are more likely to be battered by rain or sleet. Many alpines will reluctantly tolerate our winters; those that will not can be protected with panes of glass supported on wire legs, with cloches, or by being grown in a cold frame or – great luxury – in an alpine house. Hairy-leaved plants in particular suffer from damp in cold weather.

PREPARING THE SOIL

Alpines like that seemingly impossible combination, rapid drainage in winter and adequate moisture retention in summer. You can usually achieve this happy state if you perk up your existing soil. Light earth will need the addition of coarse peat (alpines don't go a bundle on lashings of manure – well, actually they do, but you'll get more foliage than flowers), and heavier soils can take both peat and sharp grit to improve their drainage. A dusting of bonemeal before planting will set your alpines on the road to establishment.

The amount of lime your soil contains (its acidity or alkalinity) will affect the plants you can grow. Most rock plants will be happy in slightly acid earth, but there are dozens (with the exception of some gentians, dwarf rhododendrons and others) that can be grown on chalk. Garden with your soil rather than against it and plant things that will be happy in your conditions.

Really go to town when you prepare the soil. Dig or fork it over, working in the appropriate enrichment and pulling out any weeds. Make sure that you eliminate every last bit or the blighters will be with you for ever once the rock garden is established. Let the soil settle for a while after cultivation; that way you can be sure it is firm and free of air pockets when construction of the rock garden begins. You'll also be able to spot any more weeds that emerge.

Spring and autumn are the customary times to plant, though alpines from pots can be established quite happily in summer provided enough attention is paid to watering. It follows that construction of a rock garden can be carried out at almost any time of the year except the middle of winter, when the soil will cling so fiercely to your spade and wellies as to make cultivation impossible.

WHICH ROCK?

You don't actually need any rock to grow rock plants; it's the state of the soil that matters most. But alpines do look good when displayed against a background of rock or when allowed to tumble over a boulder. This sets the gardener off on the road that leads to the rock-dotted mound. Steady now!

Decide which kind of rock would best fit into your garden. The answer is usually local stone, which will also be cheaper. The two kinds of stone most frequently offered are limestone and sandstone.

Westmorland limestone is that beautifully water-worn runnelled and layered stone that, to many people, typifies a traditional rock garden. Avoid buying new supplies as these will have been quarried from our endangered natural limestone pavements. Purchase only secondhand stone from old rock gardens.

Sandstone hails from all sorts of regions and is a bland, mid-brown stone that looks good in most situations.

Granite is sometimes available but is rather difficult to work with and not so easy to blend into the garden.

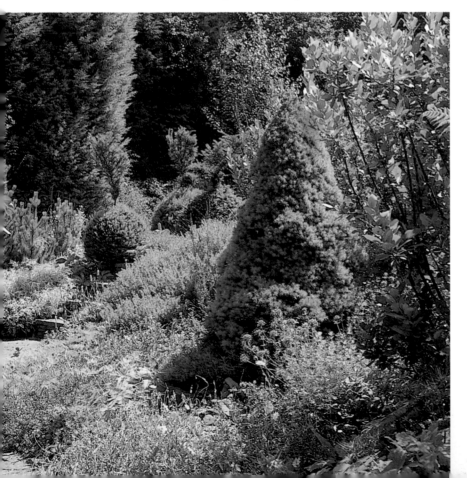

Tufa is formed from calcium carbonate deposits and is a soft, creamy white rock that rapidly becomes coated with mosses. Use single lumps of it as features (chip out holes and plant them with cushion-forming alpines) rather than incorporating it into a rock garden. It's a bit too pricey for that anyway.

All rock costs money so, if you can't afford it, settle for just one or two pieces set into a flat bed to remind you of the nature of the plants. Once they've been planted up, most rock gardens are covered with a 2.5 cm (1 in) layer of gravel, stone chippings or even pea shingle. This prevents the plants from being splashed by mud, it

This rock bank was constructed ten years ago. (See the photographs on p.169 of how it looked then and one year later.) It is now totally covered with plants and ready for renovation.

keeps their 'collars' dry, keeps down weeds, keeps in moisture and generally shows off plants to perfection.

CREATING AN ALPINE GARDEN

Rocky outcrops

If you want a traditional rock garden, the best place to build it is on a slight slope. Failing this you'll have to create a mound but, if this is the case, for goodness sake make it sizeable and make the slope gradual. Try to construct an outcrop of rock that looks almost as if it is naturally occurring, pushing up through the soil in your garden.

Look at rocks in the wild and notice how their strata (layers) all run in the same direction. Arrange your rocks similarly so the layers run almost horizontally and the rocks tilt back slightly. Put large rocks in place first – 100 kg (2 cwt) is about the largest anyone can shift on their own – and position smaller ones around them. Leave pockets of firm soil for the plants both above and below the rocks. When rock was plentiful, gardeners used to bury two thirds of it in the soil.

> "You don't need rock to grow rock plants, but alpines do look good against a rocky background or when allowed to tumble over a boulder."

There's no need to be so extravagant nowadays, just make sure that the rocks sit firm, and really ram the soil around them with your boot and an old spade handle. Jump from rock to rock and you should not detect any wobble.

When the job is finished, trample the soil to firm it so that no root-drying air pockets are left.

Rock beds

In most gardens, rock beds are easier to fit in than rocky outcrops. They're cheaper too. If your soil is sandy, the bed can be made flat on the ground. On heavier soils, it's a good idea to raise the bed up with two or three courses of brick or broken flagstone. There's no need to mortar this low wall; simply stack the bricks in a staggered fashion and make sure that they slope inwards slightly for stability. Dry-mortar the bricks with soil if you want to plant a few alpines in the crevices as you go.

Enrich the soil with peat and/or grit and add extra soil to bring the level up to within 2.5 cm (1 in) of the rim of a raised bed. One or two pieces of stone can be positioned in the surface of the bed to set the scene, but they are not essential. If your bed is too wide to lean across, lay some stepping stones through it for easy access.

Raised beds can also be built on patios but they will need to be about four bricks high and equipped with a drainage layer of rubble in the base before the soil is tipped in.

Scree beds

Plants that insist on really sharp drainage are those that grow in almost pure rock chippings at the foot of mountain slopes. In the garden they can be catered for in a rock bed that has been filled with a special sharp-draining mixture of 10 parts stone chippings, 1 part soil, 1 part peat or leaf mould (sifted), and 1 part sharp sand. They are really plants for the connoisseur and need a raised bed rather than a flat one, which may act as a sump for all rainwater in the vicinity. Mind you, it's

Plants for scree beds

- Androsace
- Erigeron
- Erodium
- Hypericum
- Leontopodium
- Nierembergia
- Origanum
- Papaver
- Sedum
- Sempervivum
- Silene
- Verbascum

amazing how many rock plants will thrive in a bed containing a scree mixture provided they are not allowed to dry out in summer: there are heavy showers even on alpine screes.

Dry walls

Where walls have to be constructed in the garden to retain banks or divide off areas, consider making them 'dry' and packing either the cavity or the rear of the wall with soil as building progresses. Pack the joints, too, and, also as the building progresses, you'll be able to insert sempervivums (house leeks), encrusted saxifrages and other alpines that are happy in vertical crevices. The key to success with dry stone walls is watering, for the plants may bake before their roots become established if you forget to turn on the hosepipe occasionally.

Creating a rock bank

1 Create a natural-looking outcrop with local rocks on slightly sloping ground. Ram the soil firmly around the rocks to make sure that there are no air pockets.

2 Water a container-grown alpine before planting. Knock it from its pot and plant without disturbing the rootball. Water it in and topdress with gravel.

3 This shows the rock bank immediately after it had been planted. The gravel topdressing helps to suppress weeds, retain moisture, and keep the plants mud-free.

4 After one year the scheme is well established, but there is room for a few more plants. Scrape away the gravel, plant the newcomer and push the gravel back.

Peat beds

Peat beds are definitely for the connoisseur. They are made to accommodate a choice group of plants that relishes moist, acid soil and usually a modicum of shade. Site your peat bed against a north-facing wall and use coir-based compost if you would rather spare the peat bogs. On chalky soil you might as well forget the whole thing, for the plants insist on acidity and need a bed that has been so enriched that it contains as much peat as soil. The edges of the bed are usually raised up with peat blocks, but to conserve peat you can use logs.

The ground must be weed-free from the outset. Peat garden plants are mainly natives of woodland, so provide them with the shade and moisture they enjoy. The peat blocks, and the peat enrichment, must be moist from the very beginning. Soak them both in a tank or tin bath of water before constructing the bed. Once in place never let them dry out. Keep a close watch to ensure no drying takes place: dry peat is virtually impossible to re-wet.

Apply a dusting of blood, bone and fishmeal over the entire area, then a 5 cm (2 in) mulch of pure peat before planting. Stepping stones can be laid over wide beds (it's not a good idea to flatten the springy mixture with your size ten wellies). An additional top-dressing of peat should be applied each spring, and any weeds removed as soon as they are seen.

SINK GARDENS

Should you have the good fortune to come across an old porcelain sink, don't kick it out of the way or smash it up for use as hardcore; instead, turn it into a sink garden. No, not a shining white one - a stone one. First clean it and remove the plug. Coat the outside with a bonding agent (an adhesive that's available from any hardware shop); while this is tacky, pat on a moistened mixture of 2 parts coir, 1 part sand and 1 part cement. A 1 cm (½ in) thick layer all over the outside and 5 cm (2 in) over

Coat an old glazed white sink with an artificial stone mixture and plant it with a selection of slow-growing alpines. The dwarf conifer and rock add height and interest.

Plants for sink gardens

- Androsace
- Armeria
- Dianthus
- Erinus
- Gentiana
- Juniperus communis 'Compressa'
- Leontopodium
- Lewisia
- Oxalis
- Saxifraga
- Sempervivum
- Thymus
- Verbascum

the lip inside is what's needed to transform the sink into a 'stone' one. The mixture is euphemistically called 'hypertufa' (trust the alpine buffs to give it a fancy handle), and when it hardens it's as tough as cement.

Stand the sink in its final position before you coat it - afterwards it will be a weighty load. It will be best stood on bricks to keep it clear of the soil, so preventing frosting and faulty drainage. Alpines in sinks need sun just as much as those in the rock garden - although you could aim to grow shade-lovers (see the list on p.173).

Leave the sink to dry and harden for about two weeks, then place a layer of rubble in the base and fill with compost: John Innes No. 2 potting compost plus half its bulk of sharp sand is a good mixture. Plant your alpines - with a piece of rock and a dwarf conifer to add a bit of height and interest - and then water them in. About 20 plants will fit into the average sink if you sensibly choose those that are dwarf and slow growing. Add a 1-2.5 cm (½-1 in) layer of stone chippings to the surface and the job is finished.

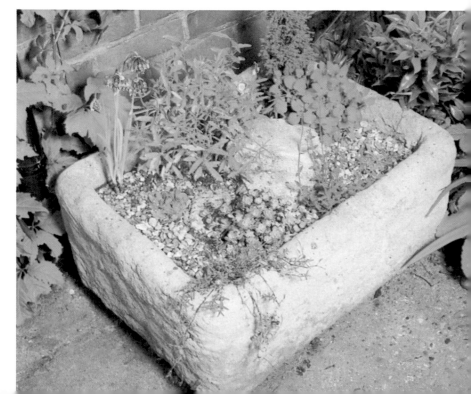

Keep a close eye on the sink during summer and soak it whenever the compost shows signs of drying out. Severe frosts may lift off parts of the 'stone' coating after a time but these can easily be patched. Replace any plants that succumb during the winter, rather than removing all the plants and starting again. Only when the sink has become really overgrown and unsightly need it be renovated and totally re-landscaped but, as a general rule, age brings even greater beauty.

PLANTING AND CARING FOR ALPINES

Planting

Now that alpines are sold almost entirely in pots, they can be planted with safety at any time between early spring and autumn. Water the plant well an hour or so before planting, tap it out of its pot and plant it without disturbing the rootball. Replace the soil and firm it down, spread the gravel mulch around the plant, then water it in. Do not plant too deeply.

Planting alpines in sinks

1 Turn an old sink into an alpine garden. Stand the sink on bricks to keep it clear of the soil. Spread a layer of drainage material over the base of the sink.

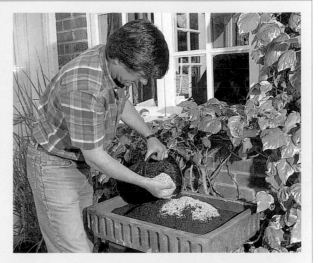

2 Fill the sink to just below the rim with a mixture of John Innes No. 2 potting compost and sharp grit to improve drainage. Firm down the compost.

3 Arrange your plants over the surface of the compost so that they are roughly 15 cm (6 in) apart.

4 Remove each plant from its pot, scoop out a hole in the compost and lower it in. Firm down the compost.

5 When planting is completed, spread a 1 cm (½ in) layer of grit over the surface of the compost.

As rocks are positioned fill the spaces between them with compost and firm it in

Leave the battens in place until the second layer of rock is stable, then remove

As you construct your rock garden, plant alpines and rock plants between layers of rock, firming a little compost around their roots. Place wooden battens between the plants to protect them while you put the second rock in position. Firm it into place then remove the battens.

To plant alpines and rock plants in vertical crevices in a rock garden, place a small stone at the base of the crevice. Position the plant on a layer of compost, cover the roots with more compost, and put a small stone on top of the compost to keep the plant in place.

Water thoroughly at the first sniff of drought. The plants are capable of coping with prolonged dry spells when they are established, but during their first year they will suffer greatly from drought.

Rock plants for gentle shade

All the rock plants in the A-Z section enjoy an open, sunny spot in well-drained soil, but the following will tolerate gentle shade:

- Ajuga
- Anemone
- Blechnum
- Epimedium
- Lewisia
- Pratia
- Saxifraga
- Trillium

Labelling

If you can't remember what your plants are, label them – but don't stud your rock garden with those white plastic markers that will make it look like a miniature graveyard. I find that those rigid plastic labels, written on in black indelible ink, can be pushed into the soil by the plant so that only the top 1 cm (½ in) is visible. This prevents the birds from pulling them out and lets you locate them when you need to, without their being

In this well-established rock garden in Dorset, the basic structure is almost hidden by the mounds of low-growing perennials, shrubs and conifers. The gravel layer between plants helps to retain moisture and keep down weeds.

blatantly obvious. You can use this method of labelling anywhere in the garden.

Aftercare and maintenance

As a general rule, all faded flowerheads of alpines can be snipped off. Exceptions occur when you consider the seedheads to be decorative or when you want to collect seed for propagation. Spring is the best time for pruning dwarf shrubs and woody alpines, for then you can cut back to a bud that is obviously growing. Dead leaves and rotting tissue can be removed at any time of year, as soon as they are seen.

Weeds should be pulled out as soon as they are seen. Annuals will come out of the gravel layer with ease, but do keep a sharp eye out for the seedling stages of tap-rooted perennials like dandelions and docks. Lift them out carefully with a knife or narrow trowel.

Feed your rock plants once a year in spring. Scatter a light dusting of blood, bone and fishmeal over the surface of the gravel and let the rain wash it in.

Rock gardens seldom need wholesale renovation; it is usually sufficient to replace worn-out plants either with new ones or with their own divisions. Spring is the best time for this.

PROPAGATION

Like border plants, alpines can be propagated by seed, cuttings or division. Details of these methods can be found in Chapter 2 Propagation.

A-Z of rock plants

THIS IS A BRIEF ALPHABET of alpines. Although most of the plants on the list are easy to grow in a wide variety of situations, I have slipped in a couple of tricky customers just to tax you a little. However, in the main you'll find them a bright, undemanding bunch.

Some plants that grow in rock gardens will also grow very happily in beds and borders and may have been included in Chapter 5 Shrubs and Chapter 9 Border Plants. I've indicated where this is the case.

Dwarf bulbs make a significant contribution to winter and spring colour on the rocks, and you'll find a list on p.154 (Chapter 11 Garden Bulbs) of a selection that look particularly good with alpines. Remember, though, that all bulbs must be allowed to produce leaves after they have flowered and that these must be left for a few weeks in order that the bulbs can flower in future years – these leaves may be a bit of a nuisance if they swamp smaller plants.

Acaena
New Zealand Burr
Carpeting

Ferny-leaved plants with burr-like flowers in summer. *A. microphylla* is the tiniest and has bronze-green leaves; *A. saccaticupula* 'Blue Haze' has blue-grey leaves and pink-flushed stems. Both spread freely.
Propagate by division.

Aethionema
Stone Cress
15 x 60 cm (6 in x 2 ft)

A. 'Warley Rose' seems to be everybody's favourite variety. It makes a spreading shrublet and is smothered in pink flowers from late spring to early summer.
Propagate by cuttings.

Ajuga See p.118

Androsace
Rock Jasmine
8 x 30 cm (3 x 12 in)

There are some lovely (and tricky) androsaces, but A. sempervivoides is not too difficult. It forms clumps of neat green rosettes over which rich pink flowers appear clustered on stalks in spring. The easiest of the cushion types is *A. cylindrica*, whose domes are smothered in white flowers in May.
Propagate by cuttings and seed.

Anemone See p.157

Arabis
Rock Cress
15 x 60 cm (6 in x 2 ft)

A favourite along with aubrieta and aurinia, this cascading plant tumbles happily down banks or walls to show off masses of blue, pink or white flowers. There is also a variegated variety.
Propagate by cuttings.

Armeria
Thrift, Sea Pink
8 x 23 cm (3 x 9 in)

Neat domes of needle-like leaves are topped in spring with drumstick tufts of rich pink, crimson or white flowers. *A. maritima* 'Düsseldorfer Stoltz' is the best red I've seen.
Propagate by cuttings.

Aubrieta
Purple Rock Cress
10 x 60 cm (4 in x 2 ft)

Another cascader, there is a host of aubrieta varieties with flowers of purple, mauve, lavender, crimson, pink and white, all set off well against the grey-green leaves in spring.
propagate by cuttings.

Blechnum See p.121

Aurinia (syn. *Alyssum*)
Gold Dust
30 x 60 cm (12 in x 2 ft)

Popular and deservedly so, *A. saxatilis* makes mounds of grey-green spatula-shaped leaves with bright yellow flower clusters in spring. Brilliant with purple aubrieta, even if it isn't exactly subtle!
Propagate by cuttings.

Campanula
Bellflower
Various sizes

There are dozens of dwarf campanulas suitable for the rock garden. Some are upright, others sprawling. Avoid those that are very invasive. Bells of blue or white are produced from spring to autumn if you choose well.
Propagate by cuttings and division.

Cerastium
Snow in Summer
15 cm x 1.2 m (6 in x 4 ft)

Don't let this glorious, grey-leaved, white-flowered trailer loose anywhere near delicate plants – it will smother them. Find a sunny bank where it can romp and delight you in spring.
Propagate by cuttings.

Chamaecyparis See p.59

Cytisus See p.62

Corydalis See p.122

Cyclamen See p.158

Dianthus
Pink

5-15 cm x 60 cm (2-6 in x 2 ft)

The daintiest and most desirable rock pink is *D. alpinus*, which makes a flat cushion topped with 5 cm (2 in) high wide-faced flowers of pale to deep pink. The hybrids of *D. deltoides* are taller at around 15 cm (6 in) but smaller flowered and best admired at a distance for their glowing colours.
Propagate by cuttings and division.

Diascia
23 cm x 1 m (9 in x 3 ft)

Diascias are very popular in pots as well as in rock gardens. *D.* 'Ruby Field' produces masses of spurred salmon-pink flowers in dainty spires over low mats of foliage nearly all summer.
Propagate by cuttings and division.

Dicentra See p.124

Dryas
Mountain Avens

8 cm x 1 m (3 in x 3 ft)

Dark green, glossy, oak-shaped leaves make a dense carpet that is spattered with nodding white wood anemone flowers in early summer. There are two species commonly grown: *D. octopetala* and *D. x suendermannii*.
Propagate by division.

Epimedium See p.126

Erigeron
Fleabane

23 x 30 cm (9 x 12 in)

Here's a lovely bright alpine daisy with prolific flowers of white or pink.

E. karvinskianus is easy to grow and blooms sporadically from late spring to autumn. Don't let it loose near dainty alpines or it will swamp them.
Propagate by division.

Erinus
10 x 15 cm (4 x 6 in)

A neat clump former with tiny saw-edged leaves and pretty pink flowers carried in clusters atop short stalks in late spring. *E. alpinus* is the true species but there is also a white variety.
Propagate by division.

Erodium
Heron's Bill

10 x 30 cm (4 x 12 in)

There are lots of erodiums valuable in the rock garden but *E. reichardii* (syn. *E. chamaedryoides*) is the most popular. White, pink-veined flowers are carried over low domes of leaves from early to late summer.
Propagate by cuttings and division.

Euphorbia
Spurge

15 x 60 cm (6 in x 2 ft)

Trailing *E. myrsinites* is a good plant to establish above a boulder or steps where it can cast its grey-leaved stems downwards. Yellow-green flowers open at the stem tips in late spring.
Propagate by cuttings and division.

Festuca See p.126

Genista See p.65

Gentiana
Gentian

15 x 30 cm (6 x 12 in)

The measurements I've given are for *G. septemfida*, a summer-flowering, blue-trumpeted gentian that is easy to grow on any soil. Species from Asia generally hate lime; the European ones don't seem to mind it. Start with *G. septemfida* and progress to others.
Propagate by division and seed.

Geranium
Cranesbill

8 x 60 cm (3 x 12 in)

You should grow as many geraniums as you can on your rock garden – they flower for such a long time. *G. sanguineum* var. *striatum* (syn. *G. s.* var. *lancastrense*) is one of the best: a sprawling mat with large, white, saucer-shaped flowers veined in pink. propagate by division.

Heathers See p.66

Dwarf conifers for rock gardens

Dwarf conifers offer year-round interest and add height and form to flat rock beds. When you buy conifers, make sure that they are dwarf or very slow growing, or they'll quickly turn your rock garden into an arboretum.

- *Abies balsamea* Hudsonia Group
- *Chamaecyparis lawsoniana* 'Gimbornii'
- *Chamaecyparis lawsoniana* 'Minima Aurea'
- *Chamaecyparis pisifera* 'Nana'
- *Cryptomeria japonica* 'Vilmoriniana'
- *Juniperus communis* 'Compressa'
- *Juniperus horizontalis* Glauca Group
- *Picea abies* 'Gregoryana'
- *Picea glauca* var. *albertiana* 'Conica'
- *Picea mariana* 'Nana'
- *Pinus mugo* 'Gnom'
- *Thuja plicata* 'Rogersii'

Helianthemum
Rock Rose
23 cm x 1 m (9 in x 3 ft)

Sun-loving summer bloomers making twiggy rugs of evergreen or evergrey leaves. The flowers may be yellow, orange, red, pink or white. 'Henfield Brilliant' is a striking mahogany-orange. The doubles hold on to their flowers longer than the singles.
Propagate by cuttings and seed.

Juniperus See p.68

Hypericum
St John's Wort
23 x 60 cm (9 in x 2 ft)

Dainty *H. olympicum* f. *minus* (syn. *H. polyphyllum*) is a treasure that makes low domes of greyish leaves that are plastered in bright yellow, shaving-brush-centred flowers during early to mid-summer. 'Sulphureum' is paler.
Propagate by cuttings, division and seed.

Iberis
Perennial Candytuft
23 cm x 1 m (9 in x 3 ft)

Dark, evergreen leaves act as an effective backdrop to the dense heads of white flowers that *I. sempervirens* produces in spring. Needs room to spread.
Propagate by cuttings and division.

Leontopodium
Edelweiss
15 x 23 cm (6 x 9 in)

From tufts of greyish leaves the starry, white-felted flowers of *L. alpinum* rise up in early summer. Soggy soil kills it.
Propagate by division.

Lewisia
15 x 15 cm (6 x 6 in)

Some lewisias are the devil to grow.

L. cotyledon hybrids are among the easiest. They make succulent rosettes from which rise branched flowerheads carrying salmon, pink or white flowers in summer. Lime-free soil is preferred, and walls and crevices are enjoyed. propagate by division.

Lithodora
Gromwell
8 x 60 cm (3 in x 2 ft)

A lime-hating trailer with narrow, hairy leaves and starry true-blue flowers in summer. It's the nearest blue to a gentian outside that family. *L. diffusa* 'Grace Ward' has replaced the old favourite 'Heavenly Blue', which is now rather lacking in vigour.
Propagate by cuttings.

Nierembergia
Cup Flower
5 x 30 cm (2 x 12 in)

A low-growing plant with a little carpet of dark green leaves through which appear large, white, cup-shaped flowers in early to mid-summer. *N. repens* (syn. *N. rivularis*) is the species offered.
Propagate by division.

Origanum
Dittany
30 x 30 cm (12 x 12 in)

Its time of flowering alone makes *O. laevigatum* worth growing – it carries tiny crimson-purple tubular flowers on branching stems in late summer and autumn. From a distance you'll see a purple haze mingled with grey-green leaves.
Propagate by cuttings and division.

Othonna
30 x 30 cm (12 x 12 in)

O. cheirifolia has fans of grey, paddle-shaped leaves and yellow daisies, carried in late spring.
Propagate by cuttings.

Oxalis
Wood Sorrel
5 x 23 cm (2 x 9 in)

Neatly pleated grey leaves rise from the tuberous root and are spiced with five-petalled, pale pink, darker-veined flowers in late spring and early summer. *O. adenophylla* is the species I describe; *O. enneaphylla* is more of a spreader: its variety 'Rosea' is also popular.
Propagate by division.

Papaver
Alpine Poppy
15 x 15 cm (6 x 6 in)

Short-lived but self-seeding, *P. alpinum* has finely cut leaves and plenty of pink, white, orange or yellow poppy flowers from early summer onwards.
Propagate by seed.

Persicaria
Knotweed
8-15 cm x 1 m (3-6 in x 3 ft)

There are two splendid plants for the rock garden: *P. affinis*, which has pink 23 cm (9 in) high pokers in summer and autumn, and *P. vacciniifolia*, which is shorter with little pink mousetail flowers that persist right into the colder weather. Both are best when allowed to tumble over rocks.
Propagate by division, or plant non-flowering cuttings in autumn.

Phlox
8 x 45 cm (3 x 18 in)

Thick mats of needle-like leaves and masses of bright, stemless flowers have made the varieties of *P. subulata*, such as 'McDaniels Cushion' (large pink flowers), justifiably popular. They are easy to grow, too, and have blooms of violet, lavender, crimson, pink, lilac and white. *P. divaricata* subsp. *laphamii* 'Chattahoochee', lavender-blue with a crimson eye is also worth growing.
Propagate by cuttings and division.

Pratia
2.5 x 45 cm (1 x 18 in)

Not showy, but nevertheless valuable, *P. angulata* 'Treadwellii' makes a rug of green leaves decorated with tiny white flowers in summer, followed by crimson-purple berries.
Propagate by division.

Primula See p.133

Pulsatilla
Pasque Flower
23 x 30 cm (9 x 12 in)

Early spring favourite with upturned bellflowers of purple, blue, crimson or white, centred with a boss of yellow stamens and swathed in silky hairs. *P. vulgaris* is the most commonly grown species. Loves chalk.
Propagate by root cuttings and seed.

Salix See p.75

Saponaria
Soapwort
15 x 45 cm (6 x 18 in)

The old favourite *S. ocymoides* is a bright plant to put where it can tumble down a boulder. It smothers itself in summer with plenty of pink flowers and as a result it can be short-lived.
Propagate by seed.

Saxifraga
Saxifrage, Rockfoil
Various sizes

You could plant up a rock garden with saxifrages and nothing else and still enjoy it for most of the year. The plants are divided into groups. Among the easiest (and the brightest) are the mossy saxifrages, with yellow, red, pink or white flowers carried in spring on 10 cm (4 in) stalks over cushions of bright green leaves; the encrusted saxifrages love crevices and have

tough leaves decorated with lime deposits; the kabschias make hard domes of leaves and usually produce short-stemmed flowers very early in spring. They like gentle shade. Try any you can get; they offer excellent value.
Propagate by division.

Sedum
Stonecrop
Various sizes

As varied as the saxifrages and even easier to grow, sedums have succulent leaves and bright starry flowers. *S. kamtschaticum* var. *kamtschaticum* 'Variegatum', 10 x 45 cm (4 x 18 in), is cheering with green and cream leaves and orange summer flowers.
Propagate by cuttings.

Sempervivum
Houseleek
5 x 30 cm (2 x 12 in)

These rosette-forming succulents are quite hardy. They are available in assorted leaf colours, from green through to deep crimson, and have starry flowers of pink, crimson, yellow or white in summer. *S. arachnoideum* is the cobweb houseleek and is covered in silvery silky hairs.
Propagate by division.

Silene
Catchfly
15 x 45 cm (6 x 18 in)

S. schafta is the one catchfly that is easy and obliging on the rock garden. It produces plenty of pinkish purple campion flowers in summer.
Propagate by cuttings, division, seed.

Sisyrinchium
23 x 30 cm (9 x 12 in)

Among tufts of small, iris-like leaves, the yellow starry flowers of *S. californicum* Brachypus Group appear from summer through to autumn.
Propagate by division and seed.

Thymus
Thyme
Carpeting

Dense little rugs of aromatic foliage studded with pinkish lilac flowers in summer. There are colour variations in both flower and leaf, some plants having variegated or golden foliage. Likes well-drained soil and full sun.
Propagate by cuttings and seed.

Trillium
Wood Lily
23-30 x 30 cm (9-12 x 12 in)

Choice woodlanders for shady, leafy pockets in the rock garden or for a peat bed. *T. grandiflorum* is the favourite species; its three broad leaves at the tip of a strong stalk set off to perfection the large white, three-petalled flowers, which are surrounded by three small green sepals.
Propagate by division.

Verbascum
Mullein
15 x 30 cm (6 x 12 in)

The neat *V.* 'Letitia' makes a mound of grey-felted leaves, topped with spires of yellow flowers from early to late summer. Protect from winter wet.
Propagate by root cuttings.

Viola See p.137

Zauschneria
Californian Fuchsia
30 x 60 cm (12 in x 2 ft)

Tricky in the colder north but usually reliably perennial in the south, *Z. californica* makes a wiry shrublet with narrow greyish leaves and tubular flowers of burning scarlet. subsp. *garrettii* 'Glasnevin' is a fraction taller and a better bet than the true species in colder areas. Both bloom from late summer into autumn.
Propagate by cuttings, division, seed.

CHAPTER 13 Water gardens

Water adds a new dimension to the garden, creating a tranquil spot to relax, enticing wildlife, and providing the environment for a host of different plants

Picture, if you can, a still summer's day by a limpid pool. Sword-leafed irises and frothy lady's mantle decorate its edges, and a water lily flaunts its shiny pads and starry flowers in the warm light. Bright goldfish dart among the shadowy water while, above the surface, dragonflies and demoiselles buzz from plant to plant, courting in the sunshine. The plate-glass surface is broken only by occasional ripples as a frog plops out of sight, or while the pond skaters dance like dervishes with a gift for walking on water. Even in the tiniest garden a sheet of water will provide spicy variety. You'll be able to grow a wider range of plants, both in the water and at its edges, and whether you like it or not you'll find that you've created a miniature nature reserve. You'll always have frogs, the occasional toad and newt, and an abundance of water-loving insects. If you don't like creepy crawlies a pond is not for you. But before you try to expel the toad population, just think of all the slugs they'll eat.

If tiny tots are at large, you'd better wait a few years before building the pond – even a few inches of water are potentially dangerous. But there's nothing to stop you from laying a pool liner, filling it with about 15 cm (6 in) of soil, planting bog plants and then laying pebbles over the earth to produce a dry river-bed effect. A hosepipe can be played into the liner occasionally to keep the soil moist. When the children are older it's a simple job to turn the river bed into a fully fledged pool – remove the bog plants, top up with water and treat the area as you would any other new water garden. But I'm racing ahead. First, here's what to do for a simple pool.

PLANNING YOUR WATER GARDEN

Choosing the right spot

Just as there's an ideal spot for every other garden feature, so there is for a pool. It should be open and sunny, not overhung by trees, but sheltered at a distance from biting winds. Under trees the water will become a mass of soggy leaf mould in autumn and your fish and aquatic plants will suffer.

If you insist on having a pool under a tree you'll have to be prepared for the task of stretching plastic netting over it every autumn before leaves start to fall, and you'll also have to put up with spindly plants that don't grow or flower as well as those in the sun. Your pool won't be so much limpid as stagnant.

What shape?

Formal pools are for formal gardens. In informal gardens (and most plots fall into that category) irregular shapes are better. I don't mean fiddly: make your pool as sweepingly curved as you can; don't go in for narrow necks and wiggly serpentine shapes.

Fit your pool into the general scheme of the garden so that its outline complements beds and borders. Make it as large as possible; the bigger the stretch of water, the more impact it will have and the easier it will be to keep in good condition - clear and not green.

How deep?

Make your pool more than 60 cm (2 ft) deep and its bottom will become a stagnant mire of lifeless mud. Make it shallower than 30 cm (12 in) and it will heat up like a pan of water on a summer's day, encouraging those algae that turn the water green. 45 cm (18 in) is the happy medium.

What lining material?

Ancient ponds were made of puddled clay but the art of constructing them went out with button boots. Concrete came next, but the work involved in making a concrete pool is amazingly arduous and life is hell when a concrete pool starts to leak. Fibreglass or rigid plastic liners may look handy little jobs when you see them stacked in the garden centre, but they are iniquitously expensive and almost always useless in the garden. Most are too small, their shapes are weird and, when filled with plant life and fish, the water nearly always turns green.

By far the best bet are the flexible liners made of butyl - a sort of luxury rubber. Thick PVC liners are the next choice (provided they're not a nasty

shade of turquoise) and finally, the cheapest liner, polythene. Polythene is also the shortest lived, but where funds are lean it's worth using, for it will almost always last for three years before it needs to be replaced. The other two types of liner will last for donkeys' years, and repair kits are available should they be encouraged to spring a leak by the clumsy placement of a garden fork.

For goodness sake calculate carefully the size of liner you'll need. Its length will be equal to the length of the pool, plus twice the depth, plus 60 cm (2 ft) to allow it to be tucked under whatever edging material you decide on. The width will be equal to the width of the pool, plus twice the depth, plus 60 cm (2 ft). There's

The handsome, bold foliage of these water plants, in all their contrasting shapes and shades of green, is reflected in the pool, creating an alluring depth and beauty in this tranquil garden feature.

Constructing a pool with a liner

1 Having decided on the shape of your pool, mark out the perimeter with pegs. Level the tops of the pegs so that they correspond with the required final level. The water should come to the top of the liner all round.

2 Excavate the pool, making it at least 60cm (2 ft) deep at the lowest point and sloping up gradually on one side. Leave shelves about 23 cm (9 in) deep all round to take pots of marginal plants.

3 To prevent the liner being pierced once it is in place, cover the hole with a layer of fibreglass insulating material, trimming it level with the top of the hole. If you prefer, use strong polythene or a layer of sand.

4 Lay the liner in the hole, checking that the material is evenly distributed and smoothing out wrinkles. Weight the edges with bricks. Slowly fill the pool with water, pulling and tugging at the liner to eliminate creasing.

5 When the pool is full to the brim, check that the water and pool edging are level all round. When you are satisfied, trim off the excess liner material, leaving about 15 cm (6 in) all round.

6 Edge the pool by laying flagstones around it, tucking the liner under them. Alternatively, use bricks, laying them so that they overlap the pool. Use fine sand or soil to bed the stones level, but don't cement them in.

nothing worse than digging out a pool and putting the liner in place only to find that it's too small. The feeling compares with buying a fitted carpet that doesn't.

CONSTRUCTING THE POOL

Preparing the hole

Once you've marked out the shape of your pool, either with a trail of sand or a curved hosepipe, you'll have to start excavating. April and May are the best months for pondmaking, so start digging in March to allow for unexpected interruptions.

The more help you can get at this stage the better. You'll be surprised how many barrowloads of soil come out of a relatively small hole, leaving you with the problem of deciding what to do with the stuff. The usual solution is to build a rock garden mound at the side of the pool. Avoid it. It will always be patently obvious that the mound is a spoil heap.

If the ground is uneven you'll need some spoil to level it off (otherwise you'll have unsightly view of the liner on the higher side), alternatively, use the stuff to build a raised bed or terrace in another part of the garden. It's the top 23-30 cm (9-12 in) of soil that's valuable for plants. Inhospitable subsoil can be used for raising up hard areas of paving and the like or it can be dumped in a hired skip and carted away.

The sides of the pool should slope gently at an angle of about 45°. Cut a step into the side if you like, just about halfway up. This will provide you with a shelf on which pots and baskets of marginal aquatic plants (those that like the shallows) can be stood.

It's tempting, at this stage, to get the liner in and fill it with water, but it might be a costly operation should any sharp stone or glass be protruding. First pat the exposed surfaces of the pool with a spade to knock any protuberances back into the soil, then line the pool with a layer of fibreglass matting; or, if you prefer, spread a 2.5 cm (1 in) layer of sand over the whole area, including a 30 cm (12 in) overlap at the pool edges. With this buffering layer in place the liner can be laid.

Fitting a liner

Unpack the liner carefully and check it for holes; they have been known to exist even before the liner is laid. Stretch it over the hole (you'll need more than one pair of hands) and gently hold the edges down with smooth stones or bricks. Check that the material is evenly distributed so that when the water is in the hole the liner will overlap an equal amount all round.

Now the pool can be filled. Lay a hosepipe on the liner and turn on the tap. This is the exciting bit – as the water flows in you'll see your pool slowly taking shape. Gradually the water's weight will push the liner flat against the soil, but you'll have to gently pull and tuck in any overlaps to avoid a mass of creases, which are potential leak areas. Turn off the hose when the pool is full. At this stage you'll be able to see the final level of the water and the level of your pool edging.

I usually incorporate a boggy area into a pool by excavating just 30 cm (12 in) of topsoil at one end, running the liner over it and up to the surface level (see p.182). The soil is then replaced before the pool is filled. Here all sorts of bog plants will be happy. Some gardeners insist on perforating the liner when it runs under a boggy area but I don't think that this is necessary. What's more, it means that you're for ever topping up the water level in the pool, and topping up encourages green scum.

Edging the pool

The most popular way of edging a pool is to lay paving (crazy or sane) around it, tucking the liner under them. I know it's hackneyed but it is the most reliable method. Mind you, bricks will do just as good a job. Lay them (or the flagstones) so that they overlap the edge of the pool by 5 cm (2 in). There's nothing worse than having to look at a strip of pool liner around what should be a clean-edged stretch of water. Lay your edging very carefully, using the surface of the water as a straight-edge and making sure that the liner slopes upwards from the water just a fraction to prevent any leakage. Fine soil or sand can be used to bed your stones or bricks level, but don't consider cementing them into place or repairs and adjustments may become difficult. Take your time over the edging and be meticulous – it will make or mar your pool.

Now comes the difficult bit. You've got to stand back and do nothing for about ten days. This will allow the water to settle down and disperse some of its undesirable chemical contents. After ten days you can introduce plants.

> "Sword-leafed irises and frothy lady's mantle decorate its edges, and a water lily flaunts its shiny pads and starry flowers in the warm light."

PLANTS FOR A WATER GARDEN

There are five basic kinds of plant that can be used in or around garden pools:

Submerged aquatics spend most of their time below the surface of the water. Many are vital oxygenating plants, keeping fish happy and preventing the water from becoming stagnant. Some produce flowering shoots above the surface, which makes them doubly valuable. No pool can become balanced and clear without oxygenators, so make sure that you have at least two bunches of them for every square metre (square yard) of the pool's surface area. You can always thin them out when they become overcrowded and give them away to pool owners anxious to clear their water.

Fixed-floating aquatics are anchored to the base of the pool (or to a basket of compost within the pool), but their leaves and flowers float on the surface. Water lilies come into this category.

Free-floating aquatics bob about merrily on the surface. Duckweed (*Lemna* spp.) is a classic example, but fairy floating moss (*Azolla*) is a more desirable plant for it is less likely to swamp the pool. In fact, it's best to avoid duckweed like the plague. It will soon plaster your pool from end to end, totally masking its reflective properties, so that it looks like a sunken lawn. Woe betide the unobservant visitor who treads on it.

Marginal aquatics like to grow in shallow water and are most at home on the shelf especially built for them, just 23 cm (9 in) or so below the surface.

Bog plants are happy in soil that stays constantly moist. It doesn't need to be really muddy but most of the plants are quite tolerant of extreme conditions.

Planting aquatics

Free floaters require no planting at all – just release them on the water's surface. Bog plants can be planted with a trowel, like any garden plant, but take care not to perforate the liner. Submerged aquatics can be tied to pebbles with fishing line and dropped to the bottom of the pool where they will soon take root in the sediment.

Marginal and fixed-floating aquatics, like water lilies, are best planted in the special plastic baskets that are made for the job. Line the basket with a bit of old sacking to prevent the compost from seeping out, and plant the lily or other aquatic plant in ordinary garden soil. This is the only occasion on which you'll hear me recommending garden soil for container-grown plants. Normally they are far better with a special potting compost, but in this case the chemical content of the compost would only help to foul the water.

Remove any tatty leaves or very long roots from the plants, then set them in the basket of soil so that their crown (junction of roots and shoots) is level with the

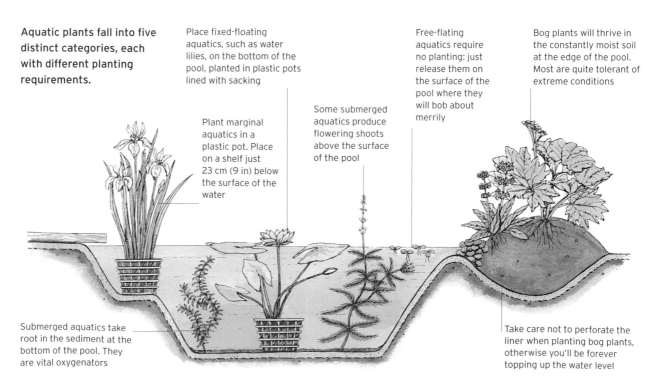

Aquatic plants fall into five distinct categories, each with different planting requirements.

Place fixed-floating aquatics, such as water lilies, on the bottom of the pool, planted in plastic pots lined with sacking

Plant marginal aquatics in a plastic pot. Place on a shelf just 23 cm (9 in) below the surface of the water

Some submerged aquatics produce flowering shoots above the surface of the pool

Free-flating aquatics require no planting: just release them on the surface of the pool where they will bob about merrily

Bog plants will thrive in the constantly moist soil at the edge of the pool. Most are quite tolerant of extreme conditions

Submerged aquatics take root in the sediment at the bottom of the pool. They are vital oxygenators

Take care not to perforate the liner when planting bog plants, otherwise you'll be forever topping up the water level surface. Firm the earth around their roots and cover its surface with gravel to prevent fish disturbing the soil and muddying the water when the plant is in place.

When the basket is planted up, perfectionists will submerge it in a tank of water so that all air can be driven out (a process that can muddy the water). Only then will they transfer the basket to the pool, standing it on bricks at first so that it rests just 15 cm (6 in) below the surface. Marginal aquatics can go straight on to their shelves, but water lilies will appreciate this gentle introduction to the water. After a couple of weeks the bricks can be removed and the basket allowed to rest on the bottom of the pool.

Never be tempted to plant aquatics in mounds of soil at the bottom of the pool. Fish will forever create havoc down there, turning the water into grey soup as they ferret around for food. All planting up is best carried out in spring, during April and May.

FISH AND OTHER WILDLIFE

No pool should be without its quota of wildlife. You'll probably attract frogs and toads whether you want them or not; newts are not so easy to entice and you may not see them very frequently even if you take the trouble to introduce them.

Iridescent dragonflies and demoiselles, or damsel flies, will doubtless come uninvited, but they are a treat to watch as they perform aerobatics over the water in summer. Other insects will abound, especially pond skaters on the surface and water boatmen beneath. Don't worry about introducing water snails: they're not essential and if you end up with the wrong ones they'll spend all their time eating your water lily leaves instead of clearing up the sediment, for which they are renowned. I've never noticed that they make any difference at all to the state of the water.

Goldfish are a must. Most experienced pond makers recommend golden orfe as being the finest fish for a garden pond. I agree that they look good in shoals, but they're not as bright as your common- or garden-pool goldfish, which move around more slowly, giving you time to admire their vivid coats. I'd settle for a mixture of the two, avoiding those expensive and revolting Koi carp, which look like a fish-breeder's nightmare. Don't overstock your pool: allow at least 30 sq cm (1 sq ft) of surface area to each fish. Introduce your fish gently about two months after planting up the pond and establishing the oxygenators.

Always buy your fish from a reputable supplier, and

Planting water lilies

1 Before planting water lilies, cut off any tatty leaves and very long roots. Plant in ordinary garden soil, in plastic baskets lined with a piece of sacking to prevent the soil from seeping out into the water.

2 Cover the soil with gravel to prevent disturbance once it is submerged. Rest the basket on bricks in the pool for two weeks before lowering to the bottom.

avoid any fish that are listless or showing signs of white fungal growth. Suspend the container in which they are supplied over the edge of the pool for a few hours so that the water temperatures can equalize. Then the fish can be allowed to swim gently out of the bag or bowl into the pool.

There's much argument about feeding fish. I've kept them going for years by dropping pelleted food into the pond once a week from April to September. Allow one pellet per fish. Drop too much food into the water as it will only cause the pool to become cloudy. Between October and March the fish will find all they need among the plants and sediment – they won't need any supplements to their diet.

Diseased or damaged fish are best removed and knocked on the head. Don't be shocked at this callousness. There are all manner of cures given for diseases, most of which involve immersing the fish in a bowl of water containing some thoroughly unpleasant solution. The fish will be miserable and is quite likely to infect the other members of the pool when he's reintroduced. I stand by my seemingly cruel solution.

You'll also have to harden your heart if your fish are speared and stolen by herons. This stately grey bird cleared my pond of all but two fish a couple of years ago. All the fish had names and were won at assorted fairgrounds with well-aimed ping-pong balls (so much for reputable suppliers). It was a heavy blow! Only plastic netting stretched over the pool will keep the big birds at bay, but who wants to look at a vista of plastic netting every day?

MAINTAINING YOUR WATER GARDEN
Green water
This is your biggest pool problem, but if you make your stretch of water large enough and deep enough it will only be a temporary nuisance. All pools turn green shortly after they are made but, if plenty of oxygenating plants are present, the water will eventually clear, though it may briefly turn pea-green each spring.

Don't be tempted to drain the pool and start again – the greening will only start again too. Leave the pool alone and only top it up with a hosepipe when the water level starts to get low. Excessive topping-up will exacerbate the problem.

Green blanket weed is easy to fish out with a wire-toothed lawn rake, but take care neither to disturb the sediment at the bottom of the pool nor to puncture the liner. Construct your pool properly, ensuring that the elements are balanced, and be patient: that way you're less likely to encounter long-term problems.

Renovation and cleaning
Just like other garden plants, aquatics and bog plants will need an annual clean-up in autumn and winter. Remove all faded leaves and chop back the stalks of deciduous kinds to within a few centimetres (inches) of soil level. Pull faded leaves from water lilies and remove any rotting vegetation from the water.

If your garden is a moving scene of fallen leaves in autumn it is definitely worthwhile covering the pool with plastic netting to catch the foliage before it falls in. Rotting leaves will cloud the water and poison the fish.

Don't clean the bottom of the pond every year; save the job up and do it when it is really necessary – say once every three years. Empty the pool and divide the plants at the same time, re-basketing those that need it. Before emptying the pool you'll have to catch and safely house your fish.

Create a water garden and it will instantly become a magnet to visitors: for humans it is a haven of tranquillity; for wildlife it forms a miniature nature reserve.

Creating a moving water feature

For a moving water feature you must provide a series of smaller pools at different heights above the main pool. Set a submersible pump on blocks at the bottom of the pool and run a hose from the pump to the header pool. Bury the hose in a trench to one side of the pool.

Pipe emerges into header pool, disguised by overlapping stones

Protect cable with armoured sleeving and fit a residual current device

Submersible pump placed on smooth blocks on pool bottom

Flexible pipe is taken out to one side and buried in trench alongside pool

Pool liner laid over protective layer of sand or fibreglass matting

In winter keep a patch of ice melted so that the fish can breathe. Don't clout it with a hammer – the sound waves will stun the fish – but pour a kettle of boiling water on the surface to make a hole. Extract a little water if you can, to leave a greater surface area from which the fish can extract oxygen.

OTHER WATER FEATURES

Moving water

Although fountains, cascades and waterfalls seldom look attractive on a small scale – and plants rarely enjoy growing in moving water – I have to admit that there is nothing more musical than the sound of moving water. The urge to add this feature to a water garden has been aided by the array of inexpensive equipment that is now available – submersible pumps for the circulation of water, preformed cascades and the like. For safety's sake, however, I would urge you to employ an electrician to install a pump or any other electrically powered feature in the garden. Pool lights, for example, bring the water alive at night and are especially worth installing adjacent to a patio or picture window to illuminate the plants, water and fish. Make sure the correct lights are chosen for the job: again rely on your tame electrician.

Tub pools

Finally, for the gardener with no garden, there's the tub pool. Half an oak beer cask, soundly coopered and painted inside with waterproofing bitumen, can be filled with water and used as a home for a pygmy water lily and three goldfish. If you can't lay your hands on a tub, find an old porcelain sink, treat it as described on p.170, put the plug in and fill it with water. The plants and fish will do just as well as in a tub. The fish will need warmer quarters in winter (a friend's pond will do nicely) but in spring and summer the pool will bring life and interest to the tiniest patio.

Pond-care calendar

■ *April/May* Check that electrics are in good order. Remove, clean and store pool heater. Reconnect pump. Lift and divide overcrowded aquatics. Feed in May with special fertilizer, directly into baskets.

■ *June/July/August* Top up water level as necessary. Remove weed from surface. Remove faded flowerheads.

■ *September/October* Clean up pond before winter. Cut down foliage and flower stems as they fade. Remove debris and made sure leaves are kept out. Remove tender aquatics to overwinter in buckets of water in cool, frost-free place. Remove, clean and store pump and replace pool heater in pond.

If space is short create a tub pool from a half barrel. Well coopered and painted inside with bitumen, it will hold a pygmy water lily and two or three fish.

A-Z of water plants

THE FOLLOWING LISTS include some of the most cheering water plants; all are easy to grow in the right situation. They're a self-sufficient little bunch who give of their best in spring and summer. Try to choose something from each of the lists to produce a healthy environment for the other water dwellers.

SUBMERGED AQUATICS

Elodea canadensis
Canadian Pondweed

This is the curly-leaved water plant that one was always given a sprig of when you bought a petshop goldfish. Its larger relative is now called *Lagarosiphon major* (syn. *E. crispa*). Both are vital oxygenators.

Hottonia palustris
Water Violet

Water violet has feathery underwater leaves and spikes of starry flowers above water in spring.

Myriophyllum species
Water Milfoil

Superbly dainty feathery leaves are the real glory of water milfoil; it also has spikes of insignificant flowers in summer.

Potamogeton crispus
Curled Pondweed

Narrow, wavy leaves. Insignificant flowers in summer.

Ranunculus aquatilis
Water Crowfoot

Feathery leaves are produced below the water, while buttercup-like leaves and white flowers appear above it in late spring.

Utricularia vulgaris
Bladderwort

A neat little insectivorous plant that catches its prey in minute bladders held among the feathery underwater leaves. Yellow snapdragon flowers appear above water in summer.

FIXED-FLOATING AQUATICS

Aponogeton distachyos
Water Hawthorn

Oval leaves sit on the water and are decorated with scented clusters of white, black-anther-dotted flowers in summer.

Nuphar lutea
Brandy Bottle, Yellow Water Lily

Water-lily-like leaves and cup-shaped yellow flowers on stalks that hold them above the water in summer.

Nymphaea species and varieties
Water Lily

The queen of the pool with those rounded, shiny pads of leaves and starry flowers of white, yellow, pink, crimson or violet-blue. I offer a selection for ponds of different sizes. All bloom for most of the summer:
N. 'Caroliniana': pale pink; small pools and tubs.
N. 'Escarboucle': rich rosy crimson; large pools.
N. 'Froebelii': rosy red; small pools.
N. 'Gladstoneana': white; large pools.
N. 'Gonnère': white; large pools.
N. 'James Brydon': rich rosy red; large or small pools.
N. 'Marliacea Chromatella': pale yellow; large pools.
N. 'Mrs Richmond': deep pink; large pools.
N. odorata var. *minor*: tiny white flowers and leaves; small pools.
N. 'Odorata Sulphurea': pale yellow; small pools.
N. 'Rose Arey': rose pink; small pools.
N. tetragona (syn. *N.* 'Pygmaea Alba'): minute white flowers and leaves; the best choice for tubs and sinks.

MARGINAL AQUATICS

Acorus calamus
Sweet Flag
75 cm (2½ ft)

Sword-shaped leaves that are sweetly scented when crushed. The variety 'Variegatus' is cream-striped and more compact.

Butomus umbellatus
Flowering Rush
90 cm (3 ft)

Grassy green leaves and umbels of lovely pink flowers in summer.

Calla palustris
Bog Arum
23 cm (9 in)

Glossy, green, heart-shaped leaves and miniature arum lily flowers of clear white in summer.

Caltha palustris
Kingcup, Marsh Marigold
30 cm (12 in)

Heart-shaped green leaves and bright yellow buttercup flowers in spring. The double-flowering variety 'Flore Pleno' is best.

Glyceria maxima var. *variegata*
Reed Meadow Grass
60 cm (2 ft)

A stunning variegated grass with leaves striped green and creamy white. Vigorous.

Houttuynia cordata 'Flore Pleno'

45 cm (18 in)

Pointed, heart-shaped leaves make a dense clump that sports white, pyramidal flowers in summer. Very handsome.

Iris laevigata
Smooth Iris

75 cm (2½ ft)

Sword-shaped leaves and handsome wide-petalled flowers of purple, blue, pink or white in early summer.

Iris pseudacorus
Yellow Flag

90 cm (3 ft)

Grey-green leaves and bright yellow iris flowers in early summer.

Juncus effusus f. *spiralis*
Corkscrew rush

45 cm (18 in)

A reed with leaves spiralled just like corkscrews – a conversation piece if nothing else.

Mentha aquatica
Water Mint

45 cm (18 in)

Green leaves and the usual lilac summer flowers of mint. Equally as aromatic as garden mint and just as useful.

Menyanthes trifoliata
Bog Bean

30 cm (12 in)

Three-lobed leaves and white early summer flowers with fringed edges.

Myosotis scorpioides
Water Forget-me-not

23 cm (9 in)

Clouds of pale blue flowers in late spring and early summer.

Orontium aquaticum
Golden Club

30 cm (12 in)

Golden-yellow flower spikes rise up from oval green leaves, early summer.

Pontederia cordata
Pickerel Weed

45 cm (18 in)

Arrow-shaped, glossy green leaves and spires of pale blue flowers in summer.

Sagittaria sagittifolia 'Flore Pleno'
Arrowhead

45 cm (18 in)

The double white flowers are carried up tall stems.

Schoenoplectus lacustris subsp. *tabernaemontani* 'Zebrinus'
(syn. *Scirpus*)
Zebra Rush

90 cm (3 ft)

Porcupine quills of green banded with creamy yellow. Very handsome.

FREE-FLOATING AQUATICS

Azolla filiculoides
(syn. *A. caroliniana*)
Fairy Floating Moss

Pale green, lacy leaves become pinky red with the onset of cold weather.

Hydrocharis morsus-ranae
Frogbit

Miniature water-lily leaves and three-petalled white flowers in summer. Sinks to the bottom in winter.

Stratiotes aloides
Water Soldier

Rosettes of green leaves float half in, half out of the water. White, three-petalled flowers open in summer.

Bog plants

The following plants are described in Chapter 9 Border Plants. They will all do well in a patch of moist soil on the pond bank.

- *Aconitum*
- *Ajuga*
- *Alchemilla*
- *Aruncus*
- *Astilbe*
- *Dicentra*
- *Gunnera* (massive bogs only!)
- *Hemerocallis*
- *Hosta*
- *Iris* (some)
- *Lobelia*
- *Lysimachia*
- *Mimulus*
- *Monarda*
- *Rheum*
- *Rodgersia*
- *Trollius*
- *Zantedeschia*

A pale blue bridge crosses a shallow pool in our garden. Variegated iris and knotweed decorate its banks.

CHAPTER 14 Wildlife in the garden

A garden is brought to life by the wildlife it attracts: by providing the right conditions, and by not being too tidy, you can encourage in a host of creatures

A garden without animals and birds, butterflies and bees is as dead as a doornail and as dull as ditchwater. Ever since I was a lad I've been just as interested in the wildlife to be found in a garden as in the plants. Serried ranks of lobelia and alyssum, salvias and French marigolds hold no joy for me, but a bank of billowing summer flowers that's perhaps a bit too overgrown for the neat-and-tidy-minded gardener offers great excitement when it's alive with butterflies and abuzz with bees.

I don't carry my love of nature to extremes though: snails and slugs are ruthlessly expelled from the rock garden and the vegetable plot – the places where they seem to do most damage – and I can't stand greenfly on roses. So how is a gardener to live with these conflicting ideas? It's not as difficult as it sounds.

The first rule is one that all lazy gardeners will enjoy putting into practice: don't be too tidy. That's not an excuse for letting all parts of the plot lie fallow for the rest of your life; it's simply a matter of selecting certain areas of the garden that can be left relatively undisturbed and where the right weeds can be encouraged to grow. There's planning to be done, even in a wilderness.

ATTRACTING BUTTERFLIES AND MOTHS

Butterflies

Most of us admire butterflies, and a few of us like moths as well. Both can be encouraged to make themselves at home in the garden if the right food plants are present. There are two distinct kinds of food plant: those that nourish the larvae or caterpillars, and those from which the adults drink nectar. You'll need patches of both so that you have vital egg-laying sites for the propagation of the species, and insect pubs where the adults can drink their fill from spring to autumn.

In a large garden, it's easy to let a sunny and sheltered corner run wild with nettles, thistles, grasses and other food-supplying weeds for egg laying; in a small garden it's more difficult to squeeze them in, but a patch of nettles alone (always in a sunny spot) will bring you a surprisingly rich harvest.

If you enjoy watching adult butterflies feeding by day, you'll be pleased to hear that there are plenty of ornamental garden plants whose nectar they love. Your entire plot does not have to be converted to (or allowed to remain) a flowerless jungle.

Plants with purple or yellow flowers are apparently the favourites, but in my own garden the following are the ones that have been as well patronized as any real-ale pub by the butterfly population. Single flowers are always better than doubles for they have large nectaries: *Ageratum*, *Agrostemma*, alyssum, *Aubrieta*, *Buddleja*, *Caryopteris*, *Centranthus*, *Echinops*, *Eryngium*, *Hebe*, honesty, *Lavatera*, lavender, *Liatris*, Michaelmas daisy, *Nepeta*, *Nicotiana*, *Petunia* (single), *Phlox*, *Phuopsis*, scabious, *Sedum*, thyme.

Moths

The moths have an equally varied diet from privet to various weeds, cabbages and lettuces. Most of them are nocturnal but they are often disturbed during the day if you brush past their resting sites among plants. In our garden we are plagued with large yellow underwings, but the occasional maiden's blush, magpie moth and hawk moth come to light too.

Finally, remember that a little shelter in the garden, in the form of a thick coat of ivy on a garage or outbuilding, or a thicket of brambles in a corner, will allow hibernating butterflies and moths to shelter through the winter and carry on their good work the following season.

BEE-ATTRACTING PLANTS

If you wave your arms around and do an impersonation of a windmill every time a bee comes near you, the last thing you'll want to do is attract them to your garden. But if you like all forms of wildlife, then the following plants will persuade the bees that your garden really is the place to visit: borage, *Buddleja*, *Echinops*, *Erica*, *Eryngium*, *Fuchsia*, godetia, *Lavatera*, lavender, lime trees, lupins, *Monarda*, nasturtium, *Nepeta*, *Nigella*, *Phacelia*, scabious.

BIRD FEEDING AND NESTING

Faded seedheads on all manner of plants, from thistles to sunflowers and Michaelmas daisies, will keep seed-eating birds such as goldfinches busy for hours, and berrying shrubs, like *Berberis*, *Pyracantha* and *Symphoricarpos*, will feed other species in winter. That's the time at which you should be making a special effort to supplement the diet of all wild birds. Outside my study and our sitting-room windows, wire-netting bird feeders, filled with bits of fat and peanuts, hang from November to March. After years of squirrels destroying flimsy models, I now have sturdy, squirrel-proof ones. The feeder is filled every morning and by evening it's almost empty, proving that the birds have a powerful hunger. The bird bath (kept thawed in winter) is patronized too and, for those species that have no head for heights (though they seem happy enough when flying), mixed wild bird food is scattered on the lawn. The centre of the lawn is the place for bird food: scatter it near beds and borders and cats will stealthily sneak through the undergrowth to wreak havoc.

> **"Butterflies can be encouraged to make themselves at home in the garden if the right food plants are present."**

We never bother with coconuts as they seem to dry up before the birds can really get stuck in. Pieces of bacon rind are ignored too; it's the softer fat or suet that goes down best. Coal tits, blue tits, great tits, nuthatches and greenfinches are regularly in evidence, and a great spotted woodpecker sometimes turns up too. Over our years here, we've had 47 species of bird appearing at one time or another.

Stop feeding the birds as soon as spring arrives; if their young are fed a diet of peanuts they'll suffer. By egg-hatching time you should be encouraging the

There are various types of bird feeder on the market. Fill them with winter snacks of suet, fat and peanuts to attract tits, nuthatches, and greenfinches to your garden.

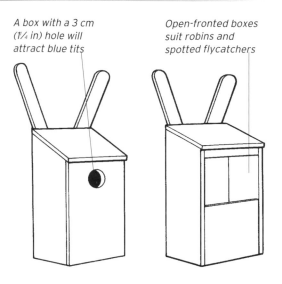

A box with a 3 cm (1¼ in) hole will attract blue tits

Open-fronted boxes suit robins and spotted flycatchers

Choose a nestbox suited to the birds you want to attract, and hang it out of the way of predatory cats.

adults to help you out with pest-control in the garden; there will be plenty of caterpillars and grubs to devour.

Some birds are irritating pests at certain times of year. Sparrows and bullfinches will strip fruit trees of their buds, often as soon as the leaves fall in autumn. Netting is really the only successful long-term deterrent. Blackbirds will adore your raspberries, but mostly the depredations can be lived with, and both you and the birds will have a substantial diet.

It's always fun to put up nestboxes, but do the job properly. Tits need a box with a hole just 3 cm (1¼ in) in diameter; make it any larger and sparrows will take over. Robins and spotted flycatchers need open-fronted boxes, and there are all manner of different permutations that can be made at home or bought from special firms. Well made from tough plywood, they are highly successful in persuading birds to nest.

The secret is to find the right place for the box. I'm no expert here, but have put all my boxes at a height of around 2 m (7 ft) - out of the way of our marauding cat. I've yet to try them in woodland, but they've lured blue tits with ease on walls facing east and south. Put your boxes up in autumn. That gives the birds a chance to do plenty of prospecting right through the winter. Sometimes they'll roost in the boxes rather than nesting in them; other years they'll ignore them completely. As well as being skilful in placing your boxes, you'll also have to rely on luck.

Don't forget that birds like the cover and nesting sites provided by shrubs, hedges and brambles. Provide these hiding places and you're bound to get more birds.

ENCOURAGING OTHER WILDLIFE

I've no room to launch into a comprehensive natural history of the back garden, but I will remind you of the joys to be had from hedgehogs, who slurp saucers of

Frogs and toads will appreciate a garden pond as a spawning site; they will repay you by devouring your slugs

Dragonflies and damselflies are a treat to watch as they perform acrobatics over the water in summer

Create a water garden and it will become an instant magnet to all manner of wildlife, such as frogs, newts, dragonflies, and pond skaters.

The plants around the pool provide a perfect habitat for all sorts of wildlife. Flowering plants will attract butterflies and bees

You may be lucky enough to entice newts to your pool for their spring breeding season. They live on land the rest of the year

Cobbles or a bog garden area at the edge of the pool make it easier for wildlife to reach the water

milk more quickly and noisily than a cat, and the mixed feelings you'll have about foxes, rabbits and deer.

There's nothing as romantic as the sight of a few deer at the top of our garden in summer or winter, but I do go up the hill with a sinking feeling, wondering what they've eaten. Once they've ring-barked a favourite tree it's curtains (for the tree, not the deer). Plastic rabbit guards are a bit of a help, but not much.

A garden pool is less of a worry and more of a magnet for all sorts of creatures from frogs and toads (valuable slug eaters) to dragonflies and demoiselles. You might be lucky enough to have newts, and you'll certainly have pond skaters whose acrobatics defy the laws of gravity. With frog-spawning sites disappearing every year, the back-garden pond is playing a vital role in their survival. (See Chapter 13 Water Gardening.)

WILD FLOWER GARDENING

Finally, don't forget the wild flowers. Only where there's space to spare for such luxuries will you want to make a patch of natural 'wild garden' or grassland where the rarer wild flowers can feel safe. But such a patch dovetails into other forms of wildlife encouragement because butterflies, moths, bees and other insects will relish the opportunity to feed in these mini-reserves. To keep the patch as grassland you'll still have to mow, but only three times a year: in early to mid-July, late August and finally in October.

One of the great things about welcoming wildlife and wild flowers into your garden is that you're creating a reserve that will replace the natural habitats decimated by modern farming and pesticides. It's a breathing space for all sorts of declining species like bumblebees. Go the whole hog and imitate nature by using only organic fertilizers

A wildflower garden provides a delightful way of encouraging the conservation of native species and attracting wildlife.

such as blood, bone and fishmeal, which encourage bacterial activity. Inorganic fertilizers like sulphate of ammonia and superphosphate supply nutrients as far as plants are concerned, but they give the bacteria – vital to soil wellbeing – nothing to break down. Avoid using herbicides altogether, and learn to live with a weedy lawn. I have! When really severe outbreaks of pests appear and desperation sets in, use an organic insecticide. They're very effective, but remember that while they're killing the pests, they may also kill smaller beneficial insects like ladybird and hover-fly larvae which feed so voraciously on aphids (possibly the very aphids you've just sprayed). Keeping the right balance between predator and pest is a ticklish business. You get rid of the pests and the predators are killed or move away in search of food. When the pests reappear, as they inevitably will, there are fewer predators to deal with them, and you're back to square one. All in all, try to tolerate pests, using insecticides as the very last resort, and always spot-treat pest outbreaks rather than spraying indiscriminately.

CHAPTER 15 Lawns

Restful on the eye, the perfect foil for surrounding plants, and a place for the whole family to play or relax – it is hardly surprising that lawns feature in most gardens

EVERY GARDEN HAS A LAWN – OR SOMETHING that passes for one. It's quite true that in tiny gardens the lawn brings with it a host of problems, but whatever the arguments against it, it has one unassailable advantage: it's cheap. It's all very well for the landscape architect to persuade you that what you really need is York stone paving, granite setts or brick paviors, but if you have to take on a second mortgage to cover the cost it's probably not worthwhile.

Mind you, he has a point about grass being a bad choice in confined spaces. It will be difficult to mow; the clippings might be difficult to dispose of; the grass is not an all-weather surface, so you'll have to steer round it when it's muddy; and you'll likely as not have problems with wear and tear, moss and fungus diseases (but then so will any lawn owner).

Grown well, all the usual compliments levelled at a lawn apply: it sets off the rest of the garden; it shows off the plants a treat; when new-mown, it makes the rest of the garden look tidy even if it isn't. And you can't play croquet on York stone paving.

THE NEW LAWN

If you're faced with the task of making a new lawn, get ready for a bit of hard graft. Whether you sow seed or lay turves the preparation of the ground is exactly the same. It should be cleared of debris, builder's rubble, long grass, all weeds and any piles of subsoil (if it's a new site), then forked or dug over. That's several weeks' work in just one sentence.

It does pay to take a bit of trouble at this stage. If you can dig out completely any tree stumps, for instance, you'll be saved the job of filling in the hole that appears years later when the stump rots. It's at this stage that fungi keep coming up on the lawn too.

A generous helping of moist compost dug into the soil during preliminary cultivations will give the grass some welcome organic matter into which it can sink its shallow roots and obtain a little resistance to drought.

Try to make the site as level as you can. Keen types will hammer pegs into the ground to the required level,

Preparing for a new lawn

1 Before sowing grass seed or laying turf, it is essential that the site is cleared of debris and weeds, forked over and enriched with organic matter. Then get the site as level as possible, using a spirit level and straightedge set between pegs marked at the required level.

2 Rake the soil so that it reaches the level marked on the pegs. Fill any hollows with added topsoil, and flatten bumps: although the lawn doesn't have to be perfectly level, these would create problems when mowing. Continue raking and levelling the entire site.

3 Once you have raked the whole site level, firm the surface by tramping over it evenly with your feet, or tamping with the back of rake. This will ensure that there are no soft spots that might later sink. Check the level again and fill any hollows as before.

4 When you are satisfied that the site is level and firm, rake it to a fine tilth and leave it for a few weeks so that any residual weeds can be dealt with. Before sowing grass seed or laying turf, scatter a general fertilizer over the site and lightly rake it in.

and check them against one another with a straightedge and spirit level. To be honest, most gardeners needn't go to this length, but it's a good idea to rake the surface as level as possible, tramp it down with your feet and rake again, crouching down and running your eye over the ground to spot any bumps and hollows that can be flattened or filled in.

When you have prepared the site it's a good idea to let it stand idle for at least a month before you sow or turf; that way any resident weeds you overlooked will

come up and show themselves and you can remove them smartly.

All in all, preparing the ground for a new lawn is a bit of a rigmarole, and if you're starting with an area that's free of perennial weeds, you could always take a short cut by rotavating rather than forking or digging. However the soil will be very fluffy when you've finished, so let it settle for a week or so then firm it well before sowing or turfing. It might be tempting to use a roller but this can flatten the surface a bit too firmly, leading to compaction. Shuffling around with your feet close together creates the ideal surface. Finally, you'll still have to take as much care over levelling as if you were using a fork or spade.

DESIGNING YOUR LAWN

When it comes to shape, that's something for you to decide, but remember that twiddly bits are hard on the eye, hard to mow, and keeping the edges trimmed is even more of a chore. Try to avoid making square or rectangular lawns unless you're going for the strictly formal look. My preference, in the average 'lawn and mixed border' situation, is for sweeping, natural lines, which will show off your plants better and look a little more romantic and restful.

Fiddle around with the shape of the lawn by laying a hosepipe on it to mark out the area. Go inside the house and check your design from windows both upstairs and down until you hit upon the right shape. An assistant comes in handy here, to save you the trouble of dashing in and out to make adjustments. When you're completely happy with the design, mark it out on the soil with a trail of sand.

SEED OR TURF?

It's tempting to turf a lawn rather than seed it because the effect is instant, but turf does have disadvantages.

> **"If the turf stays green and looks fine from a distance, then why worry if there's a bit of dock or dandelion in it?"**

It is ten times more expensive than seed; it varies in quality from supplier to supplier, and you'll have to wait for a few weeks before you can walk on it, or the un-knit turves will skid around. What's more, there's a darned sight more labour involved in laying turf evenly than there is in scattering and raking in grass seed.

The advantages of turf? Well, apart from being almost instant, you can lay it at any time of year when the soil is moist, rather than dusty, frozen or muddy. Seed is best sown in September or April and May.

Finding good turf is not easy. Look through the Yellow Pages under Turf Supplies and ring around for a few quotes. Beware of firms who offer just one type of turf – it's probably mown meadow turf, and even if it's

described as 'weed treated' you're likely to find that it's as varied in make-up as a patchwork quilt. Settle for a good, hard-wearing turf from a specialist supplier; don't be talked into having flashy 'sea-washed' stuff which is far too luxurious for a resilient lawn. Arrange for delivery on a day when you know you will be at home and ready to lay the stuff (weather permitting). Turf stacked for more than three days soon turns yellow and starts to die off. If you have to stack it yourself, remember to stack it grass to grass and soil to soil. Rolled turves can be left as they are, but do lay them quickly.

If you decide on seed, then you'll have to choose the kind of mixture you need. Don't get ideas above your station and sow a 'bowling green' type of mixture that looks good on the green-striped, pictorial packet. If you want a hard-wearing lawn that can tolerate children and picnics choose a mixture containing a dwarf variety of ryegrass. These mixtures make a dense, good-looking sward that wears well, and because the ryegrass is a dwarf strain it won't produce any of those long stems that refuse to be cut by the mower. The 'bowling green' mixtures are only suitable for lawns that won't be asked to take much wear. They don't contain ryegrass and need a much more comprehensive lawn care programme than those seed mixtures that do. They are likely to become overrun by alien grasses if not mown regularly, and they fall prey to fungus diseases more easily. On the other hand, if you want to spend every waking hour producing a velvet lawn that is the envy of your neighbours, the fine mixture is the one to go for.

Slightly shady areas can be sown with grass seed mixtures that are made up from shade tolerant grasses – look for them in the garden centre.

Whether you choose seed or turf you'll still have to calculate how much you need. Turf is sold in square metres or square yards, as a rule, and seed by weight. The recommended sowing rate is 40 g (about 1½ oz) per square metre or yard; that will allow the birds a few beakfuls without spoiling your lawn.

LAYING TURF

Once the turf is neatly stacked near the site of your lawn-to-be and the earth is waiting to receive it, scatter a light dusting of general fertilizer over the soil (a handful to the square metre or yard will do) and lightly rake it in. Don't rake for hours or you'll find more stones than you know what to do with. The soil should be

Laying turf

Start at one end of the site and lay a row of turves overlapping the intended boundary. Lay them immediately in front of your plank so that you achieve a straight line right at the start. Butt them as close together as you can and pat them firm with the back of your spade (not so hard that they turn to mud). If any of them sit too far up or down, add or subtract a little soil beneath them. If you find, as you're laying the turves, that they don't sit quite flush with one another, take a bucket of soil with you and fill any gaps.

When the first row is laid, move your plank on top of them and lay the next row, staggering the joints like those of bricks in a wall. Continue like this, overlapping the boundary of the lawn all the way round - you can trim it up later.

When the entire area is covered, remove the plank and keep every member of the family off the lawn for at least ten days; that way the turf will have a chance to settle without being buffeted around.

1 Stand on a plank placed on the turves you have already laid. Work forwards and lay in a brick pattern.

Standing on a plank to protect the newly laid turves, pat them firmly into place with the back of a spade

2 Pat down the turves so that they are firmly in contact with the levelled earth. Don't bash them

If any of the turves sit too high or too low, adjust the level of the soil beneath them

3 Adjust the level of uneven turves by adding or subtracting soil underneath them as necessary.

4 As the job progresses, brush fine soil (or a mixture of peat and sand) into any cracks between the turves.

4-6 weeks after laying turves, cut the edges to the required shape against a plank or curved hosepipe

5 The edges can be cut to the required shape with a spade or half-moon iron.

nicely moist – not so dusty it goes everywhere or so wet that it clings to your wellies.

You'll need a spade and a plank before you go any further: the spade for lifting and patting the turves into place (as well as adding and subtracting soil beneath them) and the plank to walk on.

If you're turfing in spring or summer, have a hosepipe and sprinkler handy and turn it on over the completed lawn at the slightest suspicion of dryness. Left to bake, the turf will turn brown, refuse to knit together and shrink, causing large gaps to appear.

With any luck the lawn will be ready to walk on after four to six weeks, depending on the time of year (sooner in spring and summer; later in winter). It's at this stage that you can trim the edges against a plank or a curved hosepipe. You can start to mow, too, but take it slowly and don't cut the grass too short – just remove the top 1 cm (½ in) of grass once it has grown 5 cm (2 in) high. Soon you can mow more regularly, but it's still a good idea to avoid giving the grass too much wear, and to make sure it never dries out. The kinder you are at this stage, the more quickly will your lawn establish itself.

SOWING SEED

Soil preparation is exactly the same for sowing seeds as for laying turf: scatter a handful of general fertilizer over each square metre or square yard of soil and lightly rake it in. Shuffle over the soil with your feet to firm it, then rake again. The soil should be moist, not dusty or muddy. Lawns sown in September stand the best chance of establishing quickly: there is less likely to be a sudden burst of weed growth than there is with the April and May sowings, and the earth will be nicely warmed up after the summer sunshine and gently moistened by early autumn rains. The grass will also be expected to put up with less wear and tear through autumn and winter than it would through summer, so it's likely to grow thicker more quickly.

The recommended sowing rate of 40 g (about 1½ oz) per square metre or yard will allow the birds to have a nibble, so there's no need to be neurotic and rig up Heath Robinsonian devices using little metal bottle tops and steak-and-kidney pie dishes. Sparrows will only take dust baths on the soil if it's dusty which, as far as your grass seed is concerned, is a bad thing. Keep it moist with the aid of a sprinkler. The odd bit of disturbance won't really make any difference.

Don't go to the trouble of weighing out every 40 g

(1½ oz) of the seed. Weigh one lot, put it into an old plastic yoghurt or cream carton and mark the side with a felt-tip pen. Use the measure for all your subsequent work. I've never been conscientious enough to mark out the plot into square metres, but then I kid myself that I know what a metre looks like. If you don't, check up and chalk it out on a path or patio. When it's imprinted on your mind, start sowing; for goodness sake don't mark out the entire area into little squares with canes and string.

Scatter each measure of seed evenly over its allotted area and, when the whole patch is sown, go over it with a rake, lightly raking the seed in. Don't roll it. If you've shuffled over the ground with your feet to firm it, that's all that's needed.

Turn a sprinkler on whenever the soil looks dry. It will seem ages before any grass shows, but after a few weeks, when you're bent double looking across the

The sweeping curve of the lawn, echoed by the brick path around its perimeter, draws the eye around the garden to the secluded dining area beyond, creating a pleasing sense of space and unhurried leisure.

surface of the soil, you'll detect a faint green haze. That's the youngsters pushing through. Don't worry if the effect is patchy, even when the grass is a few centimetres or inches high. The seeds germinate erratically and stragglers may still come through a few weeks after the first ones showed. Any bare patches that remain after eight weeks can be resown with seed. Rake them over, scatter the seed and rake again.

When much of the grass is about 5 cm (2 in) high, go over the lawn either with a light roller (if you have one) or with a cylinder lawn mower that can be held so that only the back roller comes into contact with the soil. This rolling will make sure that the roots of the young plants are firmly anchored to the soil before they are

Caring for your lawn

Most of us are rotten to our lawns; we cut them and bash them around without ever giving them regular meals or a wash and brush-up. Expert gardeners have complicated lawn-care programmes, but the following are the basic tasks necessary to produce a decent patch of greensward.

SCARIFYING
Scarifying involves the removal of dead grass, known as thatch, and moss. Use a wire-toothed 'springbok' rake for the job, or one of those excellent electrically powered lawn rakers. Don't worry that the lawn looks a bit bare and tatty afterwards; it will soon pull round and grow away with renewed vigour. Timing: September.

SPIKING
Spiking the lawn with a fork or a hollow-tined aerator relieves surface compaction and improves drainage and soil condition. Ram the fork in to a depth of at least 10 cm (4 in) and wiggle it around a little. Stab it in at intervals of 15 cm (6 in). Timing: September, after scarifying.

After you've scratched or scarified your lawn, aerate it by spiking with a fork or a special hollow-tined aerator to relieve compaction and to improve surface drainage.

FEEDING
This is something that shouldn't be neglected. Apply an organic lawn fertilizer once a month in summer. Because it's organic and won't 'burn' the grass, there is no need to water it in with a sprinkler if it doesn't rain within 24 hours. Timing: Monthly from May to August.

WATERING
During dry periods in spring and summer, leave a sprinkler playing over the lawn for at least two hours. Oscillating sprinklers are better than the rotating type because they cover a sensible rectangular area rather than a circle, and they can be adjusted to throw in just one direction if you're having a picnic nearby. Timing: Spring and summer.

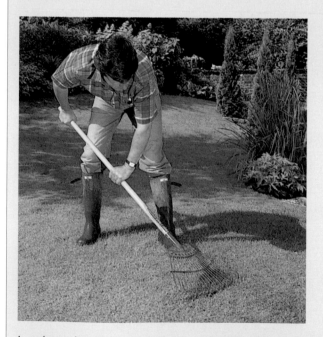

In autumn, lawns benefit from a good scratch with a wire-toothed rake to remove dead grass or 'thatch'.

pulled at by the mower.

The following day the lawn can receive its first mowing: take off just the top 1 cm (½ in) of grass, which will encourage the plants to produce sideshoots lower down, so thickening up the lawn. Cut again when the lawn has put on another 1 cm (½ in) of growth, and don't worry if there's a lot of weed growth present – most of it will be killed off by regular mowing, and any weeds that remain can be treated later with a lawn weedkiller. If you are committed to organic gardening, avoiding the use of weedkillers in particular, then you will have to settle for a weedy lawn. Some weeds, such as dandelions and plantains, can be removed by hand with an old dinner knife; others are difficult to eradicate by mechanical means.

Lawns sown in September will need few mowings before the onset of winter, but those sown in spring can be progressively mown more regularly until they are being cut once or twice a week. Keep off the area until the grass looks well established and quite thick. After about eight weeks you should be able to tread your verdant sward and park a deckchair on it, but wait a little longer before giving the go-ahead for vigorous games of football. It will be some time before the roots of the young grass plants have explored deeply into the soil.

THE IDLER'S LAWN

Any piece of ground that's fairly level and which has reasonable soil is a potential lawn. If you mow whatever grows on it – weeds, meadow- and weed-grasses – it will eventually turn into a lawn. The ironic thing is that after six or seven years you'll probably detect no difference between this type of lawn and one that was originally sown with a rye-grass mixture, unless the latter has been assiduously fed and treated against weeds. Where large areas of coarse turf are needed, under fruit trees and in paddocks, the mowing technique is well worth putting into practice.

MOWING

Everybody mows, but some mow better than others. The secret is to avoid cutting the grass too close. Far too many lawns are shaved, with the result that they wear badly and are susceptible to drought. Mowing is essential to encourage fine grasses and a thick carpet of growth, but it is far better for your grass (and for you) to mow regularly, taking off just a little, rather than to mow once a fortnight too close to the soil.

As a rule, mowing is necessary between March and October – more regularly at the height of the season than at each end. In June and July weekly or twice weekly mowing will be needed. I never mow closer than about 2 cm (¾ in), and when the weather is really dry I

LEAF SWEEPING
Removing fallen leaves is vital if your lawn is not to turn patchy and brown. Sweep all leaves from the surface as soon as possible and compost them. Timing: Autumn.

ROLLING
Rolling can help to even out bumps on a new lawn if your mower does not possess a hefty rear roller, but it's not essential. Timing: Spring.

TOPDRESSING
Topdressing is really only for the keen gardener. Scatter a mixture of sieved leaf mould and sand over the lawn and brush it in. One bucketful will do about 6 square metres (about 7 square yards). Timing: Autumn.

Topdress with a mixture of leaf mould, sand and soil. Use the back of the rake or a brush to distribute it.

prefer to leave on about 2.5 cm (1 in) of grass. Really rough areas can be left with about 4 cm (1½ in) of grass after cutting.

If you've masses of lawn and are bone idle, you can manage by mowing wide paths through it regularly, and cutting the long stuff occasionally. Not only will it save time, but it looks pleasant, too. If you don't treat your lawn with weedkiller you'll be surprised how many wild flowers it contains.

Take the clippings off the lawn when you mow, collecting them in a grassbox fitted to the mower, and compost them (taking care to mix them with other compost or they'll turn into a hot and smelly black gunge). If you can't be bothered to remove them, make sure you cut the grass regularly so that the clippings are small enough to be dried up by the sun and blown away by the wind. Left in large clods they'll kill out patches of grass and look very unsightly. Lawns from which the clippings are never removed will benefit from being scarified twice a year: once in June and once in September.

EDGING

Cutting the frayed edges from your lawn is a time-consuming and back-aching business. Use a pair of long-handled edging shears if you have lots of vertical lawn edges, but if possible try to get rid of them to save yourself some labour.

A single row of bricks laid flush with the soil at the edge of the lawn will mean that you can run the mower over them and so keep the grass in trim without resorting to shears. When the grass does start to creep over the brickwork you can give it a yearly cut back with a spade or a half-moon iron sold especially for cutting new lawn edges (see p.31).

WEEDS AND MOSS

I wish people didn't worry so much about weeds in lawns. If the turf stays green and looks fine enough from a distance then why worry that there's a bit of clover, dock or dandelion in it? If I banished all the daisies from my grass I'd be highly unpopular with both my daughters, so I'll continue to suffer the sideways glances of friends who think I ought to know better. If you feel you can't tolerate anything other than grass, then a two-pronged attack is in order. First, feed twice-yearly to promote tough vigorous growth. Then mow very regularly, when the grass is just slightly shaggy. This encourages a dense sward in which weeds will

Caring for lawn edges

Replace damaged section with the damaged piece facing inwards

Firm the replaced turf into place. Fill the gap with sandy loam and sow grass seed

If only part of the lawn edge has been damaged, cut out a section containing that part. Replace the turf with the damaged part facing the lawn. Fill the gap with sandy loam, sow grass seed and water well.

Stand on a plank to protect the lawn as you work round the edges

An annual trim with a half-moon iron will keep lawn edges smart and trim. Cut against the solid edge of a plank or against a curved hosepipe for a neat finish.

struggle to survive. Ground-hugging weeds like plantains may still be a problem but they're easy to hoick out with a daisy grubber or sharp knife. Creeping weeds like clover can be discouraged by raking them before mowing, so that they're standing in the way of

Lawn renovation

If you take on an old lawn that's knee high in grass after months of neglect, don't start digging up the ground. Instead follow this course of action. You don't have to do the lot in one day. Spread it over a period of seven weeks by doing one job each week.

1 Clear away any bricks and debris.
2 Remove the long grass to a height of 5 cm (2 in) with a scythe or rotary mower.
3 Scarify to remove dead grass and thatch.
4 Mow to a height of 2.5 cm (1 in).
5 Apply a lawn fertilizer.
6 Mow regularly.
7 Treat as a normal lawn.

the mower blades.

Moss is another *bête noir* and the only long-term solution is to remedy the conditions it finds favourable. Moss loves poorly drained, badly fed, acid soil, preferably with a bit of shade. Eliminate any of these and the moss will find it harder to survive. Spiking with a fork or lawn aerator will help to improve the drainage. Scarifying pulls out barrowloads of the long, tufted mosses that give your lawn the springiness of a mattress. Together with regular feeding, these methods will keep it under relative control. Once again, if it's green and looks all right, why worry what the neighbours think?

PESTS AND DISEASES

It's the fine lawn that is most troubled by disease; the coarser, more rugged grasses are seldom attacked by fungi apart from fairy rings. This fungus produces circles of dark green grass, often accompanied by toadstools. Only by digging out the infected turf 30cm (1ft) deep and wide will you have any chance of eradicating it. Settle instead for mowing off the toadstools and telling the children about the fairies. The grass will come to no real harm.

Toadstools that arise from old tree stumps below the lawn are also a nuisance, but it's easy enough to mow

them off or pick them out as soon as you spot them, to prevent the spores from spreading.

Brown areas may be caused by fungus diseases, but are more likely to occur as a result of fertilizer scorch (if you've applied it clumsily and too heavily) or bitch urine. In both cases a good soaking with a lawn sprinkler (or even a watering can in the case of the bitch) will help to alleviate the problem. The grass will green up later in the season.

Black or dark green areas of slime are caused by algae. If your lawn is well drained and well fed you should be able to stop them appearing. They're also most likely to appear in shady areas, so where this is caused by overhanging trees, prune back a few of the lower branches to let in light and air.

Moles are a pain in the neck and in the lawn. You'll read of umpteen old wives' cures for them, but if they infest the land around your garden there's absolutely nothing you can do to stop them coming into your plot. Traps laid in their runs will catch the individuals, and there are nasty little fuses to poison them out, but if I were you I'd enlist the help of the local mole catcher or rodent officer and enjoy using the soil from the molehills in your potting compost – it's wonderful stuff!

Worms should be positively welcomed. I know their casts are a nuisance occasionally, but a healthy worm population means a healthy soil and they do a great service by aerating the ground with their tunnels. Few lawns are really plagued by worm casts and only on really fine turf are they a severe handicap. To discourage worms from coming to the surface and leaving casts, rake off any clippings and rake up fallen leaves in autumn. Otherwise, just leave the casts to dry and sweep them off before mowing, or collect them up – like the soil from molehills, it is high quality stuff for adding to your potting compost.

You'll gather from all this that I'm not the possessor of a manicured lawn. I can still boast a patch of good-looking, fresh green turf that co-exists with a bunch of wild flowers, animals and insects, and doesn't keep me busily occupied every waking hour.

Lawn-care calendar

■ *March*	Start to mow.
■ *April*	Roll a new lawn if necessary.
■ *May*	Apply fertilizer.
■ *June/July*	Water when necessary.
■ *August*	Apply fertilizer.
■ *September*	Scarify and spike; topdress if you're keen.
■ *October/November*	Stop mowing; sweep up leaves.

16 patio gardening

Think of your patio as an outdoor room where you can relax when the weather is fine. Furnish it with tubs, baskets and small beds filled with your favourite plants

It's no use having a garden if you can't make time to sit in it, so cobble together a patio and you'll be able to sit outdoors at any time of year, regardless of conditions under foot. A patio is really any kind of stable surface on which a deckchair can be plonked. It doesn't have to be made of expensive paviors – read on!

PLANNING YOUR PATIO

The sunniest part of the garden is the most obvious place to put your pleasure patch, but it's also a good idea to position it near the house; that way the chef won't have to stagger too far with a heavy tray.

Reclining in the constant glare of summer sun palls after a while, so allow room for a parasol, a good 2 m (6 ft) in diameter, or arrange for the sun to disappear behind a tree at a certain time of day. If you're no sun worshipper then there's nothing wrong with making a patio in the shade, surrounded by a leafy canopy; but remember that if it's really overhung you're likely to be dripped on in damp weather. (I speak as a gardener who eats out in any decent fine spell, winter or summer.)

With patio gardening, the back-yard owner comes into his or her own, for it matters not a jot that there's no soil for miles; it can all be imported and put into assorted containers. But more of that later.

LAYING PATIO MATERIALS

Having decided to construct a patio and worked out where to site it, the next question is what materials you are going to use and how you are going to lay them. Whatever hard surface you decide on, buy your materials from a builders' merchant; in most cases this is a far cheaper source of supply than a garden centre. A change of texture on the patio is easy to provide if small beds are left for plants, but you can also incorporate patches of cobbles, which have a similar effect. Don't overdo it though.

Gravel is by far the cheapest stuff of which patios are made. All you need to do is level and firm the soil before spreading over it a 2.5 cm (1 in) layer of washed pea shingle. Make the layer much thicker than this and you'll find that it's difficult to walk on and soon finds its way into the house. You'll always be sweeping the odd bit of gravel out anyway, but that's the price you pay for doing things on the cheap! (My patio is made of gravel.) **Concrete** is the next most economical surface to gravel, but laying it involves much more slave labour.

You'll have to lay it over a 10 cm (4 in) layer of rubble or 'hard core' to give it stability, and large areas can look rather dull unless they're broken up by lines of brick or patches of cobbles.

Flagstones are pricey if you go for York stone or other natural materials, cheaper if they are reconstituted.

Preparing the foundations for a patio

Mark out the area with pegs and string set to the required ultimate level

Use a builder's square to check that corners form right angles

Firm down the subsoil with a plate compactor after excavating the topsoil

1 Having decided where to site your patio, the first task is to prepare a firm foundation. Mark out the area with pegs and string, with the string at the final level of the patio. Use a builder's square to make sure that corners are set accurately at right angles.

2 Dig out loose topsoil, removing any weeds or tree roots, until firm subsoil is reached. Allow for a 10 cm (4 in) layer of hardcore, covered with a 5 cm (2 in) layer of sand. Make sure that the subsoil is well packed down before adding the hardcore.

Spread a hardcore layer over the excavated area to the required level

3 Drive in pegs over the area, 2 m (6 ft) apart, using a spirit level and plank to ensure that the tops are level with the string. Adjust the pegs to allow a slight slope for surface water to drain off, lowering them by approximately 2.5 cm (1 in) for each 2 m (6 ft) run.

4 Spread a 10 cm (4 in) layer of hardcore over the entire site. On unstable soils, such as peat or heavy clay, a 15 cm (6 in) layer of hardcore is advisable. Firm it down until it is level, using the pegs as a guide. Cover the hardcore with sand to create a level surface.

Constructing patios

Laying a concrete patio

Concrete is an economical surface for a patio but it does require a lot of hard labour and a degree of DIY experience. After the site has been excavated to a depth of 20 cm (8 in) and levelled, construct a formwork of planks to hold the concrete in place until it sets. Spread hardcore 10 cm (4 in) deep and firm it down with a roller. Tip in the concrete until it is just proud of the formwork and work it well into the edges.

In large areas of concrete, put in expansion joints to prevent cracking

After levelling with the beam, fill out any hollows that appear with fresh concrete and level again

Construct a formwork by nailing planks to pegs around the edges of the patio area

Push the concrete well into corners and edges to avoid air pockets

Lay a layer of hardcore across the entire area and firm it down well

Move a tamping beam across the concrete, first to compact it and then, a second time, to remove excess material

If slabs have to be cut to fit, use a bolster chisel and club hammer, or hire a slab splitter. Wear goggles to protect the eyes

Replace slab and bed down using a block of wood and club hammer

Once the slabs are in position, lift each in turn and place five blobs of mortar on the sand below

Two days after laying the slabs, fill the gaps between them with moist mortar (pointing)

Put 2 cm (½ in) spacers between the slabs to allow for final pointing with mortar

Add a layer of sharp sand over the hardcore, levelling it and pressing down firmly

Mix the hardcore with some ballast so that all the spaces between the broken bricks and stones are filled with gravel and sand. Ram down firmly

Laying a paving slab patio

Paving slabs are an attractive choice for a patio. Prepare the site as above, excavating to the depth required for the hardcore and slabs. Add a 5 cm (2 in) layer of hardcore, followed by a 5 cm (2 in) layer of sand. Level and press down. Lay the first line of slabs along one edge marked by string. Lift each slab in turn, applying mortar to the sand below, and replace it firmly in position.

Laying a brick patio

Secondhand bricks are not just cheaper than new ones but more attractively mellowed. They do not require a hardcore or concrete base, just a firm layer of sand. First, however, you must put in a retaining edge to prevent the bricks and sand from moving outwards. This can be made of timber or, more attractively, from kerbstone blocks. Lay the bricks to your chosen pattern, butting the bricks closely together.

Tamp down the bricks with a piece of wood and a club hammer. Alternatively hire a plate compactor

Construct a retaining edge from kerbstone blocks or long concrete edgings set in mortar

After excavating the area to the depth required and firming the base, replace some of the earth and firm it down

Add a layer of sharp sand. Level and press it down with a screeding board

Lay the bricks in your chosen pattern, laying whole bricks first; go back later to fill in with cut ones. Butt the bricks closely together

Spread a thin layer of dry mortar over the surface and brush it between the joints. Sprinkle with water to set the mortar

Lay joists over the bricks with a sheet of damp-proof material between them. Use a spirit level to ensure an even base for the timber decking

Secure the planks to the joints with rust-proof nails, punching the heads below the surface

Stain the decking as required. Wooden surfaces must be dry and free of dirt before applying stain

Leave 10 mm ($^3/_8$ in) gaps between the planks to allow for drainage and expansion

Laying a timber-decked patio

A wooden patio is easy to lay. Construct a concrete foundation or footings, and lay a row of bricks spaced about one brick apart at right angles to the intended direction of the decking. Add further rows of bricks at 40 cm (16 in) intervals, checking that the bricks are level. Lay 75 x 50 mm (3 x 2 in) joists over the bricks with a sheet of plastic between them. Lay 250 x 25 mm (5 x 1 in) planks at right angles to the joists, allowing 10 mm ($^3/_8$ in) gaps for drainage.

Mortar the bricks to concrete foundation or footings, making sure that they are level with each other

Whatever you do, don't lay a patio of multicoloured pastel-shaded slabs: your sitting area should be a restful haven, not a technicolour dream. The plants will provide the colour.

Bricks are pricey if new, but quite cheap (and very good to look at) if you can find some mellowed secondhand stock. Lay both flagstones and bricks on an 8 cm (3 in) bed of sand spread over firmed and levelled soil. Use a straightedge and spirit level to make sure that your final surface is level (give it a slight 'fall' away from the house unless you want all the rain that lands on it to end up in your living room). Grout the bricks or slabs with a dry mortar mix (3 parts soft sand to 1 part cement) and allow the moisture that rises from below to set it.

> ## "Don't lay a patio of multicoloured slabs: the area should be a restful haven, not a technicolour dream."

A cautionary tale
Don't turn a hosepipe on your newly laid patio or you'll splash cement everywhere and discolour your bricks or flagstones. A mate of mine spent every weekend one year laying a brick patio and it nearly broke his heart when he washed in the grouting, only to find he had to spend days washing it out of his bricks again. If this disaster does befall you, try scattering damp coarse sand on the area and brushing it over the surface with a stiff broom (and no water). It should shift the cement deposit.

Timber patios, or decking, are quick and easy to construct. They can be bought in kit form, with all the necessary fittings, or more cheaply, made from joists and planks purchased at your local timber yard.

FURNISHING YOUR PATIO

Achieving privacy
Screens might be necessary in small gardens if you want your patio to be private. Trellis is an attractive proposition because it's cheap, but it also looks good if painted white and held firmly between posts and battens. Victorian arbours are seldom seen today, but they look delightful with flowering climbers trained over them. Solid larch-lap fencing is certainly peep-proof but rather oppressive when it encloses a small area, and concrete screening blocks look, to me, as though they've been left off a boat to Greece. If you like

them, use them and ignore my rude comments.

If wooden screening doesn't appeal, use plants. There are plenty of climbers that can be trained up simple post and wire fences, or tall shrubs and hedges that can be planted densely enough to make an effective screen.

Choosing outdoor furniture
I haven't the nerve to tell you what you should be sitting on! However, a few tips gleaned from practical experience might save you a few bob. For a start, make your patio as big as possible because furniture takes up more room than you'd think. Those beautifully upholstered recliners are the best things on earth to doze on, but they occupy a lot of space and you'll have to get them out and put them away every time you use them, which may make for storage problems. Invest in a couple by all means, but also have a pair of all-weather chairs and a table that can be left out even in winter if necessary. That way you can nip out there in a quick burst of sunshine for your morning cup of coffee without having to spend half an hour getting the posh stuff out of mothballs.

A parasol is not just decorative, it's also functional; read a book in scorching sunshine and you'll soon have a job to focus your eyes on anything else. If you do buy a parasol, go for one that's a plain colour rather than a floral print. Here I'm taking a liberty by inflicting my tastes on you, but it seems to me that the flowers in the garden should not have to compete with those on a William Morris parasol. Suit yourself!

Patio lighting
An illuminated patio is a luxury, but it becomes a bit of heaven on earth on summer evenings when you can sit out late and admire the leaves and flowers as they bask in a carefully placed spotlight. Your electrician will advise you on installation and the kind of lamps needed, but bear in mind that plants always look best when lit from the side or from below. In winter you can enjoy patio lighting from indoors if the illuminated plants are within view of your windows. If you're the outdoor type, patio lighting is a luxury worth saving for.

WHERE TO GROW PATIO PLANTS

On many plots the garden will surround the patio, bringing plants right up to the edge. In back yards or on rooftops, where a patio is all you've got, your plants will have to be grown in containers. You can plant in anything: wooden tubs, Greek urns, wall-mounted pots, large flower pots (small ones dry out too quickly), troughs, chimney pots (provided you remember they are bottomless and don't try to move them), growing bags and old porcelain sinks that have been treated to look like stone (see p.170).

Whatever your container, remember to place a layer of broken bricks, flowerpots or pebbles in the base to make for good drainage (all containers should have drainage holes) and, if the vessel is very large, stand it on a couple of bricks to keep it clear of the ground. With wooden tubs this helps to prevent rotting as well as allowing surplus water to escape unimpeded.

I would advise against the use of pots less than 23 cm (9 in) in diameter, simply because they dry out too quickly, and I would always use John Innes No. 2 potting compost in preference to the soilless types because, unlike them, if it dries out it won't shrink from the sides of the container and be difficult to re-wet. However, on rooftop and balcony gardens, peat-based composts have the advantage of being lightweight. (Always check with the appropriate authority before making a roof garden - it may save you a lot of heartache and expense later).

Leave a slight gap between the compost and the rim of all containers to allow for watering.

Windowboxes

Windows with outside sills lend themselves to being fitted with windowboxes that overflow with flowers all the year round. Spring and summer displays can be different (as with spring and summer bedding schemes) or some of the occupants can be permanent and a few bedders planted between them to vary the show from season to season.

Windowboxes are easy to make from old pieces of timber, screwed or nailed together with galvanized nails or brass screws. Treat them with a preservative such as Cuprinol - not toxic creosote which kills plants - and equip them with short legs and drainage holes. Make sure that they sit firmly on the sill. If you lack outdoor sills the boxes can be held on steel brackets screwed to the wall. Make sure they're secure or you'll crown some

---

> ## Plants for windowboxes
>
> **Permanent residents**
> - *Buxus sempervirens* **'Suffruticosa'** (dwarf box)
> - *Chamaecyparis obtusa* **'Nana'** (rounded dwarf conifer)
> - *Euonymus* **'Emerald 'n' Gold'** (variegated evergreen leaves)
> - *Festuca glauca* (blue fescue grass)
> - **Heathers** (*Erica* and *Calluna* - especially coloured-leafed varieties)
> - *Hebe pinguifolia* **'Pagei'** (until it outgrows available space)
> - *Hedera helix* varieties (common ivy)
> - *Juniperus communis* **'Compressa'** (columnar dwarf conifer)
> - *Thymus* varieties (thyme - especially coloured-leafed forms)
>
> **Temporary residents**
> Temporary residents are available in endless variety. Any spring or summer bedder that does not grow too tall will happily thrive, and dwarf bulbs will add to the spectacle in spring. Crocuses, dwarf irises and many of the compact narcissus varieties look superb, as do 'Universal' pansies, which can flower right through the winter. Dig them out before you plant the summer occupants.

Use rustproof galvanized nails or brass screws when constructing a windowbox

Construct a simple windowbox from old pieces of floorboard; make sure that it is deep enough to hold 15 cm (6 in) of compost plus drainage material.

unsuspecting passerby, who won't be able to see your floral tribute for stars.

A drainage layer is as vital in a windowbox as it is in any other container, and the compost layer should be at least 15 cm (6 in) deep. Make your box large enough to allow for both.

Hanging baskets

Made of galvanized or plastic-covered wire, hanging baskets can be slung from stout hooks or angle brackets outside doors and on plain house walls to brighten your life in summer. In winter they tend to get buffeted by the wind and the plants suffer.

To plant up the basket stand it on a large flowerpot or bucket. Line the inside with sphagnum moss (available from your florist) or old carpet underlay, or even three or four layers of newspaper cut to shape. Cut or poke holes in the liner at intervals and insert suitable trailing plants from the outside, roots first, covering their roots with compost as soon as they appear inside the basket. When all the trailers are in place, plant up the top and then water the plants in well. Bushy and trailing plants are naturally more suited to being grown in hanging baskets than stiff, upright and starchy plants.

Timber decking is an attractive choice for a patio surface, effortlessly extending the house into the garden and blending well with surrounding shrubs and trees. The timber theme in this garden includes raised beds constructed from reclaimed railway sleepers.

The secret of success with hanging baskets is watering. You'll have to soak them twice a day in midsummer, once a day even in dull weather: don't forget! Adding some water-retaining granules to the soil will help stop them drying out so quickly.

Plants for hanging baskets

It's the summer-flowering plants that make up hanging baskets. Experiment with different combinations each year, but rely on bushy and trailing plants, not those that grow tall and stiff. These are all first class:

- *Ageratum*
- *Aurinia* (Alyssum)
- *Begonia* (trailing types)
- *Begonia semperflorens*
- *Campanula isophylla* (Star of Bethlehem)
- *Centaurea cineraria* (syn. *C. gymnocarpa*)
- *Dorotheanthus* (Livingstone daisy)
- *Helichrysum petiolare*
- *Lobelia* (trailing)
- *Lysimachia nummularia* 'Aurea' (Creeping Jenny)
- *Tropaeolum* (Nasturtium)
- *Pelargonium, ivy-leaf* (ivy-leaf geranium)
- *Pelargonium, zonal* (geranium)
- *Petunia*
- *Senecio cineraria* (dusty miller)
- *Verbena*

PATIO PLANT CARE

Watering is certainly the most important job the patio gardener will undertake. All containers of compost dry out amazingly quickly on a sun-baked patch of hard standing, and plants that dry out soon die. Save your money and your temper, if not your time, by checking all containers morning and evening in summer – daily or, at the very least, every other day at other times of year.

Feed all container-grown plants once a fortnight in summer. Flowering plants love tomato fertilizer, which can be used at the same dilution as recommended for tomatoes.

Keep the basket under cover for a few weeks after planting to let its occupants establish themselves. Baskets are usually made up during late April and hung outdoors in late May or early June.

If a basket is to be hung over a door, you'd do well to invest in the kind with a built-in drip tray.

Plants that are grown in pots for a number of years should either be potted on annually in spring, or topdressed, which involves scraping away the top layer of compost and replacing it with fresh. Both operations are described in Chapter 20 House Plants.

The removal of dead and diseased plants and the controlling of pests and diseases is as vital on the patio as it is elsewhere in the garden, but at least if you're lounging on a sunbed you'll notice quite quickly if there are pests on an overhanging branch - especially if they drop into your gin and tonic. Which brings me to weeding. If you're as fidgety as I am, you'll find that your patio beds and pots are the best-weeded parts of your garden. I'm forever leaping out of the chair to pull up a bit of groundsel or hairy bittercress!

CHOOSING PLANTS FOR PATIOS

I won't give you a long list of suitable patio plants, just a selection of those that I think are especially useful, because the truth of the matter is that you can grow almost anything in a pot for a limited period of time. There are certain plants that will not like being baked in the reflected heat that comes off your patio - rhododendrons for instance - but on a shady patio they'll do well. Other plants, such as trees, will refuse to stay in a tub for more than five or ten years, but that's not a bad life for any pot plant.

The greatest boon of patio gardening is that you can try anything, and you can move your plants around to give different effects from week to week (if you feel strong enough).

Don't forget that in summer your house plants will benefit greatly from a holiday in the garden, and on the patio they will receive shelter as well as welcome sunshine. Summer showers will refresh them rather than do them any harm. Be careful to acclimatize them very gently, in shade first, to avoid leaf scorch.

Using evergreens and foliage plants
To make your potted show interesting all the year round, some of the plants should be evergreen and a lot of them should be foliage plants. Roses and other flowering shrubs will give a grand show in their season, but the evergreens will be the backbone of the display just as they are in the garden.

So long as you can give a shrub, border plant, rose or any other plant the conditions it would appreciate elsewhere in the garden, it will thrive in a container on your patio.

Potting on patio plants

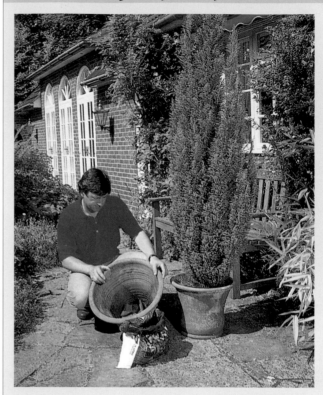

1 When plants such as this conifer have outgrown their pots, choose a new, larger container for them, and put a layer of crocks in the base to assist drainage.

Foliage plants for patios

When planning your patio display, don't forget foliage plants and shrubs: they are just as important here as elsewhere in the garden. The following plants are especially striking if grown in gravel- or cobble-covered beds. After planting, firm down the soil then cover with a stone mulch of cobbles, pebbles, gravel or washed pea shingle. It will set off the plants, keep down weeds, and help to retain moisture.

border plants for patios
(See Chapter 9 Border Plants for full details.)

- Ajuga
- Alchemilla
- Artemisia
- Asplenium
- Ballota
- Bergenia
- Blechnum
- Carex
- Cynara
- Dryopteris
- Epimedium
- Euphorbia
- Festuca
- Glyceria

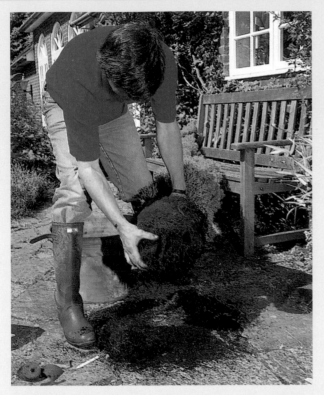

2 Knock the plant out of its old pot and tease away some of the compost from the roots. Put a layer of compost in the bottom of the new pot.

3 Set the plant in the new pot, ensuring that the top of the rootball will rest 2.5 cm (1 in) or so below the rim. Feed in compost around the rootball and firm it in.

- Heuchera
- Hosta
- Iris
- Liriope
- Matteuccia
- Milium
- Persicaria
  (syn. *Polygonum*)
- Phormium
- Polygonatum
- Rheum
- Sedum

Heuchera micrantha var. *diversifolia* 'Palace Purple' is a handsome foliage plant to grow in a patio container.

Shrubs for patios

Those marked ◆ are evergreen.
(See Chapter 5 Shrubs for full details.)

- Aralia
- Aucuba ◆
- Bamboos ◆ (some)
- Camellia ◆
- Chamaecyparis ◆ (some)
- Choisya ◆
- Cistus ◆
- Convolvulus ◆
- Cotinus
- Cotoneaster ◆ (some)
- Fatsia ◆
- Heathers ◆
- Hebe ◆
- Hedera ◆

- Ilex ◆
- Juniperus ◆
- Laurus ◆
- Lavandula ◆
- Lavatera
- Mahonia ◆
- Myrtus ◆
- Paeonia
- Pittosporum ◆
- Rhus
- Ruta ◆
- Sambucus
- Sarcococca ◆
- Yucca ◆

part IV

THE FOOD CROPS

Experience the thrill of growing
your own produce and discover
the flavour of freshly picked fruit
and vegetables

A well-tended vegetable garden is a pleasure to behold with
its neat rows of ferny carrot tops and succulent heads of
lettuce and cauliflower emerging from the fertile soil.

CHAPTER 17 Fruit growing

Even in a small garden or tiny backyard, the pleasures of fruit growing can be enjoyed, thanks to the dwarfing rootstocks and miniature varieties now available

There are few branches of gardening as confusing as fruit growing. True enough, the cultivation of raspberries and gooseberries presents few problems, but once you get on to apples and pears, cherries and peaches, the pruning alone is enough to frighten anyone off. Here then, I've tried to simplify matters a little by not telling you too much. It's amazing how many gardeners grow tons of fruits without ever laying their hands on a pair of secateurs or loppers. The pruning techniques I've described are certainly necessary to make the best of your trees, but I defer to those gardeners with lofty apple trees, coated with lichen, that groan under the weight of a heavy harvest with amazing regularity.

I've dealt with most problems and operations under the individual fruit headings, but there are one or two general comments worth making.

TIPS ON FRUIT GROWING

Site and soil Remember that most fruits are expected to go on cropping year after year. Give them the best site and soil you can to help them achieve their aims.

Pollination Tree fruits generally need to be pollinated by another variety of the same fruit so that they can produce a good crop. Try to persuade your friends and neighbours to plant a tree that complements yours if you've no room for two.

Propagation Don't propagate your own tree fruits – they are grafted on to vigour-controlling rootstocks and are best increased by the nurseryman. Two- or three-year-old trees will cost a little more than one-year-old 'maidens' but they will come into cropping more quickly and save you the complicated job of training them in the early stages.

June drop When it comes to technical terms, fruit growing has its quota. The 'June drop' is the name given to the shedding of immature tree fruits when they are quite small. It's the tree's natural way of thinning out its crop, so don't be alarmed. Just make sure that any thinning you do comes after this, otherwise you might find that the fruits you've left behind drop off too!

Setting fruit Gardeners are frequently frustrated by trees that come into flower but refuse to set fruit. The reason is usually lack of pollination, but it may also be due to frosting. Grow your trees in a sheltered spot that is not on low-lying ground.

Non-flowering If your trees refuse to flower, suspect one of the following: bird damage, frost damage, an excess of nitrogen or a lack of food in general. Faulty or very hard pruning can produce growth buds at the expense of fruit buds.

Pruning When it's time for that terrifying job, pruning, use a sharp pair of secateurs to prevent diseases from gaining a foothold through torn tissue. Always prune to just above a bud – generally an outward facing one.

Leaders, laterals and sub-laterals These are all

Heavily laden espaliered apple and pear trees provide a luscious background to this border whose colourful display includes *Nicotiana*, *Limonium* (statice), *Cosmos*, and the exotic-looking *Cleome* (spider flower).

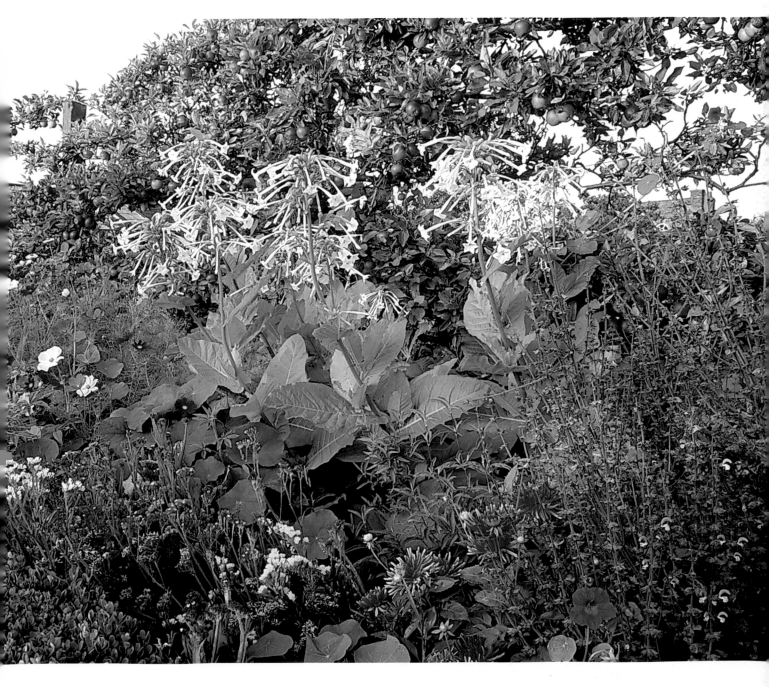

technical names for the various branches: leaders are the topmost, strongest-growing shoots; laterals are sideshoots. Sub-laterals are sideshoots that are growing from sideshoots.

Planting A fruit tree or bush is planted in exactly the same way as an ornamental tree or bush, so throughout this chapter I've referred you to Chapter 4 Trees for planting details.

Restricted forms Cordons and espaliers are usually planted against stout post and wire fences. Make sure that they are indeed stout. The posts, 10 cm (4 in) square in cross-section, should protrude 2 m (6 ft) from the ground. Treat them with a preservative other than creosote and bury to a depth of 60 cm (2 ft). They should occur every 2-2.5 m (6-8 ft) along the fence and the wire should be of a stout gauge. Spacings for the wires are recommended under individual fruits.

Fruit cage If you intend to grow plenty of fruit, it really is worth investing in a fruit cage – home-made or shop-bought. It is not much to look at and it will cost quite a few pounds to make or acquire, but it will make sure that you, not the birds, eat the fruits.

UNDERSTANDING ROOTSTOCKS

Fruit trees are not grown from pips; they are propagated in the nursery by a technique known as grafting. This involves the joining of a scion (piece of stem) from a branch of the required variety to a rootstock. The rootstock is a plant that is grown to act as the root system for a chosen variety of fruit. If allowed to grow and crop itself it would have poor fruits because it's been selected, not for its own cropping ability, but for the effect it has on the vigour and cropping ability of the scion that is attached (grafted) to it. The two are spliced together in the nursery, a natural callus forms to glue them to one another, and the scion then forms the branch framework and the rootstock the roots.

> "It's amazing how many gardeners grow tons of fruits without ever laying their hands on a pair of secateurs."

There are hundreds of rootstocks; well, perhaps not hundreds but certainly enough to thoroughly confuse you. It is recommended that you ask for a tree on a particular rootstock number, so that you can be sure of getting a tree whose ultimate size is predictable. Apple rootstocks are prefixed by the letters M or MM (which stand for Malling and Malling Merton respectively).

Rootstock m.26 is the best one for general planting in small gardens. It is reasonably dwarfing and yet not so feeble that it needs to be staked all its life. Trees on M.26 grow 2.5-4 m (8-12 ft) high.

Rootstock m.9 is the dwarfest but it needs continuous staking and is a bit miffy on very poor or very heavy soils. Trees on M.9 grow to 2 or 3 m (6 or 10 ft).

Rootstock mm.106 is not quite as dwarfing as the previous two but it still keeps trees to a reasonable size. Trees on MM.106 grow 4-6 m (12-18 ft) high.

All three rootstocks will bring the trees into bearing quite early in their lives. Choose M.26 if you can; M.9 if you want a real midget and have good soil; MM.106 if you can't find M.26.

TREE FORMS

There's an added complication: you'll have to decide what shape of tree you want. You can buy 'maidens' (one-year-old trees that consist of a single stem) and train them if you want, but it's easier, and not that much more expensive, to buy two- or three-year-old trained trees in one of several forms: standard, half-standard, bush, dwarf pyramid, cordon, or espalier.

If terror is struck into your heart by the thought of having to train or prune any fruit tree, then you can simply plant a bush, half-standard or standard tree and leave it to its own devices. You'll risk owning a tree that is not very shapely and that crops neither as heavily, nor as early in its life as a trained tree, but if you are happy to live with such a tree, that's your affair and nobody else's. If, however, you then decide to prune it later, you're in for a battle royal. Compromise by pruning it a little during its formative years to produce a good shape, then you can ignore it with less drastic results.

PLANTING FRUIT TREES

Planting distances

If you're growing more than one tree I suppose you can boast that you're planting an orchard (to an estate agent three trees constitute a small orchard). Plant bushes on M.9 and M.26 rootstocks 3 m (10 ft) apart; plant cordons 1 m (3 ft) apart with 2 m (6 ft) between rows; plant espaliers 3 m (10 ft) apart; plant dwarf pyramids 1 m (3 ft) apart in rows 2 m (6 ft) apart. You'll need to allow 6 m (20 ft) between standards and rather less between half-standards.

Fruit tree forms

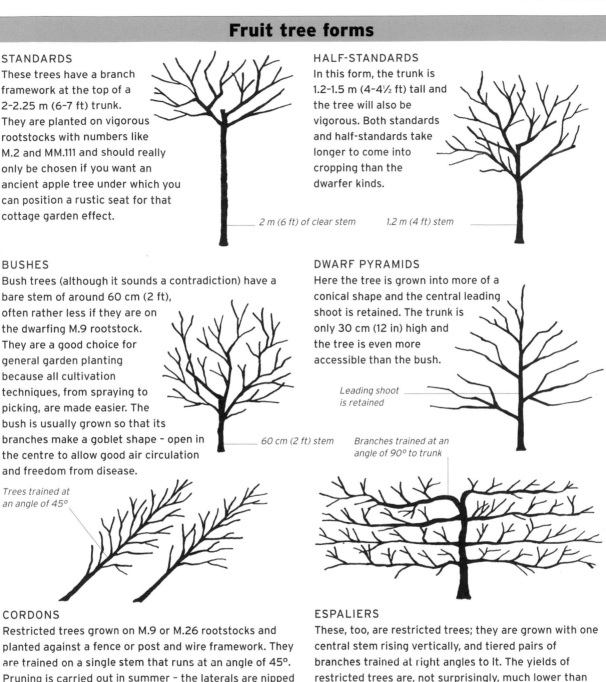

STANDARDS
These trees have a branch framework at the top of a 2–2.25 m (6–7 ft) trunk. They are planted on vigorous rootstocks with numbers like M.2 and MM.111 and should really only be chosen if you want an ancient apple tree under which you can position a rustic seat for that cottage garden effect.

2 m (6 ft) of clear stem

HALF-STANDARDS
In this form, the trunk is 1.2–1.5 m (4–4½ ft) tall and the tree will also be vigorous. Both standards and half-standards take longer to come into cropping than the dwarfer kinds.

1.2 m (4 ft) stem

BUSHES
Bush trees (although it sounds a contradiction) have a bare stem of around 60 cm (2 ft), often rather less if they are on the dwarfing M.9 rootstock. They are a good choice for general garden planting because all cultivation techniques, from spraying to picking, are made easier. The bush is usually grown so that its branches make a goblet shape – open in the centre to allow good air circulation and freedom from disease.

60 cm (2 ft) stem

DWARF PYRAMIDS
Here the tree is grown into more of a conical shape and the central leading shoot is retained. The trunk is only 30 cm (12 in) high and the tree is even more accessible than the bush.

Leading shoot is retained

Branches trained at an angle of 90° to trunk

Trees trained at an angle of 45°

CORDONS
Restricted trees grown on M.9 or M.26 rootstocks and planted against a fence or post and wire framework. They are trained on a single stem that runs at an angle of 45°. Pruning is carried out in summer – the laterals are nipped back and the central leader allowed to extend slowly.

ESPALIERS
These, too, are restricted trees; they are grown with one central stem rising vertically, and tiered pairs of branches trained at right angles to it. The yields of restricted trees are, not surprisingly, much lower than those of free-standing bushes.

When to plant
Plant bare-root trees from November to March and container-grown trees at any time of year. Planting instructions are exactly as for ornamental trees (see p.40). Cordons and espaliers are planted against a strong, 2 m (6 ft) high post and wire fence with horizontal wires at 60 cm (2 ft) intervals.

During the spring, after planting, scatter a good sprinkling of blood, bone and fishmeal around each tree and then lay a thick organic mulch. Make sure that the soil is not given a chance to dry out during establishment. Don't let grass grow up to the tree for at least three years. An annual spring feed with rose fertilizer is always appreciated.

A-Z of fruit crops

APPLE

I've always fancied having an orchard full of old varieties of apple with lovely quaint names like 'Norfolk Beefing', 'Devonshire Quarrenden' and 'Roundway Magnum Bonum' – the very sound of the names smacks of a bumper harvest. I've never yet got round to it; instead we have half a dozen hefty old trees scattered round the garden, but even these provide us with more apples than we know what to do with.

If you're keen on apples then you'll want to grow a few varieties that not only taste good but that also supply you with fruit over as long a season as possible, and that is the basis on which I have made my selection (see right). Romanticism aside, these are the varieties with some of the tastiest fruits, even if they don't have the most euphonious names. The early varieties should be eaten as soon as possible after picking; the late varieties are the best keepers.

I'm afraid I've not included 'Cox's Orange Pippin' – it requires too much spraying to keep it in good condition. 'Ribston Pippin' is easier and just as crisp and tasty. Neither have I included 'Golden Delicious'. We get far too many of these apples from France and, while they may be uniform in shape and quality and crisp of flesh, they really do not possess a flavour that can rival a decent English pippin. Now there's prejudice for you!

Where to plant Apples enjoy the classic situation: a site that's open and sunny, but sheltered at a distance from strong winds. Avoid planting in frost pockets where the blossom will be killed off. Good drainage is vital and adequate soil preparation essential; dig the ground as deeply as you can and work in plenty of compost or manure, plus a good dusting of blood, bone and fishmeal a day or two before planting. Different varieties suit different situations, and while those that I've recommended will thrive in most gardens it's a good idea to rely on the advice of your local nurseryman, who knows what thrives in your neck of the woods.

Pollination Apple pollination is complicated in theory but usually simple in practice – there are so many apple trees around that the bees can usually do a good job at cross-pollinating the flowers and ensuring a crop. Some apples won't set fruit with their own pollen so, to make sure of a good crop without having to rely on your neighbours, it's a good idea to plant two or three trees, even if they are restricted forms such as cordons and espaliers. Just make sure that they flower at the same time (see below).

Pruning This varies depending on the form of tree, but basically aims to produce a healthy framework of branches and plenty of fruiting 'spurs' (short sideshoots). Proceed thus:
Bush After planting a two- or three-year-old bush, shorten all the leading shoots by half their length, cutting back to an outward-facing bud (see right). The following winter do exactly the same, but when the tree is in its fourth year only the laterals need be pruned, back to 10 cm (4 in). Leave plenty of unpruned laterals on 'Bramley's Seedling', which is a tip-bearing variety. Aim to produce a well-spaced framework of branches, and don't be afraid to cut out damaged, very old and badly placed stems completely if they are making a nuisance of themselves. But remember, the harder you prune, the

Recommended apple varieties

VARIETY	IN SEASON	FLOWERING TIME*
EATERS		
'Discovery'	Late August/early September	1
'George Cave'	Late August/early September	1
'Ellison's Orange'	September/October	2
'James Grieve'	September/October	2
'Egremont Russet'	October/December	1
'Sunset'	October/December	2
'Ribston Pippin'	November/February	1
'Rosemary Russet'	December/March	2
'Tydeman's Late Orange'	December/March	2
COOKERS		
'Arthur Turner'	August/October	2
'Grenadier'	August/October	2
'Bramley's Seedling'	November/March	2
'Annie Elizabeth'	December/June	2
'Howgate Wonder'	November/February	2
'Lane's Prince Albert'	January/March	2

* Varieties marked **1** will flower before those marked **2**. For effective pollination, varieties within the same group should be planted together.

Pruning a newly planted bush apple tree

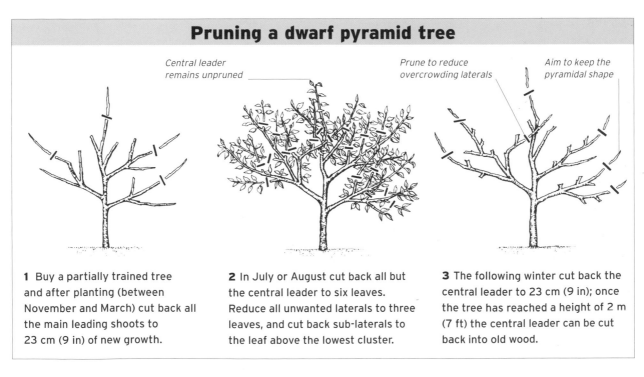

Aim to produce a well-spaced framework of branches

Laterals growing outwards from the tree can be left if there's room for them to grow

1 After planting a two-year-old bush (between November and March) shorten all the leading shoots by half their length, cutting to just above an outward-facing bud.

2 The following winter, repeat the process, cutting back the newly grown leading shoots by half. As before, cut back to just above an outward-facing bud.

3 One year later the pruning can be restricted to lateral shoots: cut them back to about 10 cm (4 in). It's a good idea to shorten some laterals every year.

Pruning a dwarf pyramid tree

Central leader remains unpruned

Prune to reduce overcrowding laterals

Aim to keep the pyramidal shape

1 Buy a partially trained tree and after planting (between November and March) cut back all the main leading shoots to 23 cm (9 in) of new growth.

2 In July or August cut back all but the central leader to six leaves. Reduce all unwanted laterals to three leaves, and cut back sub-laterals to the leaf above the lowest cluster.

3 The following winter cut back the central leader to 23 cm (9 in); once the tree has reached a height of 2 m (7 ft) the central leader can be cut back into old wood.

more growth you'll get and the fewer apples you'll harvest.

Standards Prune as for bush trees.

Half-standards Prune as for bush trees.

Dwarf pyramid Buy a partially trained dwarf pyramid tree and then you can slip into the routine of simple twice-yearly pruning.

In winter prune back all the main, leading shoots to leave just 23 cm (9 in) of new growth.

In July or August cut back all leaders except the central one, to six leaves. Any laterals not required as part of the branch framework can be reduced to three leaves, and sub-

laterals can be cut to the leaf growing above the lowest cluster (see box above for more details).

The central leader can be cut back into old wood once the tree has reached 2 m (7 ft) high. In subsequent years try to maintain the pyramidal shape of the tree; reduce overcrowded

Pruning a cordon apple tree

Buy a part-trained cordon and concentrate on summer pruning – shortening any lateral shoots to three leaves. Prune the leader once it has reached the topmost wire. The cordon can then be lowered, a little at a time and to no lower than 35°, to give it more room to grow.

Cut back any lateral shoots to leave three leaves above the basal cluster

In summer cut back to 2.5 cm (1 in) any shoots that attempt to take over from the leading shoot

When the leading shoot reaches the top wire cut it out each spring

Let the leader continue to grow

1 Maiden trees can be trained to form cordons. Plant at an angle of 45°, with the scion uppermost, and prune the lateral shoots back to four buds between November and March.

2 Remove any flowers that form one year later. Allow the leader to continue growing undisturbed, tying it in to the cane support as it extends.

3

Cut back sub-laterals to one leaf above the basal cluster

3 In subsequent years, in late July and early August, cut back any lateral shoots emerging from the main stem to leave three leaves above the basal cluster (see inset). Further growth may occur in late summer and autumn. Cut back such shoots to two leaves.

spurs and any vigorous shoots that sprout from within the framework.
Cordon See above.
Espalier Buy a trained tree and in

In late July and August, prune cordon apple trees by shortening sub-laterals to three or four buds above the basal cluster.

summer prune the branches as for cordons so that a system of spurs is built up on each 'arm'.
Thinning After the natural June drop, remove one or two fruitlets from each cluster if they look overcrowded. Always pull the central fruit out first. This is the 'king fruit', which has a deformed lump next to the stalk. Leave two fruits to each cluster.
Harvesting Pick the fruits as soon as they will part easily from the tree without tearing. The earliest will be ready from late July through August, and the later varieties in September and October. Pick any remaining apples in October and store them.
Storing The late varieties are the ones to store. It's a real fag wrapping them up in squares of greaseproof paper, so nip along to a friendly greengrocer and see if he can let you have some wooden 'Dutch trays' equipped with cardboard dividers (see right).

Store only sound fruits, and check them once a week to remove any that show signs of rotting. A cool but frostproof shed or garage is the best fruit store you'll find, unless you happen to have a cellar, where conditions will be ideal.

If you've found in the past that apples and pears shrivel while they're in store, put 1.6–1.8 kg (3–4 lb) in a polythene bag with the corners cut off and lay the bags in the trays so that they can be stacked. The polythene will keep the atmosphere around the fruits pleasantly moist. Sliced or puréed, the apples can also be frozen.
Pests and diseases Aphids, sawfly, codling moth, winter moth, apple sucker, capsid bugs, red spider mites, bitter pit, mildew, canker, scab, brown rot.

So many problems does the apple have to contend with that many gardeners adopt a spray programme.

Store apples in wooden tomato trays fitted with cardboard dividers to separate the fruits and prevent any rot spreading. Keep them in a cool, dark, frostfree place.

Coping with children and dogs, I've never felt that I could arrange for a comprehensive system of spraying. Idlers can spray with a tar oil wash such as Murphy Mortegg or ICI Clean Up in winter to remove hibernating eggs and bugs, and other infestations can be dealt with as they occur. It's not the perfectionist's way, but you'll still manage to harvest a good crop.

BLACKBERRY/ LOGANBERRY

For growing against fences, and as productive screens against post and wire supports, these two fruits will produce a succulent harvest with very little bother. I'd choose 'Bedford Giant' or 'Oregon Thornless' when selecting blackberries; 'LY 59' or the thornless 'L 654' are by far the best of the loganberries. If you've never tried loganberries you're in for a treat. Mix them up with raspberries and smother them with cream! They crop in mid- to late summer.

Where to plant Blackberries will tolerate a little shade; loganberries will too but they definitely prefer full sun. The soil should be well dug, well drained and enriched with manure or compost. Fork in a dusting of blood, bone and fishmeal just before planting.

Support Either equip a fence or wall with horizontal wires held in place by metal vine eyes at 45 cm (18 in) intervals, or make a 2 m (6 ft) post-and-wire fence with strands a similar distance apart. Each plant needs about 4 m (12 ft) of lateral fence space.

Planting Plant dormant canes between November and March – the earlier the better. Planting instructions are exactly the same as for ornamental trees and shrubs (see p.40). After planting, cut back the canes to 23 cm (9 in) above soil level, making your cuts just above a dormant bud.

Cultivation Dust the soil with blood, bone and fishmeal in February and lay a thick organic mulch in March. Tie the new canes to the support system as they grow, spacing them out in a fan formation and leaving a gap in the centre of the support system directly above the plant. Water well in dry weather. These canes will fruit in their second year while more new ones are

Space out the fruiting canes of blackberries and loganberries, training the new shoots up the centre as they grow. These can be spread out and tied in the following winter to replace the fruited stems, which are cut out at ground level.

growing. Train these up into the bare central area.

Pruning When the canes have fruited, cut them out at ground level and then space out and tie in the new canes to replace them. Repeat the process in subsequent years.

Harvesting Pick the fruits as soon as they are ripe. Hang old net curtains or muslin or close-weave plastic netting over them if birds are a problem. Pull the berries so that the 'plugs' are left behind.

Storing Make jam; freeze surplus fruits.

Pests and diseases Aphids, raspberry beetle, cane spot, cane blight, spur blight, botrytis and viruses.

Propagation During July, healthy shoot tips can be bent down and buried in the soil; hold them in place with a peg made from stout wire. Eventually a shoot will emerge. The new plant can be detached the following spring (with its own roots) and planted out where it is to grow.

BLACKCURRANT

Just the thing for vitamin C fanatics. The trouble is that blackcurrants are a bit greedy when it comes to space, but 'Ben Sarek' is compact and a heavy cropper and so the best choice for small gardens. It's a flavoursome mid-season cropper yielding its bounty during late July. Try 'Mendip Cross' for a slightly earlier crop and 'Ben Lomond' for an August harvest.

Where to plant Full sun or very gentle shade keep blackcurrants happy but, like all fruits, they can be hammered by frost if they are planted in hollows. Lime acid soil in autumn and dig it over, adding manure or compost during winter. Fork in a dusting of blood, bone and fishmeal just before planting.

Planting Two-year-old certified bushes are the best kind to buy; that way you have a guarantee that they are not infected with yield-reducing virus diseases. Plant all the varieties I've mentioned 1.5 m (5 ft) apart on the square (I told you they were a bit greedy). Planting instructions are exactly the same as for ornamental trees and shrubs (see p.40). It's a good idea to set the bushes about 5 cm (2 in) deeper than they were planted in the nursery so that the stem bases are encouraged to form roots and so give the plant more support and nourishment. Now cut all the shoots back to within 5 cm (2 in) of soil level. Use the prunings as cuttings: trim them above a bud at the top and below a bud at the base so that they are 25 cm (10 in) long. Insert them on the vegetable plot so that all but the top

> "Full sun or very gentle shade keep blackcurrants happy but, like all fruits, they can be hammered by frost if they are planted in hollows."

5 cm (2 in) is buried. They'll grow next year and can be transplanted the following autumn.

Cultivation Mulch the soil around the plants with organic matter in spring. Don't let them go short of water during their first spring and summer. No fruits will be carried during the first year. Get into the habit of repeating the mulch each spring after scattering a little blood, bone and fishmeal over the soil.

Pruning There's no need to prune after the first season's growth, but subsequently prune the bush each winter, removing any spindly stems and a few old ones. Cut them all out at ground level. Never remove more than about one third of the plant's shoots, but aim to leave a well-spaced framework of branches.

Harvesting Grow the bushes in a fruit cage or lay muslin or old net curtains over them when the fruits are coming to maturity: birds will enjoy them as much as you do. Cut off the sprigs of fruit when they are ripe – black and tender to the touch. If you can use the fruits immediately (rather than in a few days' time) pull them straight from the stalks. You should get around 4.5 kg (10 lb) fruit from one well-grown bush.

Storing Currants freeze and jam well.

Pests and diseases Birds, aphids, big bud mite, leaf spot, reversion virus, rust and American gooseberry mildew.

Propagation Already described in planting information (left).

CHERRY

It used to be that the only cherry recommended for small gardens was 'Morello' – an acid cherry that makes the most delicious pies and jam. Sweet cherries tend to make towering trees that need to be planted at least 10 m (30 ft) apart, and they are choosy as to how they perform. However, 'Stella' has changed all that. Its main advantage is that, unlike other sweet cherries, it can set a good crop of fruits with its own pollen. 'Morello' is self-fertile, too.

Where to plant Although they're tolerant of positions in the open garden, cherries are usually grown as fan-trained trees against walls. 'Morello' is often recommended for a north wall where it enjoys the cool conditions. Avoid frost pockets at all costs, and dig over and manure the ground in the autumn before planting.

Support Make sure that there are horizontal wires fastened at 30 cm (12 in) intervals up the brickwork. The stems can then be tied in and spaced out as they grow. The tree will need about 6 m (20 ft) of lateral space.

Glowing pale yellow, tinged with red, the firm-fleshed 'Bigarreau Napoleon' provides a sweet dessert cherry for cropping in late July.

Planting To make life easier (if just a little more expensive), choose a tree that has already been fan trained. It should be grafted onto a rootstock known as 'Colt', which is only semi-vigorous. Plant container-grown trees at any time of year, bare-root trees in November if possible. Planting is exactly as for trees and shrubs (see p.40). Set the tree about 30 cm (12 in) from the wall and tilt its branches towards the surface, tying the stems loosely to the wire. Cut back the stems by about one third of their length after planting, to encourage the production of laterals, which will form the basic structure of the tree. Mulch the soil around the tree with organic matter in spring after dusting the soil with blood, bone and fishmeal. A dusting of rose or tomato fertilizer can be given each April. Never let the soil dry out while the tree is establishing itself.

Pruning Prune cherries in spring or summer rather than winter. This lessens the likelihood of attack by silver leaf disease (see p.293). Acid cherries flower on one-year-old wood and it is this that pruning aims to encourage. Thin out the shoots during spring and summer, cutting out any that grow directly away from the wall and any that are weak or overcrowding. The remaining shoots should be spaced about 15 cm (6 in) apart on the wall. After fruiting, cut out the cherry-bearing laterals. This will enable them to be replaced by younger shoots that have arisen from their bases. If young growth is lacking as the tree matures, cut a few older branches back to young sub-laterals so that new shoots are encouraged. At all times keep the branch framework well spaced and not overcrowded, and keep it young.

Sweet cherries such as 'Stella' produce their fruit buds at the base of laterals that are one year old and which emerge from older wood. It follows that an older framework of branches is required on a sweet cherry than on an acid cherry, which is constantly being required to produce new wood for cropping. Pinch out the shoot tips of the new sub-laterals on sweet cherries during the summer so that they are left with just five leaves. Further shorten these shoots in autumn to three buds. These buds will carry blossom and fruits the following summer.

Harvesting There's no need to thin the fruits. 'Morello' matures in August and September, 'Stella' in July. Pick the fruits when they come to ripeness. The birds may have a go so use a large sheet of plastic netting that can be draped right over the plant. The longer the cherries are left before they are harvested, the less acid they will be, but the more likelihood there is of them being pecked.

Storing Pies can be frozen, as can the fruits themselves if they are stoned first.

Pests and diseases Aphids, birds, slugworm, winter moth, bacterial canker, brown rot, dieback, and silver leaf disease.

CURRANT, RED AND WHITE

I wish more folk were willing to plant red and white currants; they make a bright show in the flower border and possess the richest of flavours. Both can be used in jelly-making and wine-making and they fill a plump fruit pie with promise. 'Red Lake' is the best red currant for most gardens, yielding in late July. 'Laxton's Number One' is earlier and 'Rondom' later. No white currant is better than 'Versailles Blanche (syn. 'White Versailles'), but you'll also find 'White Dutch' and 'White Grape' good value.

Where to plant Plant in the same kind of spot as blackcurrants, though these two are rather less tolerant of shade.

Planting Plant one- or two-year-old plants between November and March. Buy from a reputable supplier: there is no certification scheme for red and white currants so they cannot be guaranteed free from virus diseases. Plant the bushes 1.5 m (5 ft) apart on the square and at the same level as they were growing in the nursery (look for the soil mark on the stem). Each bush should have a short trunk or 'leg' and at least three branches. Cut these back to half their length after planting, preferably to just above an outward-facing bud.

Cultivation Dust the soil around the plants with blood, bone and fishmeal in February and then lay a mulch of organic matter. Repeat this operation annually. Do not let the soil dry out during the first spring and summer, and each May scatter a handful of sulphate of potash around each bush to encourage fruit formation. Birds can eat the buds in winter and the fruits in summer if the bushes are not netted or caged.

Pruning The system is quite different from that adopted for blackcurrants. Aim to build up a goblet-shaped bush of six or eight branches: the older branches keep on fruiting for several years. Remove one or two of the most ancient branches each year in winter. Shorten all sub-laterals to six leaves in summer.

Harvesting Pick the fruits individually when they are ripe, or cut off the sprigs whole if the fruits are to be kept for a few days before being used. Like blackcurrants, each bush should produce about 4.5 kg (10 lb) of fruit.

Storing Use in jellies or freeze.

Pests and diseases Aphids, birds, red currant blister aphid, capsid bug, currant sawfly, leaf spot and coral spot.

Propagation As for gooseberries.

Damson and Gage See Plum

GOOSEBERRY

Gooseberries are not easy to prune, thanks to their thorns, but they're very easy to eat in pies, jams, stewed and in that superb dessert gooseberry fool. There are culinary and dessert kinds and even dual-purpose varieties. I reckon that those in the list below are some of the best.

Where to plant Although they are tolerant of dappled shade, gooseberries grow best in full sun on ground that does not act as a frost pocket. Dig and manure the land in autumn before planting bare-root bushes between November and March. Scatter a dusting of blood, bone and fishmeal over the soil immediately before planting.

Planting Plant to the same level as the old soil mark on the stem after removing any suckers (shoots arising from the roots or from the portion of stem that will be below ground). Like red currants, gooseberries are grown on a short 'leg'. For full planting details see the instructions on planting trees and shrubs (see p.40). Space plants 1.5 m (5 ft) from their neighbours, or plant them in flower beds and borders as shrubs. Cut back all the stems by half their length after planting, preferably to an outward-facing bud. Varieties that have a tendency to trail their stems can be cut back to an upward-facing bud. Cut out any overcrowding sideshoots: aim to produce a bush with six or eight main stems.

Cultivation Dust the soil around the bushes with blood, bone and fishmeal in spring and then lay an organic mulch. Remove any suckers that form. Water well in dry spells. In succeeding years a little sulphate of potash can be scattered around each bush in February before the general fertilizer and mulch are applied. Keep down weeds during the summer.

Pruning Prune gooseberries twice: in winter, cut back the main shoots by half and sideshoots back to three buds; completely remove one or two old stems. In summer, shorten sideshoots to about five leaves in early July.

Harvesting The first pickings can be made in May when the fruits are thinned to leave them 5 cm (2 in) apart along the stems. Early pickings can be used in a pie. When the berries are fully fattened they will gradually soften and can then be harvested in one go.

Storing All manner of preserves can be made; both the fruits themselves and pies made with them can be frozen.

Pests and diseases Aphids, birds, gooseberry sawfly, American gooseberry mildew.

Propagation Take hardwood cuttings in September or October. Shoot tips 30 cm (12 in) long can be cut above a bud at the top and below a bud at the base and relieved of all but the top four buds, which will form the branch framework of the new plant.

Insert the cuttings on the vegetable plot. The lowest bud on each cutting should be a few centimetres (inches) above ground level. Carefully lift the rooted cuttings the following autumn and transplant them to where they can be allowed to grow permanently.

Recommended gooseberry varieties

VARIETY	COLOUR	ORDER OF RIPENING	CULINARY/DESSERT
'Careless'	white	2	C
'Golden Drop'	yellow	1	D
'Keepsake'	green	1	C/D
'Lancashire Lad'	red	2	C/D
'Langley Gage'	yellow	2	D
'Leveller'	yellow	2	C/D
'May Duke'	red	1	C/D
'Whitesmith'	green	3	C/D

GRAPE

We are now blessed with a number of grapes that can be grown outdoors, but most gardeners find greater satisfaction in growing one vine in a greenhouse or conservatory, so I'm going to stay under glass.

For a start you'll need a greenhouse or conservatory at least 4 m (12 ft) long, otherwise your rampant vine will boot everything else out of the way.

Don't be tempted to try that aristocrat of grapes 'Muscat of Alexandria' unless you're prepared to take a gamble. It's a temperamental customer and not likely to perform as

well as either 'Royal Muscadine' (if you want a green grape) or 'Schiava Grossa' (syn. 'Black Hamburgh') (if you prefer black).

Preparing the soil and the house An Irishman once told me that the best thing to put under a grapevine was 'three dead dogs', but failing the availability of a canine trio I should stick to a good load of manure. Traditionally vines were always planted outside the greenhouse and the stem taken in through a hole in the wall. Today it's considered better to plant inside the house where the soil is warmer and you will have far more control over watering and feeding.

Growing happily in the border soil of this spacious conservatory, these vines are laden with tantalizingly healthy bunches of fat grapes.

Dig plenty of muck or compost into the border soil and a good sprinkling of general fertilizer. Fix training wires to the rafters of the house at 35 cm (15 in) intervals. The vine will be planted in the centre of one of the greenhouse borders and the stem or 'rod' led upwards to the eaves and then on to the ridge, which means that the growth will rest right against the glass. For this reason it's important to use 20-23 cm (8-9 in) long metal vine eyes to support the wire and allow maximum air circulation between the plant and the glass.

Planting Plant bare-root vines between November and December, container-grown vines at any time of year. Soak the soil thoroughly a few days before planting if it looks at all dry. For a bare-root vine dig a hole large enough to take the roots, trim off any damaged roots with a sharp pair of secateurs, put the plant in the hole, spread out the roots and re-firm the soil with your feet. Set the plant 15 cm (6 in) from the greenhouse wall and make sure that the old soil mark on the stem is just level with the new surface. Container-grown vines should be tapped out of their pots but otherwise disturbed as little as possible (though any roots that are obviously trying to corkscrew themselves back into the rootball should be teased out). Lower the rootball into the hole and firm back the soil. Water the plant well to settle the soil around the roots and apply a thick mulch of manure or compost.

Training and pruning There are lots of complicated methods of training a vine but this is the simplest I know (see below). Shorten the main rod (you'll have to get used to that word if you want to pass yourself off as an expert) to 60 cm (2 ft) and any lateral shoots to one bud after planting in December. When the buds start to grow, nip off all but the topmost shoot and allow this to grow to a length of 3 m (10 ft), then pinch out its tip. The shoot is most easily supported by tying it to a cane which is, in turn, tied to the wires so that it runs up the side of the house; another cane can be tied to the roof section. Sideshoots (laterals) will emerge from the new main stem. Thin them out to leave one shoot every 35 cm (15 in), to correspond with the training wires. The shoots should be trained alternately to right and left. Carefully fasten these shoots to the wires as they grow. Pinch out their tips when they are 1 m (3 ft) long, leaving five leaves on each. Pinch back any sub-laterals that form on these major sideshoots to just one leaf.

In the first autumn after planting, cut back the main laterals to two buds (this is a stub or 'spur') and shorten the main rod by two thirds of its length. In the years that follow, allow one lateral to grow from each spur and pinch out its tip two or three leaves after its flower cluster. Train the main rod as before, allowing it to retain an extra 60 cm (2 ft) each year until it is eventually pruned to just below the ridge. Don't allow all the laterals to carry fruit in the second year – only the lower pair. Another tier can be allowed to fruit each year.

Cultivation Leave the house unheated and gently ventilated right through the winter until March. The rod is cleaned while it is dormant; lower it from the support wires and scrub it down with a stiff brush to remove flaking bark. Paint it with a winter wash to kill overwintering eggs of aphids, hibernating mealy bugs, red spider mites and scale insects. Heat can be applied as early as February but most folk are content to grow their grapes in an unheated greenhouse and settle for

Pruning and training a grape vine

Pinch out any sub-laterals on these stems so that just one leaf remains

Train the laterals alternately right and left, pinching out their tips when they reach 1 m (3 ft)

Prune the laterals to leave two buds

Pinch out tip of each spur three leaves after the flower cluster

1 After planting a dormant vine, shorten the main rod to 60 cm (2 ft) and laterals to one bud.

2 Allow only the topmost bud to grow, fastening it to a cane as it extends. Laterals that emerge from this new stem should be thinned out so just one remains for each wire.

3 In the first winter after planting shorten the laterals to leave just two buds. Cut back the main rod by two thirds.

4 Allow one shoot to grow from each stub or 'spur' in subsequent years, pinching out its tip three leaves after the flower cluster. Continue to pinch out sub-laterals.

an August and September harvest. Close the ventilators in April and water the border soil well. Soon the buds will swell and training can begin. Leave the rod hanging down from the support system when you start it off, and tie it up again when the lower laterals have started to sprout.

Try to maintain a temperature of 16°C (60°F), gradually letting this rise to around 21°C (70°F) by late May (an automatic ventilating arm will be very useful here). Damp down daily in fine weather and spray the shoots with tepid rainwater once a day until the flowers open.

Shade when necessary from mid-May onwards. When the flowers open, dust over them with a fine paintbrush or a rabbit's tail to assist pollination. Try to maintain an average day temperature of 21°C (70°F) and a minimum night temperature of 13°C (55°F). Keep an eye on the border soil and really soak it before it has a chance to become dry. Apply a liquid feed (tomato fertilizer is best) every ten days once growth has started.

Thinning It's essential to thin out the fruit clusters if you want a healthy bunch of fat grapes. Thin the berries when they are pea-sized. Work from the bottom of the bunch to the top so that 1 cm (½ in) is left between all the remaining fruits. Use fine-pointed scissors and keep your fingers off the grapes or the white 'bloom' will be marked.

Harvesting When the grapes start to ripen ease off watering and stop feeding or the fruits may over-expand and split. Snip off any that do. The grapes will be ready to cut in bunches about four weeks after they have changed colour. Once harvesting is completed, ventilate well and continue to ease off watering so that the vine gradually becomes dormant once more.

Storing Grapes can't be stored, but if you grow a suitable cultivar you might like to try your hand at winemaking with your own home-grown grapes.

Pests and diseases Aphids, mealy bug, red spider mite, scale insects, scald, shanking.
propagation Tricky and not necessary if you only need one vine.

Loganberry See Blackberry

PEACH / NECTARINE

Exotic-sounding though it may be, the nectarine is nothing more than a peach without the fur coat. Grow it in exactly the same way. Don't waste your time growing a peach from a stone – it may never come to much. Instead buy a plant of a proven variety that can be relied on to produce plenty of succulent fruits. 'Peregrine' is my first choice. It ripens in August and is a good doer both under glass and in the open. 'Early Rivers' and 'Lord Napier' are among the best of the nectarines, ripening in July and August. If you insist on having peaches in July you'd better pick 'Duke of York'.

Where to plant To keep them warm and in good order, peaches and nectarines are best trained as fan-shaped trees against a south- or west-facing wall or the rear wall of a lean-to greenhouse. Dig the soil deeply, working in plenty of manure or compost and improving drainage if necessary. Acid soil should be limed a few weeks after digging and a few weeks before planting.

Support Horizontal wires should be fastened to the wall, or to a sunny fence if that's all you've got, to allow tying in. Arrange the wires at 30 cm (12 in) intervals and hold them in place with metal vine eyes screwed into wall plugs.

Planting Plant a container-grown peach for preference. It can be planted at any time of year provided the soil against the wall is not allowed to dry out. It's easiest to plant a partially trained tree with the basis of the fan formation already established, but if you're mean, or just interested in doing the job yourself, you can buy a

'maiden' (a one-year-old tree) and start from scratch. Plant the tree (after watering it well) so that its rootball rests just below the surface of the soil. (See p.40 for full planting details.) Set the plant 15–30 cm (6–12 in) away from the wall. Scatter a little blood, bone and fishmeal around it during February and then apply an organic mulch.

Training and pruning When your maiden tree is planted, wait until the shoots start to grow in spring then cut it back to 60 cm (2 ft) just above a sprouting shoot. When two healthy shoots are observed growing in opposite directions from the base of the tree, but above the graft union, cut back the central stem to just above them and remove all other shoots.

These two shoots will be taken up the wire framework in opposite directions at an angle of 45°. Fasten a cane to the wire to act as a marker and support for each shoot. Pinch out any sub-laterals that form on these main laterals.

In winter, shorten the two laterals to about 1 m (3 ft) and allow four sub-laterals to grow from each of them during the second summer. Make sure that these shoots are well spaced out on the framework, and at the end of the year cut them back to 1 m (3 ft), having pinched off their laterals during the summer.

During the third year sub-laterals are allowed to grow from the established laterals at 23 cm (9 in) intervals, but only from the top sides of the laterals. Those growing out at other angles are removed. Pinch out the tips of these shoots when they are 45 cm (18 in) long. Allow the topmost bud that remains on each to grow on and extend the framework.

Peaches are carried on wood that is one year old and the aim should be to produce as much young wood on the mature framework as possible. Mature plants should have their fruiting sideshoots cut out as soon as the fruit is picked, and new ones tied in to replace them. Thin out overcrowding shoots in spring by simply pulling them off while they are soft and green.

Under glass There's no need to heat a peach under glass; it will have a head start simply by virtue of the fact that there's glass above it. Leave the ventilators open a little right through the winter, closing them in February and ventilating only when the temperature rises to 18°C (65°F). Ideally the plants want to be kept around 10°C (50°F) at night and 16°C (60°F) during the day, but in an unheated house you'll have to rely on the weather doing this for you (and in February it's not always kind). A good sprinkling of general fertilizer, followed by a thorough watering and mulching, will help to spur the plant into action, as will a daily spray with tepid water. Damp down the floor too. Soak the soil thoroughly whenever it shows signs of drying out, and later in spring apply shading when there is a danger of sun scorch. Blinds are the best answer – they can be rolled up on dull days.

Pollination Peaches flower early, both in the open and under glass, and there are few bees around to pollinate for you. Use a soft paintbrush or a rabbit's tail to dust the pollen from flower to flower. If frost threatens, hang muslin or old net curtains over the flowering branches. When the fruitlets are the size of marbles, thin them out to leave one every 10 cm (4 in). Stop spraying the greenhouse plants with water now. When the fruits are as large as conkers, thin them to leave one every 23 cm (9 in).

Harvesting harvesting Pick the fruits as soon as they are ripe – the flesh will suddenly soften at the shoulder of the fruit (the end nearest the stalk). Once the fruits have been picked the plant can be sprayed daily with water once more.

Storing The fruits can be stored for a few days by placing them in a container lined with soft material and keeping in a cool place.

Pests and diseases Aphids, scale insects, red spider mites, mildew, peach leaf curl. The latter rarely attacks peaches under glass but almost always attacks peaches in the open. For this reason it's a good idea to give preventive sprays each year before the buds open.

PEAR

Perhaps the best all-round eating pear is 'Williams' Bon Chrétien', often known simply as 'Williams'. 'Doyenné du Comice' is certainly the juiciest and most succulent but it can be tricky in cold gardens. The long, slim 'Conference' is a good choice if you like your pears on the firm side, and if you want a good cooker try 'Catillac'.

Where to plant Warmth, sun and shelter are the keys to success with pears. Give them a well-cultivated, well-manured soil in a bright spot and they should do well. The flowers open earlier than those of the apple, so keep the trees away from frost pockets at all costs or you'll lose your blossom. As well as being grown as free-standing trees, pears can also be trained as cordons, espaliers and fans (see p.217).

Rootstocks Like the apple, the pear is grafted on to a rootstock that controls its vigour. 'Quince A' is the name of the stock most frequently used. It is relatively dwarfing and brings the tree into bearing when it's only a few years old.

Pollination It's as well to think about pollination before you plant. If your pear tree, or trees, don't receive the right kind of pollen they'll fail to set a crop. In practice there are often trees in other gardens, and the bees are able to fly between them all doing a good job. If there are no other pears in the area you'd be advised to plant two so that cross-pollination is ensured, but you'll have to plant pears that flower at the same time. 'Conference' will pollinate 'Williams', and vice versa; 'Doyenné du Comice' will pollinate 'Catillac' and that other favourite 'Beurré Hardy', and vice versa.

Planting If you are lucky enough to have room for a small orchard, plant bush trees 4 m (12 ft) apart on the square. Cordons should be planted 2 m (6 ft) apart on the support system; espaliers and fans 4.5 m (15 ft) apart. Plant pears exactly as for ornamental trees (see p.40). Scatter a good dusting of blood, bone and fishmeal over the soil during the spring after planting and then lay a thick mulch of organic matter on the soil. Don't let grass grow within 1 m (3 ft) of the tree for at least three years or the roots of the grass will rob the soil of nutrients the pear could use.

Training and pruning Pruning of established trees is similar to the pruning of apples (see p.219 for fuller details). All the varieties I've mentioned carry their fruits on short sideshoots known as 'spurs'. To encourage the production of these the main shoots are cut back by half their length during winter and the lateral shoots are shortened to three or four buds. Pears have a tendency to become overcrowded with fruiting spurs and the buds on these spurs can be reduced to three in number if you have the patience and determination.

Recommended pear varieties

VARIETY	PICK	DAYS TO RIPEN
'Williams' Bon Chrétien'	September	7-14
'Doyenné du Comice'	October	7-28
'Conference'	October	7-28
'Beurré Hardy'	Late September	14-28
'Catillac'	October	Keeps until April

It's not the end of the world if you don't prune your tree every year but it does help to keep it in shape. A yearly feed with rose fertilizer gives the tree a boost, especially in the first five years of its life. Scatter half a dozen handfuls on the soil around the trunk and lightly hoe it in during March. Thin the young fruits in mid-July to leave just two out of each cluster.

Harvesting A tricky operation. Many pears need to be picked before they are ripe and allowed to come to maturity in store. The general rule for picking is that the fruit should be removed as soon as it parts easily from the tree. 'Catillac' remains hard right through storage, softening when cooked.

Storing As for apples, but do not wrap the fruits. Keep an especially close eye on pears for they suddenly ripen and are likely to be past it if you only check them once a week. As soon as a fruit starts to soften, bring it in from the store and eat it within a day or two. The polythene bag method of storage (see p.220) is especially useful for pears - it stops them shrivelling. The early varieties will not keep for long; the later varieties last better.

Pests and diseases Aphids, red spider mite, pear midge, pear leaf blister mite, birds, codling moth, slugworm, pear sucker, pear sawfly, winter moth, canker, mildew, scab, brown rot, blossom wilt and fireblight.

PLUM / DAMSON / GAGE

These are luscious fruits that are really easy to grow. There's little to master in the way of pruning and, if you choose the right variety, you'll not need to worry about planting more than one, for the tree can set a good crop of fruits with its own pollen. If you're baffled by all the different varieties, the following are among the best: 'Victoria' is an unbeatable plum. Sometimes it's so anxious to please that the branches are snapped off by the weight of its fruits; if your penchant is for gages, try 'Early

Transparent Gage', a yellow fruit of incomparable sweetness. Both mature from mid- to late August. 'Czar' is a good culinary plum ripening earlier in the month, and 'Merryweather Damson' makes the most delectable dark red jam when it comes to maturity in September and October. Let your nurseryman tempt you with other goodies from his collection of varieties, but make sure you know whether they are dessert or culinary plums - the flavour of the culinary types is only appreciated after cooking.

Where to plant The plum is happy on deep soil; it will grow on chalky ground but seldom on really shallow stuff. Lime acid ground in the autumn before

digging and manuring. The soil needs to be well cultivated to give the roots every chance to sink and establish themselves. Compared with other fruit trees, plums are comparatively shallow rooting and an annual spring mulch of manure is especially welcome. Avoid frost pockets, and make sure the trees have plenty of sun.

Rootstocks Plums, damsons and gages are usually grafted on to one of two rootstocks: St Julien A or Myrobalan B. The latter is used for vigorous standard trees, the former

A typically heavy crop of 'Victoria' plum: the excellently flavoured, bright red fruit with golden-yellow flesh ripens in late August.

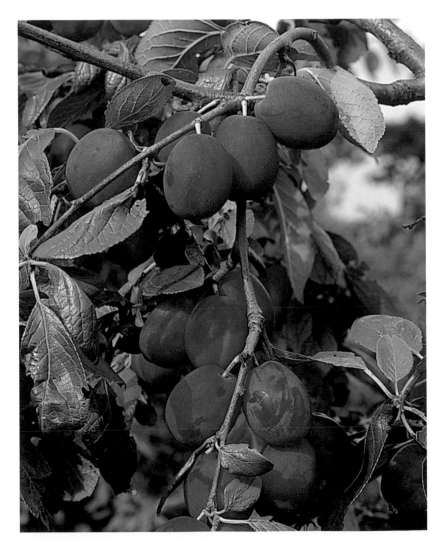

for most others. In smaller gardens St Julien A is obviously a better choice, unless you have a craving for a tree seat in which case you'll plump for a standard. The newer rootstock Pixy is more dwarfing than St Julien A but the trees are still quite large compared with bush apple trees.

Planting Having decided on a bush, pyramid, standard, half-standard or fan-shaped tree (see p.217 for details) you can think about planting. Like all trees, plums can be planted from containers at any time of year or as bare-root plants from November to March. Choose two- or three-year-old trees and plant as for ornamental trees and shrubs (see p.40). If you intend to plant them in an orchard, space bush trees 4 m (12 ft) apart, or 3 m (10 ft) apart if they are on Pixy rootstock; standards and half-standards 5.5 m (18 ft) apart. Fans should be trained against tall house walls of a southerly or westerly aspect for preference. They'll need a wire framework as recommended for peaches and acid cherries. Scatter a general fertilizer on the soil around the tree in spring and then lay a thick organic mulch. Avoid growing grass right up to plum trees: they resent the competition. Pay attention to watering during establishment.

Pruning Prune your plums in spring or summer to lessen the risk of attack by silver leaf disease, which can enter wounds in winter. Newly planted trees should be pruned in March, just as the buds are starting to break. Cut all the shoots back by half their length. Remove completely any weak or overcrowding shoots. You can do this for a couple of years and then leave the tree to its own devices if you're really lazy. Prune when necessary in spring or summer to keep the tree shapely: cut back overlong leading shoots by one third of their length and snip the tips off laterals.

Start off a fan-trained plum tree as described for peaches (see p.227). Some lateral shoots are retained as part of the framework each year; those that are not required are pinched back to five leaves in summer to encourage the production of fruiting spurs. Cut out a portion of older wood each summer and replace it with strong, younger shoots. As with all fan-trained trees, cut out any shoots that grow directly away from the wall or towards it.

Pollination Most plums (and all those I've mentioned) will set a good crop of fruits with their own pollen, though the presence of another plum tree flowering at the same time will usually make for an even heavier crop. If frost threatens at blossom time, drape wall-trained trees with old net curtains or some other fabric to offer the blooms protection.

Thinning The tree will thin its own fruits to some extent in the June drop, but you can help out after this if you like by snipping off unwanted fruits to leave the remainder 5–8 cm (2–3 in) apart. If you don't thin 'Victoria', the boughs will often snap and can allow disease to enter. A tree that bears too heavily one year will often crop lightly the next. Prop up heavily laden branches with catapult-shaped poles.

Harvesting Pick dessert plums when they are fully ripe – bite into one and see. Damsons and culinary plums can be picked with their stalks just before they are ripe. Try to harvest the fruits before birds and wasps eat their fill.

Storing Store in a cool place while you see to jam- and pie-making. They'll freeze well if you remove the stones first.

Pests and diseases Aphids, red spider mites, winter moth, pear leaf blister mite, plum sawfly, plum tortrix moth, mussel scale, wasps, silver leaf, bacterial canker, blossom wilt, brown rot.

RASPBERRY

It's a toss-up as to which is the more popular fruit in British gardens, the raspberry or the strawberry. The raspberry wins in mine. 'Malling Jewel' is easily the best flavoured of the summer fruiters, closely followed by the slightly earlier 'Malling Promise' (if you can find it). Make sure you try the autumn fruiters 'Autumn Bliss' (the best) and 'Zeva Herbsternte', which extend the season well into October. Some folk claim that these autumn crops are not as fine flavoured as the summer harvest, but I wouldn't dream of complaining at that time of year.

Where to plant Best in full sun, though the summer fruiters can take dappled shade. Choose a sheltered site on well-drained soil that has been well dug and well manured. Scatter a good dusting of blood, bone and fishmeal over the soil a few days before planting. The plants can be used as a screen and then a 45 cm (18 in) wide trench can be prepared for them rather than an entire patch of soil.

Support A 2 m (6 ft) high post and wire fence with stout horizontal wires at 45 cm (18 in) intervals is all that is necessary, or the plants can be trained against a fence fitted with wires at a similar spacing.

Planting Buy only certified raspberry canes that are free of virus diseases, which can cripple cropping. Plant from November to February. Soak the canes overnight in a bucket of water and then plant them at 45 cm (18 in) intervals along the foot of the support system, covering the roots with just 8 cm (3 in) of soil. Firm the earth well around the roots and then cut back the canes to 23 cm (9 in).

Cultivation Scatter a dusting of blood, bone and fishmeal over the soil along the row in March and then lay an organic mulch. Tie in the canes as they grow, spacing them 10 cm (4 in) apart. Cut off the old stump at ground level when the new stems grow. When the canes grow taller than the topmost wire, bend them downwards and tie them in. Cut them off level with the top wire during the winter. Keep the plants well watered at all times during the first spring and summer. Hand-weed among the plants and remove canes that emerge too far away from the row.

Pruning Summer fruiters will carry a crop in the second summer on the canes formed during their first year. The autumn fruiters will produce fruits in the first September after planting, so pruning from now on is different. All the canes of the autumn fruiters are cut out at ground level in February. As soon as the summer fruiters have been picked, the canes that carried the fruits are cut out at ground level and the new ones, which will carry next year's crop, are thinned out if necessary and tied into the framework again at 10 cm (4 in) intervals.

Harvesting Make sure it is you who get the harvest, not the birds who will be fierce competition. Net or cage the crop if you can. Pick the berries, pulling them from their plugs, as soon as they are ripe. Check the canes every few days for ripening fruits. You should be able to harvest 900 g (2 lb) from every 30 cm (12 in) run of row with summer-fruiting varieties; around 225 g (½ lb) with the autumn fruiters.

Storing The fruits freeze well.

Pests and diseases Aphids, raspberry beetle, cane spot, cane blight, spur blight, botrytis and viruses.

Propagation Dig up and transplant suckers in autumn. Only propagate from healthy, virus-free plants. Replace raspberry rows every eight years or so.

STRAWBERRY

The strawberry is more labour intensive than most fruits, but that doesn't seem to put gardeners off growing it. Don't stick by the ancient varieties, which are losing their vigour: go for some of the newcomers, but taste them before you commit yourself. I can heartily recommend the summer fruiter 'Pantagruella'. Varieties described as 'perpetual fruiting' crop late into the season; 'Aromel' is reliable even if it lacks the full flavour of 'Pantagruella'.

Where to plant An open, sunny spot in well-drained soil is what strawberries insist on. Don't whatever you do plant them in a frost pocket or you'll be lucky if you ever see a berry. Dig over the soil during spring and summer and add as much manure as you can spare. Scatter a general fertilizer over the soil a few days before planting and rake it into the surface.

Planting Buy certified strawberry plants that are guaranteed free from virus diseases. Water them well and plant while the soil is moist, during July and August and certainly no later than September. These plants can then be allowed to crop the following year. Perpetual fruiters that are not planted until spring can still be allowed to fruit in late summer and autumn, but the earlier fruiting varieties should be relieved of their flowers if they are spring planted. Conserve their strength for a bumper crop in one year's time. Plant the strawberries 45 cm (18 in) apart in rows 75 cm (2½ ft) apart. The crown of each plant should rest at soil level – not below it, nor too far above it. Water the plants in thoroughly with a sprinkler.

Cultivation Pay close attention to watering during the remainder of the summer and the following spring. I mulch my strawberry bed with pulverized bark immediately after planting. Pick off faded leaves and scatter tomato fertilizer among the plants in February at the rate of a handful to two plants; let the rain wash it in. Protect the plants from slugs and the fruits from birds: lay plastic netting over the rows or grow the plants in a fruit cage. Early in June push straw under the fruit clusters and around the plants to keep the crop clean. Bitumen strawberry mats and black plastic mulching are useful alternatives where straw is undesirable or in short supply. Remove any runners that form, unless you want to propagate from them.

If you want to hasten fruit ripening, cover a row of plants with cloches in early February. Ventilate well when the

As an alternative to straw or mats, support fruit-laden stems with loops made from lengths of galvanized wire

Strawberries are synonymous with summer, but it is possible to carry on harvesting this luscious soft fruit until late autumn. Keep fruit off the soil with clean straw or special mats.

flowers open, and remove the cloches when the crop has been picked.

Harvesting Pick the fruits, with their stalks, as soon as they are ripe. When all the fruits have been picked, chop off all the foliage and burn it along with the straw to kill pests and diseases. The perpetual fruiters will be happier if you cut off just the older leaves and remove the straw.

Storing Strawberries make good jam. The variety 'Totem' freezes well, even if it's not A1 when it comes to flavour.

Pests and diseases Aphids, birds, slugs, red spider mites, botrytis, viruses.

Propagation To keep the plants in good condition, move the strawberry bed every three years. Allow runners to form during July and August in the third year, if the plants are still healthy and virus free, and peg these into 8 cm (3 in) pots of John Innes No. 1 potting compost sunk into the soil alongside the plants. Keep the compost moist and the plantlets will quickly send out roots. Sever them from their parents and plant them out individually six weeks later. If your plants have puckered or mottled leaves, burn them and buy in virus-free stock.

18 Vegetable growing

Nothing can compare with the taste of home-grown vegetables, chosen for flavour, harvested in their prime and enhanced with a sprinkling of fresh, chopped herbs

I wish I had a penny for every time I've been asked if it's really worth growing your own vegetables. If you're going to add up labour and the cost of seeds and fertilizers I doubt if it is. But how much do you allow for flavour, convenience, the thrill of the harvest and the fact that you can choose just what variety of vegetable you grow?

Gardeners who refuse to grow vegetables because it's easier to buy them from the shops must be desperately short of imagination as well as energy. Of course some crops fail, but isn't the magic moment of picking a good crop worth all that hassle? It is to me. So no more grumbling – on with the wellies and out with the spade!

Nobody should be without a handful of herbs to add flavour and aroma to their cooking, so I've included entries for the most popular culinary herbs at the end of the A–Z section.

PLANNING YOUR VEGETABLE PLOT

Choosing the best site

You might not have much choice but, if you can, try to pick a spot that's well lit, sheltered at a distance from wind and within easy reach of the house. Avoid frost pockets – dips in the land that will collect cold air and make for a slow start and rapid finish to the growing season. Vegetables are dependent upon generous supplies of water in summer, so make sure the hosepipe will reach them. If they are allowed to dry out, all development will stop and your yields will be down. It's a good idea to start with a small plot and make it bigger as you need the space – that way you won't suddenly be faced with a massive patch of virgin soil to keep in trim.

Easy access

Paths around the plot will make access easier, and it's not a bad idea to make them out of loose-laid flagstones that can be lifted and relaid as necessary. I've divided my plot up with slabs laid on raked earth and it's easy to lift them for digging each winter. At just over one pound apiece they weren't too pricey, but I bought them a few at a time as the plot grew.

WHERE TO PLANT

I always feel a killjoy when I tell folk to plan their plots before they sow anything: most want to be out on the soil bunging in seeds for all they're worth. But if you stop to take out a pencil and paper for a few minutes you can decide which crop should go where and what can follow it. Ask yourself whether something can be grown between two other crops that will not need the space at that time. Try to position crops that need the same kind of soil preparation in the same area as this will save you humping manure to all corners of the plot. Work out when each plant needs to be sown and when it is likely to be harvested. This all sounds very grand, but a plan of campaign makes vegetable growing even more interesting.

Rotation

The rotation of crops is an ancient practice based on sound common sense. Farmers change their crops from field to field each year so that specific crop diseases do not get a chance to build up in any one area, and so that particular nutrients, which one crop might demand in quantity, do not become exhausted.

On the vegetable plot it is difficult to work out a really concrete rotation scheme (though I do try to divide my plot into three – liming one third, manuring another third and fertilizing the remainder), but it is sensible to put vegetables in a different place each year. For example, it may be more convenient, but don't keep your runner beans at the same end or your onions on one bed – even though some experts swear by this method. If disease does strike, you're in trouble, particularly with onions – it will be years before you can grow them again.

What you can do is to group together on the plot those crops that enjoy roughly the same soil conditions: those that like a freshly manured site, such as onions, leeks, peas and beans, and those that need lime if the ground is acid (most brassicas – members of the cabbage family). Vegetables that enjoy just a little fertilizer (including most root crops) can be kept to one section of the plot and that section moved yearly.

IMPROVING THE SOIL

Manuring Those patches that need manuring every year can be enriched during digging in autumn, winter, or even spring, on light soils, with well-rotted manure or garden compost. If you can't get either (though you should always make your own compost – sorry to nag)

use coarse peat laced with some general fertilizer. A bucketful to every running metre (yard) of trench will be fine (see p.15 for digging instructions).

Liming Brassicas in particular grow best on a soil that is not too acid. Soil test kits will tell you the status quo (see p.14) and a dressing of lime can be applied in winter, at least one month after manure, if necessary.

Fertilizers All crops need fertilizer. I've not mentioned its application to individual crops in the A–Z section because it should be scattered over the plot about one week before sowing any crop. Two handfuls of blood, bone and fishmeal or Growmore can be scattered over each square metre (square yard) and raked in. This is known as a base dressing.

Topdressings are given to boost growing crops. With leafy crops, fertilizers high in growth-promoting nitrogen are beneficial (sulphate of ammonia and nitrochalk, for instance). Others will prefer a more balanced fertilizer containing equal amounts of nitrogen, phosphates and potassium, such as blood, bone and fishmeal and Growmore. I've indicated which crops like which. Liquid feeds have the advantage of going straight into action and give all crops a rapid boost.

> "If there's no room for a vegetable patch, fit your vegetables among the flowers."

Mulching In flower beds and borders mulching is a common practice, but few folk mulch on the vegetable plot. That's a shame, for many crops grow better if surrounded with an organic mat. Beans and peas are especially grateful for a mulch of compost or even grass mowings in summer. Apply the mulch while the soil is moist and it will keep the moisture in as well as keeping down weeds.

WEED CONTROL

I'll speak only briefly of weed control but remember that it is vital (see Chapter 1 How to Start). If your crops have to compete with a forest of groundsel, chickweed, dandelions and couch grass they'll give up the ghost, or become spindly and not worth harvesting.

A Dutch hoe pushed between the rows on a dry day is the best means of control for most annual weeds, and that's all that should be left after your preliminary cultivations, except, perhaps, the odd persistent dandelion or nettle. Hand-weeding between the plants is a bit of a chore but there's no finer method of getting to know your crops.

SOWING AND GROWING TECHNIQUES

There are various ways of sowing seeds on the vegetable plot, and there are some vegetables that need to be sown in a greenhouse or on a windowsill before being introduced to the great outdoors. I've dealt with the techniques in Chapter 2 Propagation, but here I want to mention a few wheezes that will enable you to get the best out of your plot.

Where and when to sow
Successional sowing This is the technique of sowing small quantities of one crop at intervals so that your harvest is spread. Don't sow three rows of lettuce or

Even if your garden is too small to accommodate a full-scale vegetable plot, you can grow a few specimens in your flower beds and borders: many are handsome enough to show off flowers, such as these *Eschscholzia* 'Special Mixed' (Californian poppy), to advantage.

radish, for instance, all in one go. Sow half a row every fortnight. That way you'll have a steady succession of crops instead of an embarrassing glut.

intercropping This is where fast-growing crops such as radishes are sown between rows of slow-growing crops that will eventually need the space. The radishes will be mature by the time they are being jostled and you've managed to squeeze an extra harvest out of the soil.

Catch cropping Fast-growing vegetables are used again here: not just radishes but spring onions, turnips and non-hearting lettuce too. Sow them on land that will not be planted up with another crop until later in the year. Your first crop will have matured and been picked by then. You'll need to plan carefully.

Thinning and transplanting

Thinning Here's a job that's more vital than you think. Even the obliging radish will not grow unless it's thinned quickly. Do the job as soon as you can to give the crops that remain room to grow. You don't have to pull up the unwanted seedlings; you can simply nip them off at ground level (unless you'd rather fork them up and carefully transplant them).

Planting and transplanting When you're moving plants bear in mind a few golden rules: always water them well before transplanting and 'puddle' them in afterwards. Plant firmly and plant youngsters, not gnarled grandads. Use a trowel for most plants, a thick spade-handle dibber for brassicas if you like. Plant to the same depth as the plant was growing in the nursery bed – no shallower and no deeper.

Growing in bed systems

There's much fuss made of the modern technique of growing vegetables in beds rather than rows. It's a sensible scheme whereby several rows are spaced very close together (as close as the plants are spaced within the row) and a path left every 1 m (3 ft) or so between such blocks to allow weeding and so on.

Deep bed system Here the soil within the beds is never walked on. It's double dug during the first year and enriched with compost and manure. In subsequent winters it is forked over and any additional enrichment worked in. A friend of mine swears by the method and I aim to try it myself. The first spell of double digging is

hell on my flinty soil but I'm optimistic that the results will pay dividends.

Growing in the flower garden

Where there's simply no room for a conventional vegetable patch you'll have to fit your vegetables among the flowers. It's not as funny as it sounds. The foliage of beetroot, Swiss chard, frilly salad bowl-type lettuces, and even leeks, is good to look at and can show off flowers a treat. There are even ornamental cabbages with pink or white hearts that can be eaten. So if you're desperate to fit vegetables in, squeeze up the antirrhinums and dahlias and stick in a few runner beans and carrots, curly kale and globe artichokes.

Growing in cloches

These are the mini-greenhouses of glass or plastic that are used to give vegetable crops an early start or a late finish. Think of them as umbrellas rather than hot-houses. They will shelter early sowings from wind and rain, but should not be thought of as making sowing possible in really foul conditions. Seeds buried in cold, muddy earth under cloches will die almost as quickly as those buried in muddy earth in the open, so you'll still be governed to some degree by the weather.

Nevertheless, the greedy veg grower should not be without cloches. They come in many shapes and sizes, but all should be fitted with end pieces to prevent them from acting as wind tunnels. For best results cloches should be put in place two or three weeks before the crop is sown to ensure the soil is in good condition.

Water can be applied over the top of the cloches when necessary (it will seep through the soil to the crop roots), and don't forget to ventilate both cloches and plastic tunnels in warm weather.

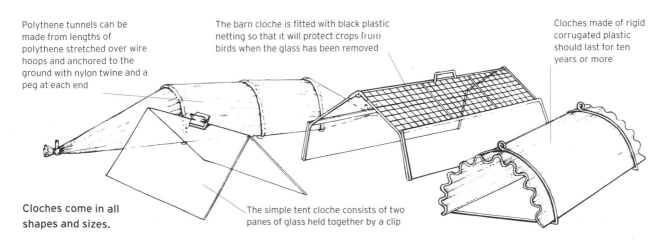

Polythene tunnels can be made from lengths of polythene stretched over wire hoops and anchored to the ground with nylon twine and a peg at each end

The barn cloche is fitted with black plastic netting so that it will protect crops from birds when the glass has been removed

Cloches made of rigid corrugated plastic should last for ten years or more

Cloches come in all shapes and sizes.

The simple tent cloche consists of two panes of glass held together by a clip

A-Z of vegetables and herbs

VEGETABLE CROPS

ARTICHOKE, GLOBE

Don't sow seeds that can yield variable plants. Instead plant rooted offshoots of a variety like 'Gros Vert de Lâon'. For patient gourmets only.

Where to plant Full sun and a very rich soil. A sheltered spot produces the biggest and best plants.

Plant in spring, spacing the youngsters I m (3 ft) apart both ways.

Cultivation Topdress with compost or manure every May. Water well in dry spells. Remove all flowers during the first year. Cut the plants down to ground level in autumn and cover with straw or bracken. Scatter fertilizer around the plants in April and feed fortnightly in summer with liquid feed. Remove side buds to let only one flower develop on each head. Divide plants every four years.

Harvest by cutting heads when firm and plump and when the scales are starting to expand. Don't wait until you can see the fuzzy flowerhead – it'll be too late. In season from July to September.

Store by cutting with 30 cm (12 in) long stalks and standing these in buckets of damp peat or sand. Globe artichokes will store for only a few days.

Problems Blackfly and slugs.

ARTICHOKE, JERUSALEM

'Fuseau' is a good, long, white variety that makes preparation a little easier.

'Boston Red' has ruddy skin. Both are dead easy to grow.

Where to plant Sunny spot on well-drained and preferably well-manured soil. A good screen or windbreak for more tender plants.

Plant tubers either in November or February and March (plant those bought from a greengrocer if you like). Set the tubers 15 cm (6 in) deep and 30 cm (12 in) apart allowing 1.2 m (4 ft) between rows or clumps. Label sites clearly.

Cultivation Water well in dry spells and earth up with soil if tubers start to push through the surface.

Harvest by chopping down dead stems in autumn and lifting the tubers as they are needed. Dig up and replant any that remain in March.

Store in the ground until required.

Problems Slugs.

ASPARAGUS

The show-off's vegetable. Previously popular varieties include 'Connover's Colossal', but now the all-male 'Lucullus' is proving a better cropper. Growing from seed is only for the very patient; buy year-old crowns for a quicker crop.

Where to plant In full sun and a sheltered spot on well-cultivated, well-manured soil. Make sure the spot is entirely weed free. Lime acid soil in the autumn before planting – but not at the same time as applying manure.

Plant one-year-old crowns in April. Plant on slight ridges made in the bottom of 10 cm (4 in) deep and 30 cm (12 in) wide trenches, spacing the crowns 30 cm (12 in) apart. Return and firm the soil. Allow 60 cm–1 m (2-3 ft) between rows.

Cultivation Never let the bed dry out. Feed with liquid fertilizer monthly from June to September during the first year. Don't harvest any shoots for the first three years, but cut off all foliage in autumn when it yellows. Apply a general fertilizer each spring, keep the bed weed free and support the fern with canes and twine. In the third year,

Plant one-year-old asparagus crowns on slight ridges made in the bottom of trenches 10 cm (4 in) deep and 30 cm (12 in) wide. Space them 30 cm (12 in) apart.

pull soil around the shoots as they start to grow; this will keep the bases white.

Harvest by cutting all stems from the third year onwards. Harvest only from late April to late June, cutting the stems 8 cm (3 in) below ground level. Allow fern to grow after the final cutting date.

Store by freezing if you have a surplus.

Problems Slugs, earwigs, asparagus beetle, violet root rot.

BEAN, BROAD

Sow 'The Sutton' and 'Optica' for spring and summer crops, both are low-growing; 'Aquadulce Claudia' is for autumn sowing.

Where to plant Full sun and a rich, well-cultivated soil. Lime acid soils in autumn.

Sow the seeds 5 cm (2 in) deep, 15 cm (6 in) apart in double rows 23 cm (9 in) apart. Sow 'Aquadulce Claudia' in November; cover with cloches if possible. Sow other varieties from February to June, or under glass in peat pots in January; plant out in March under cloches.

Cultivation Weed and water as necessary. Pinch out shoot tips to prevent blackfly infestation once five flower clusters have opened. Support with a cane and string enclosure if tall varieties are grown. Remove cloches when weather improves or when the beans hit the glass.

Harvest regularly as soon as the beans can be seen to be swollen within the pods, or pick young pods and cook as for French beans.

Store by freezing or drying beans.

Problems Blackfly, pea and bean weevil and chocolate spot.

BEAN, FRENCH

The golden oldies 'The Prince' and 'Masterpiece' are still the most popular and reliable.

Where to plant A sunny, sheltered spot in well-manured soil. Lime very acid ground in autumn.

Sow under cloches from mid-March to April; in the open from May to July. Sow the seeds at 8 cm (3 in) intervals along the bottom of a 5 cm (2 in) deep V-shaped drill. Don't sow in cold weather or soggy soil. Thin to leave one plant every 15 cm (6 in).

Cultivation Remove cloche coverings in May. Avoid drought at all costs, especially when the plants are flowering. If the plants flop, support them with brushwood.

Harvest regularly from July to October.

Store by freezing.

Problems Red spider mites and blackfly.

BEAN, RUNNER

'Butler' is a good stringless variety; the oldies 'Enorma' and 'Scarlet Emperor' will produce very long beans. 'Pickwick' is dwarf and grown without supports, like a French bean.

Where to plant A sunny, sheltered spot in very rich soil. During winter, dig a trench along the line the plants will occupy and half fill it with compost before returning the earth. Moisture and food are vital.

Sow at the foot of 2.25 m (7½ ft) high wigwams or ridge-tent-like supports in May and June, planting two seeds in

each hole. Thin to leave one plant if both seeds grow. The canes should be 30-38 cm (12-15 in) apart. Alternatively sow seeds individually in peat pots under glass in April and plant out, one to each cane, in late May.

Cultivation A single twist-tie will make sure the shoots start to climb quickly. Weed regularly between plants and rows and really soak the soil in dry spells. Drought is detested. Mulch with manure or grass clippings or compost in June.

Harvest regularly as soon as the beans are of a usable size (don't let them get too long and stringy). July to October is the runner bean season.

Store by freezing.

Problems Blackfly and birds (which nip off flowers).

BEETROOT

'Boltardy' is best for early sowings until early April. The old favourite 'Detroit Little Ball' performs well if summer sown.

Where to plant Full sun and a patch of ground that is well worked but not stony or heavily manured.

Sow seeds 8 cm (3 in) apart in drills 2.5 cm (1 in) deep and 30 cm (12 in) apart. Sow from March to July but cover all sowings made before late March with cloches until mid-April. Thin to leave one seedling at each 8 cm (3 in) station with the early sowings; one seedling every 15 cm (6 in) with later sowings (each capsule contains several beetroot seeds).

Cultivation Weed regularly and try to keep the soil evenly moist. Heavy watering during drought may split the roots.

Harvest by pulling up the roots when they are large enough to be usable but before they reach the size of tennis balls. Twist off leaves to prevent bleeding. Harvest beetroot between June and October.

Store by pickling or by placing roots in boxes of dry peat or sand in a cool, dark, frostproof place.

Make sure that climbers like runner beans (and sweet peas) are tied to supports early in their life.

Problems Blackfly and birds (which may shred young plants).

BEET, LEAF

Commonly known as Swiss chard, this is a space-saving dual-purpose vegetable. The broad leaf-stalks can be boiled for a few minutes and served with melted butter, and the leaves make a tasty spinach substitute. There are white-stemmed (Swiss chard) and red-stemmed (Ruby chard) varieties, but the white is the better culinary proposition. 'Bright Lights' has stalks in decorative shades from yellow to purple and red.

Where to plant Full sun and rich soil.

Sow the seeds 8 cm (3 in) apart in drills 2.5 cm (1 in) deep and 45 cm (18 in) apart in May and June. Thin out to leave just one plant every 30 cm (12 in).

Cultivation Keep weeded and watered. Cut out any seedheads if some of the plants bolt.

Harvest by pulling off large, outer leaves as they are needed. Harvest from August onwards.
Store under cloches or straw *in situ*. May last right through winter.
Problems Slugs and snails.

BROCCOLI / CALABRESE

Broccoli is the late winter and spring vegetable; calabrese the late summer and early autumn type, which is not reliably frost hardy. Try 'Early Purple' and 'Late White' broccoli; 'Express Corona' and 'Corvet' calabrese are the green ones.
Where to plant Full sun and a rich, well-cultivated yet firm soil. Apply lime in autumn if the ground is acid.
Sow the seeds thinly in a seedbed 1 cm (½ in) deep in small rows 23 cm (9 in) apart. Thin to leave one seedling every 8 cm (3 in). Sow broccoli in April and May; calabrese from April to June.
Plant out the youngsters when they are 8 cm (3 in) high. Space them 60 cm (2 ft) apart in rows 60 cm (2 ft) apart. Firm well and water in.
Cultivation Earth up the stems if the plants lean. Weed and water as necessary. Scatter general fertilizer among the plants in July.
Harvest calabrese from August to November (cut the central head first, then let side heads develop); broccoli from February to May.
Store by freezing.
Problems Exactly as for cabbages.

BRUSSELS SPROUT

Tangy winter vegetables. 'Peer Gynt' will be ready to pick from September onwards; 'Wellington' from December. 'Rampart' and 'Widgeon' are two excellent varieties for prolonging cropping well into the New Year, often as late as April.
Where to plant Full sun and a rich, well-cultivated and well-firmed soil. Lime in winter if the soil is acid.
sow in a seedbed under cloches during February; during March and April in an outdoor seedbed. Sow the seeds thinly in 1 cm (½ in) deep drills spaced 23 cm (9 in) apart. Thin to leave one seedling every 8 cm (3 in).
Plant out when the youngsters are 8 cm (3 in) high. Space the plants 60 cm (2 ft) apart on the square. Firm well and water in.
Cultivation Water and weed as necessary. Earth up the stems for stability as the plants grow. Stake with canes in exposed areas. Hoe in general fertilizer around the plants in summer. Remove yellow leaves in autumn.
Harvest by pulling off the sprouts when large enough to eat. Start at the bottom and gradually work upwards.
Store by leaving the sprouts on the plants through winter. End-of-season surpluses can be frozen.
Problems As for cabbage. Loose sprouts will be produced as a result of soft ground or overfeeding.

CABBAGE

A staple vegetable that can be harvested at any time of year if the sowings are planned. The chart (right) shows recommended varieties for a year-round supply of fat, firm hearts.
Where to plant Full sun on a well-cultivated, well-firmed soil that was manured for a previous crop. Lime in winter if the soil is acid.
Sow in 1 cm (½ in) deep drills on a prepared seedbed, spacing the drills 23 cm (9 in) apart. Thin to leave one seedling every 8 cm (3 in).
Plant out the seedlings when they are 8 cm (3 in) high. Firm well and puddle in. Space the plants 45 cm (18 in) apart, on the square. Spring cabbages ('April') can be spaced 15 cm (6 in) apart, in rows 30 cm (12 in) apart and thinned to leave one plant every 30 cm (12 in) as soon as their leaves touch. Use the thinnings as spring greens.
Cultivation Water and weed as necessary. Guard against drought and pigeons. Scatter a dusting of nitrochalk among the plants in

Planting out cabbages

1 Use an old spade handle as a dibber to make a hole in the prepared soil.

2 (right) Drop in the plant and push back the earth as firmly as you can.

Recommended cabbages varieties

VARIETY	SOW	PLANT	HARVEST
'Hispi'; 'Golden Acre'	February/March (frame)	April/May	June/July
'Winnigstadt'	March/May	May/July	August/October
'Celtic'; 'Christmas Drumhead'	April/May	June/July	November/January
'January King' (savoy)	April/May	June/July	October/March
'April'	July/August	September/October	April/May

summer. Remove faded leaves. Feed spring cabbages with a dusting of general fertilizer in early April.
Harvest the cabbages when they are large enough and firm enough to eat. For spring greens, cut a 'cross' shape in the stumps of harvested cabbages early in the year. Shoots will arise and can be harvested when of a decent size.
Store all varieties by leaving them *in situ* until they are needed.
Problems Aphids, caterpillars, cabbage root fly, flea beetles, pigeons,

3 Puddle in the plant, using a watering can without a sprinkler head fitted.

cabbage whitefly, clubroot, turnip gall weevil.

Calabrese See Broccoli

CARROT

A variety like 'Amsterdam Forcing' sown in a frame in March will give the earliest crops; 'Favourite' is certainly a favourite of most gardeners for April to June maincrop sowings. 'Autumn King', sown from May to early July, yields tasty late roots; the earlier you sow, the larger will be the carrots. 'Parmex' produces spherical roots that are easy to grow even on stony soil.
Where to plant Very well-worked soil that is not stony or well manured (both conditions can cause root forking). Full sun is essential. Add peat to open up heavy soil. If your soil is heavy or stony make a raised carrot bed in a 23 cm (9 in) high enclosure of old floorboards or timber. Fill the enclosure with sieved soil, sand and peat.
Sow thinly in 1 cm (½ in) deep drills spaced 5 cm (2 in) apart. Avoid thinning

the seedlings – it encourages carrot fly attack. Early crops sown in a frame or under cloches should be kept covered until mid-April.
Cultivation Weed between rows and aim to keep the soil evenly moist.
Harvest as soon as of a usable size.
Store in situ by covering with straw, or lift in October, trim off the tops and store the roots in boxes of dry peat or sand in a cool, dark, frostproof place.
Problems Carrot fly, slugs, carrot willow aphid.

CAULIFLOWER

Like cabbages, there are varieties to mature at different times of year (see p.240).
Where to plant Full sun and shelter from wind. Avoid frost pockets. The ground should be well cultivated but firm and enriched with well-rotted compost or manure.
Sow in a seedbed as for cabbages.
Plant out when 8 cm (3 in) high, spacing the summer-maturing types 45 cm (18 in) apart in rows 60 cm (2 ft) apart, and the autumn- and winter-maturing types 60 cm (2 ft) apart in rows 75 cm (2½ ft) apart. Seeds sown in heat during February can be pricked out and hardened off before being planted out in April. Firm well and puddle in.
Cultivation Weed and water cauliflowers copiously. A dusting of sulphate of ammonia will speed up the growth of slow plants in summer. Break two central leaves over the developing curds (the white centre) to protect them from muck and weather.
Harvest as soon as of a usable size.
Store whole heads in boxes of straw; divided curds can be frozen.
Problems As for cabbages. Failure to produce curds is usually caused by a check to growth, most likely lack of water or food.

Recommended cauliflower varieties

VARIETY	SOW	PLANT	HARVEST
'Snowball'; 'All Year Round'	February (in heat)	March	June/July
'Snowball'; 'All Year Round'	March/April	April/May	July/August
'Wallaby'; 'Autumn Giant'	Late April/May	June/July	August/December
'Walcheren Winter'	Late April/May	June/July	August/June

CELERIAC

These turnip-like roots are celery flavoured and superb in soup or stew. Try 'Monarch', 'Kojak' or 'Iram'.

Where to plant In full sun on rich, moisture-retentive, but not soggy, soil. The roots won't fatten in poor earth.

Sow in pots in a heated frame or greenhouse during March. Prick out the seedlings into trays as soon as they can be easily handled; harden them off before planting out. Or sow outdoors under cloches in April, sowing the seeds thinly in 1 cm (1/2 in) deep drills.

Plant out in late May or early June 30 cm (12 in) apart in rows 45 cm (18 in) apart. Don't plant too deeply. Thin the outdoor-sown seedlings to a similar spacing.

Cultivation Do not let the soil dry out. Feed with liquid fertilizer once a week. Remove a few leaves from the base of each plant as the roots start to swell; pull off sideshoots too.

Harvest from September onwards as soon as the root is fat enough to use.

Store all roots in boxes of dry peat or sand after trimming off leaves in October. Keep in a cool, dark, frost-free place.

Problems As for celery but less likely.

CELERY

Traditional 'trenched' celery is a labour-intensive crop. 'Giant White' is perhaps the most popular variety. Idlers can try self-blanchers such as 'Golden Self-blanching' or 'Latham Self-blanching'. The self-blanchers won't stand frost.

Where to plant On really rich, well-manured and moisture-retentive soil in full sun. Avoid frost pockets. Dig manure into the ground where self-blanching celery is to be grown; dig out a trench 38 cm (15 in) wide and 30 cm (12 in) deep. Spread plenty of compost or manure in the base and return the soil to within 10 cm (4 in) of the top, leaving the surplus at either side of the trench.

Sow in a heated greenhouse or frame in late March or early April. Prick out into trays and harden off.

Plant out in late May/early June. Plant the self-blanching types in blocks so the plants are 23 cm (9 in) apart. Don't

Wrap maturing celery plants in 25 cm (10 in) cardboard collars when they are 30 cm (12 in) high The protective layer keeps them clean and excludes light to blanch the leaf stalks.

plant in rows (in blocks the plants will exclude light from one another and so stay crisp). Traditional celery plants are set out in a single row at 15 cm (6 in) intervals along the trench. Water them in and never let the soil dry out

cultivation Remove any sideshoots from traditional celery and wrap the plants in 25 cm (10 in) high cylinders of cardboard when they are 30 cm (12 in) high to keep the stems clean and in the dark. Pull a little soil around the 'collars' and earth up gradually over the next few weeks until none of the card is visible. Self-blanching celery needs no such treatment, but a good wodge of straw can be spread around the outside plants early in July to exclude light even more. Both crops could do with a light dusting of general fertilizer (or a good liquid feed or two) in summer.

Harvest as soon as the leaf stalks are fat and crisp enough to eat. Start at the outside of the block with self-blanching celery, and at the end of the row with traditional types. The self-blanching celery should be harvestable from late July until October; the traditional from October to February.

Store traditional celery *in situ* by piling straw over the green tops for frost protection. Celery will freeze, but can only be served cooked afterwards.

Problems Celery fly, leaf spot and soft rot.

Courgette See Marrow

KALE

The tastiest of the greens, I reckon. Also known as borecole. 'Pentland Brig' is the most popular, but 'Fribor' is more compact at just 30 cm (12 in) high. 'Darkibor' is also very curly and certainly well worth growing.

Where to plant Full sun and a moderately rich but well drained soil. Add lime in autumn if the ground is acid.

Sow in April and May in a seedbed. Sow seeds thinly in 1 cm (½ in) deep drills spaced 23 cm (9 in) apart. Thin to leave one seedling every 8 cm (3 in).

Plant out from June to August when 10 cm (4 in) high, spacing the plants 38 cm (15 in) apart, in rows 45 cm (18 in) apart. Firm well and puddle in.

Cultivation Scatter a dusting of fertilizer around the plants during their second spring. Water and weed as necessary. Pull off faded foliage.

Harvest leaves from late autumn right through to the following May.

Store *in situ*. The plants are frost-hardy and can be harvested as required.

Problems As for cabbages.

KOHL RABI

Odd but interesting. Try the variety 'Lanro' for sowing between April and July.

Where to plant Sunny spot and a soil that's good but not freshly manured. Lime in autumn if the ground is acid.

Sow thinly in drills 1 cm (½ in) deep and 30 cm (12 in) apart. Thin to leave one plant every 15 cm (6 in).

Cultivation Weed and water as necessary. An occasional liquid feed will be appreciated.

Harvest from June to December when the roots are slightly smaller than tennis balls. Larger roots are hard and unpalatable. The leaves will cook like spinach.

Store Storage is not advisable – the roots quickly become wizened.

Problems As for cabbages.

LEEK

'Musselburgh' and 'Lyon Prizetaker' are the old favourites; 'King Richard' is a long-stemmed relative newcomer.

Where to plant Full sun and a very rich, moisture-retentive soil.

Sow thinly in March or April on a prepared seedbed in 1 cm (½ in) deep drills spaced 23 cm (9 in) apart.

Plant out in June and July when the seedlings are 15 cm (6 in) or so high. Water them well before lifting. Select the largest seedlings and shorten their leaves by one third and their roots back to 2.5 cm (1 in). Drop the plants into 15 cm (6 in) deep holes made with a piece of broom handle at 10 cm (4 in)

Plant leeks by dropping them into 15 cm (6 in) deep holes made at 10 cm (4 in) intervals with a dibber. Puddle them in.

intervals along the row. Make the rows 30 cm (12 in) apart. Puddle the plants in and leave them to it. The soil will gradually fall back on its own to blanch the stem.

Cultivation Never let the plants go short of water. Weed when necessary and apply occasional liquid feeds.

Harvest from November to May.

Store *in situ*; or if the ground they occupy is needed lift and 'heel them in' on a corner of the plot: dig out a hole, lay the leeks in at an angle and cover their roots and lower stem with soil.

Problem Leek rust.

LETTUCE

Another hearty crop that can be harvested almost all the year round. There are four basic types of lettuce: cos (with crispy upright leaves); butterhead (with soft leaves and spherical hearts); crisphead (similar but with crunchier leaves); and non-hearting (usually with frilly leaves that are cut-and-come-again).

Where to plant Sun and a good but not heavily manured soil. Lime in autumn if ground is acid. Cos lettuces tolerate a little shade.

Sow thinly in 1 cm (½ in) deep drills spaced 30 cm (12 in) apart. Double rows under cloches can be 20 cm (8 in) apart. Sow sections of a row at fortnightly intervals for a succession. Thin gradually so that eventually the developing plants are about 23 cm (9 in) apart. 'Salad Bowl' can be closer and I've even got away without thinning it at all.

Cultivation Keep the soil evenly moist to prevent 'bolting' (running to seed).

Recommended lettuce cropping plan

VARIETY	SOW	HARVEST
'Tom Thumb' (butterhead); 'Little Gem' (cos)	Early March (under cloches)	Early June
'Webb's Wonderful' (crisphead); 'Salad Bowl' (non-hearting)	March/June	June/August
'Avondefiance' (butterhead)	June/July (cloche in September)	September/December
'Winter Density' (cos)	Late August/Early September	May/June
'Unrivalled' (butterhead)	October (under cloches)	Late March/May

Weed and control slugs regularly. Winter lettuces will enjoy a sprinkling of fertilizer in March.

Harvest as soon as the plants are a reasonable size.

Store Lettuces will not store.

Problems Aphids, birds, slugs, rabbits, mildew and botrytis (the diseases are more of a winter problem).

MARROW AND COURGETTE

Courgettes are simply marrow pups, and if you grow a variety like 'Zucchini' you can make sure of having both – just leave the courgettes to mature into monsters. If you want only marrows, grow 'Green Bush', which is less space consuming than the trailing varieties.

Where to plant Prepare each planting site specially, working in masses of manure on the 45 cm (18 in) square patch that the plant will occupy. Some folk even plant on a mound of manure but I think that there's more danger of damaging drought if the spot is raised up. Marrows need full sun and shelter.

Sow seeds individually in peat pots on a windowsill or in a greenhouse. Late April is the best time. Harden off before planting out.

Plant in late June after watering the peat pot well. It should be just below the surface of the soil when planted. Water well. Allow 60 cm (2 ft) between plants.

Cultivation Never let the plants go short of water. Mulch with compost or manure in June and then feed fortnightly with liquid tomato fertilizer. Manual pollination can boost fruit setting. Remove a male flower; tear off its petals and push it into the centre of a female flower, which will possess an immature marrow behind its petals. Put pieces of slate or wood under developing marrows to keep them clean and slug-free. Lots of

male flowers and few females are often produced early in the season or in cold weather.

Harvest from July to September as soon as the fruits are large enough.

Store marrows simply by standing them on shelves in a cool but frostproof shed or garage.

Problems Slugs, mildew, botrytis, mosaic virus.

ONION

I reckon it won't be long before we have onions from the garden all the year round. See box below for recommended varieties.

Where to plant In full sun on soil that's as rich as can be. Some growers use the same rich soil on the bed every year, but there's more likelihood of disease striking with this technique. Lime acid soil in autumn.

Sow thinly in drills 1 cm (½ in) deep at the recommended time. Drills should be 30 cm (12 in) apart; 23 cm (9 in) apart for spring onions. Thin bulb onions to 10–15 cm (4–6 in) apart. Alternatively grow six rows of onions spaced 15 cm (6 in) apart and then leave wider paths from which to work. You'll save space but weeding may be more tricky. Autumn-sown onions should be thinned twice: once in autumn to 2.5 cm (1 in) and again in spring to 10 cm (4 in).

Plant onion sets (small bulbs) with a trowel so that they almost disappear from view. Space them 10 cm (4 in) apart and leave the same distance between rows as with onions raised from seeds. Sets are a convenient

means of growing onions but the bulbs are never quite as large as those grown from seeds.

Cultivation Water and weed as necessary. Don't hoe too near the plants or you'll disturb the roots. Should a few bulbs run to seed, pull them up and use them at once – they won't store. When the leaves flop naturally in midsummer, bend them all over in between the rows to allow the sun to ripen the bulbs. Fork up the bulbs in August and leave them on the soil to ripen (cover them with cloches if you can). Onions growing through the winter will appreciate any cloche protection you can give them.

Harvest at the recommended times. Only well-ripened bulbs will store. Autumn-sown and Japanese onions must be used as soon as possible.

Store by plaiting into ropes, or by hanging up in old pairs of tights – there's a novel use for them! Keep the bulbs in the light or they'll sprout.

Problems Onion fly, eelworm, mildew, neck rot and white rot.

PARSNIP

'Avonresister' has small roots resistant to canker, and 'Gladiator' is longer but also resistant. Conservative gardeners almost always stick to 'Hollow Crown Improved' and 'Tender and True'.

Where to plant On well-worked but not well-manured ground that is stone-free. Tolerant of just a little shade. Lime very acid soil in autumn.

Sow three seeds at 10 cm (4 in) intervals in 2.5 cm (1 in) deep drills spaced 30 cm (12 in) apart. Thin to

Recommended onion varieties

VARIETY	SOW SEEDS	PLANT SETS	HARVEST
'Ailsa Craig'; 'Bedfordshire Champion'	March/April	–	August onwards
'Sturon'; 'Stuttgarter Giant'	–	March/April	August onwards
'Imai Early Yellow'	August	–	Late June
'Buffalo'	August	–	July
'White Lisbon' (spring onion)	March/August	–	May/March
'Unwin's First Early'	–	September/November	July onwards

leave one seedling at each station. The seeds are slow to come up. Sow from late February (in good years) to May.

Cultivation Weed and water as necessary.

Harvest as needed from September to March.

Store *in situ*. Parsnips are as hard as nails. Mark the position of the rows for the tops to die down. In frosty weather (when lifting is difficult) it is helpful to have some roots stored in boxes of sand or peat, as for carrots. Lift any roots that remain when the land is needed for another crop and heel them in, as for leeks.

Problems Carrot fly, celery fly and parsnip canker.

PEA

If you've eaten only frozen peas since you can't remember when, it's time you tried some fresh ones. Here's how to arrange for a succession (or even just one crop to remind you of the good old days). The mangetout peas are especially recommended: harvest the pods while they're young, boil them whole for barely five minutes and serve them with melted butter: knock-out!

Where to plant Full sun on well-cultivated, well-manured soil not likely to dry out. Lime acid soil in autumn.

Sow the seeds 5 cm (2 in) apart in the bottom of 5 cm (2 in) deep and 23 cm (9 in) wide flat-bottomed drills. Never sow in cold, wet soil.

Cultivation Stake all peas with twiggy branches or cane and string enclosures when they are 10 cm (4 in) high. Water well in dry weather – copiously during flowering – and protect the plant with netting if bird damage is likely. Lawn-mowing mulches are appreciated in early summer.

VARIETY	SOW	HARVEST
'Little Marvel'	Late February/March (under cloches)	Late May/June
'Hurst Greenshaft'; 'Onward'	Late March/June	Early July/September
'Kelvedon Wonder'	Late June/July	October/November (cloche in September)
'Sugar Snap' (mangetout)	March/June	Early July/September
'Meteor'	October/November (under cloches)	May

Recommended pea varieties

Harvest as soon as the pods are filled. Don't delay.

Store by freezing.

Problems Mice, slugs, pea and bean weevil, pea moth, birds, thrips, aphids, mildew and damping off.

POTATO

Even if space is short, a row of early potatoes is very well worth growing. Nothing matches that moment when the first tender spud of the year passes your lips! There are hundreds of varieties but these, I think, are some of the best:

First Early: 'Maris Bard', 'Epicure'.
Second Early: 'Vanessa', 'Catriona'.
Maincrop: 'Desiree', 'Golden Wonder'.

Where to plant Full sun and a rich, well-cultivated soil. Spuds are often grown to break down virgin clay soils. Their roots do shatter the soil a bit but it's your earthing up that is mainly responsible.

Plant first early varieties in mid- to late March, second early and maincrop varieties in April. Sprout or 'chit' the tubers before you plant them: sprouted tubers tend to yield more heavily and rapidly than those planted with dormant 'eyes'. Stand them in egg boxes on a windowsill for six weeks prior to planting. The ends with the most buds should point upwards. When the shoots are 2.5 cm (1 in) or so long the tubers can be planted. Plant with a trowel so that the tubers are 5 cm (2 in) below the surface with their buds pointing upwards. Plant first earlies 30 cm (12 in) apart in rows 45 cm (18 in)

Stand seed potato tubers in egg boxes in good light for six weeks before planting, to encourage the shoots to grow. They will crop better as a result.

apart; second earlies and maincrop varieties 45 cm (18 in) apart in rows 60 cm (2 ft) apart.

Cultivation As soon as the shoots appear, pull some soil around them with a rake or draw hoe. Continue to earth up gently in cold weather until the ridges are 23 cm (9 in) high. If it's mild, one good earthing up can be given when the shoots have risen 15 cm (6 in) above their first earthing up. Irrigate well in any a prolonged dry spells.

Harvest first earlies in June or July; second earlies and maincrop from August onwards. Maturity often coincides with flowering.

Store If your land has a heavy slug population, lift as soon as the tubers are ready and store in thick paper sacks in a cool, dark place. Otherwise lift as required, and lift the remainder for storing in October.

Problems Slugs, wireworm, eelworm, blight, scab, virus.

Lift potatoes carefully with a fork and store in a thick paper sack in a cool dark place.

RADISH

This really is the best vegetable for impatient gardeners. Ready in six weeks during summer. Try 'Cherry Belle' or 'Crystal Ball' if you like 'em round; 'French Breakfast' if you like 'em long.

Where to plant Full sun or very slight shade in a well-worked but not freshly manured soil.

Sow sections of a row at fortnightly intervals from March to August (or from February under cloches). Sow thinly in drills 1 cm (½ in) deep between other crops to save space. Thin the seedlings to leave one every 2.5 cm (1 in).

Cultivation Water well in dry spells and weed as necessary. Be warned: slow-growing starved radishes will be as hard as bullets.

Harvest as soon as the roots are of a usable size, from April to September.

Store Storage of radishes is not to be recommended.

Problems Flea beetle.

RHUBARB

Yes, it is a vegetable and not a fruit. The variety 'Cawood Delight' is one of the best to plant.

Where to plant In full sun and a really rich soil that's been well manured. Plant in early spring, though on light soils autumn planting is often successful. Set the clumps or 'crowns' 5 cm (2 in) below the surface of the soil and 1 m (3 ft) apart. Firm the soil well.

Cultivation Don't cut anything during the first year except any flower spikes, which should always be removed as soon as they are seen. Mulch with manure every spring. Dig up and divide the plants every few years. For really early sticks, cover one plant with a bucket stuffed with straw in January. Tender pickings should be yours in March. Feed the plant well during the summer and don't force it again for a few years.

Harvest from April to July, then let the plants build up their strength.

Store by freezing.

Problems Honey fungus, crown rot.

SPINACH

You'll either love or loathe spinach. If you love it you can enjoy it all the year round with just a little bit of thoughtful sowing.

Where to plant Full sun and a rich soil. Perpetual spinach doesn't mind a bit of shade. Lime very acid ground in autumn.

Sow seeds at 8 cm (3 in) intervals in 2.5 cm (1 in) deep drills at the recommended time. Allow 30 cm (12 in) between rows. Thin to 23 cm (9 in) for winter spinach; 30 cm (12 in) for summer.

Cultivation Weed and water as necessary. Drought causes bolting: remove any flowerheads.

Harvest as soon as leaves are large enough to use.

Store by cooking and freezing.

Problems Birds, slugs, downy mildew.

SWEDE

There's nothing like a few mangels for warming you up in winter! I think 'Marian' is the best variety; it's tasty and resistant to clubroot and mildew.

Where to plant Full sun and good but not freshly manured soil. Lime acid soils in autumn.

Sow in May and June thinly in 1 cm (½ in) deep drills spaced 38 cm (15 in) apart. Thin to 23 cm (9 in) in stages.

Cultivation Weed and water as necessary; if the ground becomes dry swelling will stop.

Harvest from October onwards as soon as large enough to use. The roots should last until early spring.

Store *in situ*; the roots are quite hardy. If frosty weather looks like making harvesting difficult, lift and store a few roots as for carrots.

Problems Clubroot, brown heart and flea beetle.

SWEET CORN

It's always a bit dicey to grow sweetcorn, although you're more likely to have a successful crop in the sunny south. New varieties, bred for faster maturity, are appearing all the time. Try 'Sundance' as the best all-rounder; 'Candle' is a 'supersweet' variety, best in the south. Another good one for southerners is 'Butterscotch'.

Where to plant In full sun on a rich soil in a sheltered spot.

Sow individually in peat pots under glass during April. Harden off before planting out.

Recommended spinach varieties

VARIETY	SOW	HARVEST
'Norvak'; 'Longstanding Round'	March/May	May/November
'Broad-leaved Prickly'	August/Sepember (can cloche in October)	November/March
Perpetual spinach	March/April	June/January
Perpetual spinach	July/August	November/May

Male flower

Female flower

The female sweet corn flowers, which grow from the leaf axils, will produce the cobs. Tap the pollen from the male flower at the top to ensure fat, fully developed cobs.

Plant out in late May or early June after watering the pots thoroughly. Space the plants 45 cm (18 in) apart on the square. Water the plants well.
Cultivation Water sweetcorn copiously in dry spells and keep down weeds. The male spires of bloom open at the top of the plants and should be regularly knocked to discharge their pollen on to the ladies below. Give a dilute liquid feed once a month in summer.
Harvest when the cobs are fat and ripe. The tassels above them will turn brown and the cob will become angled away from the stem. Pull away the sheaths to see if the grains are fat and yellow. The old test of sticking a fingernail into a grain to see if it exudes milky rather than clear sap can obviously disfigure the cob.
Store by freezing.
Problems Fruit fly and slugs.

TOMATO

There are many bush varieties for outdoor growing. 'Tornado' crops well in poor summers; 'Gardeners' Delight' is tops for flavour.
Where to plant A sheltered spot in full sun on well-cultivated and rich but not freshly manured soil.

Sow seeds in a pot during March and germinate in a temperature of 18°C (65°F). Prick out seedlings into 8 cm (3 in) pots of John Innes No 1 potting compost or a peat-based equivalent.
Plant out in late May or early June after hardening the plants off. Space the plants 45 cm (18 in) apart.
Cultivation Water regularly in summer; feed fortnightly with dilute liquid tomato fertilizer once the fruits have set. Don't remove the sideshoots from bush varieties. Spread dry straw underneath them in June to keep the fruits clean.
Harvest as soon as ripe. Stand cloches over laid down plants in September to prolong the harvest.
Store unripened fruits in October; ripen in a cool place (in a drawer or on a shelf, not necessarily in bright sun). Green fruits can be used in chutney.
Problems Whitefly, red spider mite, blossom end rot, blotchy ripening, greenback, eelworm, leaf mould, stem rot, root rot, potato blight, verticillium wilt, virus. (You won't get them all!)

TURNIP

Turnip is a very underrated vegetable. I recommend 'Snowball' and 'Golden Ball'.
Where to plant Full sun and good but not freshly manured soil. Lime acid soil in winter.
Sow thinly in 1 cm (½ in) deep drills from March to September; under cloches in February. Use 'Snowball' for February to May sowings, 'Golden Ball' for later sowings. Space rows 23 cm (9 in) apart for early crops; 30 cm (12 in) apart for later crops. Thin early crops to 10 cm (4 in), later ones to 23 cm (9 in).
Cultivation Water when necessary and weed to relieve competition.
Harvest early sown crops as young as possible and before they are tennis ball sized. Late sowings can be left in the ground and pulled as needed.
Store as for carrots.
Problems Clubroot, mildew, soft rot and flea beetle.

HERBS

Shop-bought dried herbs bear no comparison to the freshly picked, home-grown variety. Grow herbs on the vegetable plot if you like, but most are handsome-enough for flower borders or as edges to paths, where they will release their fragrance when brushed against. Almost all herbs relish a warm sunny spot, which helps to bring out their full flavour.

Basil

The sweet aniseed flavour of basil is at its best on baked tomatoes and buttered carrots. Plant it in late June and pick and dry it for winter use (it will be killed by frost). Raise new plants from seed indoors in March or outdoors in May. Pinch out the shoot tips regularly and pick off any flowers.

Chives

A little clump of reed-shaped, onion-flavoured leaves. Happy in gentle shade if that's all you have to offer. Plant in spring or autumn: mature plants can be divided at that time and tired old plants cut down to ground level in early summer. Don't remove the flowers – they're lilac-pink and quite pretty. The plant is perennial.

Fennel

A hefty aniseed-flavoured herb with 1.5 m (5 ft) stems of delicate feathery leaves. Usually used in fish dishes. Plant in spring; divide mature clumps at the same time. The plant dies down in winter; the leaves don't store well.

Marjoram

Pot marjoram is the desirable perennial kind with a thyme-like flavour. Plant in spring and clip with shears when very untidy. Divide clumps in spring to propagate. Freeze or dry for winter use.

Drying and freezing herbs

DRYING

Herbs tend to have their maximum flavour just before they flower, so cut and dry them at that time for winter use. Put the shoots in brown paper bags and store them in a warm, dark place. Crush them when they are dry and put them in airtight containers from which the light can be excluded. That way they'll keep as much of their flavour as possible.

FREEZING

Herbs that lose their flavour when dried can often be successfully frozen. Sprigs of mint and parsley can be frozen in ice cubes for fruit cups; sprigs of herbs can be placed in polythene bags and put in the freezer compartment of a fridge. Although they won't keep their shape when defrosted they will often keep their flavour.

Mint

Although a useful and popular herb, mint is every gardener's bane if it gets loose, spreading like wildfire. Plant it in a bottomless bucket sunk into the ground, but with the rim protruding – that will halt its take-over bid. Plant in spring or autumn and propagate by division at those times. Dies down in winter. Dry or freeze for winter use. Make your own mint sauce with the stuff in summer and store a few bottles for winter. Can be frozen in ice cubes for use in fruit cups.

Parsley

This is an indispensable kitchen herb. Sow annually outdoors in April but be patient - seeds are slow to germinate. Cut off any flowers that form and protect with cloches in winter if you want to go on harvesting. The plant will perk up at the start of its second year but will gradually wear out. Freeze for winter use.

Rosemary

A 1.5 m (5 ft) evergreen shrub that's very useful because it can be harvested at any time of year. The leaves have a warm, savoury flavour. Plant in spring and propagate by cuttings in a propagator at the same time. Severe winters will cause die-back. Essential in stuffings and with roast lamb.

Sage

Another evergreen bush but this time it's not so hefty at around 30 cm (12 in). Plant in spring and prune in summer to encourage fresh growth. There's not much leaf in winter but sometimes enough to harvest. The variegated varieties are prettiest and just as tasty; you can also get a purple-leaved sage. Cuttings can be rooted in a propagator in summer.

Tarragon

The French variety has the best flavour. Plant it in spring in a warm, sheltered spot. Protect with cloches or straw in winter. Propagate by division in spring. Freeze for winter use. Severe winters may see it off.

Thyme

Evergreen carpeter with savoury aromatic leaves. Grow against paths and on patios. Plant in autumn or spring. Cut back in spring to promote new growth and use the clippings as cuttings. Can be gathered fresh all the year round.

Although herbs are primarily known for their aromatic or medicinal uses, many are attractive enough to be grown for their decorative qualities, as in this planting, which includes fennel, purple sage and French lavender (*Lavandula stoechas*).

part V

THE UNDER COVER GARDEN

Gardening can be enjoyed
all year round if you have a
greenhouse and a collection
of house plants to
look after

A conservatory or lean-to greenhouse bridges the gap between
house and garden, providing a pleasant retreat whatever the
weather among a lush profusion of plants.

19 Greenhouse gardening

The joy of a greenhouse is that it enables you to continue gardening through the dark winter days, as well as extending your range of flowers, fruit and vegetables

Having a greenhouse is like having a dog: you might not want to be without one, but it does tie you down. You'll need to visit it every day, morning and evening, during the growing season, and you'll not be the most popular person in the household when you dive out to water your tomatoes just as dinner is being served.

But set against all this is the pleasure you'll get from growing a wider range of plants (and the frustration of a few failures), and the fact that you'll regularly be able to make a sizeable contribution to the meal you're about to eat. You'll be able to raise potfuls of flowers nearly all the year round, if your greenhouse is kept frost free, and a few crops can be forced out of season to yield their bounty when shop prices are sky high.

So if you think you can risk the wrath of your spouse, or that you can placate it with out-of-season offerings for the table, take up the challenge and go in for gardening under cover.

CHOOSING YOUR GREENHOUSE

You'll find that there are dozens of greenhouses to choose from, all of which are capable of growing plants well. Two factors in particular will whittle down a few of the choices: price and design. You'll have to pick a greenhouse you can afford, and you're quite right to pick one that has an appealing shape. Whatever the practical qualities of a greenhouse, if you can't stand the sight of it there's not much point in owning it. Practical points are nevertheless important, so make sure that your chosen design can fulfil the following requirements:

1 Good light transmission.
2 Stability.
3 Good ventilation (one side and one ridge ventilator for every 2 m (6 ft) of the greenhouse's length).
4 Easily accessible, including a wide enough door to allow in a wheelbarrow if you feel this is necessary.

The most important consideration of all should be the use to which the house will be put. Pot plants are best in a house that has half-timbered sides, for then

The anatomy of a greenhouse

Once you have decided to get a greenhouse, you will be overwhelmed by the choices available and the decisions you have to make. You will have to decide what you want from your greenhouse, whether to go for a timber or alloy frame, glass or plastic glazing, and whether the house should be half-timbered or all glass. Here is an example of a greenhouse designed to cope with pot plants on staging and crops growing both in the soil and on ring culture.

SPAN-ROOF GREENHOUSE

This is a traditional, timber-framed span-roof greenhouse. See p.252 for a full description.

Timber frames are light, durable and very attractive. They will have to be treated with a preservative every two or three years to prolong their life

Shade is essential in summer to prevent your plants being scorched by the sun. Blinds are the most versatile: fit them externally for the maximum protection

A propagating frame allows new plants to be raised all year round

A power supply will provide for additional heating and lighting

Adequate ventilation is essential. Aim for one ridge ventilator and one side ventilator for every 2 m (6 ft) length of the greenhouse

Although expensive, glass will last virtually for ever. Compared to plastic, it is easy to clean, lets in more light, and allows less heat to escape

Tubular heaters fitted with a thermostat and installed under the staging are effective and economical

Waist-high staging allows easy access to your plants. Wooden staging, treated with timber preservative, is cheap and easy to install

For the first few years, grow crops in the soil within the greenhouse. Dig it well and work in some well-rotted manure

A sliding door has the advantage of never slamming shut – and it can be used as a ventilator. It may not fit as well as a hinged door, however, and could be draughty

A path down the centre of the greenhouse is essential to give you access to your plants. Stone slabs are easy to lay; gravel is cheaper

Here tomatoes are being grown by ring culture: bottomless pots are stood on a layer of washed pea shingle over a sheet of polythene. Water is applied to the shingle, fertilizer to the compost in the pot

Choosing a greenhouse design

Whichever design you decide on, buy the largest greenhouse you can possibly afford or accommodate – you'll soon find that it's bursting at the seams.

Span roof (See illustration on previous page)
This is the traditional greenhouse with vertical sides and two roof sections that slope down at an angle of roughly 45°. Glass-to-ground and half-timbered models are available, as are models with curved eaves. Remember that curved sections are plastic, not glass, and they will become opaque and need replacement in time. Span-roof greenhouses with a dividing partition are especially useful, for then only a portion of the house needs be heated in winter to protect frost-tender plants.

Lean-to
Designed to fit against the wall of a house, the lean-to has the advantages of being easily accessible, well insulated on one side and good to look at from inside the home if it is erected over a window. The installation of electricity and water, as well as an additional radiator from the central heating system, can be easily achieved. This design is now becoming very popular: glass-to-ground and half-timbered models are available, as well as mini versions that can be stood on patios and in back yards. A lean-to enables you to get to the greenhouse in the foulest weather without getting your feet wet.

Dome
Dome-shaped greenhouses are for lovers of space-age designs. They are costly but allow exceptionally good light transmission. Check that there are plenty of vents.

Octagonal
Rather more ornamental than useful, except to the disabled gardener who will find that many plants can be easily tended from a wheelchair. Make sure that ventilation is adequate – on some models this is not the case.

the 'understage' area can be hidden from view. Plants grown in the border soil will need a glass-to-ground greenhouse so that they receive plenty of light.

If you're intent on growing food crops, a glass-to-ground model is for you; if you aim to grow both tomatoes and pot plants then how about a house that's half glass-to-ground and half half-timbered? Manufacturers are making the decision even easier by

supplying timber panels for their glass-to-ground greenhouses so that they can be rapidly transformed.

Framework considerations
Timber houses are the romantic gardener's favourite (and that includes me). They are usually made of western red cedar, which is amazingly light, extremely durable and very handsome. They have to be painted

Dutch house

This design has been around for many years. The panes are very large – roughly 1.5 m by 60 cm (5 ft by 2 ft) – and the sides slope outwards from the eaves. Light transmission is good, but breakages are expensive.

Polytunnel

Polytunnels are cheap but nothing like as durable as their glass counterparts. Access and ventilation are achieved via the doors at either end, and a tubular steel framework supports the replaceable polythene envelope. Anchor the edges firmly for stability by burying them 30 cm (12 in) deep in the soil.

with a preservative every two or three years to prolong their life, but they look good in the garden and blend beautifully with plants.

Cedar is not cheap, and wooden houses are now more expensive to buy than those made of alloy. Greenhouses made of Baltic pine are less pricey, but I can't recommend them because they have nothing like the durability of their cedar relations.

Aluminium alloy greenhouses score because of their reasonable price, the fact that they need no maintenance other than the oiling of hinges, and because they are easy to glaze (the glass is held in position with clips or rubber strips). If you don't like the look of aluminium you can choose a model that has been coated with acrylic paint, which also stops the formation of that white powdery deposit.

Both timber and alloy houses will outlast you if they are treated well, so you pay your money and take your choice.

Glass or plastic?

If you want a permanent greenhouse, the answer has to be glass. It lasts virtually for ever, a fact that should counteract the initial expense. It allows in more light than plastic and allows heat to escape much more slowly. When it comes to cleaning, it takes little time to restore grimy glass to its former crystal-clear state, even if it has been painted with shading compounds to cut down summer glare.

Plastic has two great advantages – cheapness and safety where children are concerned – but the fact that it has to be replaced after a few years will often step up the cost. Certain plastics are now guaranteed a life of 15 years, but that's only a fraction of the time you can expect glass to last.

In time, all plastic becomes opaque and lets in less light; it loses heat rapidly, allows rapid temperature fluctuations and produces much condensation. In polytunnels ventilation is difficult and even though they are easy to erect they can be equally quickly dismantled by a gale if not securely anchored.

After all that, you could be forgiven for thinking that plastic houses are useless! They're not, and they do have a lot to recommend them where temporary and easily movable forms of protection are needed.

PUTTING UP A GREENHOUSE

Laying the foundations

Purpose-made foundations Laying foundations is a real fag. Most gardeners are anxious to get cracking with putting up their greenhouse, and all that trench digging and concrete humping is a sizeable fly in the ointment.

By far the best solution is to buy a greenhouse for which tailor-made concrete kerb foundations can also be bought. All you need to do then is lay the kerbs on firmed and levelled ground (checking that they themselves are level and square) and erect the greenhouse on top of them. Bolts will secure the base of the house to the prefabricated foundation, giving it stability in wind.

Integral base-plate Some greenhouses come equipped with an integral base-plate, which means that they can be erected straight onto firmed and levelled earth. Metal 'ground anchors' can be driven in at strategic points to offer increased wind resistance.

Digging and laying foundations

If no alternatives are available you'll just have to get out the pick and shovel. Dig a 23 cm (9 in) deep trench along the line of the foundation, ram 10 cm (4 in) of hardcore into the base and then top it with a layer of concrete shuttered between boards. A mix of 6 parts aggregate, 1 part sand and 1 part cement, mixed to a sticky consistency with water, should be tamped down between the boards, which have been checked for level and squareness. Coach bolts can be sunk into the concrete (threads uppermost) so that later the base of the house can be drilled to fit over them and the nuts screwed down to anchor the structure. It's all a real chore – you'd be better off with purpose-made foundations!

Erecting and glazing

Almost all greenhouses come with detailed instructions on erection, though the instructions very considerably in their degree of lucidity. Usually the structure is glazed after erection, though some manufacturers supply ready-glazed sections. This is a mixed blessing; it saves you the task of putting in all that glazing but it makes erection a more nail-biting job, for there's always the risk of breakage.

Some manufacturers and suppliers will offer an erection service. If your budget will stretch to it, this can be a blessing, particularly as they will be responsible for any breakages during construction.

Greenhouses that can be glazed with clips or rubber strips make glazing a doddle, but some houses still come with a large bag of putty and a smaller bag of glazing sprigs.

It's always a good idea to have somebody around to help you glaze the greenhouse, especially if putty is

---

Siting your greenhouse

I don't happen to subscribe to the idea that your greenhouse must run either north/south or east/west: it makes a difference where large commercial glasshouses are concerned, but not in your average back garden. The ideal spot for a greenhouse probably doesn't exist in a small garden, but bear the following points in mind when you're trying to shoe-horn it into the scheme.

1 Choose a spot that is well lit and not overshadowed by trees or buildings.
2 The site should be sheltered at a distance from strong winds, which will send heating bills soaring and may cause other damage.
3 Avoid frost pockets – those dips in the land where cold air collects.
4 Avoid badly drained ground, otherwise greenhouse crops that are grown in the soil will always have a late start.
5 Try to find a level site: it makes foundation laying easier.
6 Site the greenhouse where water and electricity can easily be laid on.
7 Check with your local authority to see if planning permission is required before you erect the greenhouse.

---

involved. You'll become more proficient as you progress, but at first the putty tends to get everywhere except in the channels for which it is intended. Try to glaze the whole house in one day – if it's part-glazed and a wind gets up, you could be in for a hefty bill for glass replacement.

If you do have to use putty, start by glazing the roof, strip by strip. Work putty into the rebates along the glazing bars (don't be too generous with it), and then insert the glass, starting at the bottom and leaving each pane overlapping the one below it by about 2.5 cm (1 in). Fasten the glass in position with glazing sprigs (making sure you put one under each side of the lower edge to prevent the glass from slipping) and then clean off the excess putty. Rub the glass immediately with a dry cloth to remove finger marks: you'll have a devil of a job to shift them once they're dry. Once the house is glazed you and your plants can move in without delay.

Make way for a path

Whether you grow plants in pots or on the floor, a path down the centre of the greenhouse is a must. Stone slabs are easy to lay and comfortable to walk on; gravel is cheaper and, where plants are to be grown in pots on the staging, it can be laid over the entire floor area to a depth of 2.5 cm (1 in). It looks good, keeps down weeds and holds moisture in summer when humidity is important. Buy the stuff from a builders' merchant, where it is described as washed pea shingle.

WHERE TO GROW THE PLANTS

Growing in border soil

If you plan to raise tomatoes, cucumbers, peppers and aubergines you can grow the crops in the soil within the greenhouse for a few years. Dig it well first and work in some well-rotted compost or manure. Don't grow the same crop in the same place year after year: practise a small rotation scheme and you should be able to grow good plants in the earth for three or four years. After this length of time the soil often becomes sick or exhausted and it's a good idea to move over to growing in pots, growing bags or, where tomatoes are concerned, to ring culture.

Some experts would have you ignore border soil from the outset, but I'd rather enjoy its cheapness and convenience for a couple of years before moving over to containers. You can always dig up and replace tired border soil with fresh, but it's an expensive and labour-intensive job.

Ring culture

If it's tomatoes you're growing, and the border soil becomes tired of them, turn to ring culture.

Lay a 15 cm (6 in) deep bed of washed pea shingle over a strip of polythene and retain it with boards at the edges. Alternatively, excavate a 15 cm (6 in) deep trench and lay the polythene and shingle in it. The gravel bed can stretch right down one side, or both sides, of the greenhouse.

Remove the bottoms from some 23 cm (9 in) plastic plant pots (a hacksaw will do the job), or buy special 'whalehide' rings, which are bottomless. (Conservationists please note: whalehide pots are made from bituminous paper.)

Sit the rings on the shingle, spacing them 45 cm (18 in) apart. Fill them with John Innes No. 3 potting compost and plant the young tomatoes in them. Water them well in and apply all

subsequent waterings to the shingle. Only liquid fertilizer should be applied to the compost in the pot.

The plant will develop two root systems, one for absorbing water and one for absorbing food. At the end of the growing season the plants can be removed and the gravel thoroughly washed so that it is fit to use the following year.

Staging for pot plants

Pot plants need to be grown on shelves or on benches, which the greenhouse gardener calls staging. The most luxurious staging is made from timber or alloy and supports plastic trays that can be filled with gravel. During spring and summer, the moisture evaporating from the gravel keeps the air around the plants pleasantly humid and conducive to growth. In winter it can harbour too much moisture and lead to fungus attack, but it's a time-consuming job to remove all the gravel every autumn and replace it each spring. For this

A collection of alpines happily overwinters in an all-glass greenhouse. The pots sit on slatted timber staging, and gravel on the floor helps to maintain optimum humidity.

reason I always spread gravel on the floor of the greenhouse and have plain slatted wooden staging, which can be easily and relatively cheaply built from 5 x 2.5 cm (2 x 1 in) deal and painted with a red cedar timber preservative to match a cedar greenhouse. The gravel on the floor provides sufficient buoyancy in summer without being overpoweringly moisture retentive in winter.

For ease of working, make the staging waist high and no more than 1 m (3 ft) deep, so that all plants can be reached from the front. If the house is very wide or intended to display flowering pot plants, the staging can be lower and tiered to present a bank of floral colour to the spectator. All staging should be strong. Pots full of compost may not feel very heavy on their own but collectively they weigh a ton.

Don't let the area underneath the staging lie idle. Shade-loving ferns and foliage plants will enjoy growing there.

Shelves fixed above the staging, down the sides and at the end of the greenhouse, provide more valuable space for growing pot plants. Fix them to metal angle brackets but make sure that they don't cast too much shade on the staging below. Shelves about 15 cm (6 in) wide should not cause much of a problem.

PROVIDING THE RIGHT CONDITIONS

Which type of heating?

To overwinter frost-tender plants and to make an early start with seed-raising in spring, your greenhouse will need heating. Certainly an unheated structure is valuable during the warmer months of the year and for growing winter lettuce, but a little heat will spread its usefulness over twelve months.

I'm not going to take up pages by going over all the forms of heating; instead I'll tell you quite simply that nothing beats electricity for efficiency or economy. Gone are the days when coal and paraffin offered cheap heat; thermostatically controlled electric heaters beat them hands down nowadays.

You'll have to enlist the help of an electrician to equip your greenhouse with the juice and to fit special waterproof plugs for safety. I use tubular heaters, which are slung underneath the staging and wired up to a rod-type thermostat set at 7°C (45°F) in winter (to keep my geraniums frost free) and a little higher in spring. The thermostat is the key to economy. It switches the electricity off when the required temperature is reached – a feature lacking in paraffin and solid-fuel heating systems where burning continues regardless of temperature.

The other big advantage of electricity is that it produces dry heat. This is especially important in winter when excess humidity encourages fungus diseases. Paraffin heaters give out gallons of water every day and can also cause leaf scorch. Use them as emergency measures during winter power cuts, and try to apply a little ventilation at all times so that poisonous fumes can escape. Use only those paraffin heaters expressly designed for greenhouses.

Tubular heaters are just one form of electrical air warmer; fan heaters designed for greenhouse use and air-warming cables can also be used, though the latter are really at their best in small structures where they can be clipped to the wall beneath the staging. Both types should be fitted with a thermostat for economy. Don't let a fan heater blow directly onto plants or it may brown their foliage.

Heaters running from natural gas might seem to be desirable, but they need to be connected up to the gas supply, which may be even more difficult than laying on electricity. They also produce water vapour and poisonous fumes and so cannot really compete with clean electricity.

Manufacturers will advise you on the size of heater needed for your structure. Make sure that the equipment you buy can supply the heat you need and hang a maximum and minimum thermometer in the greenhouse to check it's functioning properly.

Providing lighting

If you're investing in electrical heating you might as well fit lighting too. A single fluorescent strip fastened to the ridge will provide plenty of working light on dark evenings – and mornings, too, in winter. If you just want enough light to check that no one's run off with your plants, then an ordinary lamp socket will do.

Lean-to greenhouses that are positioned over house windows can be lit for pleasure rather than practicality. A spotlight fitted to the back wall and angled to shine on the plants will provide colourful evening scenery.

Preparing for winter

In winter, every step you take to prevent heat loss will save money. For a start check that doors and ventilators fit snugly. Stick-on household draught excluder can be used to plug any gaps. Mend all broken panes of glass before the bad weather arrives.

Keep all the glass clean so that every ray of sunlight can be utilized, and if your greenhouse is heated to a temperature of 10°C (50°F) or more, rig up some form of plastic insulation inside. Polythene sheeting or, better still, bubble polythene with built-in air pockets, should be fixed to the roof and sides of the house so that it creates an insulating layer of air. It's the 2.5 cm (1 in) gap between the polythene and the glass that does the insulating, rather than the polythene itself. Put up the insulating material in November and take it down in April. Don't cover the vents with the stuff – you'll still need them on warm days.

Double-glazed greenhouses are efficient and amazingly strong, but they're rather expensive too.

Ensuring adequate ventilation

In a stagnant atmosphere fungus diseases are rife, so try to provide plants with a little fresh air at all times except in really cold or severe weather. In summer the ventilators are vital for letting in air to prevent the plants from baking, so when you buy a greenhouse make sure that it has plenty of ventilators. As a rule of thumb look for one ridge ventilator and one side ventilator for every 2 m (6 ft) of the greenhouse's length. If there are fewer than this, ask if more can be fitted. If they can't, shop elsewhere.

Ventilators on both sides of the house will allow you to vent on the leeward and prevent howling draughts. Louvre vents are efficient but not always draughtproof; ordinary hinged vents fitted with casement stays can usually be made to fit snugly.

The one piece of equipment you should not be without is an automatic ventilating arm. These devices are fastened to a ventilator and set to open and close it at a given temperature. If you have to be out at work during the day the arm will efficiently prevent your plants from being baked alive. They are not expensive and need no power supply.

Maintaining humidity

In spring and summer, high humidity is essential to keep the plants in good health; in winter it will encourage diseases. The easiest way of maintaining a buoyant atmosphere is to damp down the floor both morning and evening – the staging too if it is covered with gravel. The moisture will evaporate into the atmosphere and keep the plants perky. Don't damp down after late summer. From autumn until late spring the atmosphere wants to be on the dry side.

Providing summer shading

In summer, additional measures have to be taken to lower temperatures and prevent plants from being scorched by the sun. Shading is the solution. The cheapest form comes in a bottle: dilute it in water and paint it on so that a white film coats the glass. There are various products: one has the advantage of being easily removed with a dry duster and yet it stays firmly in place regardless of summer downpours. Another becomes translucent when wet, so allowing in more light on dingy summer days. Shading compounds such as these cannot be used effectively on all plastics; on some they will refuse to shift however hard you wash them in autumn.

Blinds are more expensive but more versatile, for they can be raised and lowered according to the weather. External blinds are preferable to those fixed inside the house for they will intercept the sun's rays before they have a chance to heat up the greenhouse atmosphere.

> "Don't let the area beneath the staging lie idle. Shade-loving ferns and many foliage plants will enjoy growing there."

If you can't afford blinds, invest in some green plastic close-weave netting, which can be fixed to the outside of the greenhouse. Put it up in May and take it down in September.

ALL ABOUT WATERING

When I first worked in a nursery we had to water all the plants with a can. There were thousands of them. Eventually hosepipes were fitted, but the boss watched us like a hawk and came down like a ton of bricks if the hosepipe was running too fast. Whether you use a can (a long-spouted one is best) or a hosepipe, that's the secret – don't let it run too fast or the compost will be efficiently flushed out of the pot and splashed round to make a breeding ground for disease.

Tapwater or rainwater?

Tapwater does most plants no harm at all. Only if it's very hard and the plants are very sensitive will you encounter problems. In this case you can collect rainwater in a large tank. Rainwater that runs off the greenhouse roof can be channelled via the guttering into a tank sunk below the staging inside the house.

Fasten a nylon stocking over the inlet to keep out rubbish, and empty it regularly to prevent blockages. Some gardeners consider that water collected and stored in this way will spread disease. I've never found this. You can't grow plants in a sterile atmosphere and if they can't cope with a few germs in the rainwater then they are of a pretty poor constitution.

Automatic watering systems

Automatic watering saves a lot of time. It also takes some of the skill out of growing plants, but if you're busy it's worth the candle. Capillary benches are perhaps the best form of automatic watering. They are level and consist of waterproof trays on which is laid special nylon matting. This is kept constantly moist, from a reservoir or drip-feed system, and plants that are stood on it can take up just the water they need. Plastic pots with plenty of drainage holes are essential. Clay pots, unless they are fitted with a wick of the nylon material, cannot absorb the water because of the gap between the compost and the bottom of the pot. Various proprietary systems are available.

The spaghetti-tube watering system consists of a large alkathene pipe from which small-bore spaghetti tubes emerge at intervals. Each tube is pegged into a plant pot and when the tap is turned on, water is delivered to where it's needed. The trouble with this system is that it is unselective: every plant is watered when the tap is turned on and consequently there is a risk of overwatering.

When to water

The time to water any pot plant is when the surface of the compost in the pot feels dry. You can also tell by lifting the pot up and testing its weight: the drier it is, the lighter it will be. Most plants suffer no more from being allowed to dry out occasionally than we do from being a bit thirsty; however regular drought causes leaf browning and flower drop; overwatering, on the other hand, will make the plants to go into a wilt from which they seldom recover.

Watering border soil

A final tip on watering plants in the greenhouse border soil. Sink a flowerpot into the earth alongside each plant at planting time. Subsequent waterings can be applied into the pot and will get straight to the roots without running off the surface.

John Innes composts

The John Innes composts were developed in the 1930s at a research institute carrying that man's name. They are now manufactured to the original formulae by many firms (look for the seal of the John Innes Manufacturers' Association on the bag to be sure that the compost is genuine). If you want to make them up at home, here are the recipes for the five different types of composts.
Note: a box measuring 25 x 25 x 55 cm (10 x 10 x 22 in) contains 36 litres (1 bushel) when filled to the brim.

John Innes seed compost
A mixture in which all seeds can be sown.
- *2 parts by volume partially sterilized loam*
- *1 part by volume granulated peat*
- *1 part by volume coarse sand*
Plus:
- *40 g (1½ oz) superphospate of lime per 36 litres (1 bushel)*
- *20 g (¾ oz) ground limestone or chalk per 36 litres (1 bushel)*

John Innes no. 1 potting compost (JIP 1)
Prick out bedding plants into this mixture and use it when potting up rooted cuttings.
- *7 parts by volume partially sterilized loam*
- *3 parts by volume granulated peat*
- *2 parts by volume coarse sand*
Plus:
- *110 g (4 oz) John Innes base fertilizer per 36 litres (1 bushel)*
- *20 g (¾ oz) ground limestone or chalk per 36 litres (1 bushel)*

COMPOSTS FOR POT PLANTS

Pot plants won't grow in garden soil: it is neither well drained enough nor nutritious enough to support them in such a confined space. For this reason gardeners have developed a range of composts for different purposes. Originally there was a different mix for each plant, but nowadays we have just a handful of recipes that can keep most plants happy. You can buy them ready-made, but if you want to make them up at home, the recipes are given above.

The ingredients
Loam Kettering loam was originally prescribed in the formulae for composts, but by now Kettering must be in a gigantic valley. Good garden soil or, better still, soil derived from stacked turves, will do, but it should really be partially sterilized to kill harmful bacteria and weed seeds.

John Innes no. 2 potting compost (JIP 2)

Suitable for most pot plants.

- *Loam, peat and sand as for John Innes No. 1 potting compost*

Plus:

- *225 g (8 oz) John Innes base fertilizer per 36 litres (1 bushel)*
- *40 g (1½ oz) ground limestone or chalk per 36 litres (1 bushel)*

John Innes no. 3 potting compost (JIP 3)

Suitable for vigorous plants including tomatoes, chrysanthemums, cucumbers and melons.

- *Loam, peat and sand as for John Innes No. 1 potting compost*

Plus:

- *340 (12 oz) John Innes base fertilizer per 36 litres (1 bushel)*
- *60 g (2¼ oz) ground limestone or chalk per 36 litres (1 bushel)*

John Innes ericaceous compost

Suitable for lime-hating plants such as rhododendrons, azaleas and heathers.

- *Loam, peat and sand as for John Innes No. 1 potting compost*

Plus:

- *110 g (4 oz) John Innes base fertilizer per 36 litres (1 bushel)*

Proprietary electric soil sterilizers are easy to use but pricey. The soil in them should be sterilized for 10 minutes at a temperature of 82°C (180°F). If you can't afford the equipment, find a large, old saucepan and boil 1 cm (½ in) water in the base before filling it to the brim with sieved soil and letting it simmer for 15 minutes. Tip out the soil afterwards and let it cool.

Peat Moist granulated peat should be used. Pass it through a 1 cm (½ in) sieve. Peat is hard to replace in potting compost.

Sand Don't use bright yellow builder's sand. Coarse river sand is what is needed to make for good drainage.

Fertilizer John Innes base fertilizer is available ready mixed from most garden shops or nurseries. It contains:

2 parts by weight hoof and horn;
2 parts by weight superphosphate of lime;
1 part by weight sulphate of potash.

Mixing and storing composts

Measure out the ingredients and tip them into a heap. Turn the heap three or four times until the compost is well mixed. Store it in black plastic sacks or dustbins, but try to use it within two months. After this it starts to turn sour. I've used old John Innes compost on many occasions with no ill effects, but there's always a chance that some plants might not like it.

Other types of compost

Peat- and coir-based composts There are dozens of proprietary soilless composts, which at one time were based almost exclusively on peat with the addition of fertilizers. Now, due to a need to conserve our peat resources, other renewable organic resources are being experimented with. Many soilless composts today are based on coir - the fibres from coconut husks. Much has been written about the advantages and disadvantages of such composts. Only continuous experience will show us how they can best be managed, and which plants will and will not grow well in them. What all soilless composts have in common is an inability to hold on to nutrients for as long as loam-based composts, which means plants that are planted in them will need feeding regularly six weeks after potting. Because they are light, heavy plants may overbalance in them, particularly if they are allowed to dry out, so they are best kept gently moist at all times: never let them dry out as they are difficult to re-wet. Firm them only gently at potting time.

Compost for cuttings One of the simplest and most effective composts for cuttings is 1 part granulated peat or coir to 1 part coarse river sand. Use it in pots or a propagator where it will provide a well-drained medium capable of inducing root formation.

CARING FOR GREENHOUSE PLANTS

Potting

Plants in the greenhouse grow rapidly and frequently need to be given larger containers of fresh compost. There are several different techniques.

Potting up Here a rooted cutting or seedling is put in its first pot. A 9-10 cm (3½-4 in) container is usually large enough. Some compost is placed in the bottom of the pot - over a layer of crocks or other drainage material if a loam-based compost is being used in a clay pot. The plant is then dug out of its seed tray or propagator with as much compost adhering to its roots as possible.

Potting up a new arrival

1 Unpack plants obtained by mail order as soon as they arrive, and place in good light. Choose a pot large enough to hold the roots with a little room to spare.

2 Place some compost in the bottom of the pot, using a soilless potting compost or John Innes No 1 potting compost, and insert the plant.

3 Continue feeding in the compost around the plant, and then gently firm it with the fingertips to make sure there are no air pockets around the roots.

4 When potting is complete the crown of the plant should be level with the surface of the compost, which should be slightly below the rim of the pot.

Seat the plant on the compost in the new pot, and feed more compost round it, lightly firming with your fingers. When potting up is completed the plant should sit at the same level at which it grew in its previous pot, and there should be a gap of about 2 cm (¾ in) between the surface of the compost and the pot rim.

Water the plant in either by standing it in a shallow trough of water and allowing it to take up what it needs, or by gently soaking it with a can fitted with a fine rose.

Potting on Plants that have outgrown their existing container are moved on to a larger one. The technique is described fully on p.272. Plants growing in the greenhouse may require more than one new container each year if they are growing strongly prior to making flowers. Perennials that are kept for several years will usually be happy with one new pot a year, or maybe even one every second year. As a rule, pot on only during spring and summer when plants are growing actively.

Once a plant has completely filled its container with roots it should be potted on to a pot that is about 5 cm (2 in) larger in diameter.

Repotting A term that is often loosely used for any type of potting but which really indicates that a plant in a large pot is being knocked out, some of the compost removed from its rootball and replaced with fresh when the plant is returned to the same container.

Topdressing Equally useful where plants are growing in large pots. Scrape away the top 5–8 cm (2–3 in) of compost and replace it with fresh.

When to feed greenhouse plants

Greenhouse plants have what you might call a high metabolic rate, thanks to good light and relatively high temperatures. For this reason they enjoy regular feeding during the growing season. Use dilute liquid fertilizers and apply them once every ten days during the growing season. Newly potted plants need not be fed for eight weeks if they are growing in loam-based compost such as John Innes, or for six weeks if they are in a peat-based compost.

Providing support and training

Just like house plants, greenhouse plants need pinching out from time to time to keep them bushy. Simply nip out the shoot tips between your forefinger and thumbnail to encourage the production of more sideshoots. Very dwarf plants won't need pinching, nor will plants being grown on a single stem.

Fuchsias and other plants being trained as standards on a tall, single stem should have their sideshoots removed so that the main stem is encouraged to grow to the required height. Then it can be pinched out and the bushy head developed at the top.

Support single-stemmed plants with canes to which the stem can be tied with soft twine. Multi-stemmed plants can be held up with a few twiggy sticks, or by an enclosure made from split green canes and twine. All supports should be put in place before they are needed so that the plant can grow up and mask them.

Don't be frightened to cut old and straggly plants back quite hard in spring. They will often sprout vigorously and take on a new lease of life.

THE IMPORTANCE OF HYGIENE

Tidiness pays dividends in the greenhouse by keeping the risk of pest and disease attack to a minimum. Never leave dead or diseased plants among healthy ones, and always pick off faded leaves and flowers immediately you spot them.

Remove any weeds that sprout from the greenhouse floor, and act immediately when you spot a pest or disease outbreak by fumigating the house.

Once a year, in spring for preference, give the inside and outside of the house a good scrub down with horticulural disinfectant. It will remove dirt and grime as well as killing overwintering pests and their eggs. Keep the plants out of the way during the clean up – stand them under the staging and cover them with a sheet of polythene. Permanganate of potash or an algicide will shift green algal deposits from paths if a stiff brush and elbow grease are used as well.

If gravel is present on the staging, put it in a sieve and swill it clean with a hosepipe bit by bit.

A-Z of greenhouse gardening

THERE'S NO REASON WHY your greenhouse needs to be heated to tropical temperatures to keep you in flowers during winter. A minimum of 7°C (45°F) at night, and just a fraction more during the day, will keep plenty of temperate plants blooming.

GREENHOUSE FLOWERS

The list includes flowering pot plants that can be grown from seeds to give year-round colour in a cool greenhouse, as well as more extensive advice on those four confirmed favourites: carnation, chrysanthemum, fuchsia and pelargonium.

Supplement this selection with plants included in Chapter 20 House Plants, and with pot-grown bulbs described in Chapter 11 Garden Bulbs. The measurements indicate the expected ultimate height.

Begonia semperflorens **Cultorum Group** hybrids
15 cm (6 in)

Round, glossy leaves of green or brown; red, pink, salmon or white flowers from July to November.
Sow in February at 20°C (68°F).
Prick out into trays in March–April.
Pot up into 10 cm (4 in) pots in May.

Browallia speciosa **'Blue Troll'**
20 cm (8 in)

Starry flowers of sky-blue are produced from October to March, on very compact, green-leafed plants.
Sow in July at 18°C (64°F).
Pot up into 10 cm (4 in) containers in August–September.

Calceolaria hybrids
Slipper Flower
30 cm (12 in)

Soft green leaves and pouch-like flowers, often with contrasting spotting, in April to July. Biennials.
Sow in April–May at 15°C (59°F).
Prick out into trays in June.
Pot up into 8 cm (3 in) containers in July–August and into 13 cm (5 in) containers in September.

Dianthus caryophyllus hybrids
Carnation

Perpetual-flowering carnations are those that you buy from the florist for wedding buttonholes. There are dozens of varieties with blooms of red, orange, yellow, pink, white and magenta; most are called something-or-other Sim: 'Arthur Sim', 'White Sim', and so on.
Pot up young rooted cuttings into 8 cm (3 in) pots of JIP 1 in January, February or March. Specialist nurserymen will supply them at this time.
Cultivation Grow on in a temperature of 4-7°C (40-45°F): the plants insist on cool temperatures. Pot on into 13 cm (5 in) pots of JIP 2 when the plants have outgrown their previous containers, and stand them outdoors during the summer. Pot on into 20 cm (8 in) pots when necessary. Pinch out the central shoot when ten pairs of leaves have been formed, and pinch out sideshoots after eight pairs of leaves. 'Stop' the plants (pinch them out) at different times to stagger flowering. If you want winter flowers, don't stop the plants after June. Bring the pots into the greenhouse during September. The plants will grow to at least 1 m (3 ft) and will need some support. Canes and string are used by most gardeners, but special carnation supports are also available. Feed fortnightly with tomato fertilizer when the plants have

been in their final pots for six or eight weeks. When the flower buds form, remove all but the large central one. Cut the blooms with a good length of stem just before they are fully open.
Propagation Replace the plants with newly rooted cuttings every two years. Propagate them yourself by taking cuttings of sideshoots during December, January and February and rooting them in a propagator heated to 16°C (60°F).

Celosia argentea varieties
30 cm (12 in)

Plumes of orange, red or yellow flowers like waxy feathers in July to October. Annuals.
Sow in March at 20°C (68°F).
Prick out into trays in April.
Pot up into 10 cm (4 in) containers in May–June.

Chrysanthemum

The early-flowering chrysanthemums that bloom in September can be grown outdoors, but October- and later-flowering varieties are grown in pots so that they can be given greenhouse cover. Buy your chrysanths from a specialist grower who will be able to offer a wide choice of varieties.
Pot up rooted cuttings (see propagation, opposite) in March or April – allowing one plant to an 8 cm (3 in) pot of JIP 1. Grow on at a temperature of 10°C (50°F): the plants must be kept cool.
Cultivation Pot on the plants as they grow, first into 13 cm (5 in) pots and then into 20 cm (8 in) pots of JIP 3. Give each plant a 1.2 m (4 ft) cane when it is in its final pot. Pinch out the main shoot when it is 20 cm (8 in) tall and pinch out subsequent sideshoots when they, too, are 20 cm (8 in) long. Specialist nurseries will recommend precise stopping dates for each of their varieties if you want to time your blooms for a flower show. The fewer stems you leave to develop, the larger will be the individual blooms. Lightly tie the stems to

the cane with soft twine as they grow. Stand the plants outdoors on a path, patio, gravel or ash bed from late May onwards when there is no danger of frost. They should be sheltered from winds, which will blow them over, or else tied to a horizontal wire strained between two posts. Feed weekly eight weeks after planting the chrysanths in their final pots. If you want large, single blooms, remove all but the central bud on each stem. If you want sprays of flower, remove the central bud and let the rest develop. In late September bring the plants into the greenhouse, keeping them cool but frost free and in good light. Nip off any extra sideshoots and dead leaves. Either cut the open blooms with long stems, or bring the entire pot into the house if you want colour in the home. Chrysanthemum leaf miner may be a problem.

Propagation is easy from cuttings. Cut the plants down to within 5 cm (2 in) of the compost after they have finished flowering and box up these 'stools' in trays of JIP 1, having shaken most of the old compost from the roots. Keep the stools in a cool, well-lit greenhouse over the winter and they will eventually produce tough little shoots that can be taken as cuttings during January and February. Make them 5-8 cm (2-3 in) long and root them in a propagator in a temperature of 16°C (60°F).

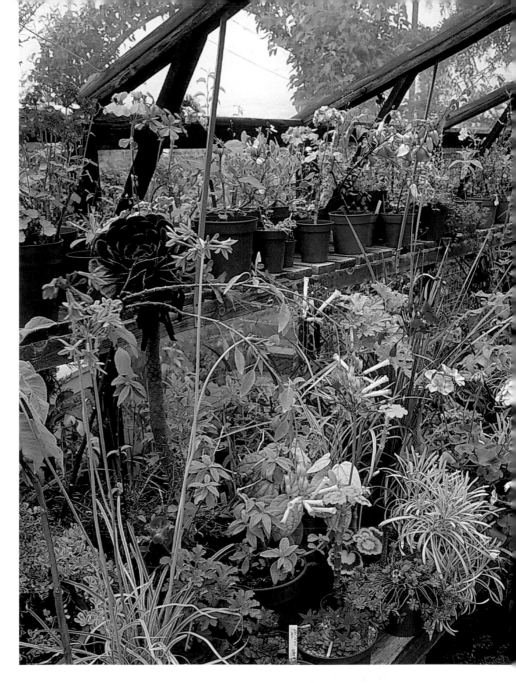

Cobaea scandens

Climber

Bells of pale blue and white in August to October, on a vigorous, vine-like plant.

Sow in March at 18°C (64°F).
Pot up into 8 cm (3 in) containers in April and into 15 cm (6 in) containers in June.

Cuphea ignea

15 cm (6 in)

Tiny, tubular red flowers tipped with purple and white in July to November.

Every inch of space in this well-stocked greenhouse is utilized to nurture a fine collection of plants, including pelargoniums, alpines, succulents and bulbs.

Sow in March at 18°C (64°F).
Pot up into 8 cm (3 in) containers in April and into 13 cm (5 in) containers in May-June.

Exacum affine

15 cm (6 in)

Tiny lilac-blue flowers in September to

March, on a neat, glossy-leaved plant.
Sow in April at 18°C (64°F).
Pot up into 8 cm (3 in) containers in May and into 13 cm (5 in) containers in June-July.

Fuchsia

Hardy fuchsias are shrubs that can be grown permanently in the garden, even though frost might cut them to the ground each winter. Tender fuchsias need frost protection and so are grown as greenhouse plants or bedded out in summer and brought under cover in autumn. There are hundreds of varieties. Some are suited to being grown as standards on a single stem; others make good hanging basket plants due to their pendulous habit; but the majority make shapely bushes.

Pot up rooted cuttings in spring or early summer in 8 cm (3 in) pots of JIP 1 or a soilless equivalent.

Cultivation Pinch the shoot tips and subsequent sideshoots to encourage bushiness. Flowering will usually commence about six or eight weeks after pinching. To produce a standard fuchsia, first check that the variety is suitable, then remove all sideshoots and fasten the main stem to a cane as it grows. When the required height is reached, pinch out the shoot tip and keep pinching the sideshoots to encourage a bushy head.

Pot on the plants in JIP 3 or a soilless equivalent as necessary. They are usually happy in 15 cm (6 in) pots. Plant pendant types in hanging baskets.

The plants will flower continuously during summer and autumn. Stand them or hang them outdoors between June and September if you wish, but bring them back inside before frosts threaten. Feed fortnightly when in flower or bud. Keep the plants on the dry side in winter. Cut the shoots back to within a few centimetres or inches of compost level in spring to encourage shoots, which can be used in propagation or pinched to produce a shapely plant once more. Repot in fresh compost at the same time. The plants will need a winter minimum temperature of 7°C (45°F); 10°C (50°F) if they are to be kept growing rather than ticking over.

Propagation is by shoot tip cuttings which can be removed and rooted in a propagator at any time during spring and summer. Maintain a temperature of 16-18°C (60-65°F) to induce rooting.

Gomphrena globosa 'Buddy'
23 cm (9 in)

Globular, crispy flowerheads of rich crimson-magenta from July to November, on compact plants. Annual.
Sow in March at 18°C (64°F).
Prick out into trays in April.
Pot up into 10 cm (4 in) container in May-June.

Hypoestes phyllostachya
23 cm (9 in)

Dark green leaves spotted with bright pink.
Sow in March at 18°C (64°F).
Pot up into 8 cm (3 in) containers in April and then into 13 cm (5 in) containers in June.

Mimulus Calypso Series
Monkey Flower
15 cm (6 in)

Trumpet blooms of red, orange and yellow covered in contrasting spots in May to July. Usually grown as annuals.
Sow at 18°C (64°F) in March.
Pot up into 10 cm (4 in) pots in April.

Pelargonium
Geranium

Geraniums are real favourites with any gardener who appreciates brilliance and good value. The zonal types are the commonest, with their attractively marked leaves and bright blooms; the miniature varieties are especially good because large numbers of them can be fitted into a small greenhouse to provide almost year-round colour. Scented-leaved pelargoniums should be tried too; their often finely cut foliage may smell of anything from peppermint to pineapples.

Pot up rooted cuttings of named varieties obtained from specialist nurseries in February or March. Put them in 12 cm (4½ in) pots of JIP 2.

Cultivation Pelargoniums, more than most plants, prefer to dry out just a

little between waterings, so don't keep them soggy. Pinch out the shoot tip of each plant when it is 10 cm (4 in) high and pinch again later on to keep plants bushy. The miniatures will grow well without pinching. Feed fortnightly from May to September, and keep the plants in brilliant light. Pick off faded flowers and leaves as soon as they are seen. Stand the plants outdoors in summer if you wish, or use them in bedding schemes. Bring them back under cover in September before the frosts. Keep the plants very much on the dry side in winter; singles may continue to flower, especially if they are disbudded during summer to save their energy, but doubles are less likely to do so. Maintain a minimum winter temperature of 7°C (45°F), though the plants can stand anything down to freezing point. Plants to be kept for a second year can be potted on into 13 or 15 cm (5 or 6 in) pots in their second spring, but most are best replaced annually from cuttings.

Propagation Take shoot tip cuttings between April and September. Make each cutting 8-10 cm (3-4 in) long and root them around the edge of a 10 cm (4 in) pot of peat and sand. Maintain a temperature of 16-18°C (60-64°F) for rooting. Pot up as soon as roots are well developed. Hybrid pelargoniums can be raised from seeds sown in a temperature of 18-21°C (64-70°F) between January and March. The plants will flower from July onwards.

Pericallis hybrids
Florist's Cineraria
30 cm (12 in)

Domes of daisy flowers of white, pink, blue, magenta or purple, often two-tone are produced from November to February. These plants are often grown as annuals.
Sow in April at 16°C (61°F).
Prick out into trays in May.
pot up into 8 cm (3 in) containers in June- July and into 13 cm (5 in) containers in August.

Primula malacoides

30 cm (12 in)

Toothed leaves held in a rosette from which rise tiered heads of pink, blue or white flowers from February to April. Often grown as an annual.
Sow at 18°C (64°F) in July.
Pot up into 8 cm (3 in) containers in August and into 13 cm (5 in) containers in September–October.

Schizanthus

Poor Man's Orchid

30 cm (12 in)

Beautifully painted flowers from July to September, atop ferny green leaves. Annuals.
Sow in April at 16°C (61°F).
Pot up into 8 cm (3 in) containers in April–May and into 13 cm (5 in) containers in May–June.

Solenostemon

Coleus, Flame Nettle

30 cm (12 in)

Colourful nettle-like leaves splashed with red, yellow, orange, green and purple.
Sow in April at 16°C (61°F).
Pot up into 8 cm (3 in) pots in May and into 13 cm (5 in) pots in June–July.

Streptocarpus hybrids

Cape Primrose

20 cm (8 in)

Long, downy leaves over which elegant trumpet flowers in a range of colours are produced on slim stems over a long season.
Sow at 18°C (64°F).
Pot up into 8 cm (3 in) containers in February–March and into 10 cm (4 in) containers in May–June.

Thunbergia alata

Black-eyed Susan

Climber

Vine-like stems clothed in green leaves and decorated with orange, black-eyed blooms from July to October. Annuals.
Sow in March at 18°C (64°F).
Pot up into 8 cm (3 in) containers in April and into 13 cm (5 in) containers in May–June.

Torenia fournieri

Wishbone Flower

30 cm (12 in)

Much-branched plants with pale blue and dark blue trumpets from July to October. Annual.
Sow in March at 16°C (61°F).
Pot up into 8 cm (3 in) containers in April–May and into 13 cm (5 in) containers in June.

Trachymene coerulea

45 cm (18 in)

Pale blue scabious flowers on tall stems in July to September. Annual or biennial.
Sow in March at 18°C (64°F).
Pot up into 8 cm (3 in) containers in April and into 13 cm (5 in) containers in May–June.

GREENHOUSE FOOD CROPS

You can grow all sorts of fruit and vegetables in a greenhouse, but here I include just the big five: tomatoes, cucumbers, aubergines, sweet peppers and melons. Grapes and peaches are included in Chapter 17 Fruit growing.

Aubergine

'Long Purple', 'Moneymaker' and 'Slice Rite' are three reliable and dark-purple-skinned varieties.
Sow thinly in a pot of seed compost in January or February and germinate in a temperature of 16–18°C (60–64°F).
Prick out individually into 8 cm (3 in) pots of soilless compost or JIP 1.
Cultivation Pot on into 13 cm (5 in) pots of JIP 3 or a soilless compost when the plants are 15 cm (6 in) high. Water well when necessary. Pinch out the shoot tip one week after potting on. Transfer to 20 cm (8 in) pots when

the plants have outgrown their 13 cm (5 in) containers. Spray open flowers with tepid water, and give a fortnightly liquid feed of tomato fertilizer from this stage on. Allow six to eight fruits to remain on each plant. Pinch out any sideshoots. Stake if necessary.
Harvest the fruits when they are a good size and while they are still shiny (they'll become tough when they turn dull). Watch out for the thorns!
Store by freezing.
Problems Aphids, red spider mites and whitefly.

Cucumber

The 'all-female' varieties, which produce very few male flowers, are well worth growing. They save you the annoyance of bitter, misshapen cucumbers if you happen to miss just one masculine bloom (they should always be pinched off to prevent fertilization). 'Femspot', 'Femdan' and 'Aidas' are all good.
Sow two seeds to an 8 cm (3 in) peat pot full of soilless compost in March or April. Push the seeds 2.5 cm (1 in) deep and germinate them in a temperature of 18°C (64°F). Should both seeds germinate, remove the weaker one and grow the remaining one on in a temperature of 18°C (64°F).
Cultivation Plant in growing bags or large pots of JIP 3 or a soilless equivalent as soon as the young plants are 23 cm (9 in) high. Equip the sides and roof of the greenhouse with horizontal wires at 30 cm (12 in) intervals

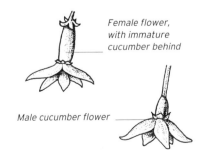

Female flower, with immature cucumber behind

Male cucumber flower

Pinch off any male cucumber flowers that occur: only female flowers have immature cucumbers behind them.

Train stems up canes and onto wires running horizontally across the roof

Plant two plants to each growing bag. Water in and keep the compost moist

immediately above the site where the cucumbers are growing. Two plants will fit in a growing bag. Water well before planting, and plant so that the rim of the peat pot is just below the surface of the compost. Water in and keep the compost constantly moist, but never soggy, from now on. Place a cane alongside each plant and train the main stem upwards; pinch out sideshoots after three leaves have formed, and subsequent sideshoots after two leaves. Pinch out the tip of the main shoot when it reaches the ridge of the greenhouse. Spray daily with tepid water and keep the atmosphere moist by damping down. Pinch off any male flowers that do occur (female flowers have immature cucumbers behind them; males do not). Keep the plants shaded from bright sun. As soon as roots appear above the compost apply a topdressing. Feed fortnightly with dilute tomato fertilizer as soon as the fruits start to swell.

Harvest the fruits as soon as they are of a decent size. The plant may continue to crop for many weeks if fruits are not allowed to mature fully.

The simplest way of training a cucumber plant is to pinch out sideshoots after three leaves have formed and subsequent sideshoots after two leaves. That way the plant

Problems Whitefly, red spider mite, aphids, mildew, stem rot and mosaic virus.

Melon

The canteloupe melons 'Charantais' and 'Sweetheart' are old favourites; I rather like the earlier maturing 'Early Sweet', which is mouthwateringly succulent.

Sow exactly as for cucumbers.
Cultivation In the early stages the same instructions apply as for cucumbers, with regard to pinching and training, but do not remove the male flowers. As soon as four or five female flowers are open at the same time (the females have miniature melons behind them), remove a male flower and push it into the centre of the females to assist pollination and subsequent fertilization. Do the job around midday when the humidity is high. If all four, or even five, fruits start to form, all well and good. If they

don't, remove all the remaining females that were fertilized and wait for another batch of four or five to come along. Melons need to develop simultaneously because far less water must be given to them as they reach maturity. If some fruits were just starting to swell when others were almost ripe, it would be difficult to give the swelling fruits the water they required without causing the mature fruits to split. Feed weekly with liquid tomato fertilizer once the fruits have set. Pinch off subsequent female flowers. Topdress the compost when roots appear above the surface. When the fruits are tennis ball-sized, support them in string bags slung from the framework of the greenhouse. Shade them from bright sunshine.

Harvest the fruits as soon as the end furthest from the stalk gives a little when pressed. Just before this happens the fruits will start to exude that long-awaited melon aroma. This is the signal to cut down on the watering and let the compost become drier. Overwatering now will cause fruit split.

Problems aphids, whitefly, red spider mite and stem rot.

Sweet Pepper
(also known as **Capsicum**)

'Canape' and 'Worldbeater' are old favourites; 'Bell Boy' is good too.
Sow seeds in a pot in March and germinate in a temperature of 16°C (60°F). Prick out individually into 8 cm (3 in) pots of JIP 1 or a soilless equivalent. Grow on in a temperature of 16–18°C (60–64°F).
Cultivation Pot on into 15 cm (6 in) pots of JIP 3 or a soilless equivalent when the plants are 15 cm (6 in) high. Pinch out the shoot tips at the same time. Keep the compost gently moist at all times and shade the plants from bright sun. Spray the flowers with tepid water daily once they have opened, and feed weekly with dilute tomato fertilizer once the fruits have set.
Harvest the fruits as soon as they are

of a usable size and while they are still shiny and green. If left to turn red, they will slow down the plant's growth rate and fewer fruits will come to maturity.

Problems Aphids and red spider mite.

Tomato

Everybody has their own favourite tomato variety; mostly 'Moneymaker'. Try 'Alicante' or 'Ailsa Craig' for a change, or the hefty-fruited 'Big Boy' if you like beefsteak tomatoes. 'Golden Boy' is a bright yellow tomato with an exquisite flavour. There is a huge number of 'heritage' tomatoes available, too.

Sow seeds in a pot during March and germinate in a temperature of 18°C (64°F). Prick out the seedlings individually into 8 cm (3 in) pots of JIP 1 or a soilless equivalent.

Cultivation Grow on the plants in a temperature of around 18°C (64°F). When they are 23 cm (9 in) high, plant them out into the border soil (spacing them 45 cm (18 in) apart); into 23 cm (9 in) diameter pots of JIP 3 or a soilless equivalent; into growing bags; or into rings (see p.255 for advice on ring culture). Water the plants well after planting and provide each one with a support – a stout cane or a string running up to the roof of the house. Remove any sideshoots as soon as they are seen. Tie the stem to the cane as it grows, or twist it carefully around the string. Try to keep the compost gently moist at all times. Sink a flowerpot into the soil alongside each border-grown plant and pour water into that instead of onto the surface of the soil: you'll prevent your tomatoes from becoming mud-spattered and the water will get straight to the roots. Spray open flowers with tepid water to encourage fruit setting. Feed weekly with diluted tomato fertilizer once the first fruits start to swell. Shade and ventilate as necessary. Pinch out the main shoot tip when six flower clusters or trusses have been formed. Cut away one or two leaves around each developing truss. Do not remove all the lower leaves as some growers do. It is not necessary and it weakens the plant.

Harvest the fruits just as soon as they are ripe. Don't leave them on the plant too long or cropping will slow down.

Store all remaining fruits in October. Strip the plants of their bounty and uproot them. The unripe fruits will slowly ripen if stored in a cool place. Put them in a drawer with a ripe banana if you want to speed up the process. Green tomatoes that refuse to blush can be used for chutney.

Problems Mindboggling, but you won't get them all: whitefly, red spider mite, blossom end rot (especially on plants in growing bags), blotchy ripening, greenback, eelworm, leaf mould, stem rot, root rot, potato blight, verticillium wilt, virus.

FOOD CROPS TO FORCE

It sounds a bit cruel, but it's not really. You're just providing plants with favourable conditions that allow them rather than force them to start growing early, yielding their crops while prices are high in the shops.

French bean

Use our old friends 'The Prince' and 'Masterpiece'.

Sow four seeds 2.5 cm (1 in) deep in a 15 cm (6 in) pot of JIP 1 during December, January or February. Keep the compost moist and maintain a temperature of 16°C (60°F). Stake with a cane and string enclosure or short twiggy pea sticks as the plants grow. Feed fortnightly with tomato fertilizer once the flowers have opened.

Harvest between 10 and 12 weeks after sowing. Pick the young pods regularly.

Potato

'Epicure' is about the best choice for forcing; 'Sharpe's Express' is also good.

Pot in January. Half fill a 20 cm (8 in) pot with equal parts JIP 3 and soilless compost. Plant three tubers 5 cm (2 in) deep. Keep the compost moist and maintain a temperature of 10°C (50°F). Topdress with more compost as the shoots grow.

Harvest during April. Deliciously early!

Rhubarb

'Timperley Early' and 'Champagne' are both good.

Plant the crowns close together in a 20 cm (8 in) deep box of moist soilless compost at any time during November or December. The crowns should have been dug up a week before planting and left on the surface of the soil exposed to frost. Keep the boxes in the dark (blacked out with sacking or black polythene) in a temperature of 13–16°C (55–60°F). Check regularly and keep the compost moist.

Harvest during January and February, cutting the pink sticks when they are about 30 cm (12 in) long. Discard the crown after cropping, unless you want to grow them on and rest them for a year before picking again.

Strawberry

'Tamella' and 'Cambridge Favourite' are both good forcers.

Plant three rooted runners to a 20 cm (8 in) pot of JIP 3 in August. Stand the plants outdoors during the autumn and early winter, watching them carefully for dryness or, more likely, waterlogging. Bring the pots in during January. Try to maintain a temperature of 10°C (50°F) during February. Feed fortnightly with liquid fertilizer once the plants come into flower. Limit the number of fruits on each plant to 12.

Harvest during April and May. Discard the plants after fruiting, or grow on in the garden if you are soft-hearted.

20 House plants

House plants have a place in every home and office, adding beauty, interest, and a vital link with nature to the environments in which we live and work

What makes a good house-plant grower? Skill? Luck? Green fingers? Usually it's a smattering of all three and a hefty helping of common sense. No plants are more at your mercy than house plants: you control the amount of heat, water and light they receive, so you're directly responsible for their health.

Too many house plants are killed with kindness and a few are murdered by neglect but, if you choose the right plant for your particular situation and learn what it likes and loathes, then it will grow happily. A plant that is put in the kind of light it enjoys and at a temperature that suits it can only be killed by faulty watering. Master all three techniques and you'll win.

DIFFERENT TYPES OF HOUSE PLANT

There are basically three kinds of house plant: the foliage types, which last almost for ever and which are grown for their leaves; the flowering pot plants, which are perennial and which keep growing after blooming; and the short-term flowering pot plants that die once their blooms have faded. Most folk like a good number of foliage pot plants that offer year-round interest, plus a few flowering ones to brighten life at intervals.

Don't think of pot plants as single pieces of furniture – often they look good and feel more at home when grouped together, provided that they all have the same heat and light requirements.

BUYING HOUSE PLANTS

Spring and summer are the best times to buy house plants; then they can be transferred to a suitable spot in your home with little check. Christmas-flowering pot plants will obviously have to be bought in winter. Make sure that they are wrapped up well for their journey home, and don't leave them in an icy car while you complete your shopping.

If you can, buy from the nursery where the plant was grown, or from a garden centre where it has been kept

Grouping several house plants together not only creates an attractive visual display, but benefits the plants by creating a higher level of humidity around them.

in the conditions it likes. Buy from chain stores and supermarkets only when the plants are known to be fresh in. Buy from greengrocers' pavement displays at your peril: most of the plants will have been chilled and blasted by icy winds. They may be cheaper, but they'll suffer as a result of their ill treatment.

What to look for
Look for a healthy, shapely plant that has plenty of stems - unless it is purposely grown on a single stem. Avoid plants that are wilting, leafless at the base (unless this is part of their charm), brown at the leaf tips or show signs of pest and disease attack. Flowering pot plants are best bought with a few blooms fully open and a few in bud. Tight buds may not develop properly in the home; fully open flowers will not last very long.

If there is a gap between the compost and the sides of the pot, leave the plant alone. It has been allowed to dry out too much and may suffer when you get it home.

LOOKING AFTER YOUR HOUSE PLANT
Starting them off
When you get the plant home, unwrap it and stand it in the room where it is to be grown. A spot that is not in full sun is best at first, even for those plants that like bright sunlight. Keep a sun-loving plant in its temporary position for two or three days before moving it into a window. Most plants prefer a spot in good, indirect light and these can be put in their final positions straightaway, as can those plants that tolerate shade. Check the plant immediately for water. If the rootball is drier than a wrung-out flannel, then water it thoroughly.

> **"A plant will recover from wilting if it's too dry. If it wilts because it is too wet, you can wave it goodbye."**

Death traps
No house plant likes to grow directly above a radiator or other heat source, in a cold draught, or sandwiched between the curtains and the window on a winter's night. Plants placed where they are constantly brushed against will soon turn brown at the edges. Spiny plants placed where they are brushed against will soon bring forth bad language and blood.

Temperatures
There's no need to alter your central heating thermostat to suit your plants; buy instead those plants that can cope with your way of life. Most plants like to be warmer during the day than they are at night, and most houses fit conveniently into this pattern.

Plants recommended for unheated rooms will grow well in temperatures around 10-15°C (50-60°F), and can sometimes tolerate a chilly 5°C (40°F) - but they will stop growing. Those recommended for centrally heated rooms will be happy in 18-24°C (64-75°F).

Light
That mystical thing called 'good, indirect light' is the kind of brightness encountered a few feet from a window. Here the plants receive plenty of light, but not the direct rays of the sun. This is the situation that most of them enjoy.

Those plants that like full sun can be stood right against a window, but take care that they are not scorched by brilliant sunshine at the height of summer. Plants recommended for shade will not grow in a pitch-dark corner. If you can't read small print at arm's length in such a spot, it's too dark even for shade lovers.

Humidity
It's amazing what a bit of atmospheric moisture can do. House-plant owners who are used to their leaves turning brown at the edges can take heart: the problem is often solved if the pot is stood on a tray or saucer of gravel that is kept constantly moist. The water evaporates around the plant and creates an environment that is much more conducive to growth than hot, dry air. Ferns, especially, will appreciate such treatment.

If you're making a plant group, try standing the pots on a large tray or bowl of moist peat, part plunging them in the stuff. This will improve the humidity, and the compost in the pots will dry out more slowly.

Large, glossy leaved plants can be sprayed with rainwater from a hand mister. Don't do this to hairy leaved plants: they'll probably rot.

Watering
Don't overdo it. Ninety-nine per cent of all household plants are killed by overwatering. Rhododendrons (Christmas azaleas), cyperus and ferns should be kept very moist at all times. All other plants need a good soak when they start to feel dry on the surface. Not

before. If the compost feels like a wrung-out flannel, it is still moist.

Nearly all pot plants are happy being watered from above. Fill the pot to the brim with water and let it soak into the compost. When water runs out of the base of the pot, the plant has had enough (unless it has been allowed to dry out so much that the compost has shrunk from the sides of the pot and is letting the water run straight through).

A plant will recover from wilting if it is dry. If it wilts because it is too wet, you can wave it goodbye.

Plants like Saintpaulia (African violet) and Cyclamen may have such a tight dome of leaves that you can neither get your finger in to feel the compost, nor penetrate the rosette with a watering can or jug. Water these from below by standing them in a shallow container for half an hour and letting them take up what they want. Check for watering by weighing the pot in your hand. You'll soon become as efficient at predicting dryness as those ladies at church bazaars who can guess the weight of a cake to the nearest gram or ounce.

Check the plants daily in summer, weekly in winter. They'll need much less water during the darker months of the year. If you still fail (and I don't really believe you can be so unlucky), invest in a plant that is growing in a hydroculture unit (see p.272). Its roots will delve through a plastic basket of gravelly granules that sits

Growing plants in a bottle garden

Small plants fond of high humidity can be grown really well in bottle gardens made in sweet jars, cider flagons, carboys and even goldfish bowls.

Spread 2.5 cm (1 in) of gravel in the base followed by 2.5 cm (1 in) of charcoal, which will prevent the compost from becoming sour. An 8 cm (3 in) layer of soilless or loam-based potting compost will keep the plants happy.

Nurseries and garden centres usually have a good selection of plants in tiny pots for bottle gardens. Look for *Chamaedorea*, *Dionaea*, *Ficus pumila*, *Hedera helix* varieties, *Maranta*, *Peperomia*, *Pilea* and *Saxifraga*. Don't introduce anything too rampant, or slower growers will soon be swamped in a miniature jungle.

Tap the plants from their pots after watering them and plant them in the compost. If the neck of the bottle is narrow, scoop out a hole in the compost with a spoon fastened to a cane. Drop the plant into the hole and re-firm the soil with a cotton reel pushed on the other end of the cane. Space plants to allow for a little growth.

Water the plants in by running water down the inside of the bottle. Place the bottle in good indirect light; that way it won't steam up too much. Leave the top off altogether if you like, or put it in place after a few days.

Stoppered bottles will need hardly any watering at all; unstoppered bottles should be checked once a month, but won't need watering every time.

1 Use a cardboard funnel to feed in a layer of gravel, then a layer of charcoal, and finally compost.

2 Dig holes in the compost with a teapoon fastened firmly to the end of a bamboo cane.

3 Water each plant before knocking it from its pot and dropping into the prepared hole.

4 Firm back the soil, with the aid of a cotton reel pushed onto the other end of the cane.

5 Settle the plants in by running water down the inside of the bottle – not too much!

Granules take up water as required

Water depth indicator

Water reservoir

A hydroculture unit consists of a plastic water reservoir fitted with a water depth indicator. The plant grows in a perforated plastic pot filled with gravelly granules, and takes up the water as it needs it.

over a water reservoir. All you have to do is keep the reservoir topped up with water. There's even a little indicator to help you out. Don't mistake a compost-filled self-watering pot for a hydroculture unit. Self-watering pots simply draw water through the compost from a reservoir below. They are difficult to manage and I've yet to see one that's full of happy plants.

Feeding

Give all pot plants a few square meals while they are growing actively. This is usually in spring and summer, but winter-flowering plants can be fed at that time too. Most vigorous plants will appreciate a fortnightly summer feed of diluted liquid pot-plant fertilizer; slow growers can be fed monthly. Flowering pot plants thrive on diluted liquid tomato fertilizer, and it's just the thing to coax shy *Saintpaulia* (African violets) into bloom.

Potting on

It's surprising how long a pot plant can carry on growing in the same container, but as we're in the business of growing plants well (rather than just keeping them alive) it's a good idea to give them a new

pot of compost every year. Spring is the best time to move them – just before growth begins with the warmer weather and improved light.

Pot on into a container that is 5 cm (2 in) larger in diameter than the existing one. Use a loam-based compost such as John Innes No. 2 or one of the proprietary soilless composts. Never use garden soil when repotting plants. It's just not good enough for them. Plastic pots have many holes in the base; clay pots have only one, so it's a good idea to lay a few pebbles in the bottom of a clay pot to prevent the hole becoming blocked by a plug of compost.

Water the plant well an hour before potting on. Place some moist compost in the bottom of the new pot (on top of the drainage layer if it is needed) and then tap the plant from its old pot so that the rootball comes out in one piece. Sit it on top of the compost in the new pot and check that the surface of the rootball rests 2.5 cm (1 in) or so below the rim. When potting is completed it should be fractionally below the surface of the new compost, yet there should still be a gap between the surface and the rim to allow for watering.

Fill in compost around the rootball, firming it lightly with your fingers. One rap with the palms of your hands on the sides of the pot will level the compost surface. Now all you need to do is water the plant well. At this stage the job is best done by standing the pot in a bowl of water; the compost can be easily displaced if it is soaked from above.

There are exceptions to all rules. A few house plants do not need repotting every year because they grow very slowly and prefer to be a little 'rootbound'. Large palms such as *Howea*, and *Aspidistra* and *Sansevieria* (mother-in-law's tongue) are three such examples, but as a general rule a plant needs a new pot when its roots are wrapped around the inside of the old one. Knock out the plant to see.

Hefty pot plants that are already in 30 cm (12 in) containers should not be repotted. Instead they can be topdressed. Scrape away the top 5 cm (2 in) of compost in spring and replace it with fresh.

GENERAL CARE

Keep them clean

When you're dusting the furniture, don't forget the plants. They collect just as much grime, and a leaf that is dirty can't manufacture food very well.

Clean hairy leaved plants with a dry paintbrush. Glossy leaves can be wiped clean with kitchen roll

In summer move house plants outdoors to a sheltered spot. Clean glossy leaves with kitchen roll dipped in a mixture of milk and rainwater.

dipped in tepid rainwater (or with a mixture of rainwater and milk if you insist on giving them a shine). Leafshine products may damage sensitive plants, although the 'wipes' seem to do a good job.

Pinching out and staking

Pinch out the shoot tips of bushy plants to keep them that way, and stake any plants that need support. Single canes and string will keep up single stems; moss-covered sticks will keep vine-like plants with aerial roots happy, and small trellis or wire supports will hold up other climbers and scramblers.

   Remove any wayward or unwanted shoots at any time of year if you're desperate to be rid of them. From the plant's point of view spring is the best time.

Summer break

All house plants except ferns will appreciate a summer break outdoors on a sheltered patio. Provide some shade at first to avoid leaf scorch. Bring them indoors early in September.

Holiday care

If you're due to go away on holiday, try to enlist the help of a neighbour and leave precise instructions on watering. If this isn't possible, plunge them in seed trays of moist peat in a shady room. They'll stay in reasonable condition for a fortnight like this.

Propagation

I've indicated in the A–Z section how each plant can best be increased. You'll find fuller details in Chapter 2 Propagation.

PESTS AND DISEASES

Relatively few pests and diseases attack house plants, but those that do make an amazing impact both on your temper and on the plant's health. I've dealt with them in Part V Pests, Diseases and Disorders, but for the record these are those most likely to attack.

Pests

Aphids (greenfly), caterpillars, earwigs, leafminers, mealy bug, red spider mite, scale insects, vine weevil, whitefly.

Diseases

Botrytis (grey mould), damping off, mildew, rust, sooty mould, viruses.

Disorders

These are caused by you. They occur as a result of unfavourable growing conditions, so take the necessary remedial action to put matters right. The most common disorders are:

Bud drop Caused by dry air, draughts, dry compost, poor light or movement of the plant during bud formation.

Failure to flower Caused by underfeeding, lack of light, unsuitable temperatures or too large a pot of compost (the plant is busy growing roots).

Leaf fall Caused by dry air, draughts, dryness at the roots or fluctuating temperatures.

Leaf spot Caused by sun scorch, splashed water, too much or too little water.

Leaf yellowing Caused particularly by overwatering and also by draughts, lack of light or nutrients. Remember that old leaves at the bottom of the plant naturally turn yellow before they fall.

Spindly shoots Caused by lack of light.

Stem rot Caused by soggy compost.

Variegation fading Caused by lack of light.

Wilting Caused by overwatering, underwatering, excessively high temperatures, vine weevil attack.

A-Z of house plants

ALMOST ALWAYS IT IS THE sight of a house plant looking beautifully seductive in the shop, garden centre or nursery that persuades you to buy it, rather than a glowing description in a catalogue. But it's what you do with it when you get it home that matters, so in this section I have concentrated on providing some information about the growing conditions that each plant prefers. Check out the guidelines given for your particular treasure so that you can find the right spot for it in your home.

Adiantum capillus-veneris
Maidenhair Fern

30 x 45 cm (12 x 18 in)

Features Foliage.
Season of interest All year round.
Likes Good indirect light, cool temperature, and high humidity.
Pot on annually, in loam-based compost.
Propagate by division.
Special information Fronds turn brown if air or compost dry; cut back dead fronds.

Aechmea fasciata
Urn Plant

45 x 45 cm (18 x 18 in)

Features Foliage/flowers. 'Urn' dies after flowering; offsets appear to replace parent plant.
Season of interest All year round.
Likes Good indirect light, warm temperature, and high humidity.

Pot on every two years in soilless compost.
Propagate by offsets.

Aphelandra squarrosa
Zebra Plant

30 x 30 cm (12 x 12 in)

Features Foliage/flowers.
Season of interest All year round.
Likes good indirect light, warm temperature, and high humidity.
Pot on annually in loam-based compost.
Propagate by cuttings.
Special information Cut off flowers as they fade, and cut back in spring.

Asparagus densiflorus
Asparagus Fern

30 x 45 cm (12 x 18 in)

Features Foliage. Good in hanging baskets and pots. Some varieties produce little white, apple-scented flowers and a few red berries.
Season of interest All year round.
Likes good indirect light or semi-shade, cool or warm temperature, and high humidity.
Pot on annually in either loam-based or soilless compost.
Propagate by division.

Asparagus setaceus
(syn. *A. plumosus*)
Asparagus Fern

30 x 30 cm (12 x 12 in)

Features Foliage.
Season of interest All year round.

Hardy house plants

The following plants will tolerate almost any condition and are notoriously hard to kill:
- *Aspidistra*
- *Billbergia*
- *Chlorophytum*
- *Cissus*
- *Cyperus*
- *Fatshedera*
- *Fatsia*
- *Impatiens*
- *Philodendron*
- *Sansevieria*
- *Tradescantia*

Likes good indirect light or semi-shade, cool or warm temperature, and high humidity.
Pot on annually in loam-based or soilless compost.
Propagate by division.
Special information Dry air or compost will cause leaf drop.

Aspidistra elatior
Cast Iron Plant

45 x 45 cm (18 x 18 in)

Features Foliage. Good in large basin-shaped containers, where it has space to spread.
Season of interest All year round.
Likes good indirect light or semi-shade, and cool temperature.
Pot on in loam-based compost only when absolutely pot bound, perhaps every three years.
Propagate by division.
Special information Do not overwater.

Asplenium nidus
Bird's Nest Fern

60 x 60 cm (2 x 2 ft)

Features Foliage.
Season of interest All year round.
Likes semi-shade, warm temperature, and high humidity.
Pot on annually in soilless compost.
special information Dry air, bright sun and draughts cause leaf scorch.

Begonia maculata
Spotted Begonia

1.2 x 1 m (4 x 3 ft)

Features Foliage/flowers.
Season of interest All year round.
Likes good indirect light, warm temperature, and high humidity.
Pot on annually in loam-based compost.
Propagate by cuttings.
Special information Cut back hard in spring when spindly.

Begonia rex
Rex Begonia
45 cm x 1 m (18 in x 3 ft)

Features Foliage. May be short-lived, and may not grow very large.
Season of interest All year round.
Likes good indirect light, warm temperature, and high humidity.
Pot on annually in loam-based compost.
Propagate by leaf cuttings.

Begonia **Semperflorens Cultorum Group**
Bedding Begonia
15 x 15 cm (6 x 6 in)

Features Flowers.
Season of interest All year round.
Likes good indirect light or direct sun, and cool to warm temperature. On a sunny windowsill will bloom through winter.
Pot on annually in loam-based compost.
Propagate by cuttings.

Begonia tuberous hybrids
60 x 60 cm (2 x 2 ft)

Features Flowers.
Season of interest Summer.
Likes good indirect light, warm temperature, and high humidity.
Pot on annually in loam-based compost.
Propagate by division.
Special information Start dry tubers in February. Flowers fall if compost becomes dry.

Billbergia nutans
Queen's Tears
60 x 60 cm (2 x 2 ft)

Features Flowers.
Season of interest Late winter.
Likes good indirect light, cool to warm temperature, and high humidity.
Pot on every two years in soilless compost.
Propagate by division.

Special information Dry atmosphere causes brown leaf tips.

Calceolaria hybrids
Slipper Flower
30 x 30 cm (12 x 12 in)

Features Flowers.
Season of interest Spring/summer.
Likes good indirect light, cool temperature, and high humidity.
Propagate by seed in soilless compost.
Special information Sow early summer for spring flowering. Discard after blooming.

Capsicum annuum
Ornamental Pepper
30 x 15 cm (12 x 6 in)

Features Fruits.
Season of interest Winter.
Likes direct sun, cool temperature, and high humidity.
Propagate by seed: sow in spring in soilless compost.
Special information Discard after winter fruiting.

Chamaedorea elegans
Parlour Palm
60 x 45 cm (2 ft x 18 in)

Features Foliage.
Season of interest All year round.
Likes good indirect light, cool to warm temperature, and high humidity.
Pot on every two years in loam-based compost.
Propagate by seed.
Special information Good in bottle gardens.

Chlorophytum comosum
Spider Plant
45 x 60 cm (18 in x 2 ft)

Features Foliage.
Season of interest All year round.
Likes good indirect light, and cool to warm temperature.
Pot on annually in loam-based compost.

Propagate by plantlets.
Special information Starved or dry plants develop brown leaf tips.

Cissus antarctica
Kangaroo Vine
1 m x 60 cm (3 x 2 ft)

Features Foliage.
Season of interest All year round.
Likes good indirect light or semi-shade, and cool temperature.
Pot on annually in loam-based or soilless compost.
Propagate by cuttings.
Special information Train over a trellis or wire framework or plant in a hanging basket.

Cissus rhombifolia
Grape Ivy
Climber

Features Foliage.
Season of interest All year round.
Likes semi-shade or good indirect light, and cool to warm temperature.
Pot on every one or two years in loam-based or soilless compost.
Propagate from cuttings.
Special information Provide a large support system. Bomb-proof.

x *Citrofortunella microcarpa*
Calamondin Orange
1 x 1 m (3 x 3 ft)

Features Fruits.
Season of interest All year round; flowers in summer; fruits follow.
Likes direct sun and cool temperature.
Pot on annually in loam-based compost.
Propagate by seed or cuttings.

Codiaeum variegatum
Croton, Joseph's Coat
1 m x 45 cm (3 ft x 18 in)

Features Foliage.
Season of interest All year round.
Likes good indirect light, warm temperature, and high humidity.

Plants for shade and sun

FOR SHADY CORNERS
- Adiantum
- Asparagus
- Aspidistra
- Asplenium
- Cissus
- Fatshedera
- Fatsia
- Maranta
- Peperomia
- Philodendron
- Pilea
- Platycerium
- Sansevieria

FOR SUNNY WINDOWSILLS
- Capsicum
- Cyclamen
- Dionaea
- Erica
- Fuchsia
- Hedera
- Impatiens
- Pelargonium
- Primula
- Rhododendron
- Saintpaulia
- Sansevieria
- Saxifraga
- Schlumbergera
- Senecio
- Solanum
- Solenostemon
- Tradescantia

Pot on every two years in loam-based compost.
Propagate by cuttings.
Special information Leaves fall if humidity in short supply.

Cordyline indivisa
Mountain Cabbage Tree

1 m x 60 cm (3 x 2 ft)

Features Foliage.
Season of interest All year round. Good outside in summer.
Likes direct sun and cool temperature.
Pot on annually in loam-based compost.
Propagate from seed.

Cordyline fruticosa varieties
Dragon Tree, Ti Tree

1 m x 45 cm (3 ft x 18 in)

Features Foliage.
Season of interest All year round.
Likes good indirect light and warm temperature.
Pot on annually in loam-based compost.
Propagate by seed or air-layering.
Special information Dry air and draughts cause leaf browning.

Cycas revoluta
Sago Palm

1 x 1 m (3 x 3 ft)

Features Foliage.

Season of interest All year round.
Likes good indirect light, cool to warm temperature, and high humidity.
Pot on every two to three years in loam-based compost.
Propagate from seed.
Pests and diseases Mealy bug and scale are common pests.

Cyclamen hybrids
Cyclamen

30 x 30 cm (12 x 12 in)

Features Flowers.
Season of interest Winter.
Likes direct sun and very cool temperature.
Pot on Dry off after flowering and repot in late summer in a loam-based compost.
Propagate from seed or tuber.
Special information Must be kept cool.

Cyperus albostriatus
Cyperus

45 x 45 cm (18 x 18 in)

Features Foliage.
Season of interest All year round.
Likes good indirect light or semi-shade, and cool to warm temperature.
special information Stand in a saucer of water that is always kept topped up.
Pot on annually in a loam-based compost.
Propagate by division.

Cyperus involucratus
(syn. *C. alternifolius*)
Umbrella Grass

1.2 m x 60 cm (4 x 2 ft)

Features Foliage.
Season of interest All year round.
Likes good indirect light or semi-shade, and cool to warm temperature.
Pot on annually in a loam-based compost.
Propagate by division.
Special information Stand in a saucer of water that is always kept topped up.

Chrysanthemum
(Florist's 'mums pot-type)

23 x 30 cm (9 x 12 in)

Features Flowers. Plant in garden after blooming, where they will then grow taller.
Season of interest Any time of year.
Likes direct sun and cool temperature.
Propagate from cuttings in soilless compost.

Dieffenbachia seguine varieties
Dumb Cane

1 m x 45 cm (3 ft x 18 in) plus

Features Foliage.
Season of interest All year round.
Likes good indirect light or direct sun, warm temperature, and high humidity.
Pot on every one or two years in soilless compost.
Propagate from cuttings.

Dieffenbachia seguine 'Amoena'
Dumb Cane

1 m x 45 cm (3 ft x 18 in) plus

Features Foliage.
Season of interest All year round.
Likes good indirect light or semi-shade, warm temperature, and high humidity.
Pot on every one or two years in soilless compost.
Propagate from cuttings.
Special information Chop back when leggy. Pull off yellow leaves. The sap is

poisonous so handle carefully. This variety needs more light than green-leaved types.

Dionaea muscipula
Venus Fly Trap
10 x 10 cm (4 x 4 in)

Features Foliage.
Season of interest All year round.
Likes direct sun, cool to warm temperature, and high humidity.
Pot on every two to three years in moss and soilless compost.
Propagate by division.
Special information Grow in live sphagnum moss under a transparent dome.

Dracaena species and varieties
Dragon Tree
1 m x 45 cm (3 x 18 in)

Features Foliage.
Season of interest All year round.
Likes good indirect light and warm temperature.
Pot on annually in loam-based compost.
Propagate from seed or by air-layering.

Special information Dry air and draughts cause leaf browning. Cut off flower spikes.

Erica 'Hyemalis'
Cape Heath
30 x 23 cm (12 x 9 in)

Features Flowers.
Season of interest Winter.
Likes direct sun, cool temperature, and high humidity.
Pot on Cut back and repot annually after flowering in soilless compost.
Propagate from cuttings.
Special information Stand outside in summer.

Euphorbia pulcherrima
Poinsettia
1 x 1 m (3 x 3 ft)

Features Bracts.
Season of interest Winter/spring.
Likes good indirect light or direct sun, and warm temperature.
Pot on Cut back annually after flowering and repot in loam-based or soilless compost.
Propagate from cuttings.

Special information Long nights induce bract formation.

---

x *Fatshedera lizei*
Ivy Tree
2 x 1 m (6 x 3 ft)

Features Foliage.
Season of interest All year round.
Likes good indirect light or semi-shade, and cool temperature.
Pot on annually in loam-based or soilless compost.
Propagate from cuttings.
Special information Needs a moss-covered stick or frame to climb up.

Fatsia japonica
False Castor Oil Palm
1 x 1 m (3 x 3 ft)

Features Foliage.
Season of interest All year round.
Likes good indirect light or semi-shade, and cool temperature.
Pot on annually in loam-based or soilless compost.
Propagate from seed or cuttings.

Ficus benjamina
Weeping Fig
2 x 1 m (6 x 3 ft)

Features Foliage.
Season of interest All year round.
Likes good indirect light, warm temperature, and high humidity.
Pot on every two years in loam-based compost.
Propagate from cuttings.
Special information A few leaves yellow and fall when first bought.

Ficus elastica varieties
Rubber Plant
3 x 1 m (10 x 3 ft) plus

Features Foliage.
Season of interest All year round.

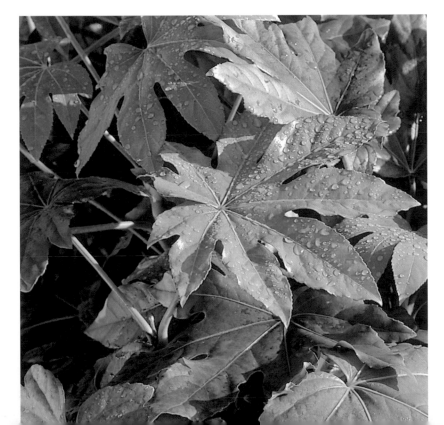

Fatsia japonica is a popular and easy-to-grow house plant, which can also be grown outdoors.

Likes good indirect light, cool to warm temperature, and fairly high humidity.
Pot on every two to three years in loam-based compost.
Propagate from leaf cuttings.
Special information Easy to overwater. Tolerant of dryness.

Ficus pumila
Creeping Fig

5 x 50 cm (2 x 20 in)

Features Foliage.
Season of interest All year round.
Likes semi-shade, warm temperature, and high humidity.
Pot on annually in soilless compost.
Propagate by cuttings.
Special information A good choice for planting in bottle gardens and suspended pots.

Fuchsia hybrids
Fuchsia

60 x 60 cm (2 x 2 ft) plus

Features Flowers.
Season of interest Summer.
Likes direct sun and cool temperature.
Pot on Cut back and repot in spring in loam-based compost.
Propagate by cuttings.
Special information Don't move in flower or buds drop. With young plants, pinch out stem tips to promote bushy growth.

Hedera helix varieties
Ivy

Climber/trailer

Features Foliage.
Season of interest All year round.
Likes good indirect light or direct sun, cool temperature, and high humidity.
Pot on annually in loam-based or soilless compost.
Propagate from cuttings.
Pests and diseases Dry air brings red spider.
Special information Shade causes loss of variegation.

Hippeastrum hybrids
Amaryllis

60 x 30 cm (2 ft x 12 in)

Features Flowers.
Season of interest Winter/spring.
Likes good indirect light or direct sun, and warm temperature.
Pot on in autumn in loam-based or soilless compost and water gingerly at first.
Propagate from seed.
Special information Dry off after flowering.

Howea belmoreana
Kentia Palm

2 x 1 m (6 x 3 ft)

Features Foliage.
Season of interest All year round.
Likes good indirect light or semi-shade, warm temperature, and high humidity.
Pot on every two or three years in loam-based or soilless compost.
Propagate from seed.
Special information Leaves turn brown in dry air or draughts.

Howea forsteriana
Kentia Palm

2 x 1 m (6 x 3 ft)

Features Foliage.
Season of interest All year round.
Likes good indirect light or semi-shade, warm temperature, and high humidity.
Pot on every two or three years in loam-based or soilless compost.
Propagate from seed.
Special information Leaves not as curly as previous species. Equally sensitive.

Hoya carnosa
Wax Plant

Climber

Features Foliage/flowers
Season of interest Spring/autumn.
Likes direct sun, warm temperature,

and high humidity. Be careful not to overwater.
Pot on every two or three years in loam-based compost.
Propagate from cuttings or by layering.
Special information Needs a support system around which to twine itself. Leave on old flower stalks – they bloom again.

Impatiens hybrids
Busy Lizzie, Balsam

60 x 60 cm (2 x 2 ft)

Features Flowers.
Season of interest All year round.
Likes direct sun, and cool to warm temperature.
Pot on Cut back and repot in spring in loam-based or soilless compost.
Propagate from cuttings taken in late spring or early summer.
Special information Plenty of food needed. When they become straggly, cut back hard.

Justicia brandegeeana
Shrimp Plant

60 x 60 cm (2 x 2 ft)

Features Flowers.
Season of interest All year round.
Likes direct sun, cool to warm temperature, and high humidity.
Pot on Cut back and repot in loam-based or soilless compost each spring.
Propagate by cuttings.

Maranta species
Prayer Plant

15 x 30 cm (6 x 12 in)

Features Foliage.
Season of interest All year round.
Likes semi-shade, warm temperature, and high humidity. Hates soggy compost.
Pot on every two years in soilless compost.
Propagate by division or cuttings.
Special information Good in bottle gardens.

Find the right spot for your house plant

All too often the house plant comes as a present, which means that you're stuck with it whether it likes your conditions or not. You'll have to do your best to find it a suitable spot. If you're buying a plant, make sure you know exactly what it likes, dislikes and tolerates, and what it is supposed to do. The following plants are suitable for the conditions indicated.

PLANTS FOR CENTRALLY HEATED ROOMS
- *Aechmea*
- *Aphelandra*
- *Begonia*
- *Codiaeum*
- *Dieffenbachia*
- *Dracaena*
- *Euphorbia*
- *Ficus*
- *Howea*
- *Monstera*
- *Peperomia*
- *Philodendron*
- *Pilea*
- *Rhoicissus*
- *Saintpaulia*
- *Sansevieria*
- *Schefflera*
- *Sinningia*
- *Stephanotis*
- *Yucca*

PLANTS FOR UNHEATED ROOMS
- *Calceolaria*
- *Cordyline*
- *Cyclamen*
- *Dendranthema*
- *Erica*
- *Fatshedera*
- *Fatsia*
- *Hedera*
- *Primula*
- *Rhododendron*
- *Saxifraga*
- *Senecio*

PLANTS FOR WARM HUMID BATHROOMS
- *Adiantum*
- *Aechmea*
- *Aphelandra*
- *Asparagus*
- *Asplenium*
- *Begonia*
- *Cyperus*
- *Dieffenbachia*
- *Dionaea*
- *Maranta*
- *Nephrolepis*
- *Peperomia*
- *Pilea*
- *Platycerium*
- *Saintpaulia*
- *Tradescantia*

Monstera deliciosa
Swiss Cheese Plant
2 x 2 m (6 x 6 ft) plus

Features Foliage. Only leaves of older, well-fed plants are perforated.
Season of interest All year round.
Likes good indirect light or semi-shade, warmth, and high humidity.
Pot on every two years in loam-based or soilless compost.
Propagate from cuttings or by air-layering.
Special information Tuck any aerial roots into the compost, where they can take up nutrients.

Nephrolepis exaltata
Ladder Fern
60 x 60 cm (2 x 2 ft)

Features Foliage.
Season of interest All year round.
Likes good indirect light or semi-shade, warmth, and high humidity.
Pot on every one or two years in soilless compost.
Propagate by division.
Special information Dry air and draughts cause leaf browning.

Nephrolepis exaltata 'Bostoniensis'
Boston Fern
60 cm x 1 m (2 x 3 ft)

Features Foliage.
Season of interest All year round.
Likes good indirect light or semi-shade, warm temperature, and high humidity.
Pot on every one or two years in soilless compost.
Propagate by division.
Special information As above. This variety is good in hanging baskets provided it can be kept moist. It will turn brown if allowed to dry out.

Pelargonium hybrids
Geranium
60 x 30 cm (2 ft x 12 in)

Features Flowers.
Season of interest Spring/autumn.
Likes some sun and cool temperature.
Pot on annually in loam-based or soilless compost.
Propagate from cuttings and seed.
Special information Bright light is vital. Leaves yellow in shade. Singles bloom in winter.

Peperomia species
Peperomia
15 x 15 cm (6 x 6 in)

Features Foliage/flowers.
Season of interest All year round.
Likes good indirect light or semi-shade, warm temperature, and high humidity. Hates soggy compost: allow to dry out before watering.
Pot on every one or two years in loam-based compost.
Propagate from leaf cuttings.
Special information Good in bottle gardens.

Pericallis hybrids
Florist's Cineraria
30 x 30 cm (12 x 12 in)

Features Flowers.
Season of interest Winter/spring.
Likes direct sun and very cool temperature.
Propagate from seed in loam-based compost.
Pests and diseases Sadly, they are loved by greenfly.
Special information Easily overwatered. Discard after flowering.

Philodendron scandens
Sweetheart Plant
Climber

Features Foliage.
Season of interest All year round.
Likes good indirect light or semi-shade, and cool to warm temperature.

Pot on every one or two years in a soilless compost.
Propagate from cuttings.
Special information Needs a large support system such as a moss-covered pole. Thrives on neglect.

Pilea cadierei
Aluminium Plant
15 x 23 cm (6 x 9 in)

Features Foliage. Good in bottle gardens.
Season of interest All year round.
Likes good indirect light or semi-shade, warm temperature, and high humidity.
Pot on annually in loam-based compost.
Propagate Renew regularly from cuttings.

Platycerium bifurcatum
Stag's Horn Fern
45 x 45 cm (18 x 18 in)

Features Foliage.
Season of interest All year round.
Likes semi-shade, warm temperature, and high humidity.
Pot on every one or two years in soilless compost.
Special information Can grow in a wad of moss wired to a piece of cork bark.

Primula obconica
German Primrose
30 x 30 cm (12 x 12 in)

Features Flowers.
Season of interest All year round.
Likes direct sun and cool temperature.
Pot on annually in a loam-based or soilless compost.
Propagate from seed or by division.
Special information Can cause a rash on sensitive skin.

Rhododendron simsii
Azalea
30 x 45 cm (12 x 18 in)

Features Flowers.

Season of interest Winter.
Likes some direct sun, very cool temperature, and high humidity.
Pot on annually in soilless compost.
Propagate from cuttings.
Special information Never let the rootball dry out. Water with rainwater.

Saintpaulia hybrids
African Violet
10 x 30 cm (4 x 12 in)

Features Flowers.
Season of interest Spring/autumn.
Likes direct sun, warm temperature, and high humidity.
Pot on every one or two years in soilless compost. Don't overpot.
Propagate from leaf cuttings.
Special information Dilute tomato fertilizer encourages flowering.

Sansevieria trifasciata 'Laurentii'
Mother-in-law's Tongue
1 m x 30 cm (3 ft x 12 in)

Features Foliage.
Season of interest All year round.
Likes sun, indirect light, or semi-shade, and cool to warm temperature.
Pot on every three or four years in loam-based compost.
Propagate by division.
Special information Almost indestructible, but do not overwater.

Saxifraga stolonifera varieties
Mother-of-thousands
Trailing

Features Foliage.
Season of interest All year round.
Likes good indirect light or direct sun, cool temperature, and high humidity.
Pot on in loam-based compost.
Propagate from plantlets.
Special information Good in hanging baskets.

Schefflera arboricola
Heptapleurum, Umbrella Tree
2 m x 45 cm (6 ft x 18 in) plus

Features Foliage.
Season of interest All year round.
Likes good indirect light, warm temperature, and high humidity.
Pot on every two years in loam-based or soilless compost.
Propagate from seed.
Special information Variegated kind needs good light.

Schefflera elegantissima
Finger Aralia
2 m x 60 cm (6 x 2 ft)

Features Foliage.
Season of interest All year round.
Likes semi-shade, warm temperature, and high humidity.

Plants for hanging pots and baskets

Trailing plants look particularly good when planted in suspended pots so that their stems can cascade into the air. Plant in soilless compost rather than the heavier soil-based types, and make sure that the pot or basket is securely fastened to the wall or ceiling. Built-in drip trays will prevent damage to furniture.

Plants in suspended pots and baskets tend to dry out more quickly than most pot plants, so check them regularly. They'll also go a bundle on extra humidity: spray them daily with tepid rainwater – but watch the furniture!

If you're short of inspiration when it comes to choosing plants try:
- *Asparagus*
- *Chlorophytum*
- *Fuchsia*
- *Hedera*
- *Hoya*
- *Nephrolepis*
- *Philodendron scandens*
- *Saxifraga*
- *Schlumbergera*
- *Tradescantia*

Pilea cadierei is an attractive foliage plant, with its distinctive silvery patterned quilted leaves.

Pot on every two years in soilless compost.
Propagate from seed.
Special information Draughts, dry air, wet or dry compost cause leaf fall.

Schlumbergera varieties
Christmas Cactus
Trailing

Features Flowers. Superb in hanging baskets.
Season of interest Winter.
Likes good indirect light, cool temperature, and high humidity.
Pot on every one or two years in loam-based compost.
Propagate from cuttings.
Special information Stand outside in summer.

Sinningia varieties
Gloxinia
23 x 30 cm (9 x 12 in)

Features Flowers.
Season of interest Summer.
Likes direct sun, warm temperature, and high humidity.

Pot on Repot tubers in spring in soilless compost.
Propagate from seed or tuber.
Special information Dry off after flowering.

Solanum capsicastrum
Winter Cherry
30 x 30 cm (12 x 12 in)

Features Fruits.
Season of interest Winter.
Likes direct sun, cool temperature, and high humidity.
Pot on Cut back and repot annually after fruiting in loam-based compost.
Propagate from seed or cuttings.
Special information A teaspoon of Epsom salts in half a litre (one pint) of water prevents leaf yellowing.

Solenostemon
Coleus, Flame Nettle
60 x 60 cm (2 x 2 ft)

Features Foliage.
Season of interest All year round.
Likes direct sun and warm temperature.
Pot on Chop back and repot in spring.
Propagate by cuttings.
Special information Tatty if light is poor in winter.

Stephanotis floribunda
Clustered Wax Flower
1 x 1 m (3 x 3 ft)

Features Flowers.
Season of interest Spring/autumn.
Likes good indirect light and warm temperature.
Pot on every two years in loam-based or soilless compost.
Propagate from cuttings.
Pests and diseases Watch out for mealy bug.
Special information Train over a support system.

Tradescantia species
Wandering Jew
Trailing

Features Foliage.
Season of interest All year round.
Likes direct sun and cool temperature.
Pot on annually in soilless compost.
Propagate Replace regularly from stem cuttings: very easy to take.
Special information Feed well.

Tradescantia zebrina
Inch Plant
Trailing

Features Foliage.
Season of interest All year round.
Likes direct sun, and cool or warm temperature. Allow surface to dry out between waterings.
Pot on annually in soilless compost.
Propagate Replace from cuttings.

Yucca aloifolia
Spanish Bayonet, Ti Tree
2 m x 60 cm (6 x 2 ft)

Features Foliage.
Season of interest All year round.
Likes direct sun, and cool to warm temperature.
Pot on every two years in loam-based compost.
Propagate from cuttings.
Special information Stand outdoors in summer. Peel off faded leaves.

part VI

PESTS, DISEASES AND DISORDERS

Give your plants the conditions
they require and problems are less
likely to arise, but when they do,
tackle them without delay

Healthy, well-tended plants, like the inhabitants of this cottage
garden in Devon, are less likely to be attacked by pests and
diseases than malnourished weaklings.

The last thing I want to do is turn you into a hypochondriac, but sooner or later your plants will be attacked by a beast or blight, and it's as well to know just how you can nurse them back to health.

METHODS OF CONTROL

Like many people, I now use no chemical spray in my own garden because I value the balance of nature that exists there – the masses of birds, insects and animals (from deer to voles) – and I'd rather not upset them. I also find that plants supplied with plenty of soil enrichment in the form of garden compost, well-rotted manure and organic fertilizer do seem to resist epidemics. My garden has not become a haven for pests and diseases because all the plants are mixed up and an epidemic cannot find sufficient concentration of any one thing to sustain it. I still get a few blighters, but I generally leave them to their own devises, and I positively enjoy seeing the mullein moth eating my verbascums and Solomon's seal sawfly munching my polygonatums. However, you may not feel the same way.

Making the most of nature

As well as growing a good mix of plants to prevent the build-up of pests and diseases, get the local wildlife on your side. Birds do a terrific job of clearing up all sorts of pests, so make them at home in your garden by providing nest boxes and putting out food in winter. Slugs are high on the menu for frogs, and even the smallest pond can support a surprisingly high population. Hedgehogs are valuable slug and snail crunchers and a pile of twigs and leaves in a quiet corner makes an inviting nesting site.

> "Healthy, well-grown plants are more resistant to attacks than feeble weaklings."

Less entertaining, but no less useful, are horticultural fleece and biological controls. Fleece presents an impenetrable barrier for pests of all sizes, and can be supported on canes or simply draped over the crop, with the edges secured against low-fliers like carrot root fly. Biological controls are invaluable in both the garden and the greenhouse, clearing up difficult pests like whitefly, mealy bugs and vine weevil. Not cheap – but worth it.

Bear in mind at all times that healthy, well-grown plants are more resistant to attacks than feeble weaklings, and some varieties have been bred for their resistance to particular diseases: these are always worth buying.

Biological pest control

Slugs Parasitic nematode *Phasmarhabditis* watered in. Kills quickly and lasts 6 weeks if soil kept moist.

Aphids (greenfly) Parasitic midge *Aphidius* or predatory midge *Aphidioletes*. For greenhouses and conservatories.

Whitefly Tiny non-stinging wasp *Encarsia* lays parasitic eggs. Ladybird relative plain *Delphastus* feeds on all stages. Greenhouse and conservatory.

Caterpillars Bacterial disease *Bacillus thuringiensis*, as contact spray. Completely safe for wildlife, pets and humans, crops safe to eat.

Vine weevil Parasitic nematode *Heterorhabditis*, watered in. For pots, baskets and open ground. Also controls chafer grubs in lawns.

Leatherjackets Parasitic nematode *Steinermena* as a lawn drench.

Chafer grubs: See Vine weevil above.

Thrips: Predatory mite *Amblyseius*. For greenhouse, conservatory, garden.

Mealy bug Predatory adults and young of *Cryptolaemus*, Australian ladybird with a voracious appetite. For greenhouses and conservatories.

Red spider mite Predatory mite *Phytoseiulus* in greenhouse and conservatory.

Sciarid fly Predatory mite *Hypoaspis* applied to soil surface. For soil and compost in greenhouses and conservatories.

* Timing and temperature can be critical for success with biological controls, so always check these with your supplier. Similarly, if you have been using insecticides, check whether this affects the timing of the release of the chosen control.

GETTING INTO GOOD HABITS

Buy disease-free plants

Buy plants from a reputable supplier and, with fruit bushes, try to buy stock that is certified disease-free. Viruses are crippling, crop-reducing diseases that are transmitted by aphids, and you'd do well to make sure that the bushes you buy are not infected with them. There's no cure once the plants are under attack.

Practise crop rotation

Crop rotation is a cultivation technique that farmers have practised down the ages – and with good reason. Even in the garden it's risky to grow one type of plant in the same spot year after year so, with the exception of trees and shrubs, aim to rotate your plantings.

Correct cultivation techniques

Some plant problems are caused neither by pests nor diseases: they are caused by you, or by the faulty growing conditions you have provided for the plant. These are known as disorders and can usually be put right if your cultivation techniques are adjusted.

Identifying plant problems

When troubles do strike, correct identification is vital so that you can tackle the problem without delay – prompt, appropriate action will prevent a minor problem from turning into a major long-term headache. Use this illustration to help you identify the problem, then turn to the relevant A–Z entry for advice on treatment.

A-Z of pests, diseases and disorders

EVERY YEAR, IN THE INTERESTS of safety and the environment fewer and fewer chemicals are made available to amateur gardeners, but there are more and more organic and biological controls; your local garden centre will be able to offer advice on the best chemicals, or organic alternatives, to use. Biological controls can be very effective, particularly in enclosed spaces such as greenhouses. Make sure what you intend to use is safe on edible crops.

Note: Organic insecticides are sold under a variety of trade names such as Bio Organic Pest Control. The active ingredient (eg. plant oils, natural fatty acids) is always clearly marked.

VEGETABLES

PESTS

Aphid (greenfly, blackfly)
CROPS ATTACKED **Wide range**

Damage/symptoms Small insects suck sap, weaken plant, transmit viruses, secrete honeydew.
Control Squash where feasible or spray with organic insecticide.

Beet leaf miner
CROPS ATTACKED **Beetroot**

Damage/symptoms Yellow or brown tunnels and blisters on leaves.
Control Pick off affected leaves. Dig ground thoroughly in winter.

Birds (sparrow, pigeon)
CROPS ATTACKED **Wide range**

Damage/symptoms The leaves, pods and flowers are torn.
Control Netting is the only reliable long-term control.

Cabbage root fly
CROPS ATTACKED **Brassicas**

Damage/symptoms Leaves wilt and turn blue; white maggots eat roots.
Control Place black felt 'collars' around plants to prevent egg laying.

Cabbage whitefly
CROPS ATTACKED **Brassicas**

Damage/symptoms Small, white, V-shaped flies suck sap and soil leaves.
Control Spray with organic insecticide. Remove badly infested leaves.

Carrot fly
CROPS ATTACKED **Carrot, parsnip**

Damage/symptoms Leaves turn reddish and wilt; roots tunnelled by grubs.
Control Avoid by not thinning the crop. Protect with horticultural fleece.

Caterpillar
CROPS ATTACKED **Wide range, especially brassicas**

Damage/symptoms Leaves eaten; caterpillars or green droppings visible.
Control Pick off or spray severe infestations with biological control *Bacillus thuringiensis*.

Celery fly
CROPS ATTACKED **Celery**

Damage/symptoms Leaves tunnelled and blistered by maggots.
Control Crush larvae in tunnels.

Eelworm
CROPS ATTACKED **Onion**

Damage/symptoms Leaves distorted and bloated; bulbs soft and deformed.
Control Destroy crops. Prevent by rotation. Keep onions, beans, parsnips and carrots off site for three years.

Eelworm (Root-knot)
CROPS ATTACKED **Tomato**

Damage/symptoms Lower leaves yellow and wilting; galls on roots.
Control Destroy plants. Replace border soil or grow in containers.

Flea beetle
CROPS ATTACKED
Radish and other seedlings

Damage/symptoms Tiny spots and holes in leaves.
Control Grow under fleece. Rotate crops. Hoe in winter to expose.

Frit fly
CROPS ATTACKED **Sweet corn**

Damage/symptoms Young plants twisted and distorted; leaves ragged.
Control Sow seed in pots indoors. Keep well watered after planting.

Gall weevil
CROPS ATTACKED
Brassicas, swede and turnip

Damage/symptoms Roots swollen and pierced by maggots; plants stunted.
Control Destroy affected roots. Dig ground thoroughly.

Leek moth
CROPS ATTACKED **Onion, leek**

Damage/symptoms Leaves tunnelled.

Control Crush caterpillars and cocoons on leaves. Clear bed of debris in winter.

Mealy cabbage aphid

CROPS ATTACKED **Brassicas**

Damage/symptoms Leaves turn yellow; grey-coloured insects on undersides.
Control Spray with organic insecticide as soon as seen.

Onion fly

CROPS ATTACKED **Onion**

Damage/symptoms Leaves wilt and turn yellowish; grubs eating roots.
Control Prevent by crop rotation. Grow from sets. Grow under horticultural fleece.

Pea and bean weevil

CROPS ATTACKED **Pea, broad bean**

Damage/symptoms Leaf edges scalloped by chewing action of small, brown weevils.
Control Encourage strong, rapid growth. Clear plant debris in winter.

Pea moth

CROPS ATTACKED **Pea**

Damage/symptoms Peas within pod found to be maggoty.
Control Sow in February or wait until May onwards.

Pea thrips

CROPS ATTACKED **Pea**

Damage/symptoms Pods blotched and spotted silvery grey.
Control Spray with organic pesticide based on plant oils.

Potato cyst eelworm

CROPS ATTACKED **Potato**

Damage/symptoms Plants stunted; lower leaves brown and shrivelled; tiny nodules but few potatoes on roots.

Control Grow resistant varieties. Do not replant infected soil with spuds for eight years.

Red spider mites

CROPS ATTACKED
French and runner bean

Damage/symptoms Leaves greyish or yellow; fine webs and tiny mites seen.
Control If severe, spray with insecticide containing natural fatty acids.

Root aphid

CROPS ATTACKED **Lettuce**

Damage/symptoms Stunted, wilting, yellow leaves; insects on roots.
Control Grow resistant varieties such as 'Iceberg'.

Slugs and snails

CROPS ATTACKED **Wide range**

Damage/symptoms Leaves and stems eaten; silvery trails visible.
Control Sink yogurt carton into soil and fill up with beer to trap. Surround susceptible plants with sharp grit. Use biological control.

Tomato moth

CROPS ATTACKED **Tomato**

Damage/symptoms Leaves and fruits eaten by fat caterpillars.
Control Prevent by weeding. Hand pick or spray with biological control *Bacillus thuringiesis*.

Wireworm

CROPS ATTACKED **Potato**

Damage/symptoms Narrow tunnels appear in tubers.
Control Earth up regularly. Control weeds. Harvest tubers quickly.

DISEASES

Anthracnose

CROPS ATTACKED
French and runner bean

Damage/symptoms Leaves, stems

and pods blotched brown.
Control Burn all infected plants. Buy seeds from a reputable source.

Blackleg

CROPS ATTACKED **Potato**

Damage/symptoms Stem bases black; leaves yellow and wilting.
Control Dig up and destroy. Store only healthy tubers.

Black rot

CROPS ATTACKED **Turnip, swede**

Damage/symptoms Leaf edges yellow; black veins; sliced root black around perimeter.
Control Destroy infected plants. Improve drainage and rotate crops.

Buckeye rot

CROPS ATTACKED **Tomato**

Damage/symptoms Grey or reddish areas on fruit, overlaid with brown concentric rings.
Control Pick off and destroy. Keep trusses away from soil.

Canker

CROPS ATTACKED **Parsnip**

Damage/symptoms Upper areas of root turn soft and brown.
Control Sow resistant varieties. Avoid over-manuring. Lime acid soils. Rotate crops.

Chocolate spot

CROPS ATTACKED **Broad bean**

Damage/symptoms Leaves blotched with brown; leaves may die.
Control Caused by too much nitrogen.

Clubroot

CROPS ATTACKED **Brassicas**

Damage/symptoms Plants stunted and weak. Roots swollen and foul-smelling.

Control Lime acid soil. Improve drainage. On infected land, grow in trenches of sterile compost.

Crown rot

CROPS ATTACKED **Rhubarb**

Damage/symptoms Buds and centre of plant brown and rotten.
Control Dig up and burn. Improve drainage. Don't replant rhubarb on infected soil.

Downy mildew

CROPS ATTACKED **Brassicas, lettuce, spinach, onion, pea, beetroot**

Damage/symptoms Leaves yellow above, whitish or purplish felted below.
Control Do not overcrowd plants. Rotate crops. Grow resistant varieties.

Dry rot

CROPS ATTACKED **Potato**

Damage/symptoms Stored tubers wrinkle at one end; white or pink fungus visible.
Control Prevent by lifting and storing tubers carefully. Destroy those that are infected.

Foot rot

CROPS ATTACKED
French bean, pea, runner bean

Damage/symptoms Leaves yellow; stem bases black and rotten.
Control Prevent by rotating crops.

Gangrene

CROPS ATTACKED **Potato**

Damage/symptoms Stored tubers develop sunken brown areas and rot.
Control Prevent by storing healthy tubers in ideal conditions.

Ghost spot

CROPS ATTACKED **Tomato**

Damage/symptoms Fruits develop white, circular spots centred with brown.
Control Caused by grey mould,

which thrives in damp conditions and poor air circulation. Prevent by ventilating well and watering carefully.

Grey mould

CROPS ATTACKED **Wide range**

Damage/symptoms Brown, rotting areas are covered with grey fur.
Control Prevent as for Ghost Spot. Pull off affected leaves.

Halo blight

CROPS ATTACKED
French and runner bean

Damage/symptoms Brown, yellow-edged blotches on leaves; soggy blotches on pods.
Control Buy seeds from a reputable supplier. Destroy infected plants.

Heart rot

CROPS ATTACKED **Celery**

Damage/symptoms Centre of plant brown and rotten.
Control Avoid damaging plants or applying too much nitrogen. Practise crop rotation.

Honey fungus

CROPS ATTACKED **Rhubarb**

Damage/symptoms Plant dies; white fungus found on roots; black 'bootlaces' may be in soil.
Control Dig up and burn. Replant new crowns on uninfected soil.

Leaf mould

CROPS ATTACKED **Tomato**

Damage/symptoms Leaves yellowish above; purplish mould visible below.
Control Destroy affected leaves. Destroy badly affected plants. Ventilate well.

Leaf spot

CROPS ATTACKED
Rhubarb, spinach, celery

Damage/symptoms Leaves spotted

with brown – centres of spots fall out. Spots on celery develop black 'pinheads.'
Control Pull off badly affected leaves.

Leek rust

CROPS ATTACKED **Leek and occasionally onion**

Damage/symptoms Leaves spotted with orange.
Control Destroy infected foliage. Practise crop rotation.

Neck rot

CROPS ATTACKED **Onion**

Damage/symptoms Stored bulbs become mouldy on upper surface.
Control Prevent by storing ripe, well-dried onions.

Potato blight

CROPS ATTACKED **Potato, tomato**

Damage/symptoms Leaves curled inwards and blotched brown. White mould on undersides. Tomato leaves brown at tips.
Control Grow resistant potato varieties.

Powdery mildew

CROPS ATTACKED **Wide range**

Damage/symptoms White powdery deposit, on leaves, shoots and pods.
Control Dust with sulphur. Sow resistant varieties. Space adequately. Improve light soils.

Powdery scab

CROPS ATTACKED **Potato**

Damage/symptoms Circular, dark brown scabs with raised edges found on tubers.
Control Destroy infected tubers. Prevent by ensuring good drainage and practising crop rotation. Plant resistant cultivars.

Rust
CROPS ATTACKED **Broad bean**

Damage/symptoms Raised orange spots on undersides of leaves.
Control Rarely crippling. Pick off affected leaves. Provide good growing conditions.

Scab
CROPS ATTACKED **Potato**

Damage/symptoms Tubers marred by rough brown scabs.
Control Prevent by avoiding over-liming. Grow resistant varieties. Infected tubers still edible.

Shanking
CROPS ATTACKED **Onion**

Damage/symptoms Central leaves turn yellow and wilt. Bulbs foul-smelling when sliced.
Control Destroy infected plants. Prevent by practising crop rotation.

Smut
CROPS ATTACKED **Onion, sweetcorn**

Damage/symptoms On onion, leaves and bulbs spotted with black; on sweetcorn, white outgrowths on cobs and stems.
Control Destroy infected plants. Keep onions off infected ground for eight years.

Soft rot
CROPS ATTACKED **Carrot, swede, turnip**

Damage/symptoms Stored or growing roots brown and rotten in centre.
Control Destroy infected roots. Prevent by ensuring good drainage and avoiding over-manuring.

Spinach blight
CROPS ATTACKED **Spinach**

Damage/symptoms Leaves roll inwards and turn yellowish.

Control Destroy infected plants. Control aphids, which transmit viruses.

Spraing
CROPS ATTACKED **Potato**

Damage/symptoms Tubers marked with red semi-circles when cut open.
Control A virus disease. Prevent by rotating crops and planting certified potatoes. Infected roots still edible.

Stem rot (*Didymella*)
CROPS ATTACKED **Tomato**

Damage/symptoms Black areas on stem bases; fruits may become brown.
Control Dig up and burn. Grow in sterile soil or rotate crop.

Verticillium wilt
CROPS ATTACKED **Tomato**

Damage/symptoms Lower leaves yellow; plant wilts in sun.
Control Try topdressing plants. Grow in sterile soil. Avoid early planting.

Violet root rot
CROPS ATTACKED **Carrot**

Damage/symptoms Roots felted with purple mould.
Control Destroy infected roots. Practise rotation. Keep carrots off infected ground for four years.

Virus
CROPS ATTACKED **Wide range**

Damage/symptoms Leaves puckered, distorted and mottled with yellow.
Control Destroy infected plants. Keep down aphids, which transmit the diseases.

Wart disease
CROPS ATTACKED **Potato**

Damage/symptoms Black, warty outgrowths on tubers of old varieties.

Control Department of the Environment, Food and Rural Affairs must be informed. Destroy infected tubers.

DISORDERS

Blossom end rot
CROPS ATTACKED **Tomato**

Damage/symptoms Black, sunken areas on undersides of fruits.
Control Caused by erratic watering. Aim to keep compost evenly moist.

Blotchy ripening
CROPS ATTACKED **Tomato**

Damage/symptoms Fruits ripen unevenly.
Control Ventilate and shade well. Ensure adequate supplies of food and water.

Bolting
CROPS ATTACKED **Wide range**

Damage/symptoms Plants form flowers and 'run to seed' prematurely.
Control Prevent dryness at the roots. Do not transplant large plants.

Brown heart
CROPS ATTACKED **Turnip, swede**

Damage/symptoms When sliced open, roots reveal brown centre.
Control Caused by boron deficiency. Apply fertilizer before sowing.

Fanging
CROPS ATTACKED
Carrot, parsnip, beetroot

Damage/symptoms Roots forked and distorted.
Control Caused by stony or over-manured soil.

Greenback
CROPS ATTACKED **Tomato**

Damage/symptoms Upper part of fruit remains green.
Control Shade from bright sun. Feed

well. Do not defoliate. Plant resistant varieties.

Green tubers

CROPS ATTACKED **Potato**

Damage/symptoms Tubers green both outside and inside.
Control Caused by sunlight. Earth up tubers adequately.

Hearts (lack of)

CROPS ATTACKED **Cabbage**

Damage/symptoms Plants remain leafy and open – no solid heart formed.
Control Plant in firm, well-manured soil that does not dry out.

Hollow heart

CROPS ATTACKED **Potato**

Damage/symptoms Tubers undamaged outside but hollow inside.
Control Caused by heavy rain or irrigation after drought.

Root split

CROPS ATTACKED **Carrot**

Damage/symptoms Roots split lengthways.
Control Caused by irrigation or heavy rain after drought. Keep evenly moist.

Scald

CROPS ATTACKED **Tomato**

Damage/symptoms Sunken, straw-coloured patches on fruits or leaves.
Control Shade from bright sunshine.

Split fruit

CROPS ATTACKED **Tomato**

Damage/symptoms Fruits split open when ripe.
Control Caused by heavy watering after dryness. Keep evenly moist.

Tip burn

CROPS ATTACKED **Lettuce**

Damage/symptoms Leaf edges

marked with brown.
Control Caused by dryness at roots.

Weedkiller damage

CROPS ATTACKED **Tomato**

Damage/symptoms Leaves narrow and distorted; stems twisted; fruits oval and hollow.
Control Keep all weedkillers away from tomatoes and use a separate watering can.

Whiptail

CROPS ATTACKED **Brassicas**

Damage/symptoms Leaves reduced to just the midrib. No pest damage.
Control Caused by a shortage of molybdenum. Increase its availability by liming acid soil to raise alkalinity.

FRUIT

PESTS

Aphid

CROPS ATTACKED **Wide range**

Damage/symptoms Sap sucked; plant weakened; viruses transmitted; honeydew secreted.
Control Attract winter predators like bluetits. Spray off with a hosepipe.

Apple sawfly

CROPS ATTACKED **Apple**

Damage/symptoms Fruitlets fall; tunnels visible. Remaining fruits possess ribbon-like scars.
Control Bin or burn fallen fruits. Cultivate soil in autumn to expose larvae.

Apple sucker

CROPS ATTACKED **Apple**

Damage/symptoms Flowers turn brown; green, aphid-like insects observed among them.
Control Attract winter predators such as blue tits. Spring-flowering plants attract insect predators.

Big bud mite

CROPS ATTACKED **Blackcurrant**

Damage/symptoms Dormant buds fat and spherical.
Control Prune out and burn infected shoots. If severe, destroy plants. Replant on new site.

Birds (sparrow, bullfinch, pigeon)

CROPS ATTACKED **Wide range**

Damage/symptoms Fruits pecked or wholly eaten.
Control Invest in a fruit cage or drape ripening crops with horticultural fleece.

Blossom weevil

CROPS ATTACKED **Strawberry**

Damage/symptoms Unopened flowers wither and turn brown; stalks eaten through.
Control Pick off and burn any infected flowers.

Brown scale

CROPS ATTACKED **Peach, grape and gooseberry**

Damage/symptoms Stems covered with small, brown, limpet-like scales.
Control Brush or wipe off. Spray adults and crawlers with insecticide based on natural fatty acids.

Capsid bug

CROPS ATTACKED **Wide range**

Damage/symptoms Tiny brown holes in leaves; raised brown areas on fruits.
Control Elusive. Gardens with a good mix of plants attract predators.

Caterpillar

CROPS ATTACKED **Wide range**

Damage/symptoms Leaves eaten; caterpillars or droppings visible.
Control Pick off or spray with biological control *Bacillus thuringiensis*.

Cherry fruit moth
CROPS ATTACKED **Cherry**

Damage/symptoms Green caterpillars eat buds, flowers and green fruits.
Control Attract winter predators such as blue tits.

Codling moth
CROPS ATTACKED **Apple, pear**

Damage/symptoms Holes tunnelled in ripe fruits; fruits are maggoty.
Control Hang codling moth traps from May to July.

Currant blister aphid
CROPS ATTACKED **Red/white currant**

Damage/symptoms Upper leaves twisted and blistered; often tinged red.
Control Attract winter predators like bluetits. Spray spring/early summer with organic insecticide.

Currant sawfly
CROPS ATTACKED **Currant**

Damage/symptoms Leaves eaten, and only veins left.
Control Pick or spray with liquid Derris.

Gooseberry sawfly
CROPS ATTACKED **Gooseberry**

Damage/symptoms Leaves eaten by larvae of sawflies, only veins left.
Control Be vigilant from April onwards. Pick off caterpillars as soon as seen.

Leaf and bud mite
CROPS ATTACKED **Raspberry**

Damage/symptoms Leaves blotched yellow on upper surface; no reduction in vigour or cropping.
Control None. Do not confuse with mosaic virus, which is accompanied by distortion and poor cropping.

Leaf midge
CROPS ATTACKED **Currant**

Damage/symptoms Shoot tips distorted and withered.
Control Spraying with organic insecticide before and after flowering may help.

Mealy bug
CROPS ATTACKED **Grape and occasionally other crops**

Damage/symptoms Small, white, mealy insects visible on stems; suck sap; secrete honeydew.
Control Brush down rods in winter. Introduce biological control *Cryptolaemus* in greenhouse/ conservatory.

Mussel scale
CROPS ATTACKED **Plum**

Damage/symptoms Tiny, mussel-shaped scales plastered on stems.
Control Brush off or wipe at first sign. Spray adult and crawlers with organic insecticide based on natural fatty acids

Pear leaf blister mite
CROPS ATTACKED
Pear and sometimes plum

Damage/symptoms Spots (pale green, then pink, then black) appear on leaves.
Control Pick off and burn infected leaves if possible. Keep tree well fed and watered.

Pear midge
CROPS ATTACKED **Pear**

Damage/symptoms Fruits fall when small. Small yellow maggots inside.
Control Destroy infected fruitlets. Fork under trees in summer to expose pupae.

Pear sucker
CROPS ATTACKED **Pear**

Damage/symptoms Flowers turn

brown; green, aphid-like insects visible.
Control Attract winter predators such as blue tits. Spring-flowering plants attract insect predators.

Plum sawfly
CROPS ATTACKED **Plum**

Damage/symptoms Fruitlets fall before they are fully developed, and are tunnelled.
Control Bin or burn fallen fruit. Cultivate soil in autumn to expose larvae.

Plum tortrix moth
CROPS ATTACKED **Plum**

Damage/symptoms Leaves bound with silken web; caterpillars inside.
Control Squash bound leaves, or pick off and destroy.

Rabbits/deer
CROPS ATTACKED **Wide range**

Damage/symptoms Leaves or bark gnawed away.
Control Difficult. Plastic tree guards help. Try suitable sonic scarer.

Raspberry beetle
CROPS ATTACKED **Raspberry**

Damage/symptoms Fruits eaten by small maggots.
Control None recommended.

Red spider mite
CROPS ATTACKED **Apple, plum, peach**

Damage/symptoms Leaves bleached and mottled; webs spun; tiny yellow, green or brown mites are visible.
Control If severe, spray with insecticide based on natural fatty acids.

Slugworm
CROPS ATTACKED **Pear, cherry**

Damage/symptoms Small, slimy,

black, slug-like creatures eating leaf surfaces.
Control Outbreaks are seldom serious and can usually be ignored.

Tortrix moth
CROPS ATTACKED **Apple**

Damage/symptoms Surface of fruit eaten; leaf stuck over damage; caterpillar may be seen.
Control Squash bound leaves, or pick off and destroy.

Wasp
CROPS ATTACKED **Wide range, especially plum**

Damage/symptoms Fruits eaten as they approach ripeness.
Control Tolerate. Where feasible protect ripening fruit with horticultural fleece or old net curtains.

Winter moth
CROPS ATTACKED **Apple, pear, plum, cherry**

Damage/symptoms Young leaves and open flowers eaten by small, green caterpillars.
Control Fasten glue or grease bands around base of trees from September to March.

Woolly aphid
CROPS ATTACKED **Wide range**

Damage/symptoms Stems covered in greyish white, wool-covered insects.
Control Brush off colonies or dislodge with jet from hose. Attract predators like blue tits

DISEASES

American gooseberry mildew
CROPS ATTACKED **Gooseberry, blackcurrant**

Damage/symptoms Leaves, shoots and fruits covered in white powder, which turns to light brown felt.

Control Prevent by pruning well. Don't use too much nitrogen. Mulch to retain moisture. Grow resistant varieties.

Bacterial canker
CROPS ATTACKED **Cherry, plum**

Damage/symptoms Gum oozes from flattened cankers on stem; leaves full of holes; tree weak.
Control Cut out and burn infected wood and treat wounds with special paint.

Blossom wilt
CROPS ATTACKED **Apple, pear, cherry, plum**

Damage/symptoms Flowers wilt and turn brown; leaves may die.
Control Cut out infected wood. Destroy any fruit infected with brown rot.

Botrytis (Grey mould)
CROPS ATTACKED **Raspberry, strawberry**

Damage/symptoms Fruits covered with fluffy grey mould.
Control Pick off infected fruits. Keep fruit bed clean and don't overwater.

Brown rot
CROPS ATTACKED **Apple, pear, plum, cherry**

Damage/symptoms Fruits develop soft brown areas on the skin, and concentric rings of buff pustules throughout the flesh.
Control Dispose of infected fruits (don't compost). Store only undamaged fruits.

Cane blight
CROPS ATTACKED **Raspberry**

Damage/symptoms Leaves wither; dark areas on canes at ground level; canes become brittle.
Control Cut out and burn infected

canes. Sterilize secateurs. Grow new plants on clean site.

Cane spot
CROPS ATTACKED **Raspberry**

Damage/symptoms Small purple spots on canes; eventually turn grey; fruits and leaves spotted later.
Control Cut out and burn infected canes.

Canker
CROPS ATTACKED **Apple, pear**

Damage/symptoms Shoots wounded and, in winter, filled with reddish fruiting bodies.
Control Prune out infected wood. Control woolly aphid.

Coral spot
CROPS ATTACKED **Wide range, especially currant**

Damage/symptoms Orange pustules appear on dead or dying stems.
Control Cut out infected wood.

Crown gall
CROPS ATTACKED **Blackberry, loganberry**

Damage/symptoms Swollen galls visible on stems at soil level or higher.
Control Cut out and burn. Replant on uninfected soil.

Fireblight
CROPS ATTACKED **Apple, pear, cherry and others**

Damage/symptoms Shoots wither and turn brown; leaves do not fall; wounds visible at stem bases.
Control Cut out damaged wood well back into healthy wood.

Honey fungus (*Armillaria*)
CROPS ATTACKED **Wide range**

Damage/symptoms Trees die back; honey-coloured toadstools may

appear; white fungal threads in soil; black 'bootlaces' in soil on occasions.
Control Dig up and burn badly infected plants. Manure others to maintain vigour.

Leaf spot
CROPS ATTACKED **Currant**

Damage/symptoms Small brown spots on leaves coagulate; leaves eventually fall.
Control Burn fallen leaves.

Peach leaf curl
CROPS ATTACKED
Peach, apricot, nectarine

Damage/symptoms Leaves become puckered and bright pink in colour.
Control Spray with foliar feed as soon as leaves open. Shelter plants from rain while buds are bursting. Destroy infected leaves.

Powdery mildew
CROPS ATTACKED **Wide range**

Damage/symptoms Leaves and shoots covered in white powder.
Control Dust all but contra-indicated fruits (noted on pack) with sulphur.

Reversion disease
CROPS ATTACKED **Blackcurrant**

Damage/symptoms Leaves distorted; flowers pinkish purple.
Control Burn. Control big bud mite, which spreads this virus disease.

Rust
CROPS ATTACKED **Plum, currant**

Damage/symptoms Leaves spotted yellow on undersides; may fall early.
Control Keep well fed and watered. Clear fallen leaves in autumn.

Shot hole
CROPS ATTACKED **Cherry, plum**

Damage/symptoms Leaves full of small holes and spotted brown. No gummosis visible.
Control Feed tree well and apply water. If gum oozing from bark, see Bacterial canker.

Silver leaf
CROPS ATTACKED **Plum and sometimes cherry, peach, nectarine**

Damage/symptoms Leaves silvery in appearance on one or more branches; wood stained brown within.
Control Cut out infected branches back to healthy tissue. Burn them. (See False silver leaf: Fruit Disorders)

Spur blight
CROPS ATTACKED
Raspberry, loganberry

Damage/symptoms Purplish areas develop around buds; buds fail to grow and soon wilt.
Control Cut out and destroy infected canes.

Stem rot (Collar rot)
CROPS ATTACKED **Melon**

Damage/symptoms Stem base turns brown and rots.
Control Prevent by not planting too deeply and by using sterilized compost.

Strawberry mildew
CROPS ATTACKED **Strawberry**

Damage/symptoms Leaves purple blotched above, white beneath.
Control Dust fortnightly with sulphur, from flower bud formation onwards.

Virus
CROPS ATTACKED **Raspberry, strawberry and others**

Damage/symptoms Leaves distorted, twisted and often mottled yellow; yields down and vigour reduced.
Control Dig up and burn affected plants. Control aphids, which spread the disease.

DISORDERS

Bitter pit
CROPS ATTACKED **Apple**

Damage/symptoms Fruits spotted dark brown; flesh affected too. Tastes bitter.
Control Keep trees well watered and mulch regularly, to improve uptake of calcium.

False silver leaf
CROPS ATTACKED **Cherry, plum**

Damage/symptoms Leaves on the entire tree turn silvery, but there is no die-back.
Control Water well and spray with foliar feed.

Frost damage
CROPS ATTACKED **Strawberry**

Damage/symptoms Centres of flowers turn black.
Control Cover flowering plants with straw, newspaper or cloches if frost threatens.

Fruit drop
CROPS ATTACKED **Apple, pear, plum**

Damage/symptoms Fruitlets fall early; no sign of insect damage.
Control There is a natural June drop in which the tree thins out its fruits. If they all drop, suspect lack of food, water or suitable pollinator.

Fruit not forming
CROPS ATTACKED **Wide range**

Damage/symptoms Flowers appear but no fruit follows.
Control Check that a suitable pollinator is present. Frost damage may produce the same symptoms.

Gummosis
CROPS ATTACKED **Cherry, plum**

Damage/symptoms Clear gum oozing from trunk or main branch; no other symptoms.
Control Cut off hardened gum. Feed tree with general fertilizer.

Nutrient deficiency
CROPS ATTACKED **Wide range**

Damage/symptoms Areas between veins on leaves become yellow. No distortion.
Control Enrich surrounding soil with general fertilizer.

Scald
CROPS ATTACKED **Grape**

Damage/symptoms Berries scorched on side nearest glass.
Control Shade and ventilate as necessary. Cut out affected fruits.

Shanking
CROPS ATTACKED **Grape**

Damage/symptoms Fruit stalks wither; berries fail to develop and turn brown.
Control Remove affected grapes. Keep soil evenly moist. Thin grape bunches.

ORNAMENTAL PLANTS

PESTS

Aphid
PLANTS ATTACKED **Wide range**

Damage/symptoms Suck sap, weaken plant, secrete honeydew, transmit viruses.
Control Squash where feasible or spray off with water.

Birds
PLANTS ATTACKED **Wide range**

Damage/symptoms Leaves, shoots, flowers and fruits pecked.
Control Netting is the only solution.

Broom gall mite
PLANTS ATTACKED **Broom**

Damage/symptoms Green or grey-brown, lumpy outgrowths appear on stems.
Control Cut off and burn galls. Destroy badly infected plants.

Bulb scale mite
PLANTS ATTACKED **Narcissus**

Damage/symptoms Bulbs in store are soft, lightweight and brown; slice open and specks are visible in tissue.
Control Destroy infected bulbs.

Capsid bug
PLANTS ATTACKED
Wide range, especially rose

Damage/symptoms Leaves punctured with brown holes and distorted.
Control Gardens with a good mix of plants attract predators.

Carnation fly
PLANTS ATTACKED **Carnation**

Damage/symptoms Maggots tunnel into stems, leaves, roots.
Control None recommended.

Caterpillar
PLANTS ATTACKED **Wide range**

Damage/symptoms Leaves eaten; caterpillars or droppings visible.
Control Pick off. Spray larger outbreaks with biological control *Bacillus thuringiensis*.

Chrysanthemum eelworm
PLANTS ATTACKED **Chrysanthemum**

Damage/symptoms Leaves turn dark brown between the veins; eventually entirely brown.
Control Burn infected plants and buy new stock. Plant in sterilized compost.

Cuckoo spit (Froghopper)
PLANTS ATTACKED **Wide range**

Damage/symptoms Green insect shelters in blob of spittle on stem.
Control Damage rarely severe. Rub off if necessary.

Earwig
PLANTS ATTACKED **Dahlia and others**

Damage/symptoms Flowers and leaves eaten.
Control Tolerate as useful predator. If damage is severe, trap in flowerpots stuffed with straw and inverted on garden canes.

Leaf cutter bee
PLANTS ATTACKED **Rose**

Damage/symptoms Large pieces cut from leaf to leave scalloped effect.
Control None. You'll just have to lump it! Leaf cutting bees are of some benefit as pollinating insects.

Leaf miner
PLANTS ATTACKED **Chrysanthemum, cineraria, holly**

Damage/symptoms Leaves tunnelled by small grubs.
Control Check plants regularly and pick off and destroy affected leaves.

Leaf rolling sawfly
PLANTS ATTACKED **Rose**

Damage/symptoms Leaves curled under; caterpillars may be inside.
Control Pick off isolated leaves. Fork soil in autumn/winter to expose larvae.

Lily beetle
PLANTS ATTACKED **Lily and relations**

Damage/symptoms Leaves eaten; scarlet beetles observed.
Control Pick off and destroy beetles and squishy brown larvae.

Narcissus fly

PLANTS ATTACKED **Narcissus**

Damage/symptoms No flowers produced, only weak, grassy leaves. Cut bulbs reveal maggot.
Control Destroy infested bulbs. Buy from reputable supplier. Rake soil into holes left when leaves die down.

Rhododendron bug

PLANTS ATTACKED **Rhododendron**

Damage/symptoms Leaves mottled yellow above, brown beneath.
Control Avoid growing in sunny, dry or exposed conditions. Grow less susceptible varieties.

Slugs and snails

PLANTS ATTACKED **Wide range**

Damage/symptoms Leaves and flowers eaten; silvery trails observed.
Control As for slugs on vegetable crops.

Stem and bulb eelworm

PLANTS ATTACKED **Narcissus**

Damage/symptoms Leaves distorted and yellow mottled; lack of flowers; brown rings within bulbs.
Control Destroy infected bulbs. Buy from reputable supplier.

Stem eelworm

PLANTS ATTACKED **Phlox**

Damage/symptoms Leaves narrow and distorted; stems split; growth stunted.
Control Dig up and burn infected plants.

Thrips

PLANTS ATTACKED **Rose, gladiolus**

Damage/symptoms Silvery grey discoloration on flowers and leaves and tiny black spots on upper leaf surface.
Control Water plants regularly. Spray with insecticide based on plant oils.

Vine weevil

PLANTS ATTACKED **Rhododendron**

Damage/symptoms Lower leaves eaten and shredded.
Control Squash adults. If severe, use biological control *Heterorhabditis*.

DISEASES

Azalea gall

PLANTS ATTACKED **Azalea**

Damage/symptoms Green, red and then white swellings appear on leaves.
Control Remove and burn galls immediately to prevent spores from spreading.

Blackleg

PLANTS ATTACKED
Pelargonium (geranium)

Damage/symptoms Base of stem becomes black and soft; grey fur develops.
Control Prevent by using sterile compost and by ventilating well. Pull off dead leaves.

Black slime

PLANTS ATTACKED **Hyacinth**

Damage/symptoms Leaves turn yellow and collapse. Black resting bodies found between scales of bulb.
Control Destroy infected bulbs. Do not replant in infected area. Use sterile composts.

Blackspot

PLANTS ATTACKED **Rose**

Damage/symptoms Large black spots appear on leaves; leaves eventually fall.
Control Pick off and burn infected leaves. Improve growing conditions. Grow resistant varieties.

Botrytis

PLANTS ATTACKED **Wide range**

Damage/symptoms Parts of plant rotting and covered with grey fur.
Control Pick off infected parts. Improve drainage. Avoid overwatering.

Bud blast

PLANTS ATTACKED **Rhododendron**

Damage/symptoms Buds turn brown and do not open; black 'pinheads' appear on them.
Control Cut off and burn infected buds. Grow pollen-rich flowers to attract predators of the leafhoppers which spread the disease.

Canker

PLANTS ATTACKED **Rose**

Damage/symptoms Rough, brown, sunken areas appear on stem.
Control Cut out and burn infected stems. Destroy plants if severe.

Carnation leaf spot

PLANTS ATTACKED **Carnation**

Damage/symptoms Purplish brown spots appear on leaves.
Control Pick off and burn badly infected leaves.

Clematis wilt

PLANTS ATTACKED **Clematis**

Damage/symptoms One or more stems wilt, then collapse completely.
Control Prune out infected shoots at ground level. New shoots may grow. Be patient.

Clubroot

PLANTS ATTACKED **Wallflower**

Damage/symptoms Plants wilt and looked stunted; swollen, knobbly roots.
Control Lime acid soil. Grow from seed to avoid importing disease.

Dutch elm disease

PLANTS ATTACKED **Elm**

Damage/symptoms Trees look burned; eventually whole tree will die.

Control None. Fell, then strip off the bark and burn it. Timber unaffected.

Grey bulb rot

PLANTS ATTACKED **Hyacinth**

Damage/symptoms Top of bulb becomes dry and grey; black fungal resting bodies found.
Control Burn infected plants. Do not plant bulbs in infected soil.

Honey fungus (*Armillaria*)

PLANTS ATTACKED **Wide range, especially trees and shrubs**

Damage/symptoms Trees or shrubs die back; honey-coloured toadstools may appear; white fungal threads and black 'bootlaces' in soil.
Control Dig up and burn infected plants. Manure to improve vigour.

Ink disease

PLANTS ATTACKED **Bulbous irises**

Damage/symptoms Black patches develop on bulb, and on leaves and flowers in wet weather.
Control Burn infected bulbs.

Leaf blight

PLANTS ATTACKED **Lily**

Damage/symptoms Leaves covered with brown blotches.
Control Remove and destroy infected growth.

Leaf spot

PLANTS ATTACKED **Dahlia, rhizomatous iris**

Damage/symptoms Brown spots appear on leaves and eventually coalesce.
Control Pull off and destroy infected leaves.

Powdery mildew

PLANTS ATTACKED **Rose, chrysanthemum and others**

Damage/symptoms Leaves and shoots covered in white powder.
Control Dust with sulphur Improve dry or light soils by mulching.

Rhizome rot

PLANTS ATTACKED **Rhizomatous irises**

Damage/symptoms Leaves turn brown from tips backwards; rhizomes rot and become slimy.
Control Dig up and burn. Control slugs. Improve drainage.

Rust

PLANTS ATTACKED **Rose, pelargonium, antirrhinum, hollyhock**

Damage/symptoms Rusty brown marks appear on underside of leaves.
Control Pick off and destroy infected leaves. Grow resistant varieties where possible.

Scab

PLANTS ATTACKED **Gladiolus**

Damage/symptoms Red-brown spots on leaves; growth may topple; black areas on corm.
Control Destroy infected plants. Keep gladioli off infected ground.

Smoulder

PLANTS ATTACKED **Narcissus**

Damage/symptoms Stored bulbs rot; growing leaves spotted and rotten; black resting bodies on bulb.
Control Destroy infected stored bulbs and garden bulbs where seen.

Tulip fire

PLANTS ATTACKED **Tulip**

Damage/symptoms Leaf tips scorched; straw-coloured streaks on leaves and flowers.
Control Burn infected bulbs. Do not plant tulips in infected soil for the next 3-4 years.

Virus

PLANTS ATTACKED **Wide range**

Damage/symptoms Leaves mottled with yellow and distorted.
Control Destroy infected plants. Control aphids, which spread virus diseases.

Wilt

PLANTS ATTACKED **Michaelmas daisy**

Damage/symptoms Leaves at stem bases wilt and shrivel; effect spreads up stem.
Control Destroy infected plants. Do not replant on infected soil.

DISORDERS

Blind shoots

PLANTS ATTACKED **Narcissus**

Damage/symptoms Leaves produced but flowers fail to appear.
Control Make sure that the bulbs don't dry out in spring. Feed after flowering.

Bud drop

PLANTS ATTACKED

Camellia and others

Damage/symptoms Flower buds fall before they have a chance to open.
Control Caused by dryness at roots - keep evenly moist and mulch.

Chlorosis

PLANTS ATTACKED **Wide range**

Damage/symptoms Leaves yellow between veins. No distortion.
Control Caused by food shortage. Feed well.

Oedema

PLANTS ATTACKED **Pelargonium**

Damage/symptoms Blisters form on the undersides of leaves; eventually burst.

A beautiful, well-planned garden, brimful of healthy plants that give year-round colour and interest, is the goal and reward of gardening.

Control Caused by overwatering and high humidity.

Peony wilt

PLANTS ATTACKED **Peony**

Damage/symptoms Tree peony: unopened buds turn grey and rot. Herbaceous peony: leaf bases turn brown and collapse.
Control Cut out and destroy infected growth.

UNDER COVER PLANTS

Hygiene is an important factor in reducing the risk of plant problems in the greenhouse (see p.261), whereas most house plant disorders can be avoided by providing your plants with the right growing conditions.

PESTS

See also under Ornamental Plants

Aphid

PLANTS ATTACKED **Wide range**

Damage/symptoms Sap sucked; plant weakened; honeydew secreted; viruses transmitted.
Control Use biological control *Aphidius* or *Aphidioletes* in greenhouse.

Caterpillars

PLANTS ATTACKED **Wide range**

Damage/symptoms Leaves eaten; caterpillars or their green droppings are visible.
Control Hand pick. Spray severe infestations with biological control *Bacillus thuringiensis*.

Earwig

PLANTS ATTACKED **Wide range**

Damage/symptoms Young leaves and flowers eaten.
Control Trap if feasible (see p.294). Scrub down greenhouse in winter.

Mealy bug

PLANTS ATTACKED **Wide range**

Damage/symptoms Oval bugs covered in white wax suck sap and secrete honeydew.
Control Wipe off with soapy water. Use biological control *Cryptolaemus* in greenhouse.

Red spider mite

PLANTS ATTACKED **Wide range**

Damage/symptoms Leaves bleached; webs spun; tiny mites visible on foliage.
Control Discourage by maintaining a humid atmosphere. Introduce biological control *Phytoseiulus* in greenhouse.

Root aphid

PLANTS ATTACKED **Small range**

Damage/symptoms Plant wilts and looks stunted; aphids found among roots.
Control Destroy isolated infections.

Scale insect

PLANTS ATTACKED **Wide range**

Damage/symptoms Brown, limpet-like scales on stems and leaves; honeydew secreted.
Control Wipe off with soapy water. Spray with insecticide based on natural fatty acids.

Slugs and snails

PLANTS ATTACKED **Wide range**

Damage/symptoms Leaves and flowers eaten; silvery trails visible.
Control Pick off pot plants. Use beer traps in greenhouse borders.

Thrips

PLANTS ATTACKED **Wide range**

Damage/symptoms Leaves and flowers speckled with white.

Control Spray with organic insecticde based on plant oils.

Vine weevil

PLANTS ATTACKED **Small range including cyclamen**

Damage/symptoms Plants wilt and look sick. Fat, 1 cm (½ in) long creamy white grubs may be found among eaten roots.
Control Destroy infected plants. Water pots and border soil with biological control *Heterorhabditis*.

Whitefly

PLANTS ATTACKED **Wide range**

Damage/symptoms White V-shaped flies on undersides of leaves; honeydew secreted.
Control In greenhouse, introduce biological control *Encarsia*.

DISEASES

Algae

PLANTS ATTACKED **Paths, pots and compost surface**

Damage/symptoms Green, slimy growth on paths, pots and compost surface.
Control Scrub off paths. Add sharp grit to improve surface drainage of compost.

Blackleg

PLANTS ATTACKED **Pelargonium (geranium)**

See under Ornamental Plants.

Damping off

PLANTS ATTACKED
Wide range of seedlings

Damage/symptoms Seedlings keel over at stem bases and die off.
Control Prevent by sowing seed thinly, ventilating well and removing infected soil and seedlings.

Sooty mould

PLANTS ATTACKED **Wide range**

Damage/symptoms Black felt appears on leaves and stems.
Control Grows on honeydew secreted by aphids etc. Control the pest; sponge off the mould.

LAWNS

It is fine lawns that are most troubled by disease: the coarser more rugged grasses are seldom attacked by fungi, Brown areas are most likely caused by fertilizer scorch or bitch urine.

PESTS

Ants

Damage/symptoms A nuisance where picnics are popular. Fine soil brought to surface to provide a spot for weeds and moss.
Control Mow over mounds to discourage nesting or destroy with boiling water and re-seed.

Birds

Damage/symptoms Only a nuisance when lawns are being sown because they eat the seeds. They also eat lawn pests.
Control Sow enough seeds for the lawn and the birds.

Dogs

Damage/symptoms Bitches in season have strong urine that burns the grass.
Control Spike area with a fork and water immediately to reduce caustic effect.

Leatherjackets

Damage/symptoms Patches of grass turn yellow. If watered and covered with polythene overnight, grey grubs

will be found on the surface in the morning.
Control Drench with biological control *Steinerma*.

Moles

Damage/symptoms Molehills appear.
Control Set traps in runs to catch offending mole - release it where it can do no harm. If adjacent to farmland there's no way of controlling moles.

Worms

Damage/symptoms Wormcasts appear on surface.
Control Brush them off. Worms are beneficial to the soil and should be tolerated.

DISEASES

Algae

Damage/symptoms Dark green slimy areas appear, usually in damp, shady spots.
Control Spike and aerate lawn to improve drainage.

Damping off

Damage/symptoms Newly germinated grass seedlings wilt, turn brown and die - especially in humid weather.
Control Water well after sowing, but only as necessary thereafter.

Dollar spot

Damage/symptoms Straw-coloured patches 2.5-5 cm (1-2 in) across appear on lawn in late summer; they enlarge and join together.
Control Feed lawn well. Use specified autumn feed after August to prevent lush, susceptible growth. Improve drainage by scariying and forking.

Fairy rings

Damage/symptoms Dark green rings appear on lawn, often accompanied by toadstools.
Control See advice under Lawns - Pests and Deseases, p.201.

Fusarium patch

Damage/symptoms Grass patches turn yellow then brown before dying off. White or pink fungus strands visible.
Control Treat as for dollar spot.

Moss

Damage/symptoms Moss colonizes areas of soil between grass - especially under trees and in shade.
Control Remove underlying causes. Improve drainage, do not mow so close, feed lawn well, relieve shady conditions, relieve acidity.

Red thread

Damage/symptoms Small patches of pale pink to red fungal growth appear on the lawn in summer and autumn, the patches later become bleached. 'Stag's horn' fruiting bodies are produced. The lawn is very rarely killed completely.
Control Spike lawn regularly and feed well to prevent attack. Use specified autumn feed after August to prevent soft, susceptible growth.

Index

Abelia x grandiflora 56
Abutilon vitifolium 92
Acaena 174
Acanthus 118
Acer griseum 46; A. japonicum
    'Vitifolium' 46; A. negundo
    'Variegatum' 46; A. palmatum 56;
    A. pseudoplatanus
    'Brilliantissimum' 46;
    A. shirasawanum 'Aureum' 56
Achillea 118
Acid soils 14
Aconite, winter 158-9
Aconitum 118
Acorus calamus 186
Actinidia kolomikta 92
Acuba japonica 84
Adam's needle 79
Adiantum capillus-veneris 274
Adonis aestivalis 142
Aechmea fasciata 274
Aethionema 174
Agapanthus 118-19
Ageratum houstonianum 147;
    A.h. 'Bavaria' 147
Agrostemma githago 'Milas' 142
Air layering 27
Ajuga 118
Alcea 118, 123
Alchemilla 110-11, 118
Alder, golden 46
Algae 201, 298, 299
Alkaline soils 14
Allium 156; A. cristophii 156
Almond 73
Alnus glutinosa 'Aurea' 46
Aloysia triphylla 92
Alpine garden 166-77
Alstroemeria 118-20
Alum root 128
Aluminium plant 280-1
Amaranthus caudatus 142;
    A. tricolor 'Illumination' 147
Amaryllis 278
Amaryllis belladonna 156-7
Amberboa moschata 142
Amelanchier canadensis 56
Anagallis 'Coerulea' 147
Anaphalis 120
Anchusa 120; A. capensis 'Blue
    Angel' 142
Androsace 174
Anemone 120, 157
Angelica tree, Japanese 56-7
Angel's fishing rod 124
Annuals 139-41, 142-50; half-hardy
    139, 140-1, 147-50
Anthracnose 287
Antirrhinum majus 147
Ants 299
Aphelandra squarrosa 273
Aphids 284-5, 286, 290, 294, 298;
    currant blister 291; root 287, 298;
    woolly 292
Aponogeton distachyos 186
Apple 218-21; cherry 48;
    Japanese crab 48
Apple sucker 290
Aquatic plants 179, 182-4, 186-7
Aquilegia 120, 123
Arabis 174
Aralia elata 56-7
Arbutus unedo 46
Arctotis 147
Argemone mexicana 142
Armeria 174

Armillaria 293, 296
Arrowhead 187
Artemisia 120
Artichoke: globe 236; Jerusalem 236
Aruncus 120
Asparagus 236
Asperula orientalis 142
Asplenium 120; A. nidus 274
Aster 120-1, 134, 147
Astilbe 121
Astrantia 121
Atriplex hortensis var. rubra 142
Aubergine 265
Aubrieta 174
Aucuba japonica 'Variegata' 57
Aurinia 174
Avens 127
Azalea 73-4, 280
Azalea gall 295
Azolla filiculoides 187

Baby blue eyes 145
Baby's breath 127
Balloon flower 133
Ballota 121
Balsam 278
Bamboos 57
Barberry 57, 84
Barrenwort 126
Basil 245
Bassia scoparia f. trichophylla 142
Beans: bog 187; broad 236-7;
    French 237, 267; runner 237
Bear's breeches 118
Bedding begonia 275
Bedding plants 138-51
Beds: greenhouse 255; ornamental
    113, 115-16, 140; raised 208-9;
    vegetables 235
Bee balm 131
Bee-attracting plants 189
Beech 85
Beet, leaf 237-8
Beetles: flea 286; lily 295;
    raspberry 291
Beetroot 237
Begonia 275; B. maculata 274; B.
    rex 25, 26, 275; B. semperflorens
    147; B.s. Cultorum Group 262, 275
Bellflower 121-2, 174
Bellis perennis 150
Bells of Ireland 145
Berberis darwinii 57, 84;
    B. x ottawensis f. purpurea 57;
    B. x stenophylla 57, 84;
    B. thunbergii 57-8
Bergamot 131
Bergenia 121
Betony 136
Betula ermanii 46; B. papyrifera
    46; B. pendula 'Laciniata' 46;
    B.p. 'Youngii' 46; B. utilis var.
    jacquemontii 46-7
Biennials 139, 141, 150-1
Billbergia nutans 274
Bindweed 18
Birch: Erman's 46; Kashmir 46-7;
    paperbark 46; pruning 43;
    Swedish 46
Birds 286, 290, 294, 299; feeding
    and nesting 189-90
Bishop's hat 126
Bitter pit 293
Black slime 295
Blackberry 221
Blackcurrant 221-2
Black-eyed Susan 134, 265
Blackleg 287, 295, 299

Blackspot 285, 295
Bladderwort 186
Blanket flower 126-7, 149
Blechnum 121
Bleeding heart 124
Blight: cane 292; halo 288; leaf
    296; potato 288; spinach 289;
    spur 293
Blind shoots 296
Blood, bone and fishmeal 14
Bluebell 160
Bog plants 187
Bolting 289
Bonemeal 15
Border plants 112-37; bulbs with
    153-4; using height 113
Boston ivy 97-8
Botrytis 285, 292, 295
Bottle garden 271
Bouncing Bet 134-5
Bowles' golden grass 131
Box 59, 84, 87; dwarf 84
Brachyscome iberidifolia 148
Bracteantha 148
Brandy bottle 186
Brassica oleracea 142
Brick patio 204-5
Broadcast sowing 21-2
Broccoli 238
Broom 62, 65
Browallia speciosa 'Blue Troll' 262
Brown heart 289
Brown scale 290
Brunnera 121
Brussels sprout 238
Bud blast 295
Bud drop 273, 296
Buddleja alternifolia 58;
    B. davidii 58-9
Bugbane 122
Bugle 118
Bulbils 27
Bulbs 152-63; propagating 27
Bull bay 97
Burning bush 142
Burr, New Zealand 174
Bush honeysuckle 79
Busy Lizzie 149, 278
Butomus umbellatus 186
Butterflies 188-9
Butterfly bush 58-9
Buxus sempervirens 59, 84;
    B.s. 'Suffruticosa' 84, 87
Buying guides 53, 81, 103, 116,
    152-3, 252-3, 268-70, 284

Cabbage 238-9; ornamental 142
Calabrese 238
Calamintha 121
Calamondin orange 275
Calandrinia umbellata 148
Calceolaria 262, 275;
    C. integrifolia 'Sunshine' 148
Calendula officinalis 142
Calla palustris 186
Calluna 66
Caltha palustris 186
Camassia 157
Camellia 25-6; C. japonica 92; C.j.
    'Tricolor' 93; C. x williamsii 59
Campanula 121-2, 174; C. medium
    150
Canary creeper 146
Candytuft 143; perennial 176
Cane spot 292
Canker 287, 292, 295; bacterial 292
Canterbury bell 150
Cape figwort 98
Cape heath 277

Capsicum 266-7; C. annuum 275
Capsid bug 285, 290, 294
Cardinal flower 130
Cardoon 123
Carex 122
Carnation 123-4, 262
Carpenteria californica 92-3
Carpinus betulus 84
Carrot 239
Caryopteris x clandonensis 59
Cast iron plant 274
Castor oil plant 149-50
Catananche 122
Catch cropping 234-5
Catchfly 177
Caterpillars 284-6, 291, 294, 298
Catmint 131
Cauliflower 239
Ceanothus 93
Celeriac 240
Celery 240; blanching 240
Celosia argentea 262
Centaurea 122; C. cineraria 148;
    C. cyanus 142-3
Centranthus 122
Cerastium 174
Ceratostigma 122
Cercis siliquastrum 47
Chaenomeles 94
Chafer grubs 284
Chamaecyparis 59;
    C. lawsoniana 47, 84
Chamaedorea elegans 275
Cheat's digging 16-17
Cherry 73, 222-3; 'Bigarreau
    Napoleon' 222-3; Japanese 49;
    purple-leaf sand 86; Sato 49;
    Tibetan 39, 49; winter 49-50, 281
Cherry laurel 73, 86
Cherry pie 149
Chilean fire bush 63
Chilean glory 95
Chilean potato tree 98
Chinese lantern flower 132
Chionodoxa forbesii 157
Chives 245
Chlorophytum comosum 275
Chlorosis 298
Chocolate spot 287
Choisya ternata 59
Christmas box 76
Christmas cactus 281
Christmas rose 127-8
Chrysanthemum 262-3, 276;
    C. carinatum 143
Cimicifuga 122
Cineraria, florist's 264
Cinquefoil 73, 133
Cissus antarctica 275;
    C. rhombifolia 275
Cistus 59-60, 61; C. 'Grayswood
    Pink' 61
x Citrofortunella microcarpa 275
Clarkia amoena 143;
    C. unguiculata 143
Clary 146
Clay soils 12
Clematis 25, 26, 94; C. montana
    'Elizabeth' 89; C.m. var. rubens
    33; pruning 94-5
Cleome spinosa 148
Climbers 88-99; roses 101, 104,
    110-11; siting 88-90
Climbing hydrangea 96-7
Cloches 235
Clubroot 285, 287-8, 296
Cobaea scandens 263
Codiaeum variegatum 275-6
Coir-based composts 259

Colchicum 157-8
Coleus 265, 281
Colour schemes 138; drifts *115;* single-colour 113
Columbine 120
Compost: making *13;* pot plants 258-9
Concrete patio *203-4*
Coneflower 134, 146; purple 125
Conifers, dwarf 175
Consolida ajacis 143
Container gardening: alpines *170-1;* bulbs *154-5;* patios *206-11;* tub pools *185*
Convallaria 122
Convolvulus cneorum 60; *C. tricolor* 'Blue Flash' 143
Coral bells 128
Coral berry 77
Coral spot 292
Cordons *216-17, 220*
Cordyline fruticosa 276; *C. indivisa* 276
Coreopsis 122; *C. tinctoria* 143
Corms *153;* propagating 27
Corn cockle 142
Cornflower 122, 142-3
Cornus alba 60; *C. kousa* 60
Cortaderia 122
Corydalis 122
Corylus avellana 'Contorta' 60; *C. maxima* 'Purpurea' 60, 84
Cosmos 148; *C. bipinnatus* 148
Cotinus coggygria 60, 62
Cotoneaster 62; *C. horizontalis* 94-5; *C. simonsii* 84
Cotton lavender 76
Couch grass *18*
Courgette 242
Crambe 123
Cranesbill 127, 175
Crataegus laevigata 'Paul's Scarlet' 47; *C. monogyna* 84
Creeping Jenny 130
Crepis rubra 143
Cress: Purple 174; Rock 174; Stone 174; Violet 143
Crocosmia 123
Crocus 158; Autumn 157-8
Crop rotation 233, 285
Croton 275-6
Crowfoot, water 186
Crown gall 292-3
Crown imperial 159
Cuckoo pint 120
Cuckoo spit *285,* 294
Cucumber 265-6
Cunninghamia lanceolata 47
Cup flower 176
Cuphea ignea 263
Cupid's dart 122
x *Cupressocyparis leylandii* 81, 84
Currant, red and white 223-4
Cuttings *23-6;* compost for 259; half-ripe 25
Cycas revoluta 276
Cyclamen 158, 276
Cydonia 94
Cynara 123
Cyperus albostriatus 276; *C. involucratus* 276
Cypress 59; Lawson 47
Cytisus 62; *C. battandieri* 95

Daffodil 161-2; winter 162
Dahlia 148, *153,* 158
Daisy: African 147; double 150; Livingstone 149; Michaelmas 120-1; Shasta 129; Swan River 148

Daisy bush 70-1; New Zealand 85
Damping off 299
Damson 229-30
Daphne 62
Davidia involucrata 47
Dawn redwood 48, 85
Deadheading: border plants 116-17; roses 104
Deadnettle 129
Delphinium 123, 130; D. grandiflorum 'Blue Butterfly' 148
Deutzia x magnifica 62
Dianthus 123-4, 175; *D. barbatus* 150; *D. caryophyllus* 148, 262; *D. chinensis* Heddewigii Group 148
Diascia 175
Dicentra 124
Dictamnus 124
Didymelia 289
Dieffenbachia seguine 276; 'Amoena' 276-7
Dierama 124
Diervilla 79
Digging *15-17;* borders 114; no-dig technique 114
Digitalis 124, 150
Dimorphotheca sinuata 143
Dionaea muscipula 277
Dipsacus fullonum 151
Diseases and disorders see Pests/diseases/disorders
Dittany 124, 176
Division 23
Dogwood 60
Dollar spot 299
Doronicum 124
Dorotheanthus 149
Double digging *15-17*
Dove tree 47
Dracocephalum moldavica 143
Dragon tree 276
Dragon's head 143
Drainage 12-13
Drills, sowing seeds *21*
Dryas 175
Dryopteris 124-5
Dumb cane 276
Dusty miller 150
Dutch elm disease 296

Earwig *285,* 294, 298
Eccremocarpus scaber 95
Echinacea 125
Echinops 125; *E. ritro* 124-5
Echium vulgare 143
Edelweiss 176
Eelworm 286; chrysanthemum *285,* 294; potato cyst 287; stem and bulb *285,* 295
Elaeagnus pungens 'Maculata' 62-3
Elder 75-6; box 46
Electrical safety, outdoors 35
Elephant's ears 121
Elodea canadensis 186
Embothrium coccineum 63
Emilia coccinea 143
Epilobium 125
Epimedium 126
Eranthis hyemalis 158-9
Eremurus 126
Erica 66; *E.* 'Hyemalis' 277
Erigeron 126, 175
Erinus 175
Erodium 175
Eryngium 126
Erysimum x allionii 151; *E. cheiri* 151
Erythronium 159

Escallonia 'Donard Star' 63; *E. rubra* var. *macrantha* 84-5
Eschscholzia californica 143; 'Special Mixed' *234-5*
Espaliers *216-17,* 220
Eucalyptus pauciflora subsp. *niphophila* 47
Eucryphia x nymansensis 'Nymansay' 63
Euonymus europaeus 64; *E. fortunei* 'Emerald 'n' Gold' 64
Euonymus japonicus 85
Euphorbia 126, 175; *E. pulcherrima* 277
Evergreens: climbers/wall plants 97; on patios *210-11;* shrubs 65
Exacum affine 263

***F**agus sylvatica* 85
Fairy rings 201, 299
Fairy wand flower 124
Fallopia 126; *F. baldschuanica* 95-6
False acacia *50*
False spikenard 136
Fanging 289
x *Fatshedera lizei* 277
Fatsia japonica 64, *277*
Feather grass 136-7
Feeding/fertilizers 14-15; bulbs 155; climbers/wall plants 91; in compost 259; greenhouse plants 261; house plants 272; lawns 198; roses 104; shrubs 55; vegetables 233
Fennel *245-7*
Fern: bird's nest 274; Boston 279; hart's tongue 120; ladder 279; maidenhair 273; male 124-5; ostrich plume 130-1; stag's horn 280
Fescue grass 126
Festuca 126
Feverfew 150
Ficus 25, 26; *F. benjamina* 277; *F. elastica* 277-8; *F. pumila* 278
Fig: creeping 278; weeping 277
Filbert, purple-leaved 60
Finger aralia 280-1
Fir, Chinese 47
Fireblight 293
Firethorn 86, 98
Fish 183-4
Fishbone cotoneaster 94-5
Flag 128; sweet 186; yellow 187
Flagstone patio *203-4*
Flame flower, Scotch 98-9
Flame nettle 265, 281
Flax 129; New Zealand 132
Fleabane 126, 175
Flies: cabbage root 286; carnation 294; carrot 286; celery 286; frit 286; narcissus 295; onion fly 287; sciarid 284; see also Blackfly; Whitefly
Florist's 'mums 276
Florist's cineraria 279
Floss flower 147
Flower borders: vegetables in *234-5;* weeding 19
Flower of a day 137
Flowering currant 74
Focal point shrubs 53, 63
Foliage plants: for patios *210-11;* shrubs 75
Foliar feeds 15
Forget-me-not 151; water 187
Forsythia x intermedia 'Lynwood' 64; *F. x intermedia* 'Spectabilis' 85

Foundations, greenhouse 253-4
Four o'clock plant 149
Foxglove 124, 150
Fragrance: climbers for 96; roses for 108; shrubs for 77
Fremontia 96
Fremontodendron californicum 96
Fritillaria 159
Frogbit 187
Froghopper 294
Frost damage 293
Fruit 214-31; pests and diseases 290-4; trees 51
Fruit drop 293-4
Fuchsia 263-4, 278; Californian 177; *F. magellanica* 64, 85
Fuller's teasel 151
Fumitory 122
Funkia 128
Furniture, patio 206
Fusarium patch *285,* 299

Gage 229-30
Gaillardia 126-7, 149
Galanthus 159
Galega 127
Galtonia candicans 159
Gangrene 288
Garrya elliptica 96
Gaultheria mucronata 65
Gazania 149
Genista 65
Gentiana 127, 175
Geranium 110-11, 127, 175, 264, 279
Germination, seeds 21
Geum 127
Ghost spot 288
Gilia capitata 143
Gilly flower 149
Ginkgo biloba 47
Gladiolus 159-60
Glazing, greenhouse 254
Gleditsia triacanthos 'Sunburst' 48
Globe flower 137
Globe thistle 125
Glory of the snow 157
Gloxinia 281
Glyceria 127; *G. maxima* var. *variegata* 186
Goat's beard 120
Goat's rue 127
Gold dust 174
Golden bells 64, 85
Golden club 187
Golden rod 136
Golden-leafed hop 96
Gomphrena globosa 'Buddy' 264
Gooseberry 224; fuchsia-flowered 98
Gorse 86
Gourd 149
Granite 167
Grape *224-5,* 225-7
Grape hyacinth 161
Grape ivy 275
Grass: grassing down 18, 19; naturalizing bulbs in *153-5;* see also Lawns
Gravel: beds 113-14; patios 200-1
Greenback 290
Greenfly *285,* 286
Greenhouse gardening *250-67;* pests and diseases 298-9
Gromwell 176
Ground elder *18*
Ground-cover 18, 19, 113, 136; roses 111; shrubs 58
Growmore 14
Gummosis 294

Gunnera 127
Gypsophila 127; *G. elegans* 143

Hamamelis mollis 65-6
Hanging baskets 207-9
Hardening off 141
Hardwood cuttings *24*, 25
Hattie's pincushion 121
Hawksbeard 143
Hawthorn 84; water 186
Hazel: corkscrew 60; purple-leafed 84
Heathers 66
Heaths 66
Heating, greenhouse 256
Hebe 66-7
Hedera 67, 96, 278
Hedges 80-7; shrub roses for 107
Helenium 127
Helianthemum 176
Helianthus annuus 143
Heliotropium arborescens 149
Helleborus 127-8
Hemerocallis 128
Heptapleurum 280
Herbs *245-7*; drying/freezing 246
Heron's bill 175
Heuchera 128
Hibiscus syriacus 67
Hippeastrum 278
Hoheria lyallii 96
Holly 68, 85
Hollyhock 118, *123*
Honesty 151
Honey fungus 288, 293, 296
Honey locust 48
Honeysuckle 97; Himalayan 70
Hornbeam 84; hop 48-9
Hosta 128
Hottonia palustris 186
House plants 268-81; air layering *27*
Houseleek 177
Houttuynia cordata 'Flore Pleno' 187
Howea belmoreana 278; *H. forsteriana* 278
Hoya carnosa 278
Humidity: greenhouse 257; house plants *268*, 270
Humulus lupulus 'Aureus' 96
Hyacinthoides 160
Hyacinthus 160
Hydrangea macrophylla 67-8; *H. paniculata* 68; *H. petiolaris* 96-7
Hydrocharis morsus-ranae 187
Hydroculture *271-2*
Hygiene, greenhouse 261
Hypericum 68, 176
Hypoestes phyllostachya 264

Iberis 143, 176
Ice plant 135
Ilex x *altaclerensis* 'Golden King' 48; *I. aquifolium* 68, 85
Impatiens 149, 278
Incarvillea 128
Inch plant 281
Ink disease 296
Intercropping 234
Ionopsidium acaule 143
Ipomoea 149
Iris 128, *130*, 151, 160-1; *I. laevigata* 187; *I. pseudacorus* 187; *I. reticulata* 160; smooth 187; variegated *187*
Ironwood, Persian 49
Ivy 67, 96, 278

Ivy tree 277

Jacob's ladder 133
Japonica 94
Jasmine: rock 174; winter 97
Jasminum nudiflorum 97
Jew's mallow 69
John Innes composts 258-9
Joseph's coat 275-6
Judas tree 47
Juncus effusus f. *spiralis* 187
June drop 214
Juniperus 68
Justicia brandegeeana 278

Kale 240-1
Kangaroo vine 275
Kansas gayfeather 129
Kerria japonica 'Pleniflora' 69
Kingcup 186
Kirengeshoma 129
Knapweed 122
Kniphofia 129
Knotweed 132, 176, *187*; Japanese 18
Kohl rabi 241

Labelling, rock plants 173
Laburnum x *watereri* 'Vossii' 48
Lad's love 120
Lady in the bath 124
Lady's mantle 118
Lamb's ears 136
Lamium 129
Land clearance 12
Landscape fabric 18-19
Larch: European 48; golden 50
Larix decidua 48
Larkspur 123
Lathyrus 129; *L. latifolius* 97; *L. odoratus* 144
Laurel, spotted 57
Laurel magnolia 97
Laurus nobilis 69
Laurustinus 86
Lavandula angustifolia 69, 85; *L. stoechas* 246-7
Lavatera x *clementii* 'Rosea' 69-70; *L. trimestris* 144
Lavender 69, 85; French *246-7*
Lawn-care tools *31*, 35
Lawns 192-201; pests and diseases 299
Lawson cypress 84
Layering *26-7*
Layia platyglossa 144
Leaf cutter bee 294
Leaf cuttings *24-6*
Leaf miner 294; beet *285-6*
Leaf spot 273, *285*, 288, 293, 296; carnation 295
Leatherjackets 284, 299
Leek 241
Legousia speculum-veneris 144
Lemon verbena 92
Leopard's bane 124
Leotopodium 176
Leptosiphon 144
Lettuce 241-2
Leucanthemum 129
Leucojum 161
Lewisia 176
Leycesteria formosa 70
Leyland cypress 81, 84
Liatris spicata 129
Lighting, patio 206
Light/lighting: greenhouse 256; house plants 270
Ligustrum ovalifolium 85
Lilac 77; Californian 93

Lilium 161
Lily 161; Arum 137; blue African *118-19*; day 128; diamond 162; foxtail 126; kaffir 162; Peruvian *118-20*; plantain 128; spire 159; sword 159-60; trout 159; wood 177
Lily of the field 162
Lily-of-the-valley 122
Lily-of-the-valley bush 72-3
Lime trees *44*
Liming 233
Limnanthes douglasii 144
Limonium sinuatum 149
Linaria 129; *L. maroccana* 'Fairy Bouquet' 144
Ling 66
Linum 129; *L. grandiflorum* 'Rubrum' 144
Liriope 129-30
Lithodora 176
Loam 258-9
Lobelia 130, 149
Lobularia maritima 144
Loganberry 221
Lonas inodora 145
Lonicera 97; *L. nitida* 85
Loosestrife 130
Lords and ladies 120
Love-in-a-mist 145
Love-lies-bleeding 142
Lunaria annua 151
Lupinus 130
Lychnis 130
Lysimachia 130

Macleaya 130
Magnolia 70; *M. grandiflora* 97
Mahonia 70
Maidenhair tree 47
Maintenance: rock gardens 173; of tools 35, 82; water gardens 184-5
Mallow 130, 144
Malope trifida 145
Maltese cross 130
Malus floribunda 48; *M.* 'John Downie' 48
Malva 130
Maple: downy Japanese 46; Japanese 56; paperbark 46
Maranta 278
Marestail *18*
Marigold: African 150; Afro-French 150; French 150; marsh 186; pot 142
Marjoram 245
Marrow 242
Masterwort 121
Matteuccia 130-1
Matthiola incana 149, 151; *M. longipetala* subsp. *bicornis* 145
Meadow rue 137
Meadow saffron 157-8
Mealy bug 284, 291, 298
Mealy cabbage aphid 287
Meconopsis 131
Megasea 121
Melon 266
Mentha aquatica 187
Mentzelia lindleyi 145
Menyanthes trifoliata 187
Metasequoia glyptostroboides 48, 85
Mexican orange blossom 59
Midges: leaf 291; pear 291
Mignonette 146

Mildew: American gooseberry 292; downy *285*, 288; powdery 288, 293, 296; strawberry 293
Mile-a-minute 95-6
Milium 131
Mimulus 131, 149; Calypso series 264
Mint 246; water 187
Mirabilis jalapa 149
Mites: big bud 290; broom gall 294; bulb scale 294; leaf and bud 291; pear leaf blister 291; red spider *284-5*, 287, 292, 298
Mock orange 72; Californian 92-3
Moles 201, 299
Moluccella laevis 145
Monarda 131
Monkey flower 131, 149, 264
Monkshood 118
Monstera deliciosa 279
Montbretia 123
Morning glory 149
Moroccan broom 95
Morus nigra 48
Moss: fairy floating 187; on lawns 200-1, 299
Mother-in-law's tongue 280
Mother-of-thousands 280
Moths 189; cherry fruit 291; codling 291; leek 286-7; pea 287; plum tortrix *285*, 291; tomato 287; tortrix 292; winter 292
Mould: grey 288, 292; leaf 288; sooty 299
Mountain ash 51
Mountain avens 175
Mountain cabbage tree 276
Mowing lawns 199-200
Mulberry, black 48
Mulching 15, 19; border plants 117; hedges 81-2; roses 104; shrubs 55; trees 43; vegetable plot 233
Mullein 137, 151, 177
Muscari 161
Mussel scale 291
Myosotis scorpioides 187; *M. sylvatica* 151
Myriophyllum 186
Myrtle *70-1*
Myrtus communis 70-1

Naked ladies 157-8
Narcissus 161-2
Nasturtium *145*, 146
Nectarine 227-8
Nectaroscordum siculum subsp. *dioscoridis* 156
Nemesia 149
Nemophila menziesii 145
Nepeta 131, *145*; *N. sibirica* 'Souvenir d'André Chaudron' *36-7*
Nephrolepis exaltata 'Bostoniensis' 279
Nerine bowdenii 162
Nicandra physalodes 145
Nicotiana 149
Nierembergia 176
Nigella damascena 145
Nolana 'Lavender Gown' 149
Nuphar lutea 186
Nymphaea 186
Nyssa sylvatica 48

Obedient plant 132-3
Oedema 298
Oenothera 131
Olearia 70-1; *O.* x *haastii* 85
Oleaster 62-3

Onion 242; ornamental 156
Orach 142
Origanum 176
Ornithogalum umbellatum 162
Orontium aquaticum 187
Osmanthus delavayi 71-2
Ostrya carpinifolia 48-9
Oswego tea 131
Othonna 176
Oxalis 176

*P*aeonia 72, 131-2
Pagoda tree 51
Painted tongue 150
Palm: Chusan 51; false castor oil 64, 277; Kentia 278; parlour 275; sago 276
Pampas grass 122
Pansy 137, 151
Papaver 132, 176; *P. nudicaule* 151; *P. rhoeas* Shirley Series 145; *P. somniferum* 'Paeony Flowered' 146
Parrotia persica 49
Parsley 246
Parsnip 242-3
Parthenocissus 97
Pasque flower 177
Passiflora caerulea 98
Passion flower 98
Paths *196-7;* greenhouse 254; vegetable plot 232
Patio gardening 202-11
Paul's scarlet thorn 47
Pea 243; everlasting 97; sweet 144
Peach 73, 227-8
Peach leaf curl 293
Pear 228-9; willow-leafed 50
Pear sucker 291
Pearl everlasting 120
Peat 259
Peat beds 170
Peaty soils 12
Pelargonium 264, 279
Penstemon 132, 149, 151, *156*
Peperomia 279
Pepper: ornamental 275; sweet 266-7
Perennials 112; tender 139, 141
Pericallis 264, 279
Perilla frutescens var. *crispa* 146
Periwinkle *78-9,* 79
Persicaria 132, 176
Pests/diseases/disorders 284-99; biological control 284; house plants 273; lawns 201; roses 105
Petunia 149
Phacelia campanularia 146
Pheasant's eye 142
Philadelphus 72
Philodendron scandens 279-80
Phlomis fruticosa 72
Phlox 119, 132, 176; *P. drummondii* 149
Phormium 132
Photinia x *fraseri* 'Red Robin' 72
Phygelius capensis 98
Physalis 132
Physostegia 132-3
Picea breweriana 49; *P. omorika* 49; *P. pungens* 'Koster' 49
Pickerel weed 187
Pieris formosa var. *forrestii* 72-3
Pilea cadierei 280, *281*
Pinching out, house plants 273
Pincushion flower 150
Pink 123-4, 148, 175
Pittosporum tenuifolium 73, 85
Planning 10-12; beds/borders 113,

115-16, 140; colour schemes 113; patios 202; vegetable plot 232; water garden 178-81
Plant names 19
Planting: alpines *171-3;* asparagus *236;* border plants 116; bulbs *153-5;* cabbages *238-9;* fruit trees 216-17; hedges 81, *81-2;* leeks *241;* shrubs 53-4; trees *40-3;* vegetables 233
Platycerium bifurcatum 280
Platycodon 133
Pleached trees *44*
Plum 73, 229-30; 'Victoria' *229*
Plumbago, hardy 122
Poached egg flower 144
Pocket handkerchief tree 47
Poinsettia 277
Polemonium 133
Pollination, sweet corn *245*
Polyanthus 133
Polygonatum 133
Polythene, black 18
Polytunnel *253*
Ponds/pools 178-87; liners *179-81;* for wildlife *190-1*
Pondweed: Canadian 186; Curled 186
Pontederia cordata 187
Poor man's orchid 265
Poplar, variegated balm of Gilead 49
Poppy 132; alpine 176; Californian 143, *234-5;* Himalayan blue 131; Iceland 151; opium 146; plume 130; prickly 142; tree 74; Welsh 131
Populus x *jackii* 'Aurora' 49
Portulaca grandiflora 149
Pot plants, care of *259-61*
Potamogeton crispus 186
Potato 243, 267
Potentilla 133; *P. fruticosa* 73, 85
Potting on *210-11,* 261, 272
Potting up *259-61*
Pratia 177
Prayer plant 278
Pricking out seedlings *23,* 141
Prickly heath *65*
Prickly rhubarb 127
Primrose: Cape 265; evening 131; German 280
Primula 133; *P. malacoides* 265; *P. obconica* 280
Privet 81, 85
Propagation 20-7; alpines 173; bulbs and corms 27, 155; cuttings *23-6;* division 23; fruit 214; hedges 83; house plants 273; layering *26-7;* roses 105; seeds *20-3;* shrubs 55
Propagators *22*
Pruning: clematis *94-5;* climbers/wall plants 91; fruit trees 215, *219-20;* grape vine *226;* hedges *82-3;* roses *103-4;* shrubs *54-5;* tools for *31-3, 44;* trees *43-5*
Prunus 73; *P.* x *cistena* 86; *P. laurocerasus* 86; *P. serrula 39,* 49; *P. serrulata* varieties 49; *P.* x *subhirtella* 'Autumnalis' 49-50
Pseudolarix amabilis 50
Pulmonaria 133-4
Pulsatilla 177
Purslane 149; rock 148
Pyracantha 98; *P. rogersiana* 86
Pyramids *217, 219*
Pyrus salicifolia 'Pendula' 50

*Q*uamash 157
Queen's tears 275
Quick 84
Quince, Japanese 94

*R*adish 244
Ramanas rose 86
Ranunculus aquatilis 186
Raspberry 230-1
Red hot poker 129
Red thread 299
Reed meadow grass 186
Renovation: border plants *117;* hedges 83; old roses 105; shrubs 55
Reseda odorata 146
Reversion disease 293
Rex begonia 275
Rheum 134
Rhizome *153*
Rhodanthe chlorocephala subsp. *rosea* 146; *R. manglesii* 146
Rhododendron 73-4; *ponticum* 86; *R. simsii* 280
Rhododendron bug 295
Rhubarb 134, 244, 267
Rhus typhina 74
Ribes R. sanguineum 74; *R. speciosum* 98
Ricinus communis 149-50
Ring culture 255
Robinia pseudoacacia 'Frisia' *50*
Rock gardens 166-77; bulbs in 154; dwarf conifers for 175
Rock rose 176
Rockfoil 177
Rodger's bronze leaf 134
Rodgersia 134
Romneya coulteri 74
Root cuttings *26*
Root-knot 286
Rootstocks, fruit trees 216
Rosa eglanteria 86; *R. rugosa* 86
Rose bay willowherb 125
Rose fertilizer 15
Rosemary 74-5, 86, *87,* 246
Roses 100-11; buying 103; care calendar 105; classifications 102
Rosmarinus officinalis 74-5, 86, *87*
Rot: black 287; blossom end 289; brown 292; buckeye 287; collar 289; crown 288; dry 288; foot 288; grey bulb 296; heart 288; neck 288; rhizome *285,* 296; soft 289; stem 273, 289, 293; violet root 289
Rowan 51
Rubber plant *25-6,* 277-8
Rudbeckia 134; R. hirta 146
Rue 75
Rush: corkscrew 187; flowering 186; zebra 187
Russian vine 95-6
Rust 289, 293, 296; leek *285,* 288
Ruta graveolens 'Jackman's Blue' 75

*S*age 134, 246; Jerusalem 72; purple *246-7*
Sagittaria sagittifolia 'Flore Pleno' 187
Saintpaulia 24-6, 280
Salix 75; *S. babylonica* var. *pekinensis* 'Tortuosa' 51; *S.* x *sepulcralis* 'Chrysocoma' 51
Salpiglossis sinuata 150
Salvia 134; *S. splendens* 150; *S. viridis* 146

Sambucus 75-6
Sand, in compost 259
Sandstone 167
Sandy soils 12
Sansevieria trifasciata 'Laurentii' 280
Santolina 76
Sanvitalia procumbens 150
Saponaria 134-5, 177; *S. vaccaria* 'Pink Beauty' 146
Sarcococca confusa 76
Savin 68
Sawfly: apple *285,* 290; currant 291; gooseberry 291; leaf rolling 295; plum 291
Saxifraga 177; *S. stolonifera* 280
Scab 289, 296; powdery 288-9
Scabiosa 135, 150
Scald 290, 294
Scale insect 298
Scarlet flax 144
Scaryfing lawns *198*
Schefflera arboricola 280; *S. elegantissima* 280-1
Schizanthus 265
Schizostylis coccinea 162
Schlumbergera 281
Schoenoplectus lacustris subsp. *tabernaemontani* 'Zebrinus' 187
Scilla 162; *S. sibirica* 160
Scree beds 168
Sea holly 126
Sea lavender 149
Sea pink 174
Sedge 122
Sedum 135, 177; *S.* 'Herbstfreude' *134*
Seedlings: hardening off 141; pricking out *23*
Seeds: annuals, biennials and bedding plants *139-41;* lawn 194, 196-9; potato tubers *243;* sowing *20-3*
Sempervivum 177
Senecio cineraria 150
Shading, greenhouse 257
Shanking 289, 294
Sheds *33*
Shoo-fly plant 145
Shot hole 293
Shrimp plant 278
Shrub roses *102,* 106-8
Shrubs 52-79; autumn/winter interest 69; for colourful foliage 75; with scented flowers 77
Sidalcea 135
Silene 177; *S. coeli-rosa* 'Blue Angel' 146
Silk tassel bush 96
Silver leaf 293; false 293
Single digging *16-17*
Sink gardens *170-1*
Sinningia 281
Sisyrinchium 177
Skimmia 76
Slipper flower 262, 275
Slugs *284-5,* 287, 295, 298
Slugworm 292
Smilacina 136
Smoke tree 60, 62
Smoulder 296
Smut 289
Snails *285,* 287, 295, 298
Snakeshead fritillary 159
Snapdragon 147
Sneezewort 127
Snowberry 77
Snowdrop 159
Snowflake 161

Snow gum 47
Snow in summer 174
Snowy mespilus 56
Soapwort 134-5, 177
Softwood cuttings 24-5
Soil 12 for borders 114; climbers
  and wall plants 90; drainage
  12-13; for fruit 214; for hedges 81;
  improving 13-15, 114; for lawns
  193; rock gardens 166-7; for roses
  102-3; tools for working 29-32;
  for trees 42; vegetable plot 233;
  weeding 19
Solanum capsicastrum 281;
  S. crispum 98
Soldiers and sailors 133-4
Solenostemon 265, 281
Solidago 136
Solomon's seal 133
Sophora japonica 51
Sorbus aucuparia 'Beissneri' 51;
  S. 'Joseph Rock' 51
Sowbread 158
Spanish bayonet 281
Spider flower 148
Spider plant 275
Spiderwort 137
Spiking lawns 198
Spinach 244
Spindle tree 64
Spiraea 76-7; blue 59
Spotted begonia 274
Spotted laurel 84
Spraing 289
Spruce: Brewer's weeping 49;
  Koster's blue 49; Serbian 49
Spurge 126, 175
Squill 162
St John's wort 68, 176
Stachys 136; S. byzantina 156
Staging, greenhouse 255-6
Stag's horn sumach 74
Star of Bethlehem 162
Star of the veldt 143
Stardust 144
Statice 149
Stem cuttings 24-5
Stephanotis floribunda 281
Sternbergia 162
Stewartia pseudocamellia 51
Stipa 136-7
Stock: Brompton 151; night-scented
  145; ten week 149
Stonecrop 135, 177
Stony soils 12
Storage, potatoes 244
Stratiotes aloides 187
Strawberry 230, 267
Strawberry tree 46
Strawflower 148
Streptocarpus 265
Successional sowing 234
Suckers: roses 104-5; trees 44
Sun rose 59-60
Sunflower 143
Supports: annuals 140; border
  plants 117; climbers 90-1;
  greenhouse plants 261, 266;
  house plants 273; runner
  beans 237; strawberry 231;
  wall plants 91
Swede 244
Sweet alyssum 144
Sweet bay 69
Sweet briar 86
Sweet corn 244-5
Sweet sultan 142
Sweet William 150
Sweetheart plant 279-80

Swiss cheese plant 278
Sycamore 46
Symphoricarpos 77
Syringa 72, 77

Tagetes 150
Tamarisk 77-8, 86
Tamarix gallica 86;
  T. ramosissima 77-8
Tanacetum parthenium 'Golden
  Ball' 150; T.p. 'Golden Moss'
  150
Tarragon 246
Tassel flower 143
Taxus baccata 86; T.b. 'Fastigiata
  Aurea' 51
Temperature: greenhouse 256;
  house plants 270
Thalictrum 137
Thinning out: annual seedlings 140;
  vegetables 235
Thrift 174
Thrips 284-5, 295, 298; pea 287
Thuja plicata 86; T.p. 'Zebrina' 51
Thunbergia alata 265
Thyme 246
Thymus 177
Ti tree 276, 281
Tickweed 122
Tidy tips 144
Timber-decked patio 205-6,
  208-9
Tithonia rotundifolia 150
Toadflax 129, 144
Tobacco plant 149
Tomato 245, 267
Tomato fertilizer 15
Tools: care of 35; cutting and
  pruning 31-4; lawn-care 31, 35;
  watering equipment 31, 34-5;
  working the soil 28-32
Topdressing lawns 199
Topiary 53
Torenia fournieri 265
Trachycarpus fortunei 51
Trachymene coerulea 265
Tradescantia 137, 281; T. zebrina
  281
Training: blackberries 221;
  climbers/wall plants 91; fruit
  trees 216-17; grape vine 226;
  greenhouse plants 261
Transplanting: shrubs 54;
  vegetables 235
Tree mallow 69-70
Tree peony 72
Tree surgery 45
Trees 38-51; staking 42, 43
Trillium 177
Trollius 137
Tropaeolum majus 145, 146;
  T. peregrinum 146; T. speciosum
  98-9
Tubers 153
Tufa 167-8
Tulipa 162-3
Tulip fire 296
Tupelo 48
Turf laying 194-6
Turnip 245

Ulex europaeus 86
Umbrella tree 280
Unbrella grass 276
Underplanting 105
Urn plant 274
Ursinia 150
Utricularia vulgaris 186

Valerian 122
Vegetables 212-13, 232-47; under
  glass 265-7; pests and diseases
  286-90
Ventilation, greenhouse 257
Venus fly trap 277
Venus's looking glass 144
Verbascum 137, 151, 177
Verbena 150
Veronica 137;
Veronica, shrubby 66-7
Vervain 150
Viburnum 78-9; V. tinus 86
Victor's laurel 69
Vinca 78-9, 79
Vine 99
Viola 137; V. x wittrockiana 151
Violet 137; African 24-6, 280; dog's
  tooth 159; water 186
Viper's bugloss 143
Virginia creeper 97-8
Virgin's bower 94
Virus diseases 289, 293, 296
Vitis 99

Wall plants 88-99
Wallflower 151; Siberian 151
Walls, dry 168
Wandering Jew 281
Wart disease 289
Wasp 292
Water gardens 178-87
Water lily 183, 186; yellow 186
Water milfoil 186
Water soldier 187
Watering 15; border plants 116;
  climbers/wall plants 91; equipment
  31, 34-5; greenhouse 257-8;
  hedges 81-2; house plants 270-2;
  lawns 198; roses 104; trees 43
Wax flower, clustered 281
Wax plant 278
Weedkiller damage 290
Weeds 12, 17-19; around roses 105;
  in lawns 200-1; 'scorched earth
  policy' 19; vegetable plot 19, 233

Weevil: blossom 290; gall 286;
  pea and bean 287; vine 284, 295,
  298
Weigela 79
Western red cedar 86; variegated
  51
Westmorland limestone 167
Wheelbarrow 35
Whiptail 290
Whitefly 284, 298; cabbage
  whitefly 286
Wild flower gardening 191
Wildlife 183-4, 188-91
Willow 75
Willow: dragon's claw 51; golden
  weeping 51
Wilt 296; blossom 292;
  clematis 295; peony 298;
  verticillium 289
Wilting 273
Wind protection, shrubs 54-5
Windflower 120, 157
Windowboxes 207
Winter care: border plants 117;
  greenhouse 256-7
Wireworm 285, 287
Wishbone flower 265
Wisteria, Chinese 99
Wisteria sinensis 99
Witch hazel 65-6
Wolfsbane 118
Wood sorrel 176
Woodbine 97
Woodruff, annual 142
Worms 201, 299

Xeranthemum annuum 146

Yarrow 118
Yew 51, 86
Yucca aloifolia 281;
  Y. filamentosa 79

Zantedeschia 137
Zauschneria 177
Zinnia 150

ACKNOWLEDGEMENTS

Illustrations by Alan Burton, Pamela Dowson and Nils Solberg

The publishers gratefully acknowledge the following for the reproduction of colour photographs

Edward Barber 2; 7.
Bob Challinor 41; 42; 65; 91; 101; 130; 138-9; 159; 160; 169; 170; 184; 238-9; 255.
Jerry Harpur 8-9; 93; 114-15; 164-5; 172;179;196-7; 208-9; 248-9; 269; 277.
Marcus Harpur 234-5.
Clive Nichols/Jonathan Baillie 33; Clive Nichols/Butterstream, Eire 119; Clive Nichols 123; Clive Nichols/Waterperry Gardens, Oxfordshire 134-5; Clive Nichols/Preen Manor, Shropshire 151; Clive Nichols/Coton Manor, Northamptonshire 156-7; Clive Nichols/Mainau, Lake Constance 163; Clive Nichols/Design:N. Hancock/Mathew Bell 246-7.
Andrew Lawson 36-7; 39; 50; 61; 66-7; 71 78-9; 87; 89; 99; 110-11; 124-5; 144; 145; 147; 148; 191; 210-11(bottom); 212-13; 215; 222-3; 224-5; 229; 263; 281; 282-3; 297.
Michael Stead 43; 44; 55; 83; 167; 171; 187; 198-9; 210; 211 (top); 220; 237; 260; 273.
Alan Titchmarsh 102.
Steve Wooster 10 Anthony Paul Design; 20 Yalding Organic Gardens; 28 Pizzoferro Garden 36 Mt Stewart, N. Ireland; 52 Beth Chatto Gardens; 80; 88; 100 Staddlecombe, Kent; 112 Green Farm Plants, Piet Oudolf Design; 138 Diana Firth's garden, NZ; 152Keukenhof, Nederlands; 164 RHS Gardens Hyde Hall; 178 Chelsea Flower Show 98, Butterfly conservation, Design Marney Hall & Paul Dyer; 188 Sticky Wicket; 192 Anthony Noel Design; 202 Gay Wilson Design; 214; 232 Woodpeckers; 250 The Lost Gardens of Heligan, Cornwall; 268.